MW01009458

Chicana/o Studies
SURVEY AND ANALYSIS

Fourth Edition

DENNIS J. BIXLER-MÁRQUEZ
CARLOS F. ORTEGA
University of Texas at El Paso

Kendall Hunt
publishing company

Cover image copyright © 2011 by Gonzalo J. Plascencia, gonzalojplascencia@gmail.com.
Reprinted by permission of the artist.

www.kendallhunt.com
Send all inquiries to:
4050 Westmark Drive
Dubuque, IA 52004-1840

Copyright © 1997, 2001, 2007, 2014 by Kendall Hunt Publishing Company

ISBN 978-1-4652-2566-5

Printed in the United States of America
10 9 8 7 6 5 4 3 2 1

Contents

Introduction:
Chicano Studies as a Discipline

Carlos F. Ortega

This anthology will begin your journey of introduction to the field of Chicano Studies. For over forty-five years, Chicano Studies has told the story of the Mexican-origin community in the United States through the perspective of activists who helped develop the field through teaching and scholarship. Designed to prepare the first-time student in Chicano Studies with a basic understanding of the research and teaching focus of the discipline, this collection provides a diverse spectrum of readings, insights, and positions. As students work through the readings, they will become familiar with the diverse experiences of the Mexican-origin community as evidenced by interdisciplinary approaches and theoretical schemes. The background will also prepare them to examine these experiences in greater depth later in their university and/or professional careers.

The preparation of any anthology is always a precarious undertaking, largely due to what is left out of the collection rather than what goes in. We as editors began this project with great enthusiasm in the mid-nineties. For one, no introductory anthology in Chicano Studies had been published in over a decade. As the need arose to have a set of standardized contemporary readings reflecting the breadth of the field, we began the process of organizing sets of readings reflecting more up-to-date findings and commentary. To that end, our primary goal was to give students a foundation, encouraging them to pursue in-depth studies on

Chicanos from the perspective of the social sciences, education, the humanities, and the arts. Pertinent knowledge of the history, culture, and major current socioeconomic and political issues affecting Chicanos is paramount to the preparation of students in various professions, especially those who intend to live and work in the Southwest and near the United States–Mexico border. It is our hope that this text will provide a fruitful experience for readers as they embark on their study of the largest ethnic minority group in the Southwest and the United States.

But what is Chicano Studies? How did it come about? What purpose does it serve? The remainder of this essay will attempt to answer these questions. By addressing the origins, intellectual focus, contributions, and current issues, the reader will better understand the role of Chicano Studies and the significance of this book. When we began the first edition of this anthology in 1996, a complete and critical history of Chicano Studies—one examining the development of Chicano Studies programs, departments, and centers, as well as assessing ideological relationships between institutions, the innovation of curriculum, and the relationship of undergraduate degrees to the workplace—did not exist. This has changed with the recent works by Michael Soldatenko and Rodolfo F. Acuña.[1] Their work will go a long way in providing much-needed critical insight to the role and function of Chicano Studies.

THE ORIGINS OF CHICANO STUDIES

The field of Chicano Studies was born during the tumultuous decade of the 1960s, during a period in US history when the very structure of society was changing, or pressured to change. Issues such as race, inequality, opportunities in education and work, health, inclusion, and the war in Viet Nam motivated groups throughout the country to question their social status and that of dominant elites.

Initially, Chicano Studies was a California product for at least two reasons: 1) the large Mexican population in the state and 2) the Chicano student movement made Chicano Studies its top priority and waged constant struggles to have programs developed and, later, to defend their existence. The push in California, however, influenced similar struggles in the Southwest and Midwest.

Politically, Chicano students were involved with organizations such as the United Mexican American Students (UMAS), the Mexican American Youth Organization (MAYO), the Mexican American Student Council (MASC), or the Movimiento Estudiantil Chicano de Aztlán (MEChA), to name only a few. Involvement with the United Farm Workers of America and local community politics, as seen with the Crusade for Justice in Denver, Colorado, laid the foundation for practical and ideological work. Racism and a legacy of discrimination in Southwestern universities also led students to confront these institutions for their lack of sensitivity.[2]

Before the 1960s there were few Chicanos enrolled in universities and fewer Chicano intellectuals with professional standing teaching and publishing. Those Chicanos who were attending college came from a small middle class. Members of the working class who attended college often did so with the help of the Catholic and Protestant clergy and, to some extent, the Mormon Church and the Young Men's Christian Association (YMCA). It was only through the GI Bill and the civil rights movement that large numbers of Mexican American working-class students were able to obtain a higher education.

The students who did attend college during the 1960s found, for the most part, no intellectual tradition with a distinct Mexican focus. It was a cultural dimension ignored in the curriculum and faculty makeup. There were, however, exceptions. At the University of Texas at Austin, George I. Sánchez was perhaps the first Mexican American scholar to wage battle against racism in the schools, starting in the 1930s when he challenged the validity of IQ tests and their bias against Mexican students. Carlos Castañeda published numerous histories, and *Our Catholic Heritage in Texas, 1519–1936,* at seven volumes, stands as a major achievement. Folklorist Américo Paredes, founder of the Mexican American Studies Center (MASC), spent his career at UT and wrote seminal studies on Chicano folklore in addition to poetry and fiction. His best-known book is *With His Pistol in His Hand* (1958).

At the University of New Mexico, Arthur Campa conducted historical and cultural studies while Sabine Ullibarrí published early Chicano literature. At the University of Notre Dame, Julián Samora, a sociologist, was the first scholar to focus attention on political leadership in the Mexican American community and the co-optation of community leaders. He also founded the Mexican American Studies Center at Notre Dame. In California, Ernesto Galarza, who came from a migrant family, received his Ph.D. in economics from Columbia University in 1929 but never pursued a university career—he did not believe universities cared about Mexican workers. Instead, he became an independent scholar and a union organizer. *Barrio Boy* (1971) and *Merchants of Labor* (1964) are some of his better-known books.

As the student movement of the 1960s came into its own, some militant students came to see the work of these first-generation scholars as too traditional, too academic, and too removed from the needs of the community. Instead, the kind of scholar in demand was one whose research would be critical of American society and, at the same time, shape the emerging consciousness based on cultural nationalism. This Chicano scholar would reject assimilation and integrationist ideologies and instead embrace a strong Mexican identity and the importance of activism. When one speaks of cultural nationalism, the focus is on the group—in this case, the Mexican community, its cultural ideas, values, and norms. Included are language, the arts, music, and any other form of expression. While there are contradictions in simply accepting any and all aspects of Mexican culture—or for that matter, any culture—it is important to recognize that many Mexican Americans know little of the culture. For the Chicano movement, it was important to embrace and understand exactly where we come from: culturally, not necessarily geographically.

Related to nationalism was the rejection of assimilation, the idea of giving up or abandoning one's cultural heritage, something that the schools worked hard to accomplish. Corporal punishment for speaking Spanish, little or nothing about the Mexican community in textbooks, and a history of denigrating Mexican culture led many Mexican Americans to reject their culture or believe they were really Americans; in short, there was confusion about identity. For this and many other reasons, the Chicano movement believed it necessary to push cultural nationalism as a way to get its members reacquainted with Mexican heritage. This is where Chicano Studies as an academic discipline comes in.

But it was not simply about cultural nationalism. The emergence of Chicano Studies was, in part, the product of mass student protest on university and college campuses throughout the southwestern United States. The radicalism of the period generated by numerous social and political issues of the time, such as poverty, civil rights, political and economic inequality, racism, and the war in Viet Nam, drove Chicano youth and community activists into the politics of change. Chicano youth were also concerned with access to institutions of higher education that traditionally excluded them. Their demands called for a university education that would 1) teach them about their culture and history and 2) offer training and knowledge needed to create change in their communities.[3]

By 1967 a Chicano student group called Quinto Sol at the University of California at Berkeley began publishing *El Grito: A Journal of Contemporary Mexican American Thought* under the leadership of Octavio Romano, a professor of anthropology at the same campus. The assumption guiding the Quinto Sol group was that Chicanos must take the responsibility of challenging the policies of assimilation promoted by the university, not to mention the dearth of Chicanos in higher education, which perpetuated racial stereotypes through its teaching and research.[4] But the work of *El Grito* was more than an intellectual exercise. The writings were a direct response to conditions in the Mexican community: bleak educational experiences, the exploitation of farm workers, and the virtual exclusion from mainstream society. Berkeley administrators, who were all to familiar with student protest, were not entirely supportive of *El Grito* and its writers, since Romano was on the faculty of anthropology and many of the staff and writers were students at the university.

During the latter part of the 1960s, especially in 1968, Chicano students applied pressure to colleges and universities to institutionalize the study of the Mexican-origin population in general and Chicanos in particular, as well as admit and retain Chicano students. Ironically, there was nothing uniform about these proposals. According to Carlos Muñoz:

> There was a consensus of the relevance and need for those programs for Chicano students but there was a lack of coherence in expectation and emphasis. Some emphasized the potential for such programs to contribute to the solution of students' cultural identity crisis caused by the assimilationist process. Others expected that these programs would develop into meaningful academic alternatives to traditional departments. Still others perceived such programs as training grounds for community organizers. Ideologically, the spectrum ran from those who identified Chicano Studies as curricula that would emphasize the contributions of Americans of Mexican descent to American culture and society to those who defined it as curricula that would focus attention on racism and the structure of class oppression.[5]

The year 1968 was tumultuous in higher education as campuses throughout the United States, caught in the middle of student strikes addressing the Viet Nam war and the civil rights movement, now had to rethink their policies and adapt to the changing society. The situation in the country, intensified by the assassination of Robert Kennedy and Martin Luther King Jr., took a turn no one could have expected. Added to this were student strikes in Europe and Mexico, the latter drawing much attention in the Chicano community, after the massacre of students in Mexico City in 1968.

Perhaps the most important development in education did not take place at a university but in public schools. In the spring of 1968, Chicano students led a mass protest against their middle and high schools. At issue was the poor quality of education, the emphasis on vocational curriculum, and the cultural dissonance that demonstrated a cultural bias by teachers and administrators toward the students. The success of the walkouts emphasized the importance of education as a political issue, and in time similar walkouts occurred at many schools throughout the Southwest.

These events shaped the demand for Chicano Studies programs. In Los Angeles, student strikes were becoming a regular occurrence, with United Mexican American Students (UMAS) leading the way. At their statewide conference that year, they discussed such topics as colonialism, international solidarity, organizational structure, legal defense, and the establishment of Chicano Studies programs. At one time, there were at least thirty-five UMAS chapters in southern California and over fifty chapters in the state with a combined membership of two thousand.[6] Their efforts and pressure led to the first Chicano Studies program in 1968 at California State College, Los Angeles.[7] By 1969, a Chicano Studies department was established at San Fernando State College (now California State University, Northridge) after students clashed with the university administration. Similarly, MEChA-orchestrated student unrest and MAYO-led community activism from 1968 to 1972 resulted in the establishment of Chicano Studies at the University of Texas, El Paso (UTEP).

Some of these programs were more successful than others due in part to their relationships with university administration, the quality of faculty and curriculum, and their relationship with the Chicano community. Evidenced by the development of programs across the country, Chicano Studies was a priority in academia, albeit a forced one. Chicano Studies programs emerged in California, New Mexico, Arizona, Texas, Colorado, and Washington in the West. Chicano and Puerto Rican students helped establish joint Chicano/Boriqua Studies programs in Indiana, Michigan, Illinois, Minnesota, and Iowa. The University of Minnesota, Notre Dame University, the University of Wisconsin, and Michigan State University still house Chicano Studies programs today.[8]

A key moment in the development of Chicano Studies came as a result of a three-day conference in Santa Barbara, California, in April of 1969. The conference, according to Mario Barrera, further developed the themes and goals discussed at the Denver Youth Conferences (1967–68). The Denver programs were a call to Mexican youth to organize themselves in order to liberate their communities through nationalism. Specifically, the resolutions called for political action, economic control of Chicano communities, and development of Chicano Studies programs. These resolutions, guided in spirit by El Plan Espiritual de Aztlán, set the stage for the future growth of Chicano Studies. The aim was to apply these goals on college campuses by developing a plan for Chicano higher education, which included the development of a Chicano student movement. The essence of El Plan was communitarian and antiassimilation.[9]

El Plan de Santa Barbara called for the creation of Chicano Studies programs, set forth curriculum approaches, and stressed the reinforcement of cultural heritage and the formation of a political community. However, while El Plan recognized that institutions of higher education were controlled by an elite, it also recognized that Chicanos who were attempting to gain access might face the reality of co-optation. While El Plan addressed these issues, how to deal with these realities was left unresolved.[10] For the most part, it would be up to individual campuses to negotiate their academic presence. The document itself asserts that the search for the American dream, achieved at the cost of assimilation, was problematic for the working class since it meant a life of cheap labor.

Thus the call for the self-determination of the community and the term Chicano[11] becomes the source of a new cultural identity. From these perspectives, Chicano Studies comes to represent the Chicano community's aspirations revolving around higher education. The focus of El Plan de Santa Barbara was a mandate to the university and college systems in California—although the directives became applicable to other areas as well. The directives called for 1) admission and recruitment of Chicano students, faculty, administrators, and staff, 2) a curriculum program and academic major relevant to the Chicano cultural and historical experience, 3) support and tutorial programs, 4) research programs, 5) publication programs, and 6) community, cultural, and social action centers.[12]

This also placed Chicano Studies within the context of political change, thus creating a link with the student movement. The resulting academic and community orientation became the cornerstone of Chicano Studies. However, the document did not define the curricula as either alternative to, or part of, the traditional university curriculum. Nor did it spell out the ideological direction other than that of "Chicanismo" or cultural nationalism. The developers of El Plan did not seem as concerned with changing the university as they were applying its resources to the needs of the Chicano community.[13] Some Chicano scholars, however, believed a significant transformation of the mission, goals, and curricula of universities was essential, particularly those in regional institutions with a substantial Chicano population base, such as the University of Texas, El Paso (UTEP). For example, in the early 1970s, Tomás Arciniega and Norma Hernández, the first Chicana dean of education, began to modify the sociocultural training of future teachers (National Teachers Corps), regional scholars, and the university's own faculty, with the scholarship developed by the Quinto Sol group. Marie Esman Barker initiated the first bilingual education program in El Paso, Texas, and its concomitant teacher-training program at UTEP. Along with prominent area educators, her organizational efforts would lead to the formation of the Southwest Association of Bilingual Education (SWABE), which later became the National Association of Bilingual Education (NABE).

Though not tied to Chicano Studies per se, or to the student activism of the early seventies that caused the faculty to take notice, the efforts developing in the College of Education became an important step in rectifying key educational issues of the day. These efforts can also be traced to the early and mid-1960s and include the seminal scholarship of Phillip D. Ortego, the first director of Chicano Studies at UTEP, who provided a voice from Texas on Chicanos. Whether discussing literature, immigration, education, or the Chicano movement, his essays were in line with the developments in California.[14] Moreover, research by Thomas Carter led to one of the early publications on Chicano education.

The focus on curricula by the authors of El Plan was on undergraduate education. It was to address the identity crisis of Mexican American youth through the teaching of Chicano culture and history and the development of Chicano activists who would return to the community.[15] The curriculum as a formal, institutionalized, and dynamic study of Chicano culture in all its diversity and unity would be an examination of the Chicano experience—from language, education, literature, aesthetics and creative arts, philosophy, folklore, and ideology to the objective conditions of its historical, social, cultural, psychological, political and economic socialization, development, and existence. To this end, several dimensions to Chicano Studies would emerge. As an institutionalized discipline, investigators would create a body of critical and empirical knowledge, there would be multidisciplinary approaches, and there would be a group of practitioners in working relation with one another. In the words of José Cuellar, Chicano Studies "was originally conceived as a part of a people's struggle for equality and justice and as a means to meet the growing need for accurate analysis of the strategic needs, progress, development, and self-determination of the Mexican community in the United States."[16]

FORMATION OF A DISCIPLINE

As Chicano Studies departments, centers, and programs took form, discussions arose calling for a Chicano paradigm reflecting a Chicano perspective of the world, and, based on new knowledge, research needed to build a Chicano consciousness that would serve to liberate the Chicano community. The discussion of paradigm centered on a model that would contribute to the restoration of human dignity, lead to the socioeconomic transformation of the Chicano community, and contribute to the fullest potential of Chicano students. An important direction came from Octavio Romano, who published a series of essays regarding the shortcomings of traditional social science, which cast a stereotyped and historically biased view of Chicanos. Romano's essays also became the foundation for the first stage of research in developing a Chicano paradigm. According to Romano, it was not just a question of Chicanos conducting social science research, but rather introducing a "Chicano image" in social science. To do so, he suggested eight preliminary steps:

1. Chicanos are creators of social systems in their own right, having laid the foundation for cooperatives, mutual aid societies, and other examples;

2. Chicanos are participants in the historical process;

3. Chicanos have created social forms like dialects or music;

4. They have engaged in social issues such as the labor movement in the Southwest and the struggle for bilingual education;

5. Chicanos are literate; having published over five hundred newspapers in the Southwest from 1848 through 1950;

6. Chicanos are capable of their own system of rationality;

7. Intellectual ability has been part of the Chicano experience; and,

8. The Chicano community has historically practiced and worked for a balance within ecosystems.[17]

This "image" became the foundation for research, teaching, and activism as well as deviating from traditional perspectives.

As the new research emerged, two important journals served as outlets for this new research literature: *El Grito*, which began publishing in 1967, and *Aztlán: A Chicano Journal of the Social Sciences and Arts* (1970), based at UCLA. *Aztlán*, in particular, strove to create not just mere critiques of social science, but also paradigms reflecting Chicano perspectives.[18] Eventually, this trend gave rise to Latino presses like the Bilingual Press and Arte Público Press and a federally funded clearinghouse (ERIC) on Mexican Americans. Also, established academic journals and university presses slowly began to publish Chicano scholarship, gradually giving access to mainstream academia.

Just as important to the growth of Chicano Studies was the influence of the cultural renaissance taking place at the time. Armando Navarro writes:

> From 1967 to 1972 Chicano student groups became increasingly supportive of Chicanismo. This cultural rebirth was predicated on Chicanos reconnecting to their Mexican roots. Rejecting assimilation and embracing cultural pluralism, Chicano students found pride, self-worth, and greatness in their mestizo heritage. The spirit and symbolism of "indigenismo," the Mexican Revolution, La Raza Cósmica, and Ché Guevara were echoed in their rhetoric, standards, and protest activities. The students embellished their vocabulary with nationalistic buzzwords, speaking of Maya, Toltec, Aztecs, Pancho Villa, the Magón brothers, Zapata, *Tierra y Libertad*, and mestizos. Chicano Studies programs were by-products of the cultural renaissance. This was manifested in numerous courses that made up the Chicano Studies curricula.[19]

But what was this new paradigm to be?

One of the key areas in developing a Chicano paradigm came from the social sciences. As more Chicanos earned doctorates, research and curriculum development came to illustrate this focus: history, labor history, sociology, politics, education, and anthropology were areas reflected in this early stage of work.[20] In time, research took on an even more diverse focus with studies published in folklore, literary criticism, biography, political economy, bilingualism, and music.[21]

With the foundation of the Chicano Studies paradigm, an attempt to conceptualize and interpret the Chicano experience began with nationalistic perspectives that addressed concerns over identity and culture. In these early years, Chicano Studies passed through two very distinct phases: First, the Chicano image in the social sciences focused on critical reviews of the literature that analyzed social science work on the Chicano written by Anglo American social scientists. It was the starting point to the development of Chicano research and subsequent paradigm. The next stage of research by Chicano scholars reflected a strong focus in the area of history. Most notable in this regard were the

publications of *Occupied America* (1972—now in its seventh edition) by Rodolfo Acuña, the essays of Juan Gómez-Quiñones, and *Furia y Muerte* (1973) by Pedro Castillo and Alberto Camarillo. These publications reflected a revisionist approach to traditional historical interpretation. Another set of articles contained such terms in their titles as "Toward," "Tentative," and "Preliminary Remarks," which reflected the early attempts at interpretation. Many of these revisionist interpretations also carried with them alternative theoretical approaches to Chicano research.[22]

In the early 1970s some Chicano scholars fell under the influence of Third World intellectuals such as Franz Fanon, Albert Memmi, and Pablo Casanova, who helped develop the idea of their people as being "internally colonized"; the colonial experiences of Third World people made more sense to them than the traditional interpretations of the time. Within the United States itself, writers such as Stokely Carmichael and Robert Blauner published widely on the notion of internal colonialism. Chicano intellectuals who asserted this view included Acuña, Carlos Muñoz Jr., Mario Barrera, and Tomás Almaguer.[23]

By 1973, the internal colony analysis generated significant literature and, in many Chicano Studies programs, was the key paradigm for teaching and research—at least in the social sciences. At the same time, many scholars, including those who supported the analysis, came to believe that the internal colony model fell short. At a UCLA symposium, participants reached an agreement whereby in order to assure relevance of the model, "it should incorporate more aspects of Marxist analysis on colonialism." The internal colony model was, in fact, an outgrowth of the Chicano movement, and its purpose had been to provide a theoretical framework for Chicano ideology. According to Carlos Muñoz:

> In the minds of the young movement scholars who developed it, internal colonization had been meaningful not only as a concept that provided an alternative interpretation of the Mexican American experience more consistent with the historical and contemporary realities of a racist society, but also with the definition of the Chicano movement as a struggle for decolonialization and antiassimilation.[24]

Mario Barrera came to see the model as a form of dialogue, not as an absolute. However, those who came to view Marxist theory and class analysis as the major influence in understanding the Chicano experience argued that the internal colonial model was too deterministic and limited to the concept of racism, ignoring class experiences of Mexican oppression in US capitalist society. Still others felt class analysis should be incorporated into the internal colonial model or rejected altogether. Viewed as limiting, many rejected the internal colonial model because the oppression of Chicanos, based on a "legacy of colonialism," had by the late twentieth century seen Chicanos become a postcolonial society.[25] While the internal colonial model still has its supporters, Chicano Studies drew from various ideological foundations as a means to interpret the Chicano experience, and the diverse expressions of this experience led to numerous debates. One thing is for certain, interpreting the Chicano experience was complex.

Originally, the basic premise of the Chicano paradigm rejected: 1) explanations of the Chicano condition based solely on genetics or cultural determinism; 2) romanticized descriptions of the Chicano; and 3) use of improper and unethical research procedures in the process of developing a body of critical and empirical knowledge and data grounded in social reality. It accepted explanations based on theories of relationships between conditions of individuals in communities of Mexican descent and the economic, political, sociocultural, and historical forces that mold and serve as their environments.[26]

Now, the concept of the internal colony was too narrow, deterministic, and unsatisfactory. By the end of the 1970s a new conceptual framework would take hold. In the meantime, researchers seemed to move along the lines of their own disciplines and, without saying so, a multidisciplinary body of literature was taking shape. One study suggests the relationship between social science and literary output:

> Each component of this creative explosion is related to all of the others in two ways. First, each negates the assumptions made by Anglo writers that Chicanos have not made and will not or cannot make significant contributions to American social, cultural, and intellectual life. Second, each is part of the Chicanos' efforts to define their own reality.[27]

The interdisciplinary and comparative focus helps to define the uniqueness of Chicano Studies. While Chicano social scientists emphasize the internal colony model, course offerings covered a wide range of topics. While the notion of cultural, social, and ideological awareness reflected the academic examination called for by El Plan de Santa Barbara, little explanation of

what one would do with a degree in Chicano Studies remained a problem. Perhaps because of the activist orientation that carried the day, it may have been assumed graduates would automatically return to the community. Regardless of the campus, curriculum approaches took on an interdisciplinary focus based on the social sciences, humanities, education, the arts, and community activism. On many campuses, such as California State University, Northridge, the curriculum also emphasized communication skills courses—writing, critical thinking, research, and public speaking. Spanish language courses were geared for first-time speakers to Chicano students. Students were also encouraged to double major in order to make the most of their professional interests. Finally, Operation Chicano Teacher (OCT), a partnership between the School of Education and Chicano Studies, was a commitment to develop a cadre of strong bilingual Chicano teachers in southern California schools. At the University of Texas, El Paso, in addition to a double-major option, academic minors, special academic areas of concentration, and leadership development programs were eventually developed to meet the needs of prospective social workers, educators, prelaw students, and students interested in graduate school.

Moreover, a necessity in bringing scholars and students together to discuss the many issues facing Chicano Studies led to the creation of the National Association for Chicana/o Studies (NACCS) in 1974. Later, Chicana feminists helped create Mujeres Activistas y Cambio Social (MALCS). These organizations sponsor annual conferences, help to create partnerships among Chicana researchers, share the latest research, and advocate for gender studies within Chicano Studies.[28]

CONTRIBUTIONS AND ISSUES IN CHICANO STUDIES

Into the late 1970s, issues surfaced bringing forth questions about the directions of Chicano Studies programs. One of the flaws emerged when Chicana feminists raised the issue of male domination. According to Cynthia Orozco, Chicanas were being undermined: "Chicano intellectuals argued that race and class were determining factors in understanding the subordinate position of Mexicans in the United States," but in the literature, or in academic programs, women are nonexistent.[29] Orozco also criticized El Plan de Santa Barbara for its lack of relevance to women in Chicano Studies.

Specifically, El Plan lacked mention of courses on Chicana Studies or awareness of sexism and the importance of gender.[30] As Alma García argues, Chicanas need to be a vital component of a Chicano Studies program, not a last-minute discussion. Chicano scholars need to develop a consciousness about the elusiveness of Chicanas in the study of the Mexican-origin community.[31] García also points out that while courses on la Chicana were developed throughout the 1970s and 1980s, providing a framework for the study of Chicanas in US society, courses often fell short due to a lack of gender analysis in Chicano Studies, "which focuses on the structure of patriarchy as a form of oppression affecting Chicanas as women."[32]

Teresa Córdova writes that to counteract the flaws in gender curriculum within Chicano Studies, gender must be placed as a central component in the study of the community. We must study the diversity of sexuality in the community, challenge patriarchy within and outside of the Chicano community, and support the pursuit of Chicana dreams and aspirations.[33]

Another set of issues revolved around the reassessment of El Plan de Santa Barbara, "not because of any fundamental inadequacy in the principles, but because of the doubt that exists within our movement concerning their applicability in Chicano Studies today."[34] Despite the soundness of the principles, El Plan fell into disuse for three reasons: 1) the co-optation of Chicano Studies programs; 2) the sellout of Chicano faculty to the world of academia; and 3) the contested value of Chicano nationalism as a driving force in Chicano Studies. The intent of regenerating the founding principles of Chicano Studies and El Plan de Santa Barbara—the necessity of self-determination, the link between Chicano Studies and the Chicano community, and the role of education in training students and developing plans, policies, and strategies—was designed to meet the needs of the community. Ironically, years earlier, Juan Gómez-Quiñones outlined the very dilemmas hindering the success of Chicano Studies, which remain evident today: the teaching, research, and structural objectives found in El Plan de Santa Barbara were based on cultural resistance and social change.[35]

As the twentieth century came to a close, concern over the preparation of a new generation of scholars arose. While many of us entered graduate school pursuing our academic interests, we did so because graduate programs in Chicano Studies did not exist. There was no choice. The strength of Chicano Studies found in its teaching components at the undergraduate level

seemed to be the only course of study. Whether at two-year institutions, state universities, or research institutions, Chicano Studies existed in some form but always at the undergraduate level. According to Rodolfo Acuña:

> The discipline itself is divided into teaching and research fields. The teaching field is much more developed than the research field, partly because research fields evolve from teaching fields and partly because of the failure of research institutions to initiate doctoral programs in Chicana/o Studies.[36]

The result of this trend continues to see the appointment of Chicano faculty to joint positions. Faculty members with doctoral degrees in, say, history will join their home department linked to the degree then split teaching time with Chicano Studies. In these situations, Chicano faculty are paid from the home department, get tenure in the home department, and in those cases where Chicano Studies programs are closed due to political and financial reasons, faculty return to full-time teaching in the home department. In these cases, there is no commitment to Chicano Studies and the research field is not fully developed. Of course, if Chicano Studies is a full department or center, then this is not an issue, because the possibility of tenure within Chicano Studies nullifies the joint appointment. In other cases, Chicano faculty completing their doctoral work in their chosen fields will teach in Chicano Studies programs where tenure-track positions are not in effect, and as soon as they complete their dissertations, they "jump ship," so to speak, by joining departments that offer tenure-track positions. It is hard to blame faculty for leaving Chicano Studies programs because, after all, the offer of tenure is one of the key benefits of teaching at a university. The result, however, is that Chicano Studies programs find it difficult to develop a core faculty committed to teaching undergraduates and willing to live in academe without tenure.

A related trend currently found on some campuses sees an attempt to develop policy where faculty must teach in departments where they earned their doctorates. If a Chicano faculty member with a doctorate in education—so the policy goes—is teaching in Chicano Studies, such a policy would force the faculty member to abandon Chicano Studies to teach in an education department—and this assuming the alternate department even has an opening or wants that faculty member.

These trends greatly affect Chicano Studies programs since they do not have the protection of department or center status. It could mean the end of Chicano Studies. It is a double-edged sword: How can one get a doctorate in Chicano Studies when research institutions do not develop graduate programs to train new faculty and practitioners in this field? While doctorates in Ethnic Studies have become one alternative, these programs do not always focus on Chicano Studies, but rather on mastering key concepts in Ethnic Studies that can later be applied to the study of different ethnic groups.

Still, Chicano Studies has made important contributions to higher education. As the demographics amongst the Latino community continue to grow, access to higher education remains an important issue for working-class Chicano youth. This point is explicit in El Plan de Santa Barbara. By the late 1980s, Chicano Studies had grown, as evidenced by its achievements. There was the accomplishment of maximizing the presence of Mexican American students, faculty, and administrative personnel; the participation in the development of professionals—teachers, lawyers, community workers, and counselors; the development of Chicano intellectuals; and the increase of knowledge in all fields from which ideological ideas, critiques, and empirical knowledge shaped perspectives and community action. Perhaps most important, Chicano Studies placed in the context of a larger historical process the political and intellectual development of an oppressed working class.[37] Finally, Chicano Studies has reached the position of a serious "regional area study" as evidenced by the interest of international scholars from Europe, not to mention Mexico.[38]

Moreover, the presence of Chicano Studies research centers has also been important. These programs provide faculty with funding, publication units, a vehicle for conducting research, and a location where researchers can concentrate on their work. Undergraduates can also benefit through internships, which can be a source of income and much-needed experience in research and program coordination. Centers at the University of California, Los Angeles; University of California, Santa Barbara; Arizona State University, University of Texas, Austin; University of Houston; and Michigan State University, among others, provide a strong base for Chicano Studies research.

The 1980s and 1990s were a period of survival and resurgence for Chicano Studies. University politics forced the closing of some programs while others became victims of administrative decisions and witnessed faculty firings that decimated programs. On another level, Chicana feminists challenged the function of Chicano Studies. Factors of race, class, gender, sexual orientation, and geographic location forced modification in interpretation of Chicano history, culture, and politics. Chicano scholars issued a direct challenge to the "us vs. them" paradigm. These factors of diversity led to the use of alternative theories: Cultural Studies, Postmodernism, and Postcolonial Studies are the current theoretical markers. This is evident in the use of the term *Chicana/o*, an indication of gender recognition and the minimizing of patriarchal perspectives. These insights have joined Marxist and nationalist perspectives in interpreting the Chicano experience. And while traditional methodologies of research remain in use, insights drawn from ethnographic and oral history offer wonderful perspectives on local experience. Some historians have embraced the internal colony model as part of the larger postcolonial concept. Some scholars have used this approach to discuss what many have termed academic colonialism as a means of analyzing the relationship of Chicano Studies to university administrations. One outgrowth of these alternate approaches can be found in Border Studies, an approach that examines the often exciting and contradictory world of life "on the line," as well as a method of analysis that theoretically offers new investigations and metaphors while explaining the world of the border.[39] Those who focus on this approach concern themselves with cultural, social, and political events as they play out at a transnational level. These and many other approaches demonstrate that Chicana/os are not a homogeneous community as once assumed. The diversity of this group provides ample space and exciting times for investigating the ever-changing social and cultural climate of the Mexican-origin community.

Recently, we have seen the development of graduate programs in Chicana/o Studies. This trend is important because the survival of any academic discipline requires training the next generation of scholars and teachers. At the university level, this means a group of scholars, trained in the field, will be able to land appointments in centers and departments of Chicano Studies, carry out research in their areas of specialization, and most important, mentor their students to become critical thinkers sensitive to the needs of their communities. Doctoral programs now in place at the University of California, Santa Barbara and Los Angeles; Michigan State University; and Arizona State University insure the development of a new generation of scholars with solid training in the field. Master's programs are located at the University of Texas, San Antonio; California State University, Northridge, San Jose, and San Diego; and the University of Arizona. The University of Texas, Austin, offers a portfolio of graduate courses focusing on Chicanos that are in use in traditional master's and doctoral programs. In a recent development, the Texas Higher Education Coordinating Board established a policy that would allow a community college to offer a field of study in Mexican American Studies that is transferable automatically to a four-year institution offering a BA in Chicana/o Studies. Depending on the institution and the commitment to such a program, we already see the articulation taking shape.

Perhaps the most important contribution of Chicano Studies is in its function as pedagogy—the art of teaching based on how teachers want their students to learn. I am not speaking here of transferring academic knowledge in the traditional manner of lecture-discussion-tests. Rather, it is the role of the faculty member as mentor that should always be at the heart of Chicano Studies.

Every year, first-generation college students begin their journey toward their undergraduate degree. Yet, many of these students lack the critical skills to navigate the university and its expectations. Chicano Studies always focused on recruiting working-class students—students who, for one reason or another, haven't developed the necessary skills and preparation for university life. Still, they arrive on campus because they see a possibility of changing the expectations and, in most cases, become the first in their families to earn an undergraduate degree. They find, however, frustration in not being able to fit in, in not having an instructor to speak with to essentially learn the ropes of the university. Faculty in general, but Chicano faculty in particular, has this responsibility. It is not enough to go home early, focus on one's research, and meet students when possible. Countless students owe their achievement to faculty who took time to mentor them, to socialize them to the skills and critical thinking necessary to comprehend the world around them.

And so, as you read the following pages, consider how Chicana/o Studies is the product of its time, specifically, the product of student activism. In its almost four decades of existence, the issues and problems confronting Chicana/o Studies have not destroyed its mission. And though problems remain, Chicana/o Studies carries on—at times in traditional academic fashion, in others, with a clear scholar/activist orientation. Recently, one of my students informed me that a student in one of her classes had asked her professor,

"Why do we need Chicano Studies? Things are not like they were in the 1960s." Unfortunately, this is not a unique sentiment. Many feel our programs grew out of political activism concerned with addressing inequality and a history of injustice. No one would doubt this. However, while things have improved, the recent events in Arizona—the draconian immigration law and the attack on Mexican American Studies—show that all is not so well and that our work is still rooted in the fight against injustice. Chicana/o Studies, then, exists to inform and guide in the understanding of these and other events. More importantly, those first-generation students continue to arrive in need of sound mentorship.

The essays herein reflect a Chicana/o Studies perspective. The research reflects current situations or conditions with implications for Chicana/o Studies. Characterized by diversity of perspective, approaches, and theoretical frameworks, the collection strives to capture the cornucopia of perspectives—although we as editors recognize it is by no means complete. The information is relevant not just to the historian but to those entering the private sector or human service professions: social work, education, and the nonprofit sector, especially in policy-making positions.

A NOTE TO STUDENTS

The book comprises five sections, each reflecting areas of research, interpretation, and analysis of the Chicana/o experience in particular and the Latino experience in general. At the end of each section one will find additional information in the form of assessment questions, suggested readings, and suggested films, videos, and websites. These materials help the student gain a deeper understanding of the Chicana/o experience. Students are also encouraged to examine the websites of key organizations that serve the Chicano population for information on current trends and initiatives.

Endnotes

1   See: Rodolfo F. Acuña. *The Making of Chicana/o Studies: In the Trenches of Academe* (New Brunswick, NJ: Rutgers University Press, 2011) and Michael Soldatenko, *Chicano Studies: The Genesis of a Discipline* (Tucson: University of Arizona Press, 2009).

2   Carlos Muñoz, Jr. *Youth, Identity, Power: The Chicano Movement* (New York: Verso Press, 1989), 127–28.

3   Muñoz, *Youth*, 130.

4   Carlos Muñoz Jr. "The Development of Chicano Studies, 1968–1981," in *Chicano Studies: A Multidisciplinary Approach*, eds. Eugene García, Francisco Lomeli, and Isidro D. Ortiz. (New York: Teachers College Press, 1984), 5.

5   Muñoz, Jr. *Development*, 9.

6   Muñoz, Jr. *Development*, 9

7   Juan Gómez-Quiñones. *Mexican Students Por La Raza: The Chicano Student Movement in Southern California, 1967–1977.* (Santa Barbara, CA: Editorial La Causa, 1978), 5.

8   See the appendix in Acuña's *Making of* for the most up-to-date listing of Chicano Studies programs. 273–298.

9   Mario Barrera. *Beyond Aztlán: Ethnic Autonomy in Comparative Perspective* (New York: Praeger Publishers, 1988), 42.

10 Barrera, *Beyond*, 42–44.

11 The term "Chicano" has always been a topic of controversy, but to some extent, this was quelled in the 1980s when the term was used interchangeably with Mexican American and vice versa. At the time of the Santa Barbara conference, "Chicano" had a specific meaning to those who identified with the term. In a seminal paper published one month after the Santa Barbara conference, Ysidro Ramón Macías characterized a Chicano as someone with a high degree of self-respect, "because this individual accepts his Mexican culture and languages"; the individual had a sense of responsibility to Chicano communities, which in part was due to the rejection of the Puritan ethic of self-improvement; that is, the Chicano did not reject the idea of self-improvement, rather the idea of self-absorption and individualism. Finally, being a Chicano meant the continued maintenance and enrichment of one's Mexican heritage. See Ysidro Ramón Macías, "Evolution of the Mind: A Plan for Political Action," *El Pocho Ché*, May, 1969 (mimeo copy).

12 Chicano Coordinating Council in Higher Education. *El Plan de Santa Barbara* (Santa Barbara, CA: La Causa Publications, 1970), 9–10. See also, Juan Gómez-Quiñones, "To Leave to Hope or Chance," in *Parameters of Institutional Change.* (Hayward, CA: Southwest Network, 1974), 154–56.

13 Muñoz Jr. *Development*, 10–14.

14 Phillip D. Ortego. "The Mexican-Dixon Line," *El Grito*, 1(4), (1963): 29–31; "Moctezuma's Children," *El Grito*, 3(3), (1970): 38–50; and "Chicano Renaissance," *Social Casework*, 52, (1971).

15 Muñoz Jr. *Youth*, 141.

16 José Cuellar, no title, no date, 8–9 (mimeo copy).

17 Octavio Romano. "Social Science, Objectivity, and the Chicano," *El Grito*, 4 (1), (1970). The writings most often mentioned in Chicano critiques of social science include, but are not limited to: Munro Edmundson. *Los Manitos: A Study of Institutional Values* (New Orleans: Middle American Research Institute/Tulane University, 1957); Celia Heller. *Mexican American Youth: Forgotten Youth at the Crossroads* (New York: Random House, 1968); Florence R. Kluckhohn and Fred L. Strodbeck. *Variations in Value Orientation.* (New York: Row, Peterson, and Co., 1961); and William Madsen. *Mexican Americans in South Texas.* (New York: Holt, Rinehart, and Winston, 1964).

18 Muñoz Jr. *Youth*, 143–46.

19 Armando Navarro. *Mexican American Youth Organization: Avant-Garde of the Chicano Movement in Texas.* (Austin, TX.: University of Texas Press, 1995), 71–72.

20 See, Isidro D. Ortiz, ed. *Chicanos and the Social Sciences: A Decade of Research and Development (1970–1980).* (Santa Barbara: Center for Chicano Studies/University of California, Santa Barbara, 1983).

21 Ricardo Romo and Raymund Paredes, eds., *New Directions in Chicano Scholarship* (La Jolla, CA: Chicano Studies Program/University of California, San Diego), 1978.

22 Tomás Almaguer. "Interpreting Chicano History: The World Systems Approach to 19th Century California," Working Paper Series #101. (Institute for the Study of Social Change/University of California, Berkeley, 1977).

23 Muñoz Jr. *Youth*, 146–48.

24 Muñoz Jr. *Youth*, 153.

25 Muñoz Jr. *Youth*, 154; Fred A. Cervantes, "Chicanos as a Postcolonial Minority: Some Questions Concerning the Adequacy of the Paradigm of Internal Colonialism," in *Perspectivas en Chicano Studies*, ed. Reynaldo Flores Macias. (Los Angeles: Chicano Studies Center/University of California, Los Angeles, 1977), 123–55.

26 Cuellar, 11–12.

27 Rudolph de la Garza and Rowena Rivera, "The Socio-Political World of the Chicano: A Comparative Analysis of Social Scientific and Literary Perspectives," in *Minority Language and Literature: Retrospective and Perspective*, ed. Dexter Fisher. (New York: Modern Language Association of America, 1977), 43.

28 Teresa Córdova, "Agency, Commitment and Connection: Embracing the Roots of Chicano and Chicana Studies," *International Journal of Qualitative Studies in Education*, 18 (2), (2005), 221–33.

29 Cynthia Orozco, "Sexism in Chicano Studies and the Community," in *Chicano Voices: Intersections of Race, Class and Gender*, ed. Norma Cantú et al (Austin: Center for Mexican American Studies/University of Texas, Austin, 1986), 12.

30 Orozco, *Sexism*, 13.

31 Alma García, "Studying Chicanas: Bringing Women into the Frame of Chicano Studies," in *Chicana Voices* (See note 29), 25–26. Also see the essays by Driscoll and Chabran in the same volume.

32 García, *Studying,* 12.

33 Reynaldo Flores Macías, "El Grito de Aztlán: Voice and Presence in Chicana/o Studies," *International Journal of Qualitative Studies in Education,* 18 (2), (2005), 174.

34 René Núñez and Raoul Contreras, "Principles and Foundations of Chicano Studies: Chicano Organizations on University Campuses in California," in *Chicano Discourse,* ed. Tatcho Mindiola (Cheney, WA: National Association for Chicano Studies, 1992), 32.

35 Gómez-Quiñones, *To Leave,* 173.

36 Rodolfo F. Acuña. *Sometimes There Is No Other Side.* (South Bend, IN: University of Notre Dame Press, 1998), 104.

37 Muñoz Jr., *Youth,* 165–67; Gómez-Quiñones, *To Leave,* 158–59.

38 In Germany, there is the work of Wolfgang Binder and Gustave Blanke; in Italy, Lia Tessarolo; in Poland, Herner Bus; in France, Genevieve Fabre, Yves-Charles Grandjeat, and Maricienne Rocard; and in Hungary, Laszlo Scholz. See, Renate von Bardeleben, Dietrich Briesmeister, and Juan Bruce Novoa, eds., *Missions in Conflict.* (Tubingen: Gunter Narr Veriag, 1988).

39 See, for example, Gloria Anzaldúa, *Borderlands: The New Mestiza.* (San Francisco: Aunt Lute Books, 1987); Carl Gutiérrez Jones, *Rethinking the Borderlands: Between Chicano Culture and Legal Discourse.* (Berkeley: University of California Press, 1995); Carlos G. Vélez-Ibáñez, *Border Visions.* (Tucson: University of Arizona Press, 1996); and José David Saldívar, *Border Matters: Remapping American Cultural Studies.* (Berkeley: University of California Press, 1997).

Historical Perspectives

It has often been said that people without knowledge of their roots are usually people without a sense of direction. People who do not know where they come from often do not know where they are going. Without a sound basis of their origins, rootless people find it harder to incorporate into their society. These insights were at the root of Chicano history during its infancy and provided a guide to the perspectives, methods, and conclusions in the late sixties. Today, Chicano history has matured and the insights are more important than ever. In this section, an understanding of the history and heritage of the Chicano is a prerequisite for learning about the contemporary dimensions of the group and its future in American society.

Due to space limitations, the historical period preceding the annexation of the Southwest by the United States is not included. However, the reader is strongly encouraged to explore that historical period, which dates back to the pre-Columbian period, via the readings and audiovisual resources suggested at the end of this section. In addition, most universities offer courses that specialize in certain segments or dimensions of relevance to the Chicano (the Mexican Revolution, the Borderlands, etc.) that would enhance the reader's background on the Chicano experience.

The five essays that comprise this section offer basic foundations for the study of Chicano history and at the same time provide specific examination of these experiences. The section is initiated by Griswold del Castillo's insights on the Treaty of Guadalupe Hidalgo and its implications for the Chicano movement. The importance of this piece is that it links the treaty to contemporary issues and restores the document's relevance to the present day. It is not a dry historical document but rather a marker for understanding the development of Chicano history.

The next four essays provide information on community studies related to El Paso, although similar narratives also describe Chicano communities throughout the Southwest. Mary Romero extends this analysis by exploring the events leading to the confrontation between an Anglo "entrepreneur" and the Mexican "salineros" near El Paso, Texas. She examines both sides of the story in order to determine if this event was a mob action or a political struggle. The essay by Mario T. García, "Border Culture," focuses on the El Paso–Ciudad Juárez borderlands and how Chicanos survived and evolved in a region of political and cultural confluence. Vicki Ruiz examines how Chicanos living in the Segundo Barrio of El Paso were also able to adjust and organize their lives in ways that enabled them to survive a period when they were essentially segregated from the rest of the city's social, political, and cultural life. Finally, Laurie Coyle and her colleagues examine an important organized labor history milestone in the Southwest, one that, to this day, reverberates among El Paso's residents: the Farah strike.

The Chicano Movement
and the Treaty

Richard Griswold del Castillo

The Treaty of Guadalupe Hidalgo is the most important document concerning Mexican Americans that exists. From it stem specific guarantees affecting our civil rights, language, culture, and religion.

Armando Rendón
Chicano Manifesto

During the 1960s and 1970s a new generation of Mexican Americans sought to redefine their position within the United States using, in part, the Treaty of Guadalupe Hidalgo. They called themselves Chicanos, a term previously used as a derogatory reference to working-class Mexican immigrants. Sparked by a growing civil rights and anti-war movement, Chicano political militants sought to focus world attention on the failed promises of the Treaty of Guadalupe Hidalgo. Beginning with an agrarian revolutionary movement in New Mexico and a farm workers' strike in California, the newly born Chicano movement resurrected the treaty as a primary document in the struggle for social justice. This generation of Mexican Americans learned of the legal basis for reclaiming their lost lands. The political aims of the Chicano movement, to gain representation and recognition, generated a more critical interpretation of the meaning of the Mexican War and the treaty. A lasting legacy of Chicano awareness in the 1960s and 1970s was a consciousness of their history dating from 1848 and the Treaty of Guadalupe Hidalgo.

THE ALIANZA MOVEMENT AND NEW MEXICAN LANDS

One of the first activists to provoke a reassessment of the treaty was Reies López Tijerina. Originally a fundamentalist preacher from Texas, Tijerina became part of the struggle of the Hispanos of New Mexico to regain the community land grants that had been taken from them after 1848 in violation of the treaty. Representing New Mexican land claimants, Tijerina traveled to Mexico City in 1959 and again in 1964 to present memorials to the Mexican authorities, including the president of Mexico. Thousands of Hispanos whose families had lost their lands in violation of the terms of the treaty signed the petitions. Tijerina and the delegation asked the government of Mexico to demand that the United States fulfill the terms of the treaty. On both occasions the Mexican government listened respectfully but did nothing.[1]

During the early 1960s Tijerina traveled throughout New Mexico, organizing La Alianza Federal de Mercedes Libres. The purpose of the organization was "to organize and acquaint the heirs of all Spanish land-grants covered by the Guadalupe Hidalgo Treaty" with their rights.[2] This organization became the catalyst for a number of militant actions by the Hispano villagers: the occupation of Kit Carson National Forest, the proclamation of the Republic of San Joaquín de Chama, the courthouse raid and shootout at Tierra Amarilla, a massive military manhunt for Tijerina and his followers, and lengthy legal battles. Lost in the sensational publicity surrounding Tijerina and the Alianza during the late 1960s was the fact that Alianza leaders justified their movement on the basis of historical and legal interpretations both of the constitutions of New Mexico and the United States and of the Treaty of Guadalupe Hidalgo. Much like the American Indian Movement of the same period, the Alianza claimed that legitimate treaty rights had been violated and demanded compensation. Tijerina's analysis of the land-grant question appeared in a booklet that the Alianza published and distributed throughout the Southwest.[3] Tijerina based his arguments for the reclamation of lost Hispano lands on two documents, the *Recopilación de leyes de las Indias*, which had been the legal framework for the Spanish land grants prior to the nineteenth century, and the Treaty of Guadalupe Hidalgo. He contended that the United States had violated Articles VIII and IX of the treaty, which had guaranteed property and citizenship rights to Mexicans. Ultimately, Tijerina's claims were presented before the U.S. Supreme Court as a class action lawsuit in 1969. Denied a hearing two times in 1970, the case finally received a favorable recommendation, but it was not presented, probably because Tijerina lacked sufficient funding to pursue the issue.[4]

One of the little-known episodes in the Alianza's history was Tijerina's effort to forge an alliance with Mexican popular and governmental organizations.

Early in January 1964 Tijerina and his wife, Rosita, went to Mexico City to meet with Mexican officials. On January 9th he met with a labor leader, Lic. Javier Rojo Gómez, who was the secretary general of the Confederación Nacional Campesina. Tijerina reported that he felt encouraged and that the interview was a great success. On January 14th he met with a secretary who worked with the Relaciones Exteriores (foreign relations) where he left a memorandum for president Adolfo López Mateos. On January 29 he sent a telegram to Lic. Donato Miranda Fonseca, secretary to the president in the National Palace, asking for a meeting, and on February 4 he met with the secretary. Tijerina had a lengthy meeting where he explained the various violations and aggressions suffered by Mexicans in the United States since the Treaty of Guadalupe Hidalgo.

Back in New Mexico, Tijerina set to work to organize a caravan to Mexico City. While doing this he began a letter-writing campaign to remind both the U.S. and Mexican governments of their obligations under the treaty.

In July, Tijerina again went to Mexico with his wife. In Chihuahua he attended a student meeting to promote the upcoming caravan. While he was speaking he was arrested by the Mexican Judicial Police. He was released from jail after a number of strategic phone calls were placed to Mexico City and Washington, D.C. He continued his journey to Mexico City undaunted, making a map for the later caravan. In Mexico City he sent a letter to Luis Echeverría, the secretary of Gobernación, along with memoranda to the president, Adolfo López Mateos, informing them of the caravan's purpose. He received a "positive impression" that the caravan would be permitted to travel to Mexico. He visited the offices of all the political parties in Mexico City, the left as well as the right, explaining his position on the treaty and "pueblo olvidado": "We, the Mexicans in the United States, only want that all Mexico, in the name of the Treaty of Guadalupe, would receive us so that the United States would know of the dear brotherhood between the Mexicans of the South and of those north of the Rio Grande."[5] Tijerina's speeches were reported in the Mexican media and he even appeared before the national syndicate of publishers in Mexico City (Sindicato Nacional de Redactores de la Prensa), where he talked about the upcoming caravan.

Tijerina held a meeting of interested Mexican officials to discuss the caravan, emphasizing that the purpose was to seek Mexican support for Chicanos and their struggles in New Mexico. Mexican federal agents also attended. The next day Tijerina was detained by the police and questioned about his activities. Finally they decided to deport him with the threat that if he returned he would be put in prison for ten years. They took him to the airport and saw him off on the plane. Tijerina was convinced that he had been set up by the U.S. government. Back in New Mexico, with a heavy heart, Tijerina called off the caravan. Tijerina's activities in attempting to gain the support of the Mexican people for the plight of the Hispano villagers had threatened the Mexican government. It was possible that the U.S. government had influenced the deportation but ultimately the Mexican government was responsible. This episode put an end to the Alianza's dream of having the Mexican government act as an advocate within the United Nations.[6]

A few years later the legal and moral issues raised by Tijerina's Alianza movement influenced domestic politics. Senator Joseph Montoya of New Mexico introduced a bill in the U.S. Senate to create a Special Commission on Guadalupe Hidalgo Land Rights. Simultaneously Representative Manuel Luján (New Mexico) introduced a similar bill in the House. Montoya proposed that the federal government establish a temporary commission that would review violations of property rights guaranteed in the treaty and make recommendations to Congress and the president regarding restitution. One of the first tasks of the commission would be to "make a comprehensive study of the provisions of the Treaty of Guadalupe Hidalgo" to determine violations of the treaty. Senator Montoya, by no means a political ally of Reies Tijerina, adopted what seemed to be a radical plan of questioning established land tenures in his home state. He justified his measure as a means of rectifying past injustices: "If certain lands have been wrongfully taken from people, we must make amends."[7] Montoya's bill reflected the degree to which the long and bitter history of land-grant conflict in New Mexico had emerged as an issue for federal concern. Senator Montoya's bill died in the Insular and Interior Affairs Committee, as did a similar bill introduced the same year by Congressman Augustus Hawkins of California.

Hawkins proposed that Congress establish a Community Land Grant Act targeted specifically at the villages of New Mexico. Like Montoya, he envisioned the establishment of a commission that would hear petitions from members of villages whose community land grants had been lost through corruption or deceit. The commission was to have the power to "reconstitute the community land-grant" under the Laws of the Indies where it was consistent with the Constitution or state laws. Additionally the Hawkins Bill provided for 10 million dollars to finance the operations of the commission.

Unfortunately there are no records of the debate surrounding either Montoya's or Hawkin's bill in these committees. That these measures were defeated is not too surprising, because any federal investigation into land tenure in New Mexico would be bound to unsettle powerful commercial and speculative interests. Nevertheless congressional interest in investigating the violations of the treaty's provisions continued. Throughout the 1970s at least three bills were introduced. In 1977 Representative Henry B. González (Texas) introduced a resolution to create a special congressional committee

"to investigate the legal, political, and diplomatic status of lands which were subject to grants from the King of Spain and the Government of Mexico prior to the acquisition of the American Southwest as a result of the Treaty of Guadalupe Hidalgo." In 1979, Representative Ronald V. Dellums (California) introduced a similar proposal, but a House committee rejected it. Finally, in 1979, as a result of lobbying by Reies Tijerina, the New Mexico legislature instructed its representatives to introduce legislation to establish a board of review to investigate the theft of communal lands in northern New Mexico.[8] This move, like others before it, was killed by conservative interests in Congress.

The motivation for the continued legislative attempts to rectify the land-grant situation in New Mexico came primarily from increased public awareness and pressure originating from a revitalized Alianza movement. Again, the public records are silent on the debates surrounding these measures, because each was squashed without a lengthy hearing.

THE URBAN CHICANO MOVEMENT

Knowledge of the treaty and its violations was widespread among New Mexicans. Collectively they had been fighting for a return of their pueblo lands for more than a century. On the other hand millions of urban Chicanos—sons and daughters of Mexican immigrants who had entered the United States after 1910—had yet to be educated about the treaty. In the 1960s and 1970s this process took place in informal meetings, discussions, and rallies.

In the spring of 1968, urban and rural Mexican American leaders found a common ground for dialog. Rudolfo "Corky" Gonzales, leader and organizer of the Denver Crusade for Justice, joined forces with Reies Tijerina to participate in the Poor People's March on Washington, D.C. Together with other urban leaders they issued a joint statement, entitled *We Demand*, listing the needs of Mexican Americans throughout the nation. These included bilingual education, adequate housing, job development, more sensitive law enforcement, economic opportunities, and agricultural reforms. The demand for agricultural reforms, inspired by Tijerina's struggle in New Mexico, called not only for a return of lands stolen from the pueblos in violation of the treaty, but also for "compensation for taxes, legal costs, etc., which pueblo heirs spent trying to save their land."[9]

The Treaty of Guadalupe Hidalgo and its implications became a topic of discussion at the first Annual Youth Conference in Denver, Colorado, which was organized by Gonzales in 1969. Knowledge of treaty violations became a driving force behind the final statement of the conference in "El Plan Espiritual de Aztlán," a document of Chicano solidarity and a declaration of independence. During the 1970s, surveys and critiques of the treaty, and especially of Articles VIII and IX, began to appear in anthologies and books being published to satisfy the demand for more printed materials dealing with Chicanos. One of the most popular of these was Armando Rendón's *Chicano Manifesto*. In the section of the book dealing with the treaty, Rendón summarized his view of the importance of the treaty: "The Treaty of Guadalupe Hidalgo is the most important document concerning Mexican Americans that exists."[10] The terms and spirit of the treaty, he said, had been systematically violated by the U.S. government. Rendón called for Chicanos to become aware of the "exact processes by which the Treaty of Guadalupe Hidalgo was made meaningless over the past century and a half." He had in mind a detailed documentary case that could be made against the federal government so that some kind of compensation could be exacted. He hinted that Chicanos could seek, as the American Indian tribes had, monetary settlements or even a return of territory to Mexico.[11] The probability that the latter would occur was nil, but the prospect of a monetary settlement did not seem wholly impossible, given the political atmosphere of the time. For many militants of the 1970s the treaty legitimized their demands for social and economic justice and provided a cause for radical action.

THE BROWN BERETS' OCCUPATION OF CATALINA ISLAND

The same year that Rendón's *Chicano Manifesto* appeared, the most dramatic attempt to publicize the importance of the treaty took place. In September 1972 the Brown Berets in California began a twenty-four-day occupation of Santa Catalina Island, claiming that it had never been included in the original treaty and thus was still part of Mexico.

The Brown Berets were founded in 1967 by David Sánchez, a former chairman of the Los Angeles Mayor's Youth Council. Eventually the Berets claimed five thousand members nationwide. The goal of the Berets

was to fulfill the ideals articulated in "El Plan Espiritual de Aztlán," that is to control or at least have a voice in the policies of major institutions in the barrio that affected Chicanos: the schools, police, welfare offices, and the immigration service. As an action-oriented militant organization, the Berets participated in and helped organize most of the major landmarks of the Chicano movement: high-school "blowouts" (walkouts) and moratorium marches in East Los Angeles, La Marcha and Caravana de la Reconquista, as well as other local actions in southern California designed to raise public awareness of oppression and racism.[12]

A particular interpretation of the meaning of the Treaty of Guadalupe Hidalgo influenced the Brown Berets' decision to stage a symbolic occupation of Santa Catalina Island. None of the nine channel islands off the coast of southern California had been mentioned in the treaty as part of the territory ceded to the United States in 1848. According to popular beliefs in Mexico and in many U.S. barrios, the islands remained part of Mexico until the 1870s, when Benito Juárez, then president of Mexico, leased Catalina Island to Americans. William Wrigley, Jr., of the chewing-gum empire, eventually acquired the ninety-nine-year lease on the property, which expired in 1970. The true history of Catalina Island's title contradicted this folk history. On July 4, 1846, Pio Pico, the last Mexican governor of California granted the island of Catalina to Tomás Robbins. Robbins sold the island to José María Covarrubias of Santa Bárbara in 1850, and Covarrubias sold it to Albert Roshard of San Francisco in 1853. Thereafter the title to the island is traceable up to Mr. Wrigley's purchase in 1919.[13]

Although the claim that Catalina had been leased from Mexico had no historical basis, the story reflected a need to keep alive the issue of the illegal seizure of community lands. The legend also reflected a real ambiguity in the treaty regarding the status of the offshore islands. This vagueness had been a source of sporadic public discussion in the 1950s and 1960s.[14]

Some legal experts in Mexico were prepared to argue that the island could be reclaimed by Mexico. A partial basis for argument was that Governor Pico's grant of the island was made after the declaration of war and hence was considered invalid by both the U.S. and the Mexican governments.[15] Late in the nineteenth century the Mexican government had considered making the ownership of the islands an international issue. In 1894 the United States asserted control over Clipperton Island in the Pacific Ocean (called Medanos or La Pasión by Mexico), a small island some thousand miles off the coast of southern Mexico. Mexican newspapers claimed that this island was rightfully Mexico's and that the Catalina Islands should be reclaimed by the Mexican government in retaliation. The issue became an item for official private correspondence but soon died for lack of presidential support.[16]

The Brown Berets did not seriously believe that they could regain Catalina for Mexico. The real purpose of the occupation was to provide a forum for discussion of the problems confronting Mexican Americans arising from their colonized status.

After several weeks of planning at a base near Lancaster, California, the offensive against the island, code named Tecolote, was ready. A primary concern was secrecy. From previous scouting expeditions the Berets knew that there was a Mexican barrio of about four hundred persons on the island. The leaders flew to Catalina and the rest of the contingent took the boat and acted as tourists. On August 30th the Berets assembled twenty-five men and one woman at the Waikiki Motel on Catalina. From there, they rented a jeep, and drove to the top of the hill above the town of Avalon Harbor. At nine o'clock the next morning the citizens of the small town awoke to see a huge Mexican flag flying from the hilltop. Campo Tecolote had been established.[17] The Beret contingent carried no arms but stood in formation, dressed in military fashion. At first some residents, recalling folktales about the controversial title to the islands thought they had been invaded by the Mexican army.[18]

The mayor of Avalon, Raymond Rydell, a former vicechancellor of the California State College system, had dealt with student militants during the 1960s. He encouraged the sheriff's department to use a low-key approach to the Beret encampment and to leave them alone as long as they caused no trouble. The vice-president of the Santa Catalina Island Company was a Mexican American named Renton. He too advised the sheriffs to leave the Berets alone; and to show his good will he sent the Beret contingent cold drinks and box lunches. David Sánchez, the Beret leader, issued a press release, which read in part: "As gentlemen who may try to understand other gentlemen, how about a peaceful resolution? . . . We have begun an occupation plan, which is by means of peaceful occupation only. By this plan, we wish to bring you the true plight of the Chicano, and the problems of the people of Mexican descent living in the United States."[19]

The occupation lasted twenty-four days. During that time the Brown Beret camp became something of a tourist attraction. The small Mexican-American population of the island helped provide food and drink for the Chicano demonstrators. Local restaurateur Mike Budd gave them a free meal at his restaurant. As the occupation stretched into weeks, the Berets had a chance to talk to some of the island's Chicano residents. Their message was that the United States was illegally occupying not just Catalina but all of the American Southwest. Mexican Americans were a colonized people, they said, victims of an unjust war of aggression. The occupation of Catalina ended peacefully on September 23, when the city council decided to enforce a local camping ordinance and threatened jail unless the Berets abandoned their campground. The Berets left, vowing to return to occupy other islands at some future date and to engage in more legal research. As it turned out, however, the Catalina occupation was the last organized action of the Brown Berets. A few weeks later their leader, David Sánchez, citing the pervasive presence of police informants within the organization, announced that the Brown Berets had been disbanded.[20]

The Treaty of Guadalupe Hidalgo provided a basis for legitimizing the occupation of Catalina Island, both for the presentation of grievances and the dramatization of *la causa.* In comparison to the Alianza's occupation of Kit Carson National Forest and the shootout at Tierra Amarilla, Catalina Island was a relatively minor incident. Nevertheless, the Santa Catalina occupation demonstrated the degree to which some were willing to take militant action based on the historical violations of the Treaty of Guadalupe Hidalgo.

INTERPRETATION BY CHICANO INTELLIGENCIA

American Indians and Mexican Americans are the only segments of U.S. society that have kept alive the issues raised by the Treaty of Guadalupe Hidalgo. Because of the popular movements of the 1960s and 1970s as well as the institutionalization of Chicano Studies classes in major universities, larger numbers of Mexican Americans have been introduced to the treaty and its significance. More often than not, however, this familiarity did not go beyond a belief that the treaty guaranteed certain rights for Mexican Americans and that these rights had been violated.

Only a few scholars writing about Chicano history have attempted to go beyond this generalized view of the implications of the treaty. Perhaps the most detailed, scholarly, and realistic appraisal of the meaning of the treaty for human rights appeared in 1978 as a doctoral dissertation by Fernando Chacón Gómez. Before Gómez, no one had analyzed how the treaty influenced subsequent court cases involving Mexican Americans. This work was a conscious blending of scholarly training and Chicano activism.

Gómez's main argument was that despite decades of "invisibility" and general neglect, the Treaty of Guadalupe Hidalgo had real legal implications for the present. He wanted to explore the legal history of the treaty after 1848 to determine "to what extent it could be used to compel enforcement of contemporary civil rights." He analyzed the cultural and historical background of the legal battles waged in the nineteenth and early twentieth centuries to secure property and civil rights for former Mexican citizens. On a case-by-case basis he pointed to the ethnocentric and racist basis of the arguments and decisions. Manifest Destiny, he concluded, had found its way into the courtroom. This was especially true in New Mexico where, because of the judge's ignorance of local tradition, "the century-old concept of flexibility of the common law may indeed have been 'bastardized.'" Elsewhere in the United States, judges relied on local precedent in making decisions. Not so in New Mexico. Thus, although the treaty was a "rights conferring document," in the courts it remained a dead letter. Chacón Gómez concluded that the most viable avenues for redress were largely in the international arena because the Supreme Court had consistently ruled against interpretations of the treaty that would protect Mexican-American rights. A legal attack on the injustices and inequalities confronted by people of Mexican origin, he thought, could best be pursued in such international forums as the United Nations and the World Court.[21] This approach is currently being followed by a handful of activists.

INTERNATIONALIZATION OF THE TREATY

Since World War II the plight of the Mexican Americans within the United States as been presented before various international forums, primarily agencies of the United Nations concerned with human rights. The Treaty of Guadalupe Hidalgo has figured prominently in these formal presentations; indeed the treaty has provided the legal rationale for discussing Mexican American rights within international bodies.

The earliest attempt to use an international forum to redress wrongs vis à vis Mexican Americans was by

the American Committee for the Protection of the Foreign Born in 1959. The committee was a leftist organization that split from the American Civil Liberties Union in 1942. Carey McWilliams, a progressive newspaper reporter, editor, author, and activist was one of its first directors during the 1940s. In the 1950s the committee fell onto the U.S. attorney general's list of subversive, communist infiltrated organizations, and committee members were questioned by the House Un-American Activities Committee in the early 1960s. In 1959 the American Committee for Protection of the Foreign Born submitted a petition to the United Nations entitled "Our Badge of Infamy: A Petition to the United Nations on the Treatment of Mexican Immigrants."[22] The petition was signed by more than sixty individuals, most of them Anglo-American professionals. They charged that the United States had violated provisions of the Universal Declaration of Human Rights, specifically Articles II, III, IV, VII, IX, XV, XXII, and XXV. In their opening statement they stated that U.S. government committees and agencies had investigated the plight of the Mexican immigrant in the United States but no change had come about. "We feel that the United Nations should consider this problem only because repeated attempts over the years by agencies of the United States government and public and private organizations have failed to overcome the serious deprivation of the human rights of the Mexican immigrants living in the United States."[23]

The petition was not limited to defending Mexican immigrants; it also dealt with the violations of the Treaty of Guadalupe Hidalgo affecting the native-born Mexican Americans. "While rights to property, especially land, were safeguarded by the provisions of the Treaty of Guadalupe Hidalgo, in practice Mexicans and Mexican Americans were cheated of most of their properties in a short while."[24] The main orientation of the petition was to present concrete evidence, in the form of historical examples, of how the human rights of Mexicans in the United States had been violated. Instances of mistreatment and murder of bracero workers were documented to show violations of Article III of the U.N. declaration guaranteeing freedoms regardless of race. Cases of wage discrimination were related to violation of Article IV, which forbade slavery and involuntary servitude. The operations of the Immigration and Naturalization Service during Operation Wetback (a repatriation program of 1954) were presented as violations of Article IX, which provided for equal protection under the law.

The significance of the committee's petition was that it was the first attempt to go beyond the domestic system to seek redress under international law. It was over twenty years before another organization attempted to internationalize the issues raised by the treaty.

During the 1980s various Native American groups discovered the Treaty of Guadalupe Hidalgo and began to forge alliances with Mexican American organizations and individuals. In July 1980, at the Sixth Annual Conference of the International Indian Treaty Council (IITC) meeting at Fort Belnap, Montana, a resolution was introduced by native delegates to support the Treaty of Guadalupe Hidalgo and Mexican-American rights to selfdetermination.[25] The International Indian Treaty Council was a San Francisco-based organization dedicated to working for the rights of native peoples throughout the Western Hemisphere. Since 1977 it had been recognized by the United Nations as a Non-Government Organization (N.G.O.) and had traveled numerous times to Geneva to present petitions and interventions on behalf of Indian people. In 1981 the IITC introduced the Treaty of Guadalupe Hidalgo as one of the North American treaties that affected Indian peoples before the International Conference of Non-Government Organizations concerning Indigenous Populations and Land. Several U.S. Indian tribes considered the treaty an important part of their claims for redress. The Hopi people, for example, presented a statement at a 1981 Geneva Conference where they cited Article IX and XI of the treaty to support their opposition to the relocation of the Navajo (Dineh) and Hopi elders from their ancestral lands near Big Mountain, Arizona.[26]

According to Hopi prophecy, "most important information" bearing on the fate of their nation would be found at the bottom of a "high stack of papers." The elders reported that they had found this "important information"—Disturnell's 1847 map, which had been appended to the Treaty of Guadalupe Hidalgo. That map contained a notation, "Los Moquis [Hopis] has conservado su independencia desde el año 1680." The meaning of this notation on the treaty map was clear: the Hopis had not been considered subjugated by the Spanish; they were independent and sovereign. In the words of the elders, "From that time forward, the power of the Hopi and our right to sovereign independence should never have been questioned."[27] The 1981 Hopi statement as delivered to the United Nations went on to assert that their rights as Mexican citizens under Article VIII of the treaty had been violated by the U.S.

courts and that their religious rights under Article IX had not been protected.

Other Indians also considered the Treaty of Guadalupe Hidalgo as bearing on their claims for compensation. The Tohono O'odham, or Papago, for example, have interpreted the treaty as bearing on their desire to reclaim lands.

The IITC continued to be active in bringing the Treaty of Guadalupe Hidalgo before international bodies. In June 1982 the position of the Chicano Caucus regarding the treaty at the IITC annual conference was presented before the General Assembly, and in September of that year Chicanos presented their case before the First American Indian International Tribunal held at D-Q University near Sacramento, California. In 1984, the IITC representatives presented the Chicano and Indian positions on the treaty before the 40th session of the U.N. Commission on Human Rights meeting in Geneva, Switzerland, and in 1985 the Treaty Council presented a document outlining the Chicano situation before a U.N. Working Group on Indigenous Populations at Geneva.

Working with the IITC during these years was a small group of Chicano and Mexican-American activists who saw a community of interest. For years the Chicano movement leaders had attempted to educate Mexican Americans regarding their indigenous roots. Almost every barrio had its contingent of nativists who strongly identified with and attempted to preserve Mexican and Southwestern Indian traditions through song, dance, paintings, and rituals. For them the spiritual lessons of the Indian peoples were all important. One statement of this position during these years was an anonymous pamphlet entitled "Aztlán vs. the United States." It argued that Chicanos in the United States were Indians by blood as well as heritage; they had suffered the same second class treatment as Indians. Aztlán, the Aztec name for their homeland, was a spiritual and biological nation that included Indians as well as Chicanos. "This is the nation of RAZA INDIGENA, and the INDIAN NATIONS, or in other words nosotros los indios de Aztlán."[28]

In the 1980s Chicano intellectuals also began to conceptualize the Treaty of Guadalupe Hidalgo in terms of its potential for mobilizing the declining activism of *el movimiento.* Armando Rendón, the noted author of *Chicano Manifesto*, wrote an essay in 1982 arguing that "the Treaty of Guadalupe Hidalgo is in fact an international human rights document, extending guarantees through the decades which have not been asserted on an international level."[29] He recommended that Chicanos seek redress in forums such as the International American Commission on Human Rights and the Inter-American Court of Human Rights. Rendón argued that the development of human rights law since the 1960s had made the treaty a viable tool for seeking justice.

Rendón's perspective found elaboration and development in the writings of Roberto Barragán, a young undergraduate at Princeton who consulted with Rendón in writing his senior thesis in the Politics Department.[30] In a lengthy, 200-page thesis Barragán argued that in light of the pronouncements of various international bodies, the treaty conferred on Chicanos particular international human rights. "Rights guaranteed by the Constitution as regards Chicanos are no longer solely of domestic character. As they are additionally protected by the Treaty, they are now of international character. As such they are under the jurisdiction of various Inter American forums."[31] Barragán's view was that the effort to protect the human rights of Mexican Americans under the treaty should be part of a three-pronged project aimed toward self-determination. The organized effort to internationalize the treaty would be known as the Treaty of Guadalupe Hidalgo Project that would integrate the various Chicano communities into an organization that would use international forums to support Chicano self determination. Among his many proposals was one that this organization could request that member states of the Organization of American States ask for an advisory opinion on the Treaty of Guadalupe Hidalgo and the status of the land grants. He also opined that the language of Article IX (relating to citizenship) could be construed to apply to Mexican immigrants in the Southwest. Barragán's thesis found a small audience because it was not published but only circulated among interested parties. It did, however, become part of the archive of contemporary thought about the international aspects of the treaty.

Recent events have shown a maturation of Indian-Chicano efforts to internationalize the issues raised by the treaty. In 1986 the IITC hosted the first National Encuentro on the Treaty of Guadalupe Hidalgo at Flagstaff, Arizona. During the three day meeting, which was attended by over 100 representatives of Indian tribes and Chicano organizations, commitments emerged that led to subsequent planning meetings the next year in Denver, Colorado, and Jemez Springs, New Mexico. The Flagstaff Encuentro also resulted in a commitment to send a delegation of Chicano observers with the IITC delegates to the Geneva U.N. Commission on Human Rights meeting in early 1987.

This was a major step in introducing a small group of Mexican Americans to international politics. For the first time a delegation of Chicano delegates spoke before a U.N. body about the Treaty of Guadalupe and contemporary problems confronting Chicanos. The IITC allowed a Chicano delegate to present an intervention before the commission. It read in part:

> That same Treaty of Guadalupe Hidalgo, in which Mexico tried to guarantee human rights to indigenous people, is continually being violated by injustices toward the Chicano indigenous people by the United States. These people have suffered since the military conquest of their indigenous land of AZTLAN. The treaty right to maintain their language and culture have been denied to Chicanos: their human rights and dignity have been subverted through racism, intended to undermine the cultural ethnicity of indigenous people.[32]

The Chicano delegates presenting formal documents also held press conferences with representatives of the media of Mexico, Brazil, Argentina, and various European nations, where they presented Chicano perspectives on the treaty and issues affecting Mexican Americans. At Geneva, the representatives learned about diplomatic protocol and lobbying to expand their views regarding the role of Mexican Americans within the world community.[33]

The first national attempt to form an organization that would regularize Chicano participation within international forums took place in Santa Cruz, California, on October 10–12, 1987. This meeting brought together international lawyers with Chicano community activists and tribal representatives. The treaty became a point of organizing a larger number of people than had previously participated. Commissions on land grants, international law, and cultural violations were established. As a result of this endeavor further Encuentros were planned to solidify the directions that were established.

The Treaty of Guadalupe Hidalgo became a focal point for claims of social and economic justice during the activist 1960s and 1970s through militant action, popular books, and scholarly studies. An important legacy of the Chicano movement is its fostering of a particular historical awareness: the Southwest is really "occupied Mexico," and Mexican Americans and Indians are a "colonized people" whose rights have been violated despite the guarantees of the treaty. In the

1980s, attempts to use the Treaty of Guadalupe Hidalgo to reach international audiences has increased, primarily through the organizing energies of the International Indian Treaty Council. The result has been that the Chicano movement has gained new international dimensions.

Endnotes

1. Patricia Bell Blawis, *Tijerina and the Land Grants* (New York: International Publishers, 1970), p. 37; see also Richard Gardner, *Grito!: Reies Tijerina and the New Mexican Land Grant Wars of 1967* (New York: Harper & Row, 1970), and Peter Nabokov, *Tijerina and the Courthouse Raid* (Albuquerque: University of New Mexico Press, 1969). For Tijerina's own account of the trip and the Alianza, see Reies Tijerina, *Mi lucha por tierra* (Mexico: Fondo de Cultura Económica, 1978).

2. Richard Gardner, p. 96.

3. Reies Tijerina, *The Spanish Land Grant Question Examined* (Albuquerque: Alianza Federal, 1966).

4. See *Tijerina et al. vs. U.S.* 396 U.S. 843; 396 U.S. 990; and 396 U.S. 922.

5. Tijerina, *Mi Lucha*, p. 106.

6. Ibid., pp. 104–110.

7. See Senate Bill 68 and House Resolution 3595 (need exact citation); *Congressional Record,* vol. 21, pt. 1, January 15, 1975, pp. 321–22.

8. The summaries of these bills were provided by the Library of Congress as follows: HR2207, 94th Congress 1/28/75; HRES 585, 95th Congress 5/18/77; HRES 16, 96th Congress 1/15/79; *Albuquerque Journal,* March 16, 1979, 8:6.

9. "We Demand," in Luis Valdez and Stan Steiner, eds., *Aztlán: An Anthology of Mexican American Literature* (New York: Alfred A. Knopf, 1972), p. 220.

10. Armando Rendón, *Chicano Manifesto* (New York: Macmillan Publishing Co., 1972), p. 81.

11. Ibid., pp. 84–85.

12. María Blanco, "A Brief History About the Brown Beret National Organization," unpublished ms., November 10, 1975, San Diego State University, Love Library, pp. 4–6.

13. Adelaide Lefert Daron, *The Ranch That Was Robbins': Santa Catalina Island, California* (Los Angeles: Arthur Clark Co., 1963), ch. 6.

14. See J. N. Bowman, "California's Off-Shore Islands," *Pacific Historical Review* 31, No. 3 (August 1962): 291–300.

15. In Mexico, J. Antonio Rosete Murgía, produced a master's thesis arguing that the islands were still part of Mexico. It is entitled "El Tratado de Guadalupe y el problema de las islas Catalina" (Master's thesis, UNAM, 1957). Rosete Murgía recommended that Mexico reopen negotiations over the status of the Catalina islands under Article 21 of the Treaty of Guadalupe Hidalgo. See *Los Angeles Times,* August 31, 1972, for details of the initial occupation.

16. Luis Zorrilla, *Historia de las relaciones entre México y los Estados Unidos de América, 1800–1958*, vol. 2. (México: Editorial Porrúa, 1977), P. 85.

17. David Sánchez, *Expedition Through Aztlán* (La Puente: Perspectiva Publications, 1978), p. 174. Sánchez provides a detailed account of the invasion in this book.

18. *Los Angeles Times,* August 31, 1972, 1, 1: 2.

19. Sánchez, pp. 180–81; *Los Angeles Times,* September 2, I, 1: 5; *Los Angeles Times,* August 31, 1972, loc. cit.

20. *Los Angeles Times,* September 23, 1972, II, 1:2.

21. Fernando Chacón Gómez, "The Intended and Actual Effects of Article VIII of the Treaty of Guadalupe Hidalgo: Mexican Treaty Rights Under International and Domestic Law," (Ph.D. diss., University of Michigan, 1977), p. 197.

22. For a history of the American Committee for the Protection of the Foreign Born, see Louise Pettibone Smith, *Torch of Liberty: Twenty-Five Years in the Life of the Foreign Born in the U.S.A.* (New York: Dwight-King Publishers, 1959); American Committee for the Protection of the Foreign Born, "Our Badge of Infamy: A Petition to the United Nations on the Treatment of Mexican Immigrants," (New York: American Committee for Protection of Foreign Born, 1959).

23. Ibid., p. 5.

24. Ibid., p. 10.

25. International Indian Treaty Council, "Plans for Treaty of Gudalupe Hidalgo Conference," 1986, Mimeograph.

26. IITC, "General Working Paper," 1986, Hopi Nation, "The Treaty of Guadalupe Hidalgo: A Native American Perspective," 1981, Mimeograph. The Indians were being relocated following an agreement that the Bureau of Indian Affairs had arranged with opposing factions with the two tribes.

27. Ibid., p. 2.

28. "Aztlán vs. the United States," 198?, Mimeograph.

29. Armando B. Rendón, "The Treaty of Guadalupe Hidalgo and its Modern Implications for the Protection of the Human Rights of Mexican Americans," 1982, p. 27, Mimeograph.

30. Roberto E. Barragán, "The Treaty of Guadalupe Hidalgo and the American Convention on Human Rights: A Political Analysis for Chicano Self Determination," Senior thesis, Politics Department, Princeton University, 1984. Barragán's thesis and Rendon's essays have

been circulated by the Tonantzin Land Institute in New Mexico as part of the Treaty of Guadalupe Hidalgo Project.

31. Ibid., p. 44.
32. International Indian Treaty Council, "Question of Violation of Human Rights or Fundamental Freedoms in Any Part of the World," Agenda Item 12, Commission on Human Rights, 43 Session, Geneva, Switzerland.
33. Ron Sandoval, "Diary," 1987, Mimeograph. Most of the xerox materials relating to the IITC and the treaty are available through the Tonatzin Land Institute, 1504 Bridge Blvd., Albuquerque, New Mexico.

El Paso Salt War: Mob Action or Political Struggle?

Mary Romero

The border area between the United States and Mexico plays an important role in popular culture. Beginning in pulp magazines and western novels, later thundering across the silver screen, the larger than life images of heroic Texans and sneaky Mexicans have played out a distorted view of American history as manifest destiny. In films like "The Alamo" and "Red River," we learn how John Wayne brought law and order to the border, subduing the Indians and pacifying the Mexicans. Only recently has the other side of the story been considered. Native American and Chicano historians have begun the laborious process of uncovering what happened from the point of view of those who were conquered. Recent films like "Little Big Man" and "The Ballad of Gregorio Cortez" have dared to suggest to the Anglo-American[1] population that a different view is possible. This essay examines a littleknown but revealing conflict between the Spanishspeaking population near El Paso, Texas and the Anglo-Americans who were seeking to move into the area.

In 1877 there were 12,000 persons living along the Rio Grande near El Paso. All but eighty were of Mexican descent. San Elizario (twenty five miles south of El Paso) had a population of 2,000 of whom only 12 to 15 were Anglo-Americans.[2] Although the Mexican population constituted the numerical majority, Anglos controlled the political positions and the majority of the wealth. Most people along the border were engaged in subsistence agriculture. Large scale cattle ranching was not yet profitable because of Indian raids and the difficulty of transporting livestock to distant markets. Salt was one of the few commodities which could be obtained locally and traded to produce supplementary income.

As long as anyone could remember there had been cattle trails to the salt licks at Guadalupe Lakes, but prior to 1824, there was no evidence of wagon tracks. The Guadalupe Lakes became an important source of salt after access to the San Andrés saline lakes, a hundred miles north of El Paso, was ended by the claim of private ownership by Anglo entrepreneurs. The *salineros* turned to the Guadalupe salt deposits as an alternative site. In 1863, a seventy-two mile road to the salt lakes was built as a cooperative undertaking by Mexicans from both sides of the border.[3]

The two cultures, Mexicano and Anglo-American, held diametrically opposed concepts of property. Prior to 1848, the area was under Spanish law. The *pueblo* or community used the land adjacent to it freely; the common land was held in trust while the *alcalde* (mayor) portioned out to each man as much land and river water as needed for his family use. Natural resources were similarly held in common; they belonged to the community and were not owned privately.[4] This crucial difference in land usage and ownership explains how

El Paso Salt War: Mob Action or Political Struggle?" by Mary Romero. Taken from *Aztlán*, Vol. 16. No. 1–2, 1985. Reprinted by permission.

Anglo developers were able to appropriate the salt beds. Under American law, they were unclaimed lands, available to anyone who filed a proper deed.

In 1877, Charles Howard, a Missouri lawyer and Texas District Judge, filed deeds and claims of ownership to the Guadalupe Salt Lakes in El Paso County. Previously the salt deposits had been communal property used by the Mexican population on both sides of the border. Howard's claim was disputed by the local population who organized to fight what they saw as a land grab and a threat to their economic survival. Although the movement was issue-oriented and lacked a specific ideology, Mexican citizens and Mexican Americans armed themselves and fought against the Texas Rangers. In the events which came to be called the El Paso Salt War, Howard was killed as were several Rangers and Mexicanos living in the border region. The event was more an insurrection or peasant revolt then a "riot" as some historians have portrayed it.

The Salt War became the object of a congressional investigation which yielded both a majority and a minority report on the causes of the disturbances. Major Jones, the governor's appointee to the committee, filed the Minority Report disputing points made by the four-member Congressional board that highly criticized the action of the Texas Rangers and local authorities. Both reports stressed cultural distinctions of land usage; however, the minority report presented the cultural interpretations of the local Mexican community as evidence of their anti-American ideology. Furthermore, the minority report analyzed the incident as an international affair in which Mexican citizens attacked the Texas Rangers and U.S. citizens. The Majority Report recommended that the United States government establish a permanent 200-man garrison to prevent further trouble over the salt beds and the usage of Rio Grande water for irrigation purposes. Fort Bliss was thus established on January 1, 1878 and still "protects" the Rio Grande Valley.

The two major histories of the El Paso Salt War have been written by Anglo-American historians. Walter Prescott Webb and C.L. Sonnichsen characterized the incident as a mob action instigated by local politicians against Charles Howard and the Texas Rangers. Both historians interpreted the event as stemming from the isolation of the region and cultural differences separating the participants. Webb emphasized that "outside agitators" were responsible for the trouble and used the terms "mob" and "riot" to describe the event. He recognized the crucial economic importance of the salt,

yet failed to understand that the private appropriation of the salt lakes was the primary cause of the event. Sonnichsen pointed out "the greed and jealousy of the Americans."[5] He disputed Webb's view that the Spanish-speaking population was "docile and stupid," by drawing attention to the different concepts of property held by the two cultures. Both historians speculated on cultural values as causing a misinterpretation of events resulting in escalation of violence.

Contemporary Chicano writers[6] have referred to the Salt War as the people's revolt rather than a mob action. They analyze the event within the context of an economy in the process of transformation from feudalism (based on common ownership of certain lands and resources) to capitalism (based on private ownership of all means of production). This perspective shifts the focus from cultural misunderstanding to structural and economic differences leading to conflict. What has been lacking in the scholarly analysis thus far is an assessment of the Mexican community's interpretation of conditions leading to the conflict. This essay will reconstruct the Mexican community's understanding and political intentions in the event by comparing testimonies made by members of the community to the testimonies of Anglos. It will also consider the relationship between the Mexican community and local politicians, and investigate the treatment of U.S. citizenship by local officials and the Mexican-American population along the border.

DESCRIPTION OF THE EVENT

In the early 1800's, El Paso's economy was mostly subsistence agriculture. Cattle ranching was unprofitable because of Indian raids and the distance to market. Mexicans from both sides of the border needed salt for their personal use. Furthermore, salt was a commodity which could be bartered in the interior of Mexico. Therefore, salt selling was an essential element of El Paso's commerce.[7] The salt lake road was completed in 1863; attempts to appropriate the lake as private property began almost immediately. In 1866, Sam Maverick of San Antonio made the first private claim to portions of the Guadalupe Lakes. Maverick's claim marked the first occasion in which a fee or duty was charged for obtaining salt. Local citizens complained about the private benefit Maverick reaped from the wagon road they had built. Mexicans on both sides of the border responded by ceasing to take salt. When they realized that Maverick claimed only a portion of the salt beds, the people began to mine salt from areas not privately owned.

Problems arose again when S.J. Fountain and W.W. Mills joined to form a "Salt Ring" to acquire possession of the salt beds in order to monopolize the salt and "collect a revenue upon each bushel or *fanega* that was taken away."[8] The founders of the Salt Ring were prominent Anglo developers and major figures in the El Paso County Company. The Salt Ring's first attempt to claim the area failed because their certificate, "known as the Jett certificate, proved defective and the company fell into two factions which carried the Salt Lakes into El Paso County Politics."[9] Sonnichsen relates the split between Mills and Fountain to divisions within the Republican party: "Fountain was a strong supporter of Radical Republicanism and Mills was a conservative."[10] Mills continued to represent the El Paso Salt Ring. Fountain led the opposition, later called the Anti-Salt Ring, whose goal became to secure the land for the people of El Paso.

In 1870, Fountain was elected state senator. His first order of business was an attempt to push a bill through the Legislature.

> calling for the relinquishment of the County of El Paso, for the use of her citizens forever, all right, title and interest of the State of Texas in and to the unlocated portion of the Guadalupe Salt Lake in El Paso County.[11]

However, a petition containing four hundred signatures against any legislation on the salt question was presented to the Texas Senate, and Fountain withdrew his bill. Apparently, disapproval was based on the desire of the local community to keep the salt beds open to Mexicans who lived on the other side of the border.

In 1872, the split in the Republican party provided Charles H. Howard, the lawyer from Missouri, the opportunity he needed to move into El Paso politics. After forming an alliance with Luis Cardis, a local stage contractor and politician, Howard campaigned for the Mexican vote and was elected to the position of county judge in 1875. Edmund Stine, a local official, proved this description of Cardis and Howard:

> both were alike ambitious, and alike unscrupulous. They worked together very harmoniously for awhile, and profited by their partnership, for, while one became district judge, the other was sent to the legislature and constitutional convention.[12]

The relationship prospered from 1872 to 1875, and then turned into a bitter feud with repeated threats of violence.

The situation was aggravated when Howard placed all the salt beds under his father-in-law's name, Zimpleman, and enforced an immediate halt to persons entering the area. When an attempt was made to collect fees for the salt removed, only three persons signed contracts with Howard. Juan Armendáriz later testified to the terms:

> Judge Howard authorized me to pay for hauling salt from the salines at the rate of $1.25 per fanega. I sold the salt after it was hauled here at $1.75 and $2 per *fanega*.[13]

Sonnichsen makes clear the seriousness of Howard's actions on the local economy:

> He might as well have told the Mexicans that he intended to sell air at so much a breath. The salt was all that stood between some of them and starvation. The river had been dry for a month; the corn drying; the people were desperate; and now the little they could pick up by hauling salt was about to be taken away from them.[14]

Angrily, the Mexican people questioned the legality of the claim. Padre Ramón Ortiz, from the parish of Paso Del Norte, testified that the Spanish government had established communal usage of the land and its resources in 1656 and the law was upheld by the Mexican authorities. The Treaty of Guadalupe Hidalgo was intended to preserve Mexican American citizens' land rights. But, after the Mexican American War, the new American citizens were unable to legitimize the same rights and privileges surrounding communal resources granted to them under Spain and Mexico. This was partly because U.S. courts did not recognize communal property, and partly because the United States delayed the demarcation of the U.S./Mexico border. The situation was further complicated by the theft of the titles of property from the El Paso and Mexican archives during the Doniphan expeditions.[15]

Local authorities responded by requesting the *salineros* to pay Howard; later, if Howard's claim was found to be illegal, their money would be returned. On September 29th, José María Juárez and Macedonio Gándara were arrested for having threatened to enter the area for salt. Judge García dismissed the case against Gándara due to lack of evidence; however, Juárez was placed under a peace bond of $200 and incarcerated for making an outburst in the courtroom.[16] Several hundred Mexicans from San Elizario and Ysleta rallied at the jail and freed Juárez. Later they held a mass meeting demanding their rights. Led by Chico Barela and León Granillo of San Elizario, they marched to Judge García's home and demanded a warrant for Howard's arrest on the basis that "it is the will of the people that he should go to jail."[17] While this argument had precedence in the Spanish legal system, the judge refused to issue the warrant. Judge García and his older brother, Porfirio García (the Justice of the Peace), were subjected to a "citizen's arrest." Later Howard and his agent, McBride, were arrested along with Sheriff Kerber. All were held prisoner for three days except Kerber, who escaped.

Padre Bourgard, the parish priest of San Elizario, and Cardis worked out a plan for the prisoner's release in which Judge García and the justice of the peace were forced to resign from public office. The terms agreed upon for Howard's release were that he:

1. relinquish all claims to the salt lakes;
2. assign claims to the people;
3. set up a $12,000 bond insuring that he would never return to the county;
4. agree not to prosecute persons involved in this incident;[18] and
5. confess to the unjust and inproper prosecution of Juárez and Gándara.[19]

In Mills' account of the event, he noted that the arrest and trial by "the people" were no more a lawless act "than defrauding people of an election fairly won, or many other things that are common."[20]

Howard agreed to the above and on October 5th he was released and fled to New Mexico where he immediately began to agitate for a counter attack with the assistance of the Texas Rangers. Howard convinced Governor Hubbard of Texas that there had been an invasion from Mexico. Major Jones of the Rangers was sent to investigate the situation. Mills characterized Howard's action as having fired the "Texas heart" with many telegrams about lawless work, war of races, invasion from Mexico, etc., etc. He charged that Cardis was the chief conspirator and marplot who had created all the trouble and had sought to have him (Howard) assassinated.[21] Although he had accused Cardis of being an assassin, Howard struck first. On his return to the salt beds, Howard shot and killed Cardis. Throughout the border region, Anglos waited for trouble to result from Howard's action. Immediately rumors began to

circulate of "midnight messengers, secret conclaves, and even some drilling in military formation."[22] To escape possible retaliation, Howard quickly placed himself under the protection of the custom-house officer.

On November 6th, a group assembled to collect the bond which had been forfeited by Howard when he returned to the area. Representatives from the Mexican community met with Major Jones and the Texas Rangers in an attempt to clarify their actions. According to Webb, the group

> produced a copy of the constitution to show that they had a right to assemble and bear arms.... They said they had the right to collect the bond. The Mexicans declared that Howard had forfeited his bond by returning to El Paso, that they had no hope of collecting it in court, and they had a right to collect it by force.[23]

Major Jones assured the Mexican community that Howard would be arrested. However, Jones's credibility eroded quickly when he organized local Anglos into a company of Texas Rangers.

Local Mexicanos were apprehensive about the neutrality of the Rangers. Another meeting was held with Jones to request that Mexicanos be allowed to form their own company of Rangers, and elect their own officers. When Jones denied the request, the people demanded that U.S. troops be called upon instead of creating a local Anglo vigilante battalion. Later reports proved the reality of community fears about the Rangers. Sonnichsen described the men selected for the company as "assembled out of holes and corners. Not one of them would have been a Ranger under normal circumstances."[24]

On November 16th, Howard voluntarily surrendered to Major Jones. With the assistance of the collector of customs, Joseph Magoffin, Howard was able to persuade the local justice of peace to set bail at $4,000. During the investigation, this action was criticized:

> the death of Cardis at the hands of Howard seems to have been premeditated murder, a crime for which there is no bail provided by law... Yet Howard, after its commission, and without being confined, or examined in the presence of a prosecuting officer, either on the part of State, district, or county, was suffered to give bail and go free.[25]

Around the first of December, a train of about sixteen carts and wagons was rumored to be moving toward the salt lakes. Howard, a murderer and illegally out on bail, was accompanied by the Texas Rangers under Lieutenant Tays, to serve "writs of sequestration on the parties having the salt."[26] Later, Captain Blair of the U.S. Army identified Howard's move towards San Elizario as the signal to awaiting Mexicans to arm themselves and prepare to fight.

On December 12, Howard and the Texas Rangers arrived at San Elizario where they were surrounded by Chico Barela and his armed followers. Tays wired for assistance to Captain Blair who had been instructed by the federal government to investigate the participation of citizens of Mexico in this struggle. Blair was intercepted by armed Mexicans who wanted to know why Howard was being protected. Blair denied a personal interest in Howard's welfare and claimed Tays was not Howard's hired protector. The Mexicans were assured that the Army would not intervene in the question of the salt bed ownership and usage, and Blair demonstrated this by returning to El Paso.

For the next week, Howard and the Texas Rangers were held under siege by local Mexican Americans and their Mexican comrades. Charles Ellis, a former sheriff and tax collector, was killed. Shortly afterwards, Sergeant E.E. Montier of the Frontier Battalion States troops was killed. Realizing that the army was not coming to rescue the tired and restless Rangers, Lieutenant Tays arranged to meet with the Mexicano leaders, who demanded Howard's surrender.

Lieutenant Tays assured Howard that the Texas Rangers would defend him to the death; nevertheless, Howard eventually surrendered. Some reports suggest that Howard's decision to surrender may have been influenced by the other besieged men who feared for their own lives. The events surrounding Howard's surrender are unclear. Tays claimed John Atkinson, one of Howard's bondsmen, negotiated a deal with the Mexican leaders behind Howard's back. Whatever the case, Atkinson returned to the Ranger quarters and instructed them to surrender. He paid eleven thousand dollars of Howard's bond on the condition that Atkinson, Howard and McBride be freed. Apparently the agreement was not kept because a public execution was called for, and Howard, McBride and Atkinson were put to death. The Ranger troops were released the following day after being "asked whether they were employed by the governor of Texas or by Howard, and then each one was required to sign a black paper."[27] Sonnichsen awarded Tays the dubious distinction of being "the only officer of the rangers who ever surrendered to an enemy."[28]

The Rangers regrouped at Franklin, New Mexico under Sheriff Charles Kerber and Captain Moore.

They were reinforced by volunteers from Silver City, New Mexico, and were authorized by the governor to return to San Elizario "to prevent further outrages, to restore peace and quiet, and to assist the civil officers in preserving and enforcing the law."[29] Their pacification program began on December 22nd.

At Ysleta, Crecencio Irigoyen and Santiago Durán were arrested during a "round up" because they had "Ranger guns" in their possession. A later report indicated they were killed while attempting to escape. The same "round up" process was used in Socorro. In the first house of the town, a man named Núñez was killed and his wife wounded. Jesús Telles, identified as a participant in the seige, was killed and Cruz Chávez was wounded. Mexicans evacuated the area in anticipation of more violence. Incidents of rape and general harassment were uncovered during the Congressional investigations. Even though many Mexicans refused to testify to the congressional committee and others had already fled across the border, state officials made the volunteers from Silver City responsible for all atrocities. On March 25th, Lieutenant Tays resigned from the Texas Rangers.

The basis for the official investigation requested by Congress and Governor Hubbard of Texas was that "Texas had been invaded by armed forces from Mexico."[30] The committee had to determine if Mexican-American land rights had been violated and whether Mexican or U.S. citizens had fought against the Texas Rangers. The actions of public officials and military personnel were also under question. Areas of dispute included the issue of the citizenship of participants, the actual date of the salt lakes' discovery, the reputation of civil law in the area, the legality of action taken by Texas Rangers and others under their command, the amount of damage, and the legality of waiving examination and permitting Howard to be released on bail. Major Jones's major concern was that "the inter-national aspect of the affair" had been ignored. He argued that the United States should demand that the Mexican government punish its own criminals and make reparations for looting. He estimated the amount of damage at $31,000 against the Board's $12,000.[31]

The issue of ownership of the salt lakes was resolved on behalf of Zimpleman who was permitted to retain his private claim. Sergeant J.D. Ford of the Texas Rangers was assigned to protect Zimpleman's private property. The local community had to submit to his authority in order to obtain the salt needed to survive.

INTERPRETATIONS OF THE EL PASO SALT WARS

A review of historians' treatment of the El Paso Salt War reveals Anglo ethnocentrism which distorts Chicano history. Both Webb and Sonnichsen identified the isolation of the region as a contributing factor permitting the incident to occur. Sonnichsen made the claim on the basis that the U.S. had pulled troops out of Fort Bliss and Fort Quitman in 1872. El Paso was in fact geographically isolated from other U.S. establishments. However, Webb's concept of isolation was restricted to Anglo Americans. The El Paso region was not isolated from Mexico. Consequently, isolation must be considered an ethnocentric term. Webb justified economic and political domination by Anglos by arguing that Mexicans were un-American, and thus not trustworthy to hold office. Webb further suggested that the Mexican population engaged in the Salt War incident were simply sheep, acting under the guidance of evil leaders. Padre Antonio Borrajo, the parish priest of San Elizario and Socorro (about ninety miles from the salt lakes), and Luis Cardis were identified as the evil leaders of the Mexican people. Webb emphasized their role by relying heavily upon Fountain's testimony given during the congressional investigation.

Fountain claimed that Padre Antonio Borrajo offered him the Mexican people's cooperation if he entered into a profit-making agreement with Borrajo over the salt beds. Borrajo suggested purchasing the land and imposing a tax on the salt obtained, thus creating a profit that could be divided between the two men. Fountain also claimed that Padre Borrajo and Luis Cardis campaigned against the passage of his bill "to have the Salt Lakes delivered to the people, under the management of a board of trustees selected by them."[32] However, it is unlikely that Padre Borrajo played a major role in the insurrection. According to Ward B. Blanchard, the deputy surveyor at the time the salt lakes were surveyed for Zimplemen, the priest had been removed from the church of San Elizario and Socorro when El Paso became part of the bishopric of Arizona.

Webb's claim of outside agitators as the cause of the Salt War was consistent with his labeling of participants of the insurrection as the "mob" and their actions as "rioting." However, Webb recognized the role of community leaders, pointing out that the governor of Texas sent a telegram to Chico Barela, the Mexican leader, demanding that he give up.

Sonnichsen also over-emphasized the role Cardis and Borrajo played in the incident. However,

Sonnichsen introduced several other items of vital background information. For instance, he pointed out the existence of different attitudes toward private property. Similarly, Webb failed to recognize the private appropriation of the salt lakes as the major cause of the El Paso Salt War. The Mexican people were not, as Webb claimed, "docile and stupid;" rather they were acting in accordance with deeply-held cultural beliefs about communal land ownership and usage. Another cultural distinction identified by Sonnichsen was the idea of participatory democracy:

> They knew that power originates in the people and they reasoned that what the people agree on must be right regardless of the law books . . . they were the people, and the people were the law. That was the argument used more than once to justify what Americans called mob action.[33]

This notion of democracy and the political participation of the Mexican community account for the fact that Luis Cardis and Padre Borrajo needed to make deals to claim the salt beds, rather than simply seizing ownership. Fountain's testimony recognized that continuing support of the Mexican people could only be maintained by manipulating their interests. In his later book, *Pass of the North,* Sonnichsen provided further information about Cardis' relationship to his Mexican constituents. For instance, when the Rio Grande flooded the farm area in El Paso in 1874, Cardis introduced a bill to provide more irrigable land for the people.[34] Therefore, the Mexican population did not follow blindly, as Webb suggested, but rather responded to economic and political circumstances.

Conflicting interpretations appearing in the House Executive Document clearly reflect interest groups involved in the incident. In order to justify the actions of the Texas Rangers, Major Jones had to establish the incident as an international affair. Notice was issued by the Mexican government warning its citizens that persons crossing the border to participate in the riot at San Elizario would be punished. Guards were placed along the border to turn back all armed persons. Since the Mexican government was obviously not involved in the conflict over the salt beds, the issue of citizenship among the participants in the rebellion was the only argument that could be made to support this perspective. Howard obtained military protection from the Texas Rangers by claiming a Mexican invasion had occurred.

Captain Blair, on the other hand, maintained throughout the investigation that this was not an international affair, thus justifying his action in retreating. Blair claimed the reports made by other officials concerning the presence of Mexican citizens were exaggerated, and noted that many Mexicans, regardless of citizenship had lived on both sides of the border. Mills commented on the argument over labeling the incident as an international affair by pointing out that "If 'all Americans' were in danger, why was only one man selected to be protected by the Rangers?"[35]

The issue of citizenship is an interesting one. The area had formerly been Mexican territory, and many Mexicans chose U.S. citizenship in order to keep their homes after the war. Testimonies and description of other political events indicate that citizenship was a distinction that was socially meaningful only to Anglos (politicians, merchants and Texas Rangers). It benefited local Anglos to recognize the border population's citizenship during a political campaign, whereas it was to their advantage to deny the border population U.S. citizenship during incidents of economic exploitation or military suppression. For instance, the establishment of El Paso as the permanent county seat in 1883 illustrates the uses of citizenship:

> When the score was in, El Paso had 2,252 votes; Ysleta had 475. Since every Mexican who could be rounded up on either side of the river had been induced to vote at least once, the number of ballots was far in excess of the number of qualified voters of the county.[36]

Very little evidence can be given to indicate that there was any practical reason for the border population to make citizenship distinctions among themselves. J.P. Hague, a Texas lawyer during the incident, described the significance of the Rio Grande as an international boundary:

> The people of one are bound to those of the other by more than ordinary obligations of race and hospitality. They have married and intermarried; their interests are in many respects identical . . . it should not be a matter of surprise that 300 armed persons, residents of Mexico . . . united with others of El Paso County and aided them in their attack upon the Rangers . . . .[37]

Remarks made during the investigation clearly show that Anglos were aware of the Mexican community's relationship on the border. Zabriskie, El Paso's district attorney at the time expressed his understanding of the community's mutual response to Howard:

It was but natural, therefore, when the dispute over the salt lakes culminated in open war, that the entire Mexican people (on both sides) should be greatly excited and deeply interested in the result. Nor is it strange that the civil authorities in El Paso, Mexico, and their supporters, being in a hopeless minority, were unable to restrain their citizens from rushing to the assistance of their brethren on this side.[38]

The Minority Report based its international affair argument on the claim that Mexican Americans opposed the U.S. method of government. For instance, the sheriff's problem in collecting taxes was cited as an example of local opposition.[39] However, the argument is weakened by several events. First of all, Mexicans requested membership in the Texas Rangers for the purpose of capturing Howard, a wanted criminal. However, Major Jones refused the offer and proceeded to recruit known Mexican haters who served to protect Howard while he was attempting to protect his capital. Therefore, the Texas Rangers were perceived as Howard's hired army. Secondly, Chico Barela clearly indicated to Captain Blair that the subject of his attack was Howard, not the United States government. As a matter of fact, the Mexican community requested the intervention of federal troops because of the lawlessness of state officials who protected Howard's interests regardless of legality. At the same time, the Texas Rangers' insistence that Mexican Americans opposed the U.S. system of government was correct. The opposition was not an attempt to overthrow U.S. imperialism in the newly conquered territory; however, they were opposed to paying tribute as a conquered people. Protection of citizenship rights had been guaranteed by the Treaty of Guadalupe Hidalgo and therefore, Mexican-Americans resisted being relegated to an inferior position.

CONCLUSION

Although land ownership and land usage were culturally defined in the Spanish and Mexican land grants, the struggle over previously community-owned lands was not a cultural conflict. The transformation from community ownership of the salt beds to private ownership changed how the salt beds were used and ultimately threatened the economic survival of the people. Howard's claim threatened the economic survival of the Mexican border population which had built the wagon road, and thus had a vested interest in the future of the salt beds. Blair described the members of the insurection as "350 sober, well-organized, well-armed determined men, with a definite purpose. Howard they wanted; nothing else, nothing less."[40] Even though the border people armed themselves and fought against the Texas Rangers, their purpose and goals were aimed at eliminating Howard, and thus alleviating economic and political oppression. At no time were border Mexican-Americans and Mexicans attacking the United States government. The *salineros* understood that private ownership of the salt beds would result in severe economic exploitation. Furthermore, the border community understood Howard to have committed criminal acts under U.S. law, and they recognized that preferential treatment of Howard (or any other Anglo) would result in further political oppression by establishing two sets of codes. The Texas Rangers were seen as a capitalist private army and not representative of the U.S. government. Acuña appropriately defined this incident as a people's revolt, rather than a riot or mob action.[41] Leaders, as well as a specific plan of action, were visible throughout the incident.

Historians and social scientists have emphasized cultural differences between Mexican and Anglo Americans and have assigned these differences as causes of land loss among the Mexican population. Historians frequently ignore the effects of transformation of land ownership on the people's economy because their evolutionary perspective of history has glossed over incidents of insurrection as "growing pains" along the road to modernization. The El Paso Salt War of 1878 is an incident of Chicano struggle against Anglo efforts to exploit natural resources on community land. Testimonies taken after the El Paso Salt War provide evidence that the local Mexican American community, with the assistance of their Mexican friends and relatives, organized and fought against Charles W. Howard's efforts to claim private ownership of salt beds formerly authorized as communal resources. The Mexican population clearly supported the insurrection as Sonnichsen noted:

> The Grand Jury of El Paso County indicted six of the leaders of the mob, and later the Governor offered rewards for Chico Barela, Sisto Luciano Frésquez, Agatón Porras, Desiderio Apodaca and Jesús García. Not a Mexican turned a finger to collect the money.[42]

Although the United States government agreed to protect the Mexican people's land rights, the grantees were subjected to new rules and laws. Legal tactics used in the judicial system supported the interests of U.S. capitalists. Mexicanos could have learned new land grant rules, but they were unable to win in a system owned by the conqueror. Frequently, taking up the gun was the last recourse in an attempt to retain usage of the community land.

Yale College

Endnotes

1. My use of the term "Anglo" follows Carey McWilliams' statement that "two or more ethnics always implies the existence of another. In most portions of the Southwest, the term 'Anglo' and 'Hispanic' are the heads and tails of a single coin, a single ethnic system; each term has meaning only as the other is implied. The terms do not define homogeneous entities; they define a relationship." Carey McWilliams, *North From Mexico* (New York: Greenwood Press, 1948) p. 8.

2. McWilliams, p. 110.

3. C.L. Sonnichsen, *Ten Texas Feuds* (Albuquerque: University of New Mexico Press, 1957) p. 123.

4. Congress, Second Session, House Executive Document No. 93 (Washington, D.C.: GPO, 1878), p. 2. Henceforth, this document will be cited as H.E.D.

5. Sonnichsen, p. 112.

6. Rodolfo Acuña, *Occupied America, The Chicano's Struggle Toward Liberation* (San Francisco: Canfield Press, 1972; second edition, 1981), p. 37–40. The August Twenty-Ninth Movement (Marxist-Leninist) organization published the pamphlet "Fan the Flames, A Revolutionary Position on the National Question," (1976) which historically documents that Chicanos are an oppressed nation. This document is largely a response to the CUPUSA's 1930s position that denied the existence of a Chicano National Movement.

7. Walter Prescott Webb, *The Texas Rangers, A Century of Frontier Defense* (Austin: University of Texas Press, 1935).

8. Ibid., p. 347.

9. Ibid.

10. C.L. Sonnichsen, *Pass of the North: Four Centuries on the Rio Grande* (El Paso: Texas Western Press, 1968) p. 181.

11. Sonnichsen, *Ten Texas Feuds,* p. 117.

12. H.E.D., p. 65.

13. Ibid., p. 112.

14. Sonnichsen, *Ten Texas Feuds,* p. 123.

15. H.E.D., p. 68.

16. Sonnichsen, *Ten Texas Feuds,* p. 128.

17. Ibid., p. 129.

18. Webb, p. 351–52.

19. Sonnichsen, *Ten Texas Feuds,* p. 131.

20. W.W. *Mills, Forty Years at El Paso, 1858-1898* (El Paso: Carl Hertozog, 1898), p. 151.

21. Ibid.
22. Sonnichsen, *Ten Texas Feuds,* p. 135.
23. Webb, p. 355.
24. Sonnichsen, *Pass of the North,* p. 138.
25. H.E.D., p. 17.
26. Ibid., p. 56.
27. Ibid., p. 57.
28. Sonnichsen, *Ten Texas Feuds,* p. 154.
29. H.E.D., p. 28.
30. Webb, p. 336.
31. Sonnichsen, *Ten Texas Feuds,* p. 155.
32. Webb, p. 348.
33. Sonnichsen, *Ten Texas Feuds,* p. 112.
34. Sonnichsen, *Pass of the North,* p. 197.
35. Mills, p. 155.
36. Sonnichsen, *Pass of the North,* p. 347.
37. H.E.D., p. 143.
38. Ibid., p. 53.
39. H.E.D., p. 143.
40. H.E.D., p. 56.
41. Acuña, p. 37.
42. Sonnichsen, *Ten Texas Feuds,* p. 155.

Border Culture

Mario T. García

Working among themselves as manual laborers and living in segregated barrios adjacent to their homeland, Mexican immigrants in El Paso and throughout the Southwest, like other newcomers to the United States, maintained native customs that helped provide a sense of community. As one historian has correctly written of the northern movement of Mexicans: "Mexican immigration bore little resemblance to the 'uprooting' experience which Oscar Handlin depicted as characteristic of European immigration. Indeed, continuity rather than alienation, marginality and social disorganization, characterized Mexican immigration." Yet, within El Paso's large Mexican population, cultural differences also existed. Mexican Americans, educated and sophisticated political refugees, and the mass of poor immigrants comprised diverse cultural enclaves although they were linked by a common language and certain Mexican traditions. Moreover, cultural continuity coexisted with some cultural change. The immigrants' adjustment to new working conditions, especially in urban areas, their relationship with more Americanized Mexican Americans, and the impact of certain gringo institutions such as the schools introduced a gradual acculturation. Cultural change among Mexican immigrants, especially children, likewise occurred because, as Ernesto Galarza indicates, working class immigration brought "no

formal institutions to perpetuate its culture." Cultural continuity as well as cultural change, the two in time developing a Mexican border culture, can be detected in the family, recreational activities, religion, and voluntary associations. The family represents the most basic cultural institution transferred by Mexican immigrants and was the most resistant barrier to American assimilation. Besides young single males who entered the United States seeking work, many families also arrived. The Dillingham Commission report of 1911 observed that a high percentage of Mexican laborers in western industries had brought their wives from Mexico. According to the commission, 81.5 percent of Mexican railroad shop workers in the survey reported their wives in the United States. Investigators discovered a similar condition in urban related work. Sixty percent of Mexicans employed as construction workers by street railways stated they had their wives with them. Although no substantial research has been done on the composition and nature of working-class or peasant families in Mexico during the late nineteenth and early twentieth centuries, nevertheless it appears that the family formed a strong social and economic unit. Galarza in his autobiography, *Barrio Boy*, recalls that his family in rural Nayarit included not only his mother (who had divorced his father prior to Galarza's birth) but also his aunt, three uncles, and two cousins. In the Galarza household the men went to labor in the fields during the day while the women and children performed the housework and cooking.

Although some Mexican women in El Paso and throughout the urban Southwest contributed to household incomes by taking in wash or lodgers, no disintegration took place in the traditional pattern of men being the chief wage earners and women doing household work (of course, certain lower-class women in Mexico were wageworkers). The 1900 El Paso census sample shows that no mothers and almost no daughters, most being too young, worked outside the home in an immigrant family headed by the father (although no data exist, some women may have worked part-time). Nevertheless, the necessity of more women having to become wage-workers over the years no doubt affected family patterns. This appears to be true as daughters grew to working age throughout the region. According to a Los Angeles survey by Paul S. Taylor in 1928, the majority of Mexican women took jobs in ministry because "of poverty, due either to irregular work of the male members of the family, or to the combination of large families, low wages, high rents. However the entrance of women into the job market constituted, as Taylor put it, a process contrary to their customs and traditions." Taylor believed that "such radical changes" in the daily lives of Mexican women could not help but produce cultural changes, especially within the family. The University of California scholar observed both older as well as younger women in industrial jobs, but he detected more profound alterations in the habits of younger Mexicans. Not only did they adapt to the work routine better, but what little education they secured in American schools, especially the learning of English, made them more productive and efficient. "They look upon some sort of industrial work" Taylor wrote, "as soon as they have completed the minimum amount of schooling as the natural course of events. Besides acquiring some new material and cultural tastes that they introduced into the home, by the 1920s young Mexican working women appear to have begun to exhibit a desire for greater independence from strict family practices. "Her parents are apt to be ignored," Taylor stressed, "she tends to break away from the old custom of parental authority." Whether Taylor's observations would also pertain to El Paso cannot be determined due to a lack of similar studies in the border city. Certainly, young Mexican women who worked in the laundries and garment factories, and possibly even as domestics, may have displayed parallel characteristics.

The economic necessity for Mexican women to find jobs likewise appears to have challenged to a degree the traditional male-dominated Mexican family structure. Although perhaps Mexican fathers could more easily accept their daughters than their wives working outside the home, a pattern not uncommon in Mexico, still Taylor noticed that Mexican men resented women working or wanting to work. One man stated that women should not work because that was a man's duty, whereas women's consisted of keeping house. Another husband told Taylor that he could not allow his wife to work because his friends would then think he could not adequately provide for his family. Another insisted that his wife could not have a job outside the home since no women in his family had ever worked; moreover, it was neither necessary nor correct. The pressure of higher living costs north of the border, however, eventually forced many Mexican women into the job market. While more research needs to be conducted into the full impact that this process had on family culture, it seems that traditional patterns slowly changed over the years. One Mexican man who had lived in the United States for over 25 years told anthropologist Manuel Gamio in the 1920s that he disliked the transformation Mexican women underwent in the Southwest. According to Carlos Ibáñez, he disliked American laws that allowed women too many rights and made them less subordinate to men. "Now the Mexican women who come here," Ibáñez emphasized, "also take advantage of the laws and want to be like the American women." Because of the change, Ibáñez concluded that if he ever married it would be in Mexico.

Within the family, Mexicans preserved many native cultural traditions that aided them in their transition to a new American setting by providing a familiar cultural environment. It is difficult to arrive at an accurate picture of family life in El Paso, but anthropologist Manuel Gamio noted certain customs being practiced in the late 1920s by Mexican immigrant families in El Paso and other southwestern locations. Gamio observed that despite the fact that Mexican immigrants accepted American material goods such as housing, clothing, domestic utensils, and machinery, they still retained earlier popular customs. These included folklore, songs and ballads, birthday celebrations, saints' days, baptisms, weddings, and funerals in the traditional style. Owing to poverty, a lack of physicians in the barrios plus traditional customs the Mexican scholar witnessed the continued use of medicinal herbs by both Mexican immigrants and Mexican Americans. "In almost all parts of America where there are Mexicans and Mexican-Americans," he stressed, "there are Mexican drug stores in which there is a great sale of every sort of medicinal plant." Mexicans along the border could also find remedies for their physical and emotional ailments by visiting Mexican healers known as *curanderos*. "I cure by means of herbs" one *curandera* in Tucson informed Gamio, "but I never promise to cure this one or that one because that is something of God. . . . I have cured many Mexicans of syphilis and tuberculosis and other diseases. I have also helped to assist at childbirth many times, when the doctors have let me. The existence of such popular traditions illustrates what scholars have discovered in studies of migration patterns: the persistence of earlier preindustrial cultural practices within an industrializing society—or what one sociologist refers to as an "urban village".

Immigrant families interviewed by Gamio further acknowledged that for the most part they continued to cook Mexican style. "I don't suffer in the matter of food," one woman told him in Los Angeles, for my mother cooks at home as if we were in Mexico. There are some dishes which are different but we generally eat Mexican style and rice and beans are almost never lacking from our table." According to a report one of Gamio's associates, however, Mexican families in certain areas purchased items such canned chile, canned sauces, and canned tomatoes from California. Obtaining food processed in the United States often led to complaints about the inadequacy and poor quality of American products in the cooking of Mexican dishes. "The foodstuffs, besides costing a lot," another woman informed Gamio, "are no good for making good Mexican food . . . so that it might be said that the food is half-Mexican and half-American, being neither the one nor the other." Most Mexican families in El Paso avoided this dietary problem by apparently purchasing much of their food in Juárez.

Outside the home, Mexicans patronized various other forms of entertainment and recreation. Men visited Mexican bars, pool halls, and gambling establishments in both El Paso and Juárez. At the turn of the century, some Mexicans sponsored horse rides in Washington Park with attendance from not only the city but the surrounding area as well. On its visits to the border the circus stood out as a special treat for Mexican children and their parents. The *Times* recorded in 1887 that many Mexicans as well as Americans had attended John Robinson's Great Circus in back of the Santa Fe depot. Elephants, camels, and other strange beasts, a reporter observed, captured the attention of the Mexican spectators. Mexicans from the adjacent territory also came in large numbers. They camped next to the circus tents, the *Times* man wrote, and everyone spent their *dinero* freely. Mexicans along with

Americans eagerly awaited the arrival of such special attractions as the Ringling Brothers' "Greatest Show on Earth" and Barnum and Bailey's circus. Besides American circuses, small Mexican traveling shows with acrobats and sideshows called *carpas* visited El Paso and performed in Chihuahuita. According to one Mexican American critic, these carpas included improvised satirical skits. "The brief, topical skits of la carpa, he proposes, "with their focus on physical movement and rapid verbal gymnastics are the progenitors of today's [Chicano] 'actos.' Mexicans also spent their limited leisure time at spectator sports that helped distract their minds from homesickness, work, and harsh living conditions. Bullfights in Juárez, for example, were a cultural link with la patria. Boxing matches on both sides of the border enticed many males. Mexican boxers such as Benny Chávez and Mexican Americans like lightweight Aurelio Herrera held special attraction for the Mexican fans. By 1900 Mexicans also began to show an interest in American baseball. In addition to its attraction as a spectator event, some Mexicans, mostly Mexican Americans, organized baseball teams of their own. The Internationals stood out as the earliest and most popular Mexican baseball team in the border city. With an all Mexican lineup and playing against Anglo-American teams, the Internationals proved to be one of the finest clubs in El Paso for several years and played games throughout the Southwest. Sportswriters considered the Mexican American players among the finest athletes. José "Curly" Villarreal, playing for a local team in 1917, was regarded as the best pitcher in the city league. One writer commented that with Curly on the pitching mound "it is a safe bet that a large number of Mexican fans will be out Sunday to see their favorite in action."

The allure of American baseball for Mexicans transcended the border and began to have a cultural impact in Mexico. "Baseball is showing promise," the *Times* proudly reported in 1908, "of becoming the national game of Mexico as well as the United States." Admitting that other foreign sports such as cricket, field hockey, and polo had some following in the neighboring republic, the *Times* believed that those cultural imports could not compare with the "grand old game." The newspaper subjectively concluded that the sport physically suited the Mexicans due to their "natural quickness." Moreover, it recognized the language influence that baseball had on Mexicans with the acceptance of baseball terms such as "You're out." The *Times* further understood the political objective American baseball served in Mexico. Baseball would create a sympathetic link between Americans and Mexicans. Two men cheering for the same team, it emphasized, would find it difficult to disagree on other matters. At the same time that the United States had become Mexico's principal trade partner and investor, the *Times* boasted that south of the border American baseball had outdistanced British, French, German, and other European sports. The border publication predicted that it would be only a matter of time before the "better classes" in Mexico would stop bullfighting and then baseball would become the national sport. "When the mob can no longer have it [bull-fighting]," the *Times* stressed, "baseball will be the national game from Central America to the Great Lakes."

In spite of strong Mexican cultural influences in El Paso owing to increased Mexican immigration and the city's proximity to the border, Mexicans underwent subtle cultural changes. After 1910, for example, they faced the acculturating influence of American mass culture through the silent movies. Although it does not appear that the early movie houses such as the Crawford, the Grand, the Little Wigwam, and the Bijou specifically excluded Mexicans, the attendance of Mexicans at the movies grew when several Mexican theaters opened by the period of World War I. The International Amusement Company of El Paso, Owned and managed by Mexican businessmen including Mexican American politico Frank Alderete, operated seven theaters in the border city. These included the Alcazar, the Eureka, the Hidalgo, the Paris, the Iris, and Rex movie houses on South El Paso Street. By 1917, these theaters showed some films produced in Mexico but for the most part Mexican audiences paid 6 or 11 cents admission, depending on where one sat, to see American movies featuring such stars as Charlie Chaplin, Mary Pickford, and Fatty Arbuckle. "Regardless of what some may say," *La Patria* commented in reviewing a Chaplin film at the Teatro Rec, "Carlos Chaplin is a magnificent artist; he is not a vulgar clown, but rather a refined and competent comic actor, whose every gesture, every graceful pose, brings forth joy not only for children, but for adults."

Besides exposing Mexicans to some American material and cultural values and mores, the movies also may have influenced their ability to understand some English. Mexicans employed by the movie houses translated English subtitles to Spanish ones, which appeared at the bottom of the screen below the original dialogue. American slang was no problem, remarked a *Times* reporter, for the translators of slapstick comedies screened at Mexican theaters. Even Americans studying Spanish took advantage of the process and visited Mexican theaters to improve their Spanish reading ability. The reporter further noted that the technique of imposing the Spanish translation on the films had been invented by a Mexican employee of the International Amusement Company and is now in use wherever American films are used for Spanish-speaking audiences. Guillermo Balderas recalls that his own brother Eduardo worked as a translator in one of the Mexican movie houses. These were 'silent movies,' Balderas remembers, "that were translated into Spanish." By the 1920s American movies were an important acculturating agent, especially on the first generation native born, on both sides of the border. As one Mexican immigrant explained in a corrido, Hollywood films had enticed him to leave Mexico for the "promised land:"

> I dreamed in my youth of being a movie star
> And one of these days I came to visit Hollywood.

For Mexican immigrants, Catholicism provided a familiar cultural environment as well as institutional support for their adjustment north of the border. The Catholic Church in El Paso, under the control of Irish Americans, recognized quite early that it would have to establish separate facilities for its Mexican members. Consequently, it organized Mexican parishes in the barrios to serve the particular religious and social needs of the immigrants. Unlike many national churches in the United States, however, those in El Paso were not staffed, for the most part, by Mexican priests, of whom there was an apparent shortage in the Southwest, but by Italian and American clergy. As a result the Church not only took into consideration Mexican cultural traditions but also became an agent of Americanization among its parishioners, especially those families, many of them political refugees, who could afford to send their children to Catholic schools. Still, the mass of Mexican immigrants retained their popular religious beliefs and practices by transferring them across the border. Regardless of economic or political background, first generation immigrants and political refugees, through their reestablishment of spiritual societies common in Mexico as well as the reenactment of native Mexican religious celebrations, successfully maintained cultural continuity and helped create a sense of community in the barrios.

As an institution, the Catholic Church in El Paso pursued a bicultural approach in its treatment of Mexican immigrants. The south-side parochial schools, for example, under the direction of the American Sisters of Loretto emphasized, as one part of their curriculum, the Americanization of their students and attempted to change what they considered to be the Mexicans' bad cultural habits.

In addition to a basic curriculum emphasizing religious and academic subjects with some industrial and domestic training, Sacred Heart School presented performances displaying both the talents of young Mexicans as well as the influences of American middle-class culture. The *Times* reported in 1895 that Sacred Heart School students would offer a musical and dramatic entertainment at the old stone church on North Oregon Street. Mainly performed in English, the school's closing exercise in 1904 took place at Myar's Opera House, where a large audience assembled. According to the *Times* critic, the entertainment not only proved to be interesting but also reflected great credit on the nuns who taught at Sacred Heart. The best acts included the singing of "The Poor Old Tramps" by a male choir and an instrumental performance by the Mandolin Club that "was rendered without a single discord, and gave promise that El Paso will have a number of skillful musicians, who, with light touch, will call forth the music that stirs men's souls." Some of the girls who presented a drama in three acts entitled The Little Waiters received round upon round of applause, and demonstrated the fact that several of the young ladies had real dramatic ability." Impressed, the *Times* gave credit to the students' teachers and praised the Catholic Church for its work among the Mexican children of the city. The performance had demonstrated, the paper concluded, "that there is an efficient and practical movement on foot to educate the Catholic youths and young girls of El Paso and teach them how to become good citizens and dutiable daughters and faithful wives."

Yet English and middle-class American customs at Sacred Heart shared the curriculum with Spanish and Mexican cultural traditions. Cleofas Calleros, who attended Sacred Heart during the first decade of the century, remembered that although there were only two Mexican teachers in a faculty of ten, both English and Spanish were used in instruction along with American and Mexican history. Years later, lecturing to the 1919 graduating girls of Sacred Heart, the Italian pastor of the parish encouraged them to adopt the best of other cultures but to never forget who they were: young Catholic Mexican girls, who were obliged to follow Christ and as Mexicans, to conserve the beautiful customs and traditions of *la raza*. Hence, Sacred Heart as well as the other Mexican parochial schools served a

two-fold purpose. They helped transmit Mexican ethnicity and, at the same time, provided lessons in English and American culture in order to assist students to adjust and hopefully succeed in the United States.

Next to Sacred Heart, the religious and cultural activities of St. Ignatius Church at Park and Second perhaps best exemplified the Church's interest in the Mexicans' adjustment. For the spiritual needs of its members, St. Ignatius sponsored a variety of religious groups popular in Mexico. In 1905 some women formed the League of the Sacred Heart and Congregation of the Daughters of Mary (Congregación de las Hijas de María). That same year a group of young people and children organized the Congregation of San Luis Gonzaga as a prayer union for youth. Care of the church sacristy led to the beginning of the Altar Society. Still other parishioners, especially women, belonged to additional religious associations such as the Society of Good Death (Buena Muerte), the Society of Our Lady of Guadalupe, the Society of Divine Providence, and the Association of Christian Mothers. Besides their specific devotions, many of these organizations assisted in the more popular religious ceremonies among the Mexican working class such as the Feast of Our Lady of Guadalupe and, of course, at Christmas, when parishioners performed the Shepherds' Play (Los Pastores). The Corpus Christi procession held every June, however, was the most impressive popular religious feast day, clearly fostering a communal spirit among the entire Mexican population of El Paso. Although this event centered around Sacred Heart Church, all Mexican parishes participated. In 1919, for example, between 10,000 and 20,000 Mexicans marched in the annual procession with thousands more watching, making the Revista Católica, the Spanish-language Jesuit newspaper in the city, declare that the Mexican colony saw Corpus Christi as an ethnic holiday.

St. Ignatius supported various other cultural and recreational activities as well. Shortly after the church opened, it hired Trinidad Concha to assemble a young women's orchestra, which by 1908 appeared in public concerts. Concha further directed the church's well-known choir. In 1912 St. Ignatius obtained the benefit of another musical group when a boys band at Sacred Heart had to leave that parish because it made too much noise and instead moved to St. Ignatius. This marked the start of the young people's band, which gained much prominence under the direction of Professor Melitón Concha. By 1918 St. Ignatius also had one of the largest Mexican athletic clubs in the city. Founded by the church to counter the success of the

Mexican YMCA, the Association of Catholic Youth (Asociación Católica de Jóvenes), better known as the Club Anahuac, sponsored both athletic and cultural events. It possessed the best baseball, football, tennis, and basketball teams in south El Paso and won several city-wide contests. Moreover, its 100 members aided in the building of athletic and playground facilities for the children of the area. And, as part of its expression of loyalty to the United States during World War I, the club held picnics and athletic exhibitions to raise money for the war fund of the Knights of Columbus. "The young members of this club," it appealed to other Mexicans, "moved by a sense of duty and humanitarianism. and not being able to contribute in any other way to relieve the suffering of our own brothers, have decided to help through this exhibition. Won't you help us by attending? *Remember:* It will benefit our brothers who are fighting on the front lines."

Indeed, the war gave St. Ignatius and the Catholic Church of El Paso another opportunity to stress the Americanization of the Mexicans, especially youth. After the United States declared war in 1917, the priests of St. Ignatius explained to their parishioners the alien registration provisions of the draft law, and urged them to cooperate with the civil and military authorities. The church also requested Mexicans to buy Liberty Bonds (Bonos de la Libertad). Yet the parish's proudest contribution to the war came when more than 40 young Mexican men, both native born and foreign born, enlisted for military service, despite the fact that most Mexicans in the city claimed draft exemptions owing to their alien status. A few of the Mexican soldiers, moreover, served with distinction. Marcos B. Armijo, who died in battle, received the Distinguished Service Cross, while the French government honored Manuel J. Escajeda with the Croix de Guerre. Marcelino Serna, however, represented not only St. Ignatius' most distinguished soldier but one of the most decorated in El Paso and Texas. Serna received the American Distinguished Service Cross, the French Croix de Guerre and Military Medal, the Italian Cross of Merit, and the British medal of Bravery. This demonstration of American patriotism on the part of St. Ignatius' youth revealed the conviction of the Catholic Church in El Paso that, regardless of native sentiments, Mexicans for their own economic benefits should learn the language, customs, and values of the United States as quickly as possible. After the war the Church strongly supported the city's Americanization program, which included night school for Mexican adults. In an editorial even the sometime Anti-American *Revista Católica*

encouraged its Mexican readers to avail themselves of this education in order to help them obtain better jobs. "The movement initiated in Washington," the Mexican Catholic paper pointed out, "to 'Americanize' all foreigners in the United States has reached El Paso, and all indicators show that it will prove more fruitful in this city than in other places. The name of this program will scare off many Mexicans and perhaps because of this fear many will not take advantage of this excellent opportunity to improve their conditions."

Hence, by 1920 the Catholic Church in El Paso through its endorsement of postwar Americanization programs as well its own efforts in the parochial schools served, along with the public schools, as a major American institution of socialization, especially for the children of Mexican immigrants. Based on a viewpoint stressing loyalty to both Church and country, which by the 1920s and 1930s increasingly meant the United States, the Catholic Church in the Southwest assisted Mexicans not only to adjust to border life but, ultimately, to believe in the American Dream. Still, the constant stream of additional immigrants into El Paso and other southwestern areas after 1920, as well as the proximity of Mexico, meant that Mexican immigrant parishes were never completely Americanized. Rather than examples of an earlier past, many of them, due to continued immigration from Mexico, remain viable through poor institutions helping to link Mexican immigrant communities in the United States with the mother country and culture.

As a form of ethnic self-protection as well as an expression of ethnicity. Mexican social organizations in El Paso revealed the Mexicans' accommodation to their new American setting. Forced to organize in a sometimes hostile society, some of El Paso's Mexicans, especially more skilled and educated ones, formed several mutual and fraternal associations that helped provide organized leadership in the Mexican settlement. Similar societies, moreover, existed in Mexico and hence were familiar forms of association. As mediating institutions the mutual and fraternal organizations, besides aiding in the preservation and encouragement of Mexican ethnic consciousness among the immigrants, helped form a more permanent and cohesive Mexican community.

As early as 1893 the Mexican newspaper *El Hispano-Americano* printed a notice from La Unión Mexicana (the Mexican Western Union), which was one of the first Mexican mutual aid societies in El Paso. "It is neither more nor less than what it's name implies a group of persons of Mexican origin," stated organizer and political exile Víctor L. Ochoa. He went on to explain that the unión had several objectives: to aid and defend its members, to unalterably maintain the Spanish language, to protect the morality of its members, and to spread fraternal bonds among Mexican nationals in the United States. In addition, when a member died, his wife and children would receive $2.50 from each unión member. One year later another mutual aid society, Los Caballeros del Progreso (the Gentlemen of Progress), stressed that the poor economic conditions of Mexicans in the United States resulted from a lack of unity and that in order to alleviate this problem Los Caballeros had been organized. *El Defensor* noted that when one of the society's members who had not kept up his dues died, Los Caballeros refused to pay the funeral costs as a lesson to other negligent members.

One Mexican newspaper also urged unity through organizations when it observed in 1899 that despite the large numbers of Mexicans in El Paso, the city's oldest Mexican mutual benefit society (1888), the Sociedad Mutualista Mexicana "La Protectora," had only 40 members. It pointed out the validity of the motto "Unity Makes Force" and informed its readers that only through organization had the United States become a great power. "'If it is true then that unity makes force," it added, "then we do not understand why Mexicans do not develop those relationships that will unite us. The Sociedad Mutualista Mexicana "La Protectora," the paper asserted, aimed to unite and protect Mexicans who lived in El Paso. Had it not been for this society, the paper believed that Mexicans in the city would have been deprived of a common meeting place where they "could exchange impressions of our beloved country." *Las Noticas* further reminded Mexicans of their obligation to one another as members of the same race" and sons of the same mother: Mexico." Among its benefits, "La Protectora assisted members who required hospitalization and paid for funeral costs. *Las Dos Américas,* another Mexican newspaper in El Paso, expressed its gratitude in 1898 to "La Protectora's" Mexican American president, A. J. Escajeda, and its vice-president C. Aguirre, for their consideration during the funeral of Antonio G. Gallardo, who had been killed by a Southern Pacific train at Deming, New Mexico. Although it appears that the membership of La Protectora remained small, it met regularly every second and fourth Monday of the month. Its leadership seems to have come from Mexican Americans like Escajeda, but the entire composition of its membership cannot be determined.

As more Mexicans arrived in El Paso by the turn of the century, several other benefit and fraternal groups appeared. The *Times* announced in 1907 that seven Mexican societies of El Paso would participate in that year's 16th of September celebrations honoring Mexican independence. These included La Benéfica patriotic society from the smelter, the Sociedad Unión Constructora, La Mutualista, Los Hijos de Hidalgo, and the Sociedad Filarmónica. Few Americans if any, a Mexican told a *Times reporter,*

are aware of the wonderful growth and activity to be found in the Mexican fraternal orders now existing in the Southwest.

While the chief element of these orders is made up of the common working class, it must be remembered that there are also affiliated with these societies many Mexicans of culture—among them professional and business men. El Paso has the distinction of having the largest number of these lodges; Tucson ranking next, it being the place where two of the most important orders, the "Sociedad Zaragoza" and the "Sociedad Hispano-Americana" have their home offices.

He further explained that the Hispano-American society paid $1,000 to the family of a deceased member and $200 to a member upon the death of his wife. In addition he declared that although the Sociedad Zaragoza had been operating for a shorter time than other societies, it had a larger membership with 28 branches throughout Arizona, New Mexico, and Texas. In El Paso it was represented by Lodge No. 18, founded that year with 90 members.

The growing numbers of Mexican immigrants and refugees in El Paso after 1910 also influenced the expansion of these societies. Mexicans in El Paso are interested in lodge work to an extent probably not generally known, member Pedro A. Candelaria stated in an interview in 1915. Candelaria observed that the Sociedad Mutualista Mexicana had a membership of 115 and La Constructora had 300 members. Both represented the two largest societies in the city and intended to protect the widows and orphans of deceased members. Each of these organizations assessed every member $3 whenever a death occurred and turned the amount over to the widow. Candelaria pointed out that still another lodge, La Benéfica, operated in East El Paso. These organizations had developed substantially in recent years, he concluded, owing to the arrival of Mexican refugees.

The sharp rise in the Mexican population of the Southwest during the years of the Mexican Revolution encouraged consolidation among Mexican mutual aid societies and increased their emphasis on insurance practices. The best example of the change can be seen in the activities of La Sociedad Alianza Hispano-Americana. Organized in 1894 in Tucson, it grew from a small numbers of lodges to 88 in 1919 with more than 4,000 members from California to Texas, and with additional lodges in northern Mexico. It hoped to unite all Mexicans and Latin Americans in the United States into one family under the principles of protection, morality, and education. According to the Alianza's historian, its membership consisted of both lower-middle-class and working-class people. In one of the largest demonstrations of Mexican social organization in the United States, El Paso hosted a national convention of the Alianza in 1910 attended by close to 200 delegates from New Mexico, Arizona, Southern California, and Texas. At their opening session the mayors of both El Paso and Juárez welcomed the delegates and assured them they would not be molested by the police of either border town. One of the main items in the convention's agenda dealt with changes in insurance payments. Every member paid a flat rate of $1 each month for $1,000 insurance without regard to age or other conditions. However, the *Times* reported that the supreme lodge had $16,790 on hand of which $14,000 had been put in the reserve fund. Although the convention voted to retain a flat rate for present members, it approved a new classified assessment for future ones but kept the amount of insurance that could be secured at $500 or $1,000, with $100 and $200 funeral benefits.

Nine years later *La Patria* published an advertisement for the Alianza containing both its insurance provisions and a list of its lodges in the Southwest. The notice emphasized that the Alianza had no political or religious qualifications for membership, that it treated every member equally, that each received the same benefits, and that it spent none of its members' funds for amusements. The Alianza also stressed that women could purchase a policy, for we believe them to be as worthy and as entitled to the same right to protect their children who depend on them. Despite the fact that most of its members were humble workers, the Alianza proudly announced that since its formation it had paid out a million and a half dollars in benefits. To share in the Alianza's protection, a Mexican had to pay $3.50 admission fee plus $1 to $2 for a medical examination. Monthly payments would then be determined by the amount of the policy and the age of its holder. We respectfully invite you and your family to join the

'Alianza,' the ad told the readers of *La Patria*. In 1919 three of its lodges, apparently located in Chihuahuita, functioned in El Paso. *La Patria* observed that members of the different lodges could attend one another's meetings. In addition Jesús M. Ortiz, who had been named Alianza organizer for Texas, believed that a new chapter could be established in East El Paso since many Mexicans there had expressed an interest in the society. Besides El Paso, lodges could be found in nearby New Mexico in Silver City, Hillsboro, Santa Rita, Las Cruces, and Hurley.

Like other immigrant organizations in the United States, the Mexican mutual and fraternal societies of El Paso provided social and cultural activities for their members. Many of these social functions consisted of dances sponsored by different lodges. In 1911, for example, the Mexican secret societies held a grand ball at the Fraternal Brotherhood Hall. The national colors of Mexico will be flying, the *Times* commented, and those who cannot have one of the most enjoyable times of their life . . . will be hard to please. In 1919 the Logia Morelos held its Second Grand Ball at Liberty Hall and in 1920 the Sociedad Mutualista Zaragoza Independiente sponsored a literary and dance show to celebrate its twelfth anniversary. That same year the Alianza hosted an artistic presentation to raise funds. Moreover, the lodges sponsored the 16th of September celebrations as well as other Mexican patriotic holidays. When William Howard Taft met Porfirio Díaz in El Paso in 1909, the city's Mexican societies turned out in force to honor both leaders and the nations they represented. As the president's carriage neared the position occupied by the Mexican societies, a reporter noticed of Taft's parade down El Paso street, there was a tumult of applause, cheers and cries of Viva Taft! Viva Taft!' After Taft had visited Díaz in Juárez, the Mexican organizations joined the parade up El Paso Street to downtown Cleveland Square. Four different Mexican societies, the *Times* observed, numbering about 1,000 men and all wearing natty uniforms comprised the divisions.

For Mexican Americans, the social activities of the lodges became quite important because participation in Anglo-Saxon society remained limited. Although the Women's Club, the El Paso Country Club, and other American social organizations had no clear policy on the exclusion of Mexican members, businessman Félix Martínez, who belonged to the Toltec Men's Club, appears to have been one of the few persons of Mexican descent throughout the period who claimed membership in an America social group. Social intercourse between Mexicans and Americans on an organized level seems to have occurred only during special political or patriotic events or the arrival of major Mexican dignitaries such as Díaz. Because of this de facto social separation as well as their own cultural affinity, Mexican Americans either formed their own clubs or joined immigrant organizations. In 1907 the Logia Fraternal No. 30, composed exclusively of Mexican Americans, held a banquet in honor of Mexican Independence Day at the Sheldon Hotel attended by 132 persons including 35 prominent American politicians. The walls of the big dining room had been decorated with a number of Mexican and American flags, while at the south end of the hall facing the toastmaster was an immense Mexican and a huge American flag leaning so close together that their folds embraced each other." After some of the American guests spoke, lodge officer Agapito Martínez emphasized that it gave him great pride to say that every member of the lodge held American citizenship and yet could also be proud of Mexico's achievements. "Freedom," said editor Lauro Aguirre, "started the fire at Philadelphia, at Paris and in Mexico." Z. M. Oriza ended the speeches by a toast to the menu motto "After All, What is Better than Friendship."

The annual 16th of September celebration proved to be not only the most important Mexican cultural event in El Paso, and throughout the Southwest, but also an indication of the level of social organization and cooperation that could occur among the different Mexican societies. The 1897 ceremonies, for example, stood out as one of the most successful holidays in El Paso and revealed the various cultural activities that often took place during this community fiesta. As early as July, the Mexican newspaper *El Monitor* announced a meeting of La Junta Patriótica Mexicana (the Mexican Patriotic Council) to select a board of directors and decide on the best format for the 16th of September celebration. One month later the paper criticized some Mexican Americans who did not believe that the 16th of September had any meaning for them and refused to support the festivities: To these 'Agringados' (Americanized Mexicans) who negate that they are Mexicans because they were born in the United States, we ask: what blood runs through their veins? Do they think they are members of the Anglo-Saxon race who only happen to have dark skins because they were born on the border! What nonsense! (Qué barbaridad!). *El Monitor* went on to add that this did not mean that Mexican Americans should not be good citizens of the United States and even fight for Tio Samuel if it went to war against a European or an Asiatic nation.

However, in the event of conflict between the United States and Mexico or a Latin American nation, *El Monitor* believed that every Mexican living north of the border should go to the defense of their "blood brothers" and the country of their parents' birth. The paper concluded by asking: "Why should there be any reason now for us to feel ashamed of being a Mexican?"

Led by the Junta Patriótica, the Mexicans of El Paso prepared to celebrate the independence of Mexico. In its September 12th edition, *El Monitor* dedicated its coverage to the Mexican workers of the city, "to whom we wish all kinds of happiness during these glorious days." It also reminded its readers of the events to be held on both the fifteenth and sixteenth, and commented that the prepared program left nothing to be desired, thanks to the work of the Junta. Similar festivities would occur in other areas of Texas, as well as in New Mexico, Arizona, and California, but the paper predicted that one of the best 16th of Septembers would be held in El Paso. To stimulate patriotic sentiments, *El Monitor* retold the story of the fathers of Mexican independence, Hidalgo and Morelos, and the independence struggle against the tyranny of Spain. Long live the illustrious Liberator, the article eulogized Hidalgo, and, 'Viva México!

Organized in honor of the Mexican colony, especially the Junta Patriótica and the Mexican consul Francisco Mallén, only rain spotted an otherwise flawless event. The celebration began on the morning of the fifteenth, when Consul Mallén dedicated the observance to Don Porfirio Díaz. That evening the Junta, the Mexican mutual benefit society "La Protectora," and the Mexican students of Sacred Heart School marched from Fifth Street, bordering the downtown area, to Sacred Heart Church in Chihuahuita preceded by a Mexican band. Throughout the route the homes and businesses of both Mexicans and Americans had been decorated with the Mexican tricolors. At 8:00 P.M. Consul Mallén and the president of the Junta, Dr. Reehy, accompanied by their wives arrived at the platform in front of the church and the program commenced by the playing of the Mexican national anthem. The more than 3,000 people who attended also heard recitations by several young people as well as songs and piano recitals. A speech in English by lawyer T.J. Beall that praised Mexican independence and Hidalgo received much applause. After several songs, Don Esteban Gómez del Campo delivered the main speech touching on various Mexican historical themes. The band then played both the Mexican and American anthems followed by two tunes originally composed by Trinidad Concha entitled

"On the Shores of the Rio Grande" and "Through El Paso." At last the secretary of the Junta read Hidalgo's act of independence (El grito de Dolores") and Consul Mallén said a few words. The program concluded with the Mexican national anthem sung by a chorus of young Mexican women. The following morning of the sixteenth, a parade through downtown El Paso containing both Mexican and American units ended the independence day celebrations.

As the 16th of September festivities partly indicated, different cultural influences touch the Mexican population of El Paso. Given diverse cultural levels within the Mexican settlement, these influences also had varied effects and responses. More acculturated than the immigrants, the minority of Mexican Americans felt the pull of both cultures much more strongly. "This civilization is American nominally," Gamio observed of Mexican Americans in the 1920s, "and exhibits the principal material aspects of modern American civilization, but intellectually and emotionally it lives in local Mexican tradition." On the other hand, the recently arrived immigrants retained to a considerable degree their native traditions in the form of language, folklore, superstitions, songs, and religious holidays, which expressed their national origins.

However, the impact of American industrialization and urbanization forced the immigrants to adjust to changed conditions. In the process many of El Paso's Mexicans formed relationships with one another through family, recreational, mutual aid, fraternal, and patriotic organizations that, on the one hand, provided a cultural security and continuity and, on the other, revealed new American conditions and influences. Moreover, the schools, both public and parochial, American material goods, and to a degree, churches represented institutions and attractions within the barrios that affected the subtle and gradual Americanization of the Mexicans.

Although their culture underwent some transformation as they adjusted to immigrant life, Mexicans, as Gamio further recognized, "never became integrally assimilated to American civilization." He believed that the problem retarding the complete Americanization of the Mexicans lay in the large gulf between what he called "purely American culture" and "purely Mexican culture." The economic discrimination and segregation aimed at Mexicans in El Paso also made it difficult to assimilate them as well as Mexican Americans because employers desired to keep them as a source of cheap labor. Furthermore, unlike European immigration, which slowed to a trickle in the 1920s, Mexican immigration persisted and reinforced a distinct Mexican presence in El Paso. Too, most Mexicans believed they would soon return to their homeland and therefore felt no strong motivation to discard their cultural traditions. Mexico, of course, was right next door. Consequently, a dialectical relationship existed between the immigrant's native culture and the attempt by American institutions and reformers to restructure earlier habits and instill a new urban-industrial discipline among the Mexicans. The eventual result: a Mexican border culture, neither completely Mexican nor American, but one revealing contrasting attractions and pressures between both cultures. Yet Mexican border culture was and is by no means monolithic because different experiences are represented. Recent arrivals display what Galarza calls "the most authentic transplant of Mexican working-class culture," whereas middle-class newcomers, such as many of the political refugees during the Revolutionary period, bring with them a more sophisticated bourgeois, one of both Mexican and European origins. Finally, Mexican Americans, especially the children and grandchildren of immigrants, have faced an erosion of their Mexican culture as American institutions, including an acculturated family environment, bring them into the fold of American mass culture.

Confronting "America"

Vicki L. Ruiz

As a child Elsa Chávez confronted a "moral" dilemma. She wanted desperately to enjoy the playground equipment close to her home in El Paso's Segundo Barrio. The tempting slide, swings, and jungle gym seemed to call her name. However, her mother would not let her near the best playground (and for many years the only playground) in the barrio. Even a local priest warned Elsa and her friends that playing there was a sin—the playground was located within the yard of the Rose Gregory Houchen Settlement, a Methodist community center.[1]

While one group of Americans responded to Mexican immigration by calling for restriction and deportation, other groups mounted campaigns to "Americanize" the immigrants. From Los Angeles, California, to Gary, Indiana, state and religious-sponsored Americanization programs swung into action. Imbued with the ideology of "the melting pot," teachers, social workers, and religious missionaries envisioned themselves as harbingers of salvation and civilization.[2] Targeting women and especially children, the vanguard of Americanization placed their trust "in the rising generation." As Pearl Ellis of the Covina City schools explained in her 1929 publication, *Americanization Through Homemaking*, "Since the girls are potential mothers and homemakers, they will control, in a large

measure, the destinies of their future families." She continued, "It is she who sounds the clarion call in the campaign for better homes."[3]

A growing body of literature on Americanization in Mexican communities by such scholars as George Sánchez, Sarah Deutsch, Gilbert González, and myself suggest that church and secular programs shared common course offerings and curricular goals. Perhaps taking their cue from the regimen developed inside Progressive Era settlement houses, Americanization projects emphasized classes in hygiene, civics, cooking, language, and vocational education (e.g., sewing and carpentry). Whether seated at a desk in a public school or on a sofa at a Protestant or Catholic neighborhood house, Mexican women received similar messages of emulation and assimilation. While emphasizing that the curriculum should meet "the needs of these people," one manual proclaimed with deepest sincerity that a goal of Americanization was to enkindle "a greater respect . . . for our civilization."[4]

Examples of Americanization efforts spanned the Southwest and Midwest from secular settlements in Watts, Pasadena, and Riverside to Hull House in Chicago. In addition, Catholic neighborhood centers, such as Friendly House in Phoenix, combined Americanization programs with religious and social services. Protestant missionaries, furthermore, operated an array of settlements, health clinics, and schools. During the first half of the twentieth century, the Methodist Church sponsored one hospital, four boarding schools, and sixteen settlements/community centers, all serving a predominately Mexican clientele. Two of these facilities were located in California, two in Kansas, one in New Mexico, and sixteen in Texas.[5] Though there are many institutions to compare, an overview, by its very nature, would tend to privilege missionary labors and thus, once again, place Mexican women within the shadows of history. By taking a closer look at one particular project—the Rose Gregory Houchen Settlement—one can discern the attitudes and experiences of Mexican women themselves. This chapter explores the ways in which Mexican mothers and their children interacted with the El Paso settlement, from utilizing selected services to claiming "American" identities, from taking their babies to the clinic for immunizations to becoming missionaries themselves.

Using institutional records raises a series of important methodological questions. How can missionary reports, pamphlets, newsletters, and related documents illuminate the experiences and attitudes of women of color? How do we sift through the bias, the self-congratulation, and the hyperbole to gain insight into women's lives? What can these materials tell us of women's agencies within and against larger social structures? I am intrigued (actually obsessed is a better word) with questions involving decision-making, specifically with regard to acculturation. What have Mexican women chosen to accept or reject? How have the economic, social, and political environments influenced the acceptance or rejection of cultural messages that emanate from the Mexican community, from U.S. popular culture, from Americanization programs, and from a dynamic coalescence of differing and at times oppositional cultural forms? What were women's real choices and, to borrow from Jürgen Habermas, how did they move "within the horizon of their lifeworld"?[6] Obviously, no set of institutional records can provide substantive answers, but by exploring these documents through the framework of these larger questions, we place Mexican women at the center of our study, not as victims of poverty and superstition as so often depicted by missionaries, but as women who made choices for themselves and for their families.

As the Ellis Island for Mexican immigrants, El Paso seemed a logical spot for a settlement house. In 1900, El Paso's Mexican community numbered only 8,748 residents, but by 1930 this population had swelled to 68,476. Over the course of the twentieth century, Mexicans composed over one-half the total population of this bustling border city.[7] Perceived as cheap labor by

Euro-American businessmen, they provided the human resources necessary for the city's industrial and commercial growth. Education and economic advancement proved illusory as segregation in housing, employment, and schools served as constant reminders of their second-class citizenship. To cite an example of stratification, from 1930 to 1960, only 1.8 percent of El Paso's Mexican workforce held high white-collar occupations.[8]

Segundo Barrio or South El Paso has served as the center of Mexican community life. Today, as in the past, wooden tenements and crumbling adobe structures house thousands of Mexicanos and Mexican Americans alike. For several decades, the only consistent source of social services in Segundo Barrio was the Rose Gregory Houchen Settlement House and its adjacent health clinic and hospital.

Founded in 1912 on the corner of Tays and Fifth in the heart of the barrio, this Methodist settlement had two initial goals: (1) provide a Christian rooming-house for single Mexican wage earners and (2) open a kindergarten for area children. By 1918, Houchen offered a full schedule of Americanization programs—citizenship, cooking, carpentry, English instruction, Bible study, and Boy Scouts. The first Houchen staff included three Methodist missionaries and one "student helper," Ofilia [sic] Chávez.[9] Living in the barrio made these women sensitive to the need for low-cost, accessible health care. Infant mortality in Segundo Barrio was alarmingly high. Historian Mario García related the following example: "Of 121 deaths during July [1914], 52 were children under 5 years of age."[10]

Houchen began to offer medical assistance, certainly rudimentary at first. In 1920, a registered nurse and Methodist missionary Effie Stoltz operated a first aid station in the bathroom of the settlement. More important, she soon persuaded a local physician to visit the residence on a regular basis and he, in turn, enlisted the services of his colleagues. Within seven months of Stoltz's arrival, a small adobe flat was converted into Freeman Clinic. Run by volunteers, this clinic provided prenatal exams, well-baby care, and pediatric services and, in 1930, it opened a six-bed maternity ward. Seven years later, it would be demolished to make way for the construction of a more modern clinic and a new twenty-two-bed maternity facility—the Newark Methodist Maternity Hospital. Health care at Newark was a bargain. Prenatal classes, pregnancy exams, and infant immunizations were free. Patients paid for medicines at cost and, during the 1940s, $30 covered the hospital bill. Staff members would boast that for less than $50, payable in installments, neighborhood women could give birth at "one of the best equipped maternity hospitals in the city."[11]

Houchen Settlement also thrived. From 1920 to 1960, it coordinated an array of Americanization activities. These included age and gender graded Bible studies, music lessons, Campfire activities, scouting, working girls' clubs, hygiene, cooking, and citizenship. Staff members also opened a day nursery to complement the kindergarten program. In terms of numbers, how successful was Houchen? The available records give little indication of the extent of the settlement's client base. Based on fragmentary evidence for the period of 1930 to 1950, perhaps as many as 15,000 to 20,000 people per year or approximately one-fourth to one-third of El Paso's Mexican population utilized its medical and/or educational services. Indeed, one Methodist from the 1930s pamphlet boasted that the settlement "reaches nearly 15,000 people."[12]

As a functioning Progressive Era settlement, Houchen had amazing longevity from 1912 to 1962. Several Methodist missionaries came to Segundo Barrio as young women and stayed until their retirement. Arriving in 1930, Millie Rickford would live at the settlement for thirty-one years. Two years after her departure, the Rose Gregory Houchen Settlement House (named after a Michigan schoolteacher) would receive a new name, Houchen Community Center. As a community center, it would become more of a secular agency staffed by social workers and at times Chicano activists.[13] In 1991 the buildings that cover a city block in South El Paso still furnish day care and recreational activities. Along with Bible study, there are classes in ballet fólklorico, karate, English, and aerobics. Citing climbing insurance costs (among other reasons), the Methodist Church closed the hospital and clinic in December 1986 over the protests of local supporters and community members.[14]

From 1912 until the 1950s, Houchen workers placed Americanization and proselytization at the center of their efforts. Embracing the imagery and ideology of the melting pot, Methodist missionary Dorothy Little explained:

Houchen settlement stands as a sentinel of friendship. . . between the people of America and the people of Mexico. We assimilate the best of their culture, their art, their ideals and they in turn gladly accept the best America has to offer as they . . . become one with us. For right here within our four walls is begun much of the "Melting" process of our "Melting Pot."[15]

The first goal of the missionaries was to convert Mexican women to Methodism since they perceived themselves as harbingers of salvation. As expressed in a Houchen report, "Our Church is called El Buen Pastor . . . and that is what our church really is to the people—it is a Good Shepherd guiding our folks out of darkness and Catholocism [sic] into the good Christian life." Along similar lines, one Methodist pamphlet printed during the 1930s equated Catholicism (as practiced by Mexicans) with paganism and superstition. Settlement's programs were couched in terms of "Christian Americanization" and these programs began early.[16]

Like the Franciscan missionaries who trod the same ground three centuries before, Houchen settlement workers sought to win the hearts and minds of children. While preschool and kindergarten students spoke Spanish and sang Mexican songs, they also learned English, U.S. history, biblical verses—even etiquette a la Emily Post.[17] The settlement also offered various after-school activities for older children. These included "Little Homemakers," scouting, teen clubs, piano lessons, dance, bible classes, and story hour. For many years the most elaborate playground in South El Paso could be found within the outer courtyard of the settlement. Elsa Chávez eventually got her playground wish. She and her mother reached an agreement: Elsa could play there on the condition that she not accept any "cookies or koolaid," the refreshments provided by Houchen staff. Other people remembered making similar bargains—they could play on the swings and slide, but they could not go indoors.[18] How big of a step was it to venture from the playground to story hour?

Settlement proselytizing did not escape the notice of barrio priests. Clearly troubled by Houchen, a few predicted dire consequences for those who participated in any Protestant-tinged activities. As mentioned earlier, one priest went so far as to tell neighborhood children that it was a sin even to play on the playground equipment. Others, however, took a more realistic stance and did not chastise their parishioners for utilizing Methodist child care and medical services. Perhaps as a response to both the Great Depression and suspected Protestant inroads, several area Catholic churches began distributing food baskets and establishing soup kitchens.[19]

Children were not the only ones targeted by Houchen. Women, particularly expectant mothers, received special attention. Like the proponents of Americanization programs in California, settlement workers believed that women held a special guardianship over their families' welfare. As head nurse Millie Rickford explained, "If we can teach her [the mother-to-be] the modern methods of cooking and preparing foods and simple hygiene habits for herself and her family, we have gained a stride."[20]

Houchen's "Christian Americanization" programs were not unique. During the teens and twenties, religious and state-organized Americanization projects aimed at the Mexican population proliferated throughout the Southwest. Although these efforts varied in scale from settlement houses to night classes, curriculum generally revolved around cooking, hygiene, English, and civics. Music seemed a universal tool of instruction. One Arizona schoolteacher excitedly informed readers of *The Arizona Teacher and Home Journal* that her district for the "cause of Americanization" had purchased a Victorola and several records that included two Spanish melodies, the "'Star Spangled Banner,' 'The Red, White, and Blue,' 'Silent Night,'. . . [and] 'Old Kentucky Home.'"[21] Houchen, of course, offered a variety of musical activities beginning with the kindergarten rhythm band of 1927. During the 1940s and the 1950s, missionaries provided flute, guitar, ballet, and tap lessons. For fifty cents a week, a youngster could take dance or music classes and perform in settlement recitals.[22] Clothing youngsters in European peasant styles was common. For instance, Alice Ruiz, Priscilla Molina, Edna Parra, Mira Gómez, and Aida Rivera represented Houchen in a local Girl Scout festival held at the Shrine temple in which they modeled costumes from Sweden, England, France, Scotland, and Lithuania.[23] Some immigrant traditions were valorized more than others. Celebrating Mexican heritage did not figure into the Euro-American orientation pushed by Houchen residents.

In contrast, a teacher affiliated with an Americanization program in Watts sought to infuse a multicultural perspective as she directed a pageant with a U.S. women's history theme. Clara Smith described the event as follows:

> Women, famous in the United States history as the Pilgrim, Betsy Ross, Civil War, and covered wagon women, Indian and Negro women, followed by the foreign women who came to live among us were portrayed. The class had made costumes and had learned to dance the Virginia Reel. . . . They had also made costumes with paper ruffles of Mexican colors to represent their flag. They prepared Mexican dances and songs.[24]

Despite such an early and valiant attempt at diversity, the teacher did not think it necessary to include the indigenous heritage of Mexican women. Indeed, stereotypical representations of the American Indian "princess" (or what Rayna Green has termed "the Pocahantas perplex"[25]) supplanted any understanding of indigenous cultures on either side of the political border separating Mexico and the United States.

Like Americanization advocates across the Southwest, Houchen settlement workers held out unrealistic notions of the American Dream as well as romantic constructions of American life. It is as if the Houchen staff had endeavored to create a white, middle-class environment for Mexican youngsters complete with tutus and toe shoes. Cooking classes also became avenues for developing particular tastes. Minerva Franco, who as a child attended settlement programs and who later as an adult became a community volunteer, explained, "I'll never forget the look on my mother's face when I first cooked 'Eggs Benedict' which I learned to prepare at Houchen."[26] The following passage, taken from a report dated February 1942 outlines, in part, the perceived accomplishments of the settlement:

> Sanitary conditions have been improving—more children go to school—more parents are becoming citizens, more are leaving Catholicism—more are entering business and public life—and more and more they are taking on the customs and standards of Anglo people.[27]

Seemingly oblivious to structural discrimination, such a statement ignores economic segmentation and racial/ethnic segregation. Focusing on El Paso, historian Mario García demonstrated that the curricula in Mexican Schools, which emphasized vocational education, served to funnel Mexican youth into the factories and building trades. In the abstract, education raised expectations, but in practice, particularly for men, it trained them for low-status, low-paying jobs. One California grower disdained education for Mexicans because it would give them "tastes for things they can't acquire."[28] Settlement workers seemed to ignore that racial/ethnic identity involved not only a matter of personal choice and heritage but also an ascribed status imposed by external sources.[29]

Americanization programs have come under a lot of criticisms from historians over the past two decades and numerous passages and photographs in the Houchen collection provide fodder for sarcasm among contemporary readers. Yet, to borrow from urban theorist Edward Soja, scholars should be mindful of "an appropriate interpretive balance between space, time and social being."[30] Although cringing at the ethnocentrism and romantic idealizations of "American" life, I respect the settlement workers for their health and child care services. Before judging the maternal missionaries too harshly, it is important to keep in mind the social services they rendered over an extended period of time as well as the environment in which they lived. For example, Houchen probably launched the first bilingual kindergarten program in El Paso, a program that eased the children's transition into an English-only first grade. Houchen residents did not denigrate the use of Spanish and many became fluent Spanish speakers. The hospital and clinic, moreover, were important community institutions for over half a century.[31]

Settlement workers themselves could not always count on the encouragement or patronage of Anglo El Paso. In a virulently nativist tract, a local physician, C. S. Babbitt, condemned missionaries, like the women of Houchen, for working among Mexican and African Americans. In fact, Babbitt argued that religious workers were "seemingly conspiring with Satan to destroy the handiwork of God" because their energies were "wasted on beings . . . who are not in reality the objects of Christ's sacrifice."[32] Even within their own ranks, missionaries could not count on the support of Protestant clergy. Reverend Robert McLean, who worked among Mexicans in Los Angeles, referred to his congregation as "chili con carne" bound to give Uncle Sam a bad case of "heartburn."[33]

Perhaps more damaging than these racist pronouncements was the apparent lack of financial support on the part of El Paso area Methodist churches. Accessible records reveal little in terms of local donations. Houchen was named after a former Michigan schoolteacher who bequeathed $1,000 for the establishment of a settlement in El Paso. The Women's Home Missionary Society of the Newark, New Jersey, Conference proved instrumental in raising funds for the construction of both Freeman Clinic and Newark Methodist Maternity Hospital. When Freemen Clinic first opened its doors in June 1921, all the medical equipment—everything from sterilizers to baby scales—were gifts from Methodist groups across the nation. The Houchen Day Nursery, however, received consistent financial support from the El Paso Community Chest and later the United Way. In 1975, Houchen's Board of Directors conducted the first community-wide fund-raising drive. Volunteers sought to raise $375,000 to renovate existing structures and build a modern day care center. The Houchen fund-raising slogan "When people pay their own way, it's your affair . . . not welfare" makes

painfully clear the conservative attitudes toward social welfare harbored by affluent El Pasoans.[34]

The women of Houchen appeared undaunted by the lack of local support. For over fifty years, these missionaries coordinated a multifaceted Americanization campaign among the residents of Segundo Barrio. How did Mexican women perceive the settlement? What services did they utilize and to what extent did they internalize the romantic notions of "Christian Americanization?"

Examining Mexican women's agency through institutional records is difficult; it involves getting beneath the text to dispel the shadows cast by missionary devotion to a simple Americanization ideology. One has to take into account the selectivity of voices. In drafting settlement reports and publications, missionaries chose those voices that would publicize their "victories" among the Spanish speaking. As a result, quotations abound that heap praise upon praise on Houchen and its staff. For example, in 1939, Soledad Burciaga emphatically declared, "There is not a person, no matter to which denomination they belong, who hasn't a kind word and a heart full of gratitude towards the Settlement House."[35] Obviously, these documents have their limits. Oral interviews and informal discussions with people who grew up in Segundo Barrio give a more balanced, less effusive perspective. Most viewed Houchen as a Protestant-run health care and after-school activities center rather than as the "light-house" [sic] in South El Paso.[36]

In 1949, the term Friendship Square was coined as a description for the settlement house, hospital, day nursery, and church. Missionaries hoped that children born at Newark would participate in preschool and afternoon programs and that eventually they and their families would join their church, El Buen Pastor. And a few did follow this pattern. One of the ministers assigned to El Buen Pastor, Fernando García, was a Houchen kindergarten graduate. Emulating the settlement staff, some young women enrolled in Methodist missionary colleges or served as lay volunteers. Elizabeth Soto, for example, attended Houchen programs throughout her childhood and adolescence. On graduation from Bowie High School, she entered Asbury College to train as a missionary and then returned to El Paso as a Houchen resident. After several years of service, she left settlement work to become the wife of a Mexican Methodist minister. The more common goal among Houchen teens was to graduate from high school and perhaps attend Texas Western, the local college. The first child born at Newark Hospital, Margaret

Holguin, took part in settlement activities as a child and later became a registered nurse. According to her comadre, Lucy Lucero, Holguin's decision to pursue nursing was "perhaps due to the influence" of head nurse Millie Rickford. According to Lucero, "The only contact I had had with Anglos was with Anglo teachers. Then I met Miss Rickford and I felt, 'Hey, she's human. She's great.'" At a time when many (though certainly not all) elementary schoolteachers cared little about their Mexican students, Houchen residents offered warmth and encouragement.[37]

Emphasizing education among Mexican youth seemed a common goal characterizing Methodist community centers and schools. The Frances De Pauw School located on Sunset Boulevard in Los Angeles, for example, was an all-girls boarding school. Frances De Pauw educated approximately 1,800 young Mexican women from 1900 to 1946 and a Methodist pamphlet elaborated on its successes. "Among [the school's] graduates are secretaries, bookkeepers, clerks, office receptionists, nurses, teachers, waitresses, workers in cosmetic laboratories, church workers, and Christian homemakers." While preparing its charges for the workaday world, the school never lost sight of women's domestic duties. "Every De Pauw girl is graded as carefully in housework as she is in her studies."[38] With regard to Friendship Square, one cannot make wholesale generalizations about its role in fostering mobility or even aspirations for mobility among the youth of Segundo Barrio. Yet it is clear that Houchen missionaries strived to build self-esteem and encouraged young people to pursue higher education.

Missionaries also envisioned a Protestant enclave in South El Paso; but, to their frustration, very few people responded. The settlement church, El Buen Pastor, had a peak membership of 150 families. The church itself had an intermittent history. Shortly after its founding in 1897, El Buen Pastor disappeared; it was officially rededicated as part of Houchen in 1932. However, the construction of an actual church on settlement grounds did not begin until 1945. In 1968, the small rock chapel would be converted into a recreation room and thrift shop as the members of El Buen Pastor and El Mesias (another Mexican-American church) were merged together to form the congregation of the Emmanuel United Methodist Church in downtown El Paso. In 1991, a modern gymnasium occupies the ground where the chapel once stood.[39]

The case histories of converts suggest that many of those who joined El Buen Pastor were already Protestant. The Dominguez family offers an example. In the words of settlement worker A. Ruth Kern:

Reyna and Gabriel Dominguez are Latin Americans, even though both were born in the United States. Some members of the family do not even speak English. Reyna was born . . . in a Catholic home, but at the age of eleven years, she began attending the Methodist Church. Gabriel was born in Arizona. His mother was a Catholic, but she became a Protestant when . . . Gabriel was five years old.[40]

The youth programs at Houchen brought Reyna and Gabriel together. After their marriage, the couple had six children, all born at Newark Hospital. The Dominguez family represented Friendship Square's typical success story. Many of the converts were children and many had already embraced a Protestant faith. In the records I examined, I found only one instance of the conversion of a Catholic adult and one of the conversion of an entire Catholic family.[41] It seems that those most receptive to Houchen's religious messages were already predisposed in that direction.

The failure of proselytization cannot be examined solely within the confines of Friendship Square. It is not as if these Methodist women were good social workers but incompetent missionaries. Houchen staff member Clara Sarmiento wrote of the difficulty in building trust among the adults of Segundo Barrio. "Though it is easy for children to open up their hearts to us we do not find it so with the parents." She continued, "It is hard especially because we are Protestant, and most of the people we serve . . . come from Catholic heritage."[42] I would argue that the Mexican community played an instrumental role in thwarting conversion. In a land where the barrio could serve as a refuge from prejudice and discrimination, the threat of social isolation could certainly inhibit many residents from turning Protestant. During an oral interview, Estella Ibarra, a woman who participated in Houchen activities for over fifty years, described growing up Protestant in South El Paso:

We went through a lot of prejudice . . . sometimes my friends' mothers wouldn't let them play with us. . . . When the priest would go through the neighborhood, all the children would run to say hello and kiss his hand. My brothers and I would just stand by and look. The priest would usually come . . . and tell us how we were living in sin. Also, there were times when my brother and I were stoned by other students . . . and called bad names.[43]

When contacted by a Houchen resident, Mrs. Espinosa admitted to being a closet Protestant. As she explained, "I am afraid of the Catholic sisters and [I] don't want my neighbors to know that I am not Catholic-minded." The fear of ostracism, while recorded by Houchen staff, did not figure into their understanding of Mexicano resistance to conversion. Instead, they blamed time and culture. Or as Dorothy Little succinctly related, "We can not eradicate in a few years what has been built up during ages."[44] Their dilemma points to the fact historians Sarah Deutsch and George Sánchez have noted: Americanization programs in the Southwest, most of which were sporadic and poorly financed, made little headway in Mexican communities. Ruth Crocker also described the Protestant settlements in Gary, Indiana, as having only a "superficial and temporary" influence.[45] Yet even long-term sustained efforts, as in the case of Houchen, had limited appeal. This inability to mold consciousness or identity demonstrates not only the strength of community sanctions, but, more significant, of conscious decision-making on the part of Mexican women who sought to claim a place for themselves and their families in American society without abandoning their Mexican cultural affinities.

Mexican women derived substantive services from Friendship in the form of health care and education; however, they refused to embrace its romantic idealizations of American life. Wage-earning mothers who placed their children in the day nursery no doubt encountered an Anglo world quite different from the one depicted by Methodist missionaries and thus were skeptical of the settlement's cultural message. Clara Sarmiento knew from experience that it was much easier to reach the children than their parents.[46] How did children respond to the ideological undercurrents of Houchen programs? Did Mexican women feel empowered by their interaction with the settlement or were Methodist missionaries invidious underminers of Mexican identity?

In getting beneath the text, the following remarks of Minerva Franco that appeared in a 1975 issue of *Newark-Houchen News* raise a series of provocative questions. "Houchen provided . . . opportunities for learning and experiencing. . . . At Houchen I was shown that I had worth and that I was an individual."[47] Now what did she mean by that statement? Did the settlement house heighten her self-esteem? Did she feel that she was not an individual within the context of her family and neighborhood? Some young women imbibed Americanization so heavily as to reject their identity. In *No Separate Refuge*, Sarah Deutsch picked up on this theme as she quoted missionary Polita Padilla: "I am Mexican, born and brought up in New Mexico, but much of my life was spent in the Allison School where we had a different training so that the Mexican way of living now seems strange to me." Others, like Estella Ibarra and Rose Escheverría Mulligan, saw little incompatibility between Mexican traditions and Protestantism.[48]

Which Mexican women embraced the ideas of assimilation so completely as to become closet Mexicans? As a factor, class must be taken into consideration. In his field notes housed at the Bancroft Library, economist Paul Taylor contends that middle-class Mexicans desiring to dissociate themselves from their working-class neighbors possessed the most fervent aspirations for assimilation. Once in the United States, middle-class Mexicanos found themselves subject to racial/ethnic prejudice that did not discriminate by class. Due to restrictive real estate covenants, immigrants lived in barrios with people they considered inferiors.[49] By passing as "Spanish," they cherished hopes of melting into the American social landscape. Sometimes mobility-minded parents sought to regulate their children's choice of friends and later marriage partners. "My folks never allowed us to be around with Mexicans," remembered Alicia Mendeola Shelit. "We went sneaking around, but my Dad wouldn't allow it. We'd always be with white." Indeed, Shelit married twice, both times to Euro-Americans.[50] Of course it would be unfair to characterize all middle-class Mexican women immigrants as repudiating their mestizo identity. Working in a posh El Paso department store, Alma Araiza would quickly correct her colleagues when they assumed she was Italian.

> People kept telling me 'You must not be Mexican.' And I said, 'why do you think I'm not?' 'Well, it's your skin color. Are you Italian?'. . . I [responded] 'I am Mexicana.'[51]

Or as a young woman cleverly remarked to anthropologist Ruth Tuck, "Listen, I may be a Mexican in a fur coat, but I'm still a Mexican."[52]

The Houchen documents reveal glimpses into the formation of identity, consciousness, and values. The

Friendship Square Calendar of 1949 explicitly stated that the medical care provided at Houchen "is a tool to develop sound minds in sound bodies; for thus it is easier to find peace with God and man. We want to help people develop a sense of values in life." Furthermore, the privileging of color—with white as the pinnacle—was an early lesson. Relating the excitement of kindergarten graduation, Day Nursery head Beatrice Fernandez included in her report a question asked by Margarita, one of the young graduates. "We are all wearing white, white dress, slip, socks and Miss Fernandez, is it alright if our hair is black?"[53] Sometimes subtle, sometimes overt, the privileging of race, class, culture, and color taught by women missionaries had painful consequences for their pupils.

Houchen activities were synonymous with Americanization. A member of the settlement Brownie troop encouraged her friends "to become 'an American or a Girl Scout' at Houchen." Scouting certainly served as a vehicle for Americanization. The all-Mexican Girl and Boy Scout Troops of Alpine, Texas, enjoyed visiting El Paso and Ciudad Juárez in the company of Houchen scouts. In a thank-you note, the Alpine Girl Scouts wrote, "Now we can all say we have been to a foreign country."[54]

It is important to remember that Houchen provided a bilingual environment, not a bicultural one. Spanish was the means to communicate the message of Methodism and Christian Americanization. Whether dressing up children as Pilgrims or European peasants, missionaries stressed "American" citizenship and values; yet, outside conversion, definitions of those values or of "our American way" remained elusive. Indeed, some of the settlement lessons were not incongruous with Mexican mores. In December 1952, a Euro-American settlement worker recorded in her journal the success of a Girl Scout dinner. "The girls learned a lot from it too. They were taught how to set the table, and how to serve the men. They learned also that they had to share, to cooperate, and to wait their turn."[55] These were not new lessons.

The most striking theme that repeatedly emerges from Houchen documents is that of individualism. Missionaries emphasized the importance of individual decision-making and individual accomplishment. In recounting her own conversion, Clara Sarmiento explained to a young client, "I chose my own religion because it was my own personal experience and . . . I was glad my religion was not chosen for me."[56]

In *Relations of Rescue*, Peggy Pascoe carefully recorded the glass ceiling encountered by "native helpers" at Protestant rescue homes. Chinese women at Cameron House in San Francisco, for example, could only emulate Euro-American missionaries to a certain point, always as subordinates, not as directors or leaders. Conversely, Mexican women did assume top positions of leadership at Methodist settlements. In 1930, María Moreno was appointed the head resident of the brand new Floyd Street Settlement in Dallas, Texas. Methodist community centers and boarding schools stressed the need for developing "Christian leaders trained for useful living."[57] For many, leadership meant ministering as a lay volunteer; for some, it meant pursuing a missionary vocation.

The Latina missionaries of Houchen served as cultural brokers as they diligently strived to integrate themselves into the community. Furthermore, over time Latinas appeared to have experienced some mobility within the settlement hierarchy. In 1912, Ofilia [sic] Chávez served as a "student helper"; forty years later Beatrice Fernandez would direct the preschool. Until 1950, the Houchen staff usually included one Latina; however, during the 1950s, the number of Latina (predominately Mexican American) settlement workers rose to six. Mary Lou López, María Rico, Elizabeth Soto, Febe Bonilla, Clare Sarmiento, María Payan, and Beatrice Fernandez had participated in Methodist outreach activities as children (Soto at Houchen) and had decided to follow in the footsteps of their teachers. In addition, these women had the assistance of five full-time Mexican laypersons.[58] It is no coincidence that the decade of greatest change in Houchen policies occurred at a time when Latinas held a growing number of staff positions. Friendship Square's greater sensitivity to neighborhood needs arose, in part, out of the influence exerted by Mexican clients in shaping the attitudes and actions of Mexican missionaries.

So, in the end, Mexican women utilized Houchen's social services; they did not, by and large, adopt its tenets of Christian Americanization. Children who attended settlement programs enjoyed the activities, but Friendship Square did not always leave a lasting imprint. "My Mom had an open mind, so I participated in a lot of clubs. But I didn't become Protestant," remarked Lucy Lucero. "I had fun and I learned a lot, too." Because of the warm, supportive environment, Houchen Settlement is remembered with fondness. However, one cannot equate pleasant memories with the acceptance of the settlement's cultural ideals.[59]

Settlement records bear out Mexican women's *selective* use of Houchen's resources. The most complete set of figures is for the year 1944. During this period,

7,614 people visited the clinic and hospital. The settlement afternoon programs had an average monthly enrollment of 362 and 40 children attended kindergarten. Taken together, approximately 8,000 residents of Segundo Barrio utilized Friendship Square's medical and educational offerings. In contrast, the congregation of El Buen Pastor included 160 people.[60] Although representing only a single year, these figures indicate the importance of Houchen's medical facilities and Mexican women's selective utilization of resources.

By the 1950s, settlement houses were few and far between and those that remained were run by professional social workers. Implemented by a growing Latina staff, client-initiated changes in Houchen policies brought a realistic recognition of the settlement as a social service agency rather than a religious mission. During the 1950s, brochures describing the day nursery emphasized that while children said grace at meals and sang Christian songs, they would not receive "in any way indoctrination" regarding Methodism. In fact, at the parents' request, Newark nurses summoned Catholic priests to the hospital to baptize premature infants. Client desire became the justification for allowing the presence of Catholic clergy, a policy that would have been unthinkable in the not too distant past.[61] Finally, in the new Houchen constitution of 1959, all mention of conversion was dropped. Instead, it conveyed a more ecumenical, nondenominational spirit. For instance, the goal of Houchen Settlement was henceforth "to establish a Christian democratic framework for—individual development, family solidarity, and neighborhood welfare."[62]

Settlement activities also became more closely linked with the Mexican community. During the 1950s, Houchen was the home of two LULAC chapters—one for teenagers and one for adults. The League of United Latin American Citizens (LULAC was the most visible and politically powerful civil rights organization in Texas.[63] Carpentry classes—once the preserve of males—opened their doors to young women, although on a gender-segregated basis. Houchen workers, moreover, made veiled references to the "very dangerous business" of Juárez abortion clinics; it appears unclear whether or not the residents themselves offered any contraceptive counseling. During the early 1960s, however, the settlement, in cooperation with Planned Parenthood, opened a birth control clinic for "married women." Indeed, a Houchen contraception success story was featured on the front page of a spring newsletter. "Mrs. G__, after having her thirteenth and fourteenth children (twins), enrolled in our birth control clinic; now for one and one half years she has been a happy and non-pregnant mother."[64] Certainly Houchen had changed with the times. What factors accounted for the new directions in settlement work? The evidence on the baptism of premature babies seems fairly clear in terms of client pressure, but to what extent did other policies change as the result of Mexican women's input? The residents of Segundo Barrio may have felt more comfortable expressing their ideas and Latina settlement workers may have exhibited a greater willingness to listen. Indeed, Mexican clients, not missionaries, set the boundaries for interaction.

Creating the public space of settlements and community centers, advocates of Americanization sought to alter the "lifeworld" of Mexican immigrants to reflect their own idealized versions of life in the United States. Settlement workers can be viewed as the narrators of lived experience as Houchen records reflected the cognitive construction of missionary aspirations and expectations. In other words, the documents revealed more about the women who wrote them than those they served. At another level, one could interpret the cultural ideals of Americanization as an indication of an attempt at what Jürgen Habermas has termed "inner colonization."[65] Yet the failure of such projects illustrates the ways in which Mexican women appropriated desired resources, both material (infant immunizations) and psychological (self-esteem) while, in the main, rejecting the ideological messages behind them. The shift in Houchen policies during the 1950s meant more than a recognition of community needs; it represented a claiming of public space by Mexican women clients.

Confronting Americanization brings into sharp relief the concept I have termed cultural coalescence. Immigrants and their children pick, borrow, retain, and create distinctive cultural forms. There is no single hermetic Mexican or Mexican-American culture, but rather permeable *cultures* rooted in generation, gender, region, class, and personal experience. Chicano scholars have divided Mexican experiences into three generational categories: Mexicano (first generation), Mexican American (second generation), and Chicano (third and beyond).[66] But this general typology tends to obscure the ways in which people navigate across cultural boundaries as well as their conscious decision-making in the production of culture. However, people of color have not had unlimited choice. Race and gender prejudice and discrimination with their accompanying social, political, and economic segmentation have constrained aspirations, expectations, and decision-making.

The images and ideals of Americanization were a mixed lot and were never the only messages immigrant women received. Local *mutualistas*, Mexican patriotic and Catholic pageants, newspapers, and community networks reinforced familiar legacies. In contrast, religious and secular Americanization programs, the elementary schools, movies, magazines, and radio bombarded the Mexican community with a myriad of models, most of which were idealized, stylized, unrealistic, and unattainable. Expectations were raised in predictable ways. In the words of one Mexican-American woman, "We felt that if we worked hard, proved ourselves, we could become professional people."[67] Consumer culture would hit the barrio full force during the 1920s, exemplified by the Mexican flapper. As we will see in the next chapter, even Spanish-language newspapers promoted messages of consumption and acculturation. Settlement houses also mixed in popular entertainment with educational programs. According to historian Louise Año Nuevo Kerr, the Mexican Mothers Club of the University of Chicago Settlement "took a field trip to NBC radio studios in downtown Chicago from which many of the soap operas emanated."[68]

By looking through the lens of cultural coalescence, we can begin to discern the ways in which people select and create cultural forms. Teenagers began to manipulate and reshape the iconography of consumer culture both as a marker of peer group identity and as an authorial presence through which they rebelled against strict parental supervision. When standing at the cultural crossroads, Mexican women blended their options and created their own paths.

Endnotes

1. Interview with Elsa Chávez, April 18, 1983, conducted by the author. *Note:* Elsa Chávez is a pseudonym used at the person's request.

2. Recent scholarship on Americanization programs aimed at Mexican communities includes George J. Sánchez, "Go After the Women: Americanization and the Mexican Immigrant Woman, 1915–1929," in *Unequal Sisters: A Multicultural Reader in U.S. Women's History*, 2nd ed., eds. Vicki L. Ruiz and Ellen Carol DuBois (New York: Routledge, 1994), pp. 284–97; Sarah Deutsch, *No Separate Refuge: Culture, Class, and Gender on the Anglo-Hispanic Frontier in the American Southwest, 1880–1940* (New York: Oxford University Press, 1987), pp. 63–86; Gilbert González, *Chicano Education in the Era of Segregation* (Philadelphia: Balch Institute Press, 1990), pp. 30–61; Ruth Hutchinson Crocker, "Gary Mexicans and 'Christian Americanization': A Study in Cultural Conflict," in *Forging a Community: The Latino Experience in Northwest Indiana, 1919–1975*, eds. James B. Lane and Edward J. Escobar (Chicago: Cattails Press, 1987), pp. 115–34; Susan Yohn, *A Contest of Faiths: Missionary Women and Pluralism in the American Southwest* (Ithaca: Cornell University Press); Vicki L. Ruiz, "Dead Ends or Gold Mines?: Using Missionary Records in Mexican American Women's History," *Frontiers: A Journal of Women's Studies*, 12:1 (1991): 33–56.

3. Pearl Idella Ellis, *Americanization Through Homemaking* (Los Angeles: Wetzel Publishing Co., 1929), preface [no page number].

4. *Ibid.*, p. 13.

5. M. Dorothy Woodruff, "Methodist Women Along the Mexican Border" (Women's Division of Christian Service pamphlet, ca. 1946) [part of an uncatalogued collection of documents housed at Houchen Community Center, El Paso, Texas; heretofore referred to as HF for Houchen Files]. This pamphlet provides brief descriptions of each of the twenty one "centers of work" operated by Methodist missionaries. For a celebratory overview of Methodist women's missionary endeavors throughout the United States, see Noreen Dunn Tatum, *A Crown of Service* (Nashville, Tenn.: Parthenon Press, 1960).

6. Steven Seidman, ed., *Jürgen Habermas on Society and Politics: A Reader* (Boston: Beacon Press, 1989), p. 171.

7. Oscar J. Martínez, *The Chicanos of El Paso: An Assessment of Progress* (El Paso: Texas Western Press, 1980), pp. 6, 17.

8. Martínez, *Chicanos*, pp. 10, 29–33. Mario García meticulously documents the economic and social stratification of Mexicans in El Paso. See Mario T. García, *Desert Immigrants: The Mexicans of El Paso, 1880–1920* (New Haven: Yale University Press, 1981). *Note:* In 1960, the proportion of Mexican workers with high white-collar jobs jumped to 3.4 percent. [Martínez, *Chicanos*, p. 10.]

9. "South El Paso's Oasis of Care," *paso del norte*, Vol 1 (September 1982); 42–43; Thelma Hammond, "Friendship Square," (Houchen Report, 1969) [HF]; "Growing with the Century" (Houchen Report, 1947) [HF].

10. García, *Desert Immigrants*, p. 145; Effie Stoltz, "Freeman Clinic: A Resume of Four Years Work" (Houchen Pamphlet, 1924) [HF]. It should be noted that Houchen Settlement sprang from the work of Methodist missionary Mary Tripp who arrived in South El Paso in 1893. However, it was not until 1912 that an actual settlement was established. ["South El Paso's Oasis of Care," p. 42].

11. Stoltz, "Freeman Clinic"; Hammond, "Friendship Square"; M. Dorothy Woodruff and Dorothy Little,

"Friendship Square (Houchen Pamphlet, March 1949) [HF]; "Friendship Square" (Houchen Report, circa 1940s) [HF]; *Health Center* (Houchen Newsletter, 1943) [HF]; "Christian Health Service" (Houchen Report, 1941) [HF]; *El Paso Times*, October 20, 1945.

12. "Settlement Worker's Report" (Houchen Report, 1927) [HF]. Letter from Dorothy Little to E. Mae Young dated May 10, 1945 [HF]. Letter from Bessie Brinson to Treva Ely dated September 14, 1958 [HF]; Hammond, "Friendship Square"; Elmer T. Clark and Dorothy McConnell, "The Methodist Church and Latin Americans in the United States" (Board of Missions pamphlet, circa 1930s) [HF]. My very rough estimate is based on the documents and records to which I had access. I was not permitted to examine any materials then housed at Newark Hospital. The most complete statistics on utilization of services are for the year 1944 in the letter from Dorothy Little to E. Mae Young. *Note:* Because of the deportation and repatriation drives of the 1930s in which one-third of the Mexican population in the United States were either deported or repatriated, the Mexican population in El Paso dropped from 68,476 in 1930 to 55,000 in 1940. By 1960 it had risen to 63,796. [Martínez, *Chicanos*, p. 6]

13. *El Paso Herald Post*, March 7, 1961; *El Paso Herald Post*, March 12, 1961; "Community Centers" (Women's Division of Christian Service Pamphlet, May 1963); *Funding Proposal* for Youth Outreach and Referral Report Project (April 30, 1974) [Private Files of Kenton J. Clymer, Ph.D.]; *El Paso Herald Post*, January 3, 1983; *El Paso Times*, August 8, 1983.

14. Letter from Tom Houghteling, Director, Houchen Community Center to the author December 24, 1990; Tom Houghteling, telephone conversation with the author, January 9, 1991.

15. Dorothy Little, "Rose Gregory Houchen Settlement" (Houchen Report, February 1942) [HF].

16. *Ibid.*; "Our Work at Houchen" (Houchen Report, circa 1940s) [HF]; Woodruff and Little, "Friendship Square"; Jennie C. Gilbert, "Settlements Under the Women's Home Missionary Society pamphlet, circa 1920s) [HF]; Clark and McConnell, "Latin Americans in the United States."

17. Anita Hernandez, "The Kindergarten" (Houchen Report, circa 1940s) [HF]; *A Right Glad New Year* (Houchen Newsletter, circa 1940s) [HF]; Little, "Rose Gregory Houchen Settlement"; "Our Work at Houchen"; Woodruff and Little, "Friendship Square." For more information on the Franciscans, see Ramón Gutiérrez, *When Jesus Came, the Corn Mothers Went Away: Marriage, Sexuality, and Power in New Mexico, 1500–1846* (Stanford: Stanford University Press, 1991).

18. Settlement Worker's Report (1927); Letter from Little to Young; letter from Brinson to Ely; *Friendship Square*

Calendar (1949) [HF]; interview with Lucy Lucero, October 8, 1983, conducted by the author; Chávez interview; discussion following presentation, "Settlement Houses in El Paso," given by the author at the El Paso Conference on History and the Social Sciences, August 24, 1983, El Paso, Texas [tape of presentation and discussion is on file at the Institute of Oral History, University of Texas, El Paso].

19. Chávez interview; discussion following "Settlement Houses in El Paso." *Note:* The Catholic Church never established a competing settlement house. However, during the 1920s in Gary, Indiana, the Catholic diocese opened up the Gary-Alerding Settlement with the primary goal of Americanizing Mexican immigrants. The bishop took such action to counteract suspected inroads made by two local Protestant settlement houses. See Crocker, "Gary Mexicans," pp. 123–27.

20. "Christian Health Service"; "The Freeman Clinic and the Newark Conference Maternity Hospital" (Houchen Report, 1940) [HF]; *El Paso Times*, August 2, 1961; *El Paso Herald Post*, May 12, 1961. For more information on Americanization programs in California, see George J. Sánchez, "Go After the Women," pp. 250–63. *Note:* The documents reveal a striking absence of adult Mexican male clients. The Mexican men who do appear are either Methodist ministers or lay volunteers.

21. Sánchez, "Go After," pp. 250–83; Deutsch, *No Separate Refuge*, "Americanization Notes," *The Arizona Teacher and Home Journal*, 11:5 (January 1923): 26. *Note:* The Methodist and Presbyterian settlements in Gary, Indiana, also couched their programs in terms of "Christian Americanization." [Crocker, "Gary Mexicans," pp. 118–20]

22. "Settlement Worker's Report" (1927); *Friendship Square Calendar* (1949) [HF]; letter from Brinson to Ely; Chávez interview.

23. "News Clipping from *The El Paso Times*" (circa 1950s) [HF].

24. Clara Gertrude Smith, "The Development of the Mexican People in the Community of Watts" (M.A. thesis, University of Southern California, 1933), p. 104.

25. Rayna Green, "The Pocahontas Perplex," in *Unequal Sisters*, pp. 15–21.

26. Sánchez, "Go After the Women," p. 260; *Newark-Houchen News*, September 1975. I agree with George Sánchez that Americanization programs created an overly rosy picture of American life. In his words: "Rather than providing Mexican immigrant women with an attainable picture of assimilation, Americanization programs could only offer these immigrants idealized versions of American life." [Sánchez, *loc. cit.*]

27. Little, "Rose Gregory Houchen Settlement."

28. García, *Desert Immigrants*, pp. 110–26; Paul S. Taylor, *Mexican Labor in the United States*, Vol. 1 (Berkeley:

University of California Press, 1930, rpt. Arno Press, 1970), pp. 79, 206–206. [Quote is from Taylor, *Mexican Labor*, p. 79.]

29. Margarita B. Melville, "Selective Acculturation of Female Mexican Migrants," in *Twice a Minority: Mexican American Women*, ed. Margarita B. Melville (St. Louis: C.V. Mosby, 1980), pp. 159–60; John García, "Ethnicity and Chicanos: Measurement of Ethnic Identification, Identity, and Consciousness," *Hispanic Journal of Behavioral Sciences*, Vol. 4 (1982): 310–11. For an insightful, brief overview of Mexican-American ethnic identification, see David Gutiérrez, *Walls and Mirrors: Mexican Americans, Mexican Immigrants, and the Politics of Ethnicity in the Southwest, 1910–1986* (Berkeley: University of California Press, 1995), pp. 1–11.

30. Edward Soja, *Postmodern Geographies: The Reassertion of Space in Critical Social Theory* (New York and London: Verso Press, 1989), p. 23. Gracias a Matthew García for bringing this text to my attention.

31. "Settlement Worker's Report" (1927); Hernandez, "The Kindergarten" [HF]; *A Right Glad New Year*; Little, "Rose Gregory Houchen Settlement"; "Our Work at Houchen"; Woodruff and Little, "Friendship Square"; "South El Paso's Oasis of Care," *loc. cit.*; *El Paso Herald Post*, March 7, 1961; *El Paso Herald Post*, March 12, 1961; *El Paso Herald Post*, May 12, 1961.

32. C.S. Babbitt, "The Remedy for the Decadence of the Latin Race" (El Paso: El Paso Printing Company) (Presented to the Pioneers Association of El Paso, Texas, July 11, 1909, by Mrs. Babbitt, widow of the author), p. 55. Pamphlet courtesy of Jack Redman.

33. George J. Sánchez, *Becoming Mexican American: Ethnicity, Culture, and Identity in Chicano Los Angeles, 1900–1945* (New York: Oxford University Press, 1993), p. 156; Robert McLean, *That Mexican! As He Is, North and South of the Rio Grande* (New York: Fleming H. Revell Co., 1928), pp. 162–63, quoted in E.C. Orozco, *Republican Protestantism in Aztlán* (Santa Barbara: The Petereins Press, 1980), p. 162. *Note*: Immigration has frequently been linked with food from the "melting pot" of assimilation to the "salad bowl" of cultural pluralism. McLean's metaphor of Uncle Sam as a diner at the immigration café follows:

Fifty and one hundred years ago Uncle Sam accomplished some remarkable digestive feats. Gastronomically he was a marvel. He was not particularly choosy! Dark meat from the borders of the Mediterranean or light meat from the Baltic equally suited him, for promptly he was able to assimilate both, turning them into bone of his bone, and flesh of his flesh—But this chili con carne! Always it seems to give Uncle Samuel the heartburn; and the older he gets, the less he seems to be able to assimilate it. Indeed, it is a question whether chili is not a condiment, to be taken in small

quantities rather than a regular article of diet. And upon this conviction ought to stand all the law . . . as far as the Mexican immigrant is concerned.

34. *Account Book for Rose Gregory Houchen Settlement* (1903–1913) [HF]; Hammond, "Friendship Square"; "Growing with the Century"; *El Paso Times*, September 5, 1975; Stoltz, "Freeman Clinic": Woodruff and Little, "Friendship Square"; *El Paso Times*, October 3, 1947; "Four Institutions. One Goal. The Christian Community" (Houchen pamphlet, circa early 1950s) [HF]; Houghteling conversation; "A City Block of Service" (Script of Houchen Slide Presentation, 1976) [HF]; *El Paso Times*, January 19, 1977; "Speech given by Kenton J. Clymer, Ph.D." (June 1975) [Clymer Files]; *El Paso Times*, May 23, 1975; *Newark-Houchen News*, September 1975. It should be noted that in 1904 local Methodist congregations did not contribute much of the money needed to purchase the property on which the settlement was built. Local civic groups occasionally donated money or equipment and threw Christmas parties for Houchen children. [*Account Book*; *El Paso Herald Post*, December 14, 1951; *El Paso Times*, December 16, 1951]

35. Vernon McCombs, "Victories in the Latin American Mission" (Board of Home Missions pamphlet, 1935) [HF]; "Brillante Historia De La Iglesia 'El Buen Pastor' El Paso," *Young Adult Fellowship Newsletter*, December 1946 [HF]; Soledad Burciago, "Yesterday in 1923" (Houchen Report, 1939) [HF].

36. This study is based on a limited number of oral interviews (five), but they represent a range of interaction with the settlement from playing on the playground to serving as the minister for El Buen Pastor. It is also informed by a public discussion of my work on Houchen held during an El Paso teachers' conference in 1983. Most of the educators who attended the talk had participated, to some extent, in Houchen activities and were eager to share their recollections. [C.f. note 13]. I am also indebted to students in my Mexican-American history classes when I taught at the University of Texas, El Paso, especially the reentry women, for their insight and knowledge.

37. Woodruff and Little, "Friendship Square"; Hammond, "Friendship Square"; *Greetings for 1946* (Houchen Christmas Newsletter, 1946) [HF]; Little, "Rose Gregory Houchen Settlement'; Soledad Burciaga, "Today in 1939" (Houchen Report, 1939) [HF]; "Our Work at Houchen"; "Christian Social Service" [Houchen Report, circa 1940s] [HF]; Interview with Fernando García, September 21, 1983, conducted by the author; *El Paso Times*, June 14, 1951; Lucero interview; Vicki L. Ruiz, "Oral History and La Mujer: The Rosa Guerrero Story," in *Women on the U.S.-Mexico Border: Responses to Change* (Boston: Allen and Unwin, 1987), pp. 226–27; *Newark-Houchen News*, September 1975.

38. Woodruff, "Mexican Women."

39. *Spanish-American Methodist News Bulletin*, April 1946 [HF]; Hammond, "Friendship Square"; McCombs, "Victories"; "El Metodismo en La Ciudad de El Paso," *Christian Herald*, July 1945 [HF]; "Brillante Historia"; "The Door: An Informal Pamphlet on the Work of the Methodist Church Among the Spanish-speaking of El Paso, Texas" (Methodist pamphlet, 1940) [HF]; "A City Block of Service" (script of slide presentation); García interview; Houghteling interview. *Note*: From 1932 to 1939, services for El Buen Pastor were held in a church located two blocks away from the settlement.

40. A. Ruth Kern, "There is No Segregation Here," *Methodist Youth Fund Bulletin* (January–March, 1953): 12 [HF].

41. *Ibid.*; "The Torres Family" (Houchen Report, circa 1940s) [HF]; interview with Estella Ibarra, November 11, 1982, conducted by Jesusita Ponce; Hazel Bulifant, "One Woman's Story" (Houchen Report, 1950) [HF]; "Our Work at Houchen."

42. Clara Sarmiento, "Lupe" (Houchen Report, circa 1950s) [HF].

43. Ibara interview.

44. Bulifant, "One Woman's Story"; letter from Little to Young.

45. Deutsch, *No Separate Refuge*, pp. 64–66, 85–86; Sánchez, "Go After the Women," pp. 259–61; Crocker, "Gary Mexicans," p. 121.

46. Sarmiento, "Lupe." In her study, Ruth Crocker also notes the propensity of Protestant missionaries to focus their energies on children and the selective uses of services by Mexican clients. As she explained, "Inevitably, many immigrants came to the settlement, took what they wanted of its services, and remained untouched by its message." [Crocker, "Gary Mexicans," p. 122.]

47. *Newark-Houchen News*, September 1975.

48. Deutsch, *No Separate Refuge*, pp. 78–79; Ibarra interview; interview with Rose Escheverriá Mulligan, Volume 27, of *Rosie the Riverter Revisited: Women and the World War II Work Experience*, ed. Sherna Berger Gluck (Long Beach: CSULB Foundation, 1983), p. 24.

49. Paul S. Taylor, "Women in Industry," field notes for *Mexican Labor in the United States*, Bancroft Library, University of California, Berkeley, Box 1. *Note*: Referring to Los Angeles, two historians have argued that "Mexicans experienced segregation in housing in nearly every section of the city and its outlying areas." [Antonio Ríos-Bustamante and Pedro Castillo, *An Illustrated History of Mexican Los Angeles* (Los Angeles: UCLA Chicano Studies Research Center, 1986), p. 135.]

50. Interview with Alicia Mendeola Shelit, Volume 37, *Rosie the Riveter Revisited*, p. 32; Mulligan interview,

p. 14. Anthropologist Ruth Tuck noted that Euro-Americans also employed the term "Spanish" to distinguish individuals "of superior background or achievement." [Ruth Tuck, *Not with the Fist* (New York: Harcourt, Brace and Co., 1946; rpt. Arno Press, 1974), pp. 142–43.]

51. Interview with Alma Araiza García , March 27, 1993, conducted by the author.

52. Tuck, *Not with the Fist*, p. 133.

53. *Friendship Square Calendar* (1949); Beatrice Fernandez, "Day Nursery" (Houchen Report, circa late 1950s) [HF].

54. "Friendship Square" (Houchen pamphlet, circa 1950s) [HF]; letter to Houchen Girl Scouts from Troop 4, Latin American Community Center, Alpine, Texas, May 18, 1951 [HF].

55. *A Right Glad New Year*; News clipping from the *El Paso Times* (circa 1950s); "Our Work at Houchen"; Little, "Rose Gregory Houchen Settlement"; "Anglo Settlement Worker's Journal" (entry for December 1952) [HF].

56. *Newark-Houchen News*, September 1975; Sarmiento, "Lupe."

57. Peggy Pascoe, *Relations of Rescue: The Search for Moral Authority in the American West, 1874–1939* (New York: Oxford University Press, 1990), pp. 112–39; Woodruff, "Methodist Women."

58. *Datebook for 1926* (entry: Friday, September 9, 1929) (Settlement Worker's private journal) [HF]; "Brillante Historia"; "Report and Directory of Association of Church Social Workers, 1940" [HF]; "May I Come In?" (Houchen brochure, circa 1950s) [HF]; "Friendship Square" (Houchen pamphlet, 1958) [HF]; Mary Lou López, "Kindergarten Report" (Houchen Report, circa 1950s) [HF]; Sarmiento, "Lupe"; "Freeman Clinic and Newark Hospital" (Houchen pamphlet, 1954) [HF]; *El Paso Times*, June 14, 1951; "Houchen Day Nursery" (Houchen pamphlet, circa 1950s) [HF]; *El Paso Times*, September 12, 1952.

59. Chávez interview; Martha González, interview with the author, October 8, 1983; Lucero interview; *Newark-Houchen News*, September 1974.

60. Letter from Little to Young; "The Door"; Woodruff and Little, "Friendship Square."

61. "Houchen Day Nursery"; "Life in a Glass House" (Houchen Report circa 1950s) [HF].

62. *Program* for First Annual Meeting, Houchen Settlement and Day Nursery, Freeman Clinic, and Newark Conference Maternity Hospital (January 8, 1960) [HF]. It should be noted that thirty years later, there seems to be a shift back to original settlement ideas. Today, Houchen Community has regularly scheduled bible studies. [Letters from Houghteling to the author.]

63. *Program* for Houchen production of "Cinderella" [HF]; letter from Brinson to Ely. For more information on LULAC, see Mario T. García, *Mexican Americans: Leadership, Ideology, and Identity, 1930–1960* (New Haven: Yale University Press, 1989).

64. Bulifant, "One Woman's Story"; *News from Friendship Square* (Spring newsletter, circa early 1960s) [HF].

65. My understanding and application of the ideas of Jürgen Habermas have been informed by the following works. Jürgen Habermas, *Moral Consciousness and Communicative Action*, trans. Christian Lenhardt and Sherry Weber Nicholsen, introd. Thomas McCarthy (Cambridge: MIT Press, 1990); Seidman, ed., *Jürgen Habermas on Society and Politics*; Nancy Fraser, *Unruly Practices: Power, Discourse, and Gender in Contemporary Social Theory* (Minneapolis: University of Minnesota Press, 1989); Seyla Benhabib and Drucilla Cornell, "Introduction: Beyond the Politics of Gender," in *Feminism as Critique*, eds. Seyla Benhabib and Drucilla Cornell (Minneapolis: University of Minnesota Press, 1987).

66. As an example of this typology, see Mario García, *Mexican Americans*, pp. 13–22, 295–302. Richard Griswold del Castillo touches on the dynamic nature of Mexican culture in *La Familia: Chicano Families in the Urban Southwest, 1848 to the Present* (Notre Dame: University of Notre Dame Press, 1984.

67. Escheverría Mulligan interview, p. 17.

68. *Louise Año Nuevo Kerr, "The Chicano Experience in Chicago, 1920–1970" (Ph.D. dissertation, University of Illinois, Chicago Circle, 1976), p. 104.*

Women at Farah: An Unfinished Story

Laurie Coyle, Gail Hershatter and Emily Honig

INTRODUCTION

When four thousand garment workers at Farah Manufacturing Company in El Paso, Texas went out on strike for the right to be represented by a union, many observers characterized the conflict as "a classic organizing battle."[1] The two-year strike, which began in May 1972 and was settled in March 1974, was similar in many ways to earlier, bloodier labor wars.

There was a virulently antiunion employer, Willie Farah, who swore in the time-honored manner that he would rather be dead than union. There was a company which paid low wages, pressured its employees to work faster and faster, consistently ignored health and safety conditions, and swiftly fired all those who complained. There was a local power structure which harassed the strikers with police dogs and antipicket ordinances, denied them public aid whenever possible, and smothered their strike and boycott activities with press silence for as long as it could. There were strikebreakers, and sporadic violence was directed at the striking workers. On the side of the strikers there

was a union, the Amalgamated Clothing Workers of America, which mustered national support for the strikers and organized a boycott of Farah pants. There was support from organized workers and sympathizers throughout the United States. Finally, there was a victory—an end to the strike and a union contract.

However, any account of the Farah strike which focuses exclusively on its "classic" characteristics misses most of the issues which make it an important and unfinished story. The Farah strikers were virtually all Chicanas. They were on strike in a town whose economy is profoundly affected by proximity to the Mexican border, in a period when border tensions were on the rise. They were workers in an industry plagued by instability and runaway shops. They were represented by a national union committed to "organize the unorganized," but which often resorted to tactics which undermined efforts to build a strong, democratic local union at Farah. Perhaps, most important, 85 percent of the strikers were women. Their experiences during and since the strike changed the way they looked at themselves—as Chicanas, as wives, and as workers—and the way they looked at their fellow workers, their supervisors, their families, and their community.

The account which follows does not focus on Willie Farah's flamboyant antiunion capers. Instead, it attempts to explore the effect of the strike on the women who initiated and sustained it. This article is based on extensive interviews (approximately seventy hours)

The authors wish to thank the real authors of this oral history—the women workers at Farah who generously shared their lives and opinions with three outsiders. Many of them asked to remain anonymous because they still live and work in El Paso, Texas.

"Women at Farah: An Unfinished Story" taken from *Mexican Women in the United States* by Coyle, Hershatter and Honig. Chicano Studies Research Center, 1980. Reprinted by permission of the authors.

conducted during the summer of 1977. In these interviews the women described their working conditions, events leading to the strike, the strike itself, the development of the union, and their lives as Mexican American women in the Southwest. In an effort to accurately place the Farah strike in perspective, this article also deals with the social and economic context in which the strike took place. The account appears here primarily as it was told by the Farah strikers themselves—eloquently, sometimes angrily, and always with humor.

BEFORE THE STRIKE

The history of the Farah Manufacturing Company exemplifies the myth and reality of the American success story. Unlike many other Southwest garment plants that ran away from the unionized Northeast, Farah got its start in El Paso. During the depression, Mansour Farah, a Lebanese immigrant, arrived in El Paso and set up a tiny shop on the South side. Farah, together with his wife and two sons, James and Willie, and a half-dozen Mexican seamstresses, began to turn out the chambray shirts and denim pants that were the uniform of the working West.

When Mansour died in 1937, James was twenty-one and Willie only eighteen, but they were well on the way to becoming kingpins of the needle trade. Winning government contracts for military pants during the war mobilization effort enabled the company to expand, and it emerged from World War II in the top ranks of the garment industry. In the postwar period, the rapid expansion of the garment industry transformed the South into the largest apparel-producing region of the United States. The Farah brothers shifted production to meet the growing demands of the consumer trade, and sold their product to the major chain stores, J.C. Penneys, Sears, and Montgomery Ward for retail under the store names. In 1950, the Farah brothers began marketing pants under their own name, and built a loyal and growing clientele in men's casual and dress slacks. The company expanded until it employed 9,500 workers in Texas and New Mexico.[2] Before the strike, it was the second largest employer in El Paso.

Farah's major role in developing El Paso's industry and expanding the employment ranks made the family prominent in town. At least among some sectors of the population, Farah had the reputation of being a generous boss who lavished bonuses on his workers, gave them turkey at Thanksgiving, bankrolled an elaborate party each Christmas, and provided health care and refreshments on the job. The company's hourly wages, however low they were, seemed generous in comparison to the piece rates which were standard in the garment world. Farah was the only garment plant in El Paso that would hire the inexperienced. In a town where the overwhelming number of unskilled Chicanas had to find work in retail or as domestic servants, many women considered themselves fortunate to work at Farah.

After the sudden death of James Farah in 1964, Willie undertook a major expansion of the company, constructing or acquiring a plant in Belgium, in Hong Kong, and five in El Paso the Gateway, Paisano, Northwest, Clark Street and Third Street plants. Within ten years, from 1960 to 1970, Farah's share of the market for men's casual and dress slacks rose from 3.3 percent to 11 percent.[3] In 1967, the company went public and qualified for the New York Stock Exchange. The booming growth, new capital investment, and increased planning and control of marketing resulted in major changes within the plant, including increased pressure on workers to produce more, higher quotas, and greater impersonality on the job.

WORKING CONDITIONS

Many workers felt that the expansion ruined what had been warm relations between management and employees. One woman remarked on the changes:

> In 1960, there were only two plants. They had time for you. But it started growing and they didn't give a damn about you, your health, or anything. They just kept pushing.

While some workers saw these changes as significant departures from happier days, many felt that the public image of Farah as one big happy family had never accorded with the reality on the shop floor. Willie ran his business like a classic patron, conducting unannounced plant inspections and instructing women in how best to do their jobs. The most minute aspects of production, down to a seamstress's technique for turning corners, were matters of near fanatical personal concern for Farah. His overbearing presence led many workers to feel that he assumed responsibility for work problems.

In fact, he would shower the workers with promises of liberal pay raises which never materialized. One woman who began working in 1953 recollected:

> I used to tell my kids, work hard and your boss will love you and treat you well. So years and

years passed, and though I was one of the fastest seamstresses, nothing was repaid, neither to me nor to the other workers. One day before the organizing drive began, I met Willie Farah and I asked him why he worked us so hard and never gave us a raise. He told me to come along to the office, and when we got there he said, "Listen, I don't know a thing about what happens to the workers on the floor. If it will make you happy, I will go myself to your supervisor and check to see if you are getting your due." Well, great, I thought, being sure of the quality of my work. Time went on and nothing happened. Seven months passed and no Willie. I asked, what happened, Willie doesn't want to give me my due?

For many, wages were never raised above the legal minimum, and workers were often misled to believe that legislated increases in the minimum wage were raises granted by management. Wages remained low under the quota system; since pay increases were based upon higher and higher production rates, workers' wages continually lagged behind spiralling quotas. Women were pitted against one another in the scramble to meet management demands and protect their jobs. As one women observed:

They would threaten to fire you if you didn't make a quota. They would go to a worker and say, "This girl is making very high quotas. It's easy, and I don't know why you can't do it. And if you can't do it, we'll have to fire you." So this girl would work really fast and if she got it up higher, they'd go to the other people and say, "She's making more. You'll get a ten cent raise if you make a higher quota than she." They would make people compete against each other. No one would gain a thing—the girl with the highest quota would make a dime, but a month later the minimum wage would come up. I knew a girl who'd been there for sixteen years, and they fired her, and another who was there for sixteen years and still making the minimum.

In the garment industry where labor comprises a major portion of a firm's expenditures, southwestern companies like Farah keep their competitive edge over unionized plants in the Northeast by these cutthroat pay practices.

Many women who were pretty and willing to date their supervisors received preferential treatment. One seamstress, who had worked on a particular job operation for twenty years, received less than the attractive young woman who had begun the operation only a year before. The less favored women were subjected to constant harassment:

Every day they would come around to your machine to see how much you'd make. If you didn't make your [quota of] 300, they would hurl things at us, yell at us like, "You don't do nothing, you don't do your job, I'm gonna fire you." Embarrass me in front of all those guys pressing seams next to me. I was so embarrassed, but I said nothing. I got to the point where I dreaded going to work.

Rather than hire Chicanos who had worked on the shop floor, it was standard practice for the company to hire Anglo males as supervisors. Their treatment of Chicana workers was frequently hostile and racist. Women were humiliated for speaking Spanish. When they could not understand a supervisor's orders, he would snap his fingers, hurl insults, bang the machines and push them. One worker remembered that:

In my department, the cafeteria, there was a supervisor. . . . This man didn't like Latinos—he had a very brusque manner when talking to us. He wasn't a supervisor; he was an interrogator! He would talk to me in English, which I can't speak, and insist upon it, even though he knew I didn't understand. The others would tell me what he said—things that offended, hurt me. But I couldn't defend myself.

The close cooperation of authorities on both sides of the border, as well as the special privileges granted to twin plants, allows for the optimum flow of labor and goods between El Paso and Juárez. The state of Texas has protected these privileges by establishing the right-to-work law. This law stipulates that no worker in a plant be required to join a union, and furthermore that all workers, whether they are union members or not, are entitled to the benefits provided by a union contract. Collective bargaining efforts have frequently been undermined by this law, and El Paso remains a largely nonunion town.

The availability of unorganized workers on the El Paso side, many of whom are Mexican nationals without rights of permanent residence, and many others who are unskilled Chicanos, has created an ideal situation for companies investing in labor-intensive operations such as electronics and garments. El Paso has become the last frontier of U.S. industry on the move south and out of the United States. "Runaways?" asked one Farah worker incredulously. "Industries in El Paso don't need to move. They have the advantage that they can get people from Juarez to work for less."

The United States government participates actively in depressing wages by manipulating the migrant work force to meet the needs of industry. The issuance of green cards, which are temporary permits for Mexicans to work in the U.S., guarantees business an abundant supply of labor which can be curtailed or expanded when necessary. In addition, the H-2 program of the U.S. Department of Labor allows an individual employer to bring in a specified number of workers from Mexico if he can prove that a labor shortage exists. This program has been used to strikebreak in the cotton industry in the South, and more recently, against union strikers in Texas. The Immigration and Naturalization Service (INS) also plays a role in regulating the presence of Mexican workers without documents. It allows them to enter during critical harvest periods or when there are labor disputes, and at the same time deports those undocumented workers who have joined strikes. "The INS knows that there are illegals," one Farah worker complained,

> . . . because when they need them, they send them in by the hundreds to the U.S. When they need them they look the other way. But when they don't need them, they get them out of there *fast*, They *know* they're there.

Even in normal times, and particularly in the last eight years with unemployment on the rise, there is intense competition for jobs in the El Paso area. The complexity of the El Paso labor market has the built-in potential for conflicts among United States-born Mexicans and Mexican nationals with or without documents. Employers in El Paso use the competition for jobs to create and exacerbate conflict among these groups whenever labor troubles arise.

Many Farah strikers maintained close ties with friends and family in Juárez. Women who had extensive personal contact with life in Mexico, either because their parents had crossed the Rio Grande or because they themselves had grown up there and come to the United States as adults, tended to see the Mexicans and Chicanos as one people. When they looked at the undocumented workers of today, they saw the experiences of their own parents. "I was born over there and raised here," one striker recalled.

I was seven when we came here. I remember, when we were living in Juárez my father had to come back and forth every fifteen days. He used to live on a farm in the U.S. I don't have any grudges against wetbacks. I do support the Texas farmworkers. If they want to sign up the whole border I don't mind. I understand how it is over there. I understand what it is to have a father as a wetback. I understand what people are trying to do with the border situation.

Many workers at Farah, as children, took part in the pilgrimage North to find work. Some of their families crossed the border illegally. "My father was a laborer," one woman recollected. "There was no work in Mexico. My parents were having a picnic one day, and zoom-they came across." Families contracted to work seasonally, harvesting cotton and pecans. Some never intended to make the United States their home, but they became permanent residents when they found that the money they earned during temporary work visits to the United States could not sustain them when they returned to the increasingly constricted economy of rural Mexico.

Other women at Farah came north as adults to seek work. Even when they succeeded in finding a stable job, the relocation entailed severe hardships and demanded major readjustments. Most of the women had grown up in the poverty-stricken rural areas of northern Mexico. They had almost no formal education, and many married very early in life. While the daily struggle to survive prepared them for the grinding labor of the factory, nothing in their backgrounds had prepared them to assume roles traditionally restricted to male heads-of-household: to leave the home, enter the industrial work force, and, for some, become the major breadwinner of the family. That the move was a radical departure from their upbringing can best be understood from the childhood recollections of the women who experienced these changes. "My childhood?" a striker reminisced:

I was born in a village where they mine silver, Cusinichi. My father worked there, as did his father and his grandfather. It was a company town. The company was American and there was a union. My family helped build the union. My father wanted to have schools, to have benefits. My father spoke to me often about how the company was very rich and that we were all making the company rich and it was just that the company give us a part for our children. My father talked a lot about this, and sometimes they would throw him out of the mine. After great fights, my father would be back in the mine.

He was a product of his times. He thought that only men should go to school, that we women should only learn to write. Men are the ones who support the family, and so the women don't need anything more.

My father named me after his mother, and even though I had two brothers and three sisters, I was my father's favorite. I was the only child until age four, when my brother arrived. Everything was for me. They took me to work, to the mines, to visit my father. He had a little office where they kept records of people injured on the job, etc. And they also took me to the paymaster. In those days they paid cash. I went everywhere with my father and uncles, to union meetings where everyone didn't stop talking shouting and discussing their problems. A child learns when it is born. When a child begins to breathe a child begins to learn.

Thus I spent all my time with my father and uncles, but when I'd learned to read and write at nine years, I was not sent to school any more. "No, Papa," I began to cry and shout. When he saw me sitting with a long face and asked me why, I said, "Why can't I go to school anymore?" So he said to go ahead. So they cut my hair and I went. I finished elementary.

Afterwards, I would look up at the mountains, so high. The mines were in the mountains. What more is there? I was dying to know. What's beyond the mountains? What are the people like? Of course my father wouldn't consider my leaving home. He wanted me to get married and have children.

One day my cousin went to the city of Chihuahua. When he returned, I asked him, "What is it like there?" Oh, the buildings are tall, very tall, and the streets-some of them are paved." Here they were made of dirt. "Imagine! The streets are wide—wide as from here to the next village." The more he said, the more I wanted to know.

I thought and thought and one day I asked my father, "Don't we have any relatives in Chihuahua?" He answered that my godfather was there. I told him, "Father, I want to meet him. Maybe I can write." "Go ahead, write him," he agreed. I wrote the letter and asked my father, "Papa, isn't it true that the mail is sacred? You can't open a sealed envelope? Right?" "Yes," he answered. So I said, "Here's the letter for my godfather," and sealed it. He could do nothing but send it. In the letter I told my godfather that I wanted to come meet him and his wife. He wrote back saying that he'd love to have me come and visit for a while. "My wife is expecting a baby and it would be fine." I wrote again asking him to ask my father for his permission, or to come if possible. He arrived. "How long it has been since we've seen each other, how great, couldn't she go with me for a while. My wife is having a baby, and it would be great if your daughter would accompany her." Since he was my godfather, my father accepted.

This woman came to the city, finished her studies and became a teacher. She married, had a family and decided once again to leave her home—this time for the United States. Hardship in Mexico pushed her, and promises of a better future for herself and her children drew her. Upon arriving in El Paso, she had to give up her teaching and enter Farah's factory. This was an immense shock to her hopes; the hardships continued. In making all of these decisions she made a radical departure from her upbringing and grew stronger as a woman. Part of this strength was her intense attachment to her origins.

Of course I still go back to Mexico frequently to see my parents in Cuateque. My father can no longer get papers to come here, but when he comes to Juárez, to visit my brother, I go to see him. My children go all the time. They love the ambiente there. I believe that this is a good country, but I don't want them to become Americanized so that they don't want to see their own people. Our roots are there. I became an American citizen by my own choice. This was my decision, but I don't want to negate my roots, or say that I don't want to be there [Mexico]. I love this country as much as I love my own [Mexico]. For that reason I live here. But my children should love both equally: the land is one and the same.

Many other women experienced profound physical and emotional changes; yet their ties to Mexico remained powerful.

A major change for those who came from Mexico involved no longer being a "native" but being stigmatized as an "alien." This identification was applied to all Mexican people regardless of citizenship, and included a population indigenous to the region and more "native" than the later white settlement.

The pride of many Farah workers in their Mexican heritage—a pride often fostered by their parents—protected them somewhat from this hostility and enabled them to stand up to it. "For not having much of an education my father was a pretty smart man," one striker remembered.

> I wish I was like him. He kept up in his history . . . He used to say, "Americanos? We are the Americanos, we're the Indians, we were the first ones here." He was an Indian. He always argued about people calling an Anglo "Americano" and a Mexican "Mexicano." That really got him mad. He'd say, "We are Americanos; *they* are Anglos." That was one thing he always argued about.

Like their sisters in Mexico, Chicanas growing up in El Paso were expected to share responsibility for la familia at an early age. They were raised in poverty, received little formal education, began working when they were still children, married young, and spent their working lives in low status, low paying jobs.

Most of the Chicana workers at Farah had grown up in the barrio in south El Paso's Second Ward. Squeezed between the downtown area and the border, residents of "El Segundo" faced street violence, police indifference, or brutality, rip-offs from slumlords, and racism from uptown whites.

The violence in the streets was inescapable. "When I grew up," one woman recalled,

> life was a lot different at that time. Everything was harder . . . At that time there were no youth centers. There was nothing to do for the kids, no recreation or things like that. So they would hang around on the corners, they would have gangs and fight against each other. You know it became a *barrio* where policemen were there all the time. That kind of reputation. I guess that's one reason why the police didn't care what happened to them because they had that reputation. So they [the police] would beat them up and a lot of times they would just be sitting there with a quart of beer and the [police] would break it and kick them and take them to jail for nothing.

The unrelieved poverty operated as brutally on residents as attacks by the police. Many a childhood ended prematurely as young girls quit school to help support their families.

> I grew up in the Second Ward. It was a poor neighborhood. We used to live in the projects. Some Mexican Americans try to help each other; others are selfish. My mother used to have three jobs: at Newark Hospital, at night, and at Levi's. After school I worked at Newberry's, babysitting, and as a maid when I was nine. With three young children and myself, I had to help my mother. It was a hard childhood. I didn't have a father. My mother had to work day and night. I told her to let me work for her at the Newark Hospital—so I cleaned the beds and floors.

While many quit school because of economic necessity, even more were driven out by systematic discrimination. They were penalized for being brown-skinned and Spanish speaking. Like the Anglo supervisors at Farah, Anglo teachers in El Paso schools instilled deepseated feelings of inadequacy, humiliation, and disaffection in their Chicano students. Chicanos were discouraged from finishing high school, and the strict tracking system prohibited college and career aspirations. "To me it was hard in school," one woman recalled.

> People making fun of you, especially the way you talked. Your English or your understanding [of English]. I believe my older brothers and sisters had the most difficulty getting adjusted here because they couldn't speak any English. Neither could I, but I was put in kindergarten so it didn't matter to me. People in that small village [outside of El Paso] didn't know how to speak English so we talked Spanish, but it was very difficult for them because they were put in the fourth or fifth grade and they were fourteen. People were making fun of them. I just went to eighth grade, then I quit and got married. I was sixteen and I'm still married to the same man. I was sixteen and I was still in eighth grade. I used to get very disappointed that most of my friends were fourteen or thirteen in the same grade. I was supposed to be in tenth grade at the age of sixteen. That used to bother me a lot. Because of the language problem I had when I came across the border [sic].

Whether at home, in the streets, at school, or on the job, there was no refuge from personal hostility or institutionalized discrimination. Mature women workers are still nursing their childhood wounds, looking back on childhood dreams which were crushed and scorned whichever way they turned.

Yet growing up Chicana in El Paso also provided these women with sources of strength, pride and courage. They drew strength from El Segundo's sense of community, which was formed in response to confrontations with the Anglo power structure of El Paso. Their families transmitted to them pride in Mexican culture, as well as countless individual examples of courage in difficult circumstances.

Whether they were raised in the U.S. or Mexico, these women by no means suffered passively. To survive they had to struggle. They responded with anger to the racism, deprivation, and systematic oppression which they experienced as Raza women. While this anger was seldom expressed openly, it was always present and potentially explosive. The advent of a unionization campaign helped to give organized expression to this anger.

EARLY ORGANIZING

Despite the fact that most workers in the El Paso region were not organized into unions, some of the women had been exposed to labor organizing drives. Women from Mexico had parents who had fled to the United States after their attempts to organize workers in Mexico had failed. They had lost everything in the process. Some women, as children, had witnessed bloody strikes in the textile mills and mines of northern Mexico. Among those women, some had even worked as children in these industries. Others had undergone the dislocation and hardship of migrant life in the United States.

Among Chicanas at Farah, some had fathers, mothers, brothers, and husbands who belonged to unions in El Paso's smelting and packing plants. There was the example of the prolonged and successful strike of garment workers for union recognition at the Top Notch clothing plant in the 1960s. But experience with organized labor was by no means widespread among workers at Farah. The overwhelming majority of the women in the plant during the day-to-day activities of a union, and virtually no examples of working women's struggles in unions to guide them. Yet, Farah workers from both sides of the border had grown up in working class families, and many had had tragic personal experiences which dramatized for them the need for unionization.

One woman recalled the early death of her father from lung cancer.

> He died when he was young, only forty-four years old. Because where he was working, they didn't have no union and he was doing dirty work, smashing cans and bumpers. When you smash them, smoke comes up and he inhaled it and that's what killed him. He didn't have no protection; they didn't even give him a mask. He put only a handkerchief to cover his face. He died of cancer because of all the things he was inhaling. That's what the doctor told us . . . He died before I turned seventeen. They operated and said he had only half a lung and wasn't going to live long. He lasted three weeks. I'd do anything for him, I was very close to him. He told me it was too late to have another job. I couldn't stand it and would go into the next room to cry so that he wouldn't hear me. He was so husky until the sickness ate him away.

This woman never lost the conviction that her father's life could have been prolonged if he'd had a union's protection on the job. "When I started to know about the union," she concluded grimly, "I joined right away because of my father."

The earliest attempt by workers at Farah to present an organized response to management attacks was a brief petition campaign among markers at the Gateway plant in 1968. A more systematic effort to address workers' grievances began in 1969 when male workers from the cutting and shipping departments contacted organizers from the Amalgamated Clothing Workers of America (ACWA).[4] They acted in spite of Farah's repeated violent tirades against unions. Farah presented films about union corruption on company time and pronounced to his workers, "See what a union does? You don't want anything to do with that!" But Farah overestimated the impact of his blitz on organizing. He was sufficiently confident of union defeat in an upcoming election that he urged cutters to vote, insisting that not to vote was to vote for the union. The cutters turned out in force for the election, and on October 14, 1970, they voted overwhelmingly to affiliate themselves with the union. Not about to accept the unexpected turn of events, Farah immediately appealed the election result with the National Labor Relations Board (NLRB). The cutting room election was tied up in court until 1972, when the election victory was set aside on grounds that the cutting room was not an appropriate bargaining unit. But by that time, organizing had long since spread to the rest of the plant.

Soon after this first election, a handful of cutters began attempts to sign up workers in other departments. Reactions to the organizing drive varied. Most women had little idea of what the activists hoped to gain from union recognition. Others were fearful—with good cause—of supervisors' retaliation. Furthermore, many workers believed what Willie Farah said about labor unions taking their money and benefits.

Even so, some women were moved by their fellow workers' persistence in the face of personal harassment and threats to their jobs. Several workers signed cards and began to talk to their coworkers about the new organizing drive. Efforts to sign up workers took place clandestinely because of the virulence of management tactics against the organizers. Women hid union cards in their purses, met hurriedly in the bathrooms and whispered in the halls to persuade the indifferent. The cafeteria was the heart of the organizing efforts. During lunch time, workers circulated among the tables to sound out each other's sentiments about the union. The first union meetings in people's homes were a completely new experience. "Oh, I did like them," a striker reminisced. "There was a lot of—you know, talking about new things, about the union. And especially, I felt that somebody was talking for us."

Management responded to organizing activities with a series of repressive measures. Supervisors were stationed in the halls to monitor sympathizers and interrogate employees concerning their union loyalties. "They would say, 'What are they saying in there?' and I would respond, 'Who? I don't know what they're saying,'" a striker recalled.

> They'd say, "Don't believe about the union, the union's a bunch of bullshit. They only want to take your money away." That's what they'd say. And I just heard them, and I didn't say anything . . . But once they knew you were involved with the union, they'd start pressuring you . . . Some of us just quit, some were fired.

All personal conversations were restricted during work time, and conditions worsened even for those not involved in organizing. "When we began organizing," one woman recalled," [the company] put even harsher supervisors who tried to humiliate people more. If there was a shortage of work on a line, they made me sweep. I refused, but other workers were afraid of being fired and obeyed. They did it to humiliate us and to assure that no organization would succeed."

Company intimidation frightened many people away. Workers treated union organizers as if they had some kind of disease. Union sympathizers were fired, among them four women. One woman described her firing, saying, "My supervisor, Héctor Romero, sent me to Salvador Ibarra's line because my line had no work."

> After lunch, Héctor Romero told me to go back to my machine because now there was work, and I worked at the machine the rest of the afternoon. About half an hour before quitting time, Ernest Boeldner, another foreman, asked me what I was doing at my machine since I had been told to work in Ibarra's line. I told him that I was only following Romero's orders. Without another word he sent me to the office where they asked me to turn in my badge and scissors. I still did not know what was going on but the bell rang and I went home. The following day when I returned to work, Victor Chamali did not let me punch in and told me I was fired. Farah says I was fired for disobedience. Some people have spread the rumor that I was fired because I was lazy or that I quit to go to work for the union. But none of this is true. I was fired to stop me from organizing and to scare other people.

The firings intimidated workers, but also angered them. As one of the women who was fired observed, "It did give them some courage. They wanted to know why I was fired after all these years, with no earlier work problems." Few workers were willing to openly confront their supervisors, but as their anger grew they discussed the union among themselves more frequently.

Organizing continued at the Gateway plant, though there were no immediate plans to take action. The activists who were fired went down to the union office and vowed to continue the struggle. One woman organized a group of students from a nearby high school to distribute leaflets in front of the Gateway, Paisano, and Third Street plants. They were insulted, their leaflets were torn up and thrown in their faces, and some of them were assaulted. But the woman came every day at 6:00 a.m. and stood her ground until the day of the walkout.

THE WALKOUT

The campaign to unionize the Farah plants intensified in the spring of 1972. In March, twenty-six workers were fired when they attempted a walkout at the

Northwest plant in El Paso. But it was a series of events in San Antonio that triggered the large-scale strike in El Paso.

One weekend, members of the union organizing committee in El Paso sponsored a march. Farah workers from San Antonio made the twelve-hour drive between the two cities to join the demonstration. Some of them did not return to San Antonio in time for work on Monday morning. On Tuesday, a supervisor confronted a worker with pictures of him marching under union banners in El Paso and then promptly fired him. Workers who objected to his dismissal were also fired. More than 500 San Antonio Farah workers walked out in protest.

Six days later, when El Paso Farah workers learned of the San Antonio strike, their frustration with working conditions and with Farah's continued suppression of union activity exploded into a spontaneous strike. On May 9, the machinists, shippers, cutters, and some of the seamstresses walked out. The walkout, which continued for almost a month, initially took the company by surprise. Women who had worked docilely at their machines for years, women who had been reduced to tears by a supervisor's reprimand, women who had never openly spoken a word in favor of the union, suddenly began to speak up.

That day that we walked out, the supervisor saw that I had a little flag on. He went over and he looked at me, sort of startled, and he said, "You?" And I said, "Yes!" And he said, "What have we done to you?" I said, "Oh, I wouldn't know where to begin." He said, "We haven't done anything to you." I said, "But you have done a lot to all of the people around me. I've seen it going on."

The startled management soon rallied with a skillful combination of promises and threats. On the first day of the walkout, as activists walked through the factory urging the workers to join them, supervisors followed them, telling the workers to let the dissidents go out on strike and suffer and lose their jobs. The loudspeaker system broadcasted "La Golondrina," a Mexican song of farewell, in a sardonic gesture to the strikers. The shop floor and the cafeteria were full of people shouting, arguing, or quietly trying to decide what to do. For many women, the decision was a difficult one which took several days to make, while the management did its best to frighten or cajole the women who were still undecided. For all of the strikers, the

day on which they decided to walk out remains a vivid and memorable one.

I remember the first time of the walkout we were all in break, eating, having some coffee. And then suddenly there was a whole bunch in the cutting room—the girls and everything. They went over to my table and said, "Alma, you've got to come out with us!" And I just looked at them. I was so scared I didn't even know what to do. What if I go and lose my thirteen years? So long, having seniority and everything. I just looked at them and said, "Yeah, yeah, I'll go. I'll go." That's all I said. And I had a whole bunch of people sitting there with me and I said, "Let's go!" And one of them said, "Well, if you go, we'll go."

So the next day I went and put pants on. I always wear dresses. I used to love to wear dresses. So I put some pants on and said, "I don't know what's going to happen. Maybe there's going to be fighting or something." You know, we were scared . . . We were scared maybe they would beat us and everything.

But I remember that day. When I was passing, the girls started yelling at me, "Alma, you'd better go out! We need you out here!" And I said, "Yeah, yeah, yeah. Wait, wait." "No, you're happy. That's what's the matter with you. You're just a happy one. The way they treat you in there, and you're still in there."

So around nine o'clock I started gathering everybody. "We're going out! Right now! When you see me get off my machine." So you should have seen all those supervisors around me. Somebody pinched a finger on me and told them I was going to go out. You should have seen them all around me. They said, "Alma, you're a good worker. We'll pay you what you want. Alma, the way you sew, the way you work, the way you help us." And I would just say, "Yeah, I know. I know." They thought I was going to stay there.

At nine o'clock I got off [the machine]. I went to the restroom and I started telling everybody, "Let's go!" So some of them just didn't go. I took a lot of people out with me.

Then I started walking through the middle of the— where all the people were working—they thought I was very happy [with work at Farah]. And they started, "Alma! Alma!" And everybody started getting off the machines. I couldn't believe it. It was something so beautiful. So exciting.

And then suddenly a supervisor got a hold of me on my shoulder, and he says, "Alma, we need you! Don't go!" So everybody started . . . I took a lot of people that were real good. I took them all out with me.

When I started walking outside, all the strikers that were out there, yelling, they saw me, and golly, I felt so proud, 'cause they all went and hugged me. And they said, "We never thought you were one of us" And I said, "What do you think? Just because I'm a quiet person?"

But it was beautiful! I really knew we were going to do something. That we were really going to fight for our rights.

As the walkout continued and spread beyond the shipping and cutting rooms, it began to include a wide variety of women. Some came from families with histories of union involvement, while others had no previous contact or experience with unions. Some who walked out had taken an active role in the union organizing campaign leading up to the strike, while others had never even signed a union card. For all of them, however, the act of walking out began a process of change in the way they looked at themselves and their work. "For me," one striker recalled,

[The day of the walkout] was something out of this world. I was pleased with myself, but at the same time I was afraid. That night I couldn't sleep. I couldn't see myself out of Farah. So many years.

THE STRIKE

The Amalgamated Clothing Workers of America quickly moved to support the Farah workers; the strike was declared an unfair labor practice strike. One month later a national boycott of Farah products was begun, endorsed by the AFL-CIO. In El Paso the strikers began to picket the Farah plants and local stores which carried Farah products. But in a town where many regarded Willie Farah as a folk hero, the strikers found that public reaction to the walkout was often hostile. One woman remembers that:

People were just very cruel. Everybody thought that Farah was a god or something. . . . I swear, they'd even turn around and spit on you if they could. There was one lady, I was handing out

some papers downtown . . . and she got her purse and started striking me. . . . When she started hitting me, she said, "Ah, you people, a bunch of dumb this and that! Farah's a great man!"

Passers-by told the picketers that they were lazy bums who just wanted welfare and food stamps. The strikers were repeatedly reminded that Farah was a major employer in an area where unemployment was high, and that they should be grateful to him for giving them jobs.

Antiunion sentiment was not limited to random comments on the street. It was also expressed in a virtual blackout in the local media. A reporter for the *El Paso Times* who wanted to write a series of feature articles on the strikers was told that the strike was a "private affair" between Farah and his workers. The editor added, "Maybe if we let Willie Farah run his business he'll let us run our newspaper." It wasn't necessary for Farah himself to exercise direct censorship. His importance in the El Paso business community ensured that no newspaper would print material which was damaging to him. A striker describing the extent of his informal influence wryly observed, "Willie Farah conquered El Paso."

There was also considerable racism in the antiunion sentiment. Some members of the Anglo community felt that Mexican Americans were "aliens" and that Mexican American strikers were ungrateful troublemakers who should be dealt with severely. One woman angrily remembers:

When we were on strike there was a program on TV and anybody could call up. You know, one man called the TV station and told them why didn't they send all the Mexicans back to Mexico? How ignorant! Here I was born in the United States and this stupid man has the nerve to say to send them all back to Mexico because we were on strike!

Racial tensions between Anglos and Chicanos, an ever-present feature of life in El Paso, were exacerbated by the strike and the political mobilization of Chicana workers which accompanied it.

However, opinions about the strike did not simply divide along racial or ethnic lines. The strike split the Chicano community. Many workers at Farah crossed picket lines and continued to keep the plant operating. They were known as the "happies" because they wore buttons which featured a smiling face and the slogan,

"I'm happy at Farah." Especially at Farah's Third St. plant, where many of the people had worked for Farah since World War II, vehement opposition to the strike was expressed.

> There was this woman who was married to one of the supervisors. . . . She even yelled at us that we were going to starve. She said, "Don't worry! We'll give you the cockroaches!"
>
> They used to call us a lot of names. . . . You should be ashamed after so many years that Willie has been supporting you with work." "Why don't you start working? All you want is to be loafing around. At your age!"

The strike divided families. Several women told of walking out while their sisters remained inside the plant. There was even one family where the husband was on strike and his wife was continuing to work at Farah. "He'd drive his wife up to the door," one striker recalled, "and get out of there as fast as he could. Now this was ridiculous!"

Striking workers were quickly replaced by strikebreakers from El Paso and the neighboring Mexican city of Juárez. There was no lack of applicants for the jobs: El Paso unemployment figures have soared as high as 14 percent in recent years, while Juarez, like much of Mexico, has a current unemployment rate of 40 percent.

Until shortly before the strike, Willie Farah, who liked to style himself as a superpatriot, had refused to hire Mexicans to work in his plant even if they had green cards. But when the strike began and he needed workers, he abruptly changed his policy, and became willing to hire Mexican nationals. Large numbers of greencarders appeared in the plant. Farah's hiring practices were partly successful in pitting workers against each other. Some Chicano strikers blamed Mexican workers for being hired by Farah, rather than blaming Farah and other employers along the border for using job competition to divide workers. However, many of the strikers recognized that the economic situation in Juarez forced people to find work wherever they could. And in spite of the economic squeeze, a small number of Juarez residents joined the strikers.

People on the picket lines faced continuing harassment from company personnel. Farah hired guards to patrol the picket line with unmuzzled police dogs. Several strikers were hit by Farah trucks, and one woman was struck by a car driven by Willie Farah's mother. Farah obtained an injunction limiting pickets to one every fifty feet; 1,008 workers were cited for violations, and many were ordered to report to the police station in the middle of the night and required to post four hundred dollar bonds. One woman was jailed six times. (The Texas law which permitted such injunctions was later declared unconstitutional, and all charges were dropped.)

Support

Although the strikers suffered physical and psychological harassment from opponents of the strike, they also discovered new sources of support. The Amalgamated Clothing Workers of America sent organizers to El Paso, gave weekly payments of thirty dollars to each striker, administered a Farah Relief Fund, and sponsored classes for the strikers on labor history and union procedures. For many workers, the films shown by the union were their first exposure to the history of labor struggles in the United States. One woman was deeply moved by a film about a strike in Chicago; another striker especially liked the movie "Salt of the Earth," because it showed the role of Chicanas in a strike in New Mexico.

Immediately after the strike began, the union organized a national boycott of Farah pants which became a crucial factor in the success of the strike. By January 1974, forty union representatives were working on boycott campaigns in more than sixty cities.[5] The Amalgamated issued leaflets, posters, and public relations kits, and worked closely with other unions, church and student groups to implement the boycott. Many Farah workers went on speaking tours to promote the boycott. All of these efforts transformed the Farah strike from an isolated local struggle to a national campaign with widespread support.

The Catholic Church was another source of help for the strikers. Father Jesse Muñoz, a priest at Our Lady of the Light Church, made church facilities available for union meetings and participated in several national speaking tours to promote the boycott of Farah products. He also came to the picket line at the Gateway plant to bless the strikers on Ash Wednesday. Bishop Sidney Metzger of El Paso publicly endorsed the boycott in a letter to his fellow bishops. Metzger said, "The fact that today over 3,000 workers are on strike is evidence that both grievances and resentment are real. And by listening to the people over the years one gradually became aware that things at Farah were not actually as they were made to appear."[6]

In El Paso, a town with a large and devout Catholic population, the approval of the church was a source of emotional as well as organizational support for the strikers and a setback for their opponents. Muñoz received threatening letters from unknown sources, and he contends that Farah hired someone to put LSD in his Coca-Cola at a union dinner.

When a group of happies announced that they planned to picket the church, the strikers quickly organized a counteraction. The happies arrived to find the church surrounded by strikers. One striker spotted the black ribbons worn by the protesters and called out, "What happened, did Willie die already?" The happies took stock of the situation and retreated.

Father Muñoz suggests that there were many reasons why the church chose to back the strikers in spite of the continuing controversy. He points out that the church has a commitment to social justice, which he personally had supported by joining the southern civil rights protests of the 1960s. "So when I came here and there was a roaring tiger in my backyard, I wasn't going to ignore it." Muñoz was also concerned that the strikers would be incited to violence by "communists from Red China, Cuba, and Berkeley," whom he charges came to town to disrupt the strike. By inviting the strikers to use church facilities, he hoped to isolate them from what he viewed as dangerous influences.

Workers at Asarco and the few other union plants in town also expressed their support for the strikers. Even more surprising to the strikers, given the prevailing mood of hostility, was the support given them by some local businesses.

> We got on that truck . . . and we went to ask everybody if they could give us some food. . . . That was when, I tell you, my life started changing. There you know who your good friends are and who cares about people. . . . We went to that fruit stand on Alameda. . . . He gave us, I guess, about twenty bags of potatoes. . . . Then we went to that Peyton [meat] packing company, and they gave us wienies. . . . Mostly we went to the stores to ask for baby food. Then we went to the *tortillería* in Ysleta [east of El Paso] . . . and that man gave us about twenty dozens of tortillas . . . and tamales, and some juice. . . . Then we went back to report to the people, to tell them that we had support.

The strikers were also encouraged by messages of solidarity and financial support from other unions around the country. Particularly important to them was the visit to El Paso of César Chávez. In addition, a variety of Chicano, student, and leftist organizations in El Paso and around the country supported the strike by publicizing the boycott and the conditions at Farah.

New Responsibilities

But the most profound changes among the Farah strikers began when they took on new responsibilities for organizing strike activities. Some women went to work for the union on a volunteer basis, writing strike relief checks, keeping records, and distributing the goods that arrived from outside El Paso. Almost immediately they began to realize that their capabilities were not as limited as they had been taught to believe. One striker asserted, "if I had not walked out, I would not have been able to realize all those things about myself."

> You know, when we used to register the people from the strike, would you believe that we organized all those cards, all those people on strike? And you know, not realizing, here you can do this anywhere! You can go to any office and sit down and work! You know, you think to yourself, "How in the world did I ever think I couldn't do anything?" This is one of the things that's held us back. We didn't think we could do it. . . . Until you actually get there and sit down and do it, and you find out, "I'm not so dumb after all!"

Other strikers went on speaking tours organized by the union or by strike support groups to publicize the boycott and raise funds.

> I had never travelled as much as I did when I was on strike. The only place I had gone was to L.A., one time, but that was about all. But I never thought that I could go to New York, or Seattle, or all these places. To me it was just like a dream, something that was just happening and I was going through, but I couldn't stop to think about it. I just had to go and talk to those people about the strike. . . . The first week it was hard [to get used to talking to groups of people]. Because over here I just used to talk to one or two persons when I was working they hardly let you talk at all. . . . Sometimes I would try to talk just as though I was talking to the strikers right here. I just didn't think that they were other people that I didn't know.

One woman observed that anti-union harassment took similar forms all over the country; when she stopped to talk to workers at a non-union plant, a supervisor appeared and shooed the workers back inside. When she spoke on the East Coast she noticed that racial and ethnic differences often kept workers isolated from one another. She returned to El Paso with a heightened perception of the difficulties involved in building a strong union.

Financial Troubles

As the months wore on, strikers faced increasing financial hardship. The union strike relief payments of thirty dollars a week were inadequate for many families. In one household both husband and wife were on strike, and there were eight children to feed and clothe. Unable to handle their house payments, the family moved in with the husband's mother. The uncertainties of the strike, the financial troubles, and the change in living arrangements were a strain on the marriage:

> My husband was worried too, because of the financial [situation], and he would start to drinking to take it off his mind. I . . . even told him to go to the hospital, because he was getting awful. And I had an operation too at that time. And he did, he went to the hospital and he got cured. . . . [Drinking was a big problem among the strikers) because there was nothing for them to do. . . . He had to be there [on the picket line] from 7:30 until 4:30 in the afternoon, because he was the [picket] captain. Mostly the kids wouldn't see him at all, and neither did I, until two in the morning when he got home.

For single women workers living with their parents, the situation was somewhat easier. Their parents supported them, and working brothers and sisters often helped with car payments and other bills. But many single women were themselves working to support widowed parents and younger siblings. For them the strike meant financial desperation.

Women who could find work in other clothing factories did so, continuing to picket at Farah before and after work and on Saturdays. Only the small number of unionized plants in El Paso were willing to hire Farah strikers. At nonunion plants, however, the jobs only lasted as long as the striker's identity was unknown.

In working-class areas, particularly in the sprawling eastern end of town, many workers felt a sense of solidarity with their neighbors.

> Here the whole neighborhood, you know, the majority of us were on strike! . . . The guy on the corner was on strike, the girl across the street, the one on the corner over there, then there was Virgie and all her sisters, and then we had one lady down the other corner that was working. . . . my neighbors in front—her father's always been fighting for unions. A lot of these things, I think, kind of made you feel good.

The Home

As women became more and more involved in running strike support activities, and as they developed new friendships among the strikers, they began to spend more time outside the home. This was a source of tension in many households.

> I was so involved that I was forgetting everything. My husband started getting very angry at me, and I was giving him a hard time. You know, at the time I didn't realize that I was hurting my kids and my husband. At the time I just felt that this was something I had to do, and if my husband liked it or didn't like it he was going to have to accept it. . . . Lucky that he was able to accept [it], because this went on and on during the strike. . . . Now I stop to think, and I tell myself, good grief, he really did put up with a lot! How would I like it if he was gone every day of the week! . . . So I'm just glad that he was able to stand behind me, and it didn't destroy our marriage, but it did destroy a lot of marriages. . . .

In some cases, differences of opinion about the merits of the walkout were fueled by financial insecurity. In other homes the husbands did not think that attending public meetings was an appropriate way for their wives to spend their time.

> Well, at the beginning they didn't like it. They thought [the women) should be at home, because here they were kind of old-fashioned, the women were always supposed to be at home. The only time she'd be working was if she had to work to keep up with the bills, and both wife and husband had to work. Otherwise there was no way that the man himself could support the house. But that's about all they thought about, just for them to work—they didn't think they could go to meetings.

But the women felt strongly enough about their involvement in the strike to put up a spirited defense of their activities.

> My ex-husband told me, "You're not gonna make it, and I'm not gonna help you!" And I said, "if God made it, and his followers made it, like Peter, he left his boat behind, his wife . . . everything, he left everything behind, all his belongings to follow God, yet he didn't die! Right now he's in better shape than we are. He's in heaven, holding that door—isn't that true!

For many women the changes in their marriages were more profound than a few disagreements over meetings or money. The strike made them more confident of their ability to make decisions, and they began to question their own attitudes toward their husbands.

> Maybe it's just the Mexican woman, maybe it's just that the Mexican woman has been brought up always to do what somebody tells you, you know, your father, your mother. And as you grow up, you're used to always being told what to do. . . .
>
> For years I wouldn't do anything without asking my husband's permission. . . . I've been married nineteen years, and I was always, "Hey, can I" or "Should I. . . ." I see myself now and I think, good grief, having to ask to buy a pair of underwear! Of course, I don't do this anymore. . . . [The time of the strike was] when it started changing. All of it. I was able to begin to stand up for myself, and I began to feel that I should be accepted for the person that I am.

Most marriages survived the ordeals of the strike, and many women feel that their growth as individuals has strengthened their relationships with their husbands. But it was also not uncommon for husbands threatened by the new eloquence, assertiveness, and political awareness of their wives simply to walk out.

The strike also transformed the relationship of women workers to their children. Many brought their children to meetings and to the picket line. "My little boy was only three months, and you should have seen me, I had him always in my arms, going everywhere," remembers one striker. Children who were slightly older took an active part in strike support work, and formed their own opinions about unionization.

> See my little boy? . . . I used to take him with me to go picket. We [adults] used to go give people . . . papers, and they would hold their papers, or throw them at us right in the face, or say "Shove it down your you-know-what." He would get them—you know, he's a small boy. People would not pay attention to him. So he would say, "Here, sir!" "OK!" He would put it in his pocket, or read it. . . . He was always out with me, always out picketing. He was about seven or eight. . . . Anybody talks about unions, he'll tell you, "Go out there and join the union." Tell him, "Unions are no good." "They're good. They educate. They educated my mother."

One teenager commented, "Mom used to be a slave. But since the strike she thinks for herself. It's a lot better."

Women also consciously reevaluated their ideas about child-rearing and their hopes for their children.

> I used to be a very nervous person when my kids were little. I almost had a nervous breakdown. . . . My husband used to drive me batty, you know. The kid couldn't be bawling over there in the other room—I had to get up and run and see what's the matter with the kid! Because my husband was an overly protective person with his children. . . . So here's the idiot wife, running like crazy to look after these kids, and it was driving me batty! . . .
>
> These are the things that I was able to begin to stand up for. It was crazy, you couldn't watch the kid constantly . . . And I've come to where now I don't feel this . . . pressure. I don't feel this anymore. I'll look out for my kids the best I can. . . .
>
> My ideas are a whole lot different than they used to be. I want my kids to be free. I never want them to feel oppressed. I want them to treat everybody as an equal. . . . I don't think they should slight someone because he's black or he's any different than they are. And this is what I want—I want them to be free people. And to be good people. . . .
>
> I want my daughter to be able to do what she's gotta do . . . and not always comply to whatever her boyfriend or her husband [wants] . . . that she should be the person that she is. And I want my boys to be the person that they are.

You know, it's very funny, when my daughter and my son were little, you know my husband wouldn't let my boy wash dishes? . . . So he grows up never washing a dish! And I tell my husband, "I think it's your fault that he doesn't know how to wash dishes . . ."

You know, I think it [the strike] has made my kids more outspoken. . . . Maybe some people would call it disrespect. I don't. I think that being outspoken is not harmful if you do it in the right way. Like my son—if someboy, if an adult, gives him a hard time, I expect him to stand up and speak for his rights.

Unidad Para Siempre

Women strikers turned a critical eye on their personal lives and their home; as they became more experienced they developed criticisms of the union campaign as well. Some women felt that the Amalgamated Clothing Workers of America was not promoting the strike and boycott actively enough, particularly in El Paso.

The union, hard-pressed to pay each striker thirty dollars a week, stopped encouraging more workers to come out on strike. (The union organizers felt that the strike could not be won unless there was a successful national boycott, and that funds should be channeled into boycott organizing rather than support of additional strikers.) There were squabbles about eligibility for emergency funds and relief payments. More important, many strikers felt that they were not being encouraged to take independent action to raise funds or publicize the strike. They wanted the process of education which had begun with the walkout to continue. One woman remembers that she and her fellow activists "were trying to get those people to reorganize not only the union, but actually to really try to stand on their own two feet . . . trying to talk things out for yourself without having somebody else talk them out."

Some strikers began to meet independently of the union, in a group which was known simply as the rank-and-file committee. (This group took the name Unidad Para Siempre—Unity Forever—when it was reactivated after the strike.) The members of the group—about forty—shared a strong sense of themselves as workers and a desire to build a strong and democratic union. They put out their own leaflets, participated in marches and rallies, helped to found the Farah Distress Fund, and talked to other strikers about the need for a strong union. "We wanted a union with action, not just words. That's why we were having meetings and going out, really doing more, making our own papers . . .

Politicization of Women

For the women on strike at Farah there was no artificial separation between personal and political change. Their experiences during the strike altered the way they looked at themselves as women and as workers.

Of course, we never did anything wrong, really. What we were fighting for was our rights, because we were very oppressed. For one thing, I was a very insecure person way back then. I felt that I was inferior to my supervisors, who were at the time only Anglo. None of this affects me anymore. I have learned that I am an equal. I have all the rights they have. I may not have the education they have, and I may not earn the money they earn. . . . But I am their equal regardless. And it's done a lot for me, it's changed a lot for me. It made me into a better person. . . .

It used to be if a supervisor got after me for anything I'd sit there and cry. Well, they don't do this to me anymore. They don't frighten me anymore. Two of them can take me into the office—it does not affect me at all. I have my say, and if they like it or not, I'm going to say so. . . . Before I wouldn't say anything. I would just hold it in and cry it out, and stay and stay. . . .

And I believe very much in fighting for your rights, and for women's rights. . . . I don't believe in burning your bra, but I do believe in our having our rights, that even if you're married you can make your marriage work. I know that sometimes we have to put up with a little bit more, but it has changed a lot of things for me. . . .

Maybe the company doesn't feel this way, but it's done a lot for us. . . .

The strike made women more conscious of political and social movements which they had regarded as "outside" and irrelevant to their own lives. These ranged from the support of local union struggles to the struggles of the UFW and Texas Farmworkers to the women's movement.

"During the strike," says one woman, "every place I turned around there'd be a strike. They [other strikers] used to go to the stores where they were selling

Farah pants, and they used to picket at the stores, and in return we used to go and help them picket." Farah workers have supported recent strikes at a local cannery and the municipal bus lines. Some of them joined the picket lines when Asarco, a nearby smelting plant, went on strike in the summer of 1977.

Recently, ex-strikers have also been involved in other unionizing drives. One woman who now works in a hospital is contemplating an organizing campaign among health care workers. Another has helped her father and uncles to begin signing up people at a bread factory. Several other women have joined a Texas Farmworkers support committee, which publicizes the working conditions of the farm workers and tries to raise funds for their unionizing campaigns.

People have also begun to discuss the women's movement in their homes. Although it is still perceived as a movement that is taking place somewhere outside of El Paso, it evokes both sympathy and support.

> Well, all of us women, we like it. And we sure would like to join them. Some of the husbands they don't like it at all. They're not happy about it. . . . [My husband] doesn't like it. . . . Sometimes [we argue] and my daughters help me, my daughters back me up. [My sons] like it too.

For all of the women, the strike made them more conscious of themselves as working people with interests distinct from other classes. One woman began to argue with her dentist, who complained to her that her strike was causing him to lose money he had invested in Farah Manufacturing Company. She commented that he could afford to lose money, and added.

> It's like I tell him, "Just because you happen to be one Mexican out of many that made it to the top—and I bet you worked your butt off to get up there. I'll respect you for your ideas as long as you respect me for mine. I happen to be of the working class, and I happen to be one of the minority (i.e. Chicana), that I feel work at the lowest type of job there is, and I feel that we have a right to fight.

For others the strike altered the way they looked at their jobs, and for the first time made them feel that their workplace was the site of an important struggle.

> For myself, I would like to continue working where I am. I think about going to school and getting a secretarial job, and I think it would be a boring thing. I like to be where the action is. For my kids, if they want a college education, I expect to give it to them. . . . I'd rather have them have a better job than me.
>
> But I like being there. I like the challenge. You don't know what the next day's going to bring you. You might get fired! . . . I don't think I could see myself sitting there in back of a desk, answering phones. When you could be fighting somewhere else, in a grievance, fighting with your supervisors, giving them hell. . . .
>
> [Before the strike] it was just a job to go to. Now it is kind of challenging, you know, you can never tell what's going to happen.

Inside the Plant: The Pressure Builds

By the beginning of 1974, the nationwide boycott organized by the ACWA was having a noticeable effect on Farah's business. Sales, which were $156 million in 1972, dropped to $126 million in 1974.[7] By the end of 1973 four Farah plants outside of El Paso had been closed, and the El Paso plants had been put on a four-day week.

The five El Paso plants, which had been operating with scab labor throughout the strike, began to resemble ghost towns. One striker who maintained a close friendship with a strikebreaker recalls:

> She told me all the things that happened in there. That sometimes there wasn't even work and they would send them home. She said sometimes they would just play tic tac toe for hours. . . . She said she used to get tired of staying waiting hours in there for material. And they would just sit down and talk, or go into a bathroom and spend thirty minutes in there. . . . I think that their orders weren't coming in [because of] the boycott.

Even among the business community in El Paso, there was concern that the city was acquiring a reputation as a bad place to invest, and there was embarrassment at the outrageous and frequently racist statements that Farah periodically made to the press. When Farah publicly blamed the Catholic Church for his problems with the union, national press coverage was not sympathetic.

The final blow came at the end of January 1974, when an Administrative Judge of the National Labor

Relations Board issued a decision which accused Farah of "flouting the (National Labor Relations) Act and trampling on the rights of its employees as if there were no Act, no Board, and no Ten Commandments." Farah was ordered to offer reinstatement to the strikers (whom the company asserted had voluntarily quit), to reinstate with back pay several workers who had been fired for union activity, and to allow the union access to company bulletin boards and employee lists.

Farah initially indicated that he would appeal the decision, but several weeks later he abruptly changed course. On February 23, apparently after preliminary discussion with union officials, he recognized the Amalgamated Clothing Workers of America as the bargaining agent for Farah employees. The union simultaneously announced that it would terminate the boycott.

The strikers, exultant and relieved, celebrated the fact that they had outlasted El Paso's major business figure.

It's like Rome. Remember, at that time, Caesar and all of them, he had a big throne. He said, "I am a god. I make these people do that and and I make these people do this." Yet his throne, his empire, crumbled down. That's what happened to Farah. It was an empire. . . . And yet, his empire came down. Farah's empire came down. . . .

However, for many strikers the feeling of triumph was marred by a confusion about who had decided to end the strike. They resented the fact that they were not involved in the discussions which preceded Farah's capitulation. Many people first heard the news on the picket line.

All of a sudden the strike was over. [We heard about it] the day before, because they said, "Nobody's gonna picket tomorrow." After I got out of the check committee I went out picketing. . . . [The picket captain] knew, I'm pretty sure he did, because he's working now as a business agent. . . .
We really didn't know what was going on. "We don't picket tomorrow." "Why don't we picket?" "I don't know. The strike is over, I guess." "Oh, really?" And then the newspaper, the headlines. . . . I didn't like it, because I thought it was something they had already made up their minds to it, you know. We were not involved. . . . I wasn't really pleased about it, but I said, "Well, at least we got the union in."

Most strikers believed that the decision to end the strike had been made in New York.

When the negotiating committee for the first contract was elected, strikers discovered to their dismay that happies were to be represented on the committee. In the few weeks before Farah recognized the union, his supervisors had been ordering people to sign union cards, telling them that if they didn't comply the factory would close. As nominal union members, these people had the right to participate in contract negotiations. The committee was thus badly split.

You know, we were strikers, and they told us we were going to have a committee for the negotiations as strikers. And I believe that as long as you're on strike, that you have the right to decide what contract you want. . . . They [the union officials] decided that it was only fair that the people that were inside [should] have another committee.
So there was the table, this side were happies, and this side was strikers. We wanted something, they voted against us. We wanted thirty cents, they wanted five cents. That's where I believe we got screwed. If we had the chance, not having that committee there, I believe we would have gotten a better . . . contract.

Other strikers on the negotiating committee felt that they were powerless, that the union officials had decided what they wanted before they held meetings with the workers. "The negotiating committee never really had much to say. . . . [The officials] say they know what is right and what isn't." If a member of the negotiating committee raised a question about a specific contract provision in negotiations, recalls one committee member, the senior union official would say: "Well, let's have a little break now." And he would talk to the people and say, "You shouldn't do that, you know. They know how much they can give you."

The final contract included pay increases of fifty-five cents an hour over three years, a medical insurance plan financed by the company, job security and seniority rights, and a grievance procedure. It also gave union representatives the right to challenge production quotas for individual operations. It was ratified at a meeting of employees on March 7.

Many workers were angry that there was little time taken to explain the contract or hear people's questions and objections.

They put us all in the cafeteria of one of the factories. And we were in there along with all the people. There was a lot of people, a lot of noise. Some of the clauses that were in there, we didn't even get to understand them very well. He [a union official would explain it in English, and Sánchez [the ACWA Joint Board Manager] would just translate it. . . . But he was going so fast with it that we didn't have a chance to really understand it. But then they said that we had to take that contract regardless because Mr. Farah had said that if that contract was not signed he wasn't about to change his mind and go for another contract. That contract had to be taken or else he would just close down the factory and that was that. . . .

So he read the contract real fast and then he asked, "Does anybody disapprove?" and then a few of the people raised their hands and they were ignored. . . . He said, "OK, this means we go back to work." . . . We didn't vote on it.

Strikers felt that two years of suffering entitled them to a stronger contract. But Farah was in financial trouble as a result of the boycott and a series of management mistakes, and his threat to close the factory was a real one. The strikers, inexperienced at contract negotiations, felt outmaneuvered by a process in which the company set the terms and the union lawyers made most of the decisions.

AFTER THE STRIKE

In spite of their misgivings about the contract, and a pervasive feeling that the situation was no longer under their control, most strikers concluded that the contract was "all right for a first try," and that it was "a beginning." They realized that their fight for better working conditions was by no means over, but at least they now had the protection of a union and a grievance procedure. They were determined that they would no longer be intimidated by supervisors; if they were mistreated they were going to climb off their machines and protest. "I'm going to say something if I have to say it," one striker insisted. "And I'll be nice if they're nice. If they're not very nice I can also be very unnice."

When they returned to work in the spring of 1974, the strikers faced tremendous obstacles. Texas was (and still is) a right-to-work state, so workers were not required to join the union. If enough workers took the benefits without joining the union, the company could

move to have the union decertified. This made the task of organizing the unorganized at Farah both very necessary and immensely difficult. It was complicated by the fact that the conclusion of the strike did not dilute Willie Farah's notorious antiunion sentiment. He had recognized the union with great reluctance, and was determined to break it. Finally, there were serious divisions among the workers in the plant. Strikers determined to build a strong union would have to overcome tensions between themselves and the "happies," as well as divisions between Chicanas and Mexicanas which had been created during the strike.

When the strikers returned to the factory, they found that the organization of production had changed dramatically during the two years of the strike. In an attempt to keep up with the changing men's clothing market, Farah was diversifying production to include men's leisure suits and jackets. Workers were placed in new production lines without adequate retraining. Women who had been sewing straight seams for ten years were suddenly expected to set sleeves. One woman said, "They just sat me on the machine and said, 'Try to do this.' That was my training."

Workers who previously had been working with a six-piece pattern for pants were now working with a thirty-piece pattern for jackets. Seamstresses accustomed to sewing cotton fabric suddenly had to adjust to sewing brushed denim, plaids and double-knits—fabrics which were much more difficult to handle. In addition, sewing collars and cuffs of jackets were much more delicate and time-consuming work than most operations involved in the production of pants.

These changes in materials, patterns and techniques were not taken into account when new production quotas were established. Women whose wages had been based on their ability to produce a certain number of pieces at one operation were expected to produce just as many at a new operation. As a result, quotas were often impossibly high. Unable to meet their new quotas within the prescribed time limit, many women suffered wage reductions and eventually were fired for low production. Some ex-strikers believe that by selectively assigning them to the most difficult new operations and establishing outrageous quotas, the company hoped gradually to weed them out of the plant.

At the same time that Farah was changing production, the company plunged into a serious financial disaster. The recession of 1974-1975 hurt the company, and in addition, Willie Farah made major miscalculations in production and marketing.[8] He had always been able to stockpile his most dependable styles and sell them on a stable market year after year. Lightning changes in styles meant that Farah could no longer predict the market. For example, one year he would corner the market in leisure suits, stockpile thousands of leisure suits, and then find that the next year no one was wearing leisure suits. In 1974 Farah decided he wanted to produce his own fabrics, and opened a textile mill in El Paso. The venture was a six million dollar flop.

Farah's financial predicament was exacerbated by marketing problems. In the past, Farah had been known for the high quality of its merchandise. But under severe pressure to meet quotas on new operations, workers were simply unable to concern themselves with perfection. "When you're pushing people they can't get their work out right," one ex-striker commented.

> So they were getting it out as fast as they could, without caring how it was coming out . . . They made all these jackets lopsided and crooked. Who are you going to sell them to once the stores see how they are? They are definitely going to return them. And that is what started happening. They were sending back truckloads of jackets, sportcoats, and pants.

In addition, retailers who disliked Farah's highhanded business practices had gladly removed Farah pants from their shelves during the boycott, and were reluctant to resume dealing with the company again after the strike.

All of these management problems resulted in a 40 percent decline in sales and a $3.5 million loss in the last quarter of 1976. Five thousand of the original 9,000 employees were laid off. Several of the Farah plants were closed, including plants in San Antonio, Victoria, and Las Cruces, New Mexico.

Union Troubles

These financial setbacks hindered the efforts of union activists to continue organizing. First, there was a visible cutback in services provided for the workers by the company. Bus service to and from the plant was curtailed, coffee and donuts no longer were served during breaks, the already inadequate medical care available to workers was cut back, and Thanksgiving turkeys and Christmas parties were no longer provided. Many workers complained that the plants were dirtier and more dust-covered than they had ever been in the past. Since these cutbacks coincided with the end of the strike, many nonunion members blamed the union, not Farah, for the decline in their working conditions.

A more serious consequence of Farah's financial setback was that it required a drastic reduction in the size of the workforce. This need to layoff workers provided Farah with an opportunity to harass and eliminate his most vocal opponents among the union activists. Some were given extremely erratic work schedules. Some days they would be required to work until noon, other days until three o'clock, and frequently they were called to work on Saturdays. They were rarely given much advance notice of their hours. Some ex-strikers were switched to production lines which were scheduled to be phased out. Others were placed on extended layoff and after one year were let go by the company.

Farah's management devised several further strategies which undercut the ability of union activists to organize. One was to isolate union members. At the end of the strike almost all of the strikers were assigned to the large Gateway plant. (By keeping them all in one place the company apparently hoped to prevent strikers from "infecting" other workers in the various plants.) After the strike, one woman recalled,

> We were closer. We didn't let our chain break. They tried to break it. At first they put us all together. And then suddenly they knew that we were so strong, they started separating us. They went to Northeast, and the other ones went to Paisano. So then suddenly you were all separated . . . Then they put "happies" with you. It was hard to make them understand.

While, in the past, an effort had been made to assign women to the plant nearest their homes, after the transfers many workers found themselves working at plants across the city from their residence.

Grievances

It is against this background of changes in production, financial setbacks, the establishment of high quotas, and transfers of workers that many grievances were filed. (During negotiations for the second contract in March 1977, union officials stated that more grievances were filed at Farah than at all other ACWA plants in the United States combined.) When workers had grievances it was up to the shop stewards to investigate the complaint, collect all the necessary information, discuss it with the immediate supervisor, fill out the forms and deliver them to the union office. If a grievance could not be resolved on the shop floor it would be turned over to a business agent.

Most of the shop stewards were inundated with
grievances. Some were responsible for lines of a hundred workers, stretched out over a quarter mile. Unlike the supervisors, they did not have roller skates
and bicycles at their disposal to traverse the distances
within the plant. They had to do all union-related
work during lunch hours and breaks. One ex-striker
said:

I'm a very active person and I love to help people. They wouldn't let you talk during work,
they wouldn't let you talk about the union or
anything. At breaktimes I would go real fast, I
would go in the plant and start talking to the
people, start going line by line.

Work for the union did not end with the end of the
working day at Farah, and most shop stewards spent
several hours each day driving to and from the union
office. "Some people don't understand the time you put
into it," one shop steward complained,

. . . the time you have to leave your kids to go
fight their cases . . . We don't get paid for being
shop stewards, we don't get gas money, we still
pay our union dues, everything. We get nothing
out of it, other than our self-satisfaction that we
are helping our people.

In addition to being overworked, shop stewards
were systematically harassed. One union activist noticed that every time she went to the bathroom a supervisor followed her, and if she took time to smoke a
cigarette, the supervisor would hurry her back to work.
Another found that whenever she had problems with
her sewing machine and signalled the supervisor, he
would consistently ignore her, and it would be hours
before the machine was repaired.

The ability of shop stewards to effectively solicit
and process grievances was further hindered by their
isolation from other union activists and from workers
in general. "They have a great big cutting room," one
shop steward commented

And on the corner where all the machines start,
that's where I'm at, on the very corner. They
kind of keep me isolated from the other people . . . I had one woman tell me-she saw me
in the bathroom. She said, "Are you the shop
steward here?" I said, "Yeah." And she said,
"You know, I'd never seen you before here." I
said, "Yes, I've been here, but I've never been

on the other side." She said, "Well, they keep
telling me there was one [shop steward, but I
never saw you."

There is at least one case of a steward being fired for
carrying out her duties. In this instance, an ex-striker
who had filed a grievance was being harassed by the supervisor. The entire production line had stopped work
to watch the argument. The shop steward stepped off
her machine and walked down the line to investigate.
The supervisor started yelling at her to return to her
machine. Outraged that she had climbed down from
her machine in the first place, and then refused to go
back, he phoned the plant manager who fired her for
disobedience. She had witnesses and was rehired after
her case went to arbitration.

A final factor which made the shop stewards less
effective than they might have been was the continuing apathy of nonunionized workers. The ex-strikers
clearly understood that they had to organize to defend
their interests, and were continually frustrated by the
complacence and lack of support from workers who
refused to act on their own behalf.

There were never enough women willing to serve
as shop stewards. When shop stewards were laid off, or
transferred from one plant to another, there was rarely
another worker willing to take their place.

The effectiveness of the grievance procedure depended largely on the resources of the union staff. The
business agents, hired by the union, were chosen from
among the ex-strikers. Inexperienced and inadequate-
ly trained, they were overwhelmed by the volume of
grievances. In addition, some ex-strikers charge that
the union carefully selected the most passive and malle-
able strikers to work full-time for the union.

Another union staff member who played a decisive
role in implementng the grievance procedure was the
union engineer. Because of the changes in production
from pants to leisure suits and the introduction of new
operations, many of the grievances dealt with allegedly
unfair quotas assigned to those operations. Quotas for
new operations were initially set by company engineers.
If they were to be challenged, a grievance had to be filed
within thirty days; then a union engineer would be sent
to the plant to determine whether or not the quota set
by the company for that operation had been reasonable.

There was only one union engineer for the five
Farah plants, and he was responsible for all the other
ACWA plants in El Paso as well. Not only was the
union engineer overworked and unable to investigate
every dispute, but all too often, ex-strikers complained,

the union engineer would back up the quotas set by the company.

One union activist, switched to a new production line and given an impossibly high quota, received a pink slip for low production. She called in the union engineer to observe the operation. She could not even produce half of the quota, and another person he observed was also not able to make the quota. Nonetheless, he agreed with the company that the quota was a reasonable one. The repeated occurrence of similar cases led many strikers to conclude that the union engineer could not be counted on as an advocate for the workers.

Many ex-strikers felt victimized by a combination of the company's determination to manipulate and undermine the union and the union's reluctance to actively challenge the company. The union seemed willing to take to arbitration only those cases in which a favorable decision was certain. Only a small percentage of all the grievances filed were taken to arbitration.

Decline of Unidad Para Siempre

Militant union members were left in a particularly vulnerable position. The rank-and-file group, Unidad Para Siempre, pushed for reforms which had not been included in the contract. These reforms included elimination of the quota system, compensation and training for shop stewards, and greater rank-and-file participation in settling grievances between workers and the company. In this way, they hoped to build a stronger and more responsive union. The continued growth of Unidad was hampered by the fact that a large number of its members—the most vocal and militant union activists—were among the first to be laid off by Farah during his cutbacks in production. Unidad members feel that the union did not actively prosecute their cases because, like the company, it felt threatened by their presence. By 1977, few members of Unidad still worked in Farah plants.

Unidad's ability to form a strong organization was further inhibited by fundamental divisions among the workers. There were differences among the ex-strikers and nonstrikers about how much and when to criticize the union. Among the workers at Farah, there were some who still actively opposed the union. They blamed the union for Farah's financial predicament; they blamed the union for the termination of services they had previously enjoyed. They did their best to aggravate union activists in the plant. "Oh, I had so many things done to me," one shop steward remarked.

They [workers hostile to the union] used to get into my car, put gum on my chair. . . . One time I was setting the cuff. People would come by and knock them all down. They would take all my union papers and leaflets. They'd take them off or throw them on the floor. . . . One time somebody cut all the threads off my machine. Can you imagine?

Other workers were simply indifferent to the union. As far as they were concerned they could take advantage of union benefits without paying dues or suffering the harassment inflicted upon union activists. Some Mexicans feared that they might lose their green cards if they became union activists.

Union members viewed the union in a variety of ways. Some uncritically supported it. In their view the major obstacle to the growth of a strong union was the apathy of the workers who refused to share the responsibility of working to improve conditions. There was another group of union activists who expressed frustration with passive, nonunion workers in the plant, but who attached equal importance to the weaknesses of the union machinery. There was still another group, many of whom belonged to Unidad, who emphasized the extent to which the union had collaborated with the company, and who saw democratizing the union as the major requirement. Finally, there was a small group of ex-strikers who became disillusioned with the union, and simply signed out.

The Second Contract

The continuing layoffs, loss of rank-and-file activists, tensions among workers in the plant, and inadequate support from the international union all combined to weaken the position of the workers during contract negotiations in early 1977.

Negotiations took place with both sides assuming that Farah was in serious financial difficulties. Workers on the negotiating committee spent several days listening to detailed descriptions of Farah's woes, and finally were told, "You can ask for the moon, but if we give it to you we'll fold tomorrow and you'll all be out on the street."

This bleak picture was accepted by union lawyers, who urged the negotiating committee to accept Farah's terms. The union officials clearly were worried about Farah's financial status, and felt that no further challenges to the company's authority should be mounted. Instead of giving an organized voice to workers' grievances, they tried to devise a strategy which would help the company back to financial health. As one union official put it, "Once Farah was a union plant, it was in the union's interest to sell pants." If selling pants more cheaply meant accepting a serious setback in working conditions, the union officials were willing to pay that price to keep Farah from going under.

The 1977 contract granted the workers a scanty thirty-cent pay raise over a three-year period. It eliminated dental benefits and retained the hated quota system. Most damaging of all, it permitted Farah to lay off experienced workers and call them back to work on a different production line-at the minimum wage. Some members of the negotiating committee reluctantly voted to accept the contract, certain that once it was taken to the workers for ratification it would be rejected.

Many workers now believe that the company exaggerated its problems so that the union would settle for a weak contract. Although it is still uncertain whether Farah Manufacturing Company will recover from its economic crisis, it is already clear that under the terms of the 1977 contract, the workers are paying for Farah's problems.

The contract was hastily presented in a short meeting held in the cafeteria at the Gateway plant. The meeting was called at the end of the working day, and most workers did not know until the last minute that the meeting was to take place. The contract was read in legalistic Spanish which few workers could understand, and questions from the floor were discouraged. When a vote was called, Tony Sánchez (the ACWA Joint Board Manager) requested that those in favor of the contract stand up. Since the room was packed, most people were already standing up. There is a great deal of controversy about what happened at this point. Many who attended the meeting say that a clear majority of workers raised their hands in opposition to the contract. No formal count was made, however, and Tony Sánchez declared that the contract had passed.

Before workers could raise their objections to the terms of the contract and the way in which the vote was conducted, the bell signalling the end of work rang. Workers swarmed out of the Gateway cafeteria, many angrily pulling their union buttons off their shirts and throwing them onto the ground. Lacking experience as well as the presence of a strong rank-and-file organization, the remaining union activists were unable to challenge the proceedings. This created even greater divisions among the workers, as many felt that they had been sold out by union militants.

Since March 1977, Farah has closed another of its El Paso plants. The number of workers at Farah, particularly union members, continues to decline.

CONCLUSION

Events at Farah since the strike show the continuing difficulty of union organizing in the Southwest. The right-to-work law, the consolidated opposition of powerful employers, the timidity of union officials, and the many incipient tensions in the border area which employers can use to divide the workforce—all of these are formidable obstacles in the way of a strong workers' organization.

The story of the ACWA at Farah also illustrates some of the problems specific to organizing workers in the garment industry. In contrast to relatively monopolized, capital-intensive industries such as auto and steel, the garment industry is highly competitive, volatile, and labor-intensive. In this context of constant business fluctuations, it is possible for a large and established company like Farah to suffer a dramatic decline within a period of several years.

The development of runaway shops during the last decade has made this instability even more pronounced. Increasing workers' organization and the relatively high cost of American labor have prompted labor-intensive industries such as garments and electronics to move south across the border, or to southeastern Asian countries, where labor is cheaper and less organized than in the United States. In border cities such as El Paso, industries have been able to take advantage of the proximity of an abundant supply of documented and undocumented workers from Mexico.

In an attempt to prevent industries from leaving the country, many unions such as the ACWA have adopted the strategy of bailing out the company in times of financial hardships. As recent events at Farah suggest, this may often be done at the expense of the workers. Although this is not a problem whose ultimate solution lies solely within the borders of the United States, current union strategy has not even provided a partial answer. Instead, it has failed to prevent runaway shops and simultaneously has helped to undermine the development of a strong union movement.

It is clear from the Farah experience that a successful unionization effort does not end when the union wins a contract. Organizing and training of workers in everything from a grievance procedure to labor history must continue on a long-term basis. In addition, workers must develop a strong rank-and-file movement-one which can overcome divisions among the workers, build a democratic local union, and encourage women workers to develop leadership skills and an analysis of their working situation.

While the Farah strike did not produce a strong, mature rank-and-file movement, it did help to create the conditions in which one can develop. The workers who made the strike were irreversibly changed by it. All of them say that they would organize and strike again; most of them recognize the need for strong support from an international union like the ACWA, as long as it does not undermine the independent organization of rank-and-file workers. "We're sticking in there and we're not going to get out and we're not giving up!" one ex-striker insisted.

In the words of one striker:

I believe in fighting for our rights, and for women's rights . . . When I walked out of that company way back then, it was like I had taken a weight off my back. And I began to realize, "Why did I put up with it all these years? Why didn't I try for something else?" Now I want to stay here and help people to help themselves.

The Chicanas who comprise the majority of strikers learned that they could speak and act on their own behalf as women and workers, lessons they will not forget.

Endnotes

1. El Paso, Texas is located on the western tip of the Texas panhandle, near the point where the boundaries of Texas, New Mexico, and Mexico intersect. In July 1975, the population was estimated by the U.S. Bureau of Census at 414,700 people, of whom 57 percent were "Spanish American." El Paso is directly across the U.S.-Mexico border from Ciudad Juárez, which has an estimated population of 600,000.

2. General Executive Board Report "Farah Boycott: Union Label," to the 1974 Convention, Amalgamated Clothing, Workers of America, p. 1.

3. Allen Pusey, "Clothes Made the Man," *Texas Monthly* (June 1977), p. 135.

4. In June 1976, ACWA merged with the Textile Workers Union of America, and became the Amalgamated Clothing and Textile Workers Union. Since the events in this article occurred before the merger, the union will be referred to as ACWA.

5. "Farah Boycott: Union Label," General Executive Board Report, op. cit.

6. Bishop Sidney Metzger to Bishop of Rochester, October 31, 1972, reprinted in *Viva La Huelga: Farah Strike Bulletin No. 15* (Amalgamated Clothing Workers of America, AFL-CIO).

7. *Moody's Industrial Manual,* 1975, p. 1099.

8. Critics of the union have blamed the strike and boycott for the company's business troubles. However, the boycott never actually destroyed Farah's profit margin. In fact, some analysts argue that the short-term effect of the strike was beneficial because it forced the company to stop overproduction. They note that "during the only full year of the boycott (1973), the company jumped from $8 million in losses to a modest $42,000 profit." Pusey, loc. cit. The losses predate the union and can be traced to management errors on Farah's part.

SECTION 1: HISTORICAL PERSPECTIVES ASSESSMENT AND APPLICATION

1. Under what pretenses were the Mexicans and their descendants in the "New American Southwest" deprived of their lands and possessions after the Treaty of Guadalupe Hidalgowas signed?

2. What are the implications of the Treaty of Guadalupe Hidalgo for Chicanos in the Southwest according to Griswold del Castillo?

3. Describe the concepts of Aztlán and Chicanismo and their major features.

4. Who were the major leaders of the Chicano movement of the late 1960s and early 1970s, their geographic area of operation, and their major political accomplishments?

5. What is the political importance for Chicanos to have established the Raza Unida Party in 1972? You can consult YouTube's La Raza Unida 40th Year Commemoration, Part 1 and Part 2. The link is in the suggested films list for section three of this book.

6. Outline the facts leading to the El Paso Salt War in 1877. In your opinion, was it a mob revolt or were the citizens of San Elizario justified in defending the salt flats from privatization?

7. What are your impressions about family life in El Paso as discussed by Mario García? What can these activities teach us about our own family experiences in the twenty-first century?

8. After reading Vicki Ruiz's chapter, locate and interview Chicanas who received social and educational services from missionary institutions as adolescents. Determine if thoseexperiences contributed to their Americanization.

9. What were the key factors, local and national, that led to the successful unionization of the Farah garment factories?

SECTION 1: SUGGESTED READINGS

Acosta, Teresa P. & Winegarten, Ruthe. (2003). *Las Tejanas, 300 Years of History*. Austin, TX: University of Texas Press.

Acuña, Rodolfo. (2007). *Corridors of Migration*. (1st ed.). Tucson, AZ: University of Arizona Press.

Acuña, Rodolfo. (2010). *Occupied America: A History of Chicanos*. (7th ed.). New York, NY: Pearson and Longman.

Barrera, Mario. (1979). *Race and Class in the Southwest: A Theory of Racial Inequality*. Notre Dame, IN: University of Notre Dame Press.

Cárdenas, Gilberto. (2004). *La Causa: Civil Rights, Social Justice and the Struggle for Equality in the Midwest*. Houston, TX: Arte Público Press.

Chávez, César & Stavans, Ilan. (2008). *An Organizer's Tale, Speeches*. New York, NY: Penguin Classics.

Chávez, Ernesto. (2002). *"¡Mi Raza Primero!" (My People First!): Nationalism, Identity, and Insurgency in the Chicano Movement in Los Angeles, 1966–1978*. Berkeley, CA: University of California Press.

Department of Defense. (1990). *Hispanics in America's Defense*. Washington, DC: US Government Printing Office.

Dorado Romo, David. (2005). *Ringside Seat to a Revolution: An Underground Cultural History of El Paso and Juárez, 1893–1923*. El Paso, TX: Cinco Puntos Press.

Driscoll, Barbara A. (1999). *The Tracks North: The Railroad Bracero Program of World War II*. Austin, TX: University of Texas Press.

Durán, Livie I. & Bernard, H. Russell. (1982). *Introduction to Chicano Studies*. (2nd ed.). Upper Saddle River, NJ: Prentice Hall College Div.

García, Ignacio M. (2003). *Héctor P. García: In Relentless Pursuit of Justice*. Houston, TX: Arte Público Press.

García, Mario T. (2008). *A Dolores Huerta Reader*. Alburquerque, NM: University of New Mexico Press.

García, Mario T. (1995). *Memories of Chicano History: The Life and Narrative of Bert Corona*. Berkeley, CA: University of California Press.

García, Mario T. (1991). *Mexican Americans: Leadership, Ideology & Identity, 1930–1960*. New Haven, CT: Yale University Press.

Gómez, Laura E. (2008). *Manifest Destinies: The Making of the Mexican American Race*. New York, NY: New York University Press.

Gonzales, Manuel G. & Gonzales, Cynthia M. (2000). *En Aquel Entonces: Readings in Mexican American History*. Bloomington, IN: Indiana University Press.

Gonzales, Manuel G. (2009). *Mexicanos: A History of Mexicans in the United States*. (2nd ed.). Bloomington, IN: Indiana University Press.

González, Gilbert G. & Fernández, Raúl E. (2003). *A Century of Chicano History: Empire, Nations, and Migration*. New York, NY: Routledge.

González, Gilbert G. & Fernández, Raúl. (1994). Chicano history: Transcending cultural models. *Pacific Historical Review, 63*(4), 469–497.

Gonzales, Rodolfo "Corky." (2001). *Message to Aztlán: Selected Writings*. Houston, TX: Arte Público Press.

Gutiérrez, David. (1998). LULAC and the Assimilationist Perspective. In Richard Delgado & Jean Stefancic, (Eds.) *The Latino Condition: A Critical Reader*. New York, NY: New York University Press.

Gutiérrez, José Angel. (1999). *The Making of a Chicano Militant: Lessons from Cristal*. Madison, WI: University of Wisconsin Press.

Gutiérrez, José Angel. (2005). *The Making of a Civil Rights Leader: José Angel Gutiérrez*. Houston, TX: Arte Público Press.

Gutiérrez, José Angel. (2006). *We Won't Back Down: Severita Lara's Rise from Student Leader to Mayor*. Houston, TX: Arte Público Press.

Jensen, Richard J. & Hammerback, John C. (2002). *The Words of César Chávez*. College Station, TX: Texas A&M University Press.

Johnson, Benjamin H. (2005). *Revolution in Texas: How a Forgotten Rebellion and Its Bloody Suppression Turned Mexicans into Americans*. New Haven, CT: Yale University Press.

Kingsolver, Barbara. (1996). *Holding the Line: Women in the Great Arizona Mine Strike of 1983*. Ithaca, NY: Cornell University Press.

Kearney, Milo & Knopp, Anthony. (1995). *Border Cuates: A History of US-Mexican Twin Cities*. Austin, TX: Eakin Press.

López Tijerina, Reies & Gutiérrez, José Angel. (2000). *They Called Me "King Tiger": My Struggle for the Land and Our Rights*. Houston, TX: Arte Público Press.

Maciel, David R. (1996). *El México Olvidado: La Historia del Pueblo Chicano Vol. I and II*. Cd Juárez, Chih.: Universidad Autónoma de Ciudad Juárez.

Mariscal, George. (Ed). (1999). *Aztlán and Viet Nam: Chicano and Chicana Experiences of the War*. Berkeley, CA: University of California Press.

Mariscal, George. (2005). *Brown-Eyed Children of the Sun: Lessons from the Chicano Movement, 1965–1975*. Albuquerque, NM: University of New Mexico Press.

Martínez, Oscar J. (Ed.). (1996). *The US-Mexico Borderlands: Historical and Contemporary Perspectives*. Lanham, MD: Rowman & Littlefield Publishers.

McWilliams, Carey. (1990). *North from Mexico: The Spanish-Speaking People of the United States*. (2nd ed.). New York, NY: Praeger Publishers.

Meier, Matt S. & Rivera, Feliciano. (1994). *The Chicano: A History of Mexican Americans*. New York, NY: Hill & Wang.

Menchaca, Martha. (2002). *Recovering History, Constructing Race: The Indian, Black and White Roots of Mexican Americans*. Austin, TX: University of Texas Press.

Moquín, Wayne & Van Doren, Charles. (1971). *A Documentary History of the Mexican Americans*. New York, NY: Praeger Publishers.

Morín, Eddie. (2006). *Valor & Discord, Mexican Americans and the Vietnam War*. Los Angeles, CA: Valiant Press.

Navarro, Armando. (2005). *Mexicano Political Experience in Occupied Aztlán: Struggles and Change*. Lanham, MD: Altamira Press.

Noriega, Chon A. Avila, Eric R. Dávalos, Karen M. Sandoval, Chela & Pérez-Torres, Rafael. (2010). *The Chicano Reader: An Anthology of Aztlán, 1970–2000*. (2nd ed.). Los Angeles, CA: UCLA Chicano Studies Research Center Publications.

Olivas, Michael A. (2013). *In Defense of My People: Alonso S. Perales and the Development of Mexican-American Public Intellectuals*. Houston, TX: Arte Público Press.

Vásquez, Enriqueta, Oropeza, Lorena & Espinoza, Dionne. (2006). *Enriqueta Vásquez and the Chicano Movement: Writings from El Grito del Norte*. Houston, TX: Arte Público Press.

Orozco, Cynthia E. (2009). *No Mexicans, Women, or Dogs Allowed: The Rise of the Mexican American Civil Rights Movement*. Austin, TX: University of Texas Press.

Perales, Mónica. (2010). *Smeltertown: Making and Remembering a Southwest Border Community*. Chapel Hill, NC: The University of North Carolina Press.

Pérez, Emma. (1999). *The Decolonial Imaginary: Writing Chicanas into History*. Bloomington, IN: Indiana University Press.

Perlmann, Joel. (2007). *Italians Then, Mexicans Now: Immigrant Origins and the Second-Generation Progress, 1890 to 2000*. New York, NY: Russell Sage Foundation.

Rendón, Armando B. (1971). *Chicano Manifesto: The History and Aspirations of the Second Largest Minority in America*. Berkeley, CA: Ollin & Associates, Inc.

Rivas-Rodríguez, Maggie; Torres, Juliana; Dipiero-D'sa, Melissa & Fitzpatrick, Lindsay. (2006). *A Legacy Greater Than Words: Stories of US Latinos & Latinas of the World War II Generation*. Austin, TX: U.S. Latino & Latina WWII Oral History Project, University of Texas at Austin.

Rosales, F. Arturo. (2007). *Dictionary of Latino Civil Rights History*. Houston, TX: Arte Público Press.

Rosales, F. Arturo. (1999). *¡Pobre Raza!: Violence, Justice, and Mobilization among México Lindo*

Immigrants, 1900–*1936.* Austin, TX: University of Texas Press.

Ruiz, Vicki L. (2008). *From Out of the Shadows: Mexican Women in Twentieth-Century America.* (10th ed.). New York, NY: Oxford University Press.

Sánchez, George J. (1993). *Becoming Mexican American: Ethnicity, Culture, and Identity in Chicano Los Angeles, 1900–1945.* New York, NY: Oxford University Press.

Sepúlveda Jr., Juan A. (2005). *The Life and Times of Willie Velásquez: Su Voto es Su Voz.* Houston, TX: Arte Público Press.

Sheridan, Thomas E. (1992). *Los Tucsonenses: The Mexican Community in Tucson, 1854–1941.* Tucson, AZ: University of Arizona Press.

Vigil, Ernesto B. (1999). *The Crusade for Justice: Chicano Militancy and the Government's War on Dissent.* Madison, WI: University of Wisconsin Press.

Vigil, James D. (2011). *From Indians to Chicanos: The Dynamics of Mexican-American Culture.* (3rd ed.). Long Grove, IL: Waveland Press, Inc.

Villanueva, Tino. (1985). *Chicanos (Selección).* México, D.F.: Fondo de Cultura Económica.

SECTION 1: SUGGESTED FILMS AND VIDEOS

Adelante Mujeres, 1992
National Women's History Project
P.O. Box 469, Santa Rosa, CA 95402

Bracero Stories, 2008
Cherry Lane Productions
600 Viplet Ave. #124, Hyde Park, NY 12538

Border Bandits, 2004
Trans-Pecos Productions
P.O. Box 4124, Dallas, TX 75208

César Chávez: The Hispanic and Latin American Heritage, 1995
Library Video Company
P.O. Box 580, Wynnewood, PA 19096

Chicano! History of the Mexican American Civil Rights Movement (parts 1–4), 1996
Check for availability at your university or local library

Harvest of Empire: The Untold Story of Latinos in America, 2012
Third World Newsreel
545 Eight Ave., Suite 550, New York, NY 10018

Harvest of Shame, 1960
CBS News Productions

Hero Street USA, 1985
Innervision Studies

The Mexican Americans, 2000
New York

One of the Hollywood Ten
Morena Films, Saltire Entertainment, ESICMA Productions, Bloom Street Productions

La Raza: History and Heritage, 1976
La Raza Series
Moctezuma Productions
McGraw-Hill Broadcasting

Latino Americans: The 500-Year Legacy that Shaped a Nation, 2013
Episode I: Foreigners in Their Own Land (1565–1880)
PBS
2100 Crystal Drive, Arlington, VA 22202

Latino Americans: The 500-Year Legacy that Shaped a Nation, 2013
Episode II: Empire of Dreams (1880–1942)
PBS
2100 Crystal Drive, Arlington, VA 22202

Latino Americans: The 500-Year Legacy that Shaped a Nation, 2013
Episode III: War and Peace (1942–1954)
PBS
2100 Crystal Drive, Arlington, VA 22202

Latino Americans: The 500-Year Legacy that Shaped a Nation, 2013
Episode IV: The New Latinos (1954–1965)
PBS
2100 Crystal Drive, Arlington, VA 22202

Mesoamerica: The Rise and Fall of the City-States, 2001
Films Media Group
132 West 31st Street, 17th Floor,
New York, NY 10001

Salt of the Earth, 1953
Independent Productions and the
International Union of Mine, Mill & Workers
Oak Forest, IL

Soldados Chicanos in Vietnam, 2003
Chusma House Publications
P.O. Box 467, San Jose, CA 95103

The American Experience: Los Mineros
PBS
2100 Crystal Drive, Arlington, VA 22202

The American Experience: Zoot Suit Riots
PBS
2100 Crystal Drive, Arlington, VA 22202
The Buried Mirror, 1991
Sogeted Productions/The Smithsonian Institute
San Antonio, TX

The Legacy of the Mexican Revolution, 1994
Films Media Group
200 America Metro Blvd, Suite 124, Hamilton,
NJ 08619

The U.S.-Mexican War, 1998
PBS
2100 Crystal Drive Arlington, VA 22202

Viva La Causa: 500 Years of Chicano History, Parts 1
& 2, 1995
Collision Course Video Productions
Southwest Organizing Project
San Francisco, CA/Albuquerque, NM

Demographics, Society, Labor, and Culture

Ana González-Barrera and Mark Hugo López in a Pew Hispanic Center report initiate this section with a concise yet highly informative portrait of the Hispanic population. As a press release for a larger report, this short document offers a concise profile of the Mexican community as of 2012. It covers a wide range of indicators that can quantitatively guide the reader in this and subsequent sections on the Hispanic presence in various sectors of American society. What follows are eight articles that examine a variety of sociological factors that currently impact the Mexican-origin community and other Latinos as well.

Marta Tienda et al showcase four major realms of social integration by Hispanics in American society: family, education, work, and health. Of the utmost importance is the structure of the family and concepts like "familismo" that inform the group's participation in the labor force, the educational arena, and other societal domains. This chapter is the result of a project by the National Research Council's Panel on Hispanics in the United States. The chapter is followed by examinations of those social and/or regional spheres.

A new article in this section is by Elizabeth Días, examining the shift from the Catholic Church to Evangelical Protestant churches by large segments of the Latino population. It illuminates the idea that simply because one is Latino, one is Catholic. The issue has become so widespread that the Catholic Church has had to take notice and the new pope realizes that how the Church deals with this shift will have a long-term effect on the Catholic Church and its members.

Pablo Vila and John Peterson reveal the environmental problems and challenges faced by the binational metroplex formed by El Paso, Texas, and Ciudad Juárez, Chihuahua, and the implications for transnational policy formulation.

David Hayes-Bautista presents keen insights on health research in the Latino community. On one level, Bautista presents a health profile of

Latinos that presents a paradox facing researchers today: although Latinos tend to be poor, have lower levels of education, and derive from immigrant backgrounds, their health tends to be better than that of non-Hispanic Whites. Bautista examines key indicators giving insight to this paradox and discusses three goals for health researchers to consider.

Two new articles provide a recent demographic profile and a discussion of social mobility and middle-class status. First, Richard Larsen discusses the growing Hispanic presence by reviewing the 2010 census. Basically, Hispanics have become "a major influence across the nation's economic, social, and political fronts." This piece gives the reader an insight as to the possibilities of influencing different levels of society. On the other hand, Harry Pachón makes evident that Latinos are not a monolithic working-class community. As more young Latinos enter university, it becomes evident a growing middle class is emerging. Pachón discusses how better educational outcomes and asset development through home owner-ship are pathways for this emerging middle class.

Finally, Arturo González presents an overview of the Mexican-origin population in the labor market. Ultimately, the Chicano rate and level of participation in the labor market determines their socioeconomic status. It is critical to determine how Chicanos interface across generations in key societal dimensions like education, home ownership, health, gender, etc. Miriam Ching Yoon Louie delves into the role of Mexican immigrant women participating in the labor force in the transnational context of the United States–Mexico border. She explores in an ethnographic man-ner the struggles and complexities of factory employment in the midst of "NAFTA the SHAFTA," job outsourcing, and inadequate government support for displaced workers, some of whom actually started their odys-sey in "maquiladoras" in Mexico.

A Demographic Portrait of Mexican-Origin Hispanics in the United States

Ana González-Barrera and Mark Hugo López

MEXICAN-ORIGIN HISPANICS IN THE UNITED STATES

A record 33.7 million Hispanics of Mexican origin resided in the United States in 2012, according to an analysis of Census Bureau data by Pew Research Center. This estimate includes 11.4 million immigrants born in Mexico and 22.3 million born in the U.S. who self-identified as Hispanics of Mexican origin.

Mexicans are by far the largest Hispanic-origin population in the U.S., accounting for nearly two-thirds (64%) of the U.S. Hispanic population in 2012.[1] Hispanics of Mexican origin are also a significant portion of the U.S. population, accounting for 11% overall.

The size of the Mexican-origin population in the U.S. has risen dramatically over the past four decades as a result of one of the largest mass migrations in modern history. In 1970, fewer than 1 million Mexican immigrants lived in the U.S. By 2000, that number had grown to 9.8 million, and by 2007 it reached a peak of 12.5 million (Pew Hispanic Center, 2011). Since then, the Mexican-born population has declined as the arrival of new Mexican immigrants has slowed significantly (Passel et al., 2012). Today, 35% of Hispanics of Mexican origin were born in Mexico. And while the

remaining two-thirds (65%) were born in the U.S., half (52%) of them have at least one immigrant parent.

Prior to the 1980s, most of the growth in the nation's Mexican-origin population came from Hispanics of Mexican origin born in the U.S. However, since the 1980s—a decade after the current wave of Mexican migration took off—and up until 2000, more growth in the Mexican-origin population in the U.S. could be attributed to the arrival of Mexican immigrants. In the decade from 2000 to 2010, that pattern reversed—births surpassed immigration as the main driver of the dynamic growth in the U.S. Mexican-origin population (Pew Hispanic Center, 2011).

Mexican immigration has also played a large role in shaping the nation's immigrant population. Today, 11.4 million Mexican immigrants live in the U.S., making them the single largest country of origin group by far among the nation's 40 million immigrants. The next largest foreign-born population, from greater China at 2 million,[2] is less than one-fifth the size of the Mexican-born population in the U.S.

In addition, Mexican migration has shaped the nation's unauthorized immigrant population. More than half (55%) of the 11.1 million immigrants who are in the country illegally are from Mexico.

Among Mexican immigrants, half (51%) are in the U.S. illegally while about a third are legal permanent residents (32%) and 16% are naturalized U.S. citizens. Overall, naturalization rates among Mexican

Figure 1

Mexican-Origin Population in the U.S., 1850-2012
(in millions)

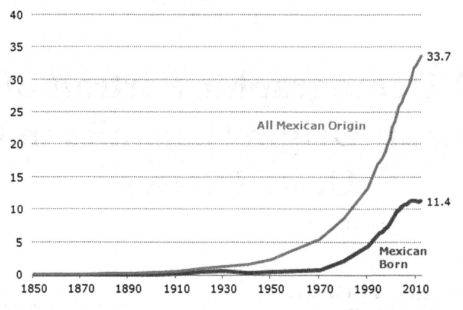

Source: For Mexican born 1850 to 1980: Gibson, Campbell and Kay Jung, "Historical Census Statistics on the Foreign-Born Population of the United States: 1850-2000," U.S. Census Bureau, Population Division, Working Paper No. 81, 2006; for Mexican born 1980 and 1990: Integrated Public Use Microdata Series (IPUMS-USA); for 1995 to 2012: Pew Hispanic Center estimates based on augmented March Current Population Surveys and 2000 Decennial Census. For Mexican population 1850-1994: Integrated Public Use Microdata Series (IPUMS-USA); for 1995 to 2012: Pew Hispanic Center estimates based on augmented March Current Population Surveys and 2000 Decennial Census.

PEW RESEARCH CENTER

Figure 2

Nativity and Legal Status of Mexican-Origin Population in the U.S., 2011
(%)

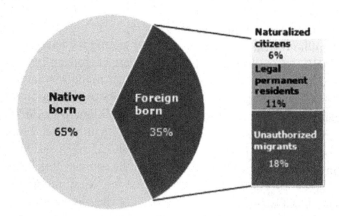

Source: Pew Hispanic Center estimates based on augmented March Current Population Survey 2011.

PEW RESEARCH CENTER

immigrants who are in the country legally are just half that of legal immigrants from all other countries combined (Gonzalez-Barrera et al., 2013).

Internationally, the U.S. is far and away the top destination for immigrants from Mexico. Fully 96% 0f Mexicans who leave Mexico migrate to the U.S. (Connor et al., 2012) Worldwide, 9% of people born in Mexico live in the U.S.[3] In addition, the U.S. has more immigrants from Mexico alone than any other country has immigrants.[4]

Mexican Immigrants Today and Two Decades Ago

The characteristics of Mexican immigrants have changed over the decades. Compared with 1990, Mexican

Table 1. Demographic Characteristics of Mexican Immigrants, 1990 and 2011

(% unless otherwise noted)

	Year		Change
	1990	**2011**	**1990–2011**
Total			
(in millions)	4.4	11.7	7.2
Gender			
Male	55	53	-2
Female	45	47	2
Age			
Median (in years)	29	38	9
Age Groups			
Younger than 18	15	7	-8
18 to 29	35	21	-14
30 to 39	24	27	3
40 to 49	13	22	10
50 to 64	9	16	8
65 or older	5	7	2
Marital Status			
Married	59	58	-1
Never married	30	29	-1
Divorced/separated/widowed	10	13	3
Education Attainment (ages 25 and older)			
Less than high school diploma	75	59	-16
High school diploma	12	24	12
Some college or more	13	17	4
Household Income			
Median (in 2012 dollars)	$38,600	$34,000	-$4,600
Medium Annual Personal Earnings (in 2012 dollars)			
Employed (ages 16 and older)	$17,900	$20,000	$2,100
Years in the U.S.			
5 years or less	30	11	-19
6 to 10 years	20	17	-3
11 to 20 years	31	33	2
More than 20 years	19	39	20

Note: All numbers and percentages are rounded after changes or shares have been computed.
Source: Pew Hispanic Center tabulations of 1990 Census and 2011 American Community Survey data.
PEW RESEARCH CENTER

immigrants in 2011 were less likely to be male (53% vs. 55%), considerably older (median age of 38 vs. 29), better educated (41% with high school or more vs. 25%), and have been in the U.S. for longer (71% had been in the U.S. for more than 10 years, compared with 50%).

On economic measures, Mexican immigrants have mixed results. Although median personal earnings increased by about $2,000 during the last two decades, the median household income of Mexican immigrants suffered a drop of more than $4,500. This reflects the effects of the recent economic recession that drove up unemployment rates in the nation, particularly among Mexican immigrants.

This demographic portrait compares the demographic, income and economic characteristics of the foreign-born and native-born Mexican-origin populations with the characteristics of all Hispanics in the U.S. It is based on tabulations from the 2011 American Community Survey by the Pew Hispanic Center, a project of the Pew Research Center. Key findings include:

- **Immigration status.** Almost two-thirds of Mexicans in the U.S. are native born (65%). About two-thirds of immigrants from Mexico (65%) arrived in the U.S. in 1990 or later.

- **Language.** Two-thirds (66%) of Mexican-origin Hispanics ages 5 and older speak English proficiently.[5] The remaining 34% report speaking English less than very well, equal to the share among all Hispanics. About nine-in-ten (89%) native-born Mexicans ages 5 and older speak English proficiently. This compares to about one-in-three (29%) among Mexican immigrants.

- **Age.** Mexican-origin Hispanics are younger than both the U.S. population and Hispanics overall. The median age of Mexicans is 25; the median ages of the U.S. population and all Hispanics are 37 and 27, respectively. U.S.-born Mexicans are considerably younger than their foreign-born counterparts. The median age of native-born Mexicans is 17, compared with 38 of the foreign born.

- **Marital status.** Among those ages 15 and older, Mexican immigrants are more likely than native-born Mexicans to be married—58% vs. 34% respectively. As a group, Mexican-origin Hispanics ages 15 and older are slightly more likely (45%) to be married than Hispanics overall (43%).

- **Fertility.** Almost one-in-ten (8%) Mexican women ages 15 to 44 gave birth in the 12 months prior to this survey. That was the same

as the rate for all Hispanic women—8%—and slightly higher than the overall rate for U.S. women—6%. More than four-in-ten (45%) Mexican women ages 15 to 44 who gave birth in the 12 months prior to the survey were unmarried. That was similar to the rate for all Hispanic women—47%—and greater than the overall rate for U.S. women—38%.

- **Regional dispersion.** More than half (52%) of Mexican-origin Hispanics live in the West, mostly in California (36%), and another 35% live in the South, mostly in Texas (26%). There is no significant difference in the regional dispersion of Mexicans by nativity.

- **Educational attainment.** Mexicans have lower levels of education than the Hispanic population overall. Some 10% of Mexicans ages 25 and older—compared with 13% of all U.S. Hispanics—have obtained at least a bachelor's degree. Mexicans born in the U.S. are almost three times more likely to have earned a bachelor's degree than those born in Mexico—15% vs. 6% respectively. About six-in-ten Mexican immigrants have not earned a high school diploma (59%), compared with 21% of Mexicans born in the U.S.

- **Income.** The median annual personal earnings for Hispanics of Mexican origin ages 16 and older was $20,000 in the year prior to the survey, the same as for U.S. Hispanics overall. U.S.-born Mexicans had higher earnings than their immigrant counterparts—a median of $22,000 vs. $19,000 respectively.

- **Poverty status.** The share of Mexicans who live in poverty, 27%, is slightly higher than the rate for Hispanics overall (25%). U.S.-born Mexicans are slightly less likely to live in poverty than their foreign-born counterparts—26% vs. 29% respectively.

- **Health insurance.** One-third of Mexicans (33%) do not have health insurance, compared with 30% of all Hispanics. More than half (57%) of Mexican immigrants are uninsured, compared with 20% of those born in the U.S.

- **Homeownership.** The rate of homeownership (49%) among Mexican-origin Hispanics is higher than the rate for all Hispanics (46%). The rate of homeownership among U.S.-born Mexicans (53%) is higher than that of Mexican immigrants (45%).

Demographics of the Mexican-Origin Population in the U.S., 2011
(Thousands, unless otherwise noted)

	Hispanics of Mexican Origin	Among Mexican-Origin Hispanics		All Hispanics
		Mexican Foreign Born	Mexican Native Born	
Total				
	33,539	11,651	21,888	51,927
Gender				
Male	17,209	6,211	10,999	26,336
Female	16,330	5,441	10,889	25,591
Age				
Median (in years)	25	38	17	27
Age Groups				
Younger than 5	3,608	47	3,561	5,141
5–17	8,534	795	7,738	12,245
18–29	6,954	2,449	4,505	10,665
30–39	5,296	3,091	2,205	8,160
40–49	4,146	2,597	1,549	6,762
50–64	3,443	1,905	1,538	6,013
65 and older	1,559	767	792	2,940
Marital Status (age 15 and older)				
Married	10,520	6,423	4,097	16,154
Never married	9,592	3,226	6,366	15,417
Divorced/separated/widowed	3,129	1,454	1,675	5,671
Fertility (women ages 15 to 44				
Total number of women	7,779	3,301	4,478	12,050
Women who had a birth in the past 12 months	637	314	323	932
Unmarried women[2] who had a birth in the past 12 months	287	111	176	435
School Enrollment (age 5 to 18)				
K-12	8,366	792	7,574	12,015
Educational Attainment (ages 25 and older)				
Less than high school diploma	7,280	5,704	1,576	10,383
High school diploma or equivalent	4,638	2,299	2,340	7,581
Some college	3,630	1,117	2,513	6,424
Bachelor's degree or more	1,659	531	1,128	3,759

Note: Numbers may not sum to the total due to rounding. [1]Unmarried women includes those who were never married, divorced or widowed. [2]For detailed information on how poverty status is determined, see http://usa.ipums.org/usa-action/variables/ POVERTY=description_tab. Due to the way in which the IPUMS assigns poverty values, these date will differ from those that might be provided by the U.S. Census Bureau.

Source: Pew Hispanic Center tabulations of the 2011 ACS (1% IPUMS sample). More information on the source data and sampling error is available at http://usa.ipums.org/usa/design.shtml and http://www.census.gov/acs/www/Downloads/data documentation/Accuracy/ACS Accuracy of Data 2011.pdf.

Demographics of the Mexican-Origin Population in the U.S., 2011 *continued...*

(Thousands, unless otherwise noted)

		Among Mexican-Origin Hispanics		
	Hispanics of Mexican Origin	Mexican Foreign Born	Mexican Native Born	All Hispanics
Median Annual Personal Earnings (in dollars)				
All (ages 16 and older with earnings)	$20,000	$19,000	$22,000	$20,000
Full-time, year-round workers	$28,000	$24,000	$33,000	$30,000
Persons in Poverty[1]				
Younger than 18	4,330	418	3,912	5,894
18–64	4,477	2,751	1,726	6,755
65 and older	282	170	112	556
Health Insurance				
Uninsured, all ages	10,910	6,583	4,327	15,572
Uninsured, younger than 18	1,737	437	1,300	2,232
Persons in Households by Type of Household[2]				
In family households	30,492	10,493	19,999	46,317
In married-couple households	19,880	7,193	12,687	29,159
In non-family households	2,480	974	1,505	4,649
Language (ages 5 and older)				
Speaks only English at home	7,546	418	7,127	11,827
Does not speak only English at home	22,386	11,186	11,200	34,959
Speaks English very well	12,102	2,992	9,110	19,051
Speaks English less than very well	10,284	8,194	2,090	15,908
Year of Entry (foreign-born only)				
Before 1990	4,057	4,057	---	6,658
1990–1999	3,576	3,576	---	5,399
2000–2005	2,729	2,729	---	4,340
2006 or later	1,289	1,289	---	2,391
Regional Dispersion				
Northeast	933	476	457	7,186
Midwest	3,599	1,319	2,279	4,772
Illinois	1,654	706	949	2,078
South	11,654	3,895	7,759	18,820
Texas	8,570	2,505	6,065	9,794
West	17,353	5,961	11,392	21,149
California	11,950	4,276	7,675	14,358
Arizona	1,777	508	1,269	1,950
Colorado	830	234	596	1,071

Note: Numbers may not sum to the total due to rounding. [1]For detailed information on how poverty status is determined, see http://usa.ipums.org/usa-action/variables/POVERTY = description_tab. Due to the way in which the IPUMS assigns poverty values, these data will differ from those that might be provided by the U.S. Census Bureau. [2]The house hold population excludes persons living in institutions, college dormitories and other group quarters.

Source: Pew Hispanic Center tabulations of the 2011 ACS (1% IPUMS sample). More information on the source data and sampling error is available at http://usa.ipums.org/usa/design.shtml and http://www.cenus.gov/acs/www/Downloads/data documentation/Accuracy/ACS Accuracy of Data 2011.pdf.

PEW RESEARCH CENTER

Household Characteristics of the Mexican-Origin Population in the U.S., 2011

(Thousands, unless otherwise noted)

| | Hispanics of Mexican Origin | Among Mexican-Origin Hispanics | | All Hispanics |
		Mexican Foreign Born	Mexican Native Born	
Total				
	8,199	4,278	3,921	13,668
Homeownership (household heads)				
In owner-occupied homes (in thousands)	3,994	1,921	2,073	6,351
In renter-occupied homes (in thousands)	4,205	2,357	1,848	7,317
Homeownership rate (%)				
Household Annual Income (in dollars)				
Median	$38,000	$34,000	$44,000	$39,000
Household Size				
Average number of persons	3.8	4.3	3.3	3.5

Note: The household population excludes persons living in institutions, college dormitories and other group quarters. Household are classified by the ethnicity of the household head. Numbers may not sum to the total due to rounding.

Source: Pew Hispanic Center tabulations of the 2011 ACS (1% IPUMS sample). More information on the source data and sampling error is available at http://usa.ipums.org/usa/design.shtml and http://www.census.gov/acs/www/Downloads/data documentation/Accuracy/ACS Accuracy of Data 2011.pdf

PEW RESEARCH CENTER

Employment Characteristics of the Mexican-Origin Population in the U.S., 2011

(Thousands, unless otherwise noted)

| | Hispanics of Mexican Origin | Among Mexican-Origin Hispanics | | All Hispanics |
		Mexican Foreign Born	Mexican Native Born	
Employment Status (civilians ages 16 and older)				
Employed	13,340	6,849	6,491	21,368
Unemployed	1,851	786	1,066	3,014
Not in labor force	7,368	3,364	4,004	11,847
Unemployment rate (%)	12.2	10.3	14.1	12.4
Industries[1]				
Construction, agriculture and mining	2,093	1,551	542	2,799
Manufacturing	1,577	998	579	2,303
Trade and transportation	2,425	1,028	1,397	4,032
Information, finance and other services	7,245	3,273	3,972	12,233
Occupation[1]				
Management, professional and related occupations	2,505	681	1,825	4,658
Services	3,242	2,055	1,187	5,138
Sales and office support	2,817	858	1,959	4,755
Construction, extraction and farming	1,868	1,437	431	2,485
Maintenance, production, transportation and material moving	2,907	1,818	1,089	4,332

Note: Number may not sum to the total due to rounding. [1]Currently employed civilians ages 16 and older.

Source: Pew Hispanic Center tabulations of the 2011 ACS (1% IPUMS sample). More information on the source data and sampling error is available at http://usa.ipums.org/usa/design.shtml and http://www.census.gov/acs/www/Downloads/data documentation/Accuracy/ACS Accuracy of Data 2011.pdf.

PEW RESEARCH CENTER

About this Report

This report examines the Hispanic population of Mexican origin in the United States by its nativity. Several data sources were used to compile the statistics shown in this report. The data for the demographic portrait tables are derived from the 2011 American Community Survey (1% IPUMS), which provides detailed geographic, demographic and economic characteristics for each group. Historical trends for the Mexican-origin and Mexican foreign-born population are based on the U.S. Census Bureau's Current Population Survey (CPS) March Annual Social and Economic Supplement conducted for 1995 to 2012 and U.S. censuses from 1850 to 2010. Estimates of the unauthorized population are based on augmented data from the March supplement of the CPS.

This report was written by Ana Gonzalez-Barrera, research associate, and Mark Hugo Lopez, associate director. Paul Taylor provided comments and editorial guidance. Jeffrey Passel provided guidance on the report's statistical analysis. Anna Brown number-checked the report. Molly Rohal was the copy editor.

A Note on Terminology

The terms "Latino" and "Hispanic" are used interchangeably in this report.

"Native born" refers to persons who are U.S. citizens at birth, including those born in the United States, Puerto Rico or other U.S. territories and those born abroad to parents at least one of whom was a U.S. citizen.

"Foreign born" refers to persons born outside of the United States, Puerto Rico or other U.S. territories to parents neither of whom was a U.S. citizen.

The following terms are used to describe immigrants and their status in the U.S. In some cases, they differ from official government definitions because of limitations in the available survey data.

"Legal permanent resident," "legal permanent resident alien," "legal immigrant" and "authorized migrant" refer to a citizen of another country who has been granted a visa that allows work and permanent residence in the U.S. For the analyses in this report, legal permanent residents include persons admitted as refugees or granted asylum.

"Naturalized citizen" refers to a legal permanent resident who has fulfilled the length of stay and other requirements to become a U.S. citizen and who has taken the oath of citizenship.

"Unauthorized migrant" refers to a citizen of another country who lives in the U.S. without a currently valid visa.

"Eligible immigrant" in this report, refers to a legal permanent resident who meets the length of stay qualifications to file a petition to become a citizen but has not yet naturalized.

"Legal temporary migrant" refers to a citizen of another country who has been granted a temporary visa that may or may not allow work and temporary residence in the U.S.

1. Percentages are computed before numbers are rounded.
2. Greater China includes immigrants from mainland China, Hong Kong and Taiwan.
3. The share of people born in Mexico who currently live in the U.S. was obtained by dividing the number of Mexican immigrants currently in the U.S. by the current population of Mexico (see www.inegi.gob.mx) and those who live in the U.S. currently.
4. Russia has 12.3 million residents who are classified as immigrants by the United Nations, but the vast majority were born in countries that had been part of the Soviet Union prior to its breakup in 1991.
5. This includes Mexicans ages 5 and older who report speaking only English at home or speaking English very well.

Realms of Integration:
Family, Education, Work,
and Health

Marta Tienda et al

This chapter examines four aspects of the Hispanic experience—family and living arrangements; schools and education; employment and economic well-being; and health status and access to care. These attributes not only portray current terms of belonging, but also highlight risks and opportunities that will ultimately define the future of the U.S. Hispanic population. A focus on features that set Hispanics apart from other groups—notably language use, youthfulness, and large shares of unskilled immigrants—helps assess whether the identified risks are likely to be enduring.

FAMILY AND LIVING ARRANGEMENTS[1]

Hispanic families are often extolled as a source of strength and cohesion that derives from their "familism"—a strong commitment to family life that values collective goals over individual well-being. Indicators of familism that differentiate Hispanics from whites include early childbearing and higher average fertility levels, large family households that often extend beyond nuclear members, and a greater overall tendency to live with kin rather than with unrelated

Reprinted with permission from *Multiple Origins, Uncertain Destinies* © 2006 by the National Academy of Sciences, courtesy of the National Academies Press, Washington, D.C.

individuals or alone. As a source of support for relatives in the extended network of kin relationships, familism can help mitigate economic and social risks in the face of adversity. These sentiments were echoed across the generational spectrum in focus groups conducted for the panel:

> Sometimes families here, white families, are not as united as Hispanic families are. We're always famous for having aunts and uncles and relatives. Americans, it's just mom and dad and kids. (Mexican immigrant. Raleigh)

> * * *

> Typically, we have close families. Family is a really big part of our culture. (third-generation Hispanic, Houston)

At the same time, consistent with their varied immigration histories and social conditions, Hispanic families are highly diverse. Specific aspects of family behavior, such as intermarriage patterns, cohesion among relatives, and the content of social exchanges, differ by nationality and generation. Mexican Americans are considered particularly familistic, possibly because the large numbers of immigrants among them bring cultural traditions into sharper relief.

Most observers agree that the positive aspects of familism are worth keeping, yet there is no consensus on what can be preserved in the face of the rapid

Americanization of second-generation youth. Whether ideals of collective support and other positive features of familism will endure and what forms family structure among Hispanics will take in the future are open questions with far-reaching implications for the evolution of group identity and social well-being.

If Hispanics follow the paths of other immigrant groups, their familism would appear to be in jeopardy as they acculturate, experience socioeconomic mobility, and adopt U.S. norms, which includes many behaviors that tend to erode kinship patterns and traditional family behavior. The rise in divorce and nonmarital childbearing among Hispanics, evident in the growth of mother-only families, signals what some scholars term "family decline."[2] In 1980, fathers were absent in 12 percent of white families, 38 percent of both Dominican and Puerto Rican families, and 40 percent of black families. By 2000, approximately 14 percent of white families had a single female head, compared with about 20 percent of Mexican and Cuban families, 25 percent of Central and South American families, 36 percent of Dominican and Puerto Rican families, and 45 percent of black families.[3] Because mother-only families are significantly more likely to be poor, this trend signals new vulnerabilities for the growing numbers of youths reared by single parents.

Generational transitions also dilute familism, although apparently not uniformly among Hispanic subgroups. For example, among Mexicans and Puerto Ricans born in the United States, the percentage of married-couple households is smaller and the percentage of female-headed households larger than among first-generation immigrants. Compared with the immigrant generation, U.S.-born Mexican Americans exhibit higher divorce rates. Only 56 percent of third-generation Mexican children (those who have American-born parents) live with both parents, compared with about 73 percent of children with Mexican-born parents. Another sign of dwindling familism is the shrinking size of extended families, which often results in reduced safety nets for related individuals.[4]

Rising nonmarital childbearing is another sign of eroding Hispanic familism. Between 1980 and 2000, the percentage of births to unmarried women more than doubled for whites (134 percent), Mexicans (101 percent), and Cubans (173 percent), and increased by more than half for Central and South Americans (64 percent) and other Hispanics (97 percent). Out-of-wedlock childbearing among Puerto Ricans rose more slowly because, as with blacks, their share of nonmarital births was already high in 1980. By 2000,

the percentage of births to unmarried Hispanic mothers was between that of whites (22 percent) and blacks (69 percent). The rate for Cubans was closer to that for whites at 27 percent, and the Puerto Rican rate was closer to that for blacks, at 59 percent. At 44 percent, the out-of-wedlock birth rate for Central and South Americans lay between the extremes.

Finally, the cultural mergers produced by rising rates of intermarriage—between Hispanics and non-Hispanics and among Hispanic nationalities—can diminish or redefine the content of familism. As a measure of social distance between groups, an indicator of assimilation, and a force that shapes racial and ethnic boundaries, intermarriage can either redefine or erode Hispanic familism over generations. For all Hispanics, the tendency to marry, cohabit, and procreate with members of their own ethnic group declines across generations, though notable differences exist across groups. Mexican Americans not only are considered to be more familistic than other Hispanics, but also, given their large numbers, are far more likely to be paired with a member of the same ethnic group in marriage, cohabitation, or parenthood than are Puerto Ricans, Cubans, Central/South Americans, or other Hispanics.[5] One possible explanation for this is that high levels of immigration, buttressed by residential segregation, help preserve Mexican familism in the face of erosion from other sources.

Whether traditional Hispanic familistic orientations will persist beyond the third generation, whether they will take the same forms, and whether they will serve similar protective functions is unknown. Trends in marriage, cohabitation, and parenthood offer provocative insights. Hispanics are more likely to partner with another Hispanic in marriage than in cohabitation and nonmarital parenthood. Although generally less common, relationships with white partners frequently involve marriage. U.S.-born Hispanics are more likely than Hispanic immigrants to have a white, or other non-Hispanic spouse.[6] Unions among partners of different Hispanic origins or between Hispanics and blacks are more likely to involve cohabitation and unmarried childbearing. Hispanic-black unions quite frequently produce children out of wedlock.

Hispanics' interethnic unions foreshadow changing ethnic boundaries through childbearing. In particular, children of mixed unions face complex identity issues: Will they retain a mixed identity, adopt the ethnic (or racial) identity of one parent, or perhaps opt for a panethnic identity? Unions between Hispanic women and white partners can facilitate assimilation into mainstream white society, because these mixed marriages are more common among the better educated. Whether and how Hispanics' ethnic mixing will redraw racial and ethnic boundaries in the United States is uncertain because the prevalence of intermarriage depends on even greater uncertainties, such as the effect of geographic dispersal on the incidence of mixed unions, future levels of immigration, and the way persons of mixed ancestry self-identity ethnically.[7] Because of their sheer numbers and relatively high residential concentration, Mexican Americans are likely to retain a relatively distinct ethnic identity, although generational transitions will blur boundaries through unions with whites. Smaller in size, other Hispanic subgroups are less likely to sustain discrete identities over time because of their higher levels of ethnic mixing with other Hispanic groups and with blacks, which creates greater ambiguity about the place of their offspring in the evolving racial spectrum. How settlement patterns recontour marriage markers will also decide the viability of Hispanicity as a panethnic identity.

SCHOOLS AND EDUCATION[8]

The United States houses some of the most outstanding universities in the world, which coexist with countless highly dysfunctional primary and secondary schools. Thousands of young Hispanics must pursue inter- and intragenerational social mobility predominantly via segregated inner-city schools that feature dropout rates well above the national average. The vastly unequal opportunities for academic achievement they confront in the lower grades contribute to widening disparities at higher levels of the education system.

Although most demographic groups have experienced significant increases in educational attainment since the 1960s, Hispanics are distinguished by their historically low levels of completed schooling, currently completing less formal schooling than any other demographic group.[9] In the context of the rising demand for skills in today's economy, this liability is cause for concern.

In 2000 working-age Hispanics averaged nearly 3 years less of formal schooling than U.S.-born whites and blacks. Moreover, there are large disparities in educational attainment among Hispanic groups, mainly between the native- and foreign-born. On average, foreign-born Hispanics of working age complete 2.5 years less of formal schooling than their U.S.-born compatriots, with negligible differences between men

and women. As figure 1 shows, the educational standing of foreign-born Hispanics has eroded since 1980 compared with both whites and blacks. By contrast, U.S.-born Hispanics have closed the school attainment gap with whites by more than half a year—from 2 to 1.3 years over the same period.

Educational disparities between foreign- and native-born Hispanics play out as inequities among national-origin groups of working age because of the changing volume and composition of immigration in recent decades. Not only do foreign-born Mexicans feature the lowest educational levels of any Hispanic subgroup, but the gap in completed schooling between the foreign and native born is larger for Mexicans than for Hispanics of other nationalities—rising from 3 years in 1980 to 4.4 years in 2000—owing to substantial educational advances among the U.S.-born rather than declining attainment of recent immigrants (see figure 2). For other Hispanics, the birthplace gap in education rose more modestly during the same period—from 1 to 1.6 years—while for Puerto Ricans it was reduced by half. Cubans are distinguished from other Hispanic ethnicities because their average education level exceeds that of other subgroups, because foreign-born Cubans average more schooling than native-born Hispanics, and because the educational attainment of U.S.-born Cubans equals (in the case of men) or surpasses (in the case of women) that of white men and women.[10]

If the schooling deficits of foreign-born Hispanics are imported from Latin America, the disparities among the native-born are produced in the United States. Scholastic disadvantages result from a myriad of social and family circumstances—mainly low parental education levels—and are compounded by schools that fail to deliver quality education.[11] Fortunately, educational disadvantages can be prevented for Hispanic youths that have not yet begun their school careers and reversed for those already enrolled.

Early Beginnings

Hispanic students' educational disadvantages begin in the early grades for two main reasons—their delayed entry into formal school settings and their limited opportunities to acquire preliteracy skills. Parents of Hispanic preschoolers are less likely than black, white, or Asian parents to be fluent in English and, because many have poor educational levels themselves, to have the resources necessary to promote their children's prescholastic literacy. This is highly significant because

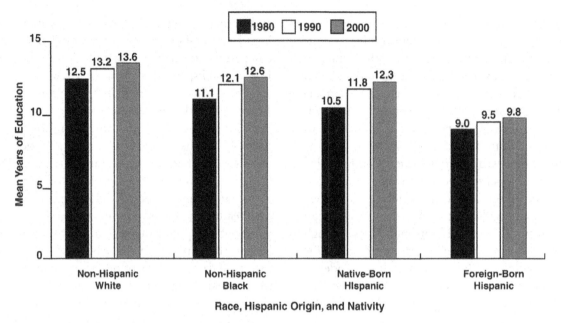

Figure 1. Mean Years of Education by Race/Ethnicity and Nativity, 1980–2000.

Note: For ages 25 to 64.

Source: U.S. Bureau of the Census (2000b), Integrated Public Use Microdata Series (IPUMS) 1 percent samples for 1980–2000.

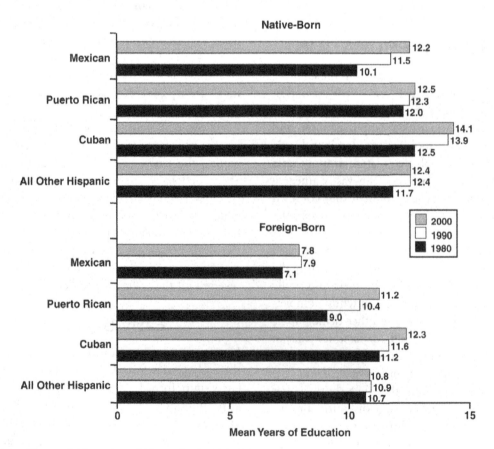

Figure 2. Mean Years of Education of Hispanics by Ethnicity.

Note: For ages 25 to 64.

Source: U.S. Bureau of the Census (2000b), Integrated Public Use Microdata Series (IPUMS) 1 percent samples for 1980–2000.

reading to preschool children fosters their language acquisition, enhances their early reading performance and social development, and may promote their future academic success.

Participation in home literacy activities such as telling stories or visiting libraries is especially low for children reared in Spanish-dominant homes. In 1999, children of Spanish monolinguals were only half as likely as white children to participate in such activities; if both parents were fluent in English, the gap was just 15 percentage points. The lack of exposure to preschool literacy activities, particularly among children from Spanish-dominant households, often creates literacy disadvantages in the early grades. A 1999 study by the U.S. Department of Education showed that Hispanic kindergarten students trailed their Asian and other non-Hispanic classmates in both reading and math skills.[12] Only Native American students had lower preschool reading literacy rates than Hispanics whose parents spoke little English (although Hispanic children exhibited lower math skills).

Household language partly reflects social class divisions and recent immigrant status—two attributes that influence children's exposure to literacy activities before kindergarten. Yet differences in school readiness between Hispanic youth reared in Spanish-dominant homes and English-dominant homes are not an indictment of Spanish-language use per se. Moreover, programs such as Head Start appear to raise Hispanic children's low average preschool literacy rates. Yet quality preschool programs often are either unavailable where the neediest children live or too costly for family budgets. Thus disadvantaged Hispanic children are left to make their way in the public schools, increasing their vulnerability to failure in the years ahead.

Primary and Middle Years

The academic achievement gap evident when Hispanics first enter school continues through the primary grades. During the first two years, teachers' perceptions of their Hispanic students' academic abilities often skew scholastic assessments, regardless of the children's actual aptitude. Results of the Early Childhood Longitudinal Study revealed that kindergarten teachers systematically rated Hispanic students below white students when first enrolled. As Hispanic children performed above their teachers' initial expectations, the gap between test-based abilities and teacher

assessments decreased by half to two-thirds during kindergarten and was eliminated by the end of the first grade. Such teacher biases are compounded by a shortage of staff who understand Hispanic children's cultural backgrounds. Nationally, Hispanic students constitute approximately 15 percent of elementary school students—and nearly 20 percent of all school-age students—yet only 4 percent of public school teachers are Hispanic.[13]

Although Hispanic elementary school children have made steady progress in reading and math, greater gains by other groups have sustained or in some cases widened Hispanic achievement gaps. A 20-year comparison of test scores reported in the National Assessment of Educational Progress shows that Hispanic students continue to lag behind whites in their scholastic achievement throughout middle and high school.[14] Evident for all Hispanic subgroups, these gaps are decidedly largest for Mexican Americans, the fastest-growing segment of the elementary school population. Carried into future grades, accumulating deficits in literacy and math competencies inhibit the learning of other academic subjects.

Middle school Hispanic students often encounter two circumstances that limit their chances for scholastic success: large, urban schools, generally considered suboptimal for learning in the middle grades,[15] and weak ties with their teachers.[16] Weak relations with teachers diminish students' motivation to pursue academic work, and in turn lower teachers' expectations in a self-perpetuating cycle of academic disengagement and underachievement. That students who become disengaged from school during the middle years cannot well appreciate the practical relevance of what is being taught in the classroom bodes ill for their academic performance in high school and dampens their aspirations for college.

Secondary School and Beyond

Even under optimal circumstances, the transition from middle to high school is a taxing experience for most students. This passage is especially difficult for Hispanic and black adolescents destined for oversized, resource-poor urban high schools staffed with many inexperienced or uncertified teachers.[17] Moreover, students whose parents lack a high school education are most in need of early guidance in course planning and preparation for college. Such guidance is in short supply in the schools these students attend. Given their parents' limited experience with the U.S. educational system and the blind trust many Hispanic parents are willing to place in teachers' authority, Hispanic eighth graders are more likely than any other demographic group to express uncertainty about the classes they will take in high school.[18] Mexican immigrant parents are especially likely to defer to teachers and administrators, rarely questioning their decisions.

High school experiences are vital in shaping students' educational expectations and occupational aspirations. Yet a recent study found that, compared with 25 percent of blacks, 31 percent of whites, and 37 percent of Asian Americans, only 23 percent of Hispanic eighth graders planned to enroll in a college preparatory curriculum.[19] These findings underscore the urgency of effective counseling on course selection in secondary school, particularly for students whose parents may be unfamiliar with the complexities of the U.S. educational system.

Despite modest improvements in recent years, rates of school failure among Hispanics remain unacceptably high. Even counting only those who actually attended U.S. high schools, the share of Hispanic high school students 16 to 19 years old who failed to graduate fell only marginally during the 1990s, from 22 to 21 percent.[20] The numbers involved are sobering because the school-age population in the United States has been growing rapidly as the children of baby boomers and recent immigrants make their way through the education system. That dropout rates for whites and blacks fell even more than for Hispanics—from 10 to 8 percent and from 14 to 12 percent, respectively—widened racial and ethnic disparities in secondary school success. Nor is the General Equivalency Diploma (GED) a viable route for Hispanics to close their high school achievement gap. In 1998, 7.9 percent of white 18- to 29-year-olds achieved high school equivalence by passing the GED test, as compared with 7 percent of Hispanics.[21] Moreover, those with exam-certified high school equivalency fare no better in the labor market than high school dropouts.[22]

Although foreign-born Hispanic youths ages 16 to 19 are significantly more likely than those who are native born to leave high school without a diploma—34 versus 14 percent in 2000—being foreign born is not the main factor explaining their failure to graduate. Many are recent arrivals who were already behind in school before arriving in the U.S.[23] Once here, they are likely to attend urban schools—such as those in Los Angeles, Chicago, and New York—that serve large numbers of low-income minority students and for which low

graduation rates are typical. Fully 40 percent of Hispanic students attend high schools that graduate less than 60 percent of entering freshmen.[24]

Popular allegations that Hispanics value education less than do other groups are contradicted by evidence that large numbers of Hispanic high school students aspire to attend college. A study conducted by Public Agenda, a New York-based nonprofit public opinion research organization, found that 65 percent of Hispanic parents, compared with 47 percent of black and 33 percent of white parents, believed a college education is the single most important factor for economic success.[25] Yet Hispanics trail all other groups in their ambitions to pursue 4-year college degrees because of their disadvantaged beginnings, limited home educational resources, concentration in scholastically weak high schools, and lack of concrete information about how to prepare for college.[26]

Compared with whites and blacks, more second-generation Hispanic youths are the first in their family to attend college. But college prospects are limited for many because they fail to take courses or exams required for college entrance—another consequence of their poor guidance counseling during high school. Compared with other subjects, achievement in mathematics is the strongest predictor of college enrollment. That Hispanic students are about 20 percent less likely than whites to complete advanced mathematics, as well as less likely than both whites and blacks to take advanced science courses, compromises their post-high school educational options.[27]

Hispanic high school graduates are also less likely than whites, Asians, and blacks to take college entrance examinations or apply to college.[28] Spanish-language use per se does not explain this gap because bilingual Hispanics are more likely than whites to complete Advanced Placement courses and to take College Board exams. And parents who are proficient in both English and Spanish often can advance their children's educational prospects by bridging cultural and language divides.[29]

Despite the above obstacles, college enrollment among Hispanics has been on the rise. There is evidence that Hispanic high school graduates are more likely than white or black students to enroll in some form of college, but Hispanics also are significantly less likely to obtain a 4-year degree because they are more likely to enroll in 2-year colleges, to attend college only part-time, or to work while enrolled full-time.[30] This is especially true for Mexicans. In 2000, Hispanics were 11 percent of high school graduates.[31] They accounted for only 7 percent of students enrolled in 4-year institutions, but 14 percent of enrollees in 2-year colleges. Differences in college attendance between native- and foreign-born Hispanics contribute somewhat to these outcomes, but they are not the driving force.

Major reasons why Hispanics are more likely than whites to enroll in 2-year rather than 4-year colleges are poor academic preparation, weak counseling, and cost. Hispanics from Spanish-speaking families (for whom the risks of dropping out of high school are higher) are nearly as likely as blacks to attend 4-year colleges if they receive adequate academic preparation.[32] Like many students who begin their college careers at community colleges, Hispanics intend to transfer to 4-year institutions, but they are less successful than other groups in making the transition.[33] Furthermore, enrollment in a 4-year institution does not guarantee a degree. Compared with other high-achieving youths who enroll in 4-year institutions, Hispanics are less likely to receive baccalaureate degrees, unless they are among the select few who attend a highly selective college.[34]

ECONOMIC WELL-BEING

As in so many other ways, Hispanics are highly diverse with respect to economic well-being. On the one hand, lacking the protections afforded by legal status, millions of undocumented Hispanics fill low-wage jobs; many make ends meet by holding multiple jobs and pooling incomes from several household members. On the other hand, rising rates of home ownership attest that both established immigrants and native-born citizens are increasingly joining the ranks of the middle class.[35] This section reviews two aspects of economic well-being—employment and earnings, and household income—among Hispanics, as well as their experience of the extremes of poverty and wealth.

Employment and Earnings[36]

Hispanics' success in the U.S. labor market depends on their propensity to work, their skills, the kinds of jobs they secure, and, because many U.S. employers discount human capital acquired abroad, where they were born (see figure 3).[37] On average, Hispanic men's employment rate (87 percent) is somewhat lower than that for U.S.-born whites (92 percent), but well above that for U.S.-born blacks (77 percent).[38] Also among men, the average employment rate for both Cubans and Mexicans (both foreign- and U.S.-born) is similar

to that for whites, but that for Puerto Rican men is appreciably lower, while that for island-born Puerto Ricans is similar to that for U.S.-born blacks.[39]

Birthplace differences in employment rates are much larger for Hispanic women than men. Overall, some 61 percent of immigrant Hispanic women were employed in 2000, compared with 76 percent of their U.S.-born counterparts. With just over one in two employed, Mexican immigrants have the lowest employment rate of all women, but the rate for island-born Puerto Ricans is only slightly higher at 61 percent. Average employment rates for U.S.-born Mexicans and Puerto Ricans are close to those for blacks (78 percent) and whites (80 percent), while Cubans have the highest rate of all, at 83 percent.

Owing to differences in educational attainment and language skills between native- and foreign-born Hispanics, the types of jobs they hold vary more on this dimension than by nationality. Foreign-born Hispanic men work disproportionately in agriculture (11 percent) and construction (18 percent), while foreign-born Hispanic women are overrepresented in manufacturing (19 percent)—mainly in production of nondurable goods.[40] Consistent with their education and English-language skills, Hispanic men and women born abroad are underrepresented in managerial/professional and technical/sales occupations, and overrepresented in service and operator/laborer occupations.

Hispanics' lower levels of education and English proficiency largely explain their lower employment rates compared with whites.[41] The 6 percentage point employment gap between native-born Mexican and white men would narrow to a mere 2 percentage points if their education and language skills were similar. With education and English proficiency levels comparable to those of whites, the employment rates of foreign-born Mexican immigrants also would be similar.[42] Foreign-born Mexican women provide an even more dramatic example, as their average employment deficit of 25 percentage points would shrink to just 3 with education and English proficiency levels comparable to those of white women. Puerto Ricans and Dominicans are an exception to this pattern because sizable employment gaps persist for them even with human capital endowments comparable to those of whites.[43]

On average, native-born Hispanic men earned 31 percent and foreign-born Hispanic men 59 percent less than whites in 1999. With similar human capital endowments, those earnings gaps would shrink to 13 and 5 percent, respectively. By comparison, and despite their higher average education levels and better

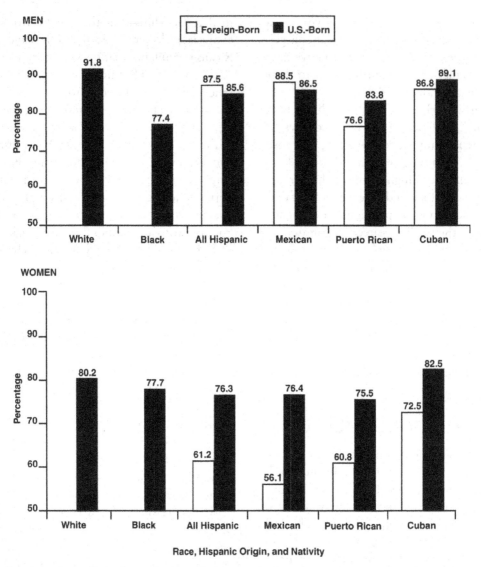

Figure 3. Employment Rates for White, Black, and Hispanic Men and Women ages 25–59 by Nativity.
Source: U.S. Bureau of the Census (2000b), 5 percent samples Integrated Public Use Microdata Series (IPUMS).

command of English relative to Hispanics, black men suffer a 44 percent earnings penalty. Foreign-born Hispanic women earn about half as much as white women on average, but this disparity, too, would shrink given comparable educational attainment and English fluency.

Hispanics' average earnings also differ by national origin. Native-born Cubans enjoy relatively high earnings: U.S.-born Cuban men earn as much as white men, and native-born Cuban women earn 20 percent *more* than white women. By contrast, both Mexicans and Puerto Ricans—especially those born abroad—exhibit large gaps compared with whites. But if Mexican and Puerto Rican women born abroad—whose average earnings trail those of white women by 63 and 28 percent, respectively— were as fluent in English and as well educated as white

women, their earnings gaps would virtually disappear.[44] Legal status also affects wages, with legal immigrants earning substantially more than those who are undocumented, and wage inequality, as discussed below.[45]

Thus unlike black men, for whom continuing discrimination in the labor market creates and augments earnings disparities, Hispanics could dramatically reduce their earnings gap with whites by closing the education gap and becoming proficient in English.[46] This does not mean that Hispanics do not experience discrimination in the labor market. There is some evidence of differences in treatment at initial contact and interview and in outcomes based on accent and phenotype.[47]

To understand the origins of earnings differentials and accurately portray Hispanic socioeconomic progress over time, one must consider changes in the birthplace composition of the Hispanic workforce. Since 1980, high rates of immigration have changed the human capital profile of Hispanic workers and widened their earnings disparities with whites. For example, the foreign-born share among Mexican men aged 25 to 59 surged from 37 percent in 1980 to 51 percent in 1990 and 63 percent in 2000. Among Hispanics, Mexicans are the largest ethnic group, average the lowest levels of human capital, and include a sizable share of undocumented workers.[48] With average educational attainment levels of 12 years for the native born and less than 9 years for the foreign born, Mexicans have faced particularly bleak labor market prospects since 1980, as the wage premiums for high skills grew and income inequality widened.

Looking back six decades, in 1940 Mexican men earned just over half (56 percent) of white men's wages. That figure rose to nearly 70 percent in the postwar decade, a period of vigorous economic growth when strong unions protected the wages of laborers. Although the Mexican-white earnings gap remained unchanged during the next two decades, by 1990 Mexican men's wages had deteriorated to 45 percent of those of white men, and this gap persisted through the following decade.[49] By contrast, earnings of black men rose between 1990 and 2000, from 50 to 56 percent of white male earnings. Larger human capital gaps since 1980, especially among the foreign born, are responsible for the stagnation of Hispanic earnings through 2000, especially as the premium placed on work-related skills has continued to rise.[50]

Previous waves of predominantly unskilled immigrants, such as the Irish and Italians, enjoyed substantial intergenerational progress that ultimately enabled their descendants to join the middle class. For most, though, this process required two or three generations to accomplish; moreover, the skill endowments of the immigrant generation were instrumental in the labor market success of their children and grandchildren.[51] Generational comparisons are particularly instructive for envisioning possible economic destinies for Hispanics. But because Hispanic immigrants are so diverse with respect to their length of U.S. residence, and because native-born Hispanics represent multiple generations, comparisons by birthplace are too coarse to portray true intergenerational progress. Snapshots of the Hispanic population taken over time can only approximate such progress, but nonetheless provide rough measures of the direction and pace of change.

Substantial educational gains realized by the U.S.-born offspring of Hispanic immigrants have narrowed the white-Hispanic earnings gap across generations, with the most sizable convergence occurring between the first and second generations. A smaller wage convergence occurs between the second and third generations, which mirrors the apparent stagnation of Hispanics' educational progress relative to whites. For example, for the 1998–2000 period, the earnings gap between Mexican and white men dropped from 66 percent for immigrants to 38 percent for the second generation and 31 percent for the third and subsequent generations combined. Second-generation Mexicans even reaped higher earnings than native-born black men with higher levels of education. Earnings deficits for Puerto Rican men were 46 percent for the first generation, 30 percent for the second generation, and 16 percent for later generations. Reflecting their higher-class origins at arrival, Cuban immigrants' 31 percent initial deficit disappeared by the second generation.[52]

The apparent slowdown in Hispanic socioeconomic progress after the second generation may be more imagined than real because it is impossible to match immigrant parents and grandparents of the first generation with their descendants in later generations.[53] In fact, substantial educational and earnings gains are evident when second-generation Hispanics are compared with their third-generation descendants 25 years later. For example, one study showed that not only are schooling gaps smaller in the second compared with the first generation, but they are always lower in the third generation.[54]

Educational gains of younger third-generation relative to older second-generation Hispanics are an encouraging sign of intergenerational progress, but they yield conservative estimates of mobility for two reasons. First, the pace of intergenerational progress may be more rapid than available data can accurately portray because of the uncertain volume, pace, and composition of immigrant flows. Decennial censuses can only approximate this highly dynamic process, which for Hispanics is further complicated by the presence of a large and growing undocumented population, whose integration prospects are highly uncertain. Second, selective opting out of Hispanic ethnicity by third and higher generations would lead to underestimation of intergenerational progress. If the most successful Hispanics are less likely to identify themselves or their children as Hispanic—either because they are more likely to marry non-Hispanics or for other reasons—available estimates of earnings gains achieved between the second and third generations are conservative. Studies focused on documenting the prevalence of such opting out of Hispanic identity are relatively recent, and consensus on this issue has not yet been established.[55]

Recent evidence for Mexicans supports the idea that the most economically assimilated Hispanics—predominantly those from the third and higher generations—may be less likely to self-identify as Hispanic.[56] U.S.-born Mexican Americans who marry non-Mexicans are substantially more educated, on average, than Mexican Americans who marry within their ethnic group (either U.S. or foreign born), as their higher employment levels and earnings attest. Moreover, the children of intermarried Mexican Americans are much less likely to self-identify as Mexican than are the children of two Mexican parents. This implies that children of Mexican-origin parents with low education, employment, and earnings may be more likely to self-identify as Mexican than the offspring of intermarriage, which would bias downward assessments of Mexican Americans' intergenerational progress beyond the second generation. The magnitude of such biases, however, has yet to be systematically assessed.[57]

Given these uncertainties, conclusions about intergenerational changes in the labor market experience of Hispanics remain tentative at best. The evidence is clear as to improvement in educational attainment and earnings growth between first- and second-generation Hispanics, both absolutely and relative to whites. But the evidence regarding progress between the second and third generations, and especially beyond the third, is less clear, because educational gains between the second and third generations are not matched by commensurate progress in earnings, particularly among younger Mexicans.[58] Less debatable is that deficiencies in education and language skills will remain a formidable obstacle to the labor market success of Hispanics, especially for immigrants, and will continue to hamper their economic progress—perhaps even more so in the years ahead than in the past—because of the higher premium placed on skills and because blue-collar jobs that traditionally served as gateways to the middle class have all but vanished. Whether the growing second generation makes sufficient progress in closing these two key obstacles to economic mobility will be decisive in the long-term positioning of the Hispanic population.

Household Income

For obvious reasons, the gaps in employment and earnings experienced by Hispanics are reflected in disparities in household income. On average, incomes of white households are larger than those of Hispanic households, just how much larger depending on the birthplace and ethnicity of the Hispanic householder. Again mirroring employment and earnings disparities, U.S.-born Hispanic householders of all national origins garner higher incomes than blacks, although this pattern does not hold for households headed by immigrants. In 1999, the median income of Hispanic households was just about 70 percent that of whites and about 10 percent higher than that of blacks.[59] At the top of the Hispanic household income ladder are South Americans and Cubans who were either born or raised in the United States.[60] Ranking lowest on median household income, as with most other measures of economic well-being, are Puerto Ricans and Dominicans, followed by Mexicans (see figure 4).

As noted, an obvious explanation for the low household incomes of immigrants, and particularly Mexicans, Dominicans, and Central Americans, is their low earnings. In addition, per capita household income depends on household size. Thus, for example, despite having higher average incomes compared with blacks, second-generation Mexicans, Puerto Ricans, and Dominicans have slightly lower median per capita incomes because of their larger households. Central Americans fare somewhat better than Mexicans because of both their higher earnings capacity and smaller average households.

Additionally, Hispanics experienced a deterioration in economic well-being over time relative to whites, whose incomes have risen more when times were good and fallen less during recessions.[61] The median household income of Hispanics averaged 74 percent of that of whites during the early 1970s, but eroded following the 1973 oil crisis-induced recession. On the heels of another economic downturn in the early 1980s, the Hispanic-white income ratio deteriorated further, falling below 70 percent in 1985–1988 and again in 1992–1998, reaching its nadir in 1995 at 61 percent.[62] Although white-Hispanic median household incomes converged during the brisk economic growth of the late 1990s, there are signs that the relative income position of Hispanics is eroding yet again.[63] Median incomes of black households were consistently lower than those of Hispanics throughout the period, but over time their income position improved relative to both whites and Hispanics. In 1972, the median black household income was 77 percent that of whites, compared with 90 percent in 2003.[64] Because these comparisons do not separate out native- and foreign-born

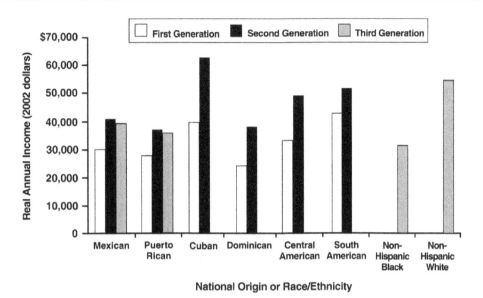

Figure 4. Median Total Household Income by Hispanic National Origin or Race/Ethnicity and Generation.

Notes: Includes only households whose head is under age 65. Results for Hispanics are shown only for cells with at least 90 observations.

Source: Pooled March CPS flies, 1998–2002.

householders, it is difficult to distinguish changes related to increased numbers of low-skill immigrants from those related to business cycle variations. Yet the Survey of Income and Program Participation, one of very few surveys that record annual variation in income, poverty, and wealth, indicates a convergence of wealth between native- and foreign-born Hispanics between 1996 and 2001.[65]

Hispanics compensate for low household income through two strategies: income pooling based on extended living arrangements and reliance on public benefits (see figure 5). Relative to both whites and blacks, Hispanic households are more likely to include relatives outside the nuclear family, and extended members' average contributions to household income are higher. Extended living arrangements are most common among immigrant generations but decline thereafter. Mexicans, Central Americans, and Dominicans of the immigrant generation are especially reliant on extended-household members for income pooling, whereas Hispanics with U.S.-born parents largely resemble blacks in their tendency to rely on other relatives for support.

To what extent complex households reflect Hispanic cultural values (familism) versus economic need is unclear. Clearly, however, reliance on this multiple-source income pooling declines over time as the rising prosperity of second and higher generations reduces the need for such compensatory income strategies.

Among Hispanic subgroups, Dominicans and Puerto Ricans under age 65 rely most heavily on public assistance, the second key source of income supplementation. In the case of Puerto Ricans, this largely reflects their high share of single female heads of household; the scarcity of jobs and relatively generous benefit programs in the northeast where many Puerto Ricans live; and the fact that as U.S. citizens, Puerto Ricans (unlike new immigrants) are eligible for public benefit programs. Although secondgeneration Puerto Ricans rely less than the first generation on income from public benefits, even those born on the mainland depend more on this source of household income compared with other Hispanic subgroups—indeed, at rates more similar to those of blacks. Puerto Ricans' high rates of welfare participation reflect their elevated poverty rates.

Poverty and Wealth Among Hispanics

Trends in median household income conceal the poverty of those at the low end and the prosperity of those at the high end of the income ladder. Indeed, poverty rates dramatize the consequences of poor employment and earnings capacities more effectively than does median household income. Although poverty rates declined during the 1990s—by 3 and 4 percentage points for Hispanics and blacks, respectively—Hispanic

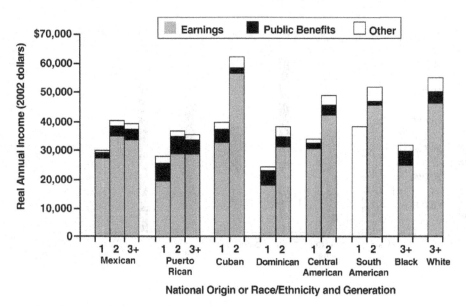

Figure 5. Sources of Median Total Household Income by Hispanic National Origin or Race/Ethnicity and Generation.

Notes: Includes only households whose head is under age 65. Means are simple averages across households, using household weights. Households with zero or negative total income or containing persons with negative income from any source are excluded. Results for Hispanics are shown only for cells with at least 90 observations.

Source: Pooled March CPS tiles, 1998–2002.

poverty held fast at more than 2.5 times the rate among whites.[66] In 1999, more than one in five Hispanics lived below the official poverty line ($16,895 for a family of four or a meager $12 per day per person).[67] Broken out by birthplace, declines in poverty were smallest for Puerto Ricans and greatest for Dominicans, who witnessed the largest drop in absolute poverty during the 1990s.[68] Central American immigrants were less likely to be poor than were Mexicans, Puerto Ricans, and Dominicans of the same generation, but their poverty rates were higher than those of South Americans.[69]

The similar overall poverty rates for first-generation Mexicans, Dominicans, and Puerto Ricans have different sources. As the least-educated group, Mexicans have the lowest overall earning capacity, a liability that persists beyond the second generation. Predominantly recent immigrants with limited skills, Dominicans are, like Puerto Ricans, further handicapped by a high incidence of female-headed households. Having only one potential earner exacerbates the effects of women's low average earnings in depressing household income. Combined, these conditions produce income shortfalls that are only minimally compensated by benefit programs.[70]

Poverty is especially pernicious for children because it is associated with many deleterious outcomes, such as low scholastic achievement, adolescent parenting, substance abuse, and violence.[71] In 1999, more than

one in four Hispanics under the age of 18 were poor, compared with nearly one in ten whites. Child poverty rates among Dominicans and Puerto Ricans—35 and 33 percent, respectively—were comparable to those of blacks. Cuban and South American youths experienced the lowest rates of poverty, between 16 and 17 percent. Child poverty rates of Mexicans and Central Americans approached the Hispanic population average—28 and 24 percent, respectively—which is well above the 17 percent overall U.S. poverty rate for those under 18.[72] Elevated Hispanic child poverty rates are particularly disturbing because the relatively young age structure of the population implies large and growing numbers of the youthful poor, and because poverty magnifies the challenges of assimilation and integration for the burgeoning second generation.

Poverty levels are also elevated among elderly Hispanics. The elderly are only a small proportion of the Hispanic population today, but their numbers will grow rapidly in the future. Today's elderly provide a glimpse of how current Hispanic workers are likely to fare at advanced ages, depending on whether the present Social Security and Medicare safety nets remain intact. Overall, about one in five elderly Hispanics was poor in 1999, compared with fewer than one in ten whites and one in four blacks. The poverty risk for Hispanic elderly varies according to national origin, reflecting incomes and types of jobs held at younger ages, as well as length of time in the U.S. labor market. Mirroring child poverty differentials, elderly poverty rates are highest for Puerto Ricans and Dominicans—24 and 29 percent, respectively—and lowest for South Americans, at 16 percent.[73] Poverty rates for other groups are close to the elderly Hispanic population average of 20 percent.

Because Hispanics tend to work for employers that do not offer pensions, elderly Hispanic householders rely more on other sources of income than do either blacks or whites. Moreover, except for Puerto Ricans and Cubans, foreign-born Hispanics rely less on Social Security than do whites and blacks because they are less likely to qualify for the benefits even if they work beyond the required 40 quarters. Until recently, the sectors in which many elderly Hispanics worked, such as agriculture and household service, were not covered by Social Security, which accounts for 42 percent of household income for elderly Central and South American immigrants, but close to 60 percent for blacks and island-born Puerto Ricans.[74]

Elderly immigrants who have not completed the required 10 years in covered jobs to qualify for Social Security benefits or whose benefits are low because of a lifetime of low-wage work often qualify for Supplemental Security Income (SSI), which offers less generous benefits than those provided by Social Security.[75] Elderly foreign-born Hispanics (with the exception of South Americans) derive a larger share of their income from SSI than do blacks, signaling their greater vulnerability to poverty, especially during inflationary periods. By qualifying for Social Security at higher rates, U.S.-born elderly Hispanics mitigate this risk to some extent and face better economic prospects relative to blacks.

Less well documented than trends and disparities in Hispanic poverty are changes at the high end of the income distribution—namely wealth. Net worth is a pertinent indicator of economic well-being because it represents assets that can be tapped in times of financial distress. Recent estimates of Hispanic wealth range from 3 to 9 percent of white median wealth.[76] Home equity constitutes the largest component of Hispanic household wealth, about 50 to 60 percent of net worth during the 1996–2002 period.[77] Less easily converted to cash than other assets in the event of financial crisis, home equity is the source of last resort to offset fluctuations in household income. The reversal of nearly two decades of wage stagnation in the late 1990s also allowed Hispanics to participate in the stock market, albeit to a much lesser extent than whites.[78]

Not only is home equity the largest component of household wealth, but it is also a key marker of middle-class status. Home ownership provides access to myriad social amenities that influence overall well-being, including school quality, neighborhood safety, recreation facilities, and access to health care organizations (see below).[79] Although Hispanic home ownership rates rose from 33 to 44 percent between 1983 and 2001, they have been relatively stagnant since the mid-1990s, even as the rates for white householders have climbed.[80] Consequently, the Hispanic-white ownership ratio, which rose from 48 to 64 percent from the mid-1980s to the mid-1990s, eroded to 60 percent by 2001.[81]

Whether the geographic dispersal of Hispanics from areas with higher to those with lower housing costs will reverse this trend remains unclear. Census data for the largest 100 metro areas indicate that both native- and foreign-born Hispanics participated in rising rates of home ownership during the 1990s owing to favorable interest rates, rising incomes, and the pace of housing construction relative to employment growth.[82] For the foreign born, however, ownership rates increased in the traditional settlement hubs while declining in the new destinations. Because the dispersal of Hispanics to new destinations is a relatively recent phenomenon that involves many recently arrived, low-skill immigrants, it is conceivable that their lower average home ownership rates will improve over time as they acculturate in their new locales.[83]

HEALTH STATUS AND ACCESS TO CARE

Like other forms of human capital, health status—both physical and psychological—is an asset that requires investments for improvement and maintenance.[84] In addition to nutritious food, regular exercise, and a toxin-free environment, health status depends on a variety of circumstances—some unique to Hispanics and others shared with populations of similar socioeconomic status, some linked to behavior that compromises or promotes health, and others associated with access to care.

Health Status and Behaviors85

Like other indicators of integration, Hispanic health status differs according to subgroup, immigrant generation, English proficiency, and degree of acculturation.

Puerto Ricans are less healthy, on average, than other Hispanic subgroups, while Mexicans, Central Americans, and South Americans often compare favorably with whites on several health indicators, despite their low average socioeconomic status. For example, the age-adjusted mortality of Hispanics is lower than that of blacks or whites; the exception is Puerto Ricans, whose mortality rates are higher than those of other Hispanic subgroups (see figure 6). Dubbed the Hispanic "epidemiological paradox" or "immigrant health paradox" by researchers, the lower mortality rates of Hispanics relative to those of whites with more favorable socioeconomic status have puzzled social and health scientists since the 1980s. Precise findings differ, but most studies show that foreign-born Mexicans, Central Americans, and South Americans are most likely to experience this advantage. One factor that contributes to their lower mortality is that healthier people are more likely to migrate than the sickly, but it is not a sufficient explanation. Why mortality rates are comparable for U.S.-born Hispanics and whites, however, remains a puzzle.

Hispanics also experience favorable birth outcomes in terms of birthweight and infant mortality, another case in which they fare much better than would be expected given their socioeconomic status. In 2001, Hispanics' infant mortality rate of 5.4 per 1,000 live births compared favorably with those of 5.7 for whites and 13.5 for blacks. Cubans (4.2), Central and South Americans (5.0), and Mexicans (5.2) all had lower infant mortality rates than whites, while Puerto Ricans (8.5) fared better than blacks but worse than whites.[86]

Experts often invoke protective cultural and social behaviors of immigrants to explain their advantage in birth outcomes relative to their U.S.-born counterparts. However, since second-generation Hispanic women also have relatively favorable birth outcomes compared with white women of comparable socioeconomic status, cultural explanations do not suffice. Other assets in the Hispanic health ledger include a lower incidence of several major cancers and relatively low rates of activity limitation (e.g., climbing stairs, getting dressed) compared with whites, along with mental health profiles that resemble those of whites. In 2000, for example, the age-adjusted death rate from cancer was 134.9 per 100,000 for Hispanics, compared with 200.6 per 100,000 for whites. Hispanics also smoke less than whites; the exception is Puerto Ricans, who smoke at similar rates.[87]

Hispanics also experience several health liabilities, diabetes and hypertension being by far the most severe. The rising prevalence of Hispanic adults considered overweight or obese likely contributes to higher rates of both conditions, as well as to cardiovascular disease. Although the U.S. epidemic of overweight and obese adults affects all racial and ethnic groups, it is

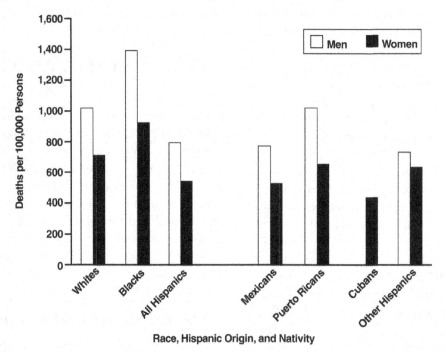

Figure 6. Age-adjusted Mortality for Whites, Blacks, and Hispanics by Sex, 2001.
Source: Arias et al. (2003).

particularly severe for Hispanics. Among Mexicans, 29 percent of men and 40 percent of women are considered obese, compared with 27 percent and 30 percent, respectively, of white men and women.[88]

Trends in overweight among Hispanic youths are particularly worrisome. Hispanic children and adolescents—Mexican and Puerto Rican girls in particular—are much more likely than whites to be overweight. Girls of Mexican origin are nearly twice as likely as white girls to be overweight, while Mexican-origin boys are more than twice as likely as white boys to be overweight. Even more troubling, rates of overweight have risen faster for Hispanic than for white youths (see figure 7). Over the last quarter century or so, the prevalence of overweight preadolescent (ages 6–11) Mexican youths doubled—rising from 13 to 27 percent for boys and from 10 to 20 percent for girls. The rate of adolescents (ages 12–19) considered overweight more than trebled for both boys (from 8 to 28 percent) and doubled for girls (from 9 to 19 percent) over the same period.[89]

Those who claim that acculturation contributes to the rise in Hispanic overweight and obesity point to immigrants' diets, which are richer in fruits and vegetables and lower in fats compared with those of native-born youths, who are more prone to consume high-fat processed and fast foods. Generational differences in diet are mirrored in the prevalence of overweight adolescents, as about one in four first-generation adolescent Hispanics is at risk of being overweight, compared

with about one in three second- and third-generation youths.[90]

Several other differences in the health circumstances of Hispanic youths are worth noting. With the exception of Puerto Ricans, Hispanic youths have low rates of asthma, the major chronic disease of childhood. This health asset is offset by their worse oral health compared with their white peers. Hispanic youths also register higher blood lead levels than white children, which places them at greater risk for the adverse effects of lead poisoning on cognitive development.[91]

Hispanic adolescents engage in many health-compromising behaviors, such as use of alcohol and illicit drugs and early sex, at rates comparable to those of white teens, although their tobacco use is lower. Cuban-origin youths have the highest levels of tobacco, alcohol, and drug use, followed by those of Mexican and Puerto Rican origin. By comparison, youths from other Hispanic subgroups have low rates of drug use—probably because larger shares of these subgroups are first-generation immigrants, which means they are less acculturated. In general, acculturated youths engage in such health-compromising behaviors more often than the less acculturated. Hispanic young people also experience poor mental health, exhibiting the highest prevalence of depression of any ethnic group. Although Hispanic adolescent girls are as likely as white adolescents to consider suicide, they are twice as likely to attempt it. Their suicide completion rate, however, is lower than that of other ethnic groups.

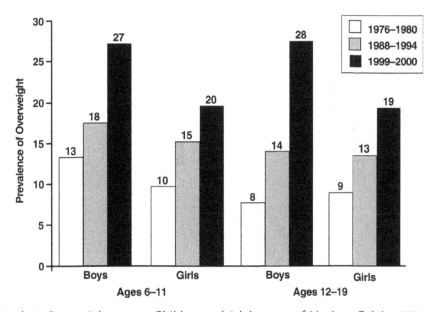

Figure 7. Time Trends in Overweight among Children and Adolescents of Mexican Origin, 1976–1980 to 1999–2000.
Source: National Center for Health Statistics (2003) (see Escarce et al., 2006).

The significance of these and other health-compromising behaviors among adolescents transcends their own physical well-being. In 2003, Hispanics had the highest teen birthrate, with 82.2 births per 1,000 adolescent females ages 15–19. In comparison, the birthrate for teens of all backgrounds was 41.7, while that for white teens was 27.5 and for black teens was 64.8.[92] Such statistics bode ill for the educational prospects of Hispanic adolescents, who are more likely than either blacks or whites to withdraw from school if they become mothers.[93] Indeed, all health conditions and behaviors that affect scholastic performance—including not only adolescent childbearing, but also drug and alcohol use and exposure to lead and other environmental contaminants—are especially worrisome because of the lifelong consequences of educational underachievement discussed above.

Access to Quality Care

Hispanics face a variety of financial and nonfinancial obstacles to obtaining appropriate health care. Low rates of insurance coverage are perhaps most notable, but limited access to providers, language barriers, and uneven quality of care exacerbate inequities in health outcomes between Hispanics and whites and between native- and foreign-born Hispanics.

The lack of insurance coverage is greater among foreign-born compared with U.S.-born Hispanics, Spanish compared with English speakers, recent compared with earlier immigrants, and noncitizens compared with citizens. Undocumented immigrants are least likely to be insured; one estimate of their uninsured rates ranges between 68 and 84 percent.[94] Owing to their large shares of recent immigrants, Mexicans and Central and South Americans have the highest uninsured rates. Puerto Ricans and Cubans have the highest insurance rates, with sources of coverage differing between the two groups. Puerto Rican children and working-age adults are much more likely than their Cuban counterparts to obtain health coverage through public insurance programs such as Medicaid and the State Children's Health Insurance Program (SCHIP), but they are less likely to obtain it through an employer (see figures 8a and 8b). For Hispanic seniors, eligibility for the Medicare program keeps insurance coverage rates relatively high.

Compared with whites, Hispanics have lower access to employer-provided health insurance because they are more likely than whites to work in small firms, in seasonal occupations, and in part-time jobs.[95] Limited eligibility for public insurance programs, such as Medicaid and SCHIP, further accentuates Hispanics' low coverage rates (with the exception of Puerto Ricans). Many Hispanics—especially Mexicans and Cubans—live in states with restrictive eligibility rules for Medicaid and SCHIP. The federal welfare reforms of 1996 placed further limitations on access to public health insurance programs for all recent legal immigrants.[96] General confusion about how the new laws affected immigrants triggered declines their overall utilization of public insurance programs.

Partly because of low rates of health insurance coverage, Hispanics are less likely than whites to have a

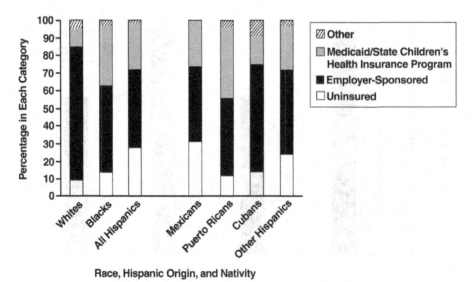

Figure 8a. Health Insurance Coverage for White, Black, and Hispanic Children, 1997 to 2001.

Source: 1997 to 2001 Medical Expenditure Panel Survey.

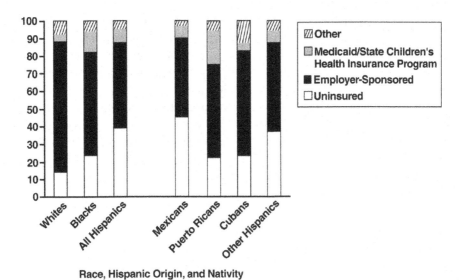

Figure 8b. Health Insurance Coverage for White, Black, and Hispanic Working-Age Adults, 1997 to 2001.
Source: 1997 to 2001 Medical Expenditure Panel Survey.

usual source of care or regular health care provider, which in turn restricts their access to more specialized forms of care. The relatively low number of Hispanic physicians, especially in Hispanics' new destinations, further hinders access to care because Hispanic physicians are more likely than their non-Hispanic counterparts to care for Hispanic patients. Given their large share of recent immigrants, Mexicans are less likely than Puerto Ricans or Cubans to have a usual source of care, as are Spanish speakers compared with English speakers. Furthermore, language barriers undermine quality health care, even among groups with similar demographic and socioeconomic characteristics, by hindering patient-provider communication; by reducing access to health information; and in the worst case, by decreasing the likelihood that sick patients will seek needed care.[97]

Hispanics' low rates of insurance and reduced likelihood of having a regular health care provider mean less preventive care, fewer ambulatory visits, and higher rates of emergency room use compared with whites, although Hispanics' rates of inpatient care are equivalent to those of whites. The preventive services on which Hispanics trail whites include pneumococcal and influenza vaccinations for seniors; mammography, pap smears, and colon cancer screening; blood pressure and cholesterol measurements; and prenatal care for the general population. In 2001, just 75 percent of Mexican and 79 percent of Puerto Rican women received prenatal care in their first trimester, compared with 92 percent of Cuban and 89 percent of white

women. Hispanic-white differences in childhood vaccination rates are trivial.[98]

Evidence on the quality of care received by Hispanics is inconclusive, partly because current assessments are based on populations that are not truly representative, such as low-income Medicaid recipients, and partly because results from satisfaction surveys are inconsistent. Nonetheless, Hispanics' reported satisfaction with health care delivery reveals large differences, depending on the degree of English proficiency. In general, Hispanics who speak only Spanish report worse experiences with health care than either whites or Hispanics who speak English. Satisfied patients are more likely to seek care when needed, to comply with provider recommendations, and to remain enrolled in health plans and with specific providers. Paradoxically, and for reasons not fully understood, Spanish-speaking Hispanics rate their physicians and health plans higher than do English-proficient Hispanics, despite admitting to worse care experiences.

To reduce language barriers to health care, the Department of Health and Human Services issued a directive in August 2000 requiring all federally funded programs and providers to offer interpreter services at no cost.[99] Yet only about half of Hispanic patients who need an interpreter receive one. In most cases, the interpreter is a staff person, relative, or friend rather than a trained medical interpreter; in such cases, reported satisfaction rates remain below those of whites.

CONCLUSION

Hispanic integration experiences are as diverse as the eclectic subgroups subsumed under the panethnic identity, but some general trends are discernible. Hispanic families converge in form and function with those of the white majority and rising intermarriage blurs the boundaries of nationality groups. The rise in divorce and nonmarital childbearing over time and across generations signal family decline. The rise of mother-only families bodes ill for economic prospects of the swelling second generation.

There are clear signs of educational progress at all levels both over time and across generations. That other groups also have improved their educational standing has widened attainment gaps, particularly at the college level. Because the fastest-growing and best-paying jobs now require at least some postsecondary education, Hispanics stand to lose economic ground even as their educational attainment rises. Still, employment and earnings trends show clear evidence of economic assimilation, with the greatest gains between the first and second generation. If the most successful third-generation Hispanics "opt out" of Hispanic identity, as available data suggest, economic progress for the third and later generations may well be understated.

Trends in Hispanic home ownership and median household income signal a growing middle class, although the dollar growth of Hispanic household assets is small compared with that recorded by white households.[100] Variation in financial status by immigrant and citizenship status, by age (favoring middle-aged over young householders) and especially by earnings capacity and educational attainment, largely explains the significant gap in economic well-being between Hispanics and whites. As long as this gap persists, however, Hispanics will remain more vulnerable to economic cycles because they have less of a cushion on which to draw during periods of financial distress.

Finally, recent health trends paint the picture of a Hispanic population burdened by the complications of obesity, diabetes, hypertension, and cardiovascular disease, which Americanization appears to worsen rather than improve. The deleterious effects of acculturation are especially evident among second-generation youths and in birth outcomes. Most striking is the high incidence of type 2 diabetes—usually a disease of adults—among young Hispanics and the increased prevalence of multiple risk factors for developing atherosclerosis among children of Mexican origin.[101] These trends foreshadow much higher rates of diabetes and its complications in the future, as large cohorts of Hispanic youths become adults.

The growing number of uninsured Hispanics will place particular stress on the health care safety net—a loosely organized system for delivering care to the uninsured that includes nonprofit organizations, government agencies, and individual providers. By default, some of the responsibility to health care delivery will shift to states and local communities, many of which are already struggling to compensate for shortfalls created by declining federal funding. Experts in both the public and private sectors consider cultural competence—the ability of health systems to provide care to patients with diverse values, beliefs, and behaviors, including tailoring delivery to meet patients' social, cultural, and linguistic needs—to be a crucial component of strategies to reduce disparities in care.[102] Compliance with the federal directive to provide interpreter services at care facilities is especially warranted in new immigrant destinations.

Endnotes

1. These findings are documented in greater detail in Landale et al., 2006.
2. Popenoe, 1993.
3. Landale and Oropesa, 2002.
4. Landale and Orepesa. 2002. The evidence for declines in familism among Central and South American nationalities is less clear than is the case for Mexicans because the generational depth is lower.
5. Landale et al., 2006.
6. Lee and Edmonston, 2005.
7. Edmonston et al., 2002, note that all population projections involve higher rates of intermarriage.
8. These findings are documented in greater detail in Schneider et al., 2006.
9. Mare, 1995.
10. See Duncan et al., 2006:Table 6-1.
11. Crosnoe, 2005; Crosnoe et al., 2004; Valencia, 2000.
12. U.S. Department of Education, National Center for Education Statistics, 1999.
13. U.S. Department of Education, National Center for Education Statistics, 1997.
14. U.S. Department of Education, National Center for Education Statistics, 2003b.
15. Carnegie Council on Adolescent Development, 1989.
16. Bryk and Schneider, 2002.
17. U.S. Department of Education, National Center for Education Statistics, 2003b; Valencia, 2002.

18. Bryk and Schneider, 2002.

19. Schneider and Stevenson, 1999.

20. Fry, 2003. This distinction is important because the Hispanic high school dropout rate has been inflated by the presence of foreign-born adolescents who withdrew from school before entering the United States.

21. U.S. Department of Education, National Center for Education Statistics, 2003a: Table 106.

22. Cameron and Heckman, 1993.

23. Fry, 2005; Hirschman, 2001.

24. Carnevale, 1999.

25. Tienda and Simonelli, 2001.

26. Kao and Tienda, 1998.

27. U.S. Department of Education, National Center for Education Statistics, 2002.

28. U.S. Department of Education, National Center for Education Statistics, 2003b.

29. Kim and Schneider, 2004; Portes and Rumbaut, 2001.

30. Fry, 2002, 2003.

31. College Enrollment and Work Activity of Year 2000 High School Graduates. Available: ftp://ftp.bls.gov/pub/news.release/History/hsgec.04132001.news [accessed December 23, 2005].

32. Schneider et al., 2006.

33. Velez, 1985.

34. Alon and Tienda, 2005; Fry, 2004.

35. Clark, 2003; Kochhar, 2004; Wolff, 2004.

36. These findings are documented in greater detail in Duncan et al., 2006.

37. Chiswick, 1978; Schoeni, 1997.

38. The annual employment rate is defined as the percentage of individuals who worked at all during the calendar year preceding the census. Similar results are obtained using annual hours of work as a measure of labor supply.

39. Dominican men also have relatively low employment rates, but nativity differentials for them are small.

40. Duncan et al., 2006: Table 6-4.

41. The estimated deficits are for persons ages 25 to 59 who worked during calendar year 1999, based on regressions by Duncan et al., 2006: Appendix Table A6-7.

42. This is not the case for black men, however, as their 15 percentage point employment deficit would shrink to only 13 percentage points if their human capital endowments were comparable to those of whites.

43. The employment gaps for Puerto Ricans and Dominicans may be due, in part, to their concentration in goods-producing industries in the northeast that have been hurt by deindustrialization, and in part to the fact that their employment patterns are more similar to those of blacks than to those of other Hispanic groups. See DeFreitas, 1991.

44. In contrast to black men, black women's modest earnings disadvantage relative to white women would disappear if they had comparable levels of human capital.

45. Phillips and Massey, 2000; Rivera-Batiz, 1999.

46. See Duncan et al., 2006.

47. Specifically, there is some evidence that darker, more Indian-looking Mexican Americans are vulnerable to discrimination based on skin color. See Allen et al., 2000.

48. Lowell and Fry, 2002.

49. Smith, 2001.

50. Duncan et al., 2006: Table 6–7.

51. Borjas, 1994; Chiswick, 1977; Neidert and Farley, 1985; Perlmann and Waldinger, 1997.

52. Duncan et al., 2006: Figure 5–8.

53. Borjas, 1993; Smith, 2003.

54. Smith, 2003, reports a 4.94-year mean education gap among all first-generation Mexicans (Table 3). This deficit fell to 2.95 years among second-generation Mexicans.

55. Alba and Nee, 1997; Duncan and Trejo, 2005; Telles et al., 2002.

56. Duncan and Trejo, 2005; Duncan et al., 2006; Reimers, 2006.

57. Edmonston et al., 2002; Rutter and Tienda, 2005.

58. Smith, 2003; see Duncan et al., 2006; Reimers, 2006.

59. U.S. Census Bureau; Income 1999. Available: http://www.census.gov/hhes/www/income/income99/99tablea.html [accessed December 27, 2005].

60. Those who were born in the United States have income levels similar to those of whites.

61. U.S. Bureau of the Census, 2004b.

62. U.S. Bureau of the Census, 2004b.

63. Wolff, 2004.

64. The Hispanic-black median income differential exceeded 90 percent between 1995 and 1997, hovering around 94 to 98 percent. See Wolff, 2004: Tables 7 and 8.

65. Kochhar, 2004.

66. Saenz, 2004: Table 11.

67. U.S. Bureau of the Census, 2000c. Poverty thresholds are not adjusted for cost-of-living differences. That large shares of Hispanics live in high-priced cities magnifies the welfare consequences of poverty-level incomes.

68. Saenz, 2004.

69. See Reimers, 2006: Table 7-2.

70. See Reimers, 2006.

71. McLanahan and Sandefur, 1994.

72. U.S. Bureau of the Census, 2000a.

73. U.S. Bureau of the Census, 2000a.

74. Reimers, 2006.

75. Social Security is an "earned" benefit that automatically increases with the cost of living, but SSI is a minimal, means-tested safety net for those elderly who have no other income. Unlike SSI, Social Security is not viewed as "welfare" by the general public. Persons who qualify for Social Security benefits by working most of their adult years in covered jobs, even at a low wage, receive more generous Social Security retirement benefits than persons forced to rely on SSI, the benefit rates of which are below the poverty line.

76. Using the Federal Reserve Board's Survey of Consumer Finances, Wolff, 2004, estimates Hispanic median net worth at 3 percent of the white median for 2001, but Kochhar, 2004, estimates the 2002 median gap at 9 percent—$8,000 versus $89,000—based on the Survey of Income and Program Participation. One source of the difference is that Wolff excludes equity in vehicles and other consumer durables from his estimate of wealth. However, both sets of estimates reveal similar trends, if not levels, for their overlapping period, namely mid-1990s to 2001–2002.

77. Kochhar, 2004:Table 9.

78. Wolf, 2004:26. Stock ownership is concentrated among households in the top quintile of the wealth distribution, accounting for 90 percent of all stock holdings.

79. Clark, 2003.

80. Wolff, 2004.

81. This estimate is close to the .62 for 2000 reported by Fischer and Tienda, 2006, on the basis of census data for the largest 100 metro areas.

82. Fischer and Tienda, 2006; Myers et al., 2005.

83. See Kochhar, 2004.

84. Grossman, 1972.

85. Our emphasis on Mexican-white comparisons reflects the paucity of research comparing other Hispanic nationalities in terms of specific health outcomes. This section draws from Escarce et al., 2006.

86. National Center for Health Statistics, 2003.

87. National Center for Health Statistics, 2003.

88. National Center for Health Statistics, 2003. National data are unavailable on the epidemiology of cardiovascular disease for Hispanics. Moreover, experts disagree about the differences in death rates from heart disease between Hispanics and whites because regional studies have yielded conflicting findings, Escarce et al., 2006.

89. National Center for Health Statistics, 2003.

90. Escarce et al., 2006.

91. Escarce et al., 2006. The Centers for Disease Control and Prevention is currently lowering the threshold blood lead level for intervention from 10 µg/dL to 5 µg/dL. More than one-fourth of preschool-age children and one-fifth of elementary school children of Mexican origin would meet the revised threshold.

92. Ryan et al., 2005.

93. Ahituv and Tienda, 2000.

94. Berk et al., 1999.

95. See Brown and Yu, 2002; Dushi and Honig, 2005; Schur and Feldman, 2001.

96. The 1996 Personal Responsibility and Work Opportunity Reconciliation Act (the Federal welfare reform law) barred legal immigrants who entered the United States after August 1996 from receiving federal Medicaid or SCHIP benefits for their first 5 years in the country. Although states can offer coverage for legal immigrants during the 5-year moratorium imposed by the federal regulations, few have elected to do so.

97. Langer, 1999; Ruiz et al., 1992.

98. Escarce and Kapur, 2006. A likely explanation for the shrinking gap in childhood vaccination rates is the Vaccines for Children program, created in 1994, which provides vaccines free of charge to eligible children, including the uninsured.

99. Department of Health and Human Services, 2000.

100. Kochhar, 2004:Tables 17 and 19.

101. Escarce et al., 2006. Other consequences of the overweight epidemic among Hispanic youth include elevated blood pressure and high rates of insulin resistance, hyperinsulinemia, glucose intolerance, and abnormalities in serum lipids. Hispanic youth also have higher triglyceride levels and lower levels of high-density lipoprotein cholesterol than white youth.

102. Betancourt et al., 2002.

¡Evangélicos!

Elizabeth Días

FROM PGS. 22–28 OF TIME SUNDAY WORSHIP AT CALVARY

Foursquare Church in Silver Spring, Md., starts in an empty parking lot. The congregants usually arrive on foot with well-worn Bibles in hand. They come in groups, Latino mothers and toddlers, grandparents and friends. *"Que Dios te bendiga"*—May the Lord bless you—each one says, offering hugs and kisses to everyone they meet. They board a refurbished school bus painted with a Bible verse and the church's Spanish name: Iglesia Cuadrangular el Calvario. When it pulls out into the busy street, I hop in my car and follow. Twenty minutes later, the bus makes a sudden left into another parking lot—this one 15 times as large, home to Trinity Assembly of God Church—and this place is packed. A dozen men in neon yellow jackets keep the cars from fighting for spaces. At least five people tumble out of every car and van, usually families of three generations, tambourines in tow. Hearing the singing from inside my car, I follow them through the sanctuary doors.

A giant flag bearing a lion with a waving mane of orange, sunbeams hangs above the nearly 500 people inside. Trumpets sound, and guitars jam the *alabanzas,* Spanish songs of praise. A dozen girls dressed in white costumes with red sequined sashes dance onstage, and teenage boys step in unison below. Little children race to the front to join. One woman waves a fan with long pink sash, and a man pounds his fist on the pew as he prays. Then a white-haired woman has a prophecy. The pastor rushes the microphone to her, and everyone falls silent as she screams. "The Lord will heal people in this room today," she cries in Spanish. *"Gloria a Dios!* Praise be to God! The Spirit of the Lord is in this place." People kneel at the altar, the ministers anoint them with oil, and then the fiesta begins again.

The faithful at El Calvario are not Catholic; they are Protestants: born-again, Bible-believing, Latino Protestants. They represent one of the fastest-growing segments among America's churchgoing millions. According to the Pew Forum on Religion and Public Life, more than two-thirds of the 52 million-plus Latinos in the U.S. are Catholic; by 2030, that percentage could be closer to half. Many are joining evangelical Protestant congregations. Among young Latinos, the drift away from the Roman Catholic Church is even more rapid. It is a migration that is forcing both the Vatican and the Southern Baptist Convention to take notice. While many Anglo churches are struggling to retain members, congregations like El Calvario are booming: 18 months ago, the suburban Washington, D.C., church had 400 members. Now more than 800 people attend an array of services each week, and its leaders are planning a 3,000-seat sanctuary. The newly converted faithful even have their own name: they call themselves *evangélicos.*

The Latino Protestant boom is transforming American religious practices and politics. *Christianity Today,* the country's leading evangelical magazine, is preparing to publish in Spanish this year. Record labels in Nashville are beginning to sign Spanish Christian-music groups. Seeing its once solidly Catholic Latino faithful shift to Protestant churches, the Vatican made a bold counterstrike in early March when it named Argentine Cardinal Jorge Bergoglio as Pope—the first Latin American Pontiff and a priest blessed with an uncommon feel for the common man. Meanwhile, the Southern Baptist Convention, the largest evangelical denomination in the U.S., hopes to make a place for these new believers, setting a goal of 7,000 Baptist Hispanic churches by 2020. Today they count 3,200, but the convention's statisticians believe the real number may be larger.

If the numbers are fuzzy, that's in part because Latino congregations are often designed to be hidden. Many start as basement prayer gatherings. Others meet in storefronts. They are often more likely to have a YouTube channel or a Facebook group than a website. Sometimes the only clues that these congregations exist are the dozens of small plastic yard signs that pop up every Sunday to guide the pilgrims. Once you start looking for them, you see them everywhere—on street corners, in yards, on the lawns of other churches. I found signs for Primera Iglesia Bautista Hispana de Maryland in Hyattsville, Md.; Iglesia de Dios del Evangelio Completo in Adelphi, Md.; Iglesia Pentecostal La Gloria de Dios; and Centra Mundial Evangelico in nearby northern Virginia.

These *iglesias,* or churches, are different in kind as well as in number. Latino Protestants are more likely to get up and dance in church than to fall asleep there. Ushers stand armed not with service bulletins but with Kleenex boxes and folded blue modesty cloths to cover women when they faint in God's presence. The intercessionary prayer list includes typical petitions for healing and comfort as well as for more earthly needs— Samuel's *papi* has been missing for a week; Maria's cousin needs immigration papers; Ernesto's friend is facing jail time. Richard Land, a former president of the Southern Baptist Convention's religious-liberty commission, told his pastors four years ago to ignore the Latin reformation at their peril: "Because if you left [Washington, D.C.] and drove all the way to L.A., there wouldn't be one town you'd pass that doesn't have a Baptist church with an *iglesia bautista* attached to it. They came here to work; we're evangelistic, we shared the Gospel with them, they became Baptist."

The *evangélico* boom is inextricably linked to the immigrant experience. *Evangélicos* are socially more conservative than Hispanics generally, but they are quicker to fight for social justice than their white brethren are. They are eager to believe in the miraculous but also much more willing to bend ecclesiastical rules to include women in church duties and invite other ethnic groups into their pews. The new churches are in many cases a deliberate departure from the countries and the faith their members left behind—but they don't look or sound anything like the megachurches of the U.S. *Evangélicos* are numerous and growing fast. And they are hiding in plain sight.

A Reformation in Maryland

JUST 10 MINUTES AWAY FROM EL CALVARIO is Iglesia Roca de la Eternidad—Rock of Eternity Assemblies of God Church. Some 700 people attend one of its three services each week. Flags from their home countries— El Salvador, Guatemala, Honduras, Ecuador, Nicaragua, Costa Rica, Panama, Mexico, Colombia—line the meeting hall. At least half the congregation, Pastor Heber David Paredes estimates, are Catholic Converts. Even more may be undocumented, he says, and about a third have trouble reading and writing in English; They call one another *hermana, hermano*—sister, brother. "Church is what they have," says Paredes, who is from Guatemala. "They don't have many places where they can feel welcome. That's what they are looking for. That's where they have a family, a place to belong."

La Roca is part of a revolution. Catholic Latin America experienced the first inklings of the 16th century European Protestant Reformation only in the 1970s and '80s, thanks largely to evangelistic Pentecostal television and radio programs. Catholics were 81% of Latin America's population in 1996, while Protestants made up only 4%, according to Latinobardmetro, a Chilean polling group. By 2010, Protestants had jumped to 13% of the population, while the percentage of Catholics dropped to 70%. Says Samuel Rodriguez, president of the National Hispanic Christian Leadership Conference in Sacramento: "We are in the first generation of the Hispanic Protestant-Reformation."

Latinos are turning not just to Protestantism but to its evangelical strain for a variety of reasons. Above all, Latinos who convert say they want to know God personally, without a priest as a middleman. More than 35% of Hispanics in America call themselves born-again, according to the Pew Forum and 9 out of 10 *evangélicos* say a spiritual search drove their conversion. "People are looking for a real experience with God," says Paredes. That direct experience comes largely from exploring the Bible; "We do the best to preach with the Bible open. When they read the Bible, they find a lot of things they didn't know before. They may have had religion, but they did not have an experience."

Among *evangélicos,* worship is adaptable and open to self-expression. You want to pray aloud in your pew? Do it at the top of your voice, even when the pastor is praying. Want to fall to your knees? Run to the altar. Sing in Spanish and switch to English at Verse 3? Go for it. "The evangelical church says this: Listen, you want to come to our church? If you are Mexican; we will show you a church where you can sing mariachi music," explains Rodriguez, "If you are Puerto Rican, we will have salsa. If you are Dominican, we will have merengue. If you are Colombian, we will have cumbia."

Like an earlier generation of immigrants from Europe, Latino Christians often see Protestantism as the path to a more genuine, more prosperous "American" life. "They see the move to Protestantism, particularly evangelicalism, as a form of upward mobility, and very often I think they associate Catholicism with what they left behind in Latin America," says Randall Balmer, the chair of Dartmouth's religion department. "They want to start anew."

Instead of the classic three-point, German-influenced sermons found in many mainline churches, the message at La Roca is theologically raw, unpolished and aimed right at the immigrant experience. Heber Paredes Jr., son of La Roca's pastor, preached one Friday evening about the example of the Apostle Paul's assistant Timothy, who was half Greek and half Jew. Timothy, he preached, had a lot in common with the young Latino men in America today. "When a young man grows up without a father, being half and half, he is mocked. Usually what you see is a troublesome child. Not Timothy... It is time that we are not just another statistic—it is time we rise up for revival."

But music and sermons alone are not enough to draw people. A hungry person, the saying goes, has no ears. "I don't want to say from the altar on Sunday, 'If someone has a need, let me know,' because I will have a line of people out the door Monday morning, needing money for rent, food. People will take advantage of that," says Paredes Sr. "But we never let people stay in need. We are not going to be able to sleep if we know a family needs food "

Like other *evangélico* churches, La Roca takes, the Bible's "feed the hungry and clothe the naked" mandate literally. At a roundtable conversation one night, a woman wept as she shared how she first met members of a La Roca family when she was a single mother.

They were cleaning her office building late one night, and when they learned she did not have an apartment, they decided to move to a two-bedroom unit so she could stay with them; The church is divided into small groups called cells that meet weekly to pray and keep tabs on everyone's needs so they can bring them to the pastor. The church has a rule: on Sunday mornings, you have to greet 10 people before you can hear the sermon.

How Choco Changed Chicago

IF ONE EVANGELICO CHURCH HAS MADE the leap from immigrant barrio to booming American megachurch, it is New Life Covenant Church in Chicago. New Life had just too members in 2000; all were Spanish Speakers. Now more, than 17,000 people attend one of the church's four campuses every Sunday, making New Life the largest Assemblies of God church in the U.S. Nine of its 11 weekly services are in English. The pastor, Wilfredo De Jesus, "has the support of evangelical giants like Rick Warren, the pastor of Saddleback Church and author of *The Purpose Driven Life,* who wrote the foreword to De Jesús' book *Amazing Faith,* published last year.

De Jesús, 48, is tall and broad-shouldered, a straight talker with a firm handshake and a deep voice. He says his nickname, Choco, comes from his love of sweets and the color of, his skin. He's of a different genre from the pastors of La Roca and El Calvario, English is his first language. He grew up in Chicago's Humboldt Park neighborhood during its gang-ridden days and then got a master's degree in Christian ministries from North Park Theological Seminary. In terms of the American Dream, he has crossed the great divide.

After he took over New Life from his father-in-law in 2000 Choco bought a farm outside the city and converted it into a home for recovering drug addicts and prostitutes. Then he purchased a liquor store near the church and turned it into a cafe to reduce loitering and crime in the neighborhood. He recalls, "We started doing English services to reach third-generation Hispanics, who love their culture, who love their rice and beans, but prefer to hear a sermon in English. I started doing that, and the church started growing."

New Life didn't just grow—it exploded. Choco leased nearby Roberto Clemente High School for Sunday use and, later transformed his original location into a new site for a Spanish-language, service for first-generation Latinos. Five months later, a second Spanish service was added. He also started to stream services online. Now people tune in from Arizona, Massachusetts, Kentucky and other states. A pastor is available to serve the needs of online congregants.

Soon even the high school became too small, so New Life bought another property in now gentrifying Humboldt Park last August. There will be 1000 seats in the main sanctuary, with overflow seating for at least 300 more. (Choco wants the sanctuary's new stage to be able to hold a live elephant and feature harnesses for flying angels—part of his sermons-as-drama series.) At the same time Chaco has branched out, opening a church in Oakwood, which is attracting a largely African-American congregation, Diversity, for New Life, is a recipe for growth. "Latino, evangelicals have forced white evangelicals to own their own deepest convictions," explains Grant Wacker, professor of Christian history at Duke Divinity School, "to embrace the neighbor, to embrace the other without regard to social, economic or ethnic distinctions."

The *Evangélico* Effect

ONE REASON THE LATINO PROTESTANT movement is important to watch is that it is largely charismatic. *Charismatic* connotes a belief in miracles, healing divine intervention, speaking in tongues and:, an active spirit world. Its most fervent extremes are enough to give even a devoted believer pause. At El Calvario, a woman was praying so hard that she vomited (or exorcised a demon)—which is not that uncommon: ushers stood prepared with plastic bags to help her. Several others collapsed on the floor in convulsions when, they felt God's presence. Sermons aren't drawn from headlines; instead, they often sound like news itself. Eliud Ruiz, El Calvario's pastor, has preached against Russia because, he believes, "Russia is going, to lead the Islamic republics against Israel. It's in the Bible."

Then there are the miracles, which can seem almost commonplace in Hispanic churches. An El Calvario woman, waved two medical reports—one from when she' was diagnosed with osteoporosis, another from the day doctors said it had disappeared. A restaurant cook testifies that God stopped her 12 years of migraines after she fasted with the Church for three days, and another woman says her internal bleeding stopped when the pastor poured oil on her forehead and the people prayed.

This kind of church treads on shaky theological ground. But it's important to remember that most *evangélico* churches are relatively new, still sorting out their place in a country where many in the congregation

aren't yet citizens. And with the exception of the rare leader like Choco, many *evangélico* pastors rely more on experience than on any formal training in college, much less divinity school. There isn't much extra cash lying around in grassroots churches for courses on biblical history, and even if there were, the pastors face more immediate needs. *Evangélico* churches are often de facto healing centers for a population with limited health care benefits. They act as food banks for people with empty refrigerators. They house people avoiding street violence. There's a lot more going on there than just saving souls.

THE LATINO PROTESTANT SURGE, SAYS RICK WARREN, IS 'THE UNTOLD STORY'

Ruiz, Paredes, and Choco all preach against premarital sex, drugs, cursing and alcohol. None of them drink, and they ask their volunteers and staff to similarly abstain. At the same time, *evangélicos* are often willing to put women in the pulpit. That's a huge advance from many of their white evangelical siblings, who still tend to relegate women to music Or children's ministries. Ruiz and his wife Lucia co-pastor El Calvario. Women solo-pastor some of the most dynamic Latino churches.

Evangélico churches often face immigration policy head-on. Choco preaches against the deportation system because it breaks up families, and Paredes is planning an immigration conference for La Roca members this Spring. Those efforts help explain why some white evangelical church leaders are quietly urging Republican lawmakers to get behind comprehensive immigration reform, "When groups appear that are similar to one's own but with some; Striking ethnic or musical or cultural differences, they can appear threatening as well as promising," explains Mark Noll, a historian of American Christianity at Notre Dame. "I think it would be very positive for the evangelical, world to look at issues of social concern—immigration, environment, employment—as theological issues."

A New Rock of Ages

THE CATHOLIC CHURCH NOW HAS 4,800 parishes with Latino programs of various kinds across the U.S. According to the U.S. Council of Catholic Bishops, up to half of Latino Catholics in America are expressing their faith much as the evangelical community does—praying with hands raised, speaking in tongues, expecting the miraculous. One attempt to keep those members in the fold has been the Catholic Charismatic Renewal movement, which has gathered steam over, the past few decades. But it may not be enough. Only 15% of all new priests ordained in the U.S. are Latino. "The challenge for the Catholic Church is to make the parish structure very flexible, very family-oriented," explains Alejandro Aguilera-Titus of the bishops' cultural-diversity office. "To the degree that we fail to do this . . . we will continue to lose a significant number of Hispanic Catholics to other religious groups, mostly Pentecostals."

The Catholics and the megachurches have little choice but to adapt. By the year 2050, Latinos will make up nearly a third of the U.S. population. By then, the first-generation *iglesias* like El Calvario and La Roca

will be third-generation churches. If they follow even part of New Life's path, their pastors will be preaching in English and merging their new strain of Protestantism with the largely white evangelical mainstream. Warren realized years ago—thanks to his ministry's location in Southern California—that the Latino influx meant he could not stand still. Over the past decade, he has helped launch 35 Spanish-speaking congregations in Orange County alone. "The greatest growth of all is coming in the Pentecostal or charismatic churches," he says. "It is the untold story."

The U.S.—and the entire Latino world—is changing. The rock on which God is building his Latino church all over America is a Blacktop parking lot in suburban Maryland and a low-income high school in Illinois Right now, they may be hard to find; But as Jesus teaches in Matthew, May they who have eyes see.

Environmental Problems in Ciudad Juárez-El Paso:
A Social Constructionist Approach

Pablo Vila and John A. Peterson

In the past few years the U.S.-Mexico border has become known as one of the most contaminated areas in the world, given the feverish industrial development that has characterized it as a result of the establishment of the twin plant industry (*maquiladoras*). Ciudad Juárez-El Paso, one of the main border industrial centers, participates fully in this characterization. The El Paso area has become a dumping ground for hazardous wastes, from toxic chemicals involved in *maquiladora* manufacturing to the Sierra Blanca Nuclear Waste Dump proposed for development within ninety miles of El Paso and only twelve miles from the Rio Grande border with Mexico. Air pollution from automobiles and point sources, including brick kilns and dust from quarries and unpaved roads, has plagued the region. Water suffers both in quality and in supply, with major groundwater sources expected to diminish within twenty-five years. Wastewater both in U.S. colonias and throughout Ciudad Juárez poisons the groundwater as well as the Rio Grande through dumping into the Aguas Negras ditch of the Lower Valley of Ciudad Juárez. If the region seems out of control, it is especially so to the low-income and immigrant communities that make up the largest population of the region, who problematize their plight quite differently from the

public and expert discourses, and whose actions and responses reflect these different perspectives.

Despite this dilemma, there has been little research until now concerning area inhabitants' perceptions about environmental issues. This absence is not by chance but is framed within a larger problematic that afflicts environmental sociology and anthropology, which has only quite recently developed a focus that prioritizes the point of view of social actors in relation to the solution of environmental problems (Hannigan 1995). Thus only in the 1980s and 1990s did sociologists and anthropologists working on environmental issues begin using a constructionist approach to the issue (Gould 1991, 1993; Kottak and Costa 1993; Krauss 1993; Cable and Benson 1993). These studies examined the interplay of environmentalist discourse and local communities largely in an effort to understand how the attitudes and risk perceptions of disenfranchised groups could be integrated into larger and global environmental concerns and movements. From this perspective arose an interest in environmental justice, where Bullard (1994), Peña (1997), and Pulido (1996) discuss landscapes of inequality and focus on the relation between labor and gender in these contexts. Their emphasis is on the roles and empowerment of social actors rather than the process of social construction.

Gould's articles basically state that whereas the visibility of the sources of environmental pollution in a region can be extremely high (in the Juárez-El Paso case, the ASARCO smokestack, heavily contaminated drainage ditches, colonia water drums, uncollected trash, vehicle emissions, brick-manufacturing smoke, etc.), the visibility of *environmental deterioration* as produced by those sources varies substantially from source to source. In addition, it is important to keep this difference in mind, given the social visibility of a particular environmental problem that makes local residents become conscious of the existence of contaminants in their city (Gould 1993). Despite this, as Gould notes, consciousness does not necessarily bring about the definition of such contamination as a "problem." Thus what for some is the "horrible stench of pollution" is for others "the sweet smell of money" (Gould 1991).

Kottak and Costa's work also proposes to investigate the relationship between ecological risk, collective perception of that risk, and the development of an environmental conscience and action. According to these authors, even though the real presence of a contaminant enhances the perception of environmental risk, such perception does not necessarily originate from a rational cost-benefit analysis of that risk. On the contrary, the perception of environmental risk arises (or does not arise) within specific cultural, political, and economic contexts that are formed at the intersection of local ethnoecologies, imported ethnoecologies (often broadcast by mass media), and the changing circumstances linked to population, industrial growth, and migrations.

> An actual threat increases risk perception, but the threat does not cause the type of reaction that follows. Hazards may be accepted or avoided, emphasized or ignored. Risk assessment emerges or languishes in particular cultural contexts, and risk is culturally constructed. Recognizing cultural variations, it is important to consider that: (1) people react to dangers they perceive; (2) risk perception is selective; (3) sets of values determine the perception of threats; (4) values are culturally and politically determined; (5) the global spread of development and environmentalism is a political and economic process that entails cultural negotiation. (Kottak and Costa 1993, 338)

If this is so, an effective environmental strategy would, for these authors, involve one that listens to those afflicted and monitors their perceptions, reactions, needs and problems (336).

Celene Krauss emphasizes a feminist perspective concerning environmental issues. On the one hand, according to Krauss, this perspective values something that is put aside by the more traditional sociological analyses,

that is, the subjective dimension of all social protest (Krauss 1993, 249). On the other hand, a feminist analysis would allow, according to Krauss, substantiation of the importance of environmental protests around specific issues (such as hazardous waste disposal in a particular community) showing how "ordinary women subjectively link the particulars of their 'private' lives with a broader analysis of power in the 'public' sphere" (249). In this manner, Krauss's article illuminates the way different groups of women, instead of constructing a *unique* truth concerning environmental problems that afflict them, construct partial visions or situational knowledge through their everyday narratives (251).

If the issue of situational knowledge is central to Celene Krauss, Sherry Cable and Michael Benson argue that the very idea of "environmental justice" is a historical and cultural construct: "Perceptions of environmental injustice arise when citizens come to believe that the state is failing to protect their lives and property from environmental pollution and that pollution costs are being unfairly imposed upon them" (Cable and Benson 1993, 464). According to these authors, local environmental action groups do not demand new environmental laws but rather press for the enforcement of already applicable laws. In this sense, these environmental activists are looking not for reform of environmental legislation but for environmental justice. This type of group arises when traditional, state-based environmental supervising mechanisms fail when trying to control what is popularly perceived as illegal and dangerous actions by local corporate actors. In this sense, these local environmental groups represent replies, initiated within the citizenship, to what is interpreted as a failure of the state to control environmental pollution (465).

If the issue of social perception of environmental issues is something relatively new within the international literature on the subject, local research in this respect is almost nonexistent. The only manuscript-length work we could find on *any environmental issue* in the early 1990s was an interesting thesis written by Héctor Padilla (1993). He points out that it was as recently as the early 1990s when environmental issues emerged as an important matter in governmental agendas and in Juárez society. From the point of view of the government, "part of the Mexican environmental policy on the Northern border, besides aiming to remodel border cities in order to maintain their attractiveness for foreign investors, responded to local-scale environmental problems which were a source of binational conflicts" (Padilla 1993, 123). Thus, he notes, the lack of an "environmental discourse" can be exemplified by the theme's absence in municipal government annual reports during the 1980s. At the same time, according to Padilla, it would seem that the Panista government seeks particularly to emphasize the environmental issue. Nonetheless, as Padilla notes:

Even though the government response to many problems arrived late, this fact did not place it totally out of concert with respect to the way civilian society demanded solutions on environmental problems. It can generally be asserted that civil society, through the action and discourse of social actors, was also late to perceive the dimension of the day-to-day problems that ail it, influenced by factors such as ignorance about the issue and its prioritization of other more pressing topics. In this sense . . . a possible explanation would be that the political agenda during the 1980s was engaged in political-electoral matters and that it was only toward the latter part of the decade when the electoral outlook was modified, that issues such as human rights, public services and the environment began to acquire political relevance. (Padilla 1993, 156)

Padilla identifies two well-defined phases in relation to civil society's participation in environmental issues. The first is characterized by a relative scarcity of "environmental" pronouncements, and the second phase outlines a discourse on the environment together with concrete action. What distinguishes both phases is also the type of ecological problem that concerned the social actors who brought them forth into the public arena. In this manner, the main points of the first phase, which would encompass 1983 to 1988, centered around the repercussions of the Cobalt 60 nuclear radiation accident, and pollution by the ASARCO smelter in El Paso. For the second phase, from 1988 to 1993, Padilla notes that the discussion centers around dwindling ecological resources, the brick-manufacturing problem, and, most of all, twin plant toxic waste disposal and its repercussions on the Juárez Valley. It is noteworthy that problems related to urban services were a constant presence in the civil society agenda during the entire 1983–1993 period (Padilla 1993, 163–64).

If on the one hand we will advance in this article a constructionist approach, on the other hand we fully realize that the "environment" has a phenomenological existence outside the perceptions of social actors in any milieu. These phenomena can sometimes be measured and monitored, and environmental discourses are replete with references to ozone, particulate matter,

and toxic elements, for example, that can and do have real-world impacts on people as well as on ecosystems. Thus the plume of smoke wafting from the ASARCO smelter tower is not just a site of human perception or representation but also dumps real toxins such as lead and other materials on the environment downwind from the source.

However, the effects of these phenomena are themselves highly contingent on the perspective of those who are part of the environment, social actors ranging from scientists to bureaucrats to residents of barrios to academics toiling away in the ivory towers of the University of Texas at El Paso, also in the plume of ASARCO. Those perspectives each generate a variety of narratives that use these "data," from scientific to olfactory, to represent their own experience of the world and their own special interests. Environmentalists and pro-industry advocates obviously have their own vested interests in constructing, analyzing, and evaluating the data and the effects of the phenomena, and this has been treated recently to good effect by Ehrlich and Ehrlich (1996) in their masterful discussion of the rhetoric of industrialists, and, less convincingly, by Bailey (1995), regarding disinformation cast by environmentalists.

RESEARCH PROJECT OBJECTIVES

Given the dearth of research on the issue of social perception of regional environmental issues in the region, it seemed important for us to contribute to this matter. Because we believe that the solution to environmental problems indubitably requires the active participation of diverse community actors, we thought that it was of great importance to be acquainted with the thoughts about the environmental problems afflicting those social actors. Thus, while there is no direct relationship between the visibility of environmental problems and social mobilization to arrive at its solution, this does not mean that social visibility of environmental problems in a region is not important. In this sense, we may argue that recognizing the existence of environmental problems is a *necessary* though not *sufficient* condition to explain the appearance and development of local environmental mobilizations (Gould 1993). If so, it should not be strange that private capital and governments often try to minimize social visibility of environmental pollution through diverse covert methods (such as ASARCO's nighttime discharge of contaminating fumes). By the same token, people who are concerned about the environment should also resort to increasing social visibility of environmental problems if they seek to enable the social mobilization that will bring about their solution.

Because of all these factors, our research project intended first to investigate the level of social visibility of environmental problems in Ciudad Juárez-El Paso. To do so, we analyzed the commonsense discourse about environmental problems of diverse social actors in the region. Second, the study sketched the different ways social actors on the border addressed environmental problems. This seemed to us of great importance, because social actors are mobilized not by problems that are defined as such by experts but rather by those their own discursive universe defines as "priority problems." In other words, people can be conscious of environmental problems in their region and even so not mobilize, since the order of their priorities does not coincide with what environmental experts dictate. A Juárez colonia leader ably expressed this idea when asked about the main problems in his colonia: he pointed out that first came the land ownership problem and, second, the lack of water. "Once we succeed with the land problem, we tackle the water head on" (quoted in Padilla 1993, 183).

MAIN RESEARCH FINDINGS

Visibility of Environmental Problems

What appears clearly in the analysis of the interviews is the high degree of social visibility of environmental problems among our interviewees. Most of the groups interviewed were generally acquainted with the principal environmental problems besetting the area.

If this was not surprising vis-à-vis officials and technicians we consulted, it was in the case of popular sectors we interviewed, who generally identified as problems the same ones singled out by the experts. Of course, our method in some respects *induces* people to identify the majority of the area's environmental problems, considering we showed them photographs that graphically illustrate those problems. Nonetheless, in most in-depth interviews, participants not only identified the problem but also demonstrated an even greater knowledge of it, referring to anecdotes, news stories, firsthand knowledge by way of family and friends, et cetera, concerning the shown photographs. In this

sense, for instance, most of our Juárez interviewees not only knew about the brick-manufacturing pollution but also knew of the plan to change their brick-baking method, foregoing burning old tires as fuel in favor of natural gas. Also, it was common to see many interviewees remember contamination episodes on the part of the ASARCO, FLOUREX, and Candados Presto companies in vivid detail, or the pollution of untreated drainage ditch sewer water (aguas negras). Something similar happened in El Paso, proving that, at least with those we interviewed, most environmental problems were highly visible. The only exception to this visibility is the possible water shortage the area might face in the future. But this exception was once again shared by experts and common folk alike.

Environmental Problem Conceptualization: Priorities and Strategies

Another issue is how the various social actors characterize environmental problems and the place these occupy within their action agenda. We frequently heard in the area comments coming from both Mexicans and Americans, claiming that environmental problems do not recognize borders, that water contamination, air pollution, toxic waste, garbage collection, and so on are not just problems for El Paso or Juárez but that they are the blight of the border area in general. It is often argued that such problems do not recognize either the political delimitation of a national border or the social delineations that divide rich and poor, adults and children, women and men, Mexicans and Anglos.

However, this affirmation does not take into account that the mere definition of *what constitutes an environmental problem* is a cultural issue. If, on the one hand, borders and social classes are permeable to different cultures, on the other hand, the conceptualization of something as a "social problem" (as a "priority environmental problem" in this particular case) originates within the limits of a particular symbolic system. This symbolic system definitely determines whether an "obvious and urgent" problem, from a technical point of view, is (or is not) considered a priority environmental problem by the actors of a historically determined social space.

In this manner, what emerges in the in-depth interviews we conducted is that, from the point of view of the construction of meaning, many El Pasoans and Juarenses do not have the same environmental problems, and if they do, they do not usually bestow the same importance on them. Consequently border residents recognize and act on those environmental issues from the point of view of what their respective symbolic universes allow them to conceptualize as *priority problems.*

Same "Technical" Environmental Problem, Different Priorities

A good example of what we are discussing here is how, in some cases, national borders substantially modify the importance of environmental problems that would, from the technical point of view, affect El Pasoans and Juarenses to the same extent. This is the case of the Sunland Park landfill, which, according to complaints by the residents of this poor New Mexico suburb, gravely affects their health. Residents have mobilized to have the landfill relocated, and some of them have organized as an environmental group that meets periodically and has begun a structured battle to attain the relocation goal. According to Sunland Park residents, the landfill pollutes not only the groundwater but also the physical environment, as well as the air. As Guadalupe Contreras pointed out:

> The landfill is so close to the residential area and the schools . . . it's only five hundred feet away! So, when the wind is blowing, all of the contaminated soil . . . all that filth comes this way, all the dust, and the trash . . . comes to the community. There have been times when the teachers send their own children (so that the school will be very pretty), so they have the children pick up the trash. Even about a month ago they had the junior high students cleaning up the trash from along all the roads, when it's the obligation of the landfill to keep this whole area, all the sides of the roads, clean; because they come through here in their trucks and drop trash, but the mayor doesn't fine them or stop them, nor do the police say anything to them because it's all the same establishment, do you know what I mean?[1]

This pollution is particularly dangerous, as residents have claimed the trash that collects there is not only household trash (as the company contends) but highly contaminated trash that comes from Mexican twin plants, as well. As Guadalupe stressed:

There are forty or fifty Juárez *maquiladoras* that bring their trash here. . . . Now, the men who run the landfill claim that it's household trash and that it's not dangerous. Then why don't they get rid of it in Juárez? We have stopped trailers, and when we opened them we found dangerous adhesives, for example, like the glue that is used for soldering; there are also different chemicals. So why don't they dispose of them in Juárez? This is the big riddle, you know what I mean?

Assorted health problems have resulted from this pollution since the landfill began operating, as documented by area residents:

> GUADALUPE: If we asked for a hearing, it was because they have to get rid of that dump, because the children complain that it always smells very bad there; that sometimes they don't even eat because of the odor, and they can't study because they have headaches, and things like that, right? So we asked for a hearing.

> AMELIA: And now I have a bunch of little bumps . . . especially on my chest and body, right? I went to the doctor, and he told me that it was a virus, but just going inside my house and not coming out makes them go away, and I just go outside to give the dog water or something and in just a little bit . . .[2]

> INTERVIEWER: The rash comes again.

> AMELIA: And I also get very itchy. The doctor told me that it was a virus; and last night I got home at ten, and when I woke up at about one in the morning, I didn't have any, and when I got up this morning at seven I didn't have even one, and now I have them again, especially on my back . . . look . . .

> INTERVIEWER: Oh! Yes, a rash . . .

Residents claim that the landfill jeopardizes not only their health but also their finances. Property values have depreciated considerably owing to the proximity of the landfill and to public knowledge about the high level of pollution it produces:

> GUADALUPE: I consider this an injustice, for example that Mr. Margarito Ibáñez, having lived here for thirty years, and having built his house and some rental apartments, so that he

could spend his later years comfortably . . . then how is it possible that a company like this, criminal, can come here and establish themselves, and then say, "Now we have contaminated your air; leave if you can." So where are all the assets the residents have worked for, will they go in the trash?

MARGARITO: I've been trying to sell that house for a year, and the people come and tell me, "Listen, I've heard about the dump, and . . . where is it located, and what's it doing to the environment?" Well, it's right up here, I tell them . . . Then they say to me, "Well, it's not worth it to me to invest ten, fifteen, or fifty thousand dollars . . . no, it's better for me to go elsewhere." Thus the dump is affecting our morals, our physical health, and our property.[3]

In the search for the cause of so much injustice, Sunland Park residents appeal to an ethnic discrimination discourse, emphasizing that it is not by chance that the landfill is located in an area with a high concentration of Hispanics.

GUADALUPE: But there is a problem; I don't know if the United States wants to get rid of Latinos, or I don't know why these companies, like the landfill, are only located where the communities are mostly Hispanic or black, why?

AMELIA: It would be good to see the dump in Coronado [the epitome of an Anglo neighborhood in El Paso]; do you believe they were going to put the landfill there? Even here the Country Club [another expression of rich and Anglo people of the city], they won't allow the toxic wastes to be transported through there, so they have to go through here, because Anglos unite and fight for what is theirs, and Mexicans tend to fight among themselves, do you know what I mean?

According to the Sunland Park residents, politics would be involved in the decision to install and maintain the landfill in their community, because they have denounced the existence of plotting between the landfill and several New Mexico authorities:

GUADALUPE: They have already run the dump out of four or five places where they've contaminated the area. If it continues here, . . . it's because now they are very well protected by the

New Mexico governor, who knows about the problem, because we've talked to people who work for him. We've asked them to help, but nothing is done because the main person, the governor, turns out to be the one who is supporting them the most!

MARGARITO: And the landfill company's attorney was our senator, who represented us, and he came to defend them!

If this is going on in Sunland Park, something very different is happening just a few blocks away, on the Mexican side. The Juárez colonia immediately facing Sunland Park is called Puerto Anapra. From the point of view of experts who have investigated the area's problematic, there is no difference between the degree of health decline that Juarenses have suffered because of the landfill's presence in Sunland Park compared to what landfill neighbors on the American side have suffered. And the Mexican residents are fully conscious of the sanitary risks to which they are exposed because of the landfill's proximity.

ENRIQUETA: And we as neighbors, it makes . . . our skin crawl, right? To realize that sometimes our kids go there to play, and we know that they even dispose of human wastes there, right? . . . Infected body parts, and it's a huge danger that we have right here.[4]

CRISTINA: And here a neighbor of ours . . . her little children . . . the youngest one, right, Suquis? He has bald spots in his hair . . . he has blemishes here [signaling the head], and they haven't gone away.[5]

INTERVIEWER: And why do you think he has those pimples in his head?

CRISTINA: Because of . . . do you know what? They said in the news that it was because the landfills are here, and when . . . let's say the cloud of smoke that comes from there, it goes way up in the air, and it all falls on our hair. That's where the infections come from.

The residents of Puerto Anapra have also organized to battle environmental problems facing their colonia. Their most important fighting cause, however, is not landfill relocation but the provision of running water, which would allow them to get rid of the annoying system of (often contaminated) barrels they use to store water that a cistern truck delivers to them once every fifteen to twenty days.

INTERVIEWER: And in the meetings that you have, do you discuss this? For example, the dead dogs, the contamination that comes over here from the American dump, et cetera. In other words, is everyone aware of this, or is it only a few people who are worried?

ENRIQUETA: It's only a few people that . . . it's a few people, right? Really, our intention in having these meetings is . . . to protect ourselves here: our piece of land, working to have water—because we don't have water. That is another problem of contamination, right? They say there are contaminated barrels, right? . . . well, we have barrels, but thank God it hasn't affected us much. We're very careful, sometimes we even try to boil the water, right? But those barrels are dangerous. So in the meetings, yes, we do discuss the landfill, but we don't set aside a special time for it . . . only once in awhile . . .

Thus, what for residents on the American side is an environmental problem of such magnitude that some even declare, "If they don't go, we're going to have to," is for Puerto Anapra residents a secondary problem in relation to the more pressing one of water supply. In this fashion, while some are thinking of leaving (the Americans), others (the Mexicans) are thinking of securing a public service improvement in order to stay, with or without the landfill. This takes place within a context where Juarenses are fully conscious of the proximity of the landfill and of the health risks and have even met with their American counterparts to find a solution to the problem. As a Sunland Park leader declared:

GUADALUPE: We wanted to know if they had the same health problems that we do. They said they did. So we sought out their leaders, and we asked them to unite with us in protest, for example, a protest on both sides, they, being from Juárez, exposing their problems. Because its the same problem; they have the same health problems, skin allergies, their hair falling out, headaches, nausea, it's all the same. And we told them, "We want your help if times arrive to protest, can you join us?" And they said yes.

However, *their* priority environmental problem is water, not the landfill. Just as Guadalupe explains: "Do

you know what happens? Water is such a huge necessity over there that they focus on that! Because what Enriqueta told me is that sometimes they go for months until the cistern trucks bring them any water, so it's a basic problem. That's why I think they focus more on the water problem, because it's a daily necessity."

Industrial Pollution: Neighbors versus Workers

Of course, we do not need to cross to the other side of the border to find divergent discourses relating to a particular environmental problem. In fact, living in such different countries as the United States and Mexico is a good reason to have environmental discourses that are not precisely alike. But such conflicting discourses can still take the form of some neighbors even denying the existence of any problem at all, while others consider that such a problem is more than unbearable. This was what occurred precisely in a couple of interviews in Juárez and some others in El Paso. In this sense, for instance, we have found that the workers in several factories that have a particularly notorious polluting history had a totally different discourse from people who live close to the plants themselves.

Hence, in Juárez, for example, people from the colonia neighboring a *maquiladora* well known for contamination problems not only had full knowledge of the source of the pollution that affects them and of the environmental problems that the plant produced but had organized around their demands as well. They even occupied the plant for a brief time.

MODESTO: A *maquiladora* was set up here, right? Then later, I noticed that they were working with toxic products, very toxic. Then time passed, years, but we couldn't find the reason for our allergies. We saw a pipe there, close to the top, that gave off a kind of lime green smoke, like . . . yellowish . . . between yellow and green, and then the allergies started. Nasal allergies, a lot of nasal dryness, a lot of itching . . . a type of rash that broke out on our heads and all over our bodies. And then the nosebleeds started, and most of us complained of severe headaches, and I had read something about that, the contamination, and, well, those are the symptoms of toxic chemicals, right? And we had not organized here in the neighborhood until the accident happened with the little girl, because the factory disposed of the chemicals right here in the street, in a very irresponsible way, right? And there was nobody to tell them anything.[6]

WALKIRIA: And that little girl was burned because they had ditches there; they would open the ditches and throw all the wastes out here, and they left that ditch open and the little girl walked by and she put her little foot in there and was burned by the acid.[7]

WALKIRIA: Think about it: is it fair that we go to bed at night and in the morning we wake up vomiting, dizzy? Because they start working at four or five in the morning. So, for example now, when it's hot weather and we turned on the air conditioner, what happened? It pulled the smoke in. Did we wake up dizzy and with headaches!

In fact, some of the neighbors (or someone in their family) used to work at the factory and told about health problems that working there had brought them.

FLORENCIA: And my great-granddaughter was born with Down's syndrome, and it was my granddaughter's first child! And she was newly wed. Her husband doesn't smoke or drink, but the company has him working with the strongest chemicals. . . . So he quit when the baby was born like that, and the hospital told him that it was from handling so many chemicals. And they were still newlyweds! Since then he has two handicapped kids, so the chemicals damaged his blood . . .[8]

IRMA: I've had this illness for a long time now, I figure since I worked at the company. At first the scars weren't very noticeable, but for a while now, very much so! I thought they were fungus, but I went to a pharmacist, and he told me they weren't fungus, that it is a skin infection or maybe allergy, but not fungus. I have even noticed that since they've reopened the factory, my daughter has diarrhea often, and Sofia's little girl too, she's very sick with diarrhea, but no amount of medicine will get rid of it.[9]

IRMA: Oh, no! . . . I am just so itchy!

INTERVIEWER: It doesn't matter [laughs].

IRMA: Now that it's just us women, I have to tell you that I don't just have it only on my legs. The other day I showed Florencia . . . I told her

I even have blood besides my streaks! But all this part is diseased; my breasts are the same way, it's not just my legs. That is the reason why I was telling you I can't sleep, my back, my butt, I won't show you that! But, can you believe it, it is not fair!

However, neither the factory owners nor the workers paid any attention to the neighbors' demands. The workers even went as far as to mock neighbors who hurt themselves because of contact with the chemicals that the factory had carelessly released into the surrounding streets. As one interviewee testified:

FLORENCIA: I have a grandson who was burned right here on the sidewalk, because they released the water with the acid here, under the door, and the acid was always coming out . . . then I sent my granddaughter . . . I sent her to the store, and she didn't notice that the little boy followed her and stepped in the water and got his feet burned—both his little feet were burned! Then, instead of helping him, they started laughing . . .

INTERVIEWER: Who started laughing? . . . The same people from . . .?

FLORENCIA: Yes, the people from the factory . . . the workers!

INTERVIEWER: But why did they laugh at your grandson's problem?

FLORENCIA: Because they saw that he was burned, that he was screaming and jumping around there. Until my granddaughter came back and picked him up and brought him to my house. He was seriously burned.

Not only that, but at the moment of greatest tension between plant and neighbors (when the latter took over the plant), the workers stood behind the owners of the plant. They also denied that the neighbors' claims held any truth, although they had similar health problems themselves. In this particular case, the digression among narratives about what was taking place came to a point of direct confrontation.

WALKIRIA: Yes, they have been rude to us, which is obvious, right? They are defending the positions they have in the factory, and we are defending our rights, no?

IRMA: When we occupied the factory, our children would pass by, and several factory workers would say, "Oh! Look at the contaminated little ones!" And then . . . they whistled at my sister-in-law and me, and then they said, "Oh, no, don't whistle at them because they're contaminated!"

FLORENCIA: "And there go the children without brains," that old hag that I was telling you about, the secretary would say, "There go the children without brains and the contaminated ones" . . . a mockery.

Consequently, as many of our interviews show, workers who labor at plants with a contamination history, when it comes to defending their source of income, often deny the truth of pollution charges. In those cases the mobilizations are usually effected by neighbors, without any support from the workers. And if it becomes extremely difficult to disavow the presence of pollution, there is always the resource of minimizing it or upholding the belief that it happened once but is not happening anymore. As a plant worker declared in another interview:

SECUNDINO: During the time that I have worked at the plant the necessity of educating the workers, providing them with adequate equipment, and modifying the machinery has been seen. All of that has greatly reduced the occupational risks and the pollution of the environment.[10]

What is odd is that many of these workers are entirely aware of the degree of environmental damage the company causes. Consequently, it is not that they support the company because they are unaware that it pollutes; rather, knowing that the company contaminates, they prioritize their source of work over the destructive effects on the environment.

INTERVIEWER: And what kinds of contaminants does the company produce?

SECUNDINO: Air pollution, because there are gaseous emissions, so mostly air pollution. And then also underground pollution. Because the factory produces acid, and due to leaks or spills the contaminated water goes underground. Or it used to go in the past.

INTERVIEWER: In other words, these days it's a little better controlled . . . and that wastewater that goes underground, would it reach the groundwater levels, or do you think that it wouldn't get that far?

SECUNDINO: Yes, it goes that deep, because the acid is very corrosive; it's contaminated water. All the chemical products are very concentrated, and the amount that goes underground depends on the size of the spill.

The economic incentives they collect from working in polluting plants are sometimes very significant and seem to outweigh not only the damage they know the company causes to the environment but also the risks to their own health.

INTERVIEWER: And, for example, in what way does the company protect you, as workers, so that you don't have problems? Or are there such good incentives that it's worth it?

SECUNDINO: Mainly that's the plant's attraction. In the past, there were barrels of applications turned in (in 1987 and 1988), because this plant was, and still is, considered high risk; so the people from this city went and made applications, as did people who came from other cities. . . . For example, they would make an application, come in and work, get to know the plant, and then leave and not come back . . . they never came back . . .

INTERVIEWER: And is it very risky for the workers to work there?

SECUNDINO: Last year, the worst accidents happened to workers when they were not working, outside the plant . . .

INTERVIEWER: But I'm referring to the risks of working with chemical substances, with the acids, and other things that can affect your health in the future.

SECUNDINO: Well, our work will definitely affect us in the future, just as many other kinds of work would . . .

We can therefore see how this interviewee is entirely conscious of the perils involved in working in such a polluting factory, and still he does not plan to change jobs. The question becomes what kind of narrative allows this worker to continue working at the plant in full knowledge of the jeopardy to his health. The logic emerges when the interviewee equates his work to his father's, who worked for years in a mine.

> SECUNDINO: My work . . . I compare it to mining, because my father worked fifteen years in a mine, and I was very happy the day he decided to retire. They paid him, and he was very happy himself to leave the mine. He worked three more years as a bricklayer, because he knew how to work in construction too. It was about five years after he left the mine that he died after being run over on the highway in San Luis Potosí. So his pleasure at having left the mine in one piece lasted a relatively short time, because he lived through the experiences of many people who died inside the mine. They stayed there, they got sick or suffered accidents in the mine; I imagine that it is still one of the places where there are more fatal accidents.

This worker develops an argument where he first recognizes the highly polluting and dangerous character of his work, because comparing his work with mining work is a kind of implicit question: what can be more dangerous and harmful to one's health than working in a mine? He then details how his father worked all his life in a mine where absolutely nothing happened to him, and how, finally, he died in a traffic accident. Therefore he wants to convince us that, for him, chance, not the kind of work you do, is the most important factor in determining people's destiny. If this is so, it does not make much difference whether one works in a dangerous place or in a nondangerous one.

National Discourses: "They Pollute More Than Us"

Another interesting aspect of the commonsense construction of environmental problems in Juárez and El Paso points to a particular attribute of the border: when it comes to finding a culprit for environmental problems, many people easily find it on the other side of the dividing line. Thus, in the majority of interviews in El Paso and Juárez, a certain logic of the "they pollute more than we do" type appeared prominently.

For this reason, many El Pasoans would, using various arguments, put almost all the burden of environmental problems that ail them on Juarenses' shoulders. Some interviewees believe that most of the pollution in the area is due to the lack of pavement in the streets of

Juárez or the use of highly pollutive fuel to heat houses in the winter.

> STEVEN: As much as the pollution, I think that in Juárez it's dust. There aren't, there aren't lawns in the neighborhoods like we have. I mean . . . Your backyard's a swimming pool, and what's gonna blow out of there? My front yard's all rocks, huh? And the roads aren't paved. I think that when you see that haze in the wintertime, you know, when it's the worst around here, it's 'cause of that. I think so. And then the other thing is they're poor people, so to heat their houses they use wood, they burn wood. And the other one really popular is the *calentones*. The little catalytic heaters with *petróleo*. Which is kerosene.[11]

Other El Pasoans interviewed argued that the most significant source of pollution on the border derives from the way Juarenses deal with their house trash, as well as the habit of burning tires to keep warm:

> JEFF: You don't find garbage disposals in Mexico. I've always heard that the people that live right across from UTEP, in Mexico, they burn tires to keep them warm, as the fuel to their fires.[12]

For Jeff, sanitary conditions in Juárez are so catastrophic that they resemble those during the Middle Ages more than they do those of a developing country: "When I go to Juárez I take the back roads there. You actually see the sewage in the middle of the roads, and when an animal dies, like a cat . . . one time a cat got hit by a bus, and the dogs were fighting over eating that cat, it was . . . uh! It was uh! . . . barbaric! [laughs].

By contrast, for other El Pasoans, Juárez's stock of notoriously old and dilapidated cars is the main cause of the areas pollution.

> SERENA: The cars over there, I don't know if they're inspected like they are here . . . to meet standards. You know, like Aníbal was telling me that I could go to Juárez and have that . . . catalytic converter removed, and they wouldn't even inspect it, and I go . . . see, I won't do that type of thing. Here in the United States you have to get your car inspected and it has to pass inspection, and I think that's important.[13]

In the account of many of our El Paso interviewees, Juarenses would be responsible not only for environmental pollution in their own city (pollution that has repercussions in El Paso's daily life as well—burning trash and tires, vehicular contamination, etc.) but also for much of the pollution generated in El Paso, prominently, the garbage generation.

> SERENA: In Mexico . . . I think people tend to litter more even in their own city. I don't want to call it an attitude, but they carry it over here.

> ETHEL: I understand the attitude she's saying, 'cause I went to the post office here and I was getting out of my car and there was this truck beside me with laborers from Mexico, I guess . . . and the guy in the front seat was gonna throw a can out the window, but he saw me and he stopped himself from doing that.[14]

This idea that Mexicans are the principal culprits for the trash present in El Paso was evident in many of our interviews. Not only that, but the issue was debated in a letter to the editor of the *El Paso Times*:

> I would like to know why people across the border always leave their garbage here. We're trying to keep our city clean, even I feel guilty when I have a gum wrapper in my hand and want to throw it away. There's a lot of tourists that stop by and shop and see all that garbage and think the worst about us. They do not know its the Mexicans who do it. The Mexicans come to shop in every one of our stores, especially Sam's, Kmart, Wal-Mart and Target. They unpack whatever they buy and leave all those big empty boxes lying all over the parking lot. Why in the world can't they put them in the garbage cans? That's one of the reasons I don't go over the border, I hate to see their dirty and filthy streets. (A. Delgado, *El Paso Times,* 26 February 1994)

As we can see, a whole arsenal of arguments was used by many El Pasoans to try to prove that, without a doubt, the greatest source of pollution came from the Mexican side.

Juarenses know very well of the "charges" against them, which is why it was not surprising to find a defensive attitude about the subject. For this reason, some of our Juarense interviewees "defended" their position, maintaining that while they admit Juárez creates a good part of the area's pollution, they also think that El Paso's pollution is much more conspicuous and dangerous than their own. In this manner, certain Juarenses argued that while it is true that brick manufacturing and other sources of air pollution are

a serious problem, they do not compare to the degree of pollution produced by American sources such as the ASARCO or Chevron refineries. The arguments went from claiming that the latter work twenty-four hours a day, whereas burning tires or trash is only an occasional practice, to pointing out that lead emissions from ASARCO constitute a larger health hazard than the brick manufacturers' wastes.

> ROBUSTIANO: I imagine that all that smoke [referring to the ASARCO refinery] pollutes more than anything else, because it's pure gas, from refineries and all that . . . it's pure, strong [dangerous] fumes. Because it's not the same as burning trash or something, the pollution from ASARCO is much worse.[15]

Other interviewees argued that vehicular contamination was not the Juarenses' fault, either. Thus they claim that even though it is true Mexican cars are very old, the source of most of the pollution would be the long waiting lines at the international crossing bridges, especially to cross to the American side, because of all the paper requirements American customs demand.

> REFUGIO: Another serious problem occurs on the bridges: you often wait more than half an hour to cross. And it's not just one car, it's several![16]

> INTERVIEWER: And in that case, who is responsible for the pollution from the bridges?

> REFUGIO: People from over there, because they don't speed up the crossing process. It's less of a hassle to come over here . . . or maybe it's that when we go over there, they don't want us, that's why they give us a free way back to Juárez. Crossing from here to there, they search your car, open the trunk, raise the hood, and look at your passport; right there you lose maybe . . . three to five minutes. For them the search is quick, but it's not just one car, it's several, and several lines . . . and not just one bridge, there are several.

Further, although the majority of our interviewees on both sides of the border agreed in identifying *maquiladora* toxic refuse as a major source of area pollution, they did not agree on who is responsible for that pollution: Mexicans or Americans. In this manner, many El Pasoans blamed the Mexican government's lack of regulation for the American twin plant industry in Juárez, while some Juarenses we interviewed placed all the blame on the American companies that operate in Juárez to evade the strict American environmental regulation while benefiting from Mexicans' need for work. As we can observe, this "they pollute more than we do" logic has countless forms of expression on both sides of the border. It might even be one of the reasons for the lack of environmental mobilization found on the border.

The "Enlightenment" Discourse among Environmental Experts

We also think that this lack of mobilization is also somewhat related to the way many "experts" address the environmental problems of the region. We think that their usual approach to those problems is not the best suited to promote public mobilization in search of environmental solutions. Thus when we interviewed the "experts" (politicians, officials, contractors, and technicians who, directly or indirectly, have an environmental discourse), the most noticeable thing we found in their discourse was what can be termed as an "enlightenment approach to environmental discourse."[17] In this type of discourse, the need to create an environmental "conscience" for the population is understood as the number one priority in environmental issues. What is forgotten in this thematizing style of environmental problematic is that often "one sees what one wants to see and one does not see what one does not want to see." In addition, it is forgotten that discourse is an appropriate tool to enforce this divide between facts and perceptions. The point we wish to underline here is this: if it is impossible to live in situations of poverty without being able to simultaneously imagine a way out of these situations, where the vision of a brighter future is automatically incorporated into a vision of the present, thus making it more bearable, it is also impossible to live in an extremely polluted situation without resorting to some mechanism that, albeit symbolically, ameliorates it.

Thus the enlightenment posture to which we are referring—*see, know, acquire conscience, act*—also overlooks the *see, construct a particular narrative about what is seen, narrowly believe such a narrative, do not act* possibility. Is there anything more visible than the pollution that often floats around Ciudad Juárez-El Paso on winter mornings? We think not. Nonetheless, to illustrate how what we call an enlightenment discourse about environmental problems fails to account for many of the people's attitudes about the environment, we shall

refer to a specific interview. In that interview, Mexican UTEP students tried by any means possible to prove the smog they were being shown in a photograph was not really smog but something else that was not really pollution.

> GRISELDA: This photograph . . . it seems to me that it isn't smog. I think that this city isn't as polluted as, say, Monterrey, where you go and it looks like this [like the photograph of Juárez]. That you can't really distinguish the . . . sometimes there are days when you can't see the mountains very clearly. So it seems to me that what the photo shows is very little . . . rather, I think . . . it's dust, or just a cloudy day or something. Because I've seen it when it's dusty, and that's how it looks.[18]

> RODRIGO: Well, El Paso doesn't meet the standard that it should . . . the "safety zone" of air and . . . the biggest pollutant many times . . . is just dust particles. And the times that El Paso has not met the standard, it's because of that. Because the carbon monoxide and all that has almost always been at the required level, but . . . what ruins everything is exactly that, the dust.[19]

> GRISELDA: I think that maybe it gives the impression that Juárez is very polluted . . . but I think it's just dust . . .

The idea of these interviewees is also to prove that smog is not really detrimental to one's health; that is, to argue that only air pollution originating from industrial or vehicular sources counts as pollution and that breathing suspended dust is not really an environmental problem. On the other hand, these students tried to remedy (although symbolically) the state of contamination they experience in the area by comparing it to other areas that supposedly are worse in that respect.

There is an additional example we would like to bring up for discussion to show how the *see, know, acquire conscience, act* logic often cannot account for why people do not organize around environmental issues even for the most grievous of them (at least from a technical point of view). What we want to mention here is how there are particular regional discourses that, although recognizing the existence of environmental problems, do not ask for any solution to them. This is the case of a religious discourse that is expanding quite rapidly on the northern border (one that comes from some Protestant denominations) that argues, among other things, that if there is pollution, it is due to God's will.

> MAFALDA: Well, for example, about the pollution, I've heard people say that "the contamination is God's will" . . .[20]

> ESTEFANÍA: Yes, a lot of people say that, that otherwise God had not allowed us to invent cars, factories, et cetera. Many people say, "If we are going to die from the pollution, it's because God wants it that way."[21]

> INTERVIEWER: But who would buy their God?

> ESTEFANÍA: Well, only they know; it's the *ecoloco* [the crazy ecologist or the toxic man] [laughs].

As we can see, the possibility of *seeing, constructing a particular narrative about what is seen, narrowly believing such narrative, not acting* has many varieties, and all of them would be impermeable to the enlightenment logic many experts apply to environmental problems.

Implications for the Implementation of Public Policy

The present work has diverse implications for the design of public policy. First, dissonance in the conceptualization of problems and priorities of environmental questions, to which we referred earlier, poses an important obstacle to the solution of the innumerable problems that trouble the border. This is especially true because the execution of solutions does require a joint focus to be effective. So we are faced on the border with a myriad of environmental problems and priorities that are differently defined culturally and locally, and they can differ because of the definition of what a problem is or because of the importance that problem, once defined as such, has to different social actors. Nonetheless they require a unique implementation—transnational and transcultural—to arrive at a solution.

As we have noted, the problem is not that the area's environmental problems have a low social visibility or that "people are not environmentally conscious" in the sense that they do not know that they should not throw trash just anywhere, or waste water, or pollute drainage ditches with toxic substances, or contribute to the proliferation of clandestine garbage dumps. We do not

want to affirm the opposite either, that is, that *all* people in the area possess an "environmental conscience." What we propose is something more complex, which has a significant effect on the design of public policy. We maintain that implementation of public policy that aims to solve environmental problems requires the active participation of the public, in one way or another. This can mean participating in a recycling program, wasting less water, disposing of industrial waste only where the law indicates, or organizing around some environmental problem that necessitates participation of the affected population (a polluting plant, an improperly located landfill, etc.). This citizen participation will only be achieved if the call for public involvement addresses the way people define which are the environmental issues that are problematic to them, and takes into account their order of priorities for their solution. In this way, people will participate or mobilize not in those issues or priorities that "technicians" define as such but rather in those the people themselves define in their own terms as problems and priorities, given their particular perspective and their current priorities. In this sense, the technicians who design public policies should have something we can call "constructionism awareness."

The second point we want to address is closely linked to the first. We believe that just as it is necessary to "listen to the people" for the implementation of effective policies, so it is also imperative to "listen to the conflicting voices" of diverse social actors and to respect their particular narratives, even if many of these voices oppose each other. What we are proposing is to transform the cacophonous chorus we have right now on the border into a more tuneful one where, through public debate and narrative exchange, an environmental consensus can be reached that may eventually lead to the implementation of environmental policies that will solve at least the most urgent and important problems that the majority of the border population can negotiate discursively.

At the same time, an emergent awareness of the connectedness of human action within a broader framework must also be incorporated into discourses at all levels regarding the environment. In the process of analyzing the perceptions and representations of the environment in local discourses, we have tried to offer some insights about how the various conflictive voices can incorporate an awareness of our role(s) as interactive players within, and not apart from, the environment. As suggested in this chapter, "local" voices are often excluded from this dialogue, both because they have been disenfranchised and because their voices are not being systematically recorded. When they are, the conflict among the various discourses is often highlighted over local perceptions and concerns. As Hannigan (1995) concludes in his discussion of environmental sociology, the site of conflict often "involves a clash between opposing cultural constructions, one rooted in a vernacular, the other in a new ecological sensibility." In this project, we seek to document the commonsense or vernacular discourse from a constructionist perspective, not only to comment on the conflicts within a larger frame, but also to understand how players perceive and work out environmental concerns in their local contexts.

Endnotes

1. Guadalupe Contreras (a pseudonym, as are the other names used in this article) is a thirty-five-year-old Mexican national born in San Esteban, Durango. She migrated first to Ciudad Juárez in 1968 and later to El Paso nine years ago. She is a divorced housewife and mother of three children. Guadalupe identifies herself as "Christian" and has completed twelve years of school. She does not own her house at Sunland Park, but rents it. She is the leader of her neighborhood grassroots organization.

2. Amelia Rosales is a thirty-one-year-old native of Ciudad Juárez who has lived in El Paso for more than twenty years. She is married, has two children, and currently is a full-time housewife. Her religion is Catholicism, and she has completed her middle school education. She owns her house in Sunland Park.

3. Margarito Ibáñez is a Mexican immigrant who was born in Chihuahua sixty-seven years ago. He migrated to El Paso in 1958 and is now retired. He is married and has two children. He does not recognize any religious affiliation and has only completed his elementary school education. He owns his own home.

4. Enriqueta Barrera is a thirty-eight-year-old Mexican national born in Sonora. She migrated to Ciudad Juárez when she was five. She is a single mother of four and a full-time housewife who has completed some secondary education. Enriqueta identifies herself as "Catholic," and she owns her house at Puerto Anapra. She is the leader of her neighborhood's grassroots organization.

5. Cristina is a thirty-five-year-old Mexican national born in Zacatecas. She is a recent migrant to Ciudad Juárez and has lived in Juárez for less than three years. She is married, has four children, and is a full-time housewife. Cristina identifies herself as "Catholic," and she owns her house in Puerto Anapra. She is illiterate.

6. Modesto is a fifty-four-year-old Mexican national born in Coahuila. He has lived in Juárez since he was twelve years old. He is married and is currently retired. Modesto is Catholic and has completed his high school education. He owns his house.

7. Walkiria is a thirty-four-year-old Mexican national born in Coahuila. She has lived in Juárez since she was two years old. She is married, and her occupation is housewife. Walkiria did not answer the question about religion, and she claimed she has completed her high school education. She owns her house.

8. Florencia is a fifty-four-year-old Mexican national born in Durango. She has lived in Juárez for the last thirty years. She is married, and her occupation is housewife. Florencia identified herself as "Christian," and she pointed out that she only went to the first three years of elementary school. She owns her house.

9. Irma is a twenty-nine-year-old native Juarense. She is married and has three children, and her occupation is housewife. Irma is Catholic and has completed her elementary school education. She owns her house.

10. Secundino is a twenty-eight-year-old native of San Luis Potosí. He migrated to Juárez four years ago to work in one of the most polluting *maquiladoras* located in the city. He is married, has three children, and listed his occupation as "worker." Secundino is Catholic and has completed less than half of his middle school education. He rents a house in a working-class neighborhood.

11. Steven is a forty-three-year-old native of New Mexico. He migrated to El Paso fifteen years ago. He is married, has two daughters, and is a manager in an American *maquiladora* in Juárez. Steven is a Baptist and has completed his high school education. He owns a house in a middle-class subdivision in west side El Paso.

12. Jeff is a twenty-seven-year-old native El Pasoan. He is single and self-employed. Jeff filled out "nonpreference" in the question about religion. He has completed his high school education and is a renter.

13. Serena was born twenty-one years ago in Costa Rica. She migrated to El Paso three years ago. She is single and currently studies at UTEP. Serena is Catholic and lives with her sister in a middle-class neighborhood on the west side of town.

14. Ethel is Serena's older sister. She is twenty-three and was also born in Costa Rica and migrated to El Paso three years ago. She is single, a student, and lives with her sister in a house that their parents own.

15. Robustiano, who is forty-three years old, came to Juárez from Parral, Chihuahua, more than twenty years ago. He lives in an extremely poor colonia in East Juárez and is self-employed. Robustiano, who never finished primary school, raises chickens on a small plot of land near his house. He used to work in the United States

illegally. He is married and has a son. Robustiano is Catholic and owns his house.

16. Refugio is a fifty-two-year-old native Juarense. He lives in a poor colonia in East Juárez and is retired (he used to work as an elementary school teacher). He is single and Catholic.

17. Because of space restrictions, we can not analyze here the different variants of the "enlightenment" discourse.

18. Griselda was born twenty-one years ago in El Paso but has lived all her life in Juárez. She is single and currently studies at UTEP. Griselda is Protestant and lives with her family in a middle-class neighborhood.

19. Rodrigo was born twenty-five years ago in Ciudad Juárez and moved to El Paso when he was ten years old. He is married and is an electric engineer. Rodrigo is Catholic and rents the apartment where he lives.

20. Mafalda was born twenty-three years ago in Durango. She migrated to Ciudad Juárez three years ago. Mafalda works at home in a house that she shares with her parents and siblings in a working-class neighborhood. She is single and answered "Catholic" to the religion question. She has completed one year of adult education.

21. Estefanía was born twenty-nine years ago in Ciudad Juárez. She works at home but also, like Mafalda, does voluntary work at a small clinic in a very poor neighborhood. She lives with her husband and two children in a working-class neighborhood. Estefanía is not Catholic but Baptist. She owns her house.

References

Bailey, Ronald. 1995. *The True State of the Planet Earth: Ten of the World's Premier Environmental Researchers in a Major Challenge to the Environmental Movement.* New York: Free Press.

Bullard, Robert. 1994. *Unequal Protection: Environmental Justice and Communities of Color.* San Francisco: Sierra Club Press.

Cable, Sherry, and Michael Benson. 1993. "Acting Locally: Environmental Injustice and the Emergence of Grassroots Environmental Organizations." *Social Problems* 40 (4): 464–77.

Ehrlich, Paul R. and Anne H. Ehrlich. 1996. *Betrayal of Science and Reason: How Anti-environmental Rhetoric Threatens our Future.* Washington, D.C.: Island Press.

Gould, Kenneth A. 1991. "The Sweet Smell of Money: Economic Dependency and Local Environmental Political Mobilization." *Society and Natural Resources* 4 (2): 133–50.

———. 1991. "Pollution and Perception: Social Visibility and Local Environmental Mobilization." *Qualitative Sociology* 16 (2): 157–78.

Hannigan, John A. 1995. *Environmental Sociology: A Social Constructionist Perspective.* New York: Routledge.

Kottak, Conrad P., and Alberto C. G. Costa. 1993. "Ecological Awareness, Environmentalist Action, and International Conservation Strategy." *Human Organization* 52 (4): 335–43.

Krauss, Celene. 1993. "Women and Toxic Waste Protests: Race, Class, and Gender as Resources of Resistance." *Qualitative Sociology* 16 (1): 247–62.

Padilla, Héctor. 1993. "Ciudad Juárez en los ochenta: Medio ambiente, acción gubernamental y participación ciudadana." Thesis, Universidad Autónoma de Ciudad Juárez.

Peña, Devon. 1997. *The Terror of the Machine: Technology, Work, Gender and Ecology on the U.S.-Mexico Border.* Austin: CMAS Books, University of Texas at Austin.

Pulido, Laura. 1996. *Environmentalism and Economic Justice: Two Chicano Struggles in the Southwest.* Tucson: University of Arizona Press.

The Latino Health Research Agenda for the Twenty-First Century

David E. Hayes-Bautista

INTRODUCTION

Until recently, medical research has been conducted overwhelmingly on non-Hispanic white male populations, with the result that baseline patterns of illnesses, behaviors, knowledge, and attitudes reflected the patterns of that population group. Under the prodding of the Report of the Secretary's Task Force on Black and Minority Health (USHHS 1987), gentle pressure has been exerted on investigators to include women and minorities in study populations. Current research guidelines now require that a principal investigator justify any exclusion of women and minorities from a research sample, and slowly these groups are becoming part of the nation's research focus. However, this prodding has been too little and too late for large states such as California, which have experienced rapid "minority" population growth in the years since the Report of the Secretary's Task Force.

In 1999 the non-Hispanic white population in the state of California became a minority population (49.7 percent), with Latinos making up the next largest group (31.3 percent), followed by Asian/ Pacific Islanders (11.8 percent), African Americans (6.7 percent), and American Indians (0.6 percent).

Among children, the changes are even more impressive. In 1998 nearly half of all the state's newborns (47.5 percent) were Latino, with non-Hispanic whites constituting barely a third (33.9 percent), Asian/ Pacific Islanders 10.7 percent, and African American 6.8 percent of the state's births.

In spite of these dramatic population changes, health and medical research in California is still largely "normed" on the non-Hispanic white population, as it is in the rest of the country. But when theoretical models that explain patterns and variations of illnesses and disease are developed on the basis of non-Hispanic white populations and then applied to Latino populations, the results are confusing, seemingly paradoxical, and of little use in creating policies and programs aimed at the Latino population. In essence, non-Hispanic white metrics have been used to craft health policies and programs in a state in which barely a third of the state's children are non-Hispanic white. This approach is no longer suitable.

The Socioeconomic Status (SES) Model

The socioeconomic status model, which undergirds much thinking on health in general and minority health in particular, is one example of how a non-Hispanic white metric has been used for health policy. This model was developed from analysis of health

From *Latinos: Remaking America* by Marcelo M. Suárez-Orozco & Mariela Páez, editors. Copyright © 2002 by the Regents of the University of California. Reprinted by permission of the University of California Press.

patterns in different economic segments of the non-Hispanic white population. In this population, low socioeconomic status (SES) leads to poor health outcomes, whereas higher SES leads to good health outcomes. In other words, "wealth equals health."

When this model is applied to minority populations, who are generally poorer than non-Hispanic whites, even poorer health outcomes may be predicted. Minority health thus may be characterized as consisting of "health disparities" with indicators consistently worse than those of non-Hispanic whites. Here, for example, is a statement from the National Center for Health Statistics: "This chartbook documents the strong relationship between race, ethnicity and various measures of socioeconomic status: income, poverty status, level of education. . . . Racial and ethnic minorities are disproportionately represented among the poor . . . only the higher socioeconomic groups have achieved the target, while lower socioeconomic groups lag farther behind." (NCHS 1998, pp. 23–25)

So consistently has the association among race, low socioeconomic status and poor health outcomes been assumed that this model serves as the justification for national health policy, such as Healthy People 2010, which sets as its goal to reduce "health disparities among racial and ethnic subgroups of the population." (NCHS 1998, p. 23)

Naturally, the SES model has been applied to Latino populations, often without the support of good data. There is a consistent bias toward assuming that because Latinos are of low SES, their health must show adverse indicators. However, as this chapter will demonstrate, Latinos, nationally as well as in California, do not exhibit these adverse indicators; Latinos exhibit patterns that are not predicted by use of conventional metrics and models. With the growth in the Latino population, this paper argues, the development of Latino-based metrics and models is crucial for the formulating of sound health policies that accurately address Latino health dynamics.

Population Metrics and Modern Medicine

Population-Based Medicine

A major shift in medical research has been away from a nearly exclusive focus on the individual (and the constituent organs and systems) to a focus on larger groups of individuals. As providers become responsible for the care of large, enrolled populations, they need to understand better the patterns of health and disease in the groups for which they are responsible so that they can be prepared to deliver the appropriate levels of care in a timely fashion. It is no longer enough to implement heroic measures after a heart attack. It is now prudent medicine to understand how, when, and why heart attacks occur, and to whom and to work with patients to minimize their occurrence. While expanding the research focus from the individual to the group, it is important to acknowledge that not all groups exhibit the same profiles. Latinos, for example, are sufficiently distinct in health issues from non-Latinos (non-Hispanic whites and African Americans) that their health patterns warrant understanding.

Evidence-Based Medicine

Over the years, medicine has developed a number of protocols for treating specific diseases and conditions. Evidence based medicine requires that treatment protocols be measured against actual results, rather than used on the assumption that if they function in one population of patients, they will function equally well in another. Such protocols were almost never developed on Latino patient populations, although they have been applied to those populations. Do results justify their use?

To answer this question, the Center for the Study of Latino Health Culture of the School of Medicine, UCLA, has been studying the relationship between health and culture, with an eye to improving medical care research and practice. Among its goals are to

- Provide data on the dynamics of Latino health.
- Provide a conceptual model of Latino risk factors so that interventions can be developed.
- Develop educational curricula to train providers.
- Create policy models to better serve the needs of the Latino communities.
- Facilitate improvements in the delivery of services.

This may appear to be an ambitious research agenda. However, the need to manage the health of Latino communities effectively requires no less than this level of effort. Furthermore, as this research is slowly implemented, its findings may well make some key intellectual contributions to the scientific basis for the existence of Latino studies.

STATISTICAL BASIS FOR LATINO METRICS

Large populations make possible the development of the statistical norms (Buttner 1996) on which policy prioritization and program setting are based. With Latinos becoming a large population, it is time now to consider developing Latino norms. Not only are there large Latino populations in many states, but these populations also present a health profile that is not consistent with the current thinking about "race/ethnic disparities" in program and policy development.

A brief overview of the Latino health profile will illustrate

- The need to understand Latino health *sui generis*—as constituting a unique phenomenon in its own right.
- The need for Latino-based norms of diseases and behaviors.
- The need for conceptual models that delineate the relationship between health and culture.

Latino Birth Outcomes

The "unpredictability" of Latino health norms is seen most comprehensively in birth outcomes. When we examine data from the National Center for Health Statistics (1998), extracted from birth certificates, the unusual contours of the Latino-based norms become clear.

Low Education

The Latinas who gave birth in 1996 were far less educated than non-Hispanic white, African American, and Asian/Pacific Islander mothers. Over half of Latina mothers (51.4 percent) had not completed high school at time of giving birth, whereas only 21.6 percent of non-Hispanic white mothers, 28.2 percent of African American mothers, and 15.0 percent of Asian/Pacific Islander mothers had not completed high school. See figure 1. A far lower percentage of Latina mothers were college graduates (6.4 percent) than were non-Hispanic white (23.9 percent), African American (10.0 percent), and Asian/Pacific Islander mothers (36.2 percent).

Low Access to Care

Numerous studies have pointed to the lower percentage of Latinos who have health insurance. This is reflected, in part, in the lower access to first-trimester prenatal care: 72.2 percent of Latina mothers received care in the first trimester of pregnancy, compared to 84.0 percent of non-Hispanic white and 81.2 percent

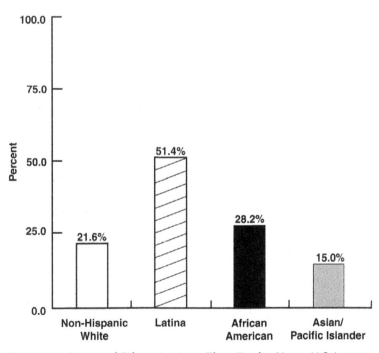

Figure 1. Maternal Education Less Than Twelve Years, U.S.A. 1996

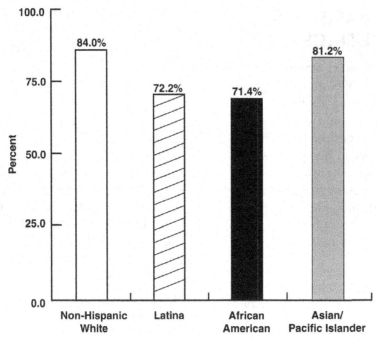

Figure 2. First-Trimester Prenatal Care, U.S.A. 1996

of Asians/Pacific Islanders. Only African American mothers received less first-trimester care (71.4 percent). See figure 2.

Low Income

Income data are not captured on the birth certificate, but data from the 1998 Current Population Survey indicate that Latinas have the highest poverty rates, and the lowest income levels, of all groups. Thus it is indisputable that Latinas giving birth have one of the worst risk-factor profiles: lowest education, lowest income, low access to care.

In the conventional wisdom, this combination of risk factors should lead to adverse birth outcomes—specifically, to a high percent of low birthweight babies and elevated infant mortality. However, the birth outcomes of Latina mothers do not fit this expectation.

Little Low Birthweight. In spite of the risk factors, Latinas give birth to comparatively few low-birthweight babies. Only 6.28 percent of Latino babies born nationally in 1996 were of low birthweight (less than 2,500 grams). This is a lower percentage than that achieved by non-Hispanic white mothers (6.34 percent), African American mothers (13.01 percent) and Asian/Pacific Islander mothers (7.07 percent). See figure 3. This pattern also holds for very-low-birthweight babies (less than 1,500 grams), where Latinas had a

percentage (1.12 percent) less than half that of African Americans (3.02 percent) and only slightly higher than non-Hispanic white (1.08 percent) and Asians/Pacific Islanders (0.99 percent).

Low Infant Mortality. Contrary to expectations, the Latina mothers, in spite of the high risk factors, have relatively low infant mortality. At 7.6 deaths per 1,000 live births, Latina infant mortality is less than half that of African Americans, at 17.1 deaths per 1,000 live births. Non-Hispanic white infant mortality is slightly lower than Latina, at 7.4. However, non-Hispanic white mothers have far more education, higher incomes, and better access to care. Asian/Pacific Islander mothers have the lowest infant mortality at 6.6 deaths per 1,000 live births. See figure 4.

This paradoxical pattern recurs in neonatal mortality (0 to 30 days after birth), where the Latino rate of 4.8 deaths per 1,000 live births is half that of the African American rate of 11.1 and only slightly higher than the non-Hispanic white rate of 4.6 and the Asian/Pacific Islander rate of 3.9. Likewise, in postneonatal mortality (31 to 365 days after birth), the Latino rate of 2.7 is half the African American rate of 6.1, equal to the non-Hispanic white rate of 2.7, and only slightly higher than the Asian/Pacific Islander rate of 2.6 deaths per 1,000 live births.

In birth outcomes alone, the need for Latino-based norms and models is obvious. In spite of the high risk

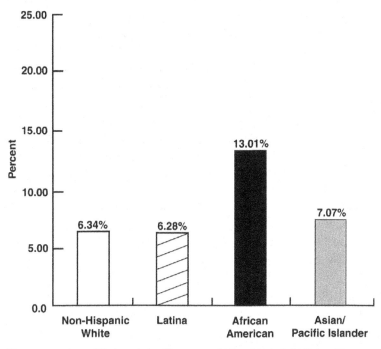

Figure 3. Low Birthweight (Percent of Live Births), U.S.A. 1996

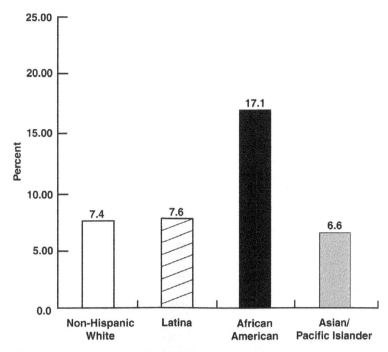

Figure 4. Infant Mortality, U.S.A. 1989–1991

factors, Latina birth outcomes more closely resemble those of the non-Hispanic white and Asian/Pacific Islander populations, which had higher income, more education, and better access to first-trimester care. None of this would be expected from the standard norms and models.

Latino "Epidemiological Paradox" or Latino Norm?

As Latinos become the majority population in many major urban areas, their health profile will become the statistical norm for those areas. If Latino health were no different from non-Hispanic white or African American health, this occurrence would be of little consequence. However, Latino health norms are distinctly at odds with the norms of those two populations.

Indeed, Latino health is so distinctive that it has received its own label: the Latino "epidemiological paradox." The paradox is this: although Latino populations may generally be described as low-income and low-education with little access to care, Latino health outcomes are generally far better than those of non-Hispanic whites. This paradox has been observed in so many Latino populations in so many regions over so many years that its existence cries out to be explained. Yet no currently conceptual models can adequately explain its existence.

With nearly half the child population of California now Latino, the Latino pattern is no longer a "paradox"; it is the norm for most of the children in the state. The question should not be "Why are Latino children doing so well in spite of high risk factors?" but instead "Why are non-Hispanic white children doing so poorly in spite of all their advantages?"

Latino health patterns become more understandable if they are analyzed, not from the perspective of "white versus minority" metrics, but from the perspective of Latino-based metrics. Once Latino-based norms are understood, variations from the Latino norms can be understood, and Latino health can be understood on its own merits.

Latino Mortality Patterns: Diseases and Norms

Mortality data from the National Center for Health Statistics for 1996 (and, occasionally, other aggregated years) provide an illustration of the need for a Latino-based norm (NCHS 1998).

The Latino "epidemiological paradox" can also be seen at the opposite end of the life spectrum, in causes of death. Latino crude death rates are around 80 percent lower than non-Hispanic white rates, but because the Latino population is so much younger than the non-Hispanic white, the age-adjusted rates provide a more meaningful comparison. In order to age-adjust rates, the Latino population is artificially "aged" and the non-Hispanic white population artificially "youthened" so that they have (artificially) the same age structure. This way, the effects of age are removed, and the death rates can be compared on a similar basis.

For all causes of death, the 1994–1996 Latino age-adjusted death rate of 376.1 deaths per 100,000 population is 20.5 percent lower than the non-Hispanic white rate of 473.6 deaths per 100,000 population. The Latino age-adjusted death rate is half (50.4 percent) that of the African American population, whose death rate is 758.7 deaths per 100,000 population. Only the Asian/Pacific Islander population rate of 282.8 deaths per 100,000 population is lower than the Latino rate, and this population has substantially higher income, more education and greater access to care. See figure 5.

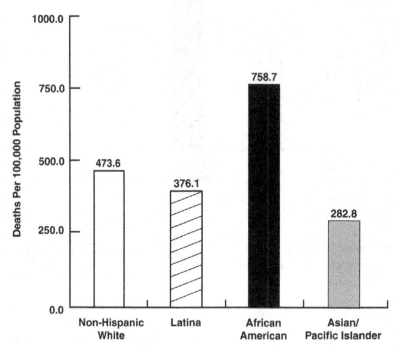

Figure 5. Age-Adjusted Death Rates, U.S.A. 1994–96

In the aggregate, the lower Latino death rate in the face of higher risk factors appears paradoxical. This holds true generally for most causes of death. In fact, of the top eleven causes of death in the United States, Latinos have age-adjusted rates equal to or lower than those of non-Hispanic white for seven, including the top three causes of death: heart disease, cancer, and stroke. Again, given rapid Latino population growth, these patterns in many areas should be considered not a paradox but the new norm.

Latino Death Rates Equal to or Lower Than

Heart Disease

The number-one cause of death in the United States is heart disease. The Latino age-adjusted death rate of 88.6 per 100,000 population is 32.4 percent lower than the non-Hispanic white rate of 131.0 and 53.7 percent lower than the African American rate of 191.5. Only the Asian/Pacific Islander rate of 71.7 is lower than the Latino rate. See figure 6.

Cancer

The number-two cause of death in the United States is cancer. The Latino age-adjusted death rate of 77.8 deaths per 100,000 population is 39 percent lower than the non-Hispanic white rate of 127.6 and 53.6

percent lower than the African American rate of 167.8. The Asian/Pacific Islander rate of 76.3 is slightly below the Latino rate. See figure 6. This lower Latino cancer mortality rate holds for most major sites.

For *lung (respiratory system) cancer*, the Latino rate of 15.4 is less than half the non-Hispanic white rate of 40.2 and is well under half the African American rate of 48.9. It is slightly lower than the Asian/Pacific Islander rate of 17.4. For *breast cancer*, the Latino rate of 12.8 is nearly one-third lower than the non-Hispanic white rate of 20.1 and is half that of the African American rate of 26.5. The Asian/Pacific Islander rate of 8.9 is somewhat lower than the Latino rate. For *prostate cancer*, the Latino rate of 9.9 is about one-third lower than the non-Hispanic white rate of 13.6. The African American rate of 33.8 is three times higher than the Latino rate. For *colorectal cancer*, the Latino rate of 7.3 deaths per 100,000 is lower than the non-Hispanic white rate of 12.1 and the African American rate of 16.8. It is also slightly lower than the Asian/Pacific Islander rate of 7.7.

Stroke

The number-three cause of death in the United States is cerebrovascular diseases. The Latino age-adjusted death rate of 19.5 deaths per 100,000 population is lower than the non-Hispanic white rate of 24.4, the African American rate of 44.2, and the Asian/Pacific Islander rate of 23.9. See figure 6.

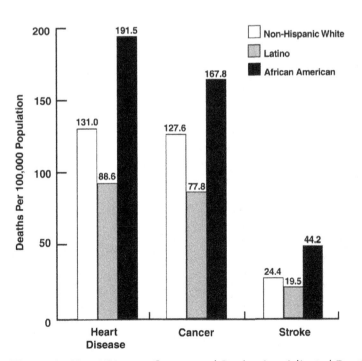

Figure 6. Heart Disease, Cancer, and Stroke, Age-Adjusted Death Rates, U.S.A. 1996

Other Causes of Death

The number-four cause of death in the United States is chronic obstructive pulmonary disease. The Latino age-adjusted death rate of 8.9 per 100,000 population is 59.7 percent lower than the non-Hispanic white rate of 22.1, and is 50 percent lower than the African American rate of 17.8. The Asian/Pacific Islander death rate of 8.6 is slightly below the Latino rate. The Latino age-adjusted death rate of 9.7 for pneumonia and influenza is 20.4 percent lower than the non-Hispanic white rate of 12.2 and is 45.5 percent lower than the African American rate of 17.8. The Latino rate is also slightly lower than the Asian/Pacific Islander rate of 9.9. The Latino death rate for suicide of 6.7 deaths per 100,000 population is 44.2 percent lower than the non-Hispanic white rate of 12.0. The African American rate of 6.6 and the Asian/Pacific Islander rate of 6.0 are slightly lower than the Latino rate.

Motor Vehicle accidents are one cause of death for which the Latino rate of 16.1 is virtually identical to the non-Hispanic white rate of 16.0 and to the African American rate of 16.7. The Asian/Pacific islander rate of 9.5 was lower than the rates for the other three groups.

Higher Latino Death Rates

There are four causes of death for which the Latino rate is higher than the rate for non-Hispanic white rate.

Diabetes

The Latino age-adjusted death rate of 18.8 per 100,000 population is 63.5 percent higher than the non-Hispanic white rate of 11. For some time, diabetes has been de-picted as the "Latino disease." However, the African American rate of 28.8 is 53.2 percent higher than the Latino rate. The Asian/Pacific Islander rate of 8.8 is the lowest of all the groups. See figure 7.

HIV/AIDS

Nationally, the Latino death rate due to HIV/AIDS is 16.3, over twice the non-Hispanic white rate of 6.0. There are sharp regional variations, however, such that in the southwestern states, the Latino death rate due to HIV/AIDS is about half the rate for non-Hispanic whites. The African American death rate of 41.4 deaths per 100,000 population is more than twice the Latino rate. The Asian/Pacific Islander rate of 2.2 is the lowest of all four groups. See figure 7.

Homicide and Legal Intervention

The Latino age-adjusted death rate of 12.4 is over three times the non-Hispanic white death rate of 3.5. This finding is gender-linked, as will be discussed below. The African American rate of 30.6 is two and one-half times higher than the Latino rate. The Asian/Pacific Islander rate of 4.6 is slightly higher than the non-Hispanic white rate. See figure 7.

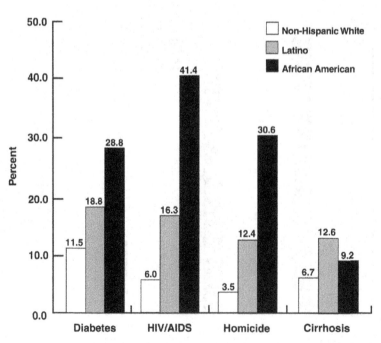

Figure 7. Diabetes, HIV/AIDS, Homicide, and Cirrhosis Age-Adjusted Death Rates, U.S.A. 1996

Chronic Liver Disease and Cirrhosis

This cause of death is the only one for which the Latino rate is simply the highest of all groups. The Latino death rate of 12.6 is nearly twice the non-Hispanic white rate of 6.7 and is 3.4 higher than the African American rate of 9.2. As will be discussed, this is due largely to male drinking patterns. See figure 7.

Illustrations could also be drawn from other data sets tracking other areas of Latino health: the hospital discharge summary, the National Health and Nutrition Evaluation Survey, the Behavioral Risk Factor Surveillance Survey, and similar population-based samples. The need for Latino-based norms is apparent in most large-scale studies; in spite of high risk factors, Latino health generally can be described as quite good.

This observation is so persistent, and so consistent, that it should no longer be viewed as a paradox, or as an interesting exception to a larger pattern. Instead, it should be considered a pattern in its own right—a pattern that is rapidly becoming the norm for large states such as California and Texas.

THE LATINO HEALTH RESEARCH AGENDA: DEVELOPING LATINO METRICS

Identifying and Documenting Latino Norms

For too long, Latino health research has been an afterthought, given attention only after the health of the non-Hispanic white and African American populations were studied. At one point, when Latinos were a small minority, this oversight might have been understandable. However, Latino births currently account for nearly half of all births in California, Texas, Arizona, and New Mexico, and their outcome profile is quickly becoming the "norm" for all births. Yet Latino norms have not been clearly established. Indeed, the fact of the Latino "epidemiological paradox" is still surprising to many health services, researchers, and providers.

The basic epidemiological work of documenting Latino norms needs to occur in a number of areas:

Causes of Death

The preceding data on causes of death give only a glimpse into the uniqueness of Latino norms. These norms need to be tracked backwards for a number of years and established for states, counties, metropolitan areas, cities, and zip codes.

Birth Outcomes

Likewise, the Latino norms in birth outcomes need to be documented for past years and broken down by state, county, metropolitan area, city, and zip code.

Behavior

Latino behavioral patterns in smoking, drinking, drug use, exercise, seat belt use, and the like are not well established. There are contradictory data from a number of small-area studies. Norms for these and related behaviors need to be documented and established.

Access to and Utilization of Health Services

Very few data exist on Latino utilization of health services, including inpatient and outpatient services and physician office visits. Some data are available from the Current Population Survey on insurance coverage, but not enough to support a detailed analysis of patterns of coverage. The private insurance and HMO worlds have very little Latino data, because they have not had any place to indicate Latino ethnicity on their records.

Identifying Variations from Latino Norms

Once the norms for Latino populations are established, the variations from the norms can be identified, and then the risk factors that cause these variations can be sought. Several important variations need to be understood. They include variations that involve gender, geography, and Latino subgroup.

Gender

Generally, females of any ethnic group have a lower death rate than males. Latina females have a death rate that is 46% lower than that of Latino males. See figure 8. However, for specific causes of death, this can vary. Nationally, the Latino male rate for firearm-related deaths is nearly ten times as high as the Latina rate. See figure 9. However, for diabetes among adults in California, the female death rate does not follow the 40 percent lower pattern we would expect but, rather, is virtually identical to the Latino male rate. See figure 9. We need to understand such gender variations.

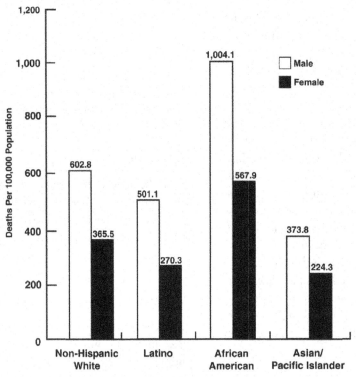

Figure 8. All Causes, Age-Adjusted Death Rates, Male and Female, U.S.A. 1994–96

Geography

In the Southwest, the norm is for Latino mortality to be lower than non-Hispanic white mortality, but this pattern is not observed in New Mexico and Colorado (NCHS 1998). See figure 10. Another variation involves HIV/AIDS. Although nationally, the Latino incidence rate is higher than the non-Hispanic white incidence, there is great regional variation. In fact, in California and Texas, the Latino rate is consistently lower than the non-Hispanic white rate and is nearly one-fifth the rate observed among Latinos in

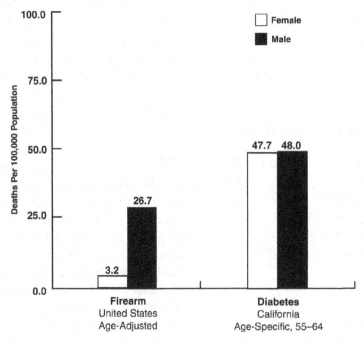

Figure 9. Latino Gender Variations: Homicide and Diabetes, 1996

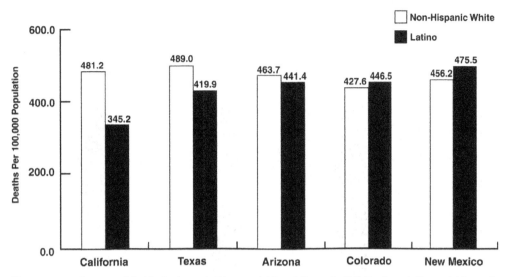

Figure 10. Geographic Variations, Latino and Non-Hispanic White Age-Adjusted Mortality, 1996

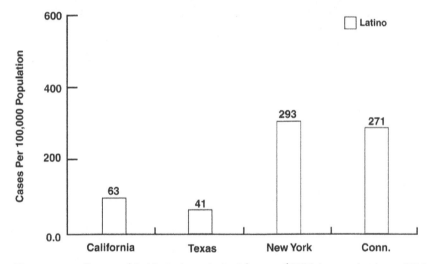

Figure 11. Geographic Variations, in Incidence of HIV Among Latinos, 1993

New York and Connecticut (CDC 1993). See figure 11. Additionally, the major mode of transmission in the Southwest for Latino non-Hispanic whites, and African Americans is male-male sex, with injection drug use being relatively minor, whereas in the Northeast, the major mode of transmission is injection drug use among Latinos, non-Hispanic whites, and African Americans, with male-male sex being relatively minor. See figure 12.

Latino Subgroup

We need to understand the differences between different Latino subgroups. In terms of birth outcomes, when we compare Mexican, Puerto Rican, Cuban, and Central/South American mothers, it is clear that mothers of Mexican origin have far lower educational levels and receive far less first-trimester prenatal care. Yet Mexican-origin Latinas also give birth to the lowest percentage of low-birthweight babies and have infant mortality 30.7 percent lower than that of mothers of Puerto Rican origin (NCHS 1998). See figure 13.

These are but a few examples of intra-Latino variation from Latino norms. Rather than comparing Latino subgroups to non-Hispanic whites or African Americans, it makes more sense to compare Latino populations to overall Latino norms. It has often been assumed that Latinos come in national-origin packages (Mexican, Cuban, etc.), but efforts to identify Latino subgroups may suggest new ways to segment Latino populations that will go further toward explaining the Latino "epidemiological paradox."

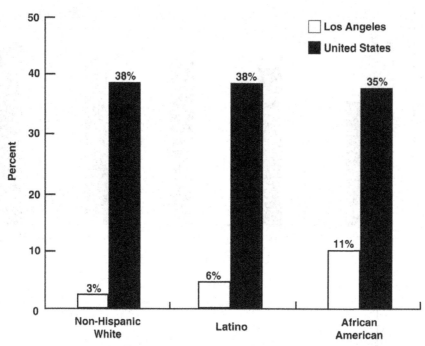

Figure 12. Geographic Variations in HIV Transmission via Intravenous Drug Use, 1996

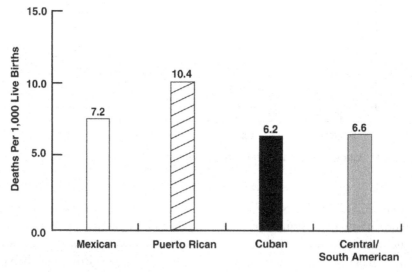

Figure 13. Latino Infant Mortality, U.S.A. 1989–1991

USING LATINO METRICS FOR LATINO POLICIES AND PROGRAMS

Although investigators in health research frequently assume that the socioeconomic status (SES) model is applicable to Latino populations, generally it is not. More Latino-specific models need to be developed that can explain the Latino "epidemiological paradox"

and harness its dynamics for better health outcomes. The relationship between culture and health needs to be understood, conceptualized, and operationalized. It may well be that the current SES-based models are but specific examples of larger, more comprehensive theoretical models that have not yet been developed.

How do Latinos achieve such good health outcomes? What do Latinos have that can be shared with non-Latino populations to reduce their risk of heart disease, cancer, and stroke? It is our hypothesis that Latino culture, in some unknown way, plays a major role in the existence of the Latino "epidemiological paradox."

The study of Latino culture has largely been the province of researchers in history, literature, the arts, and the social sciences. The university resources provided for such study have usually been meager and the research results spotty and tentative—certainly not anything that the health sciences can use to explain the Latino "epidemiological paradox." There is no commonly agreed-upon conceptual construct for Latino culture, although cultural-sensitivity curricula have attempted to reduce it to a dozen or so characteristics applied uniformly to all Latinos everywhere.

Developing Educational Models

Once the basic data have been collected and analyzed to develop the underlying theoretical models, these findings need to be worked into educational curricula, especially those of health providers. The goal of "cultural competency" has often been held as an ideal, but there is very little evidence-based research to indicate exactly what that means in medical practice. Our recent book *Healing Latinos: Realidad y Fantasía: The Art of Cultural Competence in Medicine* (Hayes-Bautista and Chiprut 1999) is an initial attempt to offer guidance to physicians and other health care providers.

In the matter of health, culture matters. In the case of Latino populations, culture's significance can be appreciated in the case of diabetes. Given the higher

Latino death rate for diabetes, this is a priority disease in California and other areas where many Latinos live. In a recent population-based survey of Latino and non-Hispanic white elderly in Los Angeles County, respondents were asked about the reasons for the onset of diabetes in adults. Latinos were as likely as non-Hispanic whites to cite the importance of heredity, diet, and overweight in the onset of diabetes. For Latinos, however, even more important than heredity, diet, and overweight was the role of *susto* (fright) in the onset of diabetes (Hayes-Bautista et al. 2000a). See figure 14.

Developing Policy Models

Health policy at the national, state, and county or municipal level needs to be informed by Latino-specific data and findings. Most health policy today is still based on assumptions about Latino norms and behavior, rather than on actual data. One such common assumption is the "minority health disparity" model, which overlooks the Latino "epidemiological paradox" and its implications for improving the health of non-Latino populations. Another common assumption is that low levels of Latino enrollment in Medicaid and other programs is due to fear of the I.N.S. However, a recent survey by the Field Institute showed that less than 9 percent of Latino respondents reported that they or any member of their family had avoided seeking services because of concerns about their immigration status. See figure 15. Far more important as barriers are the costs of care, lack of insurance coverage, and limited availability of services (California Healthcare Foundation 2000).

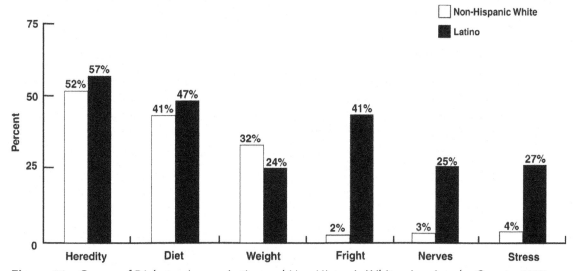

Figure 14. Causes of Diabetes Among Latino and Non-Hispanic Whites, Los Angeles County, 1997

Figure 15. Field Institute: "Avoided getting medical care for selves or someone close because of immigration status concerns." California, 2000

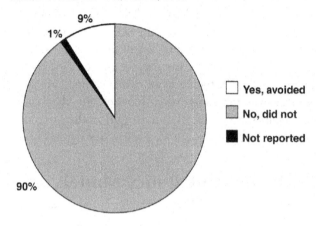

- ☐ Yes, avoided
- ☐ No, did not
- ■ Not reported

Designing the Delivery of Services

The design of delivery systems needs to reflect an understanding of Latino wants, needs, and desires. One major factor cited by Latino patients, especially immigrants, is the need for providers who speak Spanish. Recent work by our Center has confirmed this need. The shortage of Latino physicians, at least in California, is of nearly disastrous proportions. Latinos make up 30.4 percent of the state's population, but only 4.8 percent of California physicians are Latino. To express this another way, in non-Latino California, for every non-Latino physician there are 335 non-Latino Californians. In Latino California, for every Latino physician there are 2,893 Latino Californians (Hayes-Bautista et al. 2000b). This dismal ratio will get worse, in part because of declining first-year Latino matriculations.

CONCLUSIONS

The guiding maxim in health sciences research is that when the science is good, then all else follows. Latino health research is good science that can contribute in many areas: to the increased well-being of our nation's burgeoning Latino population, to the well-being of non-Latinos who can learn from the anomalies in Latino health that defy the dominant socioeconomic explanations of health, and to the scientific and intellectual foundations of Latino studies. Not only must Latinos be researched (and hence identified in records and samples) but research in Latino culture, in all its heterogeneity, must be understood, taught, and valued. Such a course might well lead to a reduction of deaths due to heart disease, cancer, and stroke in the entire population.

Latino studies does not exist just to make Latino undergraduate students feel good. Its findings are needed by all Americans.

References

Buttner, J. 1996. Biological variation and quantification of health: The emergence of the concept of normality. *Clinical Chemistry and Laboratory Medicine*, 36 (1):69–73.

California Healthcare Foundation 2000. *A Political Profile of California Latinos and Their Views on Health Issues in the 2000 Primary Elections*. Oakland: Centers for Disease Control (1993). HIV/AIDS Surveillance Report. May: 5 (1).

Hayes-Bautista, D., E. and R. Chiprut. 1999. Healing Latinos: Realidad y Fantasía: *The Art of Cultural Competence in Medicine*. Los Angeles: Cedars-Sinai Health System.

Hayes-Bautista, D., E. P. Hsu, M. Hayes-Bautista, D. Iniguez, and D. Rose 2000a. *Latino elderly diabetes knowledge, attitudes and behavior in Los Angeles County* (in preparation).

Hayes-Bautista, D., E. P. Hsu, P. Dowling, R. Stein, R. Beltran, and J. Villagomez. 2001b. "Latino physician patterns in California: Sources, locations and projections." *Academic Medicine.* 75(7): 727–736.

National Center for Health Statistics 1998. *Health, United States, 1998, with Socioeconomic Status and Health Chartbook*. U.S. Department of Health and Human Services. DHHS Publication number (PHS) 98-1232.

USHHS 1987. *Report of the Secretary's Task Force on Black and Minority Health*. Washington, DC: USDHHS.

Growing Hispanic Presence, Economic Snapshot

Richard Larsen, Deputy Managing Editor

ADVERTISEMENT

It's all in the numbers—50.5 million Hispanics, a 43 percent population increase in 10 years. One of every six people in the United States is Hispanic. Of the total Hispanic population, 17.2 million are younger than 18. One in four children in the country is Hispanic. Hispanics accounted for more than half the growth in this nation over the last decade.

The findings of the *2010 census* confirm that Hispanics have become a major influence across the nation's economic, social and political fronts. The findings also confirm that a major demographic shift is under way, the same kind of shift other ethnic groups took in the late 19th century and through a good portion of the 20th century. In fact, some people feel it is more than a shift.

In an April 1 interview on NPR, Jorge Ramos, the co-anchor of the nightly newscast "Noticiero Univision," said, "It's truly a demographic revolution . . . and it's already having enormous impact economically and politically."

Janet Murguia, president and CEO of the National Council of La Raza (NCLR), wrote in an April 22 Op-Ed piece for *The Wall Street Journal*, "Every issue that Americans care about – whether *education*, health care,

Social Security or the economy – involves the Latino community."

Increasingly, this demographic revolution comes from a younger, more involved Hispanic population.

"We are tech savvy," Hernan Lopez, president of Fox International Channels, wrote in the March 14 issue of *Advertising Age*. "We spend more time on mobile devices than our non-Hispanic peers. We use *social media* as a means to communicate, express ourselves and create, and we spend more time online than non-Hispanics."

KEY INGREDIENT TO THE ECONOMY

A younger, savvier Hispanic population has much to offer the United States in terms of the economy.

Juan Solana, chief economist for **Hispanic Business** magazine, sees in the increased Hispanic population "the potential for a future of economic growth and financial stability in the United States."

There are several major impacts Hispanics will have.

"A younger and educated labor force can contribute to mend the financial challenges that the U.S. economy will face in the coming decades," Mr. Solana said.

The Hispanic impact will not merely be on the production side, despite Hispanics becoming a growing presence in the U.S. workforce.

"Substantial potential growth lies in consumer markets due to the demographic and professional progress of Hispanics," Mr. Solana said. "Opportunities arise from seizing these emerging domestic markets, but threats come from ignoring them and allowing competitors to gain a stronghold in this segment of increasingly affluent consumers."

The Hispanic purchasing power was put at $1 trillion in 2010 and estimated by HispanTelligence, the research arm of **HispanicBusiness** magazine, to be $1.3 trillion by 2015.

But beyond the marketplace, Hispanics also will be a strong voice in other areas of the economy.

"The current debate about U.S. financial obligations as the baby-boom generation starts to retire would be more dramatic than they already are without this population growth fueled by Hispanics," Mr. Solana said.

Not only will Hispanics be a potent force in driving the material side of the economy, they will help shore up another segment that has shown a decrease over the years.

"In the decades to come," Mr. Solana said, "Hispanics will not only be emerging as a major producing and consuming force but also as a saving and investing force."

And because of Hispanics' outward migration in the United States, the benefits derived from their work, their *entrepreneurship* and their helping run the corporations of America will be more profound.

POPULATION ON THE GO

The outward migration comes as younger Hispanics move out of the states where they have predominantly lived—Arizona, California, Colorado, Florida, Illinois, New Mexico, New Jersey, New York and Texas. In 2000, 81 percent of U.S. Hispanics lived in those states. And while each of these states saw significant growth in their Hispanic population, they accounted for only 76 percent of the total Hispanic population in 2010. Two states alone, California and Texas, accounted for 50 percent of the Hispanic population in 2000. Today, they account for only 46.5 percent.

Of the nine states with the largest Hispanic population, Florida had the largest increase, 57.4 percent. The other eight states had less than 50 percent growth. Thirty-five states had a larger rate of Hispanic growth than the nine largest Hispanic states.

And where are Hispanics migrating to across the nation?

Everywhere. With one exception, the 10 states that had the largest Hispanic population growth are in the South – South Carolina, Alabama, Tennessee, Kentucky, Arkansas, North Carolina, Maryland, Mississippi and Delaware. South Dakota sneaked into the list as the ninth-fastest-growing state. The growth rate of Hispanics ranged from 96.4 percent in Delaware to 147.9 percent in South Carolina. And the nine Southern states alone now account for 5 percent of the entire Hispanic population.

STATEWIDE MIGRATION

But the migration is not just to other states but is occurring within states, as well, as Hispanics move from urban landscapes to the suburbs or to counties where the cost of living is less. In Florida, Texas and California, for example, many counties near major metropolitan areas saw the Hispanic population grow anywhere from 62.6 percent to 175.5 percent.

"The trend of more Hispanics moving to the suburban life . . . is in line with a majority of the Hispanic population that is native-born, English-dominant, middle-class, *entrepreneurial* and integrated into the U.S. society," Mr. Solana said.

In California, two counties showed exceptional growth of more than 25 percent – Kern with an increase of 26.9 percent and Riverside with an increase of 41.7 percent. Hispanic population growth in both counties was explosive. In Kern County, it jumped 62.6 percent, adding 248,612 people. Overall, Kern County only gained 177,986 people, which means without the Hispanics growth, the county would have lost population. Similarly, Riverside County's Hispanic population growth came in at 78.9 percent. Hispanics accounted for 67.6 percent of that county's growth.

In Florida, four counties around the one in which Jacksonville, the state's largest city, is located saw a growth rate of 175.5 percent, adding 178,470 people. That alone accounted for 6.7 percent of the state's growth in 10 years.

In Texas, the counties surrounding two of the state's largest cities—Houston and Dallas—and a 10-county corridor stretching northeast from San Antonio to beyond the state's capital in Austin saw growth of 25 percent or more.

Five counties near Houston, Texas' largest city, saw a combined Hispanic growth rate of 96.4 percent, which accounted for 36 percent of those counties' growth. The six counties surrounding Dallas, the state's third-largest city, had a combined Hispanic growth rate of 85.1 percent, which and made up 36.8 percent of those counties' growth.

And in the 10 counties that stretch northeast from San Antonio, Texas' second-largest city, the Hispanic population grew 64 percent and accounted for 41.7 percent of those counties' growth rate.

LOOKING FORWARD

The 2010 census showed Hispanics not only poised to have major influence throughout the nation, but to have increasing influence for decades to come.

Mark Hugo Lopez, associate director of the Pew *Hispanic Center*, said in a March 24 "PBS News Hour" interview: "One of the things that is striking about this decade for Hispanics is that more population growth among Hispanics has come from native-born births as opposed to new immigration."

NCLR's Ms. Murguia put this into perspective in her Op-Ed piece: "One out of every four children in America is Latino, and 92 percent of those children are U.S. citizens."

"It looks like, if trends continue," Mr. Lopez said, "that we will continue to see native-born births play an important role, and an increasingly important role, in Hispanic population growth through the next few decades."

And native-born births mean the youthfulness of the Hispanic population will continue, providing a strong labor pool, a potent force in the economy, a continuing influence on culture and an increasingly more diverse United States.

Increasing Hispanic Mobility into The Middle Class: An Overview

Harry P. Pachón

The Latino community has all-too-often been misconceived as a monolithic population of low-paid, blue-collar workers, agricultural laborers, and indistinguishable links in the chain holding the service economy in place. Harry P. Pachon, Ph.D., opens our eyes here to the realities of the rapidly growing Latino middle class. With the important ingredient of a heterogeneous immigrant background, challenges are considerable—the need for a better education and more financial security among these—but a successful Latino middle class is essential to the success of America's traditional and historically significant middle-class culture.

Pachon is a professor of public policy at the School of Policy, Planning and Development at the University of Southern California (USC). He also directs the Tomás Rivera Policy Institute and was one of the three cofounders of the NALEO Educational Fund. Pachon has coauthored three books and has over twenty scholarly articles on Hispanics published in the United States.

The United States has a long history of pride in itself as a middle-class society. Essential components of the American ethos include the national drive for an open and free economic system, allowing individual economic advancement, the absence of permanent social status based on heredity, the right of political equality, and the belief that individuals should enjoy the right to provide for their family through hard work and personal capability Some historians trace this cultural tradition back to the American Revolution; other scholars establish its roots in the decades just before the Civil War. Historical origins aside, enshrining this component of the American Dream in people's minds

has helped ensure the nation's political stability and has legitimized the free market system, drawing millions of immigrants to this nation in the past two centuries. It is a phenomenon that shows no sign of abating. Thus, the health and continued growth of the middle class is an important aspect of maintaining American culture. It is well within the capacity of our nation to advance this cultural idea by integrating newcomers, people who are eager to labor and integrate and realize middle-class status. In turn, hard work and belief in this ideal by continuous waves of immigrants will help strengthen and invigorate this country.

Today, Hispanics[1] attempting to realize this dream comprise the largest acknowledged ethnic minority group in the nation. Many in this country assume that the increasing presence of Hispanics is largely due to unauthorized immigration of Latino laborers and their immediate families. This view—whether true or not—is understandable given its prevalence in the media and in the recurring political dialogue on immigration. However, it is even more crucial to recognize and spotlight the fact that Hispanics constitute a rapidly growing segment of America's middle class. Much of this increase is due to the upward economic mobility of Latino legal immigrants. Popular opinion has also not yet acknowledged that Hispanics have made up two of every five *legal* immigrants to the United States for the past four decades. Legal immigration has contributed to long-established—in some cases centuries-old—Hispanic communities in the Southwest, North, and Southeast United States. Undoubtedly, the flow of unauthorized Hispanic immigrants—a group estimated to total more than 10 to 12 million—also augments the population. Interestingly, however, this number also indicates that unauthorized Hispanics actually constitute less than 25 percent of the 50 million Hispanics[2] in the nation. Birth rates overall for Hispanic immigrants—regardless of their legal status—and their children are higher than the simple replacement rate of two children, ensuring increasing numbers of native-born Hispanic U.S. citizens. This amounts to the potential of an expanding U.S. citizen/Hispanic middle class, albeit at a slower growth rate than should be expected in a nation placing so much weight and worth on achieving middle-class status.

This essay takes a step in delineating the major challenges confronted by an Hispanic community attempting to achieve the necessary economic mobility to progress into middle-class ranks. Our focus is on two major policy areas: educational capital and asset development through home ownership. To address these issues requires addressing what it means to be middle class and the characteristics of the Hispanic community that have an impact on its participation in American economy.

THE CURRENT DILEMMA OF AMERICA'S MIDDLE CLASS

Several emerging factors in the American economy complicate Hispanic mobility into U.S. society's middle class. For one, it is broadly acknowledged *that* the American middle class as a whole is facing major challenges in maintaining its traditional socioeconomic position.[3] Globalization of the economy born of substantial political developments coupled with rapidly improving information and communication technologies have delivered on the promise of opening international markets to U.S. businesses. However, market globalization has not been a one-way street. Overseas labor competition in the new world economy has also driven down the pay of American workers. U.S. workers, particularly in the production of physical goods, compete against substantially cheaper yet equally efficient foreign labor.[4] Trade agreements such as NAFTA and CAFTA have apparently exacerbated the trend.[5] This new economic reality has resulted in major industries, from the production of chocolate candies to the manufacturing of computer parts, outsourcing labor to overseas or Western Hemisphere labor sites—with a corresponding loss of these positions in the American labor market.[6] The loss of U.S. jobs that provide the basis of middle-class living has been viewed by some as evolving our nation into a bimodal labor market, in which middle-income positions grow scarce while jobs abound at the two extremes of the labor force: in the service industries with corresponding lower wages and fewer chances of economic mobility, and in the information processing fields, where higher pay eases upward mobility but also requires more education.[7]

Another factor affecting analysis of an ethnic group's middle class is the characterization of the term itself. How do we define the American middle class? There is no widely accepted formula for a status affected both by income and occupation. Although income is the widely accepted determinant, some low-paying occupations still retain middle class status: clergy and public school teachers, for example. For this essay, a simple income measure, such as the Hispanic community's position in median U.S. income range, while it does not suffice in giving a complete picture of the Latino middle class, will serve as a good beginning. Let us assume that middle-class status is delimited by an approximate annual income of $50,000 to $100,000. Although the lower end of this range may seem low, it is a conservative base point reflecting median household income in all American families.

There is a $25,000 gap between white non-Hispanic and Hispanic families. However, separating native from foreign born Hispanics demonstrates a significantly reduced income gap between the former and white non-Hispanics. Higher income growth for this community, however, does not continue unabated. As one scholar points out "The children of immigrants catch up slowly."[8] Alejandro Portes, a noted sociologist, graphically points to the clear potential problem of expanding Hispanic multigenerational poverty.

Briefly stated, he holds that, due to high immigration from Latin American countries with few employment opportunities and given the demand for low-wage labor in the United States—a significant number of second-generation Hispanics (the children of immigrants), raised in resource-poor central cities sites characterized by high crime rates, pandemic drug use, and poor schools are negatively affected in their economic mobility opportunities.[9]

Despite these sobering perspectives, other experts have found reason for optimism, especially for native-born Latinos. As one expert puts it:

> Future analyses need to acknowledge the diversity among Latinos. Relying on statistics that are substantially depressed by the low socioeconomic profile of recent Latino immigrants tend to exaggerate the extent to which native-born Latinos are economically disadvantaged and non-middle class.[10]

Further substantiating this point is that over 20 percent of Hispanics live in households earning more than the median household income of white non-Hispanics overall ($65,180) and a. segment of Hispanic households (9%) also have incomes of over $100,000.

The presence of the Hispanic middle class is a reality in American society, but adopting this perspective does not negate the undeniable issue of Hispanic poverty. The above income figures clearly show a significant income gap between Hispanics with low levels of education—particularly foreign born—and non-Hispanic whites. Other sources show 26 percent of Hispanics have zero net worth and the remaining an average net worth of $16,000, while the average white non-Hispanic household has a net worth of $88,000.[11]

THE COMPLEXITY OF THE HISPANIC COMMUNITY

Affluence cuts across acculturation, language, or life stage. This person could be an industrialist coming in from Argentina and landing his G4 in Miami. Or it could be the guy walking into the bank in paint-splattered overalls who wants to cash a $400 check. Or the guy who owns five body shops, or the woman who string of beauty salons. They may not look or speak like the affluent, but they are. They may not have a college degree or an MBA, but their business needs are the same. They need access to capital.

They need financial advice. They want to preserve and grow their wealth. They want to take care of their kids and provide for their education. They have all the same goals as everyone else, but this audience is not being well-served.[12]

So reads an excerpt from a 2007 report by the Tomás Rivera Policy Institute. Clearly, there is not one homogenous Hispanic community. Having a nuanced view of individuals and recognizing that Latinos occupy low- and middle-income categories in significant numbers more closely reflects the heterogeneous socioeconomic status of the nearly fifty million Hispanics in the United States. Although two-thirds of the community is of Mexican descent, there are significant numbers of Central Americans, Cuban Americans, Puerto Ricans, Dominicans, and other South Americans present in the nation. The heterogeneity of Hispanic origins, particularly the Cuban Americans' distinct encounters with government agencies and separate historical experience coming into the United States, also colors the socioeconomic status of Hispanic subgroups. Simply put, Latinos in small-town west Texas face different challenges to economic mobility than Latinos in Los Angeles or New York City.

Latinos also are differentiated by their length of residence in the United States. There is a tendency to think of Hispanic immigrants as frozen in socioeconomic positions determined by their economic and educational situation at the time of their arrival here.[13] Instead, significant differences in language ability and acculturation, based on length of residence and age of immigration have an impact on an individual's ability to move up the social ladder. Therefore, a Latino who enters this country at the age of four will be significantly more proficient in English after a decade than a Latino who arrives at the age of forty. Length of residence in the United States holds particular significance as a key to understanding the Hispanic community. This factor is compounded by the length of time necessary to achieve authorized status.

The overall age of foreign born Hispanics is another significant variable in understanding the economic position of this community. The average age of a Latino is over thirteen years less than the average age of a non-Hispanic white (27.3 years versus 40.6. This is significant, since most Americans' peak period of financial expenditure is between 40 and 55 years old. It's safe to assume this age range also corresponds to the period of an individual's highest income. Bear in mind that length of authorized status for foreign born

Hispanics also has an impact on an immigrant's potential. As an example, considering both age and length of authorized status, the three million Latinos alone, who gained legal status in the 1990s as a result of the Immigration and Reform Control Act of 1986, whose average age was 29, have not yet realized their full economic, earning potential.

A final factor contributing to the Latino community's heterogeneity is the presence of mixed ethnicities among third-generation Hispanics; in other words the grandchildren of Hispanic immigrants. Out-marriage rates, called exogamy by sociologists, reach 30 to 40 percent in the Hispanic community by the third generation.[14] Exogamy rates illustrate the fact that the integration of Hispanic with larger America is occurring at a most fundamental level: the mixing of blood. Today, and more so in the coming years, many third-generation Hispanic may be distinguished only by surname or be otherwise indistinguishable. In the end, when attempting to explore Hispanic middle-class growth, it is helpful to be aware of wide variations of national origin, personal background, geographic locale, length of U.S. residence, age of immigration, and the presence of non-Hispanic surnames in the household.

If it is in the nation's interest for the public and private sectors to support middle-class growth of Latinos and promote worthy life opportunities for this burgeoning U.S. population, where should the effort begin? Given the variations in this community, is it possible to recommend one-size-fits-all policies to promote and uphold Hispanic movement into the middle class?

Groundbreaking research on promoting economic mobility for low-income groups has been supported by the Ford Foundation and the Russell Sage Foundation through works such as *Assets for the Poor* and *Social Capital and Poor Communities*. Policy briefs and reports by the Demos Foundation also are providing stimulating ideas for policy makers to consider. Since moderate- and low-income Hispanics share many characteristics of other moderate- and low income groups in American society, these works are of particular relevance in understanding general factors affecting Hispanic economic mobility. We will examine selected policy recommendations here, aspects of which have been illuminated in greater depth by policy research carried out by the Tomás Rivera Policy Institute (TRPI) in the past decade and those particularly relevant to Hispanic families. Simply stated, the following issues and recommendations are meant to be components of the overall mobility agenda, complementing it by

fostering growth and economic mobility in the Hispanic community itself.

JOURNEY TO THE MIDDLE CLASS

What steps must be taken for minority households such as Hispanic families to move into the middle-income range? While there are a number of factors affecting income mobility, the acquisition of educational capital is undoubtedly the most common means of such movement. There are, however, other factors present in assisting class mobility such as, for example, engaging in micro-enterprise formation; increasing employment income over time, or leveraging credit through participation in American financial institutions. Each of these factors does not have the widespread and rapid impact provided by increased educational achievement. So that, for instance, the rate and numbers of business formations has to be considered in the context of the high number of failed business formation efforts (regardless of the ethnic background of the entrepreneur); employment mobility linked to higher income is affected by the characteristics of the present U.S. labor market, which requires an advanced level of education for many higher-level salaried positions. Finally, participation in American financial institutions, such as full use of bank/credit union and credit card services, which reduce costs for financial transactions—estimated to be close to 70 percent in savings in comparison to check cashing outlets. Further, allowing credit histories to develop is difficult for many Hispanic immigrants to achieve due to lower levels of education and legalistic barriers.

This latter point is all the more significant if one considers that the development of credit allows for income leveraging and asset development (primarily home purchasing) as well as the potential for wealth creation and transference of such wealth to future generations.

Acquiring educational capital, therefore, is one of the major factors promoting occupational mobility in American society. A well-used statistic indicates that college graduates earn one million dollars more in a lifetime than peers who do not complete a secondary education.[15] Clearly, if higher education levels are required to promote greater mobility in the American economy, then educational preparedness should be one of the highest priorities for Hispanic and other communities. As a starting point, it is important to examine the educational experiences currently afforded Hispanic children. To do this, it will be useful to consider what would constitute an ideal educational system for all children. A goal proposed by TRPI and adopted unanimously by the National Hispanic Conference of State Legislators (NHCSL) is unfortunately not enjoyed in contemporary American society by children of all backgrounds, races and ethnicities. However, imagine an educational system constructed to function in a pro-active, responsive, and seamless way for all children in the United States:

> Specifically, all children tend to be naturally curious, engaged with their environment, motivated, and excited about learning. With suitable early parenting and encouragement, cognitive enrichment, and healthy home and community environments, they will build on this framework in formal school settings, Once there, if they are provided with teachers with high expectations, proven educational tools and materials, challenging and competent instruction, and continuing encouragement by parents and family, they will rapidly acquire the basic skills and concepts of language expression and understanding, math, and science, and then move on to more detailed substantive knowledge in various disciplines and subjects. As they grow in educational attainment and achievement, and stay consistently engaged with schooling, children will expand their competencies and aspirations. They and their parents will become aware of opportunities and challenges beyond K-12, take the necessary steps to become qualified for this next level, and be encouraged and assisted in the process by teachers, counselors, and school leaders. College officials, in turn, will reach out to communities, families, and high school students and make them more aware of the need for opportunities in higher education. Students will aspire to enroll in those colleges and universities that maximize their long-term educational and career potential. While enrolled in college, they will be supported by systems of encouragement and guidance that will maintain them, and steer them to the next levels of education, as desired and appropriate. Those who are enrolled in community colleges will benefit from well-developed, smoothly functioning systems of transition with four-year colleges and universities. In fact, the entire pre-K

to "grade 18" system will work in an integrated manner, in function, if not structure.[16]

A gap exists between the ideal and actual educational prospects of Latino students, as well as an unsettling divide between real opportunities afforded Latino and other minorities and non-Latino students. These educational gaps exist at all grade levels of education in the United States. From pre-kindergarten educational experiences to post-collegiate education, each substantive field has its own challenges and complexities. Not only is it imperative to move toward doing what is right and moral by equalizing educational opportunities for Hispanic children, but the long-term prospects for maintaining the economic vitality of this country are doubtful without encouraging the full economic potential of Latino and other minority youth. In this sense, the "stakeholders" in the educational policy arena go beyond traditional educational advocacy and community based organizations. Leading-edge companies, technology-based industry, and those organizations committed to a robust and participative political economy all are aligned around this issue. In truth, this issue should be of national concern all Americans. There are cross-cutting issues and policy recommendations at play at all levels of the Hispanic educational progress. The two following basic policy recommendations serve as sketches of what should become the components of building educational capital at any level in the Hispanic community.

CULTURE VERSUS COGNITION

The first of these recommendations is that the American educational system to incorporate into its operational practices the understanding that many students hail from households with parents who have low levels of education, limited English proficiency, and experience only with other foreign educational systems, which differ significantly from the U.S. system.

Close to half of all Hispanic adults are foreign born. Basic knowledge of America's educational opportunities must be presented to immigrant parents in their native language and with an awareness of their educational backgrounds. Rather than shifting blame for Hispanic under-education to Latino culture, the system must understand that the lack of information, or cognition, may be a primary factor in Hispanic youth who are not achieving their full educational potential. For example, early childhood education (prekindergarten) does not exist in most Latin American countries, so the benefits of prekindergarten schooling must be explained in a straightforward manner. At the other end of the educational spectrum, preparation for college, the full benefits of a postsecondary education, and college financing must be explained to both parents and Hispanic youth. Studies by TRPI, for example, indicate that large numbers of Latino parents in major metropolitan areas have high aspirations for their children's college education but difficulty understanding the path of college preparedness. Many Latino parents lack understanding about basic components of the U.S. system, such as the difference between a community college and a four-year university, or between a college preparatory and a general secondary education curriculum, or the importance of the Scholastic Aptitude Test. Other TRPI studies indicate that this lack of understanding extends to college financing options, making the already intimidating prospect of paying for college even more daunting.[17]

To this end, standard procedures in immigrant school districts should include but not be limited to:

- Bilingual parental education workshops on resources parents can provide children to enhance college preparedness
- Integration of the value of a collegiate education in middle and high school curriculum
- Teacher training on educating children with limited English ability
- Basic school informational materials offered in the students' native home language
- College financing options explained at early points in secondary school

If education is a key to protecting and improving economic mobility in American society, Latino civic leaders at all levels of government and the nonprofit sector should demand accountability for Latino educational performance from teachers, school administrators, and elected officials. It truly can be said that on the issue of promoting educational opportunity, Latino leaders should remember the famous quote attributed to English statesman Lord Palmerston, "[We] have no permanent friends or allies, [we] only have permanent interests."

BUDGETING FOR EDUCATION: CRUCIAL RESOURCES

Along with a cultural approach to educational progress, it is important to state that even at a time of fiscal retrenchment, education budgets should be among the last considered for reductions by Hispanic civic leaders. State legislators and school board members in states below the national norm in per capita spending on education should become forceful advocates for bringing educational spending up to national levels. This recommendation does not underestimate the challenge and magnitude of the cost. For example, to bring just California, Florida, and Texas to the national average per capita state education spending would require each state to increase their education budget by two billion to three billion per year. Present fiscal circumstances do not bode well in the near term. A long-term strategy, however, should be developed and include a timetable for attaining funding parity. To this end, Blue Ribbon Commissions on alternate funding for state-supported education programs in locations with large Hispanic and other immigrant populations should be established.

LATINO ASSET DEVELOPMENT AND ASSET PROTECTION

The principal asset of the American middle class is home ownership. As one author so aptly says, "Owning one's own home, even if in reality the bank is truly the owner, is fundamental to the . . . American Dream."[18] Widespread, home ownership has increased the assets that American families can draw on to' start a business, pay for college, or fund retirement. Unfortunately, Latino home ownership lags a full twenty points behind white non-Hispanic rates. Granted, the overall rates of home ownership have increased in the past two decades for Latino families, but trailing so far behind remains a significant problem.

If increasing the rate of Latino home ownership is essential to helping more individuals rise into the middle class, then efforts to that end are bound to benefit not only the growing Hispanic community, but also the country as a whole. The first step in attracting more Latinos into home ownership is to concede that the process is more time-intensive and complex than a simple two-step effort.

Buying home is a multistage process in which prospective home buyers must negotiate a various and unfamiliar set of players, from realtors to lending institutions and title and escrow companies. At each stage, the home buyer confronts qualitatively distinct issues, and individuals can face a variety of barriers along the way before closing a deal.

Prospective home buyers of Latino origin encounter different kinds of barriers home ownership depending on their own unique mix of characteristics.

The particular barriers encountered are determined by a set of factors including the information they bring to the home-buying experience. For immigrants who speak little English, it is a daunting task to acquire information on and about the process. Help from others is almost certainly required. This situation would be exacerbated among recent immigrants who are not yet well placed in established community networks.[19]

As a result, there are many potential pitfalls on the way to full information about the various aspects of the home-buying process, including but not limited to:

- Starting the process
- Attempting to qualify for a mortgage, e.g., uninformed or misinformed about eligibility
- Finding a real estate agent or broker
- Finding an appropriate house
- Making offers and negotiating a sale price

While the first step may not be too difficult to launch, consider the second step of qualifying for a loan. According to one bank's CEO:

Home ownership continues to be the preferred and most stable path to the middle class and its ability to build net worth. Under FICO (Fair Isaac Corporation), Latinos do not fare well. FICO scores applicants anywhere from 350 to 850, with 620 and below being the benchmark for an "at risk" applicant. FICO looks at how long the applicant has had credit, the type of credit, the number of applications for credit, the applicant's payment history, and the amount owed in the application. This means that those who live in a cash economy and who are averse to accumulating revolving debt—both traits that are endemic to the Latino culture—are hardly a blip on the FICO radar.[20]

In this complex environment, three out of four Hispanic renters of Mexican heritage report being either somewhat or totally unfamiliar with how to qualify for a mortgage. In contrast, more than half the population studied in another TRPI study—who had either bought a home or were in the final steps of a purchase—reported familiarity with how to qualify for a mortgage. Half of this group was actively engaged in home purchasing activity despite some unfamiliarity with the mortgage qualification process. Therefore, familiarity with how to qualify for a mortgage can influence the transition to home ownership—but only in part.

Unfamiliarity with how to qualify for a loan goes hand in hand with misinformation about other aspects of participation in American financial processes, TRPI research has found that prospective Latino home buyers either have no information or, even worse, misinformation. The following issues are recommended for informational programs in both the public and private sectors to better educate and inform Latino families about the intricacies of home buying.

According to the TRPI study, the majority of Latino home buyers of Mexican origin did not know that banks and other lenders in the United States make mortgage loans to legal permanent residents who are non-U.S. citizens. One half of those planning to buy did not believe it possible, or they were not sure. A full half of respondents who were home owners were not informed about this issue. Although TRPI data do not provide evidence of a direct relationship between misinformation and the potential transition to home ownership, such a high level of misinformation among Latino home buyers certainly indicates a barrier to home ownership. The current situation holds a unique opportunity for analysis and action for the public to get the facts straight.

Poor understanding of the difference between the American financial systems and operations in a Hispanic country of origin also is present in sectors other than real estate. Highlighting the unfamiliarity with American financial issues is the concept of asset protection, or participation in the insurance industry. For example, three out of four Hispanics in California own auto insurance—a state requirement—while less than hall surveyed owned life or home owners insurance. This puts assets at risk as well as not providing income protection for spouses and children. Here again in these figures, the issues of length of residence, age, and generational status demonstrate large variations. Roughly 10 percent of the respondents in this statewide study indicated that insurance was an unnecessary expense."[21] Overall, the current situation points to a unique opportunity for analysis and future action in the public and private sectors.

IN CONCLUSION

Studies regarding public policies that promote economic mobility of Latinos into the middle class should consistently acknowledge and address issues of importance in Hispanic circles. Millions of Hispanics are foreign born with limited English-speaking ability. The need for bilingual services in the public and private sectors whenever programs to assist this community are created is evident. This includes the distribution of bilingual financial, educational, and asset protection information.

Another aspect of the Hispanic community's significant foreign born population demands attention. Foreign born status, in particular at a time of heated immigration rhetoric and anti-immigrant hostility, has far-reaching consequences in the Latino community. The presence of authorized as well as unauthorized immigrants in many Latino households raises the issue of whether household members will seek out financial institutions. Anxiety about jeopardizing legal status for legal permanent residents, individuals under temporary protected status, or individuals undergoing an adjustment of status—let alone unauthorized immigrants—may inhibit full participation in this country's economic and education systems. Public controversy regarding the use of home countries' *"matrícula consular"* by Hispanic immigrants for loan identification is a relevant example.

The Latino middle class is a growing reality in the Hispanic community. The United States has a growing number of American-born Hispanics, and demographics point to a significant population increase of this group in the next decade. Informed public and private sector policies that recognize this country's untapped potential in the faces of Hispanics can dramatically maximize the Latino middle class and reward those who are dedicated and hardworking with the reality of the American Dream, which ultimately will protect and improve the foundation on which America is built.

Trabajando:
Mexican Americans in the
Labor Market

Arturo González

Gerardo "Lalo" Medina was the road manager for Ozomatli, one of the more exciting and innovative music groups, as well as the tour manager for Dilated Peoples and Jurassic 5, both Los Angeles-based underground hip-hop groups. Medina was responsible for the everyday activities of the bands, from ensuring that their hotel reservations were correct to making sure that they made it to the next city on time to set up and prepare for the next show. He said "My job was to ensure the entire tour ran smoothly. This meant dealing with all details, large and small, and handling all the finances on the road. I was Daddy, Mommy, and friend." Medina did not set out to be a road and tour manager when he graduated from college. He graduated with a bachelor's degree from the University of California at Riverside and was an English teacher in Southern California. During this time, he was also involved in various creative activities, including contributions to the political satire group Pocho. Despite the monetary uncertainty of working in the entertainment industry, Medina thinks that the opportunities are worth the risks. The rewards have paid off: he has used his liberal arts education as well as his life experiences to make the bands' various tours successful ones—the bands consistently sell out their shows and leave a trail of happy concert-goers in their wake. Lalo is currently the road manager for the Latino music group The Mars Volta, which benefits enormously from Lalo's experience and managerial acumen.

In order to understand the underlying factors affecting the economic mobility, or lack thereof, of Mexican Americans, it is necessary to understand the labor market position of Mexican Americans, including unemployment, wages, and occupational status. This examination is the final component in the economic profile of Mexican Americans.

Workers provide their time to employers in the production of a service or product in exchange for some compensation, usually in the form of money.

The labor market is comprised of all these elements: workers, employers, and the compensation workers receive for the labor they provide. Economic theory suggests that workers who acquire skills or knowledge are more productive. Furthermore, workers who are highly productive in some measurable way will earn more because they are more valuable to employers.

In this chapter, only the supply side of the labor market is examined; that is, the labor market activity and wages of workers. In addition to providing a general portrait of Mexican American workers, it explains their various labor market outcomes. In keeping with the overall theme, the chapter provides evidence that shows an improvement in the status of Mexican Americans from one generation to the next.

Labor economists measure labor supply in different ways, including labor force participation (LFP, also termed *labor force attachment*) and the number of hours worked during a specific amount of time, such as a week or a year. The amount of income earned by workers is also of considerable interest, and much effort is devoted to understanding why workers earn the amount they do. Therefore, this chapter profiles these different areas of the labor market for Mexican Americans.

LABOR MARKET ACTIVITY

Activity in the labor market can take different forms, including part-time and full-time work, entry into and out of the labor market, search for employment, and the type of occupation workers are employed in. The majority of the working-age population not enrolled in school (that is, individuals sixteen to sixty-four years old) has two options with regard to the labor market: participate or not. Labor force participants are people who have a paying job or are looking for one. Therefore, LFP includes all unemployed people, because an unemployed person is defined as someone without a job but actively looking for one. The definition of LFP excludes workers who do not receive compensation for their labor, such as family members who work in a family business for free or persons who volunteer their time to charitable organizations. Other individuals not participating in the labor force include those who wish not to work and those unable to work, such as persons with a physical disability, for example.

Table 1 presents labor market activity during the first week of March 1999. The four possible outcomes for an individual eligible to be in the labor force are as follows: non-participation in the labor force, full-time work, part-time work, or unemployment. The total number of Mexican American workers is 10.8 million, of which 5.7 million are men and 5.3 million are women.

One of the most revealing aspects of the labor activity of Mexican American workers is the fact that Mexican American men have the highest LFP rates in the country, with 90 percent working or looking for work, compared to 87 and 89 percent of Asian and non-Hispanic white men, respectively.

Full-time work is defined as working thirty-five or more hours per week, and part-time work as working fewer than thirty-five hours a week. Although full-time work is not necessarily the preferred type of

employment, first- and second-generation Mexican American males have the highest percentage of full-time workers in their respective generations of any ethnic group (81.4 and 76.2 percent). Furthermore, third-generation Mexican Americans have the third-highest percentage of full-time workers after non-Hispanic whites and Asians. These LFP rates are consistent with those given in other studies (Borjas 1982; Borjas and Tienda 1985; DeFreitas 1985, 1991).

On the other hand, part-time employment is not a significant source of employment for Mexican American males, as only 6 percent work part time. Although this percentage is the second highest among all working men, it is not out of the ordinary compared to other groups.

In contrast to the high LFP rates of men, Mexican American women have the lowest rates of participation among women, with nearly 40 percent not being in the labor force. This is especially true among immigrant women, more than half of whom are not in the labor force. A much higher percentage of second- and third-generation Mexican American women, more than 70 percent, either work or are looking for work. Therefore, the immigrant experience, or perhaps the culture associated with the immigrant generation, is a significant factor in Mexican American females' decision about whether or not to seek employment (Segura 1992).

Yet, compared to other second- or third-generation women, Mexican American women are still less likely to be labor force participants. These generations of women in most other ethnic groups have LFP rates of around 75 percent. Non-Mexican Hispanic and white women have rates similar to these generations of Mexican American women.

Compared to men, a larger percentage of Mexican American working women have part-time jobs. Table 1 shows that 10 to 14 percent of Mexican American women work part time. Overall, table 1 shows that only white and non-Mexican Hispanic women are more likely to have part-time jobs than Mexican American women, a pattern also reported by Reimers (1992). Combined with the low labor force attachment of Mexican American women, the use of part-time employment suggests a strategic use of the labor market by Mexican American women and families (Segura 1992). That is, it is possible that Mexican American women balance economic issues with domestic and cultural expectations by working only part time. It could also be that Mexican American women have more difficulty finding work, as demonstrated by their

Table 1. Labor Force Activity, by Generation and Gender, March 1999

	MALE				FEMALE			
	First	**Second**	**Third**	**Total**	**First**	**Second**	**Third**	**Total**
MEXICAN AMERICAN								
Not in labor force	7.8%	13.2%	12.8%	10.0%	50.6%	29.1%	27.1%	39.2%
Work full time	81.4%	76.2%	75.3%	78.9%	35.1%	50.7%	53.6%	43.8%
Work part time	6.1%	6.1%	6.4%	6.2%	9.6%	13.9%	14.4%	11.9%
Unemployed	4.7%	4.5%	5.5%	4.9%	4.7%	6.3%	4.9%	5.1%
Total labor force	3,236	833	1,591	5,660	2,637	921	1,704	5,263
(in 1,000s)								
NON-HISPANIC WHITE								
Not in labor force	11.0%	13.9%	10.9%	11.1%	34.2%	27.7%	24.9%	25.4%
Work full time	76.8%	75.7%	80.9%	80.4%	49.4%	51.8%	57.0%	56.5%
Work part time	6.9%	6.8%	5.3%	5.4%	13.7%	18.2%	15.9%	16.0%
Unemployed	5.3%	3.6%	3.0%	3.1%	2.7%	2.2%	2.2%	2.2%
Total labor force	2,235	2,890	50,122	55,247	2,253	2,866	51,212	56,331
(in 1,000s)								
BLACK								
Not in labor force	13.2%	27.4%	22.7%	22.0%	26.1%	25.1%	24.7%	24.8%
Work full time	79.5%	56.9%	64.8%	65.8%	56.8%	54.9%	59.0%	58.8%
Work part time	4.7%	10.9%	5.7%	5.7%	9.4%	13.8%	10.6%	10.6%
Unemployed	2.6%	4.8%	6.8%	6.5%	7.8%	6.2%	5.7%	5.8%
Total labor force	674	134	7,581	8,389	644	148	9,419	10,212
(in 1,000s)								
OTHER HISPANIC								
Not in labor force	10.5%	13.7%	17.4%	12.1%	35.7%	18.7%	29.0%	32.7%
Work full time	79.4%	69.2%	72.1%	76.8%	47.5%	63.5%	54.1%	50.3%
Work part time	5.2%	9.0%	5.7%	5.8%	13.1%	13.7%	13.6%	13.3%
Unemployed	4.9%	8.2%	4.8%	5.3%	3.7%	4.2%	3.2%	3.6%
Total labor force	1,612	300	383	2,295	1,877	283	429	2,589
(in 1,000s)								
ASIAN								
Not in labor force	13.4%	11.1%	11.6%	13.0%	33.6%	26.2%	21.7%	31.8%
Work full time	78.2%	72.3%	77.0%	77.6%	52.4%	57.9%	63.4%	54.0%
Work part time	5.9%	11.3%	7.3%	6.5%	11.7%	13.3%	11.4%	11.8%
Unemployed	2.5%	5.4%	4.1%	2.9%	2.3%	2.5%	3.5%	2.4%
Total labor force	2,254	220	325	2,799	2,565	236	330	3,130
(in 1,000s)								

Source: Author's weighted tabulations from the March 1999 Current Population Survey.

Notes: Includes persons age sixteen to sixty-four and not attending school, living in group quarters, or serving in the armed forces.

Table 2. Average Number of Weeks Spent Looking for Work in 1998

	MALE				FEMALE			
	First	Second	Third	Total	First	Second	Third	Total
Mexican American	8.6	7.7	8.6	8.5	6.3	7.3	7.5	6.9
Non-Hispanic white	5.7	6.4	7.4	7.3	4.3	3.8	4.2	4.2
Black	15.4	16.6	11.3	11.7	4.2	6.0	8.5	8.3
Other Hispanic	8.6	5.8	8.5	8.5	7.2	4.3	4.0	6.6
Asian	5.9	7.2	10.1	7.2	3.1	10.2	4.8	4.0

Source: Author's weighted tabulations from the March 1999 Current Population Survey.

Notes: Includes persons age sixteen to sixty-four and not attending school, living in group quarters, or serving in the armed forces. Includes those who worked for part of 1998 as well as those who did not work but looked for work.

high unemployment rate and by the greater number of weeks it takes them to find a job (see table 2).

Unfortunately, one reason why Mexican Americans have a strong labor force attachment is their high unemployment rate. Table 1 shows that Mexican Americans have unemployment rates between 5 and 6 percent, whereas whites and Asians have rates ranging from 2 to 5 percent. Only blacks have higher unemployment rates (6 percent or higher), and other Hispanics have somewhat comparable rates. High levels of unemployment may result from difficulty in finding a new job after losing one or from a higher frequency of job loss. DeFreitas (1985) finds evidence that the problem of unemployment lies in the duration, rather than the frequency, of unemployment: the unemployment rate for Mexican Americans is affected nearly twice as much by an inability to find a job than by the loss of a job. Table 2 supports this finding and shows that, on average, Mexican Americans spend more weeks than non-Hispanic whites looking for a job, although not as many as black workers do. Nevertheless, the 1.2 extra weeks spent by all Mexican American males and the 2.7 extra weeks spent by Mexican American females means that, relative to whites, Mexican Americans who lose their jobs are going to be unemployed for a longer time.

EMPLOYMENT PATTERNS

Contrary to the stereotype of the "lazy Mexican" (Monroy 1999), Mexican Americans have a very strong work ethic as shown by their labor force activity. Table 3 provides further evidence that the work ethic and labor force attachment of Mexican Americans are higher than

or at least comparable to those of other ethnic groups. Among the employed, the number of weeks worked during the year and the number of hours worked per week are indicative of how much workers work. Table 3 shows that, on average, Mexican American men work the second fewest number of weeks and hours per week of all ethnic groups (less than forty-eight weeks and forty-two hours per week), but the number of hours worked per week is only 0.7 hours less than the average for the other groups. Likewise Mexican American women work the fewest number of weeks of any group of women but work a similar number of hours per week. Thus, although a high percentage of Mexican Americans work, their longer unemployment spells reduce the number of weeks and hours they are able to work.

The ability to find and maintain a full-time job, defined as thirty-five or more hours per week year-round, is also an indicator of success and stability in the labor market. Although many individuals choose not to work full time, most workers are seeking full-time work. Table 4 examines the percentage of workers aged sixteen to sixty-four who worked full time. Among men, Mexican Americans have the second lowest percentage of year-round, full-time workers, barely ahead of blacks. In all, 71.9 percent of all Mexican American men were working full time, compared to 76.2 percent of non-Hispanic white men.

First-generation Mexican American males are the least likely immigrant group to work full-time year-round. This low percentage most likely is the result of low education and employment in occupations that are seasonal in nature. The second generation has an even lower percentage of full-time, year-round workers (67.4 percent), but this percentage is the

Table 3. Average Number of Weeks and Hours per Week Worked in 1998, by Generation

	MALE				FEMALE			
	First	Second	Third	Total	First	Second	Third	Total
MEXICAN AMERICAN								
Weeks	47.6	47.8	47.4	47.6	42.4	43.6	44.7	43.5
Hours per week	41.5	42.0	41.7	41.6	37.3	37.7	36.9	37.3
NON-HISPANIC WHITE								
Weeks	48.8	48.8	49.1	49.0	46.4	46.4	46.2	46.2
Hours per week	44.9	43.9	44.2	44.2	37.7	36.8	37.4	37.4
BLACK								
Weeks	48.2	47.0	46.9	46.9	46.8	42.1	45.5	45.5
Hours per week	41.8	41.3	41.3	41.4	39.4	36.7	37.8	37.9
OTHER HISPANIC								
Weeks	48.7	48.7	48.7	48.6	45.7	46.7	47.3	45.8
Hours per week	42.5	41.8	42.0	42.2	37.6	39.2	37.8	37.8
ASIAN								
Weeks	49.2	47.0	48.0	48.7	45.9	43.2	46.0	45.6
Hours per week	42.5	39.2	43.1	42.2	39.0	37.9	39.1	38.9

Source: Author's weighted tabulations from the March 1999 Current Population Survey.

Notes: Includes persons age sixteen to sixty-four who are not attending school, living in group quarters, or serving in the armed forces.

Table 4. Percentage of Full-Time, Year-Round Workers in 1998, by Generation

	MALE				FEMALE			
	First	Second	Third	Total	First	Second	Third	Total
Mexican American	73.4%	67.4%	71.3%	71.9%	51.8%	49.9%	57.4%	53.6%
Non-Hispanic white	76.4%	75.7%	76.2%	76.2%	61.5%	54.7%	56.6%	56.7%
Black	77.4%	63.2%	70.5%	71.0%	70.2%	48.0%	61.7%	62.0%
Other Hispanic	77.7%	66.3%	74.0%	75.5%	60.6%	59.2%	59.8%	60.3%
Asian	78.3%	56.5%	70.0%	75.0%	60.5%	38.3%	62.5%	58.1%

Source: Author's weighted tabulations from the March 1999 Current Population Survey.

Notes: Includes persons age sixteen to sixty-four who worked in 1998 and were not attending school or living in group quarters. Full-time, year-round work is at least fifty weeks and more than thirty-five hours per week.

second highest among all second-generation male workers. Similarly, the percentage of full-time, year-round workers is lower for third-generation males than Mexican immigrants, but relative to other third-generation workers, Mexican American males have the third highest percentage of full-time work. Thus, among all ethnic groups, immigrant males are more commonly full-time, year-round workers than are either second- or third-generation workers.

Mexican American women, on the other hand, are generally the least likely of all women to work full-time year-round. Fewer than 54 percent work most of the year, whereas 57 to 62 percent of women of other ethnicities do so. Unlike Mexican American men, third-generation women are the most likely generation to be full-time, year-round workers.

The fact that many Mexican Americans did not work full time may be due either to an inability to find full-time work or to a preference for part-time work. Table 5 tabulates the reasons why Mexican Americans held part-time jobs in 1998. The major reason was slack work conditions, that is a reduction in work hours due to slow business. More than 50 percent of all part-time workers found themselves with part-time work because of this situation, and the second most common reason for part-time work was some unspecified reason. With the exception of the first generation, more part-time workers desired part-time work than were forced to accept it for lack of full-time employment. Nevertheless, the majority of those who work part time do so for reasons outside of their control.

Preference for part-time work grows with each generation. Among male immigrants, for example, the preference for part-time work is the lowest (2 percent) of all Mexican Americans (about 9 percent). The

difference is most striking among women, however. Only about 6 percent of the first generation desired part-time work, but 18 and 27 percent of the second and third generations, respectively, sought such work. These outcomes may result in lower wages among third-generation workers.

OCCUPATIONAL PATTERNS

The type of job an individual holds determines not only the wages he or she earns, but also long-term job stability and prospects for economic mobility. At the same time, however, a person's job type is an outcome of the interplay of human capital variables, job search and job matching, social networks, and in certain cases, timing. Human capital variables include education and training, language ability, and other traits that enhance a worker's productivity. The search for a new job entails not only actively job hunting, but also using various technologies effectively to find the appropriate job. The search may be conducted by visiting employment agencies, phoning prospective employers, or "hitting the streets." The job search is successful if the employer and employee are matched in terms of qualifications and job requirements. Only when the job is agreeable to both parties is a job offered and accepted. Many workers learn about jobs through informal means, such as when a current worker either passes along information about job vacancies to friends or relatives, or recommends friends and relatives to fill a position. The importance of some of these variables is discussed in greater detail later in the chapter.

Table 6 presents the distribution of each generation of workers in all ethnic groups across seven broadly

Table 5. Reasons for Working Part Time in 1998, by Generation

	MALE				FEMALE			
	First	Second	Third	Total	First	Second	Third	Total
Could find only part-time work	11.9%	3.8%	5.9%	9.8%	7.9%	11.9%	7.4%	8.6%
Wanted part-time work	2.0%	8.6%	9.2%	4.2%	5.5%	18.0%	26.8%	14.2%
Slack work	58.2%	62.1%	55.0%	57.9%	63.1%	52.3%	37.1%	53.4%
Other reason	27.9%	25.6%	29.9%	28.1%	23.6%	17.7%	28.7%	23.9%

Source: Author's weighted tabulations from the March 1999 Current Population Survey.

Note: Includes Mexican Americans age sixteen to sixty-four who worked part time and were not attending school or living in group quarters.

Table 6. Distribution of Occupation Type, by Generation and Gender in 1998

	MALE				FEMALE			
	First	**Second**	**Third**	**Total**	**First**	**Second**	**Third**	**Total**
PROFESSIONAL, MANAGERIAL, AND SPECIALIZED OCCUPATIONS								
Mexican American	4.1%	13.4%	14.3%	8.2%	6.2%	17.4%	22.5%	14.7%
Non-Hispanic white	42.7%	41.8%	31.0%	32.0%	36.1%	40.0%	35.6%	35.9%
Black	21.6%	20.1%	15.2%	15.9%	27.5%	45.5%	23.4%	24.0%
Other Hispanic	14.2%	32.5%	24.0%	18.0%	14.9%	33.5%	30.3%	19.9%
Asian	39.1%	30.8%	39.3%	38.5%	36.0%	45.3%	47.4%	38.1%
TECHNICAL, SALES, AND ADMINISTRATIVE SUPPORT								
Mexican American	6.4%	19.2%	17.3%	11.2%	19.5%	48.4%	42.0%	33.9%
Non-Hispanic white	16.8%	20.0%	19.7%	19.6%	31.9%	41.7%	40.9%	40.6%
Black	14.7%	34.0%	18.3%	18.2%	25.3%	32.4%	36.9%	36.2%
Other Hispanic	16.9%	34.0%	24.9%	20.2%	32.2%	47.5%	41.1%	35.7%
Asian	22.8%	30.2%	20.4%	23.2%	30.2%	43.2%	35.7%	31.9%
SERVICE								
Mexican American	16.3%	12.2%	12.5%	14.7%	34.5%	20.5%	24.9%	28.0%
Non-Hispanic white	9.5%	6.9%	7.2%	7.3%	20.1%	11.4%	14.1%	14.2%
Black	20.1%	13.7%	16.0%	16.4%	39.5%	16.0%	27.0%	27.6%
Other Hispanic	16.9%	11.5%	12.9%	15.6%	35.6%	11.6%	19.4%	29.8%
Asian	9.3%	16.3%	8.3%	9.8%	16.1%	9.9%	10.8%	15.0%
FARMING, FORESTRY, AND FISHING								
Mexican American	17.4%	6.2%	5.6%	12.6%	9.4%	2.7%	1.0%	4.8%
Non-Hispanic white	1.4%	2.1%	3.2%	3.1%	1.1%	0.5%	1.0%	1.0%
Black	2.7%	0.0%	2.7%	2.6%	0.8%	0.0%	0.2%	0.2%
Other Hispanic	4.0%	0.0%	1.4%	3.1%	0.6%	0.2%	0.2%	0.5%
Asian	1.0%	4.0%	2.9%	1.5%	0.4%	0.0%	1.7%	0.5%
PRECISION PRODUCTION, CRAFT, AND REPAIR								
Mexican American	23.5%	20.8%	22.0%	22.7%	4.3%	1.5%	1.9%	2.8%
Non-Hispanic white	16.1%	17.8%	21.1%	20.7%	2.4%	1.7%	2.1%	2.1%
Black	15.3%	9.7%	14.9%	14.9%	0.6%	2.1%	2.4%	2.3%
Other Hispanic	19.4%	7.7%	18.8%	17.9%	3.1%	1.6%	2.4%	2.8%
Asian	11.3%	7.3%	20.3%	12.0%	3.6%	0.0%	2.0%	3.1%
OPERATOR, FABRICATOR, AND LABORER								
Mexican American	32.3%	28.2%	28.3%	30.6%	26.1%	9.5%	7.7%	15.7%
Non-Hispanic white	13.5%	11.4%	17.9%	17.4%	8.4%	4.7%	6.2%	6.2%
Black	25.6%	22.5%	32.9%	32.1%	6.4%	4.0%	10.1%	9.8%
Other Hispanic	28.7%	14.3%	18.0%	25.2%	13.6%	5.5%	6.5%	11.4%
Asian	16.4%	11.5%	8.8%	15.1%	13.7%	1.7%	2.4%	11.3%

Source: Author's weighted tabulations from the March 1999 Current Population Survey.

Notes: Includes persons age sixteen to sixty-four who are not attending school and who worked in 1998. Occupation is for the job held longest in 1998. Excludes those who were unemployed or previously in the armed forces.

defined occupation types. Generally speaking, Mexican American males are concentrated in the blue-collar, labor-intensive occupations and are less visible in the white-collar, professional occupations. For example, 28 percent of second-generation Mexican Americans are operators, fabricators, or laborers, whereas only 13 percent work in professional or managerial occupations. On the other hand, the opposite is true of non-Hispanic whites and Asians—they are heavily concentrated in professional occupations.

Whereas table 6 contains a wealth of information for interethnic comparisons, figures 1 and 2 condense this information for Mexican American men and women, respectively. There are more Mexican American men in operator, fabricator, and laborer occupations (such as drilling and boring-machine operators) than in any other type of occupation, with about 30 percent of each generation of men employed in this sector. More than 20 percent of all Mexican American men work in precision production, craft, and repair occupations (such as cabinet making), making this the second most common type of occupation.

Mexican American men are least likely to work in farming, fishing, and forestry occupations. Although 17.4 percent of immigrants perform this type of labor, less than 7 percent of second- and third-generation Mexican American men do. The low percentage of Mexican American men (and women) in agriculture-related fields contradicts the stereotype of the Mexican worker as a fruit and vegetable picker.

Technical, sales, and administrative support occupations also represent another significant source of employment for Mexican American men, particularly in the second and third generations (19.2 and 17.3 percent, respectively); note that the level for immigrants is much lower, at 6.4 percent. Similarly, professional and managerial occupations account for 13 to 14 percent of second- and third-generation Mexican American male workers, but only 4.1 percent of Mexican immigrants. Lastly, significant percentages of Mexican American men also work in service occupations, with a range from 12 to 16 percent across all generations.

Figure 1 shows that there is a movement away from labor-intensive jobs and into white-collar and technical jobs from the first to the second and third generations. For example, the percentage of workers in operator, fabricator, and laborer occupations decreases from 32 to 28 percent between the first and third generations. Similarly, the percentage of workers in professional occupations rises from 4 to 14 percent from the first to third generations. Most of the movement into more prestigious occupations occurs between the first and second generations, although there continues to be an increase into the third generation. These movements are probably associated with the educational levels of each generation.

Figure 2 illustrates that Mexican American women are not as evenly distributed across occupations as men are. More than 40 percent of second- and third-generation Mexican American women work in technically oriented occupations. Another prominent occupation type for these generations is professional and managerial occupations: between 17 and 23 percent work in these types of jobs. Mexican American women

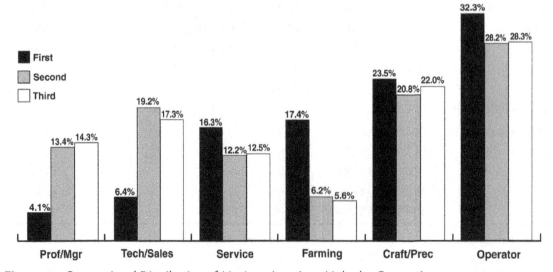

Figure 1. Occupational Distribution of Mexican American Males by Generation.

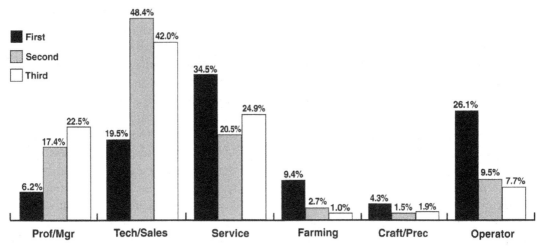

Figure 2. Occupational Distribution of Mexican American Females by Generation. Plot from data in table 18.

are also likely to be employed in service-related occupations (ranging from 21 to 35 percent). Mexican immigrant women are especially likely to be employed in service occupations. Mexican American immigrant women also differ from later generations in that a significant percentage (26 percent) are employed in operator occupations, compared to less than 10 percent for the second and third generations.

Figure 2 also illustrates a shift in occupational composition across generations of women. The movement out of blue-collar and into white-collar occupations is more pronounced among Mexican American women than among men. For example, less than 3 percent of second- and third-generation Mexican American women work in agriculture-related occupations, as opposed to nearly 10 percent of immigrant women, and the percentage of professionals and

managers increases from 6 to 23 percent between the first and third generations.

ANNUAL INCOME

The desirability of a job is often highly correlated with its wages. A person's income is generally dependent on education, training, work experience, and other worker attributes that enhance productivity. Although the information in table 7 does not adjust fir differences in these human capital characteristics, the mean annual wage information is nonetheless useful.

With a few exceptions, Mexican Americans' annual income is the lowest of all ethnic groups, ranging from roughly $19,400 to $30,000 for men and $13,000 to $18,600 for women. The annual income of Mexican American men ranges from about 50 to 100 percent

Table 7. Average Annual Salaries in 1998, by Generation

	MALE				FEMALE			
	First	Second	Third	Total	First	Second	Third	Total
Mexican American	$19,366	$29,965	$28,071	$23,276	$12,910	$18,299	$18,585	$16,194
Non-Hispanic white	$46,297	$51,306	$41,799	$42,441	$29,074	$27,961	$25,121	$25,389
Black	$27,178	$29,935	$27,081	$27,131	$20,927	$25,285	$21,127	$21,173
Other Hispanic	$27,564	$37,658	$32,672	$29,660	$17,849	$25,714	$25,299	$20,125
Asian	$41,410	$31,589	$41,318	$40,502	$25,917	$26,809	$31,098	$26,655

Source: Author's tabulations from the March 1999 Current Population Survey.

Notes: Includes persons age sixteen to sixty-four who are not attending school and who worked in 1998. Excludes persons who were self-employed, worked without pay, or lived in group quarters. Wages and salaries are top-coded by the CPS.

lower than the income of non-Hispanic white men, and the income of Mexican American women is 35 to 125 percent lower than that of white women.

Table 7 shows improvement in annual income for second- and third-generation Mexican Americans. The second generation earns an average of 35 percent more, and the third earns 31 percent more, than the first generation. The decline in income from the second to the third generation is unexpected. Comparing 1998 income to 1997 income (found in the March 1998 CPS) reveals an interesting outcome. Whereas the incomes of first- and third-generation Mexican Americans were comparable between 1997 and 1998, for unknown reasons the income of second-generation Mexican Americans grew substantially; the mean income of the second generation was $24,871 in 1997 but $29,965 in 1998, an increase of 20 percent.

WAGES, HUMAN CAPITAL, AND DISCRIMINATION

Why do Mexican Americans have lower incomes than other groups, especially non-Hispanic whites and Asians? Several possible explanations include discrimination, structural changes in the labor market, such as the loss of high-paying manufacturing jobs overseas,

less familiarity with U.S. labor markets among immigrants, lower education levels, less work experience, and other productive characteristics.

Table 8 shows several demographic differences between Mexican-origin and non-Mexican-origin populations in education, work experience, union membership, and English ability. Comparing Mexican Americans to non-Hispanic whites, it is clear that Mexican Americans average less education and less experience, and are less likely to belong to a union or speak English very well. For example, third-generation Mexican American men average 12 years of education, 18 years of work experience, 3 percent union membership, and 91 percent speak English very well. In contrast, third-generation non-Hispanic whites average 14 years of schooling, 20 years of work experience, 4.1 percent union membership, and 100 percent speak English very well. Therefore, it is not unreasonable to expect that these differences would account, at least to some extent, for the lower relative incomes of Mexican Americans.

Table 9 examines the effect of various demographic characteristics on the hourly wages of Mexican Americans and non-Mexican Americans. The Average Log Hourly Wage section gives the mean of the logarithm of hourly wage, the common economic measure of wages, and the Adjusted Log

---

Topic Highlight: Opportunities in Real Estate

Humberto López is a developer who survived the real-estate crash of the late 1980s. López is back on top as one of the most prominent dealmakers and real-estate holders in Tucson, Arizona. He owns and manages four hotels totaling 800 rooms, owns and manages about 2,600 apartment units in twelve complexes, and is managing partner of 1,000 apartments in Phoenix, Yuma, and Dallas. Among his other holdings are two California land-development deals (a 420-home development in San Marcos and a 240-home development in Carlsbad), 40 percent ownership of TransAmerica, a mail-order company in Cleveland with $65 million in sales last year, and a 50 percent interest in the Dorado Country Club in Tucson.

Born in Nogales, Arizona, in 1946, López was raised across the border in Ciudad Obregón, Sonora, until he was twelve, when his father died without a will. The family went from middle class to poor because most of its wealth was lost to lawyers and the Mexican government during probate. His mother moved the family of six back to her native Nogales, Arizona, where López began working, selling newspapers and doing yard work. Throughout high school, he worked forty hours a week at a grocery store, bagging and making deliveries. "We did pretty well in Mexico," he recalled. "But when we came back to the States, our lifestyle changed."

Despite being advised by his high-school counselor to pursue a vocational course, he went to Cochise College with friends. "My

counselor didn't think I was capable of going to college and recommended vocational school," López explained. "Several of us who had him as counselor and didn't want to go to vocational school ended up at Cochise, which was new at the time." At Cochise, he took some business courses. He seemed to learn accounting most easily, so he stuck with it and transferred to the University of Arizona. Immediately after graduation, he left Tucson and took an accounting job at Deloitte, Haskins, and Sells in Los Angeles. "When I graduated from the [University of Arizona], I didn't interview in Tucson or Phoenix," he recalled. "I wanted the biggest business with the most exposure. That's because I wanted to find the business for me." As a certified public accountant, he began requesting real-estate accounts and eventually started getting into the field himself. His first deal involved borrowing $1,000 from an uncle to buy a $3,000 lot. He later sold it for $7,000. Thus began his career in real estate.

Throughout his career, López has found time for civic activities. He has helped not-for-profit organizations raise money and is chairman of the board of advisers for the University Heart Center in Tucson. He was also named Man of the Year by City of Hope and Father of the Year by the Juvenile Diabetes Foundation in Tucson. "I like to give back because the community has been good to me," he said. "I like to give not just money, but my time." (From Higuera 1998).

Table 8. Selected Worker Characteristics, by Generation and Gender

	MALE				FEMALE			
	First	Second	Third	Total	First	Second	Third	Total
MEXICAN AMERICAN								
Schooling (years)	9.1	12.1	12.1	10.4	9.2	12.3	12.4	11.1
Work experience (years)	19.3	16.1	17.5	18.4	20.9	15.8	17.9	18.7
Union membership	1.1%	1.7%	2.7%	1.7%	0.5%	2.1%	1.4%	1.2%
Speaks English very well	18.4%	85.7%	90.6%	57.7%	—	—	—	—
NON-HISPANIC WHITE								
Schooling (years)	14.1	14.3	13.6	13.6	13.8	13.9	13.6	13.6
Work experience (years)	20.3	21.4	20.0	20.1	22.4	22.0	20.2	20.4
Union membership	2.4%	4.2%	4.1%	4.0%	2.7%	3.4%	2.8%	2.8%
Speaks English very well	75.7%	99.5%	99.9%	99.2%	—	—	—	—
BLACK								
Schooling (years)	12.6	13.7	12.7	12.7	12.8	14.2	13.0	13.0
Work experience (years)	19.8	14.7	19.0	19.0	19.4	13.0	18.9	18.8
Union membership	6.8%	0.0%	4.7%	4.9%	4.6%	6.3%	2.9%	3.1%
Speaks English very well	—	—	99.8%	—	—	—	—	—
OTHER HISPANIC								
Schooling (years)	11.4	13.6	12.7	11.9	11.9	14.1	13.0	12.3
Work experience (years)	20.6	11.2	17.3	18.9	21.3	11.2	18.9	19.6
Union membership	1.3%	2.5%	2.8%	1.7%	1.4%	1.9%	1.4%	1.5%
ASIAN								
Schooling (years)	14.3	14.0	14.3	14.3	13.9	14.7	14.4	14.1
Work experience (years)	18.4	9.4	19.1	17.7	19.8	10.8	18.1	18.8
Union membership	2.7%	2.4%	3.2%	2.7%	2.5%	0.0%	6.3%	2.8%

Sources: English proficiency data are from Trejo (1997), based on the November 1989 Current Population Survey; all other data are author's weighted tabulations from the March 1999 CPS.

Notes: Includes persons age sixteen to sixty-four who are not attending school and who worked in 1998. Excludes persons who were self-employed or worked without pay. Sample weights are used.

Hourly Wage section gives the log of hourly wage adjusted for demographic differences between non-Mexican-origin second-generation workers and all other workers. The bottom rows give the wage deficit of Mexican Americans after demographic differences between them and second-generation non-Mexican-origin workers are eliminated. Given that the average log hourly wage of non-Mexican American second-generation workers is 2.82, and second-generation Mexican Americans have a corresponding log hourly

Table 9. Average and Adjusted Hourly Wages, by Generation

	MALE			FEMALE		
	First	Second	Third	First	Second	Third
AVERAGE LOG HOURLY WAGE						
Mexican American	2.09	2.39	2.39	1.90	2.18	2.20
Non-Mexican American	2.59	2.82	2.67	2.33	2.54	2.39
ADJUSTED LOG HOURLY WAGE[1]						
Mexican American	2.58	2.68	2.64	2.43	2.43	2.42
Non-Mexican American	2.64	2.82	2.76	2.38	2.54	2.49
IMPLIED PERCENTAGE HOURLY WAGE DEFICIT[2]						
Average hourly wage	−39.7%	−34.8%	−24.5%	−14.1%	−29.4%	−18.0%
Adjusted hourly wage	−5.7%	−13.2%	−11.9%	5.4%	−11 %	−7.0%

Source: Author's weighted estimates from the March 1999 Current Population Survey.

Notes: Sample includes persons age sixteen to sixty-four who are not enrolled in school and who worked in 1998. Excludes persons who were self-employed, worked without pay, or lived in group quarters.

[1]Estimates are from regressions for males and females of log hourly wages on state of residence, central-city/MSA residence, marital status, work experience (quartic), union membership in March 1999, education, Mexican American identifier for each generation, non-Mexican American identifier for each generation, and a constant. Second-generation non-Mexican Americans are the reference group. Hourly wage is defined as total wage and salary earnings divided by the product of number of weeks worked and usual hours worked per week. Wages and salaries are top-coded by the CPS.

[2]If x is the log wage difference between Mexican Americans and non-Mexican Americans, then the implied wage differential is ex − 1.

wage of 2.39, the implied difference in hourly wages (shown in the bottom panel) is −34.8 percent ($e^{2.39-2.82} = -0.348$). In other words, second-generation Mexican Americans earn an average of 34.8 percent less than non-Hispanic whites. Similarly, first- and third-generation Mexican Americans earn 39.7 percent and 24.5 percent less than non-Mexican-origin workers of the same generation. The results show that certain demographic factors—given in the notes of the table—explain between 87 and 94 percent of the lower wages of Mexican Americans.

One reason why adjusted wages decline for Mexican Americans between the second and third generations is a difference in years of experience. As shown in table 8, second-generation Mexican Americans have less work experience than their third-generation counterparts. To calculate the adjusted wages, both generations are given the same years of experience as second-generation non-Mexican Americans (approximately 21.4 years). Doing so increases the experience of second-generation workers more than third-generation workers, resulting in a

−0.04 log point lower in adjusted wages for the second generation (2.68 compared to 2.64).

In terms of relative adjusted wages, first- and third-generation Mexican Americans make the biggest gains: first-generation men and women earn 5 to 6 percent less than comparable non-Hispanic workers, whereas third-generation workers earn about 7 to 12 percent less. These figures are considerably less than the average wage deficits.

Unfortunately, the fact is that real-world observed wages (i.e., "average" wages) stagnate from the second to the third generation for both Mexican Americans and non-Hispanic whites. However, contrary to the experience of whites, whose income is significantly lower in the third generation, the wages of Mexican Americans do not decline, and in the case of women, they actually increase. Undoubtedly, the reduction in wages is partly due to a higher percentage of part-time workers in the third generation. For this reason, the adjusted wage deficit of Mexican Americans shows improvement from the second to the third generation.

DISCUSSION

Two possible explanations exist for the wage differential between Mexican Americans and European Americans: systematic discrimination against Mexican Americans in the labor market or differences in workers' productive characteristics. Several other studies have reached the same conclusion presented here; namely, that worker characteristics explain about 95 percent of the wage differential between European Americans and Mexican Americans (Cain 1986; Ehrenberg and Smith 1994; Reimers 1985; Trejo 1997). One particularly significant characteristic distinguishing Mexican American from European American men is high English proficiency. Trejo (1997) suggests that factoring in English language proficiency further reduces the wage differential by about 5 percentage points to almost nothing. (English proficiency was not considered in the present analysis due to data limitations.) Trejo also suggests that any remaining wage difference is explained by the ethnic composition of whites—whites of British descent, for example, earn the same as Mexican Americans with the same characteristics, but both groups earn less than whites of Russian descent. He concludes that third-generation Mexican Americans earn lower wages because of lower productive characteristics, especially education and English proficiency, and that there is no evidence of systematic discrimination in wages. In contrast, he does find evidence of wage discrimination against blacks.

This evidence suggests that improving the educational levels of Mexican Americans is one of the most effective ways to reduce the wage gap between them and non-Mexican-origin workers. Improved English language proficiency will also reduce wage differentials, but this variable is highly correlated with education levels. At the same time, the maintenance of Spanish may result in highly sought-after bilingual workers; these workers may experience labor market rewards that are generally not available to monolingual English speakers.

Furthermore, improved education levels are likely to change the industrial and occupational distribution of Mexican Americans—a high-school graduate would not be expected to be an architect or engineer. The labor market can be divided into two markets, primary and secondary, with the primary market being distinguished by better wages, prestige, and stability (Cain 1986; Schiller 1989). Not surprisingly, entrance into the primary labor market is highly correlated with education. Increases in education, English ability, and work experience will more than likely result in more Mexican Americans moving out of the secondary and into the primary labor market.

Even though wage discrimination is not a significant issue for the majority of Mexican Americans, there is evidence of other types of discrimination. Delgado Bernal (1998) and Monroy (1999) provide evidence of pre-labor market discrimination in terms of Mexican American children receiving a lower-quality education. Unfortunately, no definitive study has been undertaken that measures educational discrimination in a statistically meaningful way. For example, is the lower quality of education provided to Mexican American children due simply to the fact that they are poorer, on average, than middle-class Americans? After all, poor whites also suffer from low educational levels. Poor populations live in neighborhoods that cannot fund school districts to the same extent as wealthier neighborhoods. The solution to this inequality is unclear. Attempts to equalize spending across school districts actually have had the perverse result of reducing per-pupil spending, which may end up hurting rather than helping poor students (Silva and Sonstelie 1995).

At the hiring stage, Kenney and Wissoker (1994) found that Hispanics and European Americans with nearly identical qualifications applying for entry-level jobs had different outcomes. In particular, European American applicants were more likely to be asked to file a job application, to obtain a job interview, and to be offered the job than Hispanics were. Kenney and Wissoker's study covered only two cities and was not a representative sample of employers, however, so we should be cautious in assuming that the results provide evidence of systematic job discrimination. Nevertheless, these findings indicate that it is imperative to continue enforcement of anti-discrimination laws at all levels.

SUMMARY

The labor market situation of Mexican Americans is in some ways encouraging: they are hard working and dedicated to work. On the other hand, they suffer from higher than average levels of unemployment and spend more time looking for work than most other workers. For those who are working, their occupational profile tells a mixed story. The first generation is likely to be concentrated in labor-intensive manufacturing work, but a fair percentage of the second and third generations moves out of these jobs and into white-collar occupations. Still, fewer Mexican Americans work in prestigious jobs than is true for other ethnic groups.

Mexican Americans earn more than 25 percent less than non-Mexican-origin workers, although the wage deficit decreases across generations. The adjusted averages for Mexican Americans improve into the third generation relative to non-Hispanic whites. Much of the gap can be accounted for by differences in education, English language ability, and other worker characteristics. This suggests that a prescription for attaining economic equality is to eliminate educational inequalities. Although the employment and income statistics are bleak, current education information available provides some encouraging signs that educational levels are increasing among Mexican Americans. I hope that these educational gains will continue and result in even greater economic gains for the next generation of Mexican Americans. Current Mexican American workers will also see their wages rise as they become older, acquire more work experience, maintain the same levels of labor force attachment, and continue their quest for *buenos días*.

References

Borjas, George J. 1982. The Labor Supply of Male Hispanic Immigrants in the United States. *International Migration Review* 17, 343–53.

Borjas, George J., and Marta Tienda. 1985. Introduction. In *Hispanics in the U.S. Economy*, edited by George J. Borjas and Marta Tienda. Orlando, Fla.: Academic Press.

Cain, Glen G. 1986. The Economic Analysis of Labor Market Discrimination: A Survey. In *Handbook of Labor Economics*, edited by Orley Ashenfelter and Richard Layard. Vol. 2. New York: Elsevier Science Publishers.

DeFreitas, Gregory. 1985. Ethnic Differentials in Unemployment among Hispanic Americans. In *Hispanics in the U.S. Economy*, edited by George J. Borjas and Marta Tienda. Orlando, Fla.: Academic Press.

———. 1991. *Inequality at Work: Hispanics in the U.S. Labor Force*. New York: Oxford University Press.

Delgado, Bernal, Dolores. 1998. Chicana/o Education from the Civil Rights Era to the Present. In *The Elusive Quest for Equality: 150 Years of Chicana/Chicano Education*, edited by José F. Moreno. Cambridge, Mass.: Harvard Educational Review Publishing Group.

Ehrenberg, Ronald G., and Robert S. Smith. 1994. *Modern Labor Economics: Theory and Public Policy*. 5th ed. New York: HarperCollins College Publishers.

Higuera, Jonathan J. 1998. Developer Stands Tall after Crash: Local Mogul 'Toughed' It Out, Hitting the Top of the Market. *Tucson Citizen*, May 18, p. IA.

Kenney, Genevieve M., and Douglas A. Wissoker. 1994. An Analysis of the Correlates of Discrimination Facing Young Hispanic Job-Seekers. *American Economic Review* 84, 674–83.

Monroy, Douglas. 1999. *Rebirth: Mexican Los Angeles from the Great Migration and the Great Depression*. Berkeley: University of California Press.

Reimers, Cordelia W. 1985. A Comparative Analysis of the Wages of Hispanics, Blacks, and Non-Hispanic Whites. In *Hispanics in the U.S. Economy*, edited by George J. Borjas and Marta Tienda. Orlando, Fla.: Academic Press.

———. 1992. Hispanic Earnings and Employment in the 1980s. In *Hispanics in the Workforce*, edited by Stephen B. Knouse, Paul Rosenfeld, and Amy Culbertson. Newbury Park, Calif.: Sage.

Schiller, Bradley. 1989. *The Economics of Poverty and Discrimination*. 5th ed. Englewood Cliffs, N.J.: Prentice Hall.

Segura, Denise A. 1992. Walking on Eggshells: Chicanas in the Labor Force. In *Hispanics in the Workforce*, edited by Stephen B. Knouse, Paul Rosenfeld, and Amy Culbertson. Newbury Park, Calif.: Sage.

Silva, Fabio, and Jon Sonstelie. 1995. Did Serrano Cause a Decline in School Spending? *National Tax Journal* 48, 199–215.

Trejo, Stephen J. 1997. Why Do Mexican Americans Earn Low Wages? *Journal of Political Economy* 105, 1235–68.

SECTION 2: DEMOGRAPHICS, SOCIETY AND CULTURE
ASSESSMENT AND APPLICATION

1. What are the future implications for public education given the current age distribution of Hispanics?

2. What regional settlement trends can you discern for the Hispanic population based on the article on Mexican demography in the United States?

3. Trace the academic achievement gap of Hispanics in the chapter written by Marta Tienda et al. and compare and contrast that with the achievement data in a school district in your area.

4. How would you characterize Hispanic integration in the four social realms examined in the chapter written by Marta Tienda et al.?

5. Why are Latinos joining Protestant churches in large numbers?

6. How will the shift to Protestant denominations affect Latino voting patterns in your state? Why?

7. What strategies is the Catholic Church employing to retain its members? Will they work?

8. What are some of the major environmental problems listed by Vila and Peterson that are faced by the transnational metroplex formed by El Paso, Texas-Ciudad Juárez, Chihuahua?

9. How extensively should environmental organizations include community members in the formulation of policy and specific interventions?

10. Identify a major environmental issue in a community and the principal actors involved in its public portrayal.

11. What does Hayes-Bautista identify as the leading health problems facing the Hispanic population?

12. Why is it important to develop a Latino health agenda based on Latino metrics?

13. How is the growing Hispanic presence in the nation as outlined by Larsen likely to impact the economy of your state?

14. Why is the South as a region attracting Hispanics in growing numbers?

15. Based on the economic snapshot of Hispanics 1985–2010, what is the trend for Hispanic-owned firms?

16. Has Hispanic household income in your community kept pace with the national average? Why?

17. Based on Pachón's chapter, how does home ownership affect the Hispanic population's quest for middle-class status?

18. Why is the Hispanic middle class in the nation increasing in number?

19. How do Mexican-American women in the labor force address economic and domestic issues and cultural expectations?

20. Characterize the experience of Mexican *immigrant* workers in the United States in terms of their ability to attain upward socioeconomic mobility within their generation.

21. Is the success of Mexican immigrant women worker organizations like Mujer Obrera transportable to other communities? Why?

22. Why do Mexican and Central American women predominate in the domestic worker economy?

23. How do Latina immigrant nannies view American parenting practices? Why?

24. How do Latina immigrant domestic employees manage to care for their own children while employed?

SECTION 2: SUGGESTED READINGS

Abalos, David T. (2001). *The Latino Male: A Radical Redefinition*. Boulder, CO: Lynne Rienner Publishers.

Aguirre-Molina, Marilyn & Molina, Carlos W. (2003). *Latina Health in the United States: A Public Health Reader*. San Francisco, CA: Jossey–Bass.

Aldama, Arturo J. & Quiñónez, Naomi H. (2002). *Decolonial Voices: Chicana and Chicano Cultural Studies in the 21st Century*. Bloomington, IN: Indiana University Press.

Aldama, Frederick L. (2005). *Brown on Brown: Chicano/a Representations of Gender, Sexuality, and Ethnicity*. Austin, TX: University of Texas Press.

American Cancer Society. (2003). *Cancer Facts & Figures for Hispanics/Latinos 2003–2005*. Atlanta, GA: American Cancer Society.

Anzaldúa, Gloria. (2012). *Borderlands/La Frontera: The New Mestiza*. (4th ed.). San Francisco, CA: Aunt Lute Books.

Arreola, Daniel D. (2004). *Hispanic Spaces, Latino Places: Community and Cultural Diversity in Contemporary America*. Austin, TX: University of Texas Press.

Arreola, Daniel D. (2002). *Tejano South Texas: A Mexican American Cultural Province*. Austin, TX: University of Texas Press.

Bergad, Laird W. & Klein, Herbert S. (2010). *Hispanics in the United States: A Demographic, Social, and Economic History, 1980–2005*. New York, NY: Cambridge University Press.

Bixler-Márquez, Dennis J. (2005). La Preparatoria Bowie Versus la Patrulla Fronteriza. *Aztlán: A Journal of Chicano Studies* (2nd ed., Vol. 30, pp. 157–168). Los Angeles, CA: UCLA Chicano Studies Research Center.

Bonilla, Frank, Meléndez, Edwin, Morales, Rebecca & Torres, María de Los Angeles. (1998). *Borderless Borders: U.S. Latinos, Latin Americans, and the Paradox of Interdependence*. Philadelphia, PA: Temple University Press.

Byrne, John, Glover, Leigh & Martínez, Cecilia. (2002). *Environmental Justice: Discourses in International Political Economy, Energy and Environmental Policy*. New Brunswick, NJ: Transaction Publishers.

Cafferty, Pastora San Juan & Engstrom, David W. (2002). *Hispanics in the United States: An Agenda for the Twenty-First Century*. New Brunswick, NJ: Transaction Publishers.

Castañeda, Antonia, Armitage, Susan H., Hart, Patricia & Weathermon, Karen. (2007). *Gender on the Borderlands: The Frontiers Reader*. Lincoln, NE: University of Nebraska Press.

Dohan, Daniel. (2003). *The Price of Poverty: Money, Work, and Culture in the Mexican American Barrio*. Berkeley, CA: University of California Press.

Donelson, Angela & Esparza, Adrián X. (2010). *The Colonias Reader: Economy, Housing, and Public Health in U.S.-Mexico Border Colonias*. Tucson, AZ: The University of Arizona Press.

Espinosa, Gastón & García, Mario T. (2008). *Mexican American Religions: Spirituality, Activism, and Culture*. Durham, NC. Duke University Press.

Ferguson, Kathryn, Price, Norma A. & Parks, Ted. (2010). *Crossing with the Virgin: Stories from the Migrant Trail*. Tucson, AZ: The University of Arizona Press.

Gil, Carlos B. (2012). *We Became Mexican American: How Our Immigrant Family Survived To Pursue the American Dream*. Bloomington, IN. Xlibris Corporation.

Greene Sterling, Terry. (2010). *Illegal: Life and Death in Arizona's Immigration War Zone*. Guilford, CT: Globe Pequot Press.

Jara Guerrero, Salvador, Vélez-Ibáñez, Carlos, Sánchez Benítez, Roberto & Pérez Pintor, Héctor. (2011).

Identidades Transfronterizas: Migración y Cultura Chicana. Morelia, Mich: Universidad Michoacana de San Nicolás de Hidalgo, Facultad de Derecho y Ciencias Sociales.

González, Manny J. & González-Ramos, Gladys. (2013). *Mental Health Care for New Hispanic Immigrants: Innovative Approaches in Contemporary Clinical Practice.* New York, NY: Routledge.

González, Norma. (2005). *I Am My Language: Discourses of Women and Children in the Borderlands.* Tucson, AZ: University of Arizona Press.

Griswold del Castillo, Richard. (1984). *La Familia: Chicano Families in the Urban Southwest, 1848 to the Present.* South Bend, IN: University of Notre Dame Press.

Gutiérrez, David G. (1995). *Walls and Mirrors: Mexican Americans, Mexican Immigrants, and the Politics of Ethnicity.* Berkeley, CA: University of California Press.

Jourdane, Maurice. (2004). *The Struggle for the Health and Legal Protection of Farm Workers: El Cortito.* Houston, TX: Arte Público Press.

Keefe, Susan E. & Padilla, Amado M. (1987). *Chicano Ethnicity.* Albuquerque, NM: University of New Mexico Press.

Collins, Chuck, Lui, Meizhu, Gluckman, Amy, Leodar-Wright, Betsy, Offner, Amy & Scharf, Adria. (2004). *The Wealth Inequality Reader.* Boston, MA: Dollars and Sense.

Lyons, Mark, Nixon, Leticia R. & Tarrier, August. (2004). *Espejos y Ventanas/Mirrors and Windows: Oral Histories of Mexican Farmworkers and Their Families.* Philadelphia, PA: New City Community Press.

Macías, Thomas. (2006). *Mestizo in America, Generations of Mexican Ethnicity in the Suburban Southwest.* Tucson, AZ: The University of Arizona Press.

Marquardt Friedmann, Marie, Steigenga, Timothy J, Williams, Philip J. & Vásquez, Manuel A. (2011). *Living "Illegal": The Human Face of Unauthorized Immigration.* New York, NY: The New Press.

Martínez, Oscar J. (2001). *Mexican-Origin People in the United States: A Topical History.* Tucson, AZ: University of Arizona Press.

Martínez, Oscar J. (2006). *Troublesome Border, Revised Edition.* Tucson, AZ: University of Arizona Press.

Milkman, Ruth & Wong, Kent. (2000). *Voices from the Front Lines: Organizing Immigrant Workers in Los Angeles.* Los Angeles, CA: Center for Labor Research and Education.

Ochoa, Gilda L. (2004). *Becoming Neighbors in a Mexican American Community: Power, Conflict and Solidarity.* Austin, TX: University of Texas Press.

Organista, Kurt C. (2007). *Solving Latino Psychosocial and Health Problems: Theory, Practice, and Populations.* Hoboken, NJ: John Wiley & Sons, Inc.

Passel, Jeffrey S., Cohn, D'Vera & López, Mark H. (2011). *Census 2010: 50 Million Latinos, Hispanics Account for More Than Half of Nation's Growth in Past Decade.* Washington, DC. Pew Hispanic Center.

Peña, Devon G. (1998). *Chicano Culture, Ecology, Politics: Subversive Kin.* Tucson, AZ: University of Arizona Press.

Romano, V., Octavio I. (1968). The Anthropology and Sociology of the Mexican Americans. *E1 Grito.II* (l).

Romano, V., Octavio I. (1969). The Historical and Intellectual Presence of Mexican-Americans. *El Grito. II* (2).

Romano, V., Octavio I. (1970). Social Science, Objectivity, and the Chicanos. *El Grito, IV* (1).

Russel, Joe, Corvalán, Marcos & Guadalupe, Patricia. (2006). Elite Women Series. *Hispanic Business.* Pp. 27–58.

Treviño, Roberto R. (2006). *The Church in the Barrio: Mexican American Ethno-Catholicism in Houston.* Chapel Hill, NC: University of North Carolina Press.

Saldívar, Jos David. (2012). *Trans-Americanity: Subaltern Modernities, Global Coloniality, and the Cultures of Greater Mexico.* Durham, NC: Duke University Press.

Segura, Denise A. & Pesquera, Beatriz M. (1995). Chicana Feminisms: Their Political Context and Contemporary Expressions. In Antonia Darder and Rodolfo Torres, (Eds.), *The Latino Studies Reader: Culture, Economy and Society.* Malden, MA: Blackwell Publishers.

Segura, Denise A. & Zavella, Patricia. (Eds). (2007). *Women and Migration in the U.S.-Mexico Borderlands: A Reader.* Durham, NC: Duke University Press.

Solórzano Torres, Rosalía & James Hernández, Franscisca L. (2010). *Chicana Studies, An Introduction.* (Vol. 1). Dubuque, IA: Kendall Hunt Publishing Company.

Spalding, Mark J. (1999). *Sustainable Development in San Diego-Tijuana: Environmental, Social, and Economic Implications of Interdependence.* San Diego, CA: Center for U.S.-Mexican Studies, University of California, San Diego.

Staudt, Kathleen A. (1998). *Free Trade?: Informal Economies at the U.S.-Mexico Border.* Philadelphia, PA: Temple University Press.

Tienda, Martha & Mitchell, Faith. (2006). *Multiple Origins, Uncertain Destinies: Hispanics and the American Future.* Washington, DC: National Academies Press.

Tinjacá, Mabel. (2000). *¡Visión!: Hispanic Entrepreneurs in the United States.* Pleasant Hill, MO: Heritage Publishing Company.

Tobar, Héctor. (2005). *Translation Nation: Defining a New American Identity in the Spanish-Speaking United States.* New York, NY: Penguin Group.

United States-Mexico Border Health Commission. (2003). *Healthy Border 2010: An Agenda for Improving Health on the United States-Mexico Border.* El Paso, TX: United States-Mexico Border Health Commission. www.borderhealth.org

Velásquez, Roberto J., Arellano, Leticia M. & McNeill, Brian W. (2004*). The Handbook of Chicana/o Psychology and Mental Health.* Mahwah, NJ: Lawrence Erlbaum Associates.

Vélez-Ibáñez, Carlos G., Sampaio, Anna & González-Estay, Manolo. (2002). *Transnational Latina/o Communities: Politics, Processes, and Cultures.* Lanham, MD: Rowman & Littlefield Publishers.

Vila, Pablo. (2005*). Border Identifications: Narratives of Religion, Gender, and Class on the U.S.- Mexico Border.* Austin, TX: University of Texas Press.

Williamson, Jeffrey G. (2006, September). Global migration. *Finance & Development* magazine, *43*(3), 23–27.

SECTION 2: SUGGESTED FILMS AND VIDEOS

After I Pick Up the Fruit: The Lives of Migrant Women, 2011
Nancy Ghertner Productions
www.afteripickthefruit.com

Al Otro Lado, 2004
UNICINE

An Inconvenient Truth, 2006
Paramount Pictures
5555 Melrose Avenue, Hollywood, CA 90038

Arizona: Resisting SB 1070 Immigration Law, 2011
Third World Newsreel
545 Eight Ave., Suite 550, New York, NY 10018-4971

Bill Moyers Journal: Barbara Ehrenreich on Equality, 2007
Films for the Humanities & Sciences
132 West 31st Street, New York, NY 10001

Black in Latin America, 2011
PBS
2100 Crystal Drive, Arlington, VA 22202

Bread & Roses, 2000
Lionsgate
2700 Colorado Avenua, Santa Monica, CA 90404

Cadillac Desert Series pt 1-4, 1997
PBS Home Video
2100 Cystal Drive, Arlington, VA 22202

California and the American Dream, 2006
Berkeley Media LLC
2600 Tenth Street, Suite 626, Berkeley, CA 94710

Chávez Ravine, 2004
Bullfrog Films
PO Box 149, Oley, PA 19547

Children in No Man's Land, 2008
News Day Films
190 Route 17M, Suite D, Harriman, NY 10926

De Mujer a Mujer, 1992
Women Make Movies
New York, NY

Desert Semaphore: The Chihuahuan Desert Trilogy: Part III, 1996
Chihuahuan Desert Research Institute
P.O. Box 1334, Alpine, TX 79831

Environmental Racism, 1990
Third World Newsreel
545 Eighth Ave., Suite 550
New York, NY 10018

Harvest of Loneliness: The Bracero Program, 2010
Films Media Group
132 West 31st Street, 17th Floor, New York, NY 10001

Hispanic Americans, 2000
Insight Media
2162 Broadway, New York, NY 10024-0621

Hispanic Americans: The Second Generation, 1995
Films for the Humanities and Sciences
132 West 31st Street, New York, NY 10001

I Am Joaquín! 1969
El Teatro Campesino
San Juan Bautista, CA

IMPACT: Environmental Pollution on the U.S.-Mexico Border, 1997
CNN
New York, NY

Immigration Debate, 2010
Univision

La Batalla de las Cruces: Protesta Social y Acciones Colectivas en Torno de la Violencia Sexual en Ciudad Juárez, 2005
CIESAS y Campo Imaginario
Mexico

La Bestia/The Beast, 2011
Venevision International and Visiones Films

Maquilapolis: City of Factories, 2006
California Newsreel
P.O. Box 3400, Lancaster, PA 17604

Mexican American, 2007
Amigo Films
6930 Hayvenhurst Ave, Van Nuys, CA 91406

Mixed Feelings: San Diego/Tijuana, 2002
PBS
2100 Crystal Drive, Arlington, VA 22202

Moyers & Company: Hispanic America's Turn, 2012
Films for the Humanities and Sciences
132 West 31st Street, New York, NY 10001

P.O.V.: Immigrants in New York
PBS
2100 Crystal Drive, Arlington, VA 22202

Quinceañera: Fifteen is not so sweet, 2006
Sonny Classics
10202 W. Washington Blvd.
Culver City, CA 90232

Rancho California (Por Favor), 2003
Berkeley Media LLC
2600 Tenth Street, Suite 626, Berkeley, CA 94710

SB1070: The Faces, 2011
CreateSpace

Sisters of '77, 2005
Media Projects, Inc.
5215 Homer Street, Dallas, Texas 75206

State of Latino America, 2013
C-SPAN
P.O. Box 2909, West Lafayette, IN 47996

The Changing Role of Hispanic Women, 1995
Films for the Humanities and Sciences
132 West 31st Street, New York, NY 10001

The Forgotten Americans, 2000
Galán Incorporated Television and Film
5524 Bee Caves Rd. Suite B-5 Austin, TX 78746

The Harvest (La Cosecha) 2011
Cinema Libre Studio
6634 W. Sunset Blvd, Los Angeles, CA 90028

The Hispanic Americans Series: Hispanic Entrepreneurs: Against All Odds, 2004
Films for the Humanities & Sciences
132 West 31st Street, New York, NY 10001

The Invisible Mexicans of Deer Canyon, 2006
Gatekeeper Productions
8484 Harold Way, Los Angeles, CA 90069

The Latino Family, 1993
Films for the Humanities and Sciences
132 West 31st Street, New York, NY 10001

The Three Stages of Latino Life, 1992
Films for the Humanities and Sciences
132 West 31st Street, New York, NY 10001

Under the Bridge: The Story of Chicano Park, 2011
www.hulu.com

Waging a Living, 2005
PBS
2100 Crystal Drive, Arlington, VA 22202

What's Going On?: Poverty in America, 2003
Zenger Media
P.O. Box 802, Culver City, CA 90232

Yo Soy Chicano, 1972
The Cinema Guild
115 West 30th Street, Suite 800, New York, NY 10001

Political and Socioeconomic Perspectives

This section provides an overview of selected contemporary Chicano issues in American politics and efforts to address them in a cumulative continuation of the historical, demographic, and sociocultural sections. While Chicano involvement in American politics dates back to the Mexican-American War, the contemporary orientation of this text forces a more recent point of departure—the Chicano movement.

Ignacio García initiates this section by analyzing the academic reinterpretation of the Chicano experience during the 1960s and 1970s that led to, among other things, a positive and emancipating view of Chicanos, an interpretation of the Chicano experience by Chicanos, and the academic development of Chicano Studies. Rosalía Solórzano describes the challenges faced by the Mexican-origin population in Arizona, a border state characterized by its anti-immigrant politics and oppressive immigration enforcement policy and practice. Solórzano documents the struggle for social justice undertaken by various segments of the population in this southwestern ethnic battleground—section four covers the educational dimension of that struggle. Hipsman and Meissner follow with an analysis of the economic, social, and political landscapes that would be impacted by the passage of a comprehensive reform law. The Congressional Hispanic Caucus contributes a set of guiding principles for immigration reform that would make the American dream attainable for the undocumented population. An examination of current immigration trends and politics by Mortimer B. Zuckerman concludes the immigration segment of this chapter. He portrays Hispanic immigration as a positive development for the nation due to the successful and patriotic integration of Hispanics in American society in the midst of the current immigration and national security controversies and political upheaval. He posits that the new waves of Hispanic immigrants will "enrich our nation, as million of immigrants before have."

The second segment of this section focuses on electoral politics, not at all unrelated to Hispanic immigration politics. First, Kim Geron broaches the question of what will be the face of Latino politics in the new millennium by connecting past struggles with contemporary gains. Geron examines strategies like the accommodation of other groups through coalition building and addressing class interests. Paul Taylor et al examine the strength of the Hispanic electorate and its projected impact on American elections by 2030, given its strong participation in the last two presidential elections and the anticipated growth of the Hispanic population. Steven Malanga cautions about the euphoria of this much-publicized Hispanic electorate. He challenges the assumptions by the media about its projected role and identifies voting myths of the Hispanic electorate that need to be considered in political analysis and formulation of electoral strategy. The barometric and qualitative analysis presented by Geron, Taylor et al, and Malanga may predict, with some important caveats, future levels of participation and political party affiliation in a fluid political environment that includes the variables and actors identified in this segment.

Alma M. García discusses in the third segment the development of Chicana feminist discourse, bringing into focus the origins of Chicana feminism within the context of the Chicano movement. Not only did women question traditional roles within the family, Chicana feminists drew up their own political agenda, which emerged from their own political activity and their intellectual movement. Chicana feminists were the first to question the Chicano paradigm and insist that scholars examine not only race and class, but also gender. Sonia García et al present an overview of contemporary and future Latina political leadership that delves into trends, characteristics, roles, and organization building that is generating successful Latina political leaders. The 2012 NALEO Election Profile of Latina Voters provides evidence that Latina political participation is increasingly capable of shaping the future of the nation.

Reinterpreting the Chicano Experience

Ignacio M. García

After Chicano activists rejected the liberal agenda and its prescription for integration, they set out to tackle another major obstacle to *la gente's* progress: history. They understood that the treatment of Mexican Americans was partly the result of the distorted view of them perpetuated by historians, social scientists, essayists, and the media in general. Although Mexican American middle-class reformers had taken on many of the stereotypes, few of them had ever attempted a fundamental reinterpretation of the history of Mexican Americans.[1] They had been content with emphasizing inclusion and telling "their" side of American history. Chicano activists believed, however, that for the barrios to develop the type of self-esteem and pride necessary for political action, Mexican Americans had to see themselves in a new light. They also had to shift the blame for their condition from themselves to mainstream society. Said José Angel Gutiérrez: "We're called apathetic, disorganized. We drink beer. Like to make babies. That we fight. That we're slow learners. That we're not . . . as 'ambitiously motivated' as an Anglo. That we're weird in terms of art and music. And everything that is applied to us is really a commentary on society, the Anglo. The problem is not us. The problem is white society."[2]

To Gutiérrez and other activists, the problems of the community were most often caused by external forces. Chicanos, after all, did not create low-paying jobs, did not build inadequate housing, did not set up inefficient schools, and did not write condescending or racist advertising jingles. They also did not hire policemen with violent streaks or transport powerful drugs from South America or Asia to the barrios. These problems had been forced upon a community that was faced with a relentless attack on its identity. Social scientists, according to Chicano activists, had continued to perpetuate stereotypes that were destructive to the self-esteem of the Mexican American community. Chicanos who chose to read the academic literature or the popular press came across countless references to their "apathy," "laziness," and self-victimization.[3] For many, Mexican Americans were either emotionally or intellectually unable to lift themselves up from their difficult conditions of poverty and illiteracy. They had been so socialized to accept their disadvantaged status that it had become part of the culture. This culture of poverty, argued social scientists, provided few, if any, of the tools to help Mexican Americans pull themselves out of the cycle of hopelessness in which they were caught.[4]

Chicanos also saw themselves as victims of history, though they did not see culture as at fault. Luis Valdez, founder of the Teatro Campesino, saw Mexican Americans as being treated as, and consequently acting like, a "colonized race . . . [whose] uniqueness . . . lies buried in the dust of conquest." The conquest had been not only a military one but a psychological one, since Mexican Americans had been cut off from their history.[5] The solution to this condition, according to Valdez, was to "reach into our people, in the . . . memory of their beginning."[6] Chicanos had to find a past unmarred by the conquest, and within that past find the prototype society where the early "Chicano" was unspoiled by Anglo-American society. David Sánchez, prime minister of the paramilitary group the Brown Berets, described it thus: "In the beginning . . . there were beautiful lands with all the living resources. . . . It was a paradise where the balance of nature kept everyone alive. . . . We were a proud people who perfected medicines . . . until strange ships came from an old world. . . . They came not to build, but to rule . . . at the cost of our blood."[7]

In that past, Chicanos searched for a reinterpretation of their existence that would uncover the myths and legends of the struggle for survival and provide the basis for a cultural and political renaissance. This new interpretation of the Chicano experience also sought to undo the years of biased scholarship that formed the core of what was known about the Mexican American. In 1968, Enriqueta Longeaux y Vásquez wrote: "The raza in the southwest . . . wants our history back. . . . Our cities, our mountains, and rivers were explored and settled by Indians and Spaniards, not pilgrims and wagon masters. The first cattle raisers, cowboys and farmers were raza. We weren't waiting here to be saved by the great white fathers."[8]

Octavio Romano was one of the first Chicano scholars to promote the new interpretation. An anthropologist at the University of California, Berkeley, he attacked much of the traditional scholarship on Mexican Americans by social scientists. In his most influential article, "The Anthropology and Sociology of the Mexican-American: The Distortion of Mexican-American History," Romano took on the academy: "Social science studies have dealt with Mexican Americans as an ahistoric people—with a place in history reserved for them only when they undergo some metamorphosis usually called acculturation. . . . Mexican Americans are never seen as participants in history, much less as generators of the historical process."[9] For activists, Chicano history was a recollection of events, of ideas, and of people who had resisted the American conquest of the Southwest and the subsequent colonization that followed. They believed that to "deprive man of his heritage was the worst form of oppression."[10] So they set out to uncover facts long forgotten or ignored and to debunk the Anglo-American

version of their history. To do so required more than a different retelling, it meant framing the discovered history within a new interpretation that challenged the traditional literature. This interpretation presented Chicanos as active participants in "their" history.

Romano chided social scientists who wrote that Mexican Americans had a difficult time dealing with the conflict between two cultures. This conflict, one anthropologist argued, often led them to "retreat" into their "conservative . . . world," to "escape to larger cities" or into alcoholism, or to engage in antisocial behavior. Their only hope rested on their acculturating "more and more."[11] Although offended by the belittling descriptions of Mexican Americans, Romano reacted more angrily to the implication that only acculturated Mexican Americans were active participants in their lives. Romano rebutted, "Contrary to the ahistorical views . . . Mexican Americans as well as Mexican immigrants have not . . . wallowed passively in some teleological treadmill, awaiting the emergence of an acculturated third generation before joining in the historical process."[12] He cited numerous instances when Mexican Americans had engaged in strikes in the agricultural fields and the mines of eight different states. These had been intense, even violent acts of labor resistance that had incurred a "massive counter-action" that included widespread deportations. Romano pointed to Carey McWilliams, who wrote in 1949: "Long charged with a lack of 'leadership' and talent for organization, they proved all too effectively that neither talent was lacking. . . . By 1930 the myth of the docility of Mexican labor had been thoroughly exploded."[13]

Romano took on the anthropologist Ruth Tuck, who in 1946 wrote: "For many years the (Mexican) immigrant and his sons made no effort to free themselves. They burned with resentment over a thousand slights, but they did so in private. . . . Perhaps this passivity is the mark of any minority which is just emerging."[14] With that statement, said Romano, Tuck wiped away decades of resistance and set a tone for anthropologists and sociologists to emulate in describing Mexican Americans and their condition. Romano then took on Munro Edmonson, Celia Heller, Julian Samora, Lyle Saunders, and others whose work only reaffirmed Tuck's conceptualization of the Mexican American as a victim of his or her cultural deficiencies.[15] In summarizing their work, Romano accused the aforementioned scholars of making Mexican Americans the generators of their problems, thus freeing Anglo-Americans from most responsibility. Calling upon his readers to reject these perceptions of traditional Mexican culture, he urged them to learn about the intellectual history of Mexican Americans.

That led to another important article, "The Historical and Intellectual Presence of Mexican Americans."[16] Although not as influential as his first one, this article sought to provide a picture of the pluralistic nature of the Mexican American community and to point out that there were important philosophical and ideological currents that influenced the thinking of most Mexican Americans. Romano posited that three main streams of thought permeated the Mexican American community. These were "indianist philosophy," "historical confrontation," and "cultural nationalism." "At times," wrote Romano, "they [the three philosophies] coincide with actual historical occurrences. Other times they lie relatively dormant, or appear in a poetic metaphor, a song, a short story told to children, or in a marriage pattern."[17] Indianist philosophy dealt with the indigenous origin of most Mexican Americans; historical confrontation dealt with protest and popular action against tyranny and oppression; and cultural nationalism concerned itself with the development of the cultural characteristics of being a *mexicano*.

These philosophies came from the Mexican Revolution, an event that Romano believed influenced most Mexicans who crossed the border at the turn of the century. The philosophies were passed on from generation to generation and remained an active intellectual element within an extremely diverse community. These philosophies were responsible for the resistance that Chicanos continually waged against opposition. They were also responsible for the nationalistic or ethnocentric response of the working class toward Anglo-American encroachment into their community. Romano concluded his article by warning Chicanos to avoid being "permanently entombed in the histories of the past."[18] As a young recruit to the Movement, I read Romano's first article and felt outraged over the academic scholarship on Mexican Americans. It became a hotly discussed and debated article in my "Introduction to Mexican Americans" course at Texas A & I University in Kingsville. It would be quoted over and over in Chicano newspapers, lectures, and rallies, and in other academic articles and papers during the early years of the Movement.[19] Romano had, in a few short pages, identified what most Chicano activists perceived to be the most damaging assault on the Mexican American community. Said Romano, "Mexican Americans are [seen as] simple-minded . . . children who . . . choose poverty and isolation instead of assimilating into the American mainstream."[20]

The teaching of such perceptions had served to perpetuate stereotypes and thus kept mainstream society unsympathetic and often hostile toward Mexican Americans. The racist feelings and remarks had, in part, been rationalized by liberal social scientists who saw Mexican Americans as passive, unmotivated, and responsible for accepting much of their own suffering.[21] The biased scholarship had also served to perpetuate feelings of inferiority among many Mexican Americans and to cause some of the more educated to remove themselves culturally and physically from their communities. For me, and many like me, the article revealed a condescending attitude by social scientists who—we believed—would not have written about blacks in the same manner. We were under the impression that blacks, through the civil-rights movement, were freed from much of this type of scholarship. It was a false assumption but one that led many of us to the next phase of our politicization. Although we were always conscious of discrimination, many of us often abdicated the role of "oppressed minority" to blacks because few of us had ever understood the extent of the discrimination and racism perpetrated against Mexican Americans. To find that Mexican Americans were also victims of intellectual racism, and then to realize that there was no civil-rights movement for Mexican Americans, made many of us anxious to get involved in a movement of our own. The seeming lack of Anglo-American sympathy caused the Chicano Movement to become more nationalistic and separatist in nature than it might have been.[22]

Following Romano's lead, many other Chicano college students and professors picked up the discussion of the portrayal of Mexican Americans in the academic and popular literature. Juan Gómez-Quiñones, a young scholar at the University of California at Los Angeles at the time, called for a reconceptualization of Mexican American history, arguing that the history of Chicanos was not simply a history of the "Anglo oppressor" and the "Chicano oppressed."[23] He attempted to construct the first framework for retelling the story of the Mexican American. In an article entitled "Notes on Periodization, 1900–1965," Gómez-Quiñones broke Mexican American history into several definable periods.[24] Carlos Muñoz, a graduate student at the University of California, called on Chicanos scholars and students to be more than academicians. The Chicano scholar, said Muñoz, "must commit himself to the emancipation of his people."[25] Journals such as *Aztlán, De Colores, Caracol, Regeneración, Encuentro Femenil,* and Romano's *El Grito* followed the lead of these writers and charged ahead with a scathing scholarship that sought to disprove stereotypes that had become part of the mainstream in academia.[26] All of the aforementioned were academic journals with the exception of *Caracol*, which was a popular magazine for the masses that published a hodgepodge of articles, poems, theater acts, and essays.[27] These and other periodicals became self-imposed required reading for college students and Chicano activists in the community. Whereas many Chicanos were attracted to the Movement by the rhetoric and passion of the leaders, others less passionate were attracted by the intellectual discourse on the status of Chicanos, their past, and what might lie ahead. For many students coming to universities with little knowledge of their past, it became an intellectual culture shock to read the new Chicano scholarship.[28]

If Romano's article began the debate, Rodolfo Acuña's *Occupied America* heightened its intensity. No other academic work caused the controversy that Acuña's history of Chicanos did. Beginning with the premise that Chicanos were an internal colony still suffering from the legacy of the American conquest, Acuña went on to describe in detail many of the atrocities committed against La Raza. He introduced the book in this manner: "*Occupied America* has evolved from my belief that the history of Chicanos . . . must be reexamined. . . . As my research progressed, I became convinced that the experiences of Chicanos in the United States parallel that of other Third World people who have suffered under the colonialism of technologically superior nations. Thus, the thesis of this monograph is that Chicanos . . . are a colonized people. The conquest of the Mexicans, the occupation of their land and the continued oppression they have faced document this thesis."[29]

For Chicano activists, Acuña's work was a godsend. No longer did they have to piece together accounts of discrimination and racism. In several hundred pages, Acuña documented more than enough incidents to confirm almost anything that activists chose to blame on American society.[30] Chicano academicians also quickly endorsed the book because it provided them with a text for their courses. In it they found a comprehensive and panoramic view of Chicano history. Its model of "internal-colonialism" also provided a framework by which to explain the Chicano experience. The internal-colony model posited that the Southwest had been subjected to a conquest and a ruthless process of colonization that left Mexican Americans in circumstances similar to those of nations that had been colonized by imperialist powers. A dual-wage system,

rampant segregation, exploitation of natural resources, coaptation of the native elites, and other characteristics of a foreign colony were present in the Southwest, according to Acuña. The internal-colony social structure also placed racial conflict at the center of Mexican and Anglo-American relationships.[31] Chicano students were immediately attracted to the book by the information, much of it new to them, and by its academic "legitimacy." They also liked its militancy. Far from being esoteric, it invited the reader to action, to be an active participant in history. It also provided heroes and heroines and allowed Chicano students to see that Mexican Americans had never been passive. Rather, they had resisted domination. In a time of lettuce and grape boycotts, land-grant battles, urban street militancy, and school walkouts, *Occupied America* became the intellectual bible that rationalized the heightened militancy.

In Acuña's account of the conquest of the Southwest, nothing had come by chance, or by a spontaneous desire by Anglo-American settlers to live free under a democratic government. Instead, these settlers, in collusion with merchants, land speculators, businessmen, and government officials, had plotted to take Mexico's land. "Remember the Alamo" was not the defiant cry of a ragtag army of freedom-loving men but that of a band of ruffians and outlaws who had come to Texas to engage in their own brand of frontier conquest. Acuña, in this short monograph, rewrote the histories of Texas, Arizona, California, and New Mexico, documenting the methods used to conspire for revolution and war as well as how, once attaining victory, these invaders conspired to steal the lands from the Mexicans who had chosen to stay behind. In Acuña's account there were no tough, democratically inclined cowboys who tamed the West with courage, integrity, and a single six-gun. Instead, Acuña painted a picture of fraud, violence, and lawlessness—of a time when all Mexican possessions were an open target; when the law was exclusively on the side of the Anglo-Americans; and when a heterogeneous Mexican society had, for the most part, been violently compressed into a powerless, poor rural caste. But Mexicans and their Chicano offspring fought back, wrote Acuña. In California, social bandits such as Joaquín Murrieta and Tiburcio Vásquez fought violence with violence of their own. In New Mexico, "Las Gorras Blancas" cut the wire fences of land-grabbing land barons, and the Partido del Pueblo Unido fought the Anglo-American political machines in the electoral arena. In Texas, *revolucionarios* such as Catarino Garza and Juan Cortina led several uprisings against the landed and urban elites in South Texas. The battles against the Texas Rangers and the union strikes in the mines of Arizona and the pecan factories in San Antonio became part of the border mythology. The Mexican American community had finally succumbed to oppression, but these men and numerous women became heroes through Acuña's book.

In his concluding chapter, Acuña reaffirmed the prevailing rejection of American society articulated by the leaders of the emerging movement: "Chicanos who actively participated in the political life of the nation took a hard look at their assigned role in society, evaluated it, and then decided that they had had enough, so they bid good-bye to America."[32] In this chapter, Acuña depicted the rise of a new generation of leaders who had lost hope of finding solutions through the traditional channels of protest and litigation. Although the book ended on a somber, almost pessimistic note, Acuña nonetheless succeeded in setting the tone for the intense struggle for Chicano liberation. No other book before or since has carried the powerful message that Mexican Americans are an exploited and oppressed minority but one that has fought and continues to fight back.

I would never look at American society in the same way after reading *Occupied America*. For many like myself, our historical roots had been torn from the American soil, and we set out in a quest to find identity and to learn history—"our" history. Romano and Acuña led the search for more Chicano history. The new heroes became those who resisted the American conquest of the Southwest. Mexican military men who fought against the Texas rebels or who defended Mexico against the American invasion became men to admire. Particularly admirable were men like Catarino Garza and Juan Cortina, who rose up in arms to defend their Mexican compatriots. As inspiring were Emma Tenayuca, who led the pecan shellers' strike in San Antonio in the 1930s, and Luisa Moreno, an organizer for the United Cannery, Agricultural, and Packing Workers of America and a founder of El Congreso de los Pueblos de Habla Español in 1938.[33] The search for heroes did not end with larger-than-life men and women. With time, our heroes became those individuals who survived the daily struggles in a society still foreign to them.

Romano and Acuña were not the only ones writing this new interpretation. After the initial attack on the Anglo-American academy, Chicano scholars began to write their own history. Gómez-Quiñones wrote about the labor struggles of Chicanos and their early political activism. And he provided an in-depth view of the first ideological hero of the Chicano Movement when he wrote a biography of Ricardo Flores Magón, the Mexican anarchist and intellectual precursor of the Mexican Revolution. For the more ideological radicals in the Movement, Magón became and remained the most influential historical figure in Mexican history.[34] Gómez-Quiñones also pioneered the field of Chicano studies and served as a mentor for many graduate students who wrote about Chicanos in the pages of *De Colores*, *Aztlán*, *El Grito*, and other academic journals. His influence, through his writings and the students he mentored, was felt strongly in California and on college campuses nationwide. There were others. Renato Rosaldo promoted Mexican American studies at the University of Arizona and compiled the work *Chicanos: The Beginnings of Bronze Power*, one of the first anthologies of articles on Mexican Americans produced by a major publisher. Alberto Camarillo wrote about urban Chicanos in California; Américo Paredes and José Limón wrote about folklore, *corridos*, and the Rio Grande Valley; Emilio Zamora wrote about Chicano socialist activists at the turn of the century; Margarita Melville, Adelaida del Castillo, and other women scholars wrote about Chicanas in labor, politics, and letters. Anglo-American scholars such as Stan Steiner, Joan C. Moore, and David Weber also wrote works relevant to the study of Chicanos. Still others involved in this work were amateur historians, many of them poets, dramatists, and artists who incorporated history within their art. Each of them sought to reinterpret history and to create the necessary heroes, heroines, and myths needed to add flames to the Chicano cultural renaissance. Social scientists could not fill the void on the Chicano experience fast enough, so many essayists and fiction writers contributed to the reinterpretation.

These new writers created an image of themselves and their people that did not integrate into mainstream society. In the past, Mexican American writers had struggled to force themselves into the American literary mainstream. Most wrote of their people and themselves as marginalized individuals awaiting the acculturation of their community. Marcienne Rocard has written of the contrast between these two generations: "The older Mexican American poets and short-story writers were isolated; though they sometimes attacked the dominant society harshly and felt themselves to be marginal, they were part of it in spite of themselves. They had no separate image of themselves. By contrast, Chicano writers had a will to define and assert themselves with respect to the Anglo world, a will conditioned by ethnic allegiance."[35] They were, she added, obsessed with identity.

While historians sought to discover the history of Chicanos and sociologists worked to correct the stereotypes, Chicano writers attempted to give meaning to the Chicano experience by blending the social science with folklore and mythmaking. They were at times historians, social critics, seers, and political cheerleaders. More than anyone else, Chicano writers created, expanded, and exported their "new" history as they traveled throughout the barrios of the Southwest reading their works.[36] Their topics ranged from the Aztec gods to the Mexican Revolution; from the *pachuco* to the migrant farmworker; and from the young Chicano militants to Che Guevara, Augusto Sandino, Lucio Cabañas, and Fidel Castro. Most of the poetry dealt with identity and pride in being Chicano.[37] Poetry took the Chicano mind where history could not. Whereas historians wrote of brave men and women who resisted oppression, and of short-lived victories against the Anglo-American, poems provided the ultimate victory. In them, history and the present were described not as they were but as they could and would become. It was in the realm of literature that Chicanos had full control of their lives. There were no facts to contradict Chicano liberation. In poetry Anglo-Americans were simpletons; policemen cowardly; American culture degenerate; and Chicanos organic, brave intellectuals with a rich and moral culture.[38]

Art was another form of history, since most of it depicted the Chicano's Indian heritage and the community's legacy of struggle. Many Mexican American children first learned about Pancho Villa, Emiliano Zapata, Benito Juárez, Cuauhtémoc, and other Mexican heroes from the murals in the barrio. Art was another form that transcended historical facts and provided a new view of La Raza. The murals were larger than life, and the people in them could not help but be seen as heroic. Much of the impetus for this "new" art came from the Mexican revolutionary muralists like Diego Rivera and David Alfaro Siqueiros.

Probably as important as the poetry and art was Chicano *teatro*. With the founding of the Teatro Campesino at the start of the farmworkers' struggle in the mid-1960s, theater became an important tool in the development of identity and militancy. In the case of Teatro Campesino, as well as other Chicano theater groups, the playwright and the actors were part of the social movement. Their topics were usually discrimination, racism, police brutality, workers on strike, or

Chicano culture. The goal went beyond entertainment. Theater became a way by which people came to terms with their condition. The tradition of *teatro* in the barrio had been an entrenched one up until about the 1950s. Traveling theater troupes called *carpas*, whose name referred to the tents under which they performed, were a common feature in the Mexican American communities of the Southwest.[39] The skits were usually satires that presented a working-class view of the world. It made gentle fun of people in the barrio, while being particularly cutting toward middle- and upper-class *sociedad*. Props and scenery were kept to a minimum, and most skits were improvised. Few were political in a partisan or ideological way, but they nonetheless provided commentary on people's lives. For parents, these *variedades* (variety shows)[40] were a way to keep their children immersed in the culture and to strengthen their language skills in Spanish. It was also a way to keep the family together, because parents understood that American culture and the public schools were pulling their children away from them. The theater groups kept them close to their culture and *patria*. Although some parents had left Mexico willingly and had no desire to return, they nevertheless felt estranged from their country, and the *carpas* provided some relief from the alienation that they felt in the United States.[41]

Chicano theater groups emulated many aspects of the early Mexican troupes. They were not particularly ideological as much as they were critical of American society. In its early development, Chicano theater proved to be more critical of Anglo-American culture and of those Mexican Americans who sought assimilation than of the political system. With time that changed, and the country's policies at home and abroad became the targets of Chicano satire. Its most significant function, however, remained its promotion of the "new" Chicanos.

Teatro Campesino served as the model for most of these Chicano theater groups. Founded in 1965, it sought to teach farmworkers about the union activities of César Chávez and to attract them to union membership. In 1972, Luis Valdez, the Teatro's founder, wrote the following about its use of skits and funny scenes to further *la causa*: "Our use of comedy stemmed from necessity—the necessity of lifting the strikers' morale. We found we could make social points [commentary] not in spite of the comedy, but through it. Slapstick can bring us . . . close to the underlying tragedy . . . that human beings have been wasted for generations."[42] For two years after its founding, Teatro Campesino worked alongside the union in the picket lines. Its actors performed in the fields, in the labor camps, at rallies, at union meetings, and at strike benefits. They also toured the country and at each stop publicized the union boycotts, informing Mexican American and Anglo-American audiences about the plight of the farmworkers. They advocated a rural culturalism that sought to tie all Chicanos to the land. This culturalism promoted the family as the unit of struggle, since in farmworkers families everyone worked in the fields to help out. Once unionized, all members of the family became connected to the strike, boycott, or picket line. For Teatro Campesino there existed a new Chicano, willing to work for *la causa*. This Chicano shunned materialism and looked to the land and his or her history for meaning.

The founders of Teatro Campesino, as well as those of the union, knew there existed another kind of Mexican American. He was the *vendido*, the Mexican American willing to sell out his people to the highest bidder. In the rural areas he was the Mexican labor contractor, in the urban barrios he was the *politico*, and at the university he was the acculturated Chicano who believed in the system and in education for the professional advantages it brought. The theater became the place to expose this type of character, and thus the *vendido* became one of the stock characters of most Chicano plays. It was the United Farm Workers Union (UFW)[43] that first identified the dichotomy within the Chicano community. Union organizers quickly labeled as "sell-outs" those Mexican Americans who were afraid to challenge the growers or those who worked for them. In identifying a character such as the *vendido*, Chicano theater provided a contrast for the new Chicano. It also was a way to belittle and discredit those who straddled the fence or sided against the Movement. In time, it became a way to keep discipline within the ranks, since the threat of being designated a *vendido* intimidated many a wavering Chicano activist.[44]

Chicano theater groups appeared throughout the Southwest. The Crusade for Justice had its own theater group, and so did many other organizations. But although they were supportive of the Movement, most Chicano theater groups were independent of control from activists. This freedom gave them the ability to transcend local or regional issues and allowed them artistic freedom. Much as in the Chicano Movement, their ideological base resulted from a hodgepodge of ideas and concerns. The underlying theme of all their work, and the one with which all Chicanos could identify, was the threat of cultural genocide and its economic, social, and spiritual legacy. The *teatros* provided

a simple message: Chicanos and their culture were under attack; they had to resist by knowing their history and maintaining their culture and they had to root out the *vendidos* from among them. That theme served Chicano activists from the California college campuses to the migrant shanty towns of Hidalgo County in Texas. Chicano theater, much like Chicano literature, provided a more positive view of the Mexican American community. Although the history and experience depicted in the plays often defied historical accuracy, they nevertheless projected a positive image and created new myths, something of which Chicanos seemed so much in need.

Two other institutions promoted a new interpretation of the Chicano experience: Chicano studies programs and centers, and the Chicano press. Both Chicano studies, as a political and academic movement, and the Chicano press, as a conveyor of information, proved to be crucial to the reinterpretation of the Chicano experience. More Chicanos learned about "their" history and about brown militancy from these two institutions than from any other source. Their importance to the Movimiento cannot be overemphasized.

Chicano studies programs began appearing on college campuses in the mid-1960s in response to student demands that Mexican American history and culture be taught as part of the academic curriculum. These programs first appeared in California as a result of the student strikes occurring in Los Angeles and other major cities. The main impetus for the growth of Chicano studies, however, came from a conference at the University of California at Santa Barbara in April 1969. There, over one hundred delegates from 29 campuses met under the sponsorship of the Chicano Coordinating Committee on Higher Education to develop a master plan for Chicanos in higher education.[45]

In El Plan de Santa Bárbara, which came out of the conference and became the Movement's design for educating the Chicano masses, the authors declared: "We recognize that without a strategic use of education that places value on what we value, we will not realize our destiny. . . . Throughout history the quest for cultural expression and freedom has taken the form of a struggle."[46] This "strategic use of education" meant Chicano students and faculty were to be involved in the development of curriculum and in the administration of programs. It also meant that these programs would be within what Carlos Muñoz called "the context of a politics for change."[47] The Plan's authors express this context in the following manner: "Now Chicano university students, not unmindful of the historic price of assimilation, take charge within the community as the point of departure for their social and political involvement. . . . At this moment we do not come to work for the university, but to demand that the university work for our people."[48] Many of those hired to teach and direct the programs used the classroom to expound their version of Chicano history. For those who found themselves in areas where there were no major Movement organizations, the courses in Chicano studies allowed them to participate, at least emotionally, in the Movement. Also, many of these programs sponsored trips to large protest activities, marches, and militant conferences.

In Kingsville, many joined the Movement through the efforts of José Reyna, head of the Ethnic Studies program at Texas A&I University. In his classroom, students read Romano's articles, Acuña's book, and the countless other articles, books, and periodicals that were surfacing during the early 1970s. Self-identity usually became the main topic of the courses offered there and in other places. In class environments made up mostly of Chicanos, students often discussed and debated issues that would have been deemed inappropriate in other classrooms.[49] In places such as California State University at Northridge, degrees were offered in Chicano studies, and students graduating from these programs were expected to have some fluency in both Spanish and Náhuatl (the language of the Aztecs) and to know their Mexican and Chicano history. In other places, like Kingsville, where lack of university support limited the programs, students were provided the basics of Chicano thought and were then exhorted to join community grassroots organizations that were involved in some form of activism. The Chicano studies programs provided a sense of legitimacy for many and a place in which Chicano intellectual debates were appreciated.[50] It was also for many a place where the correct "history" of La Raza could be learned. According to an editorial in *El Grito*, "The responsibility upon the shoulders of those in Chicano programs is great, for should the end product be disfigured in any way whatsoever, they will have turned victory into defeat, self-expression into self-denial, a dream into a nightmare, and a promise into . . . purposeless mouthings."[51] For Chicano academicians, Chicano studies programs were a personal responsibility. They sought to eliminate "past distortions." The "future image" was now in their hands, and they set out to craft that image.[52]

Through the efforts of Chicano studies and ethnic studies programs, many Chicanos rediscovered their culture, learned about their history, and regained an identity many had lost or had never acquired at home. Through these programs, students participated in local community activities such as Diez y Seis de Septiembre and Cinco de Mayo celebrations (Mexican patriotic holidays) and local elections and protests. It was not uncommon for groups associated with a Chicano studies program to sponsor Christmas parties, food drives, or picnics for the local Chicano community.[53] Students who had often been unaware of cultural events in their hometowns, or who had simply not been interested in participating, now became involved. With the mentoring of their professors, they saw the community in a different light. Herbal remedies, cultural traditions, and other barrio survival techniques became symbols of resistance to an alienating urban world. No longer were students ashamed of the cure-all *hierbas*, the *parteras*, the *salsa picante* and *tacos*, and *quinceañeras*, and other cultural "anomalies" in which the barrio participated. Rather than blame La Raza for its poverty, dropout rates, or juvenile delinquency, many college students, tutored by their Chicano instructors, shifted the blame to mainstream Anglo-American society. Chicano culture became all good, healthy, and moral; problems encountered were those that had been inflicted on the barrios by external forces. For many Chicano students, the Chicano experience took on a different character than even the one they had experienced themselves. Isolated in a university environment often foreign to them, they saw the community as warm and familiar. Although they were in reality separated by education and status from the community, they felt a greater connection to it than ever before. Nostalgia had become history.

For those who did not attend the university, the Chicano press served as the catalyst for intellectual discussion. "*El Gallo* was born out of frustration and determination for the truth," wrote "Corky" Gonzales of the Crusade's newspaper, in 1967.[54] One year later, the editors of *El Grito del Norte* would declare their intent to promote the "course of justice of the poor people . . . and conserve the cultural heritage of la raza."[55] Chicano newspapers carried bits of history, literature, current news, commentary, and a strong dose of cultural polemics.

There were three kinds of newspapers and magazines that formed the nucleus of the Chicano press. The first were newspapers that represented specific organizations and usually promoted particular political philosophies. There were the UFW's *El Malcriado*, La Raza Unida Party's *Para la Gente*, the Brown Berets'

Regeneración, the newspapers of other major Chicano Movement groups, and other smaller periodicals representing smaller organizations. These were initially the most influential and most scathing in their polemics. The second category of newspapers included those published by university student groups. These were mostly disseminated within the local university community and to other college campuses throughout the country. These newspapers dealt with issues of academic freedom, Chicano studies, and student politics and published a fair amount of commentary on international issues. They were often the most brash and used language deemed inappropriate for the other two categories of newspapers. Some of these were *El Chile* from Texas A & I University at Kingsville and *El Chingazo* from San Diego State University. The third kind of publication was the independent newspapers directed toward the community, even though some came from university groups or particular partisan groups. These periodicals tended to publish for a longer period of time and were as popular outside the locality where they were published as they were within. Examples were *El Grito del Norte* from Denver; *La Raza* from Los Angeles; and *Caracol* from San Antonio, Texas.

These news sheets were in essence the wire service for Chicano activists throughout Aztlán. Articles that originated in the pages of these periodicals were reprinted in other newspapers, duplicated, and passed out during rallies or political discussions. This kept the flow of ideas going and bound all of the peripheries to the centers of Chicano activism. Through them, Chicanos learned what issues were of greatest importance to the greatest number of Chicanos. From them also came word as to which leaders were rising in the Movement and which were fading. Much like radio and television for American society, the Chicano press developed a "mainstream" image of what a Chicano or Chicana in the Movement did or said.

None of the aforementioned periodicals, nor most of the others, had rigid ideological lines to present. They were nationalistic, anticapitalist, and geared toward action. *El Grito del Norte* tended to concentrate on the work of the Alianza, *El Gallo* on the politics of the Crusade for Justice, and *La Raza* on the California activities of the Chicano student movement and later La Raza Unida Party. *Caracol* tended to be the most independent. It also became the most diversified, with over half of its pages devoted to poems, autobiographical essays, plays, and short stories. These newspapers and magazines provided a view of local, national, and international events from a Chicano perspective. The

war in Vietnam was important in relation to how many Chicanos were being killed. The national liberation movements in Asia, Africa, and Latin America were analyzed to identify strategies that Chicanos could use in their own liberation. And American foreign policy received critical scrutiny to confirm the Chicano condemnation of American imperialism. Locally, the coverage revolved around daily occurrences of discrimination; local laws, ordinances, or practices that treated Chicanos as second-class citizens; and political victories by community groups.[56]

The periodicals evolved politically with time. Most went from covering the local community to commenting on national and international events. As time went by, and political victories at home became more difficult to obtain, the newspapers increased their polemical discussions on ideology and "Yankee imperialism." They also moved away from cultural events and histories that had been the mainstay of the first issues. Nevertheless, the newspapers remained the promoters of the new image of the Chicano. And they continued to interpret the Chicano experience in a separatist mode, where aggression and resistance were the main themes of that experience. Some of these newspapers later made the transition to becoming community newspapers, while others spurned more traditional periodicals that were in business to make money and not political commentary.

By the mid-1970s, for those who took time to notice, Chicanos had created a historical image for themselves. This image of a historical people with heroes, legends, intellectual foundations, and culture differed dramatically from that which came from the academic and popular literature. Mexican Americans no longer had to accept the view of the Chicano as a lazy, unambitious, violent individual with insatiable sexual desires and a culture that bred poverty and delinquency. They also did not have to accept the image of passivity. This new outlook became important as Chicano activists rejected the liberal approach to solving the problems of the community. A failure to replace the image of the nonachieving Chicano at a time when the liberal approach was rejected would have meant that Chicanos were worse off than they believed. When they had been unable to develop a mass protest movement, the liberal approach had been a safety net for Mexican Americans. The piecemeal approach had had its benefits. Once that approach was rejected, Chicanos needed a stronger self-image in order to embark on their own program of self-help. Historical identity became crucial for activists. This identity developed through the efforts of academicians, who rejected stereotypes and dug out the real history; poets and playwrights, who presented culturally militant Chicanos and Chicanas as the prototypes of the new Mexican American; Chicano studies programs, which involved students and created a reservoir of Chicano intellectuals; and newspapers and magazines, which kept Chicanos informed of what was happening in Aztlán and which served to develop a cultural and political "homogeneity" among Chicano activists.[57] The reinterpretation of the Chicano experience affected the way particular sectors within the Chicano community saw themselves. Even in segments of the community where radicalism did not dominate the mode of operations, the new view of Chicanos caused considerable change. The Church—as used here, denoting religious groups within the community, predominantly the Catholic Church—was one such entity deeply affected by the Chicano Movement's activism and its interpretation of history.[58]

For many Chicano activists, the Church had been one of those institutions that had cooperated in the oppression of the Chicano masses by teaching them subserviency and by encouraging them to be happy with their lot on Earth, as heaven would bring celestial rewards.[59] For others, the Church represented a financial and social power that refused to intervene on behalf of the poor Chicano. "The religious dollar must be invested, without return expected, in the barrios," declared an editorial in *El Grito del Norte*.[60] César Chávez, a man of deep religious loyalty, also called for a more sensitive Church. "It is our duty" to appeal to the church for the poor, he told readers of *El Grito* in 1968. "It should be as natural as appealing to government . . . and we do that often enough."[61] The Mexican American Youth Organization (MAYO) had even responded to the Church's passivity with sacrilege in 1969 when its members spray-painted brown a statue of Our Lady of the Immaculate Conception that stood on the grounds of an old seminary building in Mission, Texas. They had done so to protest the Church's refusal to give them the building for their "university without walls" and for its overall lack of support for the Movement.[62] Other activists who were Marxist-oriented, or disciples of anarchy, saw the Church as reactionary.

There were others, however, who saw that the Church was an important institution in the barrio and that many Mexican Americans remained faithful to it. "God is alive and well in the heart of the Chicano," Luis Valdez would write during the height of the grape and lettuce boycott.[63] They also saw within it a number of Chicano and Anglo-American priests

ready to join the Movement. While preaching against the Church's hierarchy, many activists united with lay leaders and clergy to promote Movement activities. In New Mexico, Reies López Tijerina, a former Pentecostal preacher, would lead the land-grant movement with a religious zeal and place it within the context of a spiritual crusade. In Robstown, Texas, a number of early Movement candidates were Baptist lay leaders. At Brigham Young University, A Chicano from San Antonio's Spanish-speaking Mormon congregation established the university's first ethnic studies club. In Tucson, a Methodist parish provided the meeting space for the Mexican American Liberation Committee. And in New York, Protestant churches, responding to lay leaders' demands, established the National Farm Workers Ministry.[64]

Chávez was the most adept at using the Church as a powerful ally. In the UFW union hall in Delano, California, a large banner reminded the farmworkers daily that "God is beside you on the picket line." In rallying the poor Chicanos to continue their strikes and their organizing amid arrests, intimidation, and seemingly unbeatable odds, Chávez continually used religious symbolism and rhetoric to inspire his followers. The march to Sacramento became a religious pilgrimage. "They [the farmworkers] hope to set themselves at peace with the Lord, so that the justice of their cause will be purified of all lesser motivations."[65] The fasts became petitions for "nonviolence and a call to sacrifice." They also became a way to attract national attention to the nobleness of the cause. For the UFW, the Virgen de Guadalupe became the patron saint of the Movement, accompanying its strikers on the picket lines, marches, and rallies. Organizations such as Católicas por La Raza, PADRES, HERMANAS, and other arose.[66]

Movement activists learned to acknowledge that religious affiliation remained important for many Mexican Americans. To make that affiliation beneficial for the Movement meant reinterpreting the Church's historical role in the community. To do so, these activists looked back in history to find those religious leaders who had sided with the oppressed and the Indians. They found Fathers Miguel Hidalgo y Costilla and José María Morelos y Pavón of the Mexican War for Independence, and they found religious revolutionaries such as Rubén Jaramillo, a lay Methodist preacher, who fought alongside the famous Mexican peasant leader of the Revolution of 1910, Emiliano Zapata. Others simply reinterpreted the role of Christ, making him a revolutionist. "For it is from him that we draw our strength," said an activist calling herself Dolores del

Grito.[67] Tijerina would compare his actions to those of an angry god: "The revolution of Tierra Amarilla was like Christ entering the temple and clearing out the Pharisees."[68] This interpretation was fanned by the development of liberation theology and the rise of guerrilla-priests in Latin America.

The moral tone of the Movement attracted a number of religious individuals to the struggle. In my own Mormon parish In San Antonio, a number of members joined La Raza Unida Party and a number of the other community organizations active at the time. The Movement to me, and many others like me, represented a variation of the social gospel. We were to work for the poor, to preach higher moral and political values, and to empower communities to challenge an evil society. Attending political masses, working with priests and lay leaders to empower poor parishioners, and placing the Movement within the context of a moral crusade served to radicalize religious life for many of us. We then interpreted many of our religious leaders' actions within a historical context of resistance against Anglo-American racism or paternalism.

The Church—as a religious entity—did not change drastically, notwithstanding many challenges to its ministries. But many Chicano followers did change. They saw the Church as having a role beyond the four walls of the chapel or the cathedral. They saw the gospel going beyond personal values to providing a framework for a just society. The moral authority of the Church was to be used to teach against the evils of poverty, discrimination, and capitalism. For activists, the changing role of the faithful in the Church, an institution that had functioned for decades as the maintainer of culture, helped in the reinterpretation of the Chicano experience. Taking the collective cultural experience of the Church as a basis, Chicano activists not only provided historicity to their struggle but also gave it a moral impetus. The intellectual dichotomy between those who accepted religion and those who rejected it remained significant throughout the Movement period, but for those who remained faithful, the new interpretation made them more adamant about working for social justice. This added to the new view of an active and resisting community.

Chicanas proved to be another sector of the community deeply affected by the reinterpretation of history. If Mexican American males suffered the burden of stereotypes, then Mexican American women suffered a double burden. What could be expected of the mothers, wives, and daughters of those men who were ahistorical, passive, lazy, and *mañana*-oriented? Arthur Rubel, one of those social scientists that Romano had taken to task for stereotyping Mexican American males, wrote about the Chicana: "[They are] ideally submissive, unworldly, and chaste."[69] They were possessions to be guarded and protected from the outside world. William Madsen went further in denigrating Mexican American women: "The Latin woman plays the perfect counterpart to the Latin male. Where he is strong, she is weak. Where he is aggressive, she is submissive. While he is condescending toward her, she is respectful toward him. A woman is expected to always display those subdued qualities of womanhood that make a man feel the need to protect her."[70] Spousal abuse, continued Madsen, was seen as deserved and as proof of profound love.

Gloria Molina de Pick argued that Chicanas suffered from the depiction of being chaste and submissive as well as seductive and representing the "most provocative of sexual adventures."[71] This contradiction, wrote Adaljiza Sosa Riddell, served to free American society from any responsibility for the Chicanas' oppression, and it kept Chicanas "preoccupied" with their "shortcomings." This conflictive dichotomy blamed Chicanas "for not being good mothers, for not keeping the family together, for working instead of staying home, or conversely, for being too oriented to their family, for having too many children, for not working, for staying home."[72] Mexican American women simply could not win. Either seen as submissive and passive or as seductive and responsible for familial shortcomings, they were even less a rational entity than their husbands, fathers, or sons.

Initially, the Movement's interpretation of women centered on their relationships to the family. At the Chicano Youth Liberation Conference, Chicanas, anxious to be seen as part of a united front, voted to declare that they did not want to be "liberated."[73] But the Movement, notwithstanding the chauvinism of some of its leaders, could not help but challenge patriarchy through its liberation rhetoric and through the opportunity it gave women to become involved in protest activities. Women, through their clerical skills, their willingness to do tedious jobs well, and their ability to follow through on assignments, became the organizational backbone of the Movement.

When Movement activities began in the early 1960s, precursors were few. Although they tended to be predominantly male, there were a significant number of women. A few women were known Movement-wide, but many others were part of the rank and file, whose influence remained at the local and regional level.

These women, once in the Movement, began to argue for inclusion in the new interpretation. "When we talk equality," wrote Longeaux y Vásquez, "we better be talking about total equality."[74] But rather than wait for the men to dominate the process, they set out to do the interpretation. Chicano activists often saw the historical Mexican woman as self-sacrificing—as the *abuelita*, or the Adelita who followed the man during times of upheaval. The poet José Montoya wrote:

When I remember the *campos* [fields]
. . . I remember my *jefita's* [mother's]
palote [rolling pin]
(I swear, she never slept)
Es tarde mi hijito [it's late my son]
cover up
. . . a maternal reply mingled with
the hissing of the hot *planchas* [iron]
. . . *y la jefita* slapping tortillas
. . . *y en el fil* [in the field], pulling
her *cien* [one hundred]
libras del algodón [pounds of cotton]
. . . that woman—she only complains
in her sleep.[75]

Chicanas saw themselves as more than self-sacrificing spouses or mothers. Like the male activists, they saw themselves as having a strong historical legacy but a diverse one. They accepted the role of the self-sacrificing woman as a legitimate part of the Chicana experience but complemented it with that of the labor leader who fought for the rights of working people, of the *soldadera* who fought with guns and rifles for freedom, and of the ideologue who wrote and spoke against injustices. Women were to be found wherever there was struggle.[76]

Most Chicana activists felt a need to remain within the mainstream of the Movement. They saw the liberation of community as the first goal. They argued, at least initially, that Chicanas first became ideologically conscious of discrimination as Chicanas rather than as women. But within the Movement, they demanded the room to deal with issues that affected them as mothers and as women. And they also sought an influential role in defining the direction of the community's liberation. Many men responded to the women's concerns positively. Activist scholar Martha Cotera remembered that most of the male leaders in La Raza Unida Party tended to be supportive. "I don't really remember the men as obstacles," she would say years later.[77]

The women's dialogue, first among themselves and then publicly in the publications such as *Regeneración*, *Encuentro Femenil*, and other Chicano journals of the time, sought to define a new place for Chicanas. The new Chicana would stand alongside her man as the *soldadera* of the Mexican Revolution did, but she expected the partnership to be equal. And the definition of liberation now had to include freedom from *machismo* and the full freedom to participate in all aspects of the Chicano community's decision making. The political agenda had to concern itself with child care, employment and training for women, and a redefinition of familial roles.[78] Chicano activists, faced with a need for dedicated workers and confronted with their own "ideologically progressive" rhetoric, found themselves forced to open the Movement to women. Although the opening oftentimes seemed scarcely a crack to many, the women took advantage of it and reinterpreted their historical role within the Chicano community. If the men had struggled and resisted conquest and discrimination, then Chicanas had done the same. Chicana scholars, artists, essayists, and poets made sure that those within and without the Movement did not forget.

Chicanas also began exploring the special burden that they carried as women. Declared the platform of La Raza Unida Party in Colorado: "For our women . . . there exists a triple exploitation, a triple degradation; they are exploited as women, as people of *La Raza*, and they suffer from the poverty that straitjackets all of *La Raza*. We feel that without recognition . . . of their special form of oppression . . . our movement will suffer greatly."[79] Like their black counterparts, these Chicanas sought to expand beyond the ideological boundaries set for them by male activists and white feminists. Chicanas saw their struggle in terms of community and family, even as they fought for equality at the personal level. Unbridled by the males' concept of honor, which saw political defeat as humiliating, these women continued to push for an end to racism and for collective empowerment in the face of strong opposition. Once they reinterpreted the Chicana experience as positive and heroic, they found the historical impetus to continue their activism.

Scholarly works of high quality, with a few exceptions, would come after the decline of the Movement. Some of them would even contradict the romanticism of the Movement-inspired histories. But most continued to offer a new and positive interpretation of the Chicano experience. Chicano Movement historians, trained or otherwise, had engaged in a historical discourse to discredit stereotypes and to combat the crisis of identity that many Mexican

Americans confronted. Their history often worked chronologically backward. Their premise was that Chicanos were a strong and courageous people who had survived conquest, colonization, and racial brutality. Working back from that premise meant interpreting the "facts" to support the thesis. This new view of history allowed Chicanos to become the evaluators and legitimizers of their history and provided them the opportunity to define their historical significance and importance. Historical reinterpretation would be one of the most significant products of the Chicano Movement.

Endnotes

1. One who did was Carlos E. Castañeda, who wrote what historian Mario T. García calls a "complementary history" of the Mexican American. This history attempted to underscore the similarities between Mexican Americans and Anglo-Americans. It also sought to dispel the stereotypes that Anglo-Americans had about Mexican Americans. For a further explanation of Castañeda's work, see Mario T. García, *In Search of History: Carlos E. Castañeda and the Mexican American Generation*, Renato Rosaldo Lecture Series Monograph 4 (Tuscon: Mexican American Studies and Research Center, University of Arizona, 1988), 1–20.

2. John C. Hammerback, Richard J. Jensen, and José Angel Gutiérrez, *A War of Words* (Westport, Conn.: Greenwood Press, 1985), 51.

3. See the following works for an example of this type of scholarship: Celia S. Heller, *Mexican-American Youth: Forgotten Youth at the Crossroads* (New York: Random House, 1968); William Madsen, *Mexican-Americans of South Texas, Case Studies in Cultural Anthropology* (New York: Holt, Rinehart and Winston, 1964); Ruth Tuck, *Not with the Fist* (New York: Harcourt, Brace and Co., 1946); and Edmonson S. Munro, *Los Manitos: A Study of Institutional Values* (New Orleans: Middle American Research Institute, 1957).

4. "Poverty of culture" was developed as a concept from the writings of men like Oscar Lewis, Michael Harrington, and Daniel Moynihan. Ironically, all three authors claimed to write on behalf of the disadvantaged but ended up coining concepts that were used to blame the victims of poverty. See Oscar Lewis, *La Vida: A Puerto Rican Family in the Culture of Poverty* (New York: Random House, 1966); and Michael Harrington, *The New American Poverty* (New York: Penguin Books, 1984).

5. Valdez referred to the Spanish Conquest of Mexico, but other activists would us the term "conquest" to describe the occupation of the American Southwest

by the U.S. military, which is what it refers to here. Whereas Anglo-American scholars often describe the Spanish Conquest as having created a legacy of problems for Mexicans, Chicano scholars would see the later conquest as being more significant.

6. Luis Valdez and Stan Steiner, eds., *Aztlán: An Anthology of Mexican American Literature* (New York: Alfred A. Knopf, 1972), xiii, xiv.

7. See David Sánchez, "Chicano Power Explained" (mimeographed booklet), Special Collections, Stanford University Libraries, 1.

8. Enriqueta Longeaux y Vásquez, "Despierten hermanos," *El Grito del Norte*, August 24, 1968, p. 6.

9. Octavio Romano, "The Anthropology and Sociology of the Mexican American: The Distortion of Mexican-American History," *El Grito* 2 (1968): 13–14.

10. Enriqueta Longeaux y Vásquez, "A nuestros lectores," *El Grito del Norte*, September 15, 1968, p. 2.

11. William Madsen, *The Mexican American in South Texas* (New York: Holt, Rinehart and Winston, 1964), 109.

12. Romano, "Anthropology and Sociology," 14.

13. Carey McWilliams, *North from Mexico: The Spanish-Speaking People of the United States* (New York: Greenwood Press, 1968), as quoted in Romano, "Anthropology and Sociology."

14. Tuck, *Not with the Fist*, 198.

15. Interestingly, Julian Samora was both praised and criticized during this period.

16. Octavio Romano, "The Historical and Intellectual Presence of Mexican Americans," *El Grito* (winter 1969): 32–46.

17. Ibid., 40–44.

18. Ibid., 46.

19. Romano's articles and his publication *El Grito* became required reading for Chicano activists. A Chicano student would have been hard pressed to discuss Chicano identity and history without discussing Romano's work.

20. Editorial, *El Grito* 1, no. 1 (fall 1967): 4.

21. Many liberal scholars, in trying to empathize, often added to the stereotypes of being overly sensitive about Chicano issues to the point of condescension. See Américo Paredes, "On Ethnographic Work among Minority Groups," in *New Directions in Chicano Scholarship*, ed. Raymond Romo and Raymond Paredes (La Jolla, Calif.: Chicano Studues Monograph Series, 1978). See also Octavio Romano, "Minorities, History and Cultural Mystique," *El Grito* 1, no. 1 (1967).

22. It is also because of the scarcity of Anglo-American liberal supporters that the Chicano Movement has not been a major theme explored by Anglo-American academicians. Few Anglo-American activists or scholars

ever received training in the struggles of Chicanos for equal rights as many did in the black civil-rights battles. See Renato Rosaldo, Jr., *When Natives Talk Back: Chicano Anthropology Since the Late Sixties*, Renato Rosaldo Lecture Series Monograph 2 (Tucson: Mexican American Studies and Research Center, University of Arizona, 1986), 3–20, for a discussion of the early abandonment of Chicano scholarship by Anglo-American scholars, who were unwilling to face Chicano critique of their work.

23. See Juan Gómez-Quiñones, "Toward a Perspective on Chicano History," *Aztlán* (fall 1971): 1–49.

24. Juan Gómez-Quiñones, "Notes on Periodization, 1900–1965," *Aztlán* (spring 1970): 115–118.

25. See Carlos Muñoz, "Toward A Chicano Perspective of Political Analysis," *Aztlán* (fall 1970).

26. Many of the articles published in these journals were reprinted in numerous community and underground newspapers and magazines and thus became accessible to those communities and campuses where the journals were not available.

27. *Caracol* is in itself a work worthy of study, since it is served as a vehicle for many artists and essayists to get started. Everything that was submitted was published, and so it encouraged many to continue to pursue their dreams of writing, drawing, and publishing. Headed by Cecilio García-Camarillo, *Caracol* proved to be the most important popular literary magazine of the Movement.

28. More research has to be conducted on those who rediscovered their ethnicity during the years of the Chicano Movement. Many of these "born-again" Chicanos became the most passionate of all the activists.

29. See Acuña, introduction to *Occupied America*, 1st ed.

30. The other book to appear at about the same time was by Matt S. Meier and Feliciano Rivera, *The Chicanos: A History of Mexican Americans* (New York: Hill and Wang, 1972), which was a milder version popular among Anglo-American historians who chose to include the history of Mexican Americans in their courses. That book never quite gained a place in Chicano studies.

31. The theory would eventually come under attack from Chicano Marxist scholars for having no class-analysis component. Other mainstream Chicano historians would also question the model. As mentioned above, by the second edition of his *Occupied America* in 1981, Acuña had also rethought his political model and so did not include it. Still, the internal-colony model remains influential even today, much in the same manner that Frederick Jackson Turner's discredited theory of the development of the West remains influential among western historians. For a more in-depth explanation of

the internal-colony model, see Mario Barrera, Carlos Muñoz, and Charles Ornelas, "The Barrio as Internal Colony," *Urban Affairs Annual Review* 6 (1972): 465–98; see also Tomás Almaguer, "Toward the Study of Chicano Colonialism," *Aztlán* 2, no.1 (spring 1971): 7–20.

32. Acuña, *Occupied America*, 3d. ed., chapter 11.

33. For information on Emma Tenayuca and Luisa Moreno, see Carlos Larralde, *Mexican American Movements and Leaders* (Los Alamitos, Calif.: Hwong, 1976); for information on El Congreso de los Pueblos de Habla Español, see M.T. García, *Mexican Americans*, 145–74.

34. Juan Gómez-Quiñones, *Sembradores, Ricardo Flores Magón y el Partido Liberal Mexicano: A Eulogy and Critique* (Los Angeles: Aztlán Publications, Chicano Studies Center, University of California, 1973).

35. Marcienne Rocard, *Children of the Sun*, 213.

36. Ibid.

37. Ibid., 213–15.

38. In the works of the Teatro Campesino, La Raza would win its economic battle; in Nephthali De Leon's plays, the Chicano struggle had the blessings of Che Guevara and other fallen revolutionaries; in Rudy Anaya's novels, all answers came from within the Chicano family; and in Evangelina Vigil's poems, the Chicana won her struggles against Anglo society and Chicano men.

39. Nicolas Kanellos, *Mexican American Theater Then and Now* (Houston: Arte Público Press, 1983), 41–51.

40. Most working-class drama was composed of a series of skits and musical numbers; thus they were called variety shows. See Kanellos, *Mexican American Theater*, 19–40.

41. Kanellos deals with this type of sociological dilemma facing Mexican Americans in his discussion of Chicano theater groups; see *Mexican American Theater*, 35–38.

42. Luis Valdez, "Notes on Chicano Theater," in *Aztlán: An Anthology of Mexican American Literature*, ed. Luis Valdez and Stan Steiner (New York: Alfred A. Knopf, 1972), 353–54.

43. The NFWA had become the United Farmworkers Union, or UFW.

44. The taxonomy or lexicon, as some called it, of the Chicano Movement served a useful purpose for activists seeking to change the way the community perceived itself and Anglo-American society. See Valdez, "Notes on Chicano Theater," 354–59.

45. Carlos Muñoz, *Youth, Identity, Power*, 134–35.

46. Ibid., 191–202.

47. Ibid., 138.

48. Ibid., 192.

49. It is important to note that, unlike today, when many Anglo-American students are "forced" to take these

courses because of degree requirements, few Anglo-American students took them when they first became part of the college curriculum.

50. In Kingsville, the Chicano Movement depended on the limited facilities of the ethnic studies program and used students to do much of the campaigning, leafleting, and protest marching.

51. Editorial, *El Grito* 3, no. 3 (spring 1970): 2.

52. Ibid.

53. In Kingsville, La Raza Unida Club sponsored Christmas parties for children, Cinco de Mayo celebrations for the community, lectures series, art exhibits, Tejano music concerts, and Chicano plays.

54. Editorial, *El Gallo*, July 28, 1967, p. 2.

55. Longeaux y Vásquez, "A nuestros lectores," 2.

56. For a discussion of Chicano newspapers, see Stephen Casanova, "La Raza Unida Press," 1986, personal collection of I.M. García.

57. This homogeneity did not spill over into political strategies or even rigid ideologies, but it did provide an image of Chicanos deeply committed to struggle for liberation.

58. For a discussion of the changes that took place in the American Catholic Church after the activism of the 1960s and 1970s, see Jay P. Dolan and Allan Figueroa Deck, S.J., eds., *Hispanic Catholic Culture in the U.S.: Issues and Concerns* (Notre Dame, Ind.: University of Notre Dame Press, 1994).

59. See "Católicos por la raza," *La Raza* (February 1970).

60. Editorial, *El Grito del Norte*, February 11, 1970, p. 2.

61. César Chávez, "The Mexican Americans and the Church," *El Grito* 2, no. 4 (summer 1968).

62. Navarro, "El Partido," 250–52.

63. Luis Valdez, "The Church and the Chicanos," in *Aztlán: An Anthology of Mexican American Literature*, ed. Luis Valdez and Stan Steiner (New York: Alfred A. Knopf, 1972), 387–88.

64. Leo D. Nieto, "The Chicano Movement and the Churches in the United States," *Perkins Journal* (fall 1975).

65. See "Peregrinación, Penitencia, Revolución," by César Chávez (mimeographed; reprinted in Luis Valdez and Stan Steiner, eds., *Aztlán: An Anthology of Mexican American Literature* [New York: Alfred A. Knopf, 1972], 389–90.)

66. See Dolan and Deck, *Hispanic Catholic Culture*, 224–36.

67. See "Jesus Christ as a Revolutionist," *El Grito del Norte*, February 11, 1970.

68. "Day of Triumph in Tierra Amarilla," *El Grito del Norte*, January 1969, p. 7.

69. Arthur Rubel, "The Family," in *Mexican Americans in the United States*, ed. John H. Burman (New York: Shenkman Publishing Co., 1970), 214.

70. William Madsen, *Mexican American*, 20.

71. Gloria Molina de Pick, "Reflexiones sobre el feminismo y la raza," *La Luz* (August 1972): 58.

72. Adaljiza Sosa Riddell, "Chicanas and el Movimiento," *Aztlán* 5, nos. 1 and 2 (1974): 160.

73. Enriqueta Longeaux y Vásquez, "The Woman of La Raza," in *Aztlán: An Anthology of Mexican American Literature*, ed. Luis Valdez and Stan Steiner (New York: Alfred A. Knopf, 1972), 272.

74. Enriqueta Longeaux y Vásquez, "The Women of La Raza," *El Grito del Norte*, July 6, 1969.

75. José Montoya, "La Jefita," in *El Espejo—The Mirror: Selected Mexican American Literature*, ed. Octavio V. Romano (Quinto Sol Publications: 1969).

76. See "Our Feminist Heritage," in Martha P. Cotera's *The Chicana Feminist* (Austin, Tex.: Information Systems Development, 1977), 1–7.

77. Martha Cotera made this statement on September 12, 1994, in Austin, Texas at a training session for producers and writers of an upcoming Public Broadcasting System special on the Chicano Movement.

78. Enriqueta Longeaux y Vásquez, "Woman of La Raza," 274–77.

79. "La Chicana," *El Grito del Norte, June 5, 1971,* special section.

Border Challenges and Ethnic Struggles for Social Justice in Arizona: Hispanic Communities Under Siege

Rosalía Solórzano Torres

This chapter focuses on border challenges, ethnic straggles, and the responses of Latina/o communities in Arizona. The Arizona's immigration reform, SB 1070, And the anti-ethnic studies law, HB 2281, attempt to streamline undocumented migration and the erasure of La Raza and Mexican-American Studies at the Tucson united School District. The dissemination of political hateful discourses guides the militarization of the border as an important social location and the creation communities under siege. These laws dehumanize and create misguided and a blatant climate of racial hostility against Mexican and Hispanic communities, particularly those situated on the US-Mexico border. This chapter concludes a brief examination of the repercussions of Republican political vitriol, a dissemination of an "ecology of fear," and the assassination attempt launched against Congresswoman Gabrielle Giffords, which brutally ended the lives of six individuals and left 14 others wounded in Tucson, Arizona.

R.S. Torres
Pima Community College, Tucson; Arizona, USA
e-mail: solorzanoros@hotmail.com

M. Lusk et al. (eds.), *Social Justice in the U.S. -Mexico Border Region*,
DOI 10.1007/978-94-007-4150-8-13, © Springer Science+Business Media
B.V. 2012

BORDER CHALLENGES

The border is a dynamic space where social, cultural, economic, and a political multiplicity of paradoxical scenarios emerge and are recycled only to reemerge again (James Hernandez 2007). It is critical to acknowledge and focus on the borderscapes of paradox: the points of emergence, sustenance, and connection, but those of discontinuities and fragmentation between and within the border, but form perspective of the people who live there, as a "shared community and united space" (James Hernandez 2007, p. 21). The US-Mexico border becomes the site of people's reactions to binational dictates at local and state levels. I focus on the SB 1070 and the HB 2281 particularly from the impacts upon Mexican and Hispanic communities and how these and dominant communities at large engage in the paradoxes brought about by political and cultural challenges to all people. "The border is not only the place of danger, pollution, violence, and transgression of dominant representations. Here, collective and individual efforts to heal, rehabilitate, and celebrate also renew community ties daily" (James Hernandez 2007, p. 21). At the core of this metaphor, the fluidity of social interaction, human resources, and capital are continually enforced by a binational diversity of complex levels of bureaucracies and institutions. The issues of immigration and border economies are woven into complex national political scenarios where individuals become involved in the forging and creation of laws, and the ways that these laws are also prioritized and then enacted.

The US-Mexico border becomes a space of transformation and resistance. It is also a compelling social and political location for "marginalizing and unifying practices that constitute the border as paradox" (James Hernandez 2007, p. 22). Although the US-Mexico border is socially located at the "margins – the edge, it may also be conceptualized as a center of global and political economic change" (Staudt 1998, p. 10). The border, as a borderscape of paradox and a localized entity, becomes a most fluid social and cultural spatial entity defining the situated lives of its border citizens' lives. Through daily social and economic interaction, individuals sustain their cultural and political identities on both sides of the border.

Mexicans, Chicanas, and Chicanos historically have become ethno-racially denned, politically disempowered, and economically marginalized communities throughout the Southwest, and especially on the US-Mexico border (see Chap. 1). Mexicans, Chicanas, and Chicanos have continued a history of struggles and resisted the "melting pot" and cultural erasure designed and guided by Anglo-American ideology. The historical experiences of conquest, whether as internal colonies, annexation, or as a result of a war, have deeply affected and weakened the sociopolitical and economic lives of minority groups in the United States.

Currently, some of the most salient social structural issues impacting US-, Mexico border communities are national and state security. These issues have become a top priority for the state of Arizona legislators since the aftermath of September 11. Protecting the safety of the US-Mexico border has become one of the most heated political, social, and economic debates of this century. In terms of national security and political economic discourses, some of the most salient issues impacting Mexican and Hispanic communities on the US-Mexico border are immigration regulation of undocumented migrants by the Department of Homeland Security, Immigration and Customs Enforcement (ICE), the building of walls and fences, virtual and human surveillance, national nativism and xenophobia, a national environment of political vitriol (the proliferation of hate and violence scripted into Republican political campaigns), federal militarization of the border, economic issues, crime, drug trafficking vigilantism of paramilitary groups like the Minutemen, education, international commerce and trade.

In this chapter, I focus on the impact of the militarization and the political discourses formulated by Arizona legislators in creating a militarized border zone between the US-Mexico through the immigration reform law, SB 1070.1 recur to research findings that seem to indicate Arizona legislators have been successful in creating inflammatory policies fueled by insecurity and xenophobia targeting and maintaining Mexican and Hispanic communities under siege, particularly those closer to the US-Mexico border. Arizona's anti-immigrant legislation creates an apparatus of control targeting minority groups and harassing Mexican and Latino communities. The new immigration law SB 1070 and the anti-ethnic studies law HB 2281 enacted by politicians in the state of Arizona demonstrate the negative impacts of policies aiming to discredit, label, and ostracize Mexican and Latina/o communities.

Crucial in our understanding of borderscape paradoxes is that for Mexicans, Chicanas, and Chicanos, the US-Mexico Southwest and the borderlands are primordial cultural, demographic, and geographic spaces: a homeland. I agree that at the core of complex social structural subordinating dynamics driven by state economic, demographic, and political processes lie the possibilities of political transformation and agency by the less powerful (Staudt 2009). The study of these borderscapes of paradox creates long-term heuristic impacts and, at the short term, immediate responses to local, state, and national control imposed on individuals and communities.

THE EFFECTS OF THE IMMIGRATION REFORM LAW AND THE ANTI-ETHNIC STUDIES LAW IN ARIZONA

On April 23, 2010, governor of Arizona, Jan Brewer, signed SB 1070, the immigration reform law that became effective in 2011. The passage of this law crystallizes political interests espoused by the right-wing agenda in Arizona. SB 1070, and much like HB 2281, aims to eliminate ethnic studies in schools and universities (National Institute for Latino Policy 2010). Other states such as Alabama and Georgia have followed Arizona with similar and even more draconian laws.

Three years before the passage of this law, Prince William County, Virginia, introduced a similar bill and created an environment of fear in the communities of color, as well as negatively impacting all the community. "Our county was severely hurt economically. Many, many people left this county," said Nancy Lyall, a Mexicans without Borders member. "Prince William County has had some of the biggest depreciation of homes of anywhere in this area" (McCarren 2010, p. 1).

National social and political elements have been very important in facing up to the Republican imposition of SB 1070. There is national discontentment and preoccupation of the citizenry on the various "unresolved" issues created by immigration legislative disputes. The Hispanic communities have historically voted in support of the Democratic Party, perhaps with the exception of the Cuban contingency which has tended to vote Republican. For Hispanics, the fact that Democrats have failed to prioritize Hispanic issues and that President Obama has failed, so far, to create and enact a national immigration law addressing amnesty and legalization" of undocumented migrants in the country has constituted a serious concern. Early in his administration, President Obama shifted his call for bipartisan collaboration, particularly in addressing immigration issues, the creation of job and the budget deficits.

In Arizona, the perceived "uncontrolled" undocumented immigration in the United States and the militarization of the US-Mexico border has been the core center of SB 1070. The perception by politicians of the "invasion of the border by undocumented migrants" both at the national and state levels has resulted in a "flooding" of border patrol agents, surveillance vehicles, and top-of-the-line technology—cameras and stadium lights, all along the 2,000 miles shared between Mexico and the United States. During a testimony to the Senate Committee on Homeland Security last year, Dennis Burke, US attorney for Arizona, noted that Arizona now has more than 6,000 federal law-enforcement agents, with the majority of them employed by the Border Patrol representing nearly ten agents for every mile of international line between Arizona and Sonora. The Border Patrol presence has been backed by increases in counter-smuggling technology and intelligence the establishment of permanent highway checkpoints, and a dramatic increase in customs inspectors at US ports (Wagner 2010).

Wagner (2010) asserts that DHS has reported the construction of 347 miles of pedestrian fences and 299 miles of "vehicles barriers." Over 660 miles of border have been built along the US-Mexico border. These physical obstacles are constructed to disrupt and discourage undocumented migration. At the Same time, these *borderscapes of paradox* have engaged in a

potentially irreversible destruction of endangered species through partitioning their ecological habitat by the construction of walls and fences. Let us look at the findings that conclusively invalidate the "invasion of the border" position and its pro-militarization of the border arguments.

Doris Meissner (2010), senior fellow at the Migration Policy Institute, who served as a commissioner of the US Immigration and Naturalization Service, debunks the argument that immigration is at an all-time high, and that most new immigrants arrive in the country without documents. She calls these arguments "fabrications" against immigrants which "daily resonate" within legislative sessions Today, about two-thirds of immigrants are documented, either as naturalized citizens as lawful permanent residents. Of approximately 10.8 million of unauthorized immigrants who are in the country, about 40% arrived with authorization but overstayed their visas. Although the unauthorized immigrant population includes more people from Mexico than from any other country, Mexicans are also the largest group of lawful migrants.

The issues of militarizing and shutting off the border in order to keep us communities "safe" have also been contested by research. One of the most important findings presented is that ". . . apprehensions along the U.S.-Mexico border have declined by more than 50% over the past 4 years while increases in the size of the undocumented population continue and had been growing by about 50,000 a year" (Meissner 2010, p. 1). Although undocumented migration and anti-immigrant sentiments have been increasing throughout Arizona, the US-Mexico border has never been more secure. Sheriff Dupnik, responding to the militarization of the border, argued that "This is a media-created event." Dupnik said, "I hear politicians on TV saying the border has gotten worse. Well, the fact of the matter is that the border has never been more secure" (Wagner 2010).

The enactment of draconian laws, SB 1070 and HB 2281, had significant electoral consequences within Arizona. Sheriff Dupnik has denounced the Arizona's immigration reform law. This law has become a model for the rest of the country of "what not to do" (Dupnik 2010). Yet, there is an opposite reaction created by the alarming issues of militarizing and shutting off the border in order to keep its communities safe, an environment of fear and terror created by the media and the legislation. The immigration reform law, SB 1070, has mobilized anti-immigrant sentiment, not only at a state but also at national levels. The anti-immigrant policies endorsed by the governor of Arizona, Jan Brewer, have triggered a momentum for what I call the *cloneglom-erization,* or the increased cloning and dissemination of SB 1070 throughout the United States by various states. A triggering effect of the immigration reform law is likely to have a multiplying effect during the next decade. Texas Representative Debbie Riddle is one of the politicians who lined up to be the first to file an Arizona style immigration bill for Texas. She filed on November 8, 2010 (Johnson 2010).

This cloneglomerization effect goes hand in hand and is likely an effect of the recent unprecedented national electoral power gained by the Republican Party. According to Johnson (2010), the following states are likely to consider SB 1070 policies in upcoming legislative sessions: Ohio, Tennessee, Colorado, Georgia, Mississippi, Oklahoma, South Carolina, Minnesota, Missouri, Nebraska, New Mexico, Pennsylvania, and Utah. Wessler (2010) contends that white anxiety about the rapidly growing Latina/o population may also fuel anti-immigrant laws. The manner by which extremist legislation operates is by labeling, blaming, ostracizing, and demonizing the immigrant. This modus operandi becomes the venue by which various counties, cities, and states have been crafting and passing equally draconian legislation across the country. The SB 1070 and HB 2281 laws have been crucial for the reelection of Arizona's Governor Jan Brewer to a second term in office.

THE ANTI-IMMIGRATION "SCAPEGOAT" EFFECT

Migrants have been blamed for a gamut of problems such as the high unemployment in the nation. What are the evidence-based findings in refusing this assertion? Research findings show that although immigrants account for 12.5% of the population, they make up 15% of the workforce. They are overrepresented among workers largely because the rest of the population is aging. For over decades, migrants and their children have accounted for 58% of the US population. Immigrants tend to be concentrated in high- and low-skilled occupations that complement—rather than compete with—jobs held by native workers (Meissner 2010, p. 1). There is a widely shared belief among minority groups that SB 1070 leads to an expansion of invasive political control strategies used by the state apparatus in order to "control and cleanse" the border. The argument yields for protecting the region from potential national security attacks, crime, delinquency, the smuggling of drugs, and finally "shutting off or sealing" the US-Mexico border with walls, fences, surveillance and the National Guard. In enacting all of these national safety measures, national and state governments target immigrant communities, which become under siege through the sum operation of all of these invasive processes. Latinas/os become scapegoats for the state.

ETHNIC STRUGGLES FOR SOCIAL JUSTICE: RESPONSES FROM COMMUNITIES UNDER SIEGE

Numerous rallies and marches at local and state levels and national, political economic, religious, educational, as well as law enforcement leaders from both sides of the border have denounced this law and have formed national and international coalitions to oppose it. MALDEF, ACLU, ACLU of Arizona, LULAC, and NTLLC are among a coalition of organizations legally challenging the immigration reform law (de La Torre 2010). Coalitions of civil rights groups and activists have condemned HB 2281 and the immigration reform law.

About 200 groups joined an economic boycott against Arizona including African American and Jewish organizations. They asked members and supporters not to endorse conferences, or planning conventions in Arizona, and to abstain from buying goods. Alessandra Soler Meetze, executive director of American Civil Liberties Union of Arizona stated that "If these laws were implemented, citizens would effectively have to carry 'their papers' at all times to avoid arrest. It is a low point in modern America when a state law requires police to demand documents from people on the street" (de La Torre 2010).

On May 6, 2010, an issue of the *New York Times* entitled "Latino Groups Urge Boycott of Arizona over the New Law" by Julia Preston informed the public that the National Council of La Raza, or NCLR, the League of United Latin American Citizens, or LULAC, as well the National Puerto Rican Coalition announced a business boycott against the state of Arizona. US Representative Raul Grijalva Democrat from Arizona, joined the boycott at a cost of receiving numerous death threats on his life. Janet Murgufa, president of the NCLR, announced that "The new (immigration reform) law is so extreme, and its proponents appear so immune to an appeal to reason, nothing short of these extraordinary measures is required" (Preston 2010).

The faculty administrators, and staff of three of Arizona's universities—Arizona State University, Northern Arizona University, and the University of Arizona—voiced their strong opposition to SB 1070. Similarly, NACCS, the National Association of Chicana and Chicano Studies, and MALCS, *Mujeres Activas en Letras y Cambio Social,* publicly denounced SB 1070 and HB 2281. NACCS and HACU joined and endorsed the economic boycott against Arizona.

At the University of Arizona, the Faculty Senate denounced SB 1070, and in a letter written by the president of the University of Arizona, Robert N. Shelton criticized SB 1070 as "flawed public policy that sends all the wrong messages about our state." He wrote, "The anger that has been generated by SB 1070 is understandable. Many on our campus-whether international students and visitors, or faculty and staff who fear their ethnicity will make them targets-are anxious about its implementation. It is the expectation of most legal experts that SB 1070 will be overturned by the courts. Whether or not this happens, I am certain that no one on our campus should fear that because of their ethnicity or national origin they will be accosted by our police" (Shelton 2010).

In Arizona, the *racialized* discourses brought about by SB 1070 and HB 2281 endorsed by Republicans, right-wing groups, administrators, and legislators continue to stir a collective awareness and actions from people across the nation (Rogers 2010). Ethnic Studies Week was a nationally coordinated event aimed to defend ethnic studies in Arizona and inspired by opposition to the passage of the HB 2281 in Arizona's Public Schools and the May 21 passage of new social sciences standards by the Texas State Board of Education. As of August 12, 2010, the group had over 1,300 members from across the nation. The University of Arizona Gender and Women Studies Department served as an organizational and leadership umbrella for the various community organizations, educators, and activists who organized and participated in celebrating Ethnic Studies Week in Tucson, Arizona, from October 4 to 10, 2010.

THE DEHUMANIZATION EFFECT OF THE IMMIGRATION REFORM LAW

Arizona Senator Russell Pearce, author of SB 1070, has predicted that the law would discourage, stop, and eradicate undocumented migration and crime in order to *secure* neighborhoods throughout Arizona. However, a statistic disregarded by Mr. Pearce provided by the American Immigration Council of the Immigration Policy Center (IPC) shows that crime rates have systematically fallen in Arizona since 2005. Research findings gathered by the IPC on undocumented immigrants show that immigrants are less likely to commit crimes than native-born individuals (Immigration Policy Center [IPC] 2010). This report concludes that immigration policies are not effective ways of addressing crimes because the majority of those committing crimes are not immigrants.

The immigration reform law has been contested on the fact that some of its regulations seemed to be "unconstitutional" and restrictive of individuals' freedom. Pima County Sheriff Clarence W. Dupnik, in a guest opinion on May 6, 2010, harshly criticized and pointed to two stances by which the law would delegate the enforcement to in demanding documents from those individuals stopped when there may be "reasonable suspicion" that they may be undocumented (Dupnik 2010). The criminalization and dehumanization of communities of color is evident. They are likely to become under siege through the enforcement of this law, through physical, psychological, cultural, and political control.

Last year in Phoenix, Arizona, Sheriff Joe Arpaio of Maricopa County directed his officers to raid a local company, Lasermasters, and arrested 24 immigrants. The workers were charged with felony identity theft for working with false documents (Preston 2010). Opposition to the immigration reform law immediately triggered the responses of Latina/o communities throughout Arizona and created nationwide coalitions denouncing SB 1070. Communities of color launched rallies, protests, marches, and an economic boycott against the state of Arizona. In Los Angeles, California, more than a dozen protesters were arrested by police officers for chaining themselves together and blocking traffic in front of a federal immigration center for protesting against the Arizona law (Preston 2010). These forms of resistance are likely to increase in Arizona in the future, particularly before a new presidential election.

THE CURRENT STATE OF THE IMMIGRATION REFORM LAW, SB 1070

The immigration reform law went through litigation processes in challenging the legality and validity of its language and its impacts on communities of color and other communities as well. Arizona had spent over a million dollars defending its law in court by July of 2010. SB 1070 became a law on July 29, 2010.

President Obama won an injunction against most of the SB 1070 law, except for the employer provisions. In November of 2010, Supreme Court arguments made it likely that the injunction against the law would be sustained (Johnson 2010). US District Court Judge Susan Bolton issued a preliminary injunction preventing several sections of Arizona's new immigration law from becoming law. Her decision impacts the immigration reform law by removing:

- The portion of the law that requires an officer to make a reasonable attempt to determine the immigration status of a person stopped, detained, or arrested if there is reasonable suspicion that they are in the country illegally

- The section that creates a crime of failure to apply for or carry "alien-registration papers." The portion that makes it a crime for illegal immigrants to solicit, apply for, or perform work. (This does not include the section on day laborers.)

- The section that allows for a warrantless arrest of a person where there is a probable cause to believe they have committed a public offense that makes them removable from the United States

The Arizona court decision affirmed the following aspects of the law: The ruling says that law enforcement still must enforce federal immigration laws to the fullest extent of the law when SB 1070 went into effect on Thursday, July 29, 2010. Individuals will still be able to sue an agency if they adopt a policy that restricts such enforcement. That section of the law creates misdemeanor crimes for harboring and transporting illegal immigrants. Her ruling followed hearings on three of seven federal lawsuits challenging SB 1070. Judge Susan Bolton also denied legal requests by Governor Jan Brewer, Maricopa County Sheriff Joe Arpaio, and several other defendants seeking to have the lawsuits dismissed because, they argued, the plaintiffs did not prove that they would be harmed by the law if it went into effect (Rau et al. 2010).

MORE OF THE SAME POLITICAL RHETORIC OF FEAR AND CULTURAL ERASURE

On May 2010, Governor Brewer signed HB 2281 and the bill became a law on December 31, 2010. HB 2281 is widely interpreted as the banning of ethnic studies in the public schools of the state of Arizona. This law specifically targets the Raza and Mexican-American or Chicana/o Studies Program at the Tucson Unified School District The author of this law is Tom Home who at the time was the State Superintendent of Public Instruction. Although nearly half of Arizona's public school classrooms are filled by Hispanics, HB 2281 makes it illegal for these students to learn about the richness of their history and culture.

This law also includes the firing or reassignment of language teachers with "heavy accents" and "ungrammatical English." The law states: "That any course, class, instruction, or material may not be primarily designed for pupils of a particular ethnic group as determined by the State Superintendent of Instruction. State aid will be withheld from any school district or charter school that does not comply" (Calefati 2010).

HB 2281 is also a political interest disguised as an educational reform, an "Americanization" reform much like the ones established by the Federal Government in the beginning of the twentieth century for assimilating all people of color. Tom Horne argues, "Traditionally, the American public school system has brought together students from different backgrounds and taught them to be Americans and to treat each other as individuals, not on the basis of their ethnic backgrounds" (Calefati 2010). Under this statement lies the foundation of cultural erasure, as effective political right-wing rhetoric in creating collective historical amnesia and separating specifically Mexicans and Hispanics from their ethnic and cultural roots. It is a mechanism of racial supremacy and control. Delegitimizing the histories of individuals through economic control, instilling fear and xenophobia, creates subjugation and repression.

Tom Horne, Republican, won the seat for attorney general for the state of Arizona in 2010 defeating Democrat Felicia Rotellini. He is a strong supporter of the immigration reform law. The HB 2281 law also denies Hispanics their right to define the most important pedagogies to educate their youth. This borderscape of paradox juxtaposes the roles and rights that pedagogues have in educational institutions with those of politicians, individuals like Horne, and Huppenthal who use their political appointments and political power attempting to interpret educational pedagogies, as well as dictating erasure at those teachings perceived to be a threat to the status quo. Hence, Horne's interpretations of Raza and Mexican American Studies as a threat to American values shows a political "ethnic chauvinism" against Mexican American Studies.

Certainly under HB 2281, it is politicians in Phoenix who will issue the sanctions impacting not only students but pedagogues as well. The anti-ethnic studies law is yet another distinct manifestation of an "ecology of fear." Extreme right-wing, xenophobic politicians become the executors of education by exercising the law to censure educational materials—"legally mandating" administrators to enforce a racist law and enforcing sanctions on those who refuse to follow these mandates. Home argued that students will still be exposed to other cultures and traditions within the state standards and dictated by the politicians (Strauss 2010).

Hence, it is not educators but politicians who will micromanage the teaching processes and say, what, who, when, and how to teach the children of minority groups (not only Hispanics) their cultural heritage. These are effective ways of cultural erasure through the removal of ethnic identity and cultural pride, or a "whitewashed" process impacting the future generations of educated Hispanic youth. The National Institute for Latino Policy announced on October 20, 2010, that 11 teachers were suing Arizona over the new "anti-Latino" schools law. According to Martinez and Gutierrez (2010), 11 Tucson, Arizona, educators sued the state board of education and the superintendent for what the teachers consider an "anti-Hispanic" ban looming on Mexican-American Studies. The teachers are suing because HB 2281, which went into law May of 2010, violates free speech, equal protection, and due process.

Meyers and Orozco (2010) of Oregon State University have studied educational gains by minority students. They argue that there is multidisciplinary evidence concluding that student learning is positively correlated to student success when students are offered culturally relevant and community-minded curriculum. These scholars argue that when students are encouraged to think critically from cultural differences to gender equity and transnational relations, they are more likely to be educationally engaged for higher levels of education (Meyers and Orozco 2010). In addition, targeting Raza and Chicana/o Studies program, in the Tucson Unified School district, could potentially negatively affect students' academic achievement and reverse the academic gains they have made over the last several years.

Grado (2010) reports that Senator John Huppenthal intends to take his fight against ethnic studies programs as elected superintendent of Public Instruction in Arizona, a position previously held by Tom Horne. Political xenophobia and educational micromanagement permeate in defining the content and approaches of what types of instruction are permitted at local and state levels in Arizona. The banning of ethnic studies continues the hostilities against the Mexican and Latina/o and people of color communities. Although the immigration reform and the anti-ethnic studies laws are effective in the state of Arizona, collective organization of Mexican and Latina/o groups is crucial in creating resistance in structuring counter-hegemonic transformation not only at local, state, but also at national levels. For the next decade, it is likely that public disobedience and transformative political coalitions will increase and continue providing strength resisting and increasing the struggles for representation and social justice. The more intense these hostilities are throughout Arizona, the more likely communities will continue the resistance and struggle against them. The more laws are created aiming to control and repress communities, the more likely these struggles for social justice would intensify beyond 2011.

TOWARD POLITICAL REPRESENTATION OF HISPANIC COMMUNITIES

Currently, Mexican and Latina/o communities continue to legally challenge, confront, and resist the socioeconomic structural inequalities affecting their living standards. They are proactively paving the way for increasing their political participation at local and national levels. According to the US Census (2009), the number of Hispanic citizens who reported voting in the 2008 presidential election reached 9.7 million. The most important priority for Mexican-Americans in Arizona is challenging and changing the present authoritarian and unconstitutional environments created by its legislation through a political voter agenda that includes and unites all Latino and Latina ethnic and national groups in the United States. The organized efforts create a direct and well structured, inclusive, political voter agenda for the future elections.

Historically, Hispanics have been voting overwhelmingly Democratic, particularly Puerto Ricans and Mexicans. For the right-wing Republican extremists, the Hispanic vote threatens their political control. Rodríguez et al. (2010) remind us that Republicans are threatened by the possibility of the Hispanic vote turning Arizona into a blue state. Hence, the rationale of the immigration reform and the anti-ethnic studies laws aim at minimizing and preventing the number of Hispanics who become US citizens, creating a displacement and removal of the Hispanic population, and the developing policies aiming to minimize and restrict social, health delivery systems in order to minimize the Hispanic political participation in Arizona.

The Hispanic vote is shifting electoral power and reinforcing national political representation. The way to electoral power is to choose from the "lesser of two evils" and move forward to structuring and gaining political representation and power within the Democratic Party. For example, the "Tequila Party" created by various business entrepreneurs, industrialists, educators, and professionals would "ideally" organize to influence the Democratic Party in order to advance Hispanic leadership, interests, pro-immigrant rights, and strengthening interethnic solidarity among Hispanic groups.

Transformative political coalitions are empowered with representation through leadership coalitions making Latina/o communities a priority on the national agenda. Currently, the level of political harassment and antagonism against immigrant communities throughout the United States would likely increase. This represents a serious concern for the Democratic Party in upcoming elections. Collective organization is necessary for resistance and to attempt social justice against state or global economic forces. The decade from 2010 to 2020 is undoubtedly a ripe historical time for Hispanics to become politically engaged, particularly for social demographic and economic issues—a decade to fulfill their own public political agendas.

THE ECOLOGY OF FEAR AND THE REPERCUSSIONS OF POLITICAL VITRIOLIC RHETORIC

Professor Gerardo Devón Pena's concept "ecology of fear" illustrates the Arizona political climate and how "the manipulation and creation of story lines which have a political and civic climate, deliberately manipulated by politicians, produce a climate of intolerance, fear, insecurity, and hatred that is hostile to any one appearing 'foreign' to the self-image of 'white Americans'— whether immigrants or people of color in general" (Peña 2010, p. 2).

Congresswoman Gabrielle Giffords is not separate from Hispanic communities because of her political priorities on health care and immigration. Since the attack on her person, a multiplicity of media sources has reported on her wellness process. Congresswoman Giffords' political labor on behalf of equitable representation for people potentially could have made her a "target" and a real threat to the Republican Party, Tea Party members, and its extreme Christian right wing which is vehemently anti-populist and antidemocratic, despite their political rhetoric and discourses.

There are social, cultural, and political consequences affecting Arizona's political environment as an aftermath of the shootings. Congresswoman Giffords's future representation in the Senate has been removed and stopped from a pathway of bipartisan civil dialogue and political momentum. Giffords is well loved by her constituents and is perceived by many as a leader who was attempting to bridge and connect the differences between constituents. She has tried to reach between the liberal and conservatives by weaving mutual political, economic, social, and cultural understandings that would ultimately serve for the benefit of the community at large.

The assailant, Jared Lee Loughner, shot Congresswoman Giffords at point blank. Although seriously wounding her, miraculously Giffords survived the attack. Loughner's shooting rampage that left six people dead and wounded 14 others changed the history of Arizona and the people of Tucson forever. Who is culpable for this atrocious act of violence? Whether the assailant is perceived as an isolated mental illness or insanity case, psychiatrists argue that it is entirely possible for such an individual with bizarre behavior, psychotic behavior, antisocial behavior, and "the belief that one's mind is being externally controlled could be provoked to violence by rising levels of vitriol in political discourse" (Billeaud and Watson 2011).

Dissemination of an "ecology of fear" by political extremist right-wing vitriol is likely to be correlated with the shootings. Gun imagery, talk of "targeting" elected officials and "taking out political opponents" espoused by individuals like Glenn Beck or Sarah Palin's March 2010 web graphic targeting congressional districts, among them Congresswoman Gabrielle Giffords, trigger real violent consequences. Tea Party Iraq veteran Jesse Kelly held an event advertised with a vocabulary of destruction creating a warlike environment, the words "Get on Target for victory in November. Help remove Gabrielle Giffords from office. Shoot a fully automatic M16 with Jesse Kelly," in taking the district for Republicans. This scenario depicts a warlike environment which is deliberately engineered to create terror and violence. It is irresponsible political vitriol rhetoric with a vocabulary of bellicose metaphors of fear and physical threats, psychological intimidation, and violent imagery.

Giffords had previously addressed the violence issue in an interview with Chuck Todd of MSNBC. She said that Palin had put the "crosshairs of a gun sight over our district" and that "when people do that, they have got to realize there are consequences to that action." According to Rich (2011), at least three others of the 20 members of Congress on Palin's map were also hit with vandalism or death threats. Palin's map read, *"Don't retreat, Instead-Reload!"*

The following two acts of violence were also happening in Tucson, Arizona, in what became one of the "most venomous campaign seasons in recent history" (Brodesky 2011). After the House passing of the health-care bill, vandals smashed the front door of Gifford's office in Tucson, Arizona, Seven months before Giffords' office had been vandalized, one of the attendees dropped a gun on the floor during a *Congress on your Corner* session as she addressed health-care issues in a gathering in the town of Douglas, Arizona.

White powder was sent to Congressman Raul Grijalva's congressional office last year during the month of October. He was compelled to temporarily close his Phoenix office as a result of increasing threats to his life. These threats resulted after the called for an economic boycott against the state of Arizona. His support of the boycott came as a direct opposition to SB 1070.

Since 2008, other violent acts of hatred have appeared at a national level. Rich (2011) argues that since Obama's ascension to the presidency, there have been repeated incidents of political violence, for example, the 2009 killing of three Pittsburgh law enforcement officers by a neo-Nazi Obama hater, and an attack on and an IRS office in Austin, Texas.

There has been a multiplicity of news coverage of the Tucson's tragedy joined by community voices challenging the continuing spreading of fear, terror, and the state of siege that was created by the shooting rampage that impacted all the community of Tucson, Arizona, and the state of Arizona as well. On Saturday, January 8, 2011, 75-year-old Sheriff Clarence W. Dupnik, a Democrat with more than three decades of law enforcement experience in Arizona's second most populous Pima County, linked the Tucson rampage to inflammatory conservative political rhetoric during a nationally televised news conference.

"When you look at unbalanced people, how they respond to the vitriol that comes out of certain mouths about tearing down the government. The anger, the hatred, the bigotry that goes on in this country is getting to be outrageous. And unfortunately, Arizona I think has become the capital. We have become the Mecca of bigotry and prejudice" (Riccardi 2011). This remark created a swift response from the right wing, Republicans, extremists, the Christian right, and Tea Party members. They started to discredit and partially blame Sheriff Dupnik for the shootings because he did not provide security to cover Congresswoman Giffords' event (Fischer 2011).

Another crucial issue of contemporary discontentment among people in Arizona is that Arizona currently is one of three states at a national level allowing people to carry concealed weapons without a permit. Goodman (2011) interviewed Sheriff Dupnik as he declared Arizona's gun law "insane." "We are the Tombstone of the United States of America ... I have never been a proponent of letting everybody in this state carry weapons under any circumstances that they want. And there is almost where we are."

Sheriff Dupnik call for civility on political issues currently resonates not only in the state of Arizona but throughout the nation as a result of President Obama's speech during his visit to Tucson, Arizona, on Wednesday, January 12, 2011.

TOGETHER WE THRIVE

On Wednesday 12, 2011, President Obama and his wife Michelle Obama attended a memorial event at the University of Arizona McKale Center. The President offered the nation's condolences to the victims of the shootings calling to "... usher in a new era of civility in their honor." President Obama's speech was nationally praised as a compassionate and powerful address. The city of Tucson and the state of Arizona were grieving the losses caused by the ominous act of hatred that left families without their loved ones. Many vigils and marches have been taking place outside of Gabrielle Giffords' office, and a memorial has been set outside of the University Medical Center for the citizenry to express their sentiments, grieving for the fallen and the actions of the heroes.

President Obama urged the citizenry to look inward but also prompted a collective response against "reflexive ideological and social conflict" (Cooper and Zeleny 2011). Thousands of people at the McKale Center sat silent listening and cheered at several points during President Obama's address. "It's important for us to pause for a moment and make sure that we are talking with each other in a way that heals, not a way that wounds," the President said. He added "let us remember that it is not because a simple lack of civility caused this tragedy. It did not. But rather because only a more civil and honest public discourse can help us face up to our challenges as a nation, in a way that would make them proud," referring to all those remembered in his eulogy: US Judge John M. Roll, Gabe Zimmerman, Dorwan Stoddard, Dorthy Murray, Phyllis Schneck, and 9-year-old Christina Taylor Green.

In conclusion transformative political and economic coalitions are empowering options for Latino communities in making "visible" their political participations through leadership on the national agenda. Currently, the levels of political harassment and antagonism against immigrant communities throughout the United States would likely increase, as well as the cloneglomerization of SB 1070 across the nation. This becomes a serious concern for President Obama and the Democratic Party in upcoming elections for 2012 and 2014. Collective organization of the Latino community is crucial for representation and social justice in a global economy. The decade from 2010 to 2020 is undoubtedly a ripe historical time for Latinos and Mexicans to culturally, socially, economically, and politically engage in a decade of change and representation in the United States.

References

Billeaud, J., & Watson, J. (2011, January 11). *Arizona Giffords shooting: Parents of suspect devastated, neighbor says.* Retrieved from Arizona Central: http://www.azcentral.com/news/articles/2011/01/11/20110111gabrielle-giffords-arizona-shooting-suspect-neighbors.html

Brodesky, J. (2011, February 13). *While AZ circles the drain, legislators dream up ways to keep us laughing.* Retrieved from *Arizona Daily:* http://azstarnet.com/news/local/govt-and-politics/article_15815925330a-5el6-ac7b-78a5c87aab2c.html

Calefati, J. (2010, May 12). *Arizona bans ethnic studies.* Retrieved October 7, 2010, from *Mother Jones:* http://momerjones.com/mojo/2010/05/ethnic-studies-banned-arizona

Cooper, H., & Zeleny, J. (2011, January 11). *Obama calls for a new era of civility in U.S. politics.* Retrieved January 13, 2011, from *The New York Times:* www.nytimes.com

de la Torre, A. (2010, April 29). *National Immigration Law Center, MALDEF, ACLU, ACLU of Arizona will challenge Arizona racial profiling law in court.* Retrieved

from National Immigration Law Center. News Releases: www.nilc.org/pubs/news-releases/nr012.htm

Dupnik, D. (2010, May 5). Arizona's immigration mistake: Those who look suspiciously like illegal immigrants will find their liberty in severe jeopardy. *Wall Street Journal,* pp. Guest Opinion, 1.

Ethnic Studies in Arizona. (2010, September 16). *University of Arizona faculty senate unanimously passes resolution opposing House bill 2281!!!* Retrieved from http://www.ethnicstudiesarizona.com/2010/09/university-of-arizona-faculty-senate.html

Fischer, H. (2011, January 11). Dupnick's remark stir political debate. *Arizona Daily Star.* Tucson, AZ, p. A5.

Goodman, A. (2011, January 11). *A tale of two sheriffs.* Retrieved January 12, 2011, from Truthdig: http:///truthdig.com/report/item/a_tale?of-two-Sheriffs-20110111

Grado, G. (2010, October 29). *Senator Huppenthal would seek to restrict ethnic studies at the University of Arizona.* Retrieved January 11, 2011, from *Arizona Capitol Times.* Dolan Media Newswire Story: http://www.dolanmedia.com/view/cfm?recrD=644652

Immigration Policy Center [IPC]. (2010, June 22). *Arizona's punishment doesn't fit the crime: Studies show decrease in Arizona crime rates over time.* Retrieved October 7, 2010, from American Immigration Council: http://www.immigrationpolicy.org/just-facts/arizona%E2%80%99s-punishment-doesn%%E2%80%99t-fit-crime-studies-show-decrease-arizona-crime-rates

James Hernandez, F. (2007, August). Marginalities and the democratic imaginary of the global borderlands. *Dissertation UMI 3281863.* Stanford University, Palo Alto, CA.

Johnson, L. (2010, December 28). *Many states look to Arizonas SB1070 as a model for new immigration legislation.* Retrieved January 20, 2011, from *Washington Independent:* http://washingtonindependent.com/104713/many

Martinez, M., & Gutierrez, T. (2010, October 20). *11 teachers sue Arizona over new 'antiHispanic' schools law.* Retrieved from CNN Story Highlights: http://www.sodahead.com/united-states/teachers-sue-arizona-over-anti-hispanic-schools-law/question-1290837/

McCarren, A. (2010, April 30). *Virginia official: Similar immigration law worked.* Retrieved from WUSA-TV, Washington, DC: http://www.azcentral.com/news/articles/2010/04/30/20100430arizona-immigration-law-virgnia-law-similar.html

Meissner, D. (2010, May 2). *5 myths about immigration.* Retrieved May 7, 2010, from *The Washington Post:* http://www.washingtonpost.com/wpdyn/content/article/2010/04/30/AR2010043001106.html?wspisrc=nl_pmopinions

Meyers, S., & Orozco, R. (2010, May 12). *New Arizona law could be detrimental to students, according to OSU researchers.* Retrieved from Oregon State University [OSU]: http://oregonstate.edu/ua/ncs/archives/2010/may/new-arizona-law-could-be-detrimental-students-according-osu-researchers

National Institute for Latino Policy. (2010, April 30). *Arizona ethnic studies classes banned, teachers with accents can no longer teach English.* Retrieved from Huffpost Politics: http://www.huffingtonpost.com/2010/04/30/arizona-ethnic-studies-cl_n_558731.hlml

Peña, G. (2010, May 4). Letter to Gov. Honorable Jan Brewer on behalf of the National Association of Chicana and Chicano Studies. *National Association of Chicana and Chicano Studies.* San Jose, CA: http://www.naccs.org/images/naccs/ltrs/SB_1070.pdf

Preston, J. (2010, May 6). *Latino groups urge boycott of Arizona over new law.* Retrieved May 6, 2010, from *The New York Times:* http://www.nytimes.com/2010/05/07/us/07immig.html

Rau, A., Rough, G., & Hensley, J. (2010, July 28). *Arizona immigration law: Key parts struck down by judge.* Retrieved from Arizona News from *The Arizona Republic:* http://tucsoncitizen.com/arizona-news/2010/07/28/arizona-immigration-law-key-parts-struck-down-by-judge/

Riccardi, N. (2011, January 10). *After shootings, Clarence Dupnik is Arizona's new sheriff in town.* Retrieved from *Los Angeles Times:* http://articles.latimes.com/print/2011/jan/10nation/la-na-arizona-shooting-sheriffs-201101. Retrieves 11 Jan 2011.

Rich, F. (2011, January 16). *No one listened to Gabrielle Giffords.* Retrieved January 18, 2011, from *The New York Times:* http://www.nytimes.com/2011/01/16/opinion/16rich.html?_=language

Rodriguez, R., Mendez-Negrete, J., & Peña, D. (2010, May 27). *Deep impact: Three Mexican-American scholars discuss Arizona's immigration law and its ramifications on the state's colleges and universities.* Retrieved from http://goliath.ecnext.com/coms2/gi_019912949942/ Deep-impact-three-Mexican-American.html

Rogers, I. (2010, June 22). *Assessing Arizona,* Retrieved January 11, 2011, from Issues in Higher Education: http://diverseeducation.com/article/13900/

Shelton, R. (2010, May 6). *Thank you. To the campus community.* Retrieved from The University of Arizona. Office of the President: http://president.arizona.edu/memos_letters/thank-you

Staudt, K. (1998). *Free trade: Informal economies on the U.S.-Mexico border.* Philadelphia: Temple University Press.

Staudt, K. (2009). Violence at the border: Broadening the discourse to include feminism, human security, and deeper democracy. In K. A. Staudt, T. Payan, & Z. A. Kruszewski (Eds.), *Human rights along the U.S.-Mexico border: Gendered violence and insecurity* (pp. 1-27). Tucson: University of Arizona Press.

Strauss, V. (2010, May 17). *Arizona officials go after Mexican studies program.* Retrieved from *The Washington Post:* http://www.washingtonpost.com/wp-dyn/content/article/2010/0516/AR2010051603094.html?nav=emailpage

U.S. Census Bureau News. (2009, July 15). *Facts for features: Hispanic heritage month 2009.* Retrieved April 29, 2010, from Report CB09-FF.17: http://www.census.gov/mewsroom/releasest/pdf/cb09-ff7.pdf

Wagner, D. (2010, May 2). *Violence is not up on Arizona border despite Mexican drug war.* Retrieved from *The Arizona Republic:* http://www.azcentral.com/news/articles/2010/05/02/20100502arizona-border-violence-Mexico-html

Wessler, S. (2010, November 12). *White anxiety fuels anti-immigrant laws.* Retrieved from *Color Lines.* News for Action: http://colorlines.com/archives/2010/11/in_the_shadows_of_arizonas.html

Immigration in the United States: New Economic, Social, Political Landscapes with Legislative Reform on the Horizon

By Faye Hipsman and Doris Meissner
Migration Policy Institute

Immigration has shaped the United States as a nation since the first newcomers arrived over 400 years ago. Beyond being a powerful demographic force responsible for how the country and its population became what they are today, immigration has contributed deeply to many of the economic, social, and political processes that are foundational to the United States as a nation.

Although immigration has occurred throughout American history, large-scale immigration has occurred during just four peak periods: the peopling of the original colonies, westward expansion during the middle of the 19th century, and the rise of cities at the turn of the 20th century. The fourth peak period began in the 1970s and continues today.

These peak immigration periods have coincided with fundamental transformations of the American economy. The first saw the dawn of European settlement in the Americas. The second allowed the young United States to transition from a colonial to an agricultural economy. The industrial revolution gave rise to a manufacturing economy during the third peak period, propelling

America's rise to become the leading power in the world. Today's large-scale immigration has coincided with globalization and the last stages of transformation from a manufacturing to a 21st century knowledge-based economy. As before, immigration has been prompted by economic transformation, just as it is helping the United States adapt to new economic realities.

For a nation of immigrants and immigration, the United States adjusts its immigration policies only rarely, largely because the politics surrounding immigration can be deeply divisive. As a result, immigration policy has often been increasingly disconnected from the economic and social forces that drive immigration. When changes have been made, they have generally taken years to legislate.

Today, the United States may be on the threshold of major new reforms that would address longstanding problems of illegal immigration, as well as those in the legal immigration system, which has not been updated since 1990. The impetus for comprehensive immigration reform (CIR) has returned to the congressional stage, with bipartisan groups in the House and Senate engaged in significant negotiations to craft legislation that would increase enforcement at the nation's borders and interiors, legalize the nation's estimated 11 million unauthorized immigrants, and provide legal avenues for employers in the United States to access future workers they need. CIR, in one form or another, has been under consideration since at least 2001, with major debates in the Senate in 2006 and 2007. After the failure of CIR legislation in the Senate in 2007, the effort to reform the nation's immigration laws was sidelined. The results and voting patterns of the 2012 presidential election gave both political parties new reasons to revisit an immigration reform agenda.

This country profile examines key legislative events that form the history of the US immigration system, the size and attributes of the immigrant population in the country, the characteristics of legal and illegal immigration streams, US policies for refugees and asylum seekers, immigrant integration efforts, postrecession immigration trends, immigration enforcement, immigration policies during President Obama's administration, and prospects for reform legislation.

EARLY HISTORY

In the decades prior to 1880, immigration to the United States was primarily European, driven by forces such as industrialization in Western Europe and the Irish potato famine. The expanding frontiers of the American West and the United States' industrial revolution drew immigrants to US shores. Chinese immigrants began to arrive in large numbers for the first time in the 1850s after gold was discovered in California in 1848.

Federal oversight of immigration began in 1882, when Congress passed the Immigration Act. It established the collection of a fee from each noncitizen arriving at a US port to be used by the Treasury Department to regulate immigration. Arriving immigrants were screened for the first time under this act, and entry by anyone deemed a "convict, lunatic, idiot, or person unable to take care of himself or herself without becoming a public charge" was prohibited.

As the mining boom in the West began to subside, animosity toward the large populations of Chinese laborers and other foreigners surged, and so began a series of legislative measures to restrict immigration of certain racial groups, beginning with nationals of China. The Chinese Exclusion Act of 1882 was the first such law. It halted immigration of Chinese laborers for ten years, barred Chinese naturalization, and provided for the deportation of Chinese in the country illegally. In a follow-on bill, Congress passed the 1888 Scott Act and banned the return of Chinese nationals with lawful status in the United States if they departed the country. In 1892, the Geary Act extended the ten-year bar on

Chinese labor immigration, and established restrictive policies toward Chinese immigrants with and without legal status.

Between 1880 and 1930, over 27 million new immigrants arrived, mainly from Italy, Germany, Eastern Europe, Russia, Britain, Canada, Ireland, and Sweden. This peak immigration period—the last large-scale immigration wave prior to the current period—also led to new restrictions.

In an expansion of racial exclusion, and by overriding a presidential veto, Congress passed the 1917 Immigration Act which prohibited immigration from a newly drawn "Asiatic barred zone" covering British India, most of Southeast Asia, and nearly all of the Middle East. It also expanded inadmissibility grounds to include anarchists, persons previously deported within the past year, and illiterate individuals over the age of 16.

Nativist and restrictionist sentiment continued through the 1920s, prompting the United States to introduce numerical limitations on immigration for the first time. The Immigration and Naturalization Act of 1924 established the national-origins quota system, which set a ceiling on the number of immigrants that could be admitted to the United States from each country. It strongly favored northern and western European immigration. The 1952 Immigration and Nationality Act continued the national-origins quota system but for the first time allocated an immigration quota for Asian countries.

THE POST-1965 ERA

Although the discriminatory nature of the national-origins quota system had become increasingly discredited, it took until the Kennedy era and the ripple effects of the nation's civil-rights movement for a new philosophy guiding immigration to take hold. The resulting Immigration and Nationality Act Amendments of 1965 repealed the national-origins quota system and replaced it with a seven-category preference system based primarily on family unification. Overall, the legislation set in motion powerful forces that are still shaping the United States today.

The 1965 act increased numerical limits on immigration from 154,000 to 290,000. A ceiling on immigration from the Americas (120,000) was imposed for the first time, and a per-country limit of 20,000 was set for Eastern Europe. The new caps did not include "immediate family members" of US citizens (spouses, minor children, and parents). In 1976, the 20,000 per county limit was applied to the Western Hemisphere.

The year before the 1965 Act, Congress terminated the Bracero program, which it had authorized during World War II to recruit agricultural workers from Mexico to fill farm-labor shortages in the United States. In the wake of these and other sweeping changes in the global economy, immigration flows that had been European-dominated for most of the nation's history gave way to predominantly Latin American and Asian immigration.

Today's large-scale immigration began in the 1970s, and has been made up of both legal and illegal flows. Prior periods of large-scale immigration occurred before visas were subject to numerical ceilings, so the phenomenon of "illegal immigration" is a relatively recent element of immigration policy history and debates.

The largest source country of legal admissions, Mexico, has also accounted for the largest share of illegal immigrants who cross the southwest land border with the United States to seek the comparatively higher wages available from US jobs.

By the mid-1980s, an estimated 3 to 5 million noncitizens were living unlawfully in the country. To address illegal immigration, Congress passed the Immigration Reform and Control Act of 1986 (IRCA), which was intended to act as a "three-legged stool." IRCA included the following:

- Sanctions against employers who knowingly hired unauthorized workers, including fines and criminal penalties intended to reduce hiring of unauthorized immigrants;
- Increased border enforcement designed to prevent the entry of future unauthorized immigrants; and
- Legalization that granted legal status to unauthorized immigrants who had lived in the United States for at least five years (with a more lenient measure for agricultural workers) in an effort to "wipe the slate clean" of illegal immigration for the future. The combined programs granted lawful status to 2.7 million individuals (out of 3 million applicants).

Ultimately, IRCA failed for several reasons. First, the legalization program excluded a significant slice of the unauthorized population that had arrived after the five-year cutoff date but stayed in the United States and became the core of a new unauthorized population. Second, improvements in border enforcement did not begin in earnest until the 1990s. And the heart

of the law—employer sanctions—had weak enforcement provisions that proved ineffective at checking hiring practices of sizable numbers of unauthorized immigrants.

Four years later, Congress passed the Immigration Act of 1990 to revamp the legal immigration system and admit a greater share of highly-skilled and educated immigrants. It raised legal immigration caps, modified the temporary nonimmigrant visa system, and revised the grounds of inadmissibility and deportation. The law also established Temporary Protected Status (TPS), creating a statutory footing for permission to live and work in the United States to nationals of countries deemed unsafe for return because of armed conflict or natural disaster.

Overall, IRCA and its enforcement mechanisms were no match for the powerful forces that drive illegal migration. Both IRCA and the 1990 Act failed to adequately foresee and incorporate measures to provide and manage continued flows of temporary and permanent immigrants to meet the country's labor market needs, especially during the economic boom years of the 1990s.

As a result, illegal immigration grew dramatically and began to be experienced not only in the six traditional immigration destination states of New York, New Jersey, Florida, Texas, Illinois, and California, but also in many other areas across the southeast, midwest, and mountain states that had not had experience with large-scale immigration for up to a century. Although immigration served as a source of economic productivity and younger workers in areas where the population and workforces were aging, a large share of the immigration was comprised of illegal immigration flows. Thus, the challenge to deeply-held rule-of-law principles and the social change represented by this immigration generated progressively negative public sentiment about immigration that prompted Congress to pass a set of strict new laws in 1996, as follows:

- The Personal Responsibility and Work Opportunity Reconciliation Act (PRWORA), commonly known as the Welfare Reform Act, denied access to federal public benefits, such as Medicaid, Supplemental Security Income (SSI), and food stamps to categories of authorized and unauthorized immigrants. Some states later chose to reinstate some of these benefits for authorized immigrants who lost eligibility under PRWORA.
- The Illegal Immigration Reform and Immigrant Responsibility Act (IIRIRA) bolstered

immigration enforcement, increased penalties for immigration-related crimes, provided for expedited removal of inadmissible noncitizens, barred unlawfully present immigrants from re-entry for long periods of time, and set income requirements for immigrants' family sponsors at 125 percent of the federal poverty level. IIRIRA also required the government to track foreign visitors' entries and exits, which became a key element in the government's security strategy after the 9/11 terrorist attacks.

- The Anti-Terrorism and Effective Death Penalty Act (AEDPA) made it easier to arrest, detain, and deport noncitizens.

Subsequently, Congress returned to shoring up legal immigration measures in 2000 by enacting the American Competitiveness in the Twenty-First Century Act to meet demand for skilled immigrants—especially in science, math, and engineering specialties—and enable employers to fill technology jobs that are a critical dimension of the post-industrial, information age economy. The act raised the annual number of H-1B visas given to high-skilled workers in specialty occupations to 115,000 in fiscal year (FY) 2000, then to 195,000 for FY 2001, 2002, and 2003. At present, 65,000 H-1B visas per year are available, with an additional 20,000 H-1B visas (due to a law passed in late 2004) for foreign-born individuals with advanced US degrees.

The 1990s saw the longest period of sustained economic and job growth the United States had experienced since at least World War II. Immigration—at both high and low ends of the labor market, both legal and illegal—was an important element in achieving the productivity and prosperity of the decade. Immigration also contributed to the economic transformation required for the United States to compete in a global economy. With more than 14 million newcomers (legal and illegal), the 1990s reached numerical levels that out-numbered the previous all-time high set during the first decade of the 20th century. The trend has continued into the 2000s with more than 16 million newcomers from 2000–10.

THE LASTING IMPACT OF 9/11 ON IMMIGRATION POLICY

No recent event has influenced the thinking and actions of the American public and its leaders as much as the terrorist attacks of September 11, 2001. In the almost-12 years since 9/11, many aspects of the US immigration enforcement system have become dramatically more robust. The national security threat posed by international terrorism led to the largest reorganization of the federal government since World War II. The overhaul brought about the merger of 22 federal agencies to create the Department of Homeland Security (DHS) in 2003.

Because the 9/11 hijackers obtained valid visas to travel to the United States, despite some being known by US intelligence and having been encountered by law enforcement agencies, the immigration system came under particular scrutiny. The Immigration and Naturalization Service (INS), which had been part of the Department of Justice since 1941, was dissolved and its functions were transferred to three newly created agencies within DHS, as follows:

- Customs and Border Protection (CBP) oversees the entry of all people and goods at all ports of entry and enforces laws against illegal entry between the ports.
- Immigration and Customs Enforcement (ICE) is responsible for enforcement of immigration and customs requirements in the interior of the United States, including employer requirements, detention, and removals.
- US Citizenship and Immigration Services (USCIS) adjudicates immigrant benefit applications, such as visa petitions, naturalization applications, and asylum and refugee requests, and administers the E-Verify program.

An additional new post-9/11 immigration entity has been US-VISIT, which is housed in the National Protection and Programs Directorate (NPPD) of DHS. It manages the IDENT biometric fingerprint information system used by all immigration agencies—including consulates abroad in visa screening—to confirm the identity of noncitizens entering the country.

9/11 also led to the passage of a series of new national security laws with far-reaching implications for noncitizens seeking to travel to or living in the United States. The most well-known is the USA Patriot Act. With regard to immigration, the act expanded the authority of law enforcement agencies to search, monitor, detain, and remove suspected terrorists, and allowed for the detention of foreign nationals for up to seven days before the government files criminal or immigration charges. It also strengthened border enforcement, especially along the northern border with Canada.

Laws that followed include the Enhanced Border Security and Visa Entry Reform Act of 2002 (EBSVERA), which tightened visa screening, border inspections, and tracking of foreign-born persons, including foreign students, particularly through broad use of biometric fingerprint records. It also served as an impetus to create the US-VISIT program, as the bill mandated information-sharing systems that made national security data available to immigration officers responsible for issuing visas, making removal or admissions decisions, and for investigations and identification of noncitizens.

In June 2002, the US Attorney General began the National Security Entry-Exit Registration System (NSEERS), a program that placed extra travel screening requirements on nationals from a list of 25 countries associated with an Al Qaeda presence (and North Korea). Additionally, males over the age of 16 who were nationals of designated NSEERS countries and already living in the United States were required to register with the federal government and appear for "special registration" interviews with immigration officials. The program was discontinued in 2011.

In 2005, the REAL ID Act prohibited states from issuing driver's licenses to unauthorized individuals, and expanded terrorism-related grounds of inadmissibility, removal, and ineligibility for asylum. One year later, the Secure Fence Act of 2006 authorized the completion of 700 miles of fencing along the southwest border with Mexico.

Heightened security and data-sharing measures adopted after the attacks has enabled the government to meet a post-9/11 goal of "pushing the border out." By screening individuals seeking to enter the United States more times and against more databases than ever before, those who pose a threat to the country can be prevented from ever reaching US soil, often times before they even board a plane. This objective is being bolstered by increased collaboration with foreign governments in law enforcement matters and through international agreements that allow bilateral sharing of information such as Passenger Name Records (PNRs).

One immediate result of tightened screening procedures was a dramatic drop in the number of visas the government issued to individuals wishing to visit, work, and live in the United States. Between 2001 and 2002, the number of nonimmigrant visas fell by 24 percent. Present visa issuances have returned to pre-9/11 levels, but it has taken ten years to rebound.

A PROFILE OF TODAY'S IMMIGRANT POPULATION

The US foreign-born population (legal and illegal) is 40.4 million, or 13 percent of the total US population of 311.6 million, according to 2011 American Community Survey estimates. Although this is a numerical high historically, the foreign born make up a smaller percentage of the population today than in 1890 and 1910 when the immigrant share of the population peaked at 15 percent. The foreign-born share fell to a low of 5 percent (9.6 million) in 1970. About 20 percent of all international migrants reside in the United States, which, as a country, accounts for less than 5 percent of the world's population.

The foreign-born population is comprised of approximately 42 percent naturalized citizens, 31 percent permanent residents (green card holders), and 27 percent unauthorized immigrants. Roughly 11.7 million, or 29 percent of the immigrant population is from Mexico, the largest immigration source country. Chinese and Indian immigrants make up the second and third largest immigrant groups, with 1.9 million or 5 percent of the foreign-born population each. In 2010, India replaced the Philippines as the third largest source country (see Table 1). The top three regions of origin of the foreign-born population are Latin America, Asia, and Europe (see Figure 1).

The foreign-born population is geographically concentrated, with 65 percent residing in the six states that have long been the country's main immigrant destinations—about 25 percent in California alone (in 2011). The other immigrant-heavy states are New York (11 percent of all foreign born), Texas (10 percent), Florida (9 percent), Illinois (4 percent), and New Jersey (5 percent). The proximity of several of these states to Mexico and longstanding, continuous immigration to traditional metropolitan destinations in New York, New Jersey, and Illinois created strong networks that have grown over time.

While these states continue to draw and represent the bulk of the foreign-born population, newcomers—particularly unauthorized immigrants from Mexico—began to settle in many additional destinations during the 1990s. Employment opportunities—particularly in agriculture, food manufacturing and construction—mainly fueled the new settlement patterns. They combined with lower costs of living and "hollowing out", i.e. depopulation of certain areas of the country due to aging and internal migration. As a result, states like Georgia, Nevada, and many others have become known as

Table 1. Immigrant Population by Country of Birth Residing in the United States, 1960 to 2011

Sending Country	Estimate	Percentage
Mexico	11.7 million	29
China (inc. Hong Kong)	1.9 million	5
India	1.9 million	5
Philippines	1.8 million	4
El Salvador	1.3 million	3
Vietnam	1.3 million	3
Cuba	1.1 million	3
Korea	1.1 million	3
Dominican Republic	900,000	2
Guatemala	851,000	2

Source: MPI Data Hub, available online.

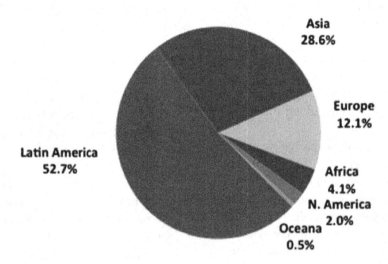

Figure 1. Foreign Born Population by Region of Origin, 2011

Note: Latin America includes: South America, Mexico, and the Caribbean; Northern America includes Canada, Bermuda, Greenland, and St. Pierre and Miquelon

the "new growth" or "new destination" immigration states.

Ten states, mostly in the south and west, have experienced over 270 percent immigrant population growth since 1990. They are North Carolina, Georgia, Tennessee, Arkansas, Nevada, South Carolina, Kentucky, Nebraska, Utah, and Alabama. These changes and patterns help to explain why immigration has become an issue of national political concern and debate.

HOW THE IMMIGRATION SYSTEM WORKS

The guiding principles, and different ways to immigrate to the United States were largely established by the 1965 Immigration and Nationality Act and take place through three primary immigration streams. They are family (re)unification for US citizens and lawful permanent residents (LPRs or "green card" holders) with close family members; meeting legitimate labor market needs; and refuge for those in need of humanitarian protection (see next section). The most common ways to immigrate are through the family-based or employment-based channels.

Family-based immigration rests on the principle of family unity. Immediate family members of US citizens—defined as their spouses, minor children, and parents—can join their US families without numerical limitations. US citizens can also (re)unify with their adult married and unmarried children, as well as with their siblings, but the waiting times for such (re)unifications are lengthy, as is the case with family reunification for most LPRs. Family-based immigrants must

be sponsored by a qualifying relative under any of six categories of relatives. Family-sponsored immigration has accounted for about two-thirds of all permanent immigration to the United States over the last decade.

Employment-based visas for permanent immigration are dedicated to the nation's economic and labor market needs. Employment-based immigration is limited to 140,000 visas per year, and has accounted for between 12 percent (in 2003) and 22 percent (in 2005) of legal immigration in the last decade. In FY2011, it was 13 percent. Employment-based green cards are available for five categories of workers, the majority of whom must be sponsored by their employer.

Additionally, each year, approximately 50,000 individuals are granted permanent residency through the diversity visa lottery. Under the Immigration Act of 1990, 55,000 applicants from countries that are underrepresented in US immigration streams are granted

Table 2. Family and Employment-Based Immigration Channels and Numerical Limits

Category Name	Composition	Annual Cap
FAMILY CHANNEL		
Immediate Relatives of US Citizens	Spouses and minor children (under 21) of US citizens, and parents of US citizens who are 21 or older	No numerical limit
1st Preference	Unmarried adult sons and daughters (21 and over) of US citizens	23,400
2A Preference	Spouses and minor children of lawful permanent residents	114,200* shared between the 2A and 2B categories
2B Preference	Unmarried adult sons and daughters of lawful permanent residents	
3rd Preference	Married adult sons and daughters of US citizens	23,400
4th Preference	Siblings of US citizens who are 21 and older	65,000
EMPLOYMENT CHANNEL**		
1st Preference	Foreign nationals of "extraordinary ability;" outstanding professors and researchers; multinational executives and managers	40,040
2nd Preference	Foreign nationals who hold advanced degrees or demonstrate exceptional ability in the sciences, arts, or business	40,040
3rd Preference	"Skilled workers" (foreign nationals capable of performing skilled labor, requiring at least two years of experience); "professional workers" (foreign nationals who hold at least a baccalaureate degree); and "other workers" (foreign nationals capable of performing unskilled labor)	40,040; but no more than 10,000 visas are available for the sub-category of "other workers"++

(Continued)

Table 2. *(Continued)*

Category Name	Composition	Annual Cap
4th Preference	"Special Immigrants," including Afghan/Iraqi translators, international organization employees, and religious workers	9,940
5th Preference	Immigrant investors	9,940

* At least 77 percent of the total visas available to the 2nd Family Preference (2A and 2B) must be allocated within the 2A category.
** Under the Immigration and Nationality Act (INA) 203(b), the statutory caps for the employment-based categories are listed as percentages of the worldwide level of employment-based visas. Table 1 calculates the actual number of visas allocated in each category in accordance with the current 140,000 annual "floor" of employment-based visas.
++ The *Nicaraguan and Central American Relief Act* (NACARA), Pub. L. 105-100 (November 19, 1997), further limited the number of visas that may be issued in the 3rd preference "other" category, by allowing a reduction of up to 5,000 of the 10,000 visas allocated to this category to offset visas issued to NACARA beneficiaries.
Source: Immigration and Nationality Act (INA) 201, 203, 204.

immigrant visas each year (5,000 are reserved for applicants under the Nicaraguan and Central American Relief Act [NACARA] of 1997).

Noncitizens must qualify for a family-based or employment-based visa, be a refugee or asylee, or be selected in the diversity visa lottery in order to become LPRs, i.e. immigrants. LPRs can permanently live and work in the United States, are eligible to naturalize after a certain number of years, and are subject to removal if they commit a serious crime.

With the exception of spouses, minor children, and parents of US citizens, the number of individuals who can become permanent residents each year is limited in statute by numerical ceilings and per-country limits. However, the demand to immigrate greatly exceeds the number of visas Congress authorizes the government to grant. Additionally, no more than 7 percent of immigrant visas can be issued to nationals of a single country. The result has been delays in granting applications for eligible green card

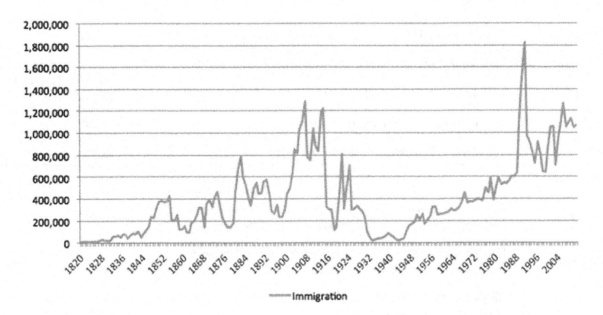

Figure 2. Legal Immigration to the United States, FY 1820 to 2011

Note: The 1990 spike in LPR admissions reflects the one-time adjustment of newly legalized immigrants under IRCA.
Note: These data represent persons admitted for legal permanent residence during the 12-month fiscal year ending September 30 of the year designated. The total for 1976 includes both the fiscal year and transitional quarter data.
Source: Department of Homeland Security, Office of Immigration Statistics, Yearbook of Immigration Statistics (various years). Available online.

petitioners that frequently span many years, especially for immediate family members from Mexico or the Philippines, for example, which are among the top five source countries for legal immigration but face severe delays in getting a green card.

Over the past 150 years, the levels of legal immigration have varied, from over 1 million people per year during the early 20th century to a trickle during the Great Depression and World War II (see Figure 2). Immigrants legalized under IRCA caused the number of authorized immigrants to peak in the late 1980s. The 1990s and 2000s, until the recession, have registered historic highs in overall immigration levels.

REFUGEE AND ASYLUM ADMISSIONS

The United States has long been the world's leading country of refuge, providing protection to victims of political, ethnic, religious and other forms of persecution through asylum and refugee resettlement. Humanitarian protection has been an abiding, albeit sometimes controversial, tenet of US immigration policy.

The statutory determination to qualify as a refugee or asylee is the same. However, the terminology differs: refugees are granted humanitarian relief in a foreign country and travel to the United States for resettlement, while asylees apply for humanitarian status having already reached or are living in the country.

Refugee policy includes a flexible ceiling on admissions that the president and Congress set each year. Slots are allotted regionally to refugees from East Asia, Near East/South Asia, Africa, Europe/Central Asia, and Latin America and the Caribbean. Admissions may also be made from an "unallocated reserve."

The United States admitted large numbers of refugees after World War II, in response to migration waves that occurred in the war's aftermath and in accord with international refugee protocols adopted by the United Nations. In 1980, Congress passed the Refugee Act, a measure that adopted the definition of a refugee in US refugee law with international standards. It established, for the first time, a permanent and systematic procedure for admitting refugees, created a formal refugee resettlement process, and provided a statutory base for asylum for the first time.

Beginning that same year and throughout the 1980s, US refugee and asylum laws became the subject of considerable controversy, when massive numbers of Central Americans from Guatemala, El Salvador, and Nicaragua began to flee civil war and repression in their home countries and apply for political asylum in the United States. Offering protection to these refugees, however, was at odds with the Reagan administration's cold war strategy of providing support to Central American governments being challenged by left-wing rebels. As a result, Salvadoran and Guatemalan asylum claims were approved at extremely low rates, while between 1981 and 1990, almost one million Salvadorans and Guatemalans are estimated to have entered the United States unlawfully.

During the same period as the Cold War ended, large resettlement programs for refugees from Southeast Asia and the former Soviet Union have been replaced with admissions from a more diverse set of countries. One exception is Cuba, a communist country from which hundreds of thousands have fled since its 1959 revolution. This massive emigration led to a 1994 agreement intended to prevent Cubans from trying to reach the United States by boat under life-threatening conditions. In FY 2011, there were 36,452 new immigrants from Cuba, the vast majority entering as refugees.

In the 1970s and 1980s, refugee and humanitarian emergencies led to annual admissions of more than 200,000 during some years. During the last decade and half, and especially since 9/11, both the size of the refugee program and annual asylum grants have decreased (see Figure 3). FY 2011 saw 56,384 refugee arrivals, down from 73,293 in FY 2010. Burma (16,972) Iraq (9,388) Bhutan (14,999), Somalia (3,161), and Cuba (2,920) were the top five refugee-sending countries of FY 2011. That year, 24,988 individuals were granted asylum (defensive and affirmative), a slight uptick from FY 2010 after about ten years of steady decline. There is no cap on asylum approvals.

TEMPORARY VISITORS

Noncitizens who enter the United States for tourism, work, or study reasons are admitted with a temporary nonimmigrant status. There are over 70 categories of visas for nonimmigrants, including tourists, business visitors, foreign students, H-1B workers, religious workers, intracompany transferees, diplomats, and representatives of international organizations. Nonimmigrant visas typically have strict terms and conditions, and allow for periods of stay ranging from a few weeks or months to

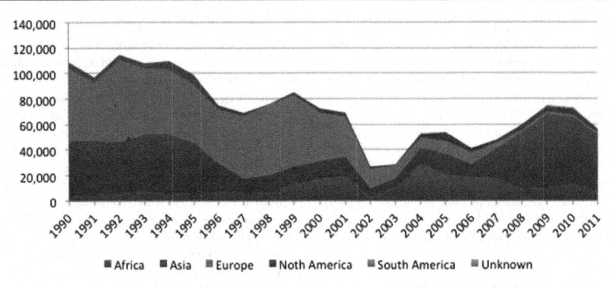

Figure 3. Refugee Arrivals by Region of Origin, 1990 to 2011

Source: DHS, Yearbook of Immigration Statistics, 1990–2011

six or more years. A small number of nonimmigrant visas allow for eventual permanent residency.

In 2011, 7.5 million nonimmigrant visas were granted. Temporary tourism and business visitors represent the vast majority of nonimmigrant visa holders. Nonimmigrant visas issued to foreign students have increased significantly during the last decade. The 447,410 student visas issued in 2011 is more than 50 percent greater than the number issued in 2001. Much of this growth has been driven by the exponential rise in students from China, who now represent 35 percent of all foreign students. South Korea, Saudi Arabia, and India also send students to the United States in high numbers.

ACQUIRING US CITIZENSHIP

Under the 14th amendment of the US constitution, persons born on US soil are American citizens. Citizenship can also be acquired through naturalization. US citizens are entitled to rights and privileges not extended to noncitizens, such as the right to vote, protection from deportation, ability to apply for immigration of family members, and eligibility for federal assistance programs.

Permanent residents are eligible for US citizenship once they are have lived continuously in the country for five years (three years if they are married to a US citizen), are at least 18 years old, have not committed any serious crimes, have good moral character, and have knowledge of the English language and US civics, demonstrated

by passing a citizenship test. The current exam emphasizes US history and government, and was introduced in 2008 after years of design, evaluation, and testing.

The average annual number of naturalizations increased from less than 120,000 during the 1950s and 1960s to 210,000 during the 1980s, up to 500,000 during the 1990s, and again to 680,000 between 2000 and 2009. In 2012, there were 757,434 naturalizations, up from 694,193 in 2011 and 619,913 in 2010. As of FY 2011, 8.5 million LPRs were eligible to naturalize but had not applied. A combination of reasons, including inadequate language skills needed to pass the citizenship exam, fear of the exam, an expensive filing fee of $680, and lack of knowledge about the naturalization process, can all discourage potential applicants.

Since the 1990s, a series of new laws and policies have affected naturalization trends. IRCA brought about historically high naturalizations in the mid-1990s as the 2.7 million unauthorized immigrants who obtained LPR status under the law's legalization program became eligible for naturalization. The growing eligibility pool further grew with passage of the 1996 laws described above. They reduced noncitizens' access to federal benefits and legal protections, thus incentivizing naturalization. Between 1994 and 1997, the number of naturalization petitions filed nearly tripled, from 543,353 to 1,412,712.

Naturalization spiked again in 2008 as a result of citizenship outreach campaigns ahead of the 2008 presidential election, coupled with a scheduled increase in the naturalization application fee that many eligible applicants attempted to beat.

In 2012, Mexico accounted for the highest share of naturalizations (13.7 percent), followed by the Philippines (5.9 percent), India (5.7 percent), the Dominican Republic (4.4 percent), and China (4.2 percent). The largest number of new citizens lived in California (21 percent), Florida (13.3 percent), and New York (12.4 percent), according to DHS statistics.

UNAUTHORIZED IMMIGRANTS

Unauthorized immigrants enter the United States by crossing the land border clandestinely between formal ports of entry, using documents fraudulently for admission at a port of entry, or overstaying a valid temporary visa.

Illegal immigration began to build and reach relatively high levels in the early 1970s. Immigration policymaking in the United States has been preoccupied with the issues it represents for much of the four decades since. The numbers of unauthorized immigrants who were not eligible for IRCA's legalization but remained in the United States, in addition to immigration spurred by rapid job creation in the 1990s and early 2000s, combined with powerful push factors in Mexico, have caused the unauthorized population to grow by 300,000 to 500,000 per year between 1990 and 2006. After reaching an estimated peak of 12 million in 2007, the unauthorized population has declined in recent years, to 11.1 million in 2011, according to the Pew Hispanic Center.

Illegal immigration is a bellwether of economic conditions, growing substantially in a strong economy with high demand for low-skilled labor (the 1990s and early 2000s), and tapering off with economic contraction (since 2008) (see Figure 4). The arrival of unauthorized immigrants in large numbers has revitalized certain communities and contributes to local economic growth. At the same time, rapid and unchecked social change and pressure on public services brought about by individuals here illegally has sparked anger and resentment, making immigration a hotly contested issue of national concern.

DHS estimates that 59 percent of unauthorized residents are Mexican born; with El Salvador accounting for 6 percent, Guatemala 5 percent, Honduras 3 percent, and China 2 percent. The ten leading countries of origin also include the Philippines, India, Korea, Ecuador, and Vietnam, which represented 85 percent of the unauthorized immigrant population in 2011.

Roughly 46 percent of unauthorized adult immigrants are parents of young children. As of 2010, there were 5.5 million minors with at least one unauthorized parent. While 1 million of these minors are also unauthorized, the vast majority—4.5 million—are US-born, and are, therefore, American citizens.

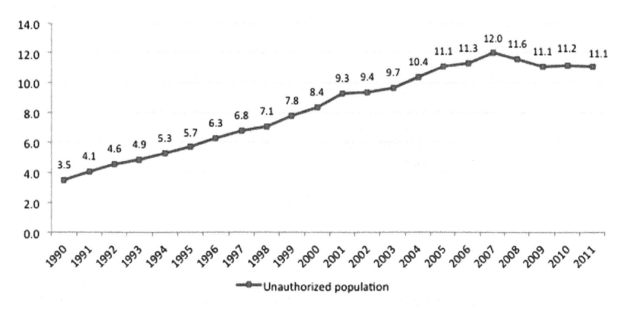

Figure 4. Estimated Unauthorized Population, 1990 to 2011 (millions)

Source: Pew Hispanic Center, Bob Warren

IMMIGRANT INTEGRATION

While the public debate tends to focus disproportionately on questions of who, how many, and what kind of noncitizens should be admitted to the United States, many see immigrant integration as the true test of a successful immigration system. Unlike other traditional immigration countries, such as Canada and Australia, for example, the United States does not have a federally-driven immigrant integration policies or an agency responsible for making sure immigrants effectively become part of US society. Instead, integration policies are limited, underfunded, largely ad hoc, and often target narrow immigrant groups, such as refugees or migrant workers.

Historically, schools, churches, employers, and community-based groups have taken the lead at the local level to spearhead immigrant integration efforts that include English classes, job training, and health care clinics. In recent years, several states and cities have launched integration initiatives aimed at improving opportunities and services available to immigrants.

Federal policies that affect immigrant integration outcomes include the No Child Left Behind Act passed in 2001 that required schools and funding for states to ensure that limited English proficient (LEP) children become proficient in English. In 2009, the Children's Health Insurance Program (CHIP) was expanded to cover authorized immigrant children. Additionally, the federal Adult Education program funds English education and GED preparation.

Access to basic rights and mainstream institutions in American society like most jobs in the labor market, public education, community and emergency health care systems, and citizenship have been the pillars of successful integration, despite that fact that they do not represent explicit, formal policy efforts. Integration is commonly measured by comparing indicators such as income, education, health, and living standards for foreign and native-born populations. Despite the absence of broad immigrant integration policies, the foreign born have historically become well integrated in the United States. At the same time, today's large numbers of foreign born, especially the sizable unauthorized population who may gain legal status if CIR is enacted, pose substantial immigrant integration challenges for all levels of government and society—as well as for the individuals themselves—in the years ahead.

IMMIGRATION ENFORCEMENT

As illegal immigration intensified during recent decades, immigration enforcement has been the dominant focus of the federal government's response to immigration for at least 25 years. Enforcement involves visa screening; land border enforcement between ports of entry; land, air, and sea ports of entry admissions, employer enforcement, detention and removal of criminals and others who have violated immigration laws, and immigration administrative courts. Nonetheless, the dominant focus of immigration enforcement has been the southwest land border enforcement.

The US-Mexico border is a diverse area that spans more than 1,900 miles. For most of the period since the Border Patrol was created in 1924, chronic lack of funding and adequate resources prevented it from carrying out its mission of preventing illegal border crossings. That began to change with stepped up border enforcement during the 1990s.

Since then, the federal government has invested billions of dollars into personnel, infrastructure, and technology on the border. The Border Patrol now has more than 21,000 agents, having doubled in size since just 2005; 651 miles of border fencing has been built (mandated in the 2006 Secure Fence Act); and a vast array of cameras, ground sensors, aircraft, and drones are in place. More than $11 billion was spent on border enforcement in FY 2011.

As a result, crossing points that were traditionally used by people entering illegally into the country have been largely closed off, making it difficult, dangerous, and expensive to cross. The number of apprehensions the Border Patrol makes has decreased from nearly 1.7 million in 2000 to 365,000 in 2012.

Immigration enforcement capabilities in the country's interior have also been significantly strengthened. Deportations, federal partnerships with state and local law enforcement agencies, and efforts to discourage hiring of unauthorized immigrants are all parts of the equation.

Since 1986, the government has carried out more than 4 million deportations (or removals). Almost half have occurred since 2007. Annual removals have climbed steeply for the last 15 years, from roughly 30,000 in 1990 to 188,500 in 2000, to over 400,000 in 2012. Deportation levels are largely governed by Congress, which provides the enforcement agencies with levels of funding that specify the numbers to be detained and removed each year.

While some argue that historically high removals enhance national security, public safety, and the rule of law, others contend that the system carries severe human costs to families, children, communities, and tears at the social fabric of the United States.

Cooperation between Federal and State Agencies

Immigration enforcement has been seen as the responsibility of the federal government since at least the late 1800s. However, in 1996, as part of IIRIRA, Congress created a provision called section 287 (g) which established cooperation between federal and state agencies to enforce immigration laws.

This cooperation has been carried out through two widely used but controversial programs: the 287 (g) program and Secure Communities. 287 (g) deputizes state and local law enforcement officers to enforce immigration laws, and is being phased out after peak use in 2010. In its place, Secure Communities is being used in almost every jurisdiction in the country. Through the program, fingerprints taken during the arrest process are automatically checked against federal immigration records and arrestees can then be detained by ICE. These programs reflect important technological advances in identification and data sharing made in recent years, in addition to a goal of the Obama administration to focus enforcement actions on criminals.

Some states, particularly those that experienced rapid immigrant population growth during the past two decades, became increasingly frustrated with what they perceived as inadequate federal enforcement of immigration laws. They began enacting their own enforcement legislation. Arizona's SB1070, which passed in 2010, was the first and best known of these measures. It required state and local police officers to inquire into the immigration status of anyone stopped or arrested if an officer has "reasonable suspicion" that the individual is an unauthorized immigrant. In 2011, five more states—Utah, Indiana, Georgia, Alabama, and South Carolina—enacted similar laws.

Legal challenges to SB1070 as an unconstitutional pre-emption of federal authority moved quickly through the federal courts. In June 2012, the Supreme Court struck down all but one of the provisions of the Arizona law in a landmark decision that upheld federal primacy in immigration enforcement.

Employer Enforcement

Employer enforcement has been the weakest element of US immigration enforcement strategy. Large-scale worksite enforcement raids, such as the one of a meatpacking plant in Postville, Iowa, in 2008 have been supplanted with a new focus by the Obama administration on auditing employers and punishing those who violate hiring laws, rather than the workers who are improperly employed. At the same time, the voluntary online E-Verify system developed by DHS to check the immigration status of new hires has gained traction. In 2009, the Obama administration mandated its use by all federal contractors. Many states have established similar requirements. By 2012, 400,000 employers were enrolled in the program compared to 24,463 five years before.

In its early years, E-Verify was criticized heavily for inaccuracy. While many improvements have been made, concerns remain over the program's inability to validate identity, detect identity theft, and the possibility that its use can lead to discrimination and unfair labor practices.

At nearly $18 billion in FY2012, federal spending for immigration enforcement is now 24 percent greater than spending for all other principal criminal federal law enforcement agencies combined. Public sentiment that called for strengthened enforcement as a necessary pre-condition for broader immigration reform measures has both driven the build-up and succeeded in accomplishing it.

A NEW ERA OF LOWER LEVELS OF IMMIGRATION?

Despite the large numbers of unauthorized immigrants residing in the United States, numerous indicators suggest that changing migration dynamics have set in that will reduce levels of illegal immigration in the future, even as the US economy rebounds. After growing annually for several decades, the size of the unauthorized population has begun to decline since 2007. Furthermore, the number of migrants arrested while attempting to cross the border has fallen dramatically during the last decade, especially since 2008. The Pew Hispanic Center estimates that immigration from Mexico has reached net zero and has possibly reversed, meaning that inflows and outflows are approximately equal or outflows are greater.

A combination of factors is responsible for the new trends. First, sectors that typically employ unauthorized immigrants—including construction, hospitality, and tourism—experienced deep job loss in the recession, so job demand for lower-skilled workers has diminished. Second, the buildup of immigration enforcement at the border and in the US interior has raised the costs, risks, and difficulty of migrating illegally. Finally, structural changes in Mexico—sustained economic growth, improved rates of high school graduation, falling fertility rates, a decline in the size and growth of the prime working-age population, and the emergence of a strong middle class—have slowed emigration.

Taken together, these changes represent significant, lasting new developments that are likely to remain in place during the near-term future.

THE OBAMA ADMINISTRATION AND IMMIGRATION

President Obama was unsuccessful in obtaining immigration reform legislation during his first term, although he identified it as among his top legislative priorities. Many immigrant voters and communities charged him with having broken a promise and not worked hard enough on the issue with Congress. At the same time, Congress has been deeply divided on immigration legislation and showed no appetite to take up the issue again after the repeated failures of 2005–2007.

In the face of legislative inaction, the administration took a series of executive actions to establish new policies and initiatives that have led to important shifts in US immigration policy.

The most significant new policy the administration created has been the Deferred Action for Childhood Arrivals (DACA) program, which was announced in June 2012. The program grants deferred action (protection from deportation) and work authorization to certain young unauthorized immigrants who came to the United States as children, have pursued an education, and have not committed serious crimes or pose no national security threat. In a further step, DHS deemed DACA status to constitute "lawful presence," which makes individuals eligible for driver's licenses and other state-determined benefits where states choose to grant them.

According to Migration Policy Institute estimates, 1.7 million individuals are eligible for the DACA program. As of March 2013, the program's rolling application process has seen 469,530 requests and USCIS has approved 245,493 cases.

Other policy shifts under the Obama administration include the following:

- In July 2010, the Department of Justice brought a lawsuit against Arizona challenging the constitutionality of its immigration law SB1070. The administration also challenged immigration laws passed in Alabama, South Carolina, and Utah.

- In 2010, DHS announced an updated prosecutorial discretion directive. The new policy called for prioritizing certain noncitizens (serious criminals, national security threats, immigration law violators, and recent border crossers) over others for removal from the United States.

LOOKING AHEAD

The 2012 election fundamentally changed the political calculus of immigration reform. More than 12 million Latino voters went to the polls, making up 10 percent of the American electorate. Seventy-three percent of them supported President Obama, representing a crucial margin that played a key role in his re-election victory. Other smaller immigrant groups, such as Asians, also overwhelmingly supported the president's re-election. With the Latino electorate slated to grow to 28 million by 2016, both the Republican and Democratic parties have strong incentives to court Latino and other immigrant-group voters, for whom immigration reform is a threshold issue to win their allegiance.

The new political forces that were pivotal in returning President Obama to the White House almost immediately led to key voices in the Republican Party beginning to talk about new approaches to immigration.

The Republican Party's increasing support for immigration reform has combined with a growing recognition within the Democratic Party that it must deliver on an urgent issue for millions of its supporters. And with business, faith-based communities, and others turning out in support for a major overhaul of the country's immigration laws to deal with unauthorized immigrants and create new channels for future legal workers, the prospects for action in the 113th Congress appear, at this writing, to be brighter than they have been in more than a decade.

Sources

Bergeron, Claire. 2013. Going to the Back of the Line. Washington, DC: Migration Policy Institute. **Available online**.

Britz, Emma and Jeanne Batalova. 2013. Frequently Requested Statistics on Immigrants and Immigration in the United States. *Migration Information Source*, January 2013. **Available online**.

Customs and Border Protection. 2013. *US Border Patrol Statistics*. **Available online**.

Fix, Michael, ed. 2007. *Securing the Future: US Immigrant Integration Policy*. Washington, DC: Migration Policy Institute.

Gzesh, Susan. 2006. Central Americans and Asylum Policy in the Reagan Era. *Migration Information Source*, April 2006. **Available online**.

Hoefer, Michael, Nancy Rytina, and Bryan Baker. 2012. Estimates of the Unauthorized Immigrant Population Residing in the United States: January 2011. Washington, DC: Department of Homeland Security, Office of Immigration Statistics. **Available online**.

Immigration and Customs Enforcement. 2013. *Removal Statistics*. Available online.

Ji, Qingqing and Jeanne Batalova. 2012. Temporary Admissions of Nonimmigrants to the United States. *Migration Information Source*, November 2012. **Available online**.

Office of Immigration Statistics. Various Years. Yearbook of Immigration Statistics. Washington, DC: Department of Homeland Security. **Available online**.

McCabe, Kristen and Doris Meissner. 2010. Immigration and the United States: Recession Affects Flows, Prospects for Reform. *Migration Information Source*, January 2010. **Available online**.

Meissner, Doris, Deborah W. Meyers, Demetrios G. Papademetriou, and Michael Fix. 2006. *Immigration and America's Future: A New Chapter*. Washington, DC: Migration Policy Institute.

Meissner, Doris, Kerwin, Donald M., Chishti, Muzaffar, and Claire Bergeron. 2013. *Immigration Enforcement in the United States: The Rise of a Formidable Machinery*. Washington, DC: Migration Policy Institute. **Available online**.

Migration Policy Institute. 2011 American Community Survey and Census Data on the Foreign Born by State. **Available online**.

Migration Policy Institute. US Historical Immigration Trends. **Available online**.

Motel, Seth and Eileen Patten. 2013. Statistical Portrait of the Foreign-Born Population in the United States, 2011. Washington, DC: Pew Hispanic Center. **Available online**.

Passel, Jeffrey, D'Vera Cohn, and Ana Gonzalez-Barrera. 2013. Net Migration from Mexico Falls to Zero-and Perhaps Less. Washington, DC: Pew Hispanic Center **Available online**.

Passel, Jeffrey and D'Vera Cohn. 2012. Unauthorized Immigrants: 11.1 Million in 2011. Washington, DC: Pew Hispanic Center. **Available online**.

Rytina, Nancy. 2012. Estimates of the Legal Permanent Resident Population in 2011. Washington, DC: DHS, Office of Immigration Statistics. **Available online**.

Russell, Joseph and Jeanne Batalova. 2012. Green Card Holders and Legal Immigration to the United States. *Migration Information Source*, October 2012. **Available online**.

Russell, Joseph and Jeanne Batalova. 2012. *Refugees and Asylees in the United States*. **Available online**.

One Nation: Principles on Immigration Reform and Our Commitment to the American Dream

Congressional Hispanic Caucus
The Honorable Charles Gonzalez, Chair November 28, 2012

Today, we declare our commitment to the American people to work tirelessly toward common-sense, comprehensive immigration reform that serves America's interests, promotes fairness and the rule of law and contributes effectively and meaningfully to our economic well-being and recovery.

America has always been a nation of immigrants. In order to preserve our history, national identity and culture we must create a modern, 21st century legal immigration system that reflects our legacy. Therefore, we commit to fighting for principled, comprehensive immigration reform that:

1. Requires the estimated 11 million undocumented immigrants in the U.S. to register with the federal government, submit to fingerprinting and a criminal background check, learn English and American civics, and pay taxes to contribute fully and legally to our economy and earn a path to permanent residency and eventual citizenship;

2. Protects the unity and sanctity of the family, including the families of bi-national, same-sex couples, by reducing the family backlogs and keeping spouses, parents, and children together;

3. Attracts the best and the brightest investors, innovators, and skilled professionals, including those in science, technology, engineering, and math (STEM) studies, to help strengthen our economy, create jobs, and build a brighter future for all Americans;

4. Builds on the extraordinary success of the Deferred Action for Childhood Arrivals (DACA) program and incorporates DREAMers— those who were brought to the U.S. at a young age and are Americans but for a piece of paper— into the mainstream of life in the United States through a path to citizenship so that America benefits from their scholastic achievements, military service and pursuit of their dreams;

5. Includes a balanced, workable solution for the agriculture industry that ensures agricultural workers have a route to citizenship and employers have the workers and American agriculture continues to lead in our global economy;

6. Ends the exploitation of U.S. and immigrant workers by providing sufficient, safe, and legal avenues for foreign workers to fill | legitimate gaps in our workforce, with full

Source: Congressional Hispanic Caucus, November, 28, 2012 by The Honorable Charles Gonzalez, Chair.

labor rights, protection from discrimination, and a reasonable path to permanency that lifts up wages and working conditions for both native and foreign-born workers and their families;

7. Ensures smart and reasonable enforcement that protects our borders and fosters commerce by targeting serious criminals and real threats at our northern and southern borders and promotes the safe and legitimate movement of people and goods at our ports of entry and which are essential to our economy;

8. Establishes a workable employment verification system that prevents unlawful employment and rewards employers and employees who play by the rules, while protecting Americans' right to work and their privacy; and

9. Renews our commitment to citizenship, to ensure all workers pay their fair share of taxes,

fully integrate into our way of life and bear the same responsibilities as all Americans and reaffirms our shared belief that the Citizenship Clause of the Constitution is a fundamental freedom that must be preserved.

Our immigration laws ought to reflect both our interests and our values as Americans and we believe these principles are consistent with our nation's commitment to fairness and equality. We commit to adhering to the above principles as we negotiate on behalf of all Americans in good faith with both parties and all stakeholders in the immigration reform debate. We acknowledge that the time to reform the system is long past due. We ask all sides to set aside the vitriol and gamesmanship that is often a part of this debate and that blocks our ability to truly solve the problem. The American people deserve nothing less.

Land of Opportunity

Mortimer B. Zuckerman

We are a nation of immigrants, neatly epitomized in Franklin Delano Roosevelt's ironic remark to the Daughters of the American Revolution: "Welcome, fellow immigrants." Immigrants come to America for many reasons, but mainly they come because it's the land of opportunity and upward mobility where achievement is more important than inheritance. Uprooting themselves from the familiarity of family, community, and even language and culture, they are self-selected risk-takers, which is why they tend to be hardworking, self-starting, creative, and smart. It's also why immigration has been such an economic plus for America and why so many of us look so favorably on legal immigrants.

Some Americans, however, have reservations, and some, perhaps driven by nativist, anti-immigrant sentiment or concern over the cost of illegal immigrants, decry the huge waves of legal and illegal Hispanic immigration we've seen over the past 50 years: Eleven million illegals live in a shadow world within our borders, reinforced annually by an influx of hundreds of thousands more. They are mainly from Mexico, just a car ride away, so they can maintain real and emotional ties to their home country. The anxiety is that Hispanics will retain their language and culture and

thus remain separate from and isolated within America. The popular phrase is that they will acculturate rather than assimilate, for Hispanics can remain within their own culture given the easy accessibility to Spanish TV networks, newspapers, and radio stations—and the fact that many tend to live in large Spanish-speaking enclaves, in places like California—all of which raises the concern that we might become a bilingual country.

Roots. The concerns are understandable, but the thing to really watch is not how much Hispanics are changing America but how much America is changing Hispanics. They are learning English as fast as any immigrant group. True, they are retaining their native language longer, but the transition from Spanish to English is virtually completed in one generation, on average. Of the children born here to immigrants, only 7 percent rely on Spanish as their primary language, and nearly half have no Spanish skills at all. Of the third generation, that is, Latinos born of U.S.-born parents, virtually none speak only Spanish, and less than a quarter are bilingual. According to the Pew Hispanic Center poll of 2004, 96 percent believe English is fundamental to their future. By the third generation, 60 percent of Mexican-American children speak only English at home.

When Hispanics have children in America, they tend to sink deeper roots here and lose touch with the homes they left behind. That's why there is little difference, for example, between Mexican-American lifestyles and other American lifestyles. Hispanics are embracing the American way. Their goals are the essence of the American dream: economic opportunity and security, health and education, and home ownership. They place as much emphasis on the American values of hard work and family as any group in America.

They are also intermarrying at a rate similar to that of other immigrant groups. By the third generation, a third of Hispanic women marry non-Latinos. They serve and die in the military as much as any other group in proportion to their population and now compose about 10 percent of the U.S. military. They have also done relatively well financially for a community that came here with virtually nothing. Nearly 80 percent live above the poverty line, and 68 percent of those who have lived here for 30 years or more own their own homes. Their culture of hard work, in other words, has enabled them to climb out of poverty, and they are going through the same powerful process of change as any of the immigrant groups that have come to the United States, melting gradually but inexorably into our middle and working classes.

The one area where they lag is education. Roughly 60 percent of Hispanics graduate from high school, compared with 90 percent of nonimmigrant Americans; only 8 percent get college degrees, compared with 26 percent of whites. Their strong work ethic compounds the problem by drawing many young Latinos into the workforce before they finish high school, keeping high school graduation rates lower and trapping too many in low-wage service jobs. In fairness, the urban public schools that they typically attend have failed them, as they have failed so many others, for these are no longer the best schools with the best teachers, as they were a century ago.

Yes, the challenges of this wave of Hispanic immigration are daunting, especially the illegals. But there's no reason to be pessimistic. The evidence suggests strongly that we will be able to absorb the Hispanics—as we have earlier generations from Europe—and weave them into a dynamic American society. Not only that. Every new wave of immigrants has taught our nation something new and enriched our culture. This, in other words, is an opportunity, not a problem.

Latino Politics in the New Millennium

Kim Geron

The aim of this book is twofold: to describe the transi-tion by Latinos from disenfranchised outsiders to political leaders and policymakers, and to explain to what degree Latino elected officials are sensitive to ethnic community concerns and seek to deliver policy benefits to their communities. Stated another way, the story that has been presented explored the historical struggle of Latinos to overcome discriminatory barri-ers to full participation and to achieve political incor-poration and obtain policy benefits. This book makes a contribution to the larger study of Latino politics. First, it shows through case studies the different ways Latino communities have mobilized to achieve and consolidate Latino political incorporation. Second, it explores the demographics of Latino political lead-ers, the pathways they used to win elective office, and their views on contemporary policy matters. Third, it has summarized the more than 150 years of struggle by Latinos to receive, in the words of the Voting Rights Act, "an equal opportunity to participate in elections and to elect a candidate of their choice." This struggle is far from over for Latinos. Discriminatory barriers have been made illegal, yet high rates of noncitizenship, low voter registration and turnout rates, combined with continuing racially polarized voting patterns, have limited Latinos' access, full participation, and election to office. Relative to the majority population, Latinos still do not have equal opportunity to participate in the electoral process.

While some argue that Latinos have entered a post-civil rights era in which they are no longer victims of the political system and no longer in need of legal pro-tection through court-ordered boundaries, others con-tend that Latinos still need the protection of the Voting Rights Act and its amendments to obtain their fair share of elected positions in a society that remains bounded by racial politics. One thing that is not in dispute is the fact that Latinos continue to live in residentially segregated areas that are densely populated and have underfunded schools, and that they have lower average levels of education and income than the average Ameri-can. Social struggles are still required for Latinos and other racial minorities to achieve full equality in our democracy. These battles must continue to be waged, while others in the Latino community push forward the boundaries of who can be elected and where they can be elected.

The core of majority-Latino districts that have elected Latinos should be viewed as a base, not a ceiling, for Latino electoral aspirations. The dilemma faced by Latino political strategists is how to expand the num-ber of districts in each state where Latinos will have the opportunity to elect the representative of their choice. Should a certain percentage of majority-minority

districts be broken up and district lines redrawn to create more non-Latino-majority electoral districts where
Latino candidates can compete? This assumes that non-
Latino voters will vote for Latinos. While there is some
evidence for this in certain areas of the country, the
legacy of prejudice and discrimination against Latinos
still hangs heavy over the political process. As the Mexican American Legal Defense Fund (MALDEF) noted
recently about one state: "Unfortunately, racially polarized voting persists in California, thus demonstrating
the continued need for and enforcement of the Voting
Rights Act. MALDEF's consultants have conducted
preliminary racial polarization analysis of elections
occurring during the decade and have found evidence
of polarization, particularly in Southern California."[1]

While for the foreseeable future the preservation of
existing Latino-majority districts is a necessary part of
Latino efforts for equal opportunity in the political
process, this should not restrict Latino attempts to win
elections in areas and regions where historically they
have had only a limited presence. How to hold on to
existing seats and expand into new electoral districts
has become a controversial issue.

DRAWING CONCLUSIONS AND SEEKING CLARITY FROM LATINO POLITICS

Latinos have overcome enormous barriers to achieve
elected office and are now institutionalized in the very
structures that previously excluded them. This seeming contradiction between societal biases toward Latinos and Latino electoral successes has mainly occurred
through the group efforts of Latinos to modify electoral structures to allow them to elect candidates of
their choice. Before the 1980s, in most cases, only Latinos elected Latinos to office. By the 1990s, this pattern
was beginning to break down as non-Latinos in some
locations began to help elect Latinos to office. The election of Latinos in diverse locations has allowed for a
more systematic study of the attitudes and patterns of
Latino officeholders and their policy beliefs. This chapter will suggest some tentative conclusions that can be
drawn from an analysis of the history of Latino political efforts and the case studies of contemporary Latino
political incorporation efforts, and it will offer some
suggestions for students and activists involved in the
study and practice of Latino politics.

In spite of attempts to exclude them from participating in fundamental political activities such as

voting and running for office, Latinos have overcome
marginalization and discriminatory practices by the
dominant majority to achieve numerous political
milestones. Beginning in the eighteenth and nineteenth centuries, pioneer Latino politicians became
involved in American-style electoral politics. During
the Jim Crow segregation era, from the late 1800s
to the 1950s, nonwhites in most communities were
prevented from voting, seeking office, and fully participating in the democratic process, yet Latinos
remained active in political affairs, built middle-class
civil rights groups, and organized labor and political
activities.

Beginning in the 1960s, Latinos organized outside
the mainstream political arena, built alternative organizations, and framed new political ideologies that
reflected the militancy of the times. They also used
legal methods and insider politics within the political
parties and at the grassroots level to have a voice in
mainstream American politics. Longtime Latino ethnic groups such as Mexicans and Puerto Ricans and
new immigrants from the Caribbean Islands, Central
America, and South America became more engaged
in domestic and homeland politics. Foreign policy
in Latin America became not just an issue for U.S.
foreign policy planners; now Latin American governments and their supporters and critics within the
Latino Diaspora are more actively engaged. Several
Latin American nations have established dual nationality provisions for their former residents who live in
the United States. Remittances from Latinos to their
families and towns of origin in Latin America have
become a multibillion-dollar effort and are critical for
the economic development of our neighbors in the
Western Hemisphere.

The stakes are high in a globalized economy. With
the U.S. Hispanic market already larger than all but
the eleven richest countries, there is potential for economic and political influence. The interrelationships
between the United States and Latin America is illustrated by recent events: the Elian Gonzalez controversy
in 2000, the efforts of George W. Bush and Vicente
Fox to regularize Mexican immigrants to the United
States, and U.S. government involvement in the internal politics of Venezuela. The U.S. government also
provided $1.3 billion in foreign aid to the Colombian
government (third largest after Israel and Egypt at
the time) as part of Plan Colombia in 2000.[2] Eighty
percent of the aid was earmarked for the military and
police, which helped fuel Colombia's long civil war
whose victims were almost all civilians. The growing

interrelationships among the nations and peoples of the Western Hemisphere require ongoing attention and the active involvement of the Latino community and its leadership.

LEARNING FROM THE INCORPORATION PROCESS

A few general conclusions can be drawn regarding how the process of political incorporation unfolds and how political governing coalitions are constructed at the local level. The first conclusion is that a singular major event that sparks protests and demands for change, leading to movements for political representation, is not required. In our case studies, usually several events combined to trigger a reaction leading to movements for political incorporation. In Salinas, there was not one decisive trigger event but a string of events that culminated in political incorporation.

Another conclusion that can be drawn from these case studies relates to the role of community organizations in the incorporation process. Community organizations that mobilized to achieve the inclusion of Latinos have had an important impact on the character of the political incorporation process in various places. Community-led efforts to win district elections in San Antonio, Miami-Dade County, and Salinas built a strong foundation to carry forward the demand for full political incorporation. In Los Angeles, while district elections already existed when Latinos began to seek inclusion, the struggle took the form of drawing district boundaries that enabled Latinos to have a fair chance at winning elected office. In Salinas, the strength of Latino political incorporation was due to a strong grassroots community organization, the Alisal Betterment Committee (ABC), that fought to win district elections for community representatives who would reflect the values and beliefs of the Latino community. The formation of this organization and the mobilization of the Chicano community, combined with the sophistication of Chicano community activists, were indispensable to the campaigns to win district elections.

Another conclusion that can be drawn is that a biracial coalition to achieve political incorporation is a tactic, not a strategic necessity. Where Latinos are a minority of the population, Latino politicians will continue to work with an array of allies, including labor, African Americans, Asian and Pacific Islanders, and Native Americans, to build electoral coalitions. Where

Latinos are the dominant majority in locations such as Miami and Salinas, the role of white liberals was not critical in Latinos' ascent to political leadership, and sometimes other potential allies were not evident. In Salinas, the political incorporation efforts of Latinos were carried out without strong support from the white community, yet there was a critical minority that consistently supported Latino efforts. In Miami, white liberals and the conservative Cuban American community were at odds over many issues and failed to work together. A biracial coalition was not necessary in the political incorporation efforts within either of these communities.

This finding is similar to conclusions others have drawn regarding some Latino-majority cities in the Southwest. The point is that where Latinos are the majority of voters, they are less likely to seek or need the assistance of white liberals, although they will want to work closely with whites and with other minority groups where there is agreement on policy aims and goals. This certainly was the case with the 2001 Ed Garza mayoral victory in San Antonio, where Garza won the support of both white and Mexican American voters. In many other cities, the achievement of political incorporation for Latinos and other racial minorities was based on the forging of biracial and multiracial coalitions.[3]

POLITICAL INCORPORATION AND CLASS INTERESTS

Another conclusion that can be drawn from the efforts of Latinos to achieve political incorporation is that governing coalitions encompass multiple class interests. Urban government involves a complex mix of influences as commercial development, labor, neighborhood, environmental, and Latino and other minority community interests seek to steer local policy. The dominant governing coalition in cities where Latinos have been electorally successful does contain Latinos, often as members of the city council and as city bureaucrats; however, a combination of factors has limited the level of policy benefits being delivered to the working poor in the Latino community. These factors include slow economic investment, systemic poverty in the Latino community produced by a low-wage labor market, and differing land use and environmental policy agendas of elected Latinos and other local elected officials. Issues such as crime reduction, public safety, and no-growth versus progrowth tend to receive the most attention and budgetary consideration in cities; meanwhile, services desperately needed in the Latino community, such as more varied employment opportunities, training for better-paying jobs, easing of school overcrowding, improved educational services, and after-school programs have received inadequate resources.

Latino political incorporation has meant, for the first time, not only the representation of Latinos in general but, more specifically, the inclusion of low-wage Latino workers and the urban poor in the dialogue in some communities. Latino worker interests are usually involved in the electoral coalition that elects Latinos to office. Previously, local governments rarely addressed labor issues. Today, these concerns are likely to be openly discussed and debated, since they relate to water issues, housing, education, and other social policies. In many cities, policies have been created that have benefited the working poor in Latino communities; these policies appear to be much stronger than those of previous governing coalitions, which were dominated exclusively by downtown business interests. For example, the city of Los Angeles passed a living-wage ordinance in 1997 after a community coalition that included numerous Latino worker organizations carried out a grassroots campaign. The ordinance requires that any contractor doing business with the city provide health benefits and pay salaries that are substantially higher than the state's current minimum wage of $6.75 per hour.

Another observation from the case studies and history of political incorporation efforts is that Latino community stakeholders and officeholders have not always acted with a common vision. The need for an ongoing community-based movement of Latinos that can articulate demands for policy equity, hold city leaders (including Latino council members) accountable for their actions, and push for a greater share of policy benefits in the future was an important lesson learned by community activists in places like San Antonio and Los Angeles. However, Latinos are not the dominant economic players in most communities, and thus they remain economically dependent on the same economic interests that have controlled local and regional politics for decades. In cities such as Salinas and San Antonio, where Latinos are the majority of the governing coalition, the Latino community must negotiate a relationship with the dominant economic forces that shape the policy agenda. In these locations, the governing coalition must deal with the dual pull of corporate influences and the need to redistribute resources to the working poor in Latino and other communities.

In Miami, where Latino business interests are quite powerful, Cuban American politicians are also brokers for the wealth and power of their community's members in the business world. Here there appears to be a more equitable relationship between race and class forces; however, this is highly unusual. In most cities, the role of Latino politicians is to negotiate policy benefits for the Latino community in the context of supporting large economic development projects. This usually involves obtaining agreements from private developers to build affordable housing, hire from the community, and fund urban education or parks and recreation areas in Latino communities as part of development efforts.

Economic interests will remain significant where there are investment opportunities. This requires that they deal with the political forces that occupy the seats of power. Economic interests must find ways to compromise to achieve their financial goals or use their economic strength to negotiate a deal most favorable to them. This is the logic of the market system. Latinos in power in local and higher levels of government should continue to leverage their political power to obtain the best possible economic deals for their communities and for others in need of community development and social services.

LEVELS OF POLITICAL INCORPORATION AND POLICY BENEFITS

The results of these case studies indicate that the level of political incorporation is not an accurate predictor of the strength of Latino political power. The more important question is, how does political power manifest itself in the strength of policy benefits returning to local Latino communities? The level of political incorporation alone does not determine the answer to this question. Particularly in cities that use district elections, where candidates are elected from different neighborhoods with widely divergent socioeconomic conditions and issue formation, there are different types of Latino officeholders.

At least in cities with district elections, the number of Latinos on a city council does not fully explain differences in policy formation among cities. Even in cities with at-large electoral systems, the ability of Latinos to get elected stems from the support of different voter bases. This will, in turn, affect the character and type of governing coalition that is created. A 1990s study of California Latina officeholders found that almost 100 percent of them were of working-class origins and "given [this], these elected officials may introduce policy perspectives more responsive to the needs of poor and working-class people."[4]

Not only is who is elected significant, but what type of administrators are hired into key positions, such as city manager, police chief, and head of economic development, are also important in the construction of a governing coalition. Those holding these positions, in conjunction with elected officeholders, have a powerful role at the local level. They shape local policy decisions and can steer cities in a variety of directions. These usually nonelected local government leaders can provide leadership regarding key issues and direct resources to solve long-standing problems.

A final conclusion of the case studies is that in addition to the important roles of economic interests, Latino politicians, and city administrators, an ongoing, organized community-led movement of Latinos must be vigilant to ensure that policy benefits are returned to the community. The key lesson from the many political incorporation efforts is the need for the Latino community to continue to mobilize to receive its fair share of resources and highlight broader social issues *after* Latinos are elected to office. This can take the form of a well-organized interest group such as Communities Organized for Public Service (COPS) in San Antonio, Texas, that regularly meets with elected officials and holds them accountable for the stands they take on local issues. Where it is absent, there is no mechanism other than electing different political actors to keep local government accountable to the needs of the Latino community. Latino politicians, even if they have run for office on a program to implement a Latino agenda, may soon lapse into a business-as-usual mentality that is disconnected from the most pressing needs of the community. This situation existed for a time in Los Angeles, where elements of the Latino elected leadership had grown removed and insulated from the grassroots needs of their communities.[5] This is a dangerous trend and adds to cynicism in the Latino community that elections are an ineffective and counterproductive arena for democratic action.

In a representative democracy, an overreliance on the electoral arena, on elected Latino officeholders, and on achieving the maximum numbers of Latinos in office will not solve the complex problems of Latino communities. In addition to maintaining the accountability of political leaders, issue-based neighborhood organizing in Latino communities is vital to address structural inequalities. Understanding the interplay between political incorporation efforts and empowerment efforts at the grassroots level is important for the study of Latino politics.

Community initiatives usually begin as small and seemingly insignificant actions but form the basis for later large-scale changes, such as the dramatic changes in the cities we explored. These efforts are difficult to maintain, as movements ebb and flow; yet the existence and maintenance of organized interest groups, neighborhood-based organizations, community activists, and local residents can extend inclusion in a governing coalition or force changes in policies of cities as small as Salinas and as large as Los Angeles.[6] More often than not, it is these efforts that provide the spark that ultimately leads to reevaluation of public policy, institutional changes, and the election of new leaders.

FINAL THOUGHTS

The diversity of the political experiences of Latinos makes broad generalizations difficult. For example, the rapid rise to local political power of Cuban Americans in south Florida is due to the combination of a favorable U.S. government policy and local political and economic underdevelopment in Miami that enabled Cubans to overcome the discriminatory obstacles created by the city's Anglo establishment.[7] The Cuban experience reflects a different process of political incorporation from that of Puerto Ricans, who are citizens by decree of the U.S. government; of Mexican Americans in the Southwest and Midwest, who have suffered a much longer history of entrenched structural discrimination and social ostracism; and of recent immigrants and refugees from Central and South America, who have only recently begun to achieve electoral office.

Latinos do not share an identical political experience in this country, and no one method is adequate to study such a diverse group of people. Although Latinos have a common history of conquest and colonization, their diverse paths to political officeholding and political power reflect a multiplicity of factors—the conditions they entered as ethnic immigrants, their social and political status upon entering this new environment, and the sorts of efforts they made to change their status. For these reasons, this book did not attempt to capture the totality of Latino political experience; rather, it is a more focused exploration of how racial politics have unfolded in the post-civil rights era, where racial identities, economics, and political power have been contested in various ways. While I did analyze the political conflicts with whites in some cities and the transition of power away from those who had held it for many decades, the book did not fully explore the dynamics of black and Latino political relationships. This is an important topic that others have more fully examined.[8]

This book sought to capture the contemporary thinking of Latino elected officials. The results of the survey of Latino elected officials demonstrate that LEOs exhibit significant concern for the needs of the Latino community in their political behavior. The interviews conducted with LEOs confirmed the initial finding of the mail survey that most Latino political leaders were committed to being substantive representatives of the Latino community. They consciously sought to set policy that would benefit this community.

With Latinos achieving political office, and in some cases dominating the local political power structure, have the limitation of Latinos' collective economic fortunes and lack of economic control reduced their officeholding to window dressing, merely giving the appearance that they have gained equality with whites? It is my belief that Latino politics, as it is played out in numerous locations, has the potential to create partnerships for the economic development of Latino communities. This will not be easy, as the Latino community does not control most of the economic resources in its regions; yet the sheer number of Latino voters is forcing global economic interests to address their needs. The U.S. Hispanic market is enormous, and the Latino community has the potential to shape economics and politics in the hemisphere. Within the constraints of an unequal economic system, Latino political power can at opportune moments redirect economic resources to solve some long-standing social problems.

As the numbers of Latinos continue to grow in urban, suburban, and rural communities, different pathways to political empowerment are becoming available. There will undoubtedly be a wider variety of Latino candidates from both major parties and as independents. More important, the ongoing poverty and social inequality in many communities will require the construction of new and varied forms of social movements to respond to new conditions. As many U.S.-born Latinos move away from the barrios to the suburbs, the growth of middle-class enclaves of Latinos and the integration of Latino families into non-Latino areas will also create new challenges and new voting patterns. Furthermore, the continuing growth of anti-immigrant forces that fan racial and cultural wars will also prompt new and varied responses within the Latino and other immigrant communities. As old alliances fray, new ones may emerge.

Undoubtedly this chapter is but one piece of a much larger puzzle. The types of electoral districts and candidates seeking office can be explored more systematically and compared in other qualitative studies. As part of the growing body of literature on racial politics in American cities, however, this study helps to validate the development of Latino politics at the local and national level. Latino politics is still a relatively new subfield of social science investigation, and as various social theories are tested in the context of the experiences of Latinos, and in interaction with others, these theories will be enriched.

In a society as diverse as the United States, equality for all remains an elusive goal. In a nation where physical and cultural differences have been used by a dominant majority to discriminate against and marginalize groups of people, symbolic and substantive representation are necessary steps in a long process of gaining full equality for historically underrepresented groups. The political representation of people of color, however, is not exclusively the responsibility of those of that particular racial or ethnic group. The historical divisions among peoples of color in this country require continued exploration of how minority representatives act to represent their own historically underrepresented group members and others. As Melissa Williams (1998) notes, "Although representation for marginalized groups is not in itself a cure for injustice, there is good reason to believe it is at least a healing measure."[9]

Endnotes

1. MALDEF (2001).
2. G. Leech (2000).
3. R. Hero (1997), p. 257.
4. P. C. Takash (1993).
5. J. Regalado (1997).
6. R. Rosales (2000); J. Regalado (1998); J. Anner (1996); P. Medoff and H. Sklar (1994).
7. D. Moreno (1997).
8. N. Vaca (2004); E. Morales (2004); J. Jennings (1994); C. P. Henry (1980); J. Miles (1992).
9. M. Williams (1998), p. 243.

References

Anner, John, ed. 1996. *Beyond Identity Politics: Emerging Social Justice Movements in Communities of Color.* Boston: South End.

Henry, Charles P. 1980. "Black-Chicano Coalitions: Possibilities and Problems." *Western Journal of Black Studies* 4: 202–232.

Hero, Rodney. 1997. "Latinos and Politics in Denver and Pueblo, Colorado: Differences, Explanations, and the 'Steady-State' of the Struggle for Equality." In *Racial Politics in American Cities*, 2nd ed., edited by Rufus P. Browning, Dale R. Marshall and David H. Tabb. New York: Longman.

Jennings, James, ed. 1994. Blacks, *Latinos, and Asians in Urban America: Status and Prospects for Politics and Activism.* Westport, CT: Praeger.

Leech, Gary. 2000. "Plan Colombia: A Closer Look." Colombia Journal Online, www.colombiajournal.org/plancolombia.html (accessed January 10, 2005).

Medoff, Peter, and Holly Sklar. 1994. *Streets of Hope: The Fall and Rise of an Urban Neighborhood.* Boston: South End.

Mexican American Legal Defense and Education Fund (MALDEF). n.d. "About Us: The Founding of MALDEF." http://www.maldef.org/about/index.htm (accessed December 8, 2001).

Miles, Jack. "Blacks vs. Browns." 1992. *Atlantic Monthly*, October, pp. 41–68

Morales, Ed. 2004. "Brown like Me? Book Review." *Nation*, February 19. www.thenation.com/doc (accessed February 8, 2005).

Moreno, Dario. 1997. "The Cuban Model: Political Empowerment in Miami." In *Pursuing Power: Latinos in the Political System*, edited by F. Chris Garcia. Notre Dame, IN: Notre Dame University Press.

Regalado, Jaime. 1998. "Minority Political Incorporation in Los Angeles: A Broader Consideration." In *Racial and Ethnic Politics in California*, edited by Michael B. Preston, Bruce E. Cain, and Sandra Bass, 2: 381–409. Berkeley: Institute of Government Studies Press.

Rosales, Rodolfo. 2000. *The Illusion of Inclusion: The Untold Political Story of San Antonio. Austin*: University of Texas Press.

Takash, Paula Cruz. 1993. "Breaking Barriers to Representation: Chicana/Latina Elected Officials in California." *Urban Anthropology* 22, no. 3-4 (fall-winter): 325–360.

Vaca, Nicolás C. 2004. *The Presumed Alliance: The Unspoken Conflict between Latinos and blacks and What It Means for America.* New York: HarperCollins.

Williams, Melissa S. 1998. *Voice, Trust, and Memory: Marginalized Groups and the Failing of Liberal Representation.* Princeton, NJ: Princeton University Press.

An Awakened Giant:
The Hispanic Electorate is Likely to Double by 2030

by Paul Taylor, Ana González-Barrera, Jeffrey Passel and Mark Hugo López

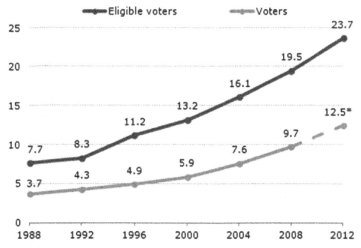

Figure 1

Latino Participation in Presidential Elections, 1988-2012
(in millions)

—— Eligible voters   —— Voters

Note: Eligible voters are U.S. citizens ages 18 and older.

Source: For 1988 through 2008, Pew Hispanic Center tabulations of the Current Population Survey November Supplements; for 2012 number of eligible voters, Pew Hispanic Center tabulations of the August Current Population Survey; * for 2012 number of voters, Pew Hispanic Center estimate based on the National Election Pool national exit poll and number of votes tallied as reported by media outlets and election turnout experts.

PEW RESEARCH CENTER

The record number[1] of Latinos who cast ballots for president this year are the leading edge of an ascendant ethnic voting bloc that is likely to double in size within a generation, according to a Pew Hispanic Center analysis based on U.S. Census Bureau data, Election Day exit polls and a new nationwide survey of Hispanic immigrants.

The nation's 53 million Hispanics comprise 17% of the total U.S. population but just 10% of all voters this year, according to the national exit poll. To borrow a boxing metaphor, they still "punch below their weight."

However, their share of the electorate will rise quickly for several reasons. The most important is that Hispanics are by far the nation's youngest ethnic group. Their median age is 27 years—and just 18 years among native-born Hispanics—compared with 42 years for that of white non-Hispanics. In the coming decades, their share of the age-eligible electorate will rise markedly through generational replacement alone.

According to Pew Hispanic Center projections, Hispanics will account for 40% of the growth in the eligible electorate in the U.S. between now and 2030, at which time 40 million Hispanics will be eligible to vote, up from 23.7 million now.[2]

Moreover, if Hispanics' relatively low voter participation rates and naturalization rates were to increase to the levels of other groups, the number of votes that Hispanics actually cast in future elections could double within two decades.

Table 1 Age- and Citizen Voting-Eligible Population, Actual and Projected: 2012 and 2030 (in millions)

	2012	2030	Share of growth (%)
All	215	256	100
Hispanic	24	40	40
White	154	163	23
Black	27	35	21
Asian	9	16	15

Note: "White" "Black" and "Asian" include only the non-Hispanic components of those populations. American Indian/Alaska Native not shown. "Share" calculated before rounding. Source: Pew Hispanic Center tabulations of the August 2012 Current Population Survey and Pew Research Center projections, 2012

If the national exit poll's estimate proves correct that 10% of all voters this year were Hispanic, it would mean that as many as 12.5 million Hispanics cast ballots. But perhaps a more illuminating way to analyze the distinctive characteristics of the Hispanic electorate—current and future—is to parse the more than 40 million Hispanics in the United States who did not vote or were not eligible to vote in 2012. That universe can be broken down as follows:

- **11.2 million** are adults who were eligible to vote but chose not to. The estimated 44% to 53% turnout rate of eligible Hispanic voters in 2012 is in the same range as the 50% who turned out in

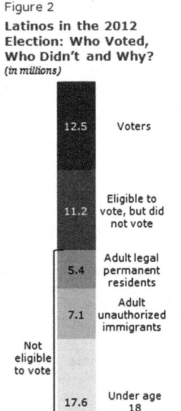

Figure 2

Latinos in the 2012 Election: Who Voted, Who Didn't and Why?
(in millions)

12.5	Voters
11.2	Eligible to vote, but did not vote
5.4	Adult legal permanent residents
7.1	Adult unauthorized immigrants
17.6	Under age 18

(5.4, 7.1, and 17.6 are marked "Not eligible to vote")

Source: Pew Hispanic Center tabulations of the March 2011 and August 2012 Current Population Surveys and Pew Hispanic Center Hispanic vote estimate based on the National Election Pool national exit poll and the number of votes tallied as reported by media outlets and election turnout experts

PEW RESEARCH CENTER

2008. But it still likely lags well below the turnout rate of whites and blacks this year.[3]

- **5.4 million** are adult legal permanent residents (LPRs) who could not vote because they have not yet become naturalized U.S. citizens. The naturalization rate among legal immigrants from Latin America and the Caribbean trails that of other legal immigrants by a sizable margin—49% versus 72%, according to a Pew Hispanic analysis of the 2011 March Current Population Survey (CPS). The new Pew Hispanic survey finds that a major reason Hispanic immigrants naturalize is to gain civil and legal rights, including the right to vote. The flexing of electoral muscle by Hispanic voters this year conceivably could encourage more legal immigrants to become naturalized citizens.

- **7.1 million** are adult unauthorized immigrants and would become eligible to vote only if Congress were to pass a law creating a pathway to citizenship for them. Judging by the immediate post-election comments of leading Democratic and Republican lawmakers, the long-dormant prospects for passage of such legislation appear to have been revived by Latinos' strong showing at the polls.

- **17.6 million** are under the age of 18 and thus too young to vote—for now. That vast majority (93%) of Latino youths are U.S-born citizens and thus will automatically become eligible to vote once they turn 18. Today, some 800,000 Latinos turn 18 each year; by 2030, this number could grow to 1 million per year, adding a potential electorate of more than 16 million new Latino voters to the rolls by 2030.

Thus, generational replacement alone will push the age- and citizen-eligible Latino electorate to about 40 million within two decades. If the turnout rate of this electorate over time converges with that of whites and blacks in recent elections (66% and 65%, respectively, in 2008), that would mean twice as many Latino voters could be casting ballots in 2032 as did in 2012.

This turnout could rise even more if naturalization rates among the 5.4 million adult Hispanic legal permanent residents were to increase over time—and/or if Congress were to pass a comprehensive immigration reform bill that creates a pathway to citizenship for the more than 7 million unauthorized Hispanic immigrants already living in the U.S.

The Pew Hispanic Center survey finds that more than nine-in-ten (93%) Hispanic immigrants who have not yet naturalized say they would if they could. Of those who haven't, many cite administrative costs and barriers, a lack of English proficiency and a lack of initiative. For example, according to the survey, only 30% of Hispanic immigrants who are LPRs say they speak English "pretty well" or "very well."

In addition to all these factors, there is the as-yet-unknowable size and impact of future immigration. About 24 million Hispanic immigrants have come to U.S. in the past four decades—in absolute numbers, the largest concentrated wave of arrivals among any ethnic or racial group in U.S. history. Some 45% arrived in the U.S. legally, and 55% arrived illegally.[4]

Assuming Hispanic immigration continues into the future—even at the significantly reduced levels of recent years—the Hispanic electorate will expand beyond the numbers dictated by the growth among Hispanics already living in the U.S. And because immigrants tend to have more children than the native born, the demographic ripple effect of future immigration on the makeup of the electorate will be felt for generations.

In 2008, the Pew Research Center projected that the Hispanic share of the total U.S. population would be 29% by 2050 (Passel and Cohn, 2008). Since that projection was made, the annual level of Hispanic immigration has declined sharply (Passel, Cohn and Gonzalez-Barrera, 2012). Because of this decline, the share of Hispanics in 2050 now appears unlikely to reach 29%. However, the 2008 projection also included a "low immigration scenario" that showed the Hispanic share of the U.S. population would be 26% by mid-century (Passel and Cohn, 2008)—still much higher than today's 17%.

WHO NATURALIZES AND WHO DOESN'T

A record 15.5 million legal immigrants were naturalized U.S. citizens in 2011, according to a Pew Hispanic Center analysis of Census Bureau data. In addition, the share of the nation's legal immigrants who have become U.S. citizens has reached its highest level in three decades—56%. However, naturalization rates among legal immigrants from Latin America and the Caribbean (49%), especially Mexican legal immigrants (36%), remain below those of other immigrants (72%).

In the new Pew Hispanic Center survey, when asked in an open-ended question why they decided to naturalize, almost one-in-five (18%) naturalized

Figure 3

What Is the Main Reason You Have Not Yet Naturalized?

(% of Latino legal permanent residents who say ...)

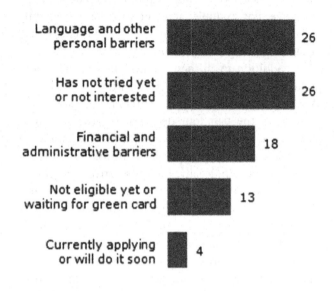

Language and other personal barriers	26
Has not tried yet or not interested	26
Financial and administrative barriers	18
Not eligible yet or waiting for green card	13
Currently applying or will do it soon	4

Notes: Based on foreign-born Latino legal permanent residents (n=243). Other reasons, "Don't know" and "Refused" answers not shown.

Source: Pew Hispanic Center, 2012 National Survey of Latinos

PEW RESEARCH CENTER

Hispanic immigrants said that acquiring civil and legal rights—including the right to vote—was the main reason. This response was closely followed by an interest in having access to the benefits and opportunities derived from U.S. citizenship (16%) and family-related reasons (15%). Other reasons included viewing the U.S. as home (12%) and wanting to become American (6%).

The Pew Hispanic survey also explored the reasons Hispanic immigrants who are legal permanent residents haven't yet tried to become citizens. According to the survey, when asked in an open-ended question why they had not naturalized thus far, 45% identified either personal barriers (26%), such as a lack of English proficiency, or administrative barriers (18%), such as the financial cost of naturalization.

ABOUT THIS REPORT

This report explores the growing size of the Hispanic electorate and the reasons Hispanic immigrants give for naturalizing to become a U.S. citizen—and for not naturalizing.

The report uses several data sources. Latino vote shares are based on the National Election Pool national exit poll as reported on November 6, 2012, by CNN's Election 2012 website. Data on Latino immigrants' views of naturalization are based on the Pew Hispanic Center's 2012 National Survey of Latinos (NSL). The NSL survey was conducted from September 7 through October 4, 2012, in all 50 states and the District of Columbia among a randomly selected, nationally representative sample of 1,765 Latino adults, 899 of whom were foreign born. The survey was conducted in both English and Spanish on cellular as well as landline telephones. The margin of error for the full sample is plus or minus 3.2 percentage points. The margin of error for the foreign-born sample is plus or minus 4.4 percentage points. Interviews were conducted for the Pew Hispanic Center by Social Science Research Solutions (SSRS).

For data on the legal status of immigrants, Pew Hispanic Center estimates use data mainly from the Current Population Survey (CPS), a monthly survey of about 55,000 households conducted jointly by the U.S. Bureau of Labor Statistics and the Census Bureau. It is best known as the source for monthly unemployment statistics. Each March, the CPS sample size and questionnaire are expanded to produce additional data on the foreign-born population and other topics. The Pew Hispanic Center estimates make adjustments to the government data to compensate for undercounting of some groups, and therefore its population totals differ somewhat from the ones the government uses. Estimates of the number of immigrants by legal status for any given year are based on a March reference date. For more details, see Passel and Cohn (2010).

This report was written by Director Paul Taylor, Research Associate Ana Gonzalez-Barrera, Senior Demographer Jeffrey S. Passel and Associate Director Mark Hugo Lopez. Ana Gonzalez-Barrera took the lead in developing the survey questionnaire's naturalization section. Passel and D'Vera Cohn provided comments on earlier drafts of the report. The authors also thank Scott Keeter, Leah Christian, Cohn, Richard Fry, Cary Funk, Rakesh Kochhar, Rich Morin, Seth Motel, Kim Parker, Passel, Eileen Patten and Antonio Rodriguez for guidance on the development of the survey instrument. Motel provided excellent research assistance. Fry, Morin and Patten number-checked the report text and topline. Marcia Kramer was the copy editor.

A NOTE ON TERMINOLOGY

The terms "Latino" and "Hispanic" are used interchangeably in this report.

"Foreign born" refers to persons born outside of the United States, Puerto Rico or other U.S. territories to parents neither of whom was a U.S. citizen.

The following terms are used to describe immigrants and their status in the U.S. In some cases, they differ from official government definitions because of limitations in the available survey data.

Legal permanent resident, legal permanent resident alien, legal immigrant, authorized migrant: A citizen of another country who has been granted a visa that allows work and permanent residence in the U.S. For the analyses in this report, legal permanent residents include persons admitted as refugees or granted asylum.

Naturalized citizen: Legal permanent resident who has fulfilled the length of stay and other requirements to become a U.S. citizen and who has taken the oath of citizenship.

Unauthorized migrant: Citizen of another country who lives in the U.S. without a currently valid visa.

Eligible immigrant: In this report, a legal permanent resident who meets the length of stay qualifications to file a petition to become a citizen but has not yet naturalized.

Legal temporary migrant: A citizen of another country who has been granted a temporary visa that may or may not allow work and temporary residence in the U.S.

1. According to the National Election Pool national exit poll, 10% of all voters in 2012 were Hispanic. And according to media reports and election turnout experts, an estimated 125 million votes were cast in 2012. However, the resulting estimate of 12.5 million Hispanics voters should be treated with caution. If history is a guide, it will likely differ—possibly substantially—with the demographic breakdown of the vote that will be reported next spring based on data drawn from the U.S. Census Bureau's 2012 November Current Population Survey (CPS), conducted after the presidential election. For example, in 2008, according to the National Exit Pool national exit poll, 9% of voters were Hispanic. But according to the 2008 November CPS, 7.4% of voters were Hispanic (Lopez and Taylor, 2009). If the gap in the Hispanic share between the National Exit Pool national exit poll and the CPS is as large as in 2012 as it was in 2008, the number of Hispanic voters could range from a low of 10.5 million to a high of 12.5 million.

2. This projection is based on assumptions about future levels of fertility, mortality, and immigration. The projections subdivide the population by age, sex, race/Hispanic origin and generation (foreign-born, U.S.-born with immigrant parent(s) and U.S.-born with native parents). See Passel and Cohn (2008) for details on methodology and assumptions. The figures cited here are from the "middle" projection which assumes slight increases in immigration levels through 2030. The future voting-eligible population includes the U.S.-born population ages 18 and older plus the foreign-born population ages 18 and over who have become U.S. citizens by naturalization. The estimates of naturalized citizens in the future are based on extrapolation of trends in naturalization rates by race/Hispanic origin observed for 1995–2010.

3. In 2008, according the Census Bureau's November CPS, 50% of age- and citizen-eligible Hispanics voted, compared with 65% of blacks and 66% of whites (Lopez and Taylor, 2009).

4. Some of those who arrived as unauthorized immigrants in the 1970s and 1980s subsequently became legal immigrants (and some naturalized) as a result of the Immigration Reform and Control Act of 1986.

More Hispanic Voting Myths: Why the Media's Emphasis on Race and Ethnicity is Wrong

Steven Malanga

Many a *postmortem* of Mitt Romney's defeat has focused on his poor showing among Hispanics and argued that Republicans won't do better in national elections until they find a way to appeal to this growing voting bloc, especially by modifying the party's stance on immigration. Yet these analyses often rely on faulty data that overstate the impact that Hispanic voters have on elections. They also typically ignore the fact that, as exit polls show, Latinos are almost certainly voting, like everyone else, on major issues—especially the economy—not on narrow ethnic lines. Latinos are just like other voters, history suggests: they're more likely to vote for Republicans when the party puts forward a good candidate with broad appeal.

Most of the analyses that I've read begin by noting the rapid growth of America's Hispanic population. But one-third of adult Hispanics are not U.S. citizens and consequently can't vote. Even Latinos who are citizens don't vote as reliably as whites or blacks do, and as a result, their population growth rate doesn't translate into commensurate voting power. According to U.S. Census data for the 2010 midterm elections (the most recent national data available), adult Hispanics numbered 32.5 million in the U.S. population, but only 10.9 million were registered to vote and only 6.6 million

From *City Journal*, http://www.city-journal.org/2012/eon1113sm.html by Steven Malanga, Senior Editor. Copyright © 2012 by City Journal. Reprinted by permission.

actually voted (up from 5.6 million in the 2006 midterms). By contrast, of the 155.5 million adult white residents in the United States in 2010, 104 million were registered to vote and 74.3 million did vote. In other words, nearly half of the country's adult whites participated in the 2010 elections; only 20 percent of adult Latinos did.

Sure, as Latinos become more assimilated into American society, their participation rates may increase—but their voting patterns will probably change as well. One recent *analysis* warns that Latinos' share of the population by 2050 will be so large as to permanently damage Republicans' prospects. Such scenarios, however, assume a static electorate that, in 40 years, votes the same way it does today. If in 1940, say, I had constructed a similar chart projecting the growth rate of the country's Italian-American population, based on its having a higher birthrate than that of the Anglo-American population, I could have issued the same warning to Republicans. Americans of Italian descent were voting heavily Democratic back then. By 1980, they had become a key component of the Reagan coalition.

The argument that Latinos are moving away from Republican candidates relies on the contrast between the number of Hispanic votes that successful GOP candidates like Ronald Reagan and George W. Bush received and the less impressive results of John McCain in 2008 and Mitt Romney this year. On the surface, that argument seems compelling, but it ignores a couple of important points. For one thing, it generally overstates Bush's numbers among Latino voters, thanks to some bad exit polling in 2004 long since *discredited*. Today, the media persist in claiming that Bush received somewhere between 41 percent and 45 percent of the Latino vote against John Kerry, a sharp contrast with the 27 percent that Romney captured. Yet subsequent academic *analyses* of the 2004 elections estimate that Bush actually received about 35 percent of the Latino vote. That wasn't a "historic" high, as Bush political advisor Karl Rove still claims; rather, it was in line with what Reagan, another victorious Republican, had achieved.

Also, there's the stubborn fact that McCain and Romney did worse than Reagan and Bush among many other demographic groups, including traditionally strong Republican ones. Romney, for instance, won the vote among those who say they attend religious services regularly, but not by as wide a margin as Bush did. Once we have better data, the larger issue in the 2012 election may turn out to be a sharp decline in white voters, which cannot be explained merely by demographic shifts. It's possible that 5 million or more eligible whites *didn't vote*, perhaps because of a lack of enthusiasm for either candidate.

What's more likely than race to account for Hispanic voting trends is income, a decisive factor in this election. The Obama campaign did a good job of portraying Romney as a Wall Street multimillionaire whose policies would favor the rich. Despite some conservatives' belief that the Republican Party is capturing blue-collar America, Romney lost decisively among lower-income voters, who continue to vote Democratic in large numbers. Hispanic households fit into this demographic group: on average, their incomes are about 35 percent lower than the national average. Even more to the point is that Romney did terribly among voters who earned less than $50,000 a year, capturing just 38 percent of their votes—and over 60 percent of Hispanic households fit that income profile.

The media like to focus on race and ethnicity in voting patterns, because those factors seem to demand great changes in parties' political strategies. Since your race or ethnic background doesn't change, the thinking goes, it's the party that must change to reach out to you. That this emphasis on race is often mistaken doesn't mean that Republicans don't need to work with Democrats on, for example, comprehensive immigration reform that fixes our broken system. Today's status quo—more like a stalemate—isn't good for anyone.

But in most cases, income is a far better determinant of voting patterns than race is (blacks are an exception, for historical reasons). The voting of ethnic groups evolves significantly as their incomes change. The ancestors of millions of today's ethnic voters came to America in the great immigration wave of the early twentieth century and voted reliably Democratic for generations. Over the last 30 years or so, their descendants' voting allegiances shifted significantly. Many were first attracted to the Republican Party by an optimistic presidential candidate who campaigned on a convincing pro-growth agenda. That won over voters in 1980; it would do so today, too.

The Development of Chicana Feminist Discourse

Alma M. García

Between 1970 and 1980 a Chicana feminist movement developed in the United States that addressed the specific issues that affected Chicanas as women of color. The growth of the Chicana feminist movement can be traced in the speeches, essays, letters, and articles published in Chicano and Chicana newspapers, journals, newsletters, and other printed materials.

During the sixties American society witnessed the development of the Chicano movement, a social movement characterized by a politics of protest. The Chicano movement focused on a wide range of issues: social justice, equality, educational reforms, and political and economic self-determination for Chicano communities in the United States. Various struggles evolved within this movement: the United Farmworkers unionization efforts, the New Mexico Land Grant movement, the Colorado-based Crusade for Justice, the Chicano student movement, and the Raza Unida Party.

Chicanas participated actively in each of these struggles. By the end of the sixties, Chicanas began to assess the rewards and limits of their participation. The 1970s witnessed the development of Chicana feminists whose activities, organizations and writings can be analyzed in terms of a feminist movement by women of color in American society. Chicana

feminists outlined a cluster of ideas that crystallized into an emergent Chicana feminist debate. In the same way that Chicano males were reinterpreting the historical and contemporary experience of Chicanos in the United States, Chicanas began to investigate the forces shaping their own experiences as women of color.

The Chicana feminist movement emerged primarily as a result of the dynamics within the Chicano movement. In the 1960s and 1970s, the American political scene witnessed far-reaching social protest movements whose political courses often paralleled and at times exerted influence over each other. The development of feminist movements have been explained by the participation of women in larger social movements. Macías, for example, links the early development of the Mexican feminist movement to the participation of women in the Mexican Revolution. Similarly, Freeman's analysis of the white feminist movement points out that many white feminists who were active in the early years of its development had previously been involved in the new left and civil rights movements. It was in these movements that white feminists experienced the constraints of male domination. Black feminists have similarly traced the development of a Black feminist movement during the 1960s and 1970s to their experiences with sexism in the larger Black movement. In this way, then, the origins of Chicano feminism parallel those of other feminist movements.

Alma M. García. From Gender & Society, Vol. 3, No. 2, June 1989, pages 217–238. Reprinted by permission of Sage Publications.

ORIGINS OF CHICANA FEMINISM

Rowbotham argues that women may develop a feminist consciousness as a result of their experiences with sexism in revolutionary struggles or mass social movements. To the extent that such movements are male dominated, women are likely to develop a feminist consciousness. Chicana feminists began the search for a "room of their own" by assessing their participation within the Chicano movement. Their feminist consciousness emerged from a struggle for equality with Chicano men and from a reassessment of the role of the family as a means of resistance to oppressive societal conditions.

Historically, as well as during the 1960s and 1970s, the Chicano family represented a source of cultural and political resistance to the various types of discrimination experienced in American society. At the cultural level, the Chicano movement emphasized the need to safeguard the value of family loyalty. At the political level, the Chicano movement used the family as a strategic organizational tool for protest activities.

Dramatic changes in the structure of Chicano families occurred as they participated in the Chicano movement. Specifically, women began to question their traditional female roles. Thus, a Chicana feminist movement originated from the nationalist Chicano struggle. Rowbotham refers to such a feminist movement as "a colony within a colony." But as the Chicano movement developed during the 1970s, Chicana feminists began to draw their own political agenda and raised a series of questions to assess their role within the Chicano movement. They entered into a dialogue with each other that explicitly reflected their struggles to secure a room of their own within the Chicano movement.

DEFINING FEMINISM FOR WOMEN OF COLOR

A central question of feminist discourse is the definition of feminism. The lack of consensus reflects different political ideologies and divergent social-class bases. In the United States, Chicana feminists shared the task of defining their ideology and movement with white, Black, and Asian American feminists. Like Black and Asian American feminists, Chicana feminists struggled to gain social equality and end sexist and racist oppression. Like them, Chicana feminists recognized that the nature of social inequality for women of color was multidimensional. Like Black and Asian American feminists, Chicana feminists struggled to gain equal status in the male-dominated nationalist movements and also in American society. To them, feminism represented a movement to end sexist oppression within a broader social protest movement. Again, like Black and Asian American feminists, Chicana feminists fought for social equality in the 1970s. They understood that their movement needed to go beyond women's rights and include the men of their group, who also face racial subordination. Chicanas believed that feminism involved more than an analysis of gender because as women of color, they were affected by both race and class in their everyday lives. Thus, Chicana feminism, as a social movement to improve the position of Chicanas in American society, represented a struggle that was both nationalist and feminist.

Chicana, Black and Asian American feminists were all confronted with the issue of engaging in a feminist struggle to end sexist oppression within a broader nationalist struggle to end racist oppression. All experienced male domination in their own communities as well as in the larger society. Ngan-Ling Chow identifies gender stereotypes of Asian American women and the patriarchal family structure as major sources of women's oppression. Cultural, political, and economic constraints have, according to Ngan-Ling Chow, limited the full development of a feminist consciousness and movement among Asian American women. The cross-pressures resulting from the demands of a nationalist and a feminist struggle led some Asian American women to organize feminist organizations that, however, continued to address broader issues affecting the Asian American community.

Black women were also faced with addressing feminist issues within a nationalist movement. According to Thornton Dill, Black women played a major historical role in Black resistance movements and, in addition, brought a feminist component to these movements. Black women have struggled with Black men in nationalist movements but have also recognized and fought against the sexism in such political movements in the Black community. Although they wrote and spoke as Black feminists, they did not organize separately from Black men.

Among the major ideological questions facing all three groups of feminists were the relationship between feminism and the ideology of cultural nationalism or racial pride, feminism and feminist baiting within the larger movements, and the relationship between their feminist movements and the white feminist movement.

CHICANA FEMINISM AND CULTURAL NATIONALISM

Throughout the seventies and in the eighties, Chicana feminists have been forced to respond to the criticism that cultural nationalism and feminism are irreconcilable. In the first issue of the newspaper, *Hijas de Cuauhtémoc*, Anna Nieto Gómez stated that a major issue facing Chicanas active in the Chicana movement was the need to organize to improve their status as women within the larger social movement. Francisca Flores, another leading Chicana feminist, stated:

> [Chicanas] can no longer remain in a subservient role or as auxiliary forces in the [Chicano] movement. They must be included in the front line of communication, leadership and organizational responsibility. . . . The issue of equality, freedom and self-determination of the Chicana—like the right of self-determination, equality, and liberation of the Mexican [Chicano] community—is not negotiable. Anyone opposing the right of women to organize into their own form of organization has no place in the leadership of the movement.

Supporting this position, Bernice Rincón argued that a Chicana feminist movement that sought equality and justice for Chicanas would strengthen the Chicano movement. Yet in the process, Chicana feminists challenged traditional gender roles because they limited their participation and acceptance within the Chicano movement.

Throughout the seventies, Chicana feminists viewed the struggle against sexism within the Chicano movement and the struggle against racism in the larger society as integral parts of Chicana feminism. As Nieto Gómez said:

> Chicana feminism is in various stages of development. However, in general, Chicana feminism is the recognition that women are oppressed as a group and are exploited as part of *"La Raza"* people. It is a direction to be responsible to identify and act upon the issues and needs of Chicana women. Chicana feminists are involved in understanding the nature of women's oppression.

Cultural nationalism represented a major ideological component of the Chicano movement. Its emphasis on Chicano cultural pride and cultural survival within an Anglo-dominated society gave significant political direction to the Chicano movement. One source of ideological disagreement between Chicana feminism and this cultural nationalist ideology was cultural survival. Many Chicana feminists believed that a focus on cultural survival did not acknowledge the need to alter male-female relations within Chicano communities. For example, Chicana feminists criticized the notion of the "ideal Chicana" that glorified Chicanas as strong, long-suffering women who had endured and kept Chicano culture and the family intact. To Chicana feminists, this concept represented an obstacle to the redefinition of gender roles. Nieto stated:

> Some Chicanas are praised as they emulate the sanctified example set by [the Virgin] Mary. The woman *par excellence* is mother and wife. She is to love and support her husband and to nurture and teach her children. Thus, may she gain fulfillment as a woman. For a Chicana bent upon fulfillment of her personhood, this restricted perspective of her role as a woman is not only inadequate but crippling.

Chicana feminists were also skeptical about the cultural nationalist interpretation of machismo. Such an interpretation viewed machismo as an ideological tool used by the dominant Anglo society to justify the inequalities experienced by Chicanos. According to this interpretation, the relationship between Chicanos and the larger society was that of an internal colony dominated and exploited by the capitalist economy. Machismo, like other cultural traits, was blamed by Anglos for blocking Chicanos from succeeding in American society. In reality, the economic structure and colony-like exploitation were to blame.

Some Chicana feminists agreed with this analysis of machismo, claiming that a mutually reinforcing relationship existed between internal colonialism and the development of the myth of machismo. According to Sosa Riddell, machismo was a myth "propagated by subjugators and colonizers, which created damaging stereotypes of Mexican/Chicano males." As a type of social control imposed by the dominant society on Chicanos, the myth of machismo distorted gender relations within Chicano communities, creating stereotypes of Chicanas as passive and docile women. At this level in the feminist discourse, machismo was seen as an Anglo myth that kept both Chicano and Chicanas in a subordinate status. As Nieto concluded:

> Although the term "machismo" is correctly denounced by all because it stereotypes the Latin man . . . it does a great disservice to both men and women. Chicano and Chicana alike must be free to seek their own individual fulfillment.

While some Chicana feminists criticized the myth of machismo used by the dominant society to legitimate racial inequality, others moved beyond this level of analysis to distinguish between the machismo that oppressed both men and women and the sexism in Chicano communities in general, and the Chicano movement in particular, that oppressed Chicana women. According to Vidal, the origins of a Chicana feminist consciousness were prompted by the sexist attitudes and behavior of Chicano males, which constituted a "serious obstacle to women anxious to play a role in the struggle for Chicana liberation."

Furthermore, many Chicana feminists disagreed with the cultural nationalist view that machismo could be a positive value within a Chicano cultural value system. They challenged the view that machismo was a source of masculine pride for Chicanos and therefore a defense mechanism against the dominant society's racism. Although Chicana feminists recognized that Chicanos faced discrimination from the dominant society, they adamantly disagreed with those who believed that machismo was a form of cultural resistance to such discrimination. Chicana feminists called for changes in the ideologies responsible for distorting relations between women and men. One such changes was to modify the cultural nationalist position that viewed machismo as a source of cultural pride.

Chicana feminists called for a focus on the universal aspects of sexism that shape gender relations in both Anglo and Chicano culture. While they acknowledged the economic exploitation of all Chicanos, Chicana feminists outlined the double exploitation experienced by Chicanas. Sosa Riddell (1974, p. 159) concluded: "It was when Chicanas began to seek work outside of the family groups that sexism became a key factor of oppression along with racism." Francisca Flores (1971a, p. 4) summarized some of the consequences of sexism:

It is not surprising that more and more Chicanas are forced to go to work in order to supplement the family income. The children are farmed out to a relative to baby-sit with them, and since these women are employed in the lower income jobs, the extra pressure placed on them can become unbearable.

Thus, while the Chicano movement was addressing the issue of racial oppression facing all Chicanos, Chicana feminist argued that it lacked an analysis of sexism. Similarly, Black and Asian American women stressed the interconnectedness of race and gender oppression. Hook (1984, p. 52) analyzes racism and

sexism in terms of their "intersecting, complementary nature." She also emphasizes that one struggle should not take priority over the other. White (1984) criticizes Black men whose nationalism limited discussions of Black women's experiences with sexist oppression. The writings of other Black feminists criticized a Black cultural nationalist ideology that overlooked the consequences of sexist oppression (Beale 1975; Cade 1970; Davis 1971; Joseph and Lewis 1981). Many Asian American women were also critical of the Asian American movement whose focus on racism ignored the impact of sexism on the daily lives of women. The participation of Asian American women in various community struggles increased their encounters with sexism (Chow 1987). As a result, some Asian American women developed a feminist consciousness and organized as women around feminist issues.

CHICANA FEMINISM AND FEMINIST BAITING

The systematic analysis by Chicana feminists of the impact of racism and sexism on Chicanas in American society and, above all, within the Chicano movement was often misunderstood as a threat to the political unity of the Chicano movement. As Marta Cotera (1977, p. 9), a leading voice of Chicana feminism pointed out:

The aggregate cultural values we [Chicanas] share can also work to our benefit if we choose to scrutinize our cultural traditions, isolate the positive attributes and interpret them for the benefit of women. It's unreal that *Hispanas* have been browbeaten for so long about our so-called conservative (meaning reactionary) culture. It's also unreal that we have let men interpret culture only as those practices and attitudes that determine who does the dishes around the house. We as women also have the right to interpret and define the philosophical and religious traditions beneficial to us within our culture, and which we have inherited as our tradition. To do this, we must become both conversant with our history and philosophical evolution, and analytical about the institutional and behavioral manifestations of the same.

Such Chicana feminists were attacked for developing a "divisive ideology"—a feminist ideology that was frequently viewed as a threat to the Chicano movement as a whole. As Chicana feminists examined their roles as women activists within the Chicano movement, an ideological split developed. One group active in the Chicano movement saw themselves as "loyalists" who believed that the Chicano movement did not have to deal with sexual inequities since Chicana men as well as Chicano women experienced racial oppression. According to Nieto Gómez (1973, p. 35), who was not a loyalist, their view was that if men oppress women, it is not the men's fault but rather that of the system.

Even if such a problem existed, and they did not believe that it did, the loyalists maintained that such a matter would best be resolved internally within the Chicano movement. They denounced the formation of a separate Chicana feminist movement on the grounds that it was a politically dangerous strategy, perhaps Anglo inspired. Such a movement would undermine the unity of the Chicano movement by raising an issue that was not seen as a central one. Loyalists viewed racism as the most important issue within the Chicano movement. Nieto Gómez (1973, p. 35) quotes one such loyalist:

> I am concerned with the direction that the Chicanas are taking in the movement. The words such as liberation, sexism, male chauvinism, etc., were prevalent. The terms mentioned above plus the theme of individualism is a concept of the Anglo society; terms prevalent in the Anglo women's movement. The *familia* has always been our strength in our culture. But it seems evident . . . that you [Chicana feminists] are not concerned with the *familia*, but are influenced by the Anglo woman's movement.

Chicana feminists were also accused of undermining the values associated with Chicano culture. Loyalists saw the Chicana feminist movement as an "anti-family, anti-cultural, anti-man and therefore an anti-Chicano movement" (Gómez 1973, p. 35). Feminism was, above all, believed to be an individualistic search for identity that detracted from the Chicano movement's "real" issues, such as racism. Nieto Gómez (1973, p. 35) quotes a loyalist as stating:

> And since when does a Chicana need identity? If you are a real Chicana then no one regardless of the degrees needs to tell you about it. The only ones who need identity are the *vendidas*, the *falsas*, and the opportunists.

The ideological conflicts between Chicana feminists and loyalists persisted throughout the seventies. Disagreements between these two groups became exacerbated during various Chicana conferences. At times, such confrontations served to increase Chicana feminist activity that challenged the loyalists' attacks, yet these attacks also served to suppress feminist activities.

Chicana feminist lesbians experienced even stronger attacks from those who viewed feminism as a divisive ideology. In a political climate that already viewed feminist ideology with suspicion, lesbianism as a sexual lifestyle and political ideology came under even more attack. Clearly, a cultural nationalist ideology that perpetuated such stereotypical images of Chicanas as "good wives and good mothers" found it difficult to accept a Chicana feminist lesbian movement.

Cherrie Moraga's writings during the 1970s reflect the struggles of Chicana feminist lesbians who, together with other Chicana feminists, were finding the sexism evident within the Chicano movement intolerable. Just as Chicana feminists analyzed their life circumstances as members of an ethnic minority and as women, Chicana feminist lesbians addressed themselves to the oppression they experienced as lesbians. As Moraga (1981, p. 28) stated:

> My lesbianism is the avenue through which I have learned the most about silence and oppression[1] . . . . In this country, lesbianism is a poverty—as is being brown, as is being a woman, as is being just plain poor. The danger lies in ranking the oppressions. The danger lies in failing to acknowledge the specificity of the oppression.

Chicana, Black, and Asian American feminists experienced similar cross-pressures of feminist-baiting and lesbian-baiting attacks. As they organized around feminist struggles, these women of color encountered criticism from both male and female cultural nationalists who often viewed feminism as little more than an "anti-male" ideology. Lesbianism was identified as an extreme deviation of feminism. A direct connection was frequently made that viewed feminism and lesbianism as synonymous. Feminists were labeled lesbians, and lesbians as feminists. Attacks against feminists—Chicanas, Blacks, and Asian Americans—derived from the existence of homophobia within each of these communities. As lesbian women of color published their writings, attacks against them increased (Moraga, 1983).

Responses to such attacks varied within and between the feminist movements of women of color. Some groups tried one strategy and later adopted another. Some lesbians pursued a separatist strategy within their own racial and ethnic communities (Moraga and Anzaldúa 1981; White 1984). Others attempted to form lesbian coalitions across racial and ethnic lines. Both strategies represented a response to the marginalization of lesbians produced by recurrent waves of homophobic sentiments in Chicano, Black, and Asian American communities (Moraga and Anzaldúa 1981). A third response consisted of working within the broader nationalist movements in these communities and the feminist movements within them in order to challenge their heterosexual biases and resultant homophobia. As early as 1974, the "Black Feminist Statement" written by a Boston-based feminist group—the Combahec River Collective—stated (1981, p. 213): "We struggle together with Black men against racism, while we also struggle with Black men against sexism." Similarly, Moraga (1981) challenged the white feminist movement to examine its racist tendencies; the Chicano movement, its sexist tendencies; and both, their homophobic tendencies. In this way, Moraga argued that such movements to end oppression would begin to respect diversity within their own ranks.

Chicana feminists as well as Chicana feminist lesbians continued to be labeled *vendidas* or "sellouts." Chicana loyalists continued to view Chicana feminism as associated, not only with melting into white society, but more seriously, with dividing the Chicano movement. Similarly, many Chicano males were convinced the Chicana feminism was a divisive ideology incompatible with Chicano cultural nationalism. Nieto Gómez said that "[with] respect to [the] Chicana feminist, their credibility is reduced when they are associated with [feminism] and white women." She added that, as a result, Chicana feminists often faced harassment and ostracism within the Chicano movement. Similarly, Cotera stated that Chicanas "are suspected of assimilating into the feminist ideology of an alien [white] culture that actively seeks our cultural domination."

Chicana feminists responded quickly and often vehemently to such charges. Flores answered these antifeminist attacks in an editorial in which she argued that birth control, abortion, and sex education were not merely "white issues." In response to the accusation that feminists were responsible for the "betrayal of [Chicano] culture and heritage," Flores said, "Our culture hell"—a phrase that became a dramatic slogan of the Chicana feminist movement.

Chicana feminists' defense throughout the 1970s against those claiming that a feminist movement was divisive for the Chicano movement was to reassess their roles within the Chicano movement and to call for an end to male domination. Their challenges of traditional gender roles represented a means to achieve equality. In order to increase the participation of and opportunities for women in the Chicano movement, feminists agreed that both Chicanos and Chicanas had to address the issue of gender inequality. Furthermore, Chicana feminists argued that the resistance that they encountered reflected the existence of sexism on the part of Chicano males and the anti-feminist attitudes of the Chicana loyalists. Nieto Gómez, reviewing the experiences of Chicana feminists in the Chicano movement, concluded that Chicanas "involved in discussing and applying the women's question have been ostracized, isolated and ignored." She argued that "in organizations where cultural nationalism is extremely strong, Chicana feminists experience intense harassment and ostracism."

Black and Asian American women also faced severe criticism as they pursued feminist issues in their own communities. Indeed, as their participation in collective efforts to end racial oppression increased, so did their confrontations with sexism. Ngan-Ling Chow describes the various sources of such criticism directed at Asian American women:

> Asian American women are criticized for the possible consequences of their protests: weakening the male ego, dilution of effort and resources in Asian American communities, destruction of working relationships between Asian men and women, setbacks for the Asian American cause, co-optation into the larger society, and eventual loss of ethnic identity for Asian Americans as a whole. In short, affiliation with the feminist movement is perceived as a threat to solidarity within their own community.

Similar criticism was experienced by Black feminists.

CHICANA FEMINISTS AND WHITE FEMINISTS

It is difficult to determine the extent to which Chicana feminists sympathized with the white feminist movement. A 1976 study at the University of San Diego that examined the attitudes of Chicanas regarding the white feminist movement found that the majority of Chicanas surveyed believed that the movement had affected their lives. In addition, they identified with such key issues as the right to legal abortions on demand and access to low-cost birth control. Nevertheless, the survey found that "even though the majority of Chicanas . . . could relate to certain issues of the women's movement, for the most part they saw it as being an elitist movement comprised of white middle-class women who [saw] the oppressor as the males of this country."

Nevertheless, some Chicana feminists considered the possibility of forming coalitions with white feminists as their attempts to work within the Chicano movement were suppressed. Since white feminists were themselves struggling against sexism, building coalitions with them was seen as an alternative strategy for Chicana feminists. Almost immediately, however, Chicana feminists recognized the problems involved in adopting this political strategy. As Longeaux y Vásquez acknowledged, "some of our own Chicanas may be attracted to the white woman's liberation movement, but we really don't feel comfortable there. We want to be a Chicana *primero* [first]." For other Chicanas, the demands of white women were irrelevant to the Chicana movement.

Several issues made such coalition building difficult. First, Chicana feminists criticized what they considered to be a cornerstone of white feminist thought, an emphasis on gender oppression to explain the life circumstances of women. Chicana feminists believed that the white feminist movement overlooked the effects of racial oppression experienced by Chicanas and other women of color. Thus, Del Castillo maintained that the Chicana feminist movement was "different primarily because we are [racially] oppressed people." In addition, Chicana feminists criticized white feminists who believed that a general women's movement would be able to overcome racial differences among women. Chicanas interpreted this as a failure by the white feminist movement to deal with the issue of racism. Without the incorporation of an analysis of racial oppression to explain the experiences of Chicanas as well as of other women of color, Chicana feminists believed that a coalition with white feminists would be highly unlikely. As Longeaux y Vásquez concluded: "We must have a clearer vision of our plight and certainly we cannot blame our men for the oppression of the women."

In the 1970s, Chicana feminists reconciled their demands for an end to sexism within the Chicano movement and their rejection of the saliency of gender oppression by separating the two issues. They clearly identified the struggle against sexism in the Chicano

movement as a major issue, arguing that sexism prevented their full participation. They also argued that sexist behavior and ideology on the part of both Chicano males and Anglos represented the key to understanding women's experiences that focused exclusively on gender oppression.

Chicana feminists adopted an analysis that began with race as a critical variable in interpreting the experiences of Chicano communities in the United States. They expanded this analysis by identifying gender as a variable interconnected with race in analyzing the specific daily life circumstances of Chicanas as women in Chicano communities. Chicana feminists did not view women's struggles as secondary to the nationalist movement but argued instead for an analysis of race and gender as multiple sources of oppression. Thus, Chicana feminism went beyond the limits of an exclusively racial theory of oppression that tended to overlook gender and also went beyond the limits of a theory of oppression based exclusively on gender that tended to overlook race.

A second factor preventing an alliance between Chicana feminists and white feminists was the middle-class orientation of white feminists. While some Chicana feminists recognized the legitimacy of the demands made by white feminists and even admitted sharing some of these demands, they argued that "it is not our business as Chicanas to identify with the white women's liberation movement as a home base for working for our people."

Throughout the 1970s, Chicana feminists viewed the white feminist movement as a middle-class movement. In contrast, Chicana feminists analyzed the Chicana movement in general as a working-class movement. They repeatedly made reference to such differences, and many Chicana feminists began their writings with a section that disassociated themselves from the "women's liberation movement." Chicana feminists as activists in the broader Chicano movement identified as major struggles the farmworkers movement, welfare rights, undocumented workers, and prison rights. Such demands of the white feminist movement, and Chicana feminists could not get white feminist organizations to deal with them.

Similar concerns regarding the white feminist movement were raised by Black and Asian American feminists. Black feminists have documented the historical and contemporary schisms between Black feminists and white feminists, emphasizing the socioeconomic and political differences. More specifically, Black feminists have been critical of the white feminists who advocate a female solidarity that cuts across racial, ethnic, and social class lines. As Thornton Dill states:

> The cry "Sisterhood is powerful!" has engaged only a few segments of the female population in the United States. Black, Hispanic, Native American, and Asian American women of all classes, as well as many working-class women, have not readily identified themselves as sisters of the white middle-class women who have been in the forefront of the movement.

Like Black feminists, Asian American feminists have also had strong reservations regarding the white feminist movement. For many Asian Americans, white feminism has primarily focused on gender as an analytical category and has thus lacked a systematic analysis of race and class.

White feminists organizations were also accused of being exclusionary, patronizing, or racist in their dealings with Chicanas and other women of color. Cotera states:

> Minority women could fill volumes with examples of put-down, put-ons, and out-and-out racism shown to them by the leadership in the [white feminist] movement. There are three major problem areas in the minority-majority relationship in the movement: (1) paternalism or materialism, (2) extremely limited opportunities for minority women . . . , (3) outright discrimination against minority women in the movement.

Although Chicana feminists continued to be critical of building coalitions with white feminists toward the end of the seventies, they acknowledged the diversity of ideologies within the white feminist movement. Chicana feminists sympathetic to radical socialist feminism because of its anticapitalist framework wrote of working-class oppression that cut across racial and ethnic lines. Their later writings discussed the possibility of joining with white working-class women, but strategies for forming such political coalitions were not made explicit.

Instead, Del Castillo and other Chicana feminists favored coalitions between Chicanas and other women of color while keeping their respective autonomous organizations. Such coalitions would recognize the inherent racial oppression of capitalism rather than universal gender oppression. When Longeaux y Vásquez stated that she was "Chicana *primero*," she was

stressing the saliency of race over gender in explaining the oppression experienced by Chicanas. The word *Chicana* however, simultaneously expresses a woman's race and gender. Not until later—in the 1980s—would Chicana feminist ideology call for an analysis that stressed the interrelationship of race, class, and gender in explaining the conditions of Chicanas in American society, just as Black and Asian American feminists have done.

Chicana feminists continued to stress the importance of developing autonomous feminist organizations that would address the struggles of Chicanas as members of an ethnic minority and as women. Rather that attempt to overcome the obstacles to coalition building between Chicana feminists and white feminists, Chicanas called for autonomous feminists organizations for all women of color. Chicana feminists believed that sisterhood was indeed powerful but only to the extent that racial and class differences were understood and, above all, respected. As Nieto concludes:

> The Chicana must demand that dignity and respect within the women's rights movement which allows her to practice feminism within the context of own culture. . . . Her approaches to feminism must be drawn from her own world.

CHICANA FEMINISM: AN EVOLVING FUTURE

Chicana feminists, like Black, Asian American and Native American feminists, experience specific life conditions that are distinct from those of white feminists. Such socioeconomic and cultural differences in Chicano communities directly shaped the development of Chicana feminism and the relationship between Chicana feminists and feminists of other racial ethnic groups, including white feminists. But dialogue among all feminists will require mutual understanding of the existing differences as well as the similarities. Like other women of color, Chicana feminists must address issues that specifically affect them as women of color. In addition. Chicana feminists must address those issues that have particular impact on Chicano communities, such as poverty, limited opportunities for higher education, high school dropouts, health care, bilingual education, immigration reform, prison reform, welfare, and, most recently, United States policies in Central America.

At the academic level, an increasing number of Chicana feminists continue to join in a collective effort to carry on the feminist legacy inherited from the 1970s. In June 1982, a group of Chicana academics organized a national feminist organization called Mujeres Activas Letras y Cambio Social (MALCS) in order to build a support network for Chicana professors, undergraduates, and graduate students. The organization's major goal is to fight against race, class, and gender oppression facing Chicanas in institutions of higher education. In addition, MALCS aims to bridge the gap between academic work and the Chicano community. MALCS has organized three Chicana/Latina summer research institutes at the University of California at Davis and publishes a working paper series.

During the 1982 conference of the National Association for Chicano Studies, a panel organized by Mujeres en Marcha, a feminist group from the University of California at Berkeley, discussed three major issues facing Chicana feminists in higher education in particular and the Chicano movement in general. Panelists outlined the issues as follows:

1. For a number of years, Chicanas have heard claims that a concern with issues specifically affecting Chicanas is merely a distraction/diversion from the liberation of Chicano people as a whole. What are the issues that arise when women are asked to separate their exploitation as women from the other forms of oppression that we experience?

2. Chicanas are confronted daily by the limitations of being a woman in this patriarchal society; the attempts to assert these issues around sexism are often met with resistance and scorn. What are some of the major difficulties in relations amongst ourselves? How are the relationships between women and men affected? How are the relationships of women to women and men to men affected? How do we overcome the constraints of sexism?

3. It is not uncommon that our interests as feminists are challenged on the basis that we are simply falling prey to the interests of white middle-class women We challenge the notion that there is no room for a Chicana movement within our own community We, as women of color, have a unique set of concerns that are separate from white women and from men of color.

While these issues could not be resolved at the conference, the panel succeeded in generating an ongoing discussion within the National Association for Chicano Studies (NACS). Two years later, in 1984, the national conference of NACS, held in Austin, Texas, adopted the theme "Voces de la Mujer" in response to demands from the Chicana Caucus. As a result, for the first time since its founding in 1972, the NACS national conference addressed the issue of women. Compared with past conferences, a large number of Chicanas participated by presenting their research and chairing and moderating panels. A plenary session addressed the problems of gender inequality in higher education and within NACS. At the national business meeting, the issue of sexism within NACS was again seriously debated as it continues to be one of the "unsettled issues" of concern to Chicana feminists. A significant outcome of this conference was the publication of the NACS 1984 conference proceedings, which marked the first time that the association's anthology was devoted completely to Chicanas and Mexicanas.

The decade of the 1980s has witnessed a rephrasing of the critical question concerning the nature of the oppression experienced by Chicanas and other women of color. Chicana feminists, like Black feminists, are asking what are the consequences of the intersection of race, class, and gender in the daily lives of women in American society, emphasizing the simultaneity of these critical variables for women of color. In their labor-force participation, wages, education, and poverty levels, Chicanas have made few gains in comparison to white men and women and Chicano men. To analyze these problems, Chicana feminists have investigated the structures of racism, capitalism, and patriarchy, especially as they are experienced by the majority of Chicanas. Clearly, such issues will need to be explicitly addressed by an evolving Chicana feminist movement, analytically and politically.

Endnotes

1. For bibliographies on Chicanas see Balderama (1981); Candelaria (1980); Loeb (1980); Portillo, Ríos, and Rodríguez (1976); and Baca Zinn (1982, 1984).

References

Almaguer, Tomás. 1974. "Historical Notes on Chicano Oppression." *Atlas* 5:27–56.

Baca Zinn, Maxine. 1975a. "Political Familism: Toward Sex Role Equality in Chicano Families." *Aztlán* 6:13–27.

———. 1975b. "Chicanas: Power and Control in the Domestic Sphere." *De Colores* 2/3:19–31.

————. 1982. "Mexican-American Women in the Social Sciences." *Signs: Journal of Women in Culture and Society* 8:259–72.

————. 1984. "Mexican Heritage Women: A Bibliographic Essay." *Sage Race Relations Abstracts* 9:1–12.

Balderama, Sylvia. 1981. "A Comprehensive Bibliography on La Chicana." Unpublished paper, University of California, Berkeley.

Barrera, Mario. 1974. "The Study of Politics and the Chicano." *Aztlán* 5:9–26.

————. 1979. *Race and Class in the Southwest.* Notre Dame, IN: University of Notre Dame Press.

Beale, Frances. 1975. "Slave of a Slave No More: Black Women in Struggle." *Black Scholar* 6:2–10.

Cade, Toni. 1970. *The Black Woman.* New York: Signet.

Candelaria, Cordelia. 1980. "Six Reference Works on Mexican American Women: A Review Essay." *Frontiers* 5:75–80.

Castro, Tony. 1974. *Chicano Power.* New York: Saturday Review Press.

Chapa, Evey. 1973. "Report from the National Women's Political Caucus." *Magazín* 1:37–39.

Chávez, Henri. 1971. "The Chicanas." *Regeneracion* 1:14.

Cheng, Lucie. 1984. "Asian American Women and Feminism." *Sojourner* 10:11–12.

Chow, Esther Ngan-Ling. 1987. "The Development of Feminist Consciousness Among Asian American Women." *Gender & Society* 1:284–99.

Combahee River Collective. 1981. "A Black Feminist Statement." Pp. 210–18 in *This Bridge Called My Back: Writings by Radical Women of Color*, edited by Cherrie Moraga and Gloria Anzaldúa. Watertown, MA: Persephone.

Córdova, Teresa et al. 1986. *Chicana Voices: Intersections of Class, Race, and Gender.* Austin, TX: Center for Mexican American Studies.

Cotera, Marta. 1973. "La Mujer Mexicana: Mexicano Feminism." *Magazín* 1:30–32.

————. 1977. *The Chicana Feminist.* Austin, TX: Austin Information Systems Development.

————. 1980. "Feminism: The Chicana and Anglo Versions: An Historical Analysis." Pp. 217–34 in *Twice a Minority: Mexican American Women*, edited by Margarita Melville. St. Louis, MO: C.V. Mosby.

Davis, Angela. 1971. "Reflections on Black Women's Role in the Community of Slaves." *Black Scholar* 3:3–13.

————. 1983. *Women, Race and Class.* New York: Random House.

Del Castillo, Adelaida. 1974. "La Vision Chicana." *La Gente*: 8.

Dill, Bonnie Thornton. 1983. "Race, Class, and Gender: Prospects for an All-Inclusive Sisterhood." *Feminist Studies* 9:131–50.

Dunne, John. 1967. *Delano: The Story of the California Grape Strike.* New York: Strauss.

Fallis, Guadalupe Valdés. 1974. "The Liberated Chicana—A Struggle Against Tradition." *Women: A Journal of Liberation* 3:20.

Flores, Francisca. 1971a. "Conference of Mexican Women: Un Remolino. *Regeneración* 1(1):1–4.

————. 1971b. "El Mundo Femenil Mexicana." *Regeneración* 1(10):i.

Fong, Katheryn M. 1978. "Feminism Is Fine, But What's It Done for Asia America?" *Bridge* 6:21–22.

Freeman, Jo. 1983. "On the Origins of Social Movements." Pp. 8–30 in *Social Movements of the Sixties and Seventies*, edited by Jo Freeman. New York: Longman.

————. 1984. "The Women's Liberation Movement: Its Origins, Structure, Activities, and Ideas." Pp. 543–56 in *Women: A Feminist Perspective*, edited by Jo Freeman. Palo Alto, CA: Mayfield.

García, Alma M. 1986. "Studying Chicanas: Bringing Women into the Frame of Chicano Studies." Pp. 19–29 in *Chicana Voices: Intersections of Class, Race, and Gender*, edited by Teresa Córdova et al. Austin, TX: Center for Mexican American Studies.

García, F. Chris and Rudolph O. de la Garza. 1977. *The Chicano Political Experience.* North Scituate, MA: Duxbury.

Gómez, Anna Nieto. 1971. "Chicanas Identify." *Hijas de Cuauhtémoc* (April):9.

————. 1973. "La Femenista." *Encuentro Femenil* 1:34–47.

————. 1976. "Sexism in the Movement." *La Gente* 6(4):10.

González, Sylvia. 1980. "Toward a Feminist Pedagogy for Chicana Self-Actualization." *Frontiers* 5:48–51.

Hernández, Carmen. 1971. "Carmen Speaks Out." *Papel Chicano* l (June 12):8–9.

Hooks, Bell. 1981. *Ain't I a Woman: Black Women and Feminism.* Boston: South End Press.

————. 1984. *Feminist Theory: From Margin to Center.* Boston: South End Press.

Joseph, Gloria and Jill Lewis. 1981. *Common Differences: Conflicts in Black and White Feminist Perspectives.* Garden City, NY: Doubleday.

Kushner, Sam. 1975. *Long Road to Delano.* New York: International.

LaRue, Linda. 1970. "The Black Movement and Women's Liberation." *Black Scholar* 1:36–42.

Loeb, Catherine. 1980. "La Chicana: A Bibliographic Survey." *Frontiers* 5:59–74.

Longeaux y Vásquez, Enriqueta. 1969a. "The Woman of La Raza." *El Grito del Norte* 2(July):8–9.

————. 1969b. "La Chicana: Let's Build a New Life." *El Grito del Norte* 2(November):11.

———. 1970. "The Mexican-American Woman." Pp. 379–84 in *Sisterhood Is Powerful*, edited by Robin Morgan. New York: Vintage.

———. 1971. "Soy Chicana Primero." *El Grito del Norte* 4(April 26):11.

Macías, Anna. 1982. *Against All Odds*. Westport. CT: Greenwood.

Márquez, Evelina and Margarita Ramírez. 1977. "Women's Task Is to Gain Liberation." Pp. 188–94 in *Essays on La Mujer*, edited by Rosaura Sánchez and Rosa Martínez Cruz. Los Angeles: UCLA Chicano Studies Center.

Martínez, Elizabeth. 1972. "The Chicana." *Ideal* 44:1–3.

Matthiesen, Peter. 1969. *Sal Si Puedes: César Chávez and the New American Revolution*. New York: Random House.

Meier, Matt and Feliciano Rivera. 1972. *The Chicanos*. New York: Hill & Wang.

Moraga, Cherrie. 1981. "La Guera." Pp. 27–34 in *This Bridge Called My Back: Writings by Radical Women of Color*, edited by Cherrie Moraga and Gloria Anzaldúa. Watertown, MA: Persephone.

———. 1983. *Loving in the War Years*. Boston: South End Press.

Moraga, Cherrie and Gloria Anzaldúa. 1981. *This Bridge Called My Back: Writings by Radical Women of Color*. Watertown, MA: Persephone.

Moreno, Dorinda. 1979. "The Image of the Chicana and the La Raza Woman." *Caracol* 2:14–15.

Mujeres en Marcha. 1983. *Chicanas in the 80s: Unsettled Issues*. Berkeley, CA: Chicano Studies Publication Unit.

Muñoz, Carlos, Jr. 1974. "The Politics of Protest and Liberation: A Case Study of Repression and Cooptation." *Aztlán* 5:119–41.

Nabokov, Peter. 1969. *Tijerina and the Courthouse Raid*. Albuquerque, NM: University of New Mexico Press.

Navarro, Armando. 1974. "The Evolution of Chicano Politics." *Aztlán* 5:57–84.

Nelson, Eugene. 1966. *Huelga: The First 100 Days*. Delano, CA: Farm Workers Press.

Nieto, Consuelo. 1974. "The Chicana and the Women's Rights Movement." *La Luz* 3(September):10–11, 32.

———. 1975. "Consuelo Nieto on the Women's Movement." *Interracial Books for Children Bulletin* 5:4.

Orozco, Yolanda. 1976. "La Chicana and 'Women's Liberation.'" *Voz Fronteriza* (January 5):6, 12.

Piven, Frances Fox and Richard A. Cloward. 1979. *Poor People's Movements: Why They Succeed, How They Fail*. New York: Vintage.

Portillo, Cristina, Graciela Ríos, and Martha Rodríguez. 1976. *Bibliography on Writings on La Mujer*. Berkeley, CA: University of California Chicano Studies Library.

Riddell, Adaljiza Sosa. 1974. "Chicanas en el Movimiento." *Aztlán* 5:155–65.

Rincón, Bernice. 1971. "La Chicana: Her Role in the Past and Her Search for a New Role in the Future." *Regeneración* 1(10):15–17.

Rowbotham, Sheila. 1974. *Women, Resistance and Revolution: A History of Women and Revolution in the Modern World*. New York: Vintage.

Ruiz, Vicki L. 1987. *Cannery Women, Cannery Lives: Mexican Women, Unionization, and the California Food Processing Industry*, 1930–1950. Albuquerque: University of New Mexico Press.

Segura, Denise. 1986. "Chicanas and Triple Oppression in the Labor Force." Pp. 47–65 in *Chicana Voices: Intersections of Class, Race and Gender*, edited by Teresa Córdova et al. Austin, TX: Center for Mexican American Studies.

Shockley, John. 1974. *Chicano Revolt in a Texas Town*. South Bend, IN: University of Notre Dame Press.

Vidal, Mirta. 1971. "New Voice of La Raza: Chicanas Speak Out." *International Socialist Review* 32:31–33.

White, Frances. 1984. "Listening to the Voices of Black Feminism." *Radical America* 18:7–25.

Wong, Germaine Q. 1980. "Impediments to Asian-Pacific-American Women Organizing." Pp. 89–103 in *The Conference on the Educational and Occupational Needs of Asian Pacific Women*. Washington, DC: National Institute of Education.

Woo, Margaret. 1971. "Women + Man = Political Unity." Pp. 115–16 in *Asian Women*, edited by Editorial Staff. Berkeley, CA: University of California Press.

Zavella, Patricia. 1987. *Women's Work and Chicano Families: Cannery Workers of the Santa Clara Valley*. Ithaca, NY: Cornell University Press.

Understanding Latina Political Leadership

Sonia García, Valerie Martínez-Ebers, Irasema Coronado,
Sharon R. Navarro, and Patricia Jaramillo

Latinas,[1] especially those of Mexican descent, have a long history as political actors dating at least as far back as the Texas revolution in 1836, when Francisca Alvarez, the so-called "Angel of Goliad," persuaded Mexican officers to defy the execution orders given by their president, General Antonio López de Santa Anna, thus saving the lives of numerous Texas soldiers held as prisoners of war. Since 1959, when Norma Zuniga Bénavides successfully ran for school board trustee in Laredo, Texas, Latinas have served in public office in the United States (Cotera 1976; Gomez-Quiñones 1990; Acosta and Winegarten 2003). Only recently, however, have scholars begun to examine the complexity and contributions of Latina leadership in the American political context.

What motivates Latinas to become involved in political activity, and what barriers do they confront in their efforts? Do they typically follow the conventional paths of men and women of other races and ethnic groups? As elected leaders, do they have unique political perspectives and/ or skills gleaned from their cultural background or life experiences? Finally, how does their leadership influence public policy? To answer these central questions, this book presents case studies of the first elected and appointed Latina public officials in various levels of offices in the state of Texas.

Specifically, we describe and analyze the political stories of women who have reached public office as the "first state legislator," the "first state senator," the "first mayor of a major Texas city," and so on.

These detail-rich case studies, derived primarily from personal interviews, are intended to provide readers with a multidimensional understanding of Latinas' political leadership. As Alessandro Portelli, a leading scholar utilizing oral history, explains, "Oral sources tell us not just what people did, but what they wanted to do, what they believed they were doing and what they now think they did" (in Stille 2001). As much as possible, we substantiate their subjective stories with archival data and other sources. We also examine and compare these stories in light of conclusions drawn from earlier studies of women in politics. Our methods make these case studies both descriptive and theory-building.

Undoubtedly, the numbers and influence of Latina political leaders are increasing at the national level and in states other than Texas. However, taking a case study approach within one state is a first step towards fully understanding the efforts and impacts of Latina public officials. It is our hope that future research will continue our approach by examining Latina leadership in other states.

Examining the first Latinas elected to specific positions in Texas has important implications. First of all, since Latinas are underrepresented, these first Latina public officials have already paid a price in crossing the barriers to their entry into politics; pressure is increased when she is the first one, or the only one, because of society's tendency to stereotype her as representative of all Latinas. Second, Texas leads the country with respect to the largest number of Latinas (and Latinos) elected to public office. Third, as the demographic makeup of the state and the country changes, we all benefit from understanding how an inclusive and diverse democracy should work. Fourth, with the 2000 Census pronouncement of Latinos as the largest ethnic group in the United States, we can expect that this population will continue to seek political representation at. all levels of government. With that as a given, it is essential to examine Latinas, specifically Mexican American women, and their role in politics.

NATIONAL ATTENTION TO LATINAS

Events prompting this study of Latina trailblazers started in the late 1980s, when Latinas achieved a new presence and level of visibility in the national political arena. Ileana Ros-Lehtinen (R-FL), a Cuban American, received national attention in 1982 as the first Latina to be elected to the U.S. Congress. Ten years later, in 1992, two additional Latinas were elected to the U.S. House of Representatives: Lucille Roybal-Allard (D-CA), the first Mexican American representative from California, and Nydia Velásquez (D-NY), the first Puerto Rican representative from New York.

In 1996, Loretta Sánchez, a businesswoman from Orange County, California, brought further public attention as well as notoriety to Latinas in politics when she narrowly defeated Republican incumbent Robert Dornan in a bitterly fought election. The controversial longtime incumbent Dornan was targeted as "out of touch" with his constituency, especially after a distracting run for the 1996 Republican presidential nomination. The 46th District had always had a slight Democratic majority, but it became even more Democratic after the 1990 Census, which showed a considerable increase in Hispanics living in the district. Sánchez won by only 984 votes on the strength of support from Hispanics and blue-collar workers. Dornan contested the election, alleging that some of the registered voters were not U.S. citizens, but the results were upheld. Sánchez handily defeated Dornan in a 1998-rematch and has not since faced serious opposition.

In a short period of time, three other Latina Democrats, were sent to the U.S. House from California: former state legislator Grace Napolitano (1998), former

state senator Hilda Solis (2000), and lawyer and activist Linda Sánchez (2003), the sister of Loretta Sánchez. The Sánchez sisters received national acclaim as the first "sister act" in the Congress. As of 2006, seven Latinas were serving in Congress, all in the House of Representatives. No Latina has ever run for or been elected to the U.S. Senate. In 2006 Patricia Madrid, attorney general of New Mexico, ran for Congress in one of the most competitive races for the Democratic Party nationwide, hoping to be the first Latina congresswoman from New Mexico. U.S. Representative Heather Wilson (R) edged out Madrid by 879 votes.[2]

Although numerous Latinas have sought Texas congressional seats, the Lone Star State has yet to elect a Latina to the thirty-two-member delegation to the U.S. Congress. Two prominent Latinas ran in Texas Democratic primaries in 1996 for the House of Representatives: Dolores Briones, who was elected as county judge in 1998, campaigned unsuccessfully for an open seat in El Paso, while Mary Helen Berlanga, the first Latina on the State Board of Education, unsuccessfully challenged the incumbent in Corpus Christi on the Gulf Coast. Four years later, Latinas tried again. Although attorney and community activist Diana Rivera-Martinez unsuccessfully challenged the incumbent in the Democratic primary in Mercedes in south Texas, Regina Montoya Coggins won the Democratic nomination in Dallas, but was unsuccessful in her bid to unseat the Republican incumbent in the general election.

Other more recent, albeit unsuccessful, stories regarding Latina congressional candidates are demonstrative of their continuing emergence. These candidacies are also indicative of the tough challenges these women face in the Lone Star State. In 2004, state judge Leticia Hinojosab from McAllen unsuccessfully challenged incumbent Lloyd Doggett in the Democratic primary in the newly constructed 25th Congressional District, which stretches more than 350 miles from Austin to McAllen. Some would argue that the new configuration was intentionally designed by the Republican majority in the state legislature to defeat Representative Doggett. Interestingly, the former chair of the Texas Public Utilities Commission, Rebecca Armendariz Klein, won the Republican nomination but could not defeat Doggett in the restructured district. In another newly restructured district, Houston businesswoman and attorney Arlette Molina won the Republican primary but was unable to defeat the Democratic challenger, Al Green, a former justice of the peace and president of the local NAACP chapter.

Texas Latinas, like Latinas nationwide, are notably more successful in winning elections for state legislative seats.[3] For example, Polly Baca-Barragan was the first Latina elected to both the Colorado House of Representatives and the Colorado Senate, in 1974 and 1978, respectively. The first Latina ever elected to a state legislature in the United States, Baca-Barragan served for twelve years. She also was the first Latina to be nominated by a major political party for the U.S. House of Representatives, in 1980, and the first Latina to serve in a state party leadership role (Senate Democratic Caucus), in 1985-1986. Other significant Latina firsts include the late Texas state representative Irma Rangel, who was first elected in 1976 and served fourteen consecutive terms prior to her death in 2003.

Gloria Molina was California's first Latina state legislator, elected in 1982. She resigned in 1987 and successfully ran for the Los Angeles City Council. In 1991, Molina became the first Mexican American of either sex to be elected to the Los Angeles County Board of Supervisors. As the first Latina on the board, Molina was also the first Latina elected to local office to receive national publicity.

The increasing number of Latina candidates in hotly contested elections at county, city, and school district levels in prominent urban areas such as San Francisco and Pasadena, California; Phoenix, Arizona; San Antonio, Houston, and Dallas, Texas; and Santa Fe, New Mexico, has continued to focus national media attention on the importance of Latina leadership in local arenas. Interestingly, from our perspective as Texas scholars, a local Latina leader making national news in 2004 was Dallas County sheriff Lupe Valdez. A retired federal law enforcement officer, Valdez outpolled three opponents in the 2004 Democratic primary and then went on to narrowly defeat the Republican challenger, a thirty-year veteran of the Sheriff's Department. It is important to note that Valdez is making history as the first woman, the first Hispanic, and the first openly gay person to serve in this capacity (Moreno 2004).

PATTERNS OF REPRESENTATION FOR LATINAS

Although Latinas have made gains in politics in recent years, there are still relatively few in office, and for the most part they are unrecognized as political actors. Since the 1980s, many organizations and scholars have tracked the level of political involvement of Latinos and Latinas. According to the National Association for Latino Elected and Appointed Officials (NALEO), there were 3,128 Latino/a elected officials nationwide in 1984, 4,625 in 1994, and ten years later that number had risen to 5,041. As of 2005, there were more than 6,000 elected and appointed Latino/a officials, an almost 100 percent increase in representation over the past twenty years.[4]

As the importance of gender in electoral politics increased, greater scholarly attention was given to disaggregating Latino and Latina elected officials.[5] Sierra and Sosa-Riddell (1994) reported 592 Latina elected officials in 1987, and that total increased to 744 in 1989. By 1992, Latinas comprised more than 30 percent of all Latino/a elected officials, when women as a whole constituted only 17.2 percent of all elected officials in the country. Significantly, Latina officials were most prominent on local school boards and in municipal governments (Pachon and DeSipio 1992, cited in Montoya et al. 2000).

As of 2004, Latinas held 27.4 percent of all elected positions held by Latinos and Latinas nationwide, a slight drop in their relative proportion, but Latinas had the highest representation in state senates of all Latino/a elected officials (40 percent), followed by 33 percent in county offices, 32 percent in Congress, 32 percent on school boards, 26 percent in state houses, 24 percent in municipal offices, and 23 percent in judicial/law enforcement offices. One study, covering 1990 to 2002, shows that Latinas made significant progress in the Congress (from one to seven representatives) and in state offices (increasing from sixteen to sixty-one). Latina increases still outpaced increases in Latino/a representation overall, as well. as increases among white women (Fraga and Navarro 2004).

Regarding Latina representation in Texas, in 1991 Texas led all other states with significant Hispanic populations, with 361 Latina elected officials, followed by California (163) and New Mexico (135). By 1999, Texas led the country in the total number of Latinos elected to public office, but when the numbers were disaggregated by gender, Texas ranked only sixth out of the states with significant Hispanic populations. Arizona and California—followed by Florida, Colorado, and New York—ranked above Texas.[6] In 2005, NALEO reported that there were 2,137 Latino elected officials in Texas, 591 of them (over 30 percent) women. As mentioned above, Texas Latinas once again rank first in the country in the number of public officials, followed by California, New Mexico, Arizona, and Colorado. The majority of Texas Latina elected officials can be found in municipal and county offices and on school boards.

THE STATUS OF U.S. LATINAS

To fully understand the significance of Latinas achieving some prominence in elected office, it is necessary to acknowledge the struggles that U.S. Latinas have faced and continue to face. Research in history and the social sciences has documented and illustrated the discrimination and oppression experienced by Mexican American women (Melville 1980; Cordova et al. 1986). These early studies underscore the complexity of Latinas' experiences in the United States. A growing area of research addresses the legal issues faced by and impacting Mexican American women and Latinas in general (Hernandez 1976; Ontiveros 1993; Valencia et al. 2004). The host of issues affecting Latinas range from reproductive rights, pregnancy discrimination, workplace discrimination, equal pay, educational attainment, and affirmative action to sexual harassment, domestic violence, and sexual violence. Mexican American women have played a pivotal role in the struggle for equality and justice for Latinos. Organizations such as Comisión Femeníl Mexicana Nacional (established in 1973), the Mexican American Legal Defense and Education Fund (MALDEF) Chicana Rights Project (established in 1974), and other women's legal organizations played key roles in bringing cases in the courts (Valencia et al. 2004, 41).

With regard to reproductive rights, "the issue of voluntary consent for sterilization is an area of particular relevance" to Latinas (Valencia 2004, 43). In *Madrigal v. Quilligan* (1981), a federal court in California heard a challenge by Mexican and Mexican American women who alleged that the University of Southern California, Los Angeles County Medical Center performed illegal and unwanted sterilizations upon them without their consent (ibid.). Although the trial court in *Madrigal* denied the women's claims, reasoning that the sterilizations resulted because of the women's limited English abilities and their "cultural background," the case resulted in stricter federal regulations requiring medical consent in one's native language.

With regard to workplace discrimination, Valencia and colleagues also point out how the challenges that all women face are compounded for Latinas, especially "when one considers the intersection of various factors, including gender, race and ethnicity, class, language ability, and immigrant status" (2004, 48). As a result of the cumulative effect of these factors, Latinas are more likely to work in traditionally segregated jobs, as secretaries, custodians, maids, nannies, and garment workers. They are also more likely to be the lowest paid workers in comparison to men and other related groups of women. The U.S. Department of Labor and the U.S. Equal Employment Opportunity Commission reported in 1999 that while women earn only seventy-five cents for every dollar that a man earns, African American women earn just sixty-five cents, and Hispanic women earn fifty-five cents for each dollar that white men earn.

In addition, given the realities of the country's segregated workforce, Latino/a undocumented immigrants, legal residents, and U.S. citizens often work side by side. In *EEOC v. Tortilleria La Mejor* (1991), the Equal Employment Opportunity Commission and a Latina plaintiff "successfully argued in federal court that the protections under Title VII of the Civil Rights Act of 1964 were applicable to all workers irrespective of their legal status" (Valencia et al. 2004,49) Earlier, Mexicans and Mexican Americans who worked as maids in a hotel in California successfully challenged the discrimination and sexual harassment they faced in federal court in the 1989 case *EEOC v. Hacienda Hotel*.

In sum, Latinas have been at the forefront of legal battles in the fight for equality and justice for Mexican American women—and for all women. Latinas "have had to struggle with the dual challenge of being both Mexican American and female" (Valencia et al. 2004, 61). The intersection of these two forces means that they, and Latinas in general, face unique issues, as in the realm of reproductive rights and workplace discrimination.

LATINA ORGANIZATIONS

One factor contributing to the increased political representation of Latinas is the early involvement and support of Latina organizations. In many cases, Latinas in political office received their initial training from community-based organizations and activities (Takash-Cruz 1993; Hardy-Fanta 1993; Prindeville 2002). One recent study shows how Latinas, like women from other races and ethnic groups, are creating their own paths of leadership development and advocacy by forming various Latina-based organizations (Garcia and Marquez 2005). National organizations that have helped to prepare Latina women for political office include the League of United Latin American Citizens (LULAC) Ladies Auxiliary, which established chapters as early as the 1930s; the Mexican American National Association (MANA), established in 1974; and Comisión Femenil Mexicana Nacional, established in 1973.

Other Latino/a-based organizations established in the 1970s and 1980s—such as the National Hispana Leadership Institute, MALDEF, and Southwest Voter Registration and Education Project (SWVREP)—offer leadership training for Latinos in politics. Similarly, the National Women's Political Caucus (NWPC), established in 1971, and specifically the Hispanic Steering Committee have sponsored candidate development conferences for Latinas, and NWPC currently provides resources for female candidates of color. Regional organizations established in the 1980s and 1990s also target and assist potential political candidates) the Hispanic Women's Political Coalition in Denver, Colorado, the Hispanic Women in Leadership in Houston, Texas; and Hispanas Organized for Political Empowerment in California are a few examples.

Political action committees have also been formed to foster Latinas running for office. Although technically not a formal political action committee, the Latina Political Action Committee (LPAC) (established in the mid-1980s and based in Sacramento, California) was formed to elect more Latinas and raise money for Latina candidates. Formal PACs such as the Florida Hispanic Women's Pact and the Latina P.A.C. in Houston raise money for Latina candidates and others who support their issues. Latina P.A.C., in particular, established in 1991, supports qualified Latina candidates for elected and appointed positions, regardless of political affiliation.

LATINAS IN TEXAS

Given this book's focus on Latinas in Texas politics, a review of their political role in a historical context is necessary. Generally speaking, Texas women in the 1990s experienced less than average status compared to women in the other forty-nine states. Studies show that Texas ranked thirtieth in terms of the number of women in the state legislature in 1996. A report on the status of women in Texas by the Institute for Women's Policy Research indicates that Texas ranked seventeenth in the nation in terms of the number of women elected to state and national offices in 2,000.[7]

Mexican American women have served in various public offices (Acosta and Winegarten 2003). As mentioned earlier, since 1955 Mexican American women have served in elected positions. Research also documents Mexican American women's involvement in securing women's right to vote in the 1900s, and in forming *mutualistas,* or mutual aid societies, beginning

in the 1920s. These societies were informal networks that provided assistance and services to recent Mexican immigrants. Mexican American women were also involved in the Chicano civil rights movement and the women's movement during the 1960s and 1970s. They have been involved in party politics, registering voters and collecting poll taxes, and during the 1960s, many were involved in Viva Kennedy Clubs. Some women formed organizations within the two major parties: the Mexican American Democrats (MAD) (later the Tejano Democrats) and the Mexican American Republicans of Texas (MART). Many women also got involved in third party politics, specifically La Raza Unida in the 1960s and 1970s. In many cases, Chicanas ran for public office as La Raza Unida candidates. As early as 1964, Virginia Muzquiz did so, running for the Texas state legislature. Likewise, Tejana candidates Alma Canales and Marta Cotera ran for statewide offices in 1972.

Latinas have also been involved in other political organizations, such as the American GI Forum Women's Auxiliary, the Political Association, of Spanish-speaking Organizations (PASSQ), and the Texas Women's Political Caucus. These groups and the women associated with them often helped launch Tejanas' ascension to public office (Acosta and Winegarten 2003).

THEORETICAL FRAMEWORK

Although Latinas have gained visibility in the national political arena and have clearly demonstrated leadership in U.S. politics, very few studies document their significance and potential as elected officials. Latina scholars have begun to fill the void In this area of research. Sierra and Sosa-Riddell contend that "Latina activity is highly complex and comprised of many diverse forms of political practice and intervention" (1994, 307). Motivated by the desire to solve problems in their neighborhoods, schools, and communities, Latinas are more likely to be active in grassroots political organizing. However, some Latinas have a more general commitment to the notion of public service, a motivation that leads them to activities in electoral politics. Political participation is typically viewed as being divided into two separate spheres, electoral and grassroots, and political scholars often confine their research to a single sphere. Latina leaders, however, frequently remain active or at least maintain connections in both spheres simultaneously (Sierra and Sosa-Riddell 1994; Pardo 1990; Takash-Cruz 1993; Montoya et al. 2000; García and Márquez 2001). We expect to find evidence of this interconnectedness and overlapping activity among the Latinas in our study.

The sense of a strong Mexican cultural identity, with its traditions and ties to religion and spirituality, is also important to Latinas in politics. Because of this strong connection to their culture, Latinas are also likely to retain their traditional gender roles while advocating for their community. The literature on Chicana feminism suggests that Latinas do not separate politics from the needs of the family and the Latino community as a whole (Pesquera and Segura 1993). Perhaps due to family responsibilities and traditional cultural sex roles, Latinas are more likely to develop policy priorities and direct their activities to the needs of women and families, and their particular ethnic communities. These important elements of their political socialization and orientations are shaped by their unique experiences and political history as minority women (García and Márquez 2001). Thus, we expect the Latinas in our study to demonstrate a strong cultural identity as well as a focus or emphasis on policies that assist families and Latino communities.

Some scholars of race/ethnicity politics find that Latinas demonstrate "a vision of politics" that is more participatory or inclusive (Hardy-Fanta 1993). Latinas are also able to transform traditional networks, resources, and relationships based on family and culture and use them as political assets (Pardo 1990). Equally important, Latinas demonstrate a capacity to overcome barriers of race, class, gender, and culture largely because they are able to draw from their experiences as longtime community activists (Takash-Cruz 1993; Sierra 1997; García and Márquez 2001).

Research also addresses how Latinas are politically motivated by various reasons, incentives that combine traditionally relevant, political goals with specific community-oriented objectives (García and Márquez 2001). They exhibit a commitment to getting particular candidates elected and certain policies addressed, as well as a commitment to their individual communities (influenced by the demographic makeup of the district or city) and the Chicano/Latino community at large. Latinas manifest abilities to bridge traditional and community motivations for their political involvement (García and Márquez 2001). As they enter traditional mainstream politics, Latinas bring with them their experiences from grassroots politics and from cultural networks and resources (García and Márquez 2001). Similarly, we expect that the Latinas in our study will demonstrate these attitudinal characteristics, as well as draw from their families and cultural networks.

Finally, recent scholarship theorizes that Latinas are well positioned as powerbrokers and have the potential to play key roles in American politics. Given their multiple identities as women, women of color, members of an ethnic minority, and part of a growing immigrant constituency, Latinas have a unique perspective and ability to advocate for multiple constituencies as well as adapt to different contexts (Fraga et al. 2005; Fraga and Navarro 2004). This intersectionality of identities provides Latinas with resources and skills to negotiate and form coalitions. In particular, they have the capacity to bridge the barriers between women of different ethnic and racial groups, as well as between men and women of different racial and ethnic groups. Similarly, we expect to find that the Latinas in our study demonstrate the capacity to negotiate, form coalitions, and adapt to differing political contexts.

Although Latinas share certain experiences as women of color, it is also important to note that they are not homogenous. There are various differences among Latina candidates and public officials that are based on many-factors. Some of these cleavages are common among all people in politics, such as educational levels, class, ideological differences, feminist orientations, religion, partisanship, marital status, gender, motherhood, and sexuality. Other differences, however, impact Latinos and Latinas specifically, such as language, immigrant status, ancestry, cultural orientations, degree of assimilation, historical experiences, and regional backgrounds. These differences highlight the importance of coalitions and compromise within the larger Latino community. Coalitions are especially important today, given the increasing concern for immigrant rights within the Latino community.

A related point is that in most other contexts, the ability to advocate for multiple constituencies may not be viewed positively. Representatives that advocate for multiple groups may be viewed as not being loyal, as "flip-flopping," or as "sitting on a fence." However, in electoral politics, given the dynamics and necessity of compromise and coalitions, advocating with an understanding of multiple constituencies should be considered a unique strength. Democratic theory suggests that politics centers on conflict, compromise, cooperation, and coalitions. Effective representatives need certain skills, including the ability to form coalitions and mobilize communities, to negotiate differences, and to view politics as inclusive and participatory. The strategies that Latinas employ provide an excellent model to broaden our understanding of U.S. electoral politics.

FORMAT AND AREAS OF INQUIRY

As mentioned, this book provides case studies of the first elected and appointed Latina public officials in Texas, and it is dedicated to Latinas in statewide office, in the Texas State House, and in the Texas Senate, and to those who are judges, city mayors, and city council members. With regard to municipal offices, Latinas were selected by city, based on the city's size or historical significance. It is important to note that, although it is beyond the scope of this particular project, the authors recognize that many Latinas hold county positions in Texas.

The objectives of the book are as follows: 1) to present an overview of Latinas' participation in electoral politics, 2) to provide case studies, of specific Latina public officials in Texas; 3) to contribute to a theoretical framework on Latina politics, and 4) to provide a basis of useful information and resources on Latinas in public office for students, practitioners of electoral politics, and aspiring public officials.

Given that the women presented in this book are the first Latinas to hold a particular office, it is essential to understand their backgrounds and initiation into politics, as well as their ascendance to public office. Four areas of inquiry bring us a step closer to understanding why there are so few: 1) political socialization; 2) the initial decision to seek public office and the experiences and barriers faced; 3) leadership style, and 4) perceptions of representational roles and advocacy priorities.

The areas addressed in the book are in some respects relevant to all public officials, to all female elected officials, and all minority public officials. However, we believe that Mexican American women as public officials, particularly "the first ones" appointed or elected to specific public offices, have unique perspectives and/or experiences. Identifying their perspectives and sharing their experiences will provide readers with a broader understanding of American politics, civic participation, and electoral politics.

With, respect to political socialization, several key questions are examined. What factors influenced the socialization of the Latinas in our study? Were they raised in political families, or did they experience political socialization as adults? How does culture influence Latinas' socialization? Some of the literature on Latinas' political socialization suggests that Latinas are influenced by traditional gender roles similar to those of women in other race or ethnic groups, but they are also affected by cultural traditions that may impede or enhance political participation (Hardy-Fanta 1997; Pardo 1990).

Regarding these women's bids for public office, some of the questions include: How did they decide whether or not to run for public office? What factors do they consider in deciding whether or not to run for public office? And, how do they run their campaigns? Latinas tend to link individuals, family, friendship networks, and community relationships when running for public office (Hardy-Fanta 1993). The literature also suggests that Latinas manifest a unique form of campaigning—one that is more personal (Hardy-Fanta 1993). Gender, context, and political resources play a role in shaping the organization, message, and style of the campaigns (Garcia and Berberena 2004).

Other questions center on the routes these women took to holding office. Do Latinas follow the same paths to office as other elected officials? The literature suggests that Latinas do not follow conventional routes. The informal requirements for elective office are usually a college education and high-status occupation, which Latinas, in general, may not have, perhaps because of deliberate and systematic discrimination. Instead, Latinas gain their political experience from community activism and participation in political campaigns (Takash-Cruz 1993; Sierra 1997; Fraga et al. 2003). Equally important is the relationship between their early political socialization and the decision to seek public office.

Related to this area of running for office are the potential obstacles for Latina candidates. The literature suggests that Latinas face barriers based on race, class, and gender (Takash-Cruz 1993; Gutiérrez and Deen 2000; García and Márquez 2001), and also that Latina public officials are able to overcome these barriers (Takash-Cruz 1993; García and Márquez 2001), including the media stereotype of Latinas as political novices. Other important challenges Latinas face are cultural and societal factors that demand traditional familial responsibilities.

The third and fourth areas of inquiry relate to leadership, advocacy, and types of representation. Do Latinas make a difference after they are elected? As leaders? As representatives of Latinas and the larger Latino community? The literature suggests that Latinas demonstrate an ability to advocate for gendered agendas and Latino-based agendas. Among their strengths is the ability to use their experiences as women and as Mexican Americans to build coalitions, and to advocate for multiple interests simultaneously (Fraga et al. 2003; Fraga and Navarro 2004).

Equally important to these areas of inquiry is demonstration of the significance of increased Latina representation. Why is it important to have more Latinas in office? Many would argue that the reason we would want more Latinas in public office is to advocate for the issues that most affect Latinas and the larger Latino community. Issues such as child care, equal pay, domestic violence, breast cancer research, and reproductive rights affect women generally, but affect women of color in different ways. Latinas clearly play a role in representing and advocating for their communities. Electing more Latinas also brings this country closer to a true representative democracy.

2012 Election Profile
Latina Voters

TOTAL U.S. FEMALE POPULATION (2010): 156,964,212

LATINA POPULATION (2010): 24,858,794

PROJECTED LATINA VOTE IN 2012: 6,367,000
PROJECTED LATINA SHARE OF ALL FEMALE VOTERS: 8.4%

During the last decade, the Latina population was the nation's fastest-growing female population group, and Latina growth exceeded half of the overall increase in the female population. In the last four presidential elections, Latinas have comprised slightly more than half of all Latino voters, and have thus contributed significantly to the decisive impact of the Latino electorate.

This 2012 Election Profile also highlights:

- The NALEO Educational Fund's projected Latina vote for Election 2012, both nationally, and for the nine states that together account for 77% of the U.S. Latina population (page 3);
- The number of Latinas registered to vote in six key states (page 3);
- A comparison of the number of Latino and non-Latino voters in the last four presidential elections, by gender (page 4), and the voter turnout rates of adult U.S. citizens in each group (page 5);
- The Latina share of the female vote in the last four presidential elections (page 5); and
- A comparison of the potential Latina eligible electorate and Latina registration and voting (page 6).

A REPORT OF THE NALEO EDUCATIONAL FUND

The nation's leading non-profit organization that facilitates full Latino participation in the American political process, from citizenship to public service.

THE LATINA POPULATION AND POPULATION GROWTH

Between 2000 and 2010, the nation's female population grew from 143.4 million to 157.0 million, an increase of 9.5%. During the same period, the Latina population grew from 17.1 million to 24.9 million, an increase of 45.0%.

The Latina population growth between 2000 and 2010 significantly exceeded the growth in other female population groups, and Latina growth during the

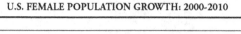

U.S. FEMALE POPULATION GROWTH: 2000-2010

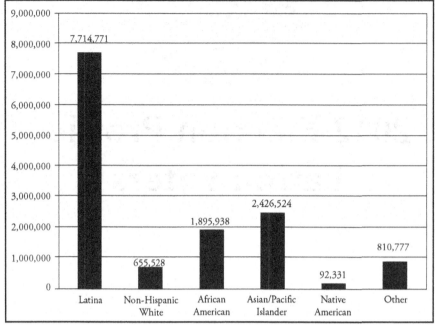

U.S. LATINA POPULATION: 2010

	2010 Census		2010 ACS*	
	Population	**Share of Total Female Population**	**Population**	**Share of Total Female Population**
All Latinas	24,858,794	15.8%	25,007,598	15.9%
Latina Adults	16,483,192	13.7%	16,604,976	13.7%
Latina Adult U.S. Citizens	N/A		11,122,368	10.0%

*2010 American Community Survey, 1-year estimates. See "Sources" below for an explanation of the differences between 2010 Census and ACS data.

decade exceeded half of the total female population growth (56.7%).

2012 PROJECTED LATINA VOTE AND LATINA REGISTERED VOTERS

Projected Latina Vote

The NALEO Educational Fund projects that 6.4 million Latinas will cast ballots in the November 2012 presidential election, and that more than one in every 12 female voters (8.4%) will be Latina. The table below presents projections of the Latina vote for the nine states which together include 77% of the Latina population.

The NALEO Educational Fund projects that the greatest percentage increases in 2012 Latina turnout from 2008 will occur in Illinois (35%) and Florida (35%). Our projections estimate that more than 1 million Latinas will cast ballots in California (nearly 2 million) and Texas (1.0 million), and that the Latina share of the female vote will range from 7% in Illinois to 31% in New Mexico.

Female Registered Voters (2012) for Selected States

The table below presents the number of female and Latina registered voters in six states which together include 61% of the Latina population.

State	Projected Latina Voters	Increase from 2008	Latina Share of Female Voters (Projected)
NATIONAL	6,367,000	24.0%	8.4%
Arizona	1,54,000	17.7%	10.2%
California	1,992,000	27.2%	24.9%
Colorado	126,000	17.7%	9.5%
Florida	853,000	34.6%	17.7%
Illinois	220,000	34.9%	7.2%
New Jersey	210,000	14.4%	10.4%
New Mexico	153,000	10.4%	30.9%
New York	487,000	12.6%	11.6%
Texas	1,047,000	17.5%	20.5%

State*	Total Female	Total Latina	Latina Share of Female Registered Voters
Arizona	1,778,281	314,550	17.7%
California	8,877,430	2,269,998	25.6%
Illinois	3,903,807	319,994	8.2%
New Jersey	2,759,499	325,427	11.8%
New York	6,268,859	778,998	12.4%
Texas	6,847,673	1,477,735	21.6%

*Data for Colorado, Florida and New Mexico are not available.

States with more than 1 million Latina registered voters include California (2.3 million) and Texas (1.5 million). The Latina share of female registered voters in the foregoing six states ranges from 8% in Illinois, to 26% in California, where more than in one in four female registered voters is Latina.

Latina Voting In Presidential Elections

Between the 1996 presidential election and the 2008 presidential election, the number of Latina voters nearly doubled, growing from 2.7 million to 5.1 million, an increase of 90.5%. While the number of Latina voters in each election exceeded the number of male Latino voters, the number of male Latino voters increased at a faster rate over the entire period. Between 1996 and 2008, the male Latino vote grew from 2.2 million to 4.6 million, an increase of 106.4%.

In contrast, between 1996 and 2008, the non-Latino vote for both females and males increased more slowly than the Latino vote, and there was not a significant difference over the period between the increase in female voters (22.2%) and male voters (20.2%).

Latina Share of Female Voters

In the last four presidential elections, the Latinal share of all female voters has increased from 4.8% in 1996 to 7.3% in 2008.

Latino Vote in Presidential Elections: 1996 - 2008

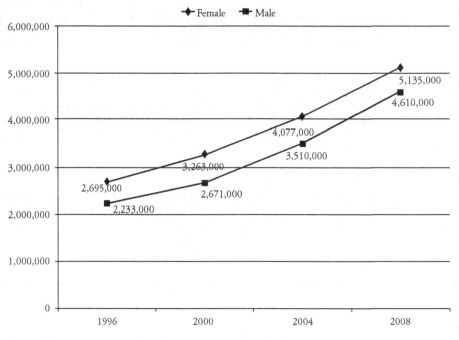

Non-Latino Vote in Presidential Elections: 1996 - 2008

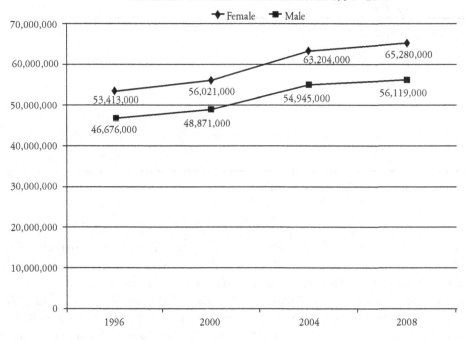

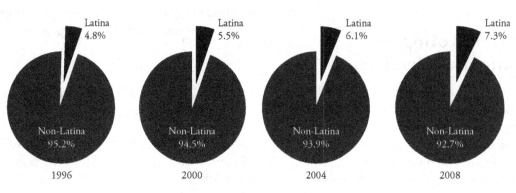

Year	Latina Share of Latino Vote	Female Share of Non-Latino Vote
1996	54.7%	53.4%
2000	55.0%	53.4%
2004	53.7%	53.5%
2008	52.7%	53.8%

In the last four presidential elections, the female share of both the Latino and non-Latino vote slightly exceeded half of all voters.

Latino Turnout

In the last four presidential elections, the turnout rate of Latina adult U.S. citizens ranged from 46% to 52%, and slightly exceeded the turnout rate of Latino males. A comparison of the turnout rate of non-Latino

Turnout of Adult U.S. Citizens

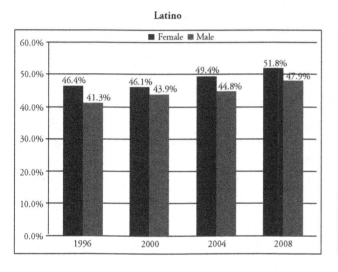

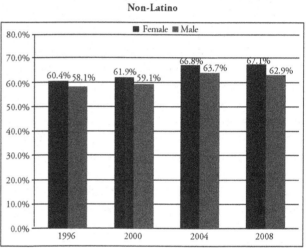

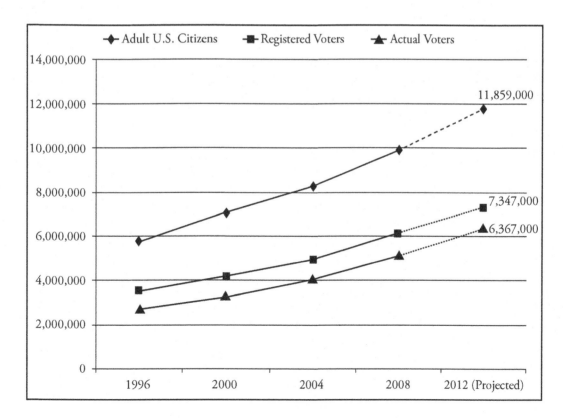

females and males reveals a similar pattern; in addition for both genders, non-Latino turnout rate are higher than those of Latinos.

Eligible Population, Latina Registered Voters and Actual Voters

While the number of Latina voters and the Latina share of female voters have increased during the last four presidential elections, this increase has not kept pace with the growth in the number of Latina adult U.S. citizens - those Latinas who are essentially eligible to register and vote, and thus comprise the potential Latina electorate. In 2008, 4.8 million eligible Latinas did not cast ballots, and had they done so, the number of Latina voters would have nearly doubled from 5.1 million to 9.9 million. The NALEO Educational Fund projects that if current trends continue, this gap will continue to grow, and it highlights the ongoing need for effective strategies by political parties, candidates, election officials and non-profit organizations to reach and engage Latina voters.

For more information about the NALEO Educational Fund's Election 2012 publications, please contact Rosalind Gold at rgold@naleo.org or (213) 747-7606, ext. 4420.

Sources

This report uses data from the U.S. Census Bureau's 2010 American Community Survey (ACS), 1-year estimates, and the 2010 Census Summary File 1. The ACS is conducted every year and is an on-going survey of a sample of the population which produces estimates of various population characteristics. The 2010 Census provides data from the official count of the entire population that is conducted every 10 years. Differences in the two data sources' universes, reference periods, and the way in which the data are tabulated may affect the comparability of data from the sources.

U.S. Census Bureau, Current Population Survey (CPS), *Voting and Registration in the Elections of November: 1996–2008.* The CPS data used in this report and the survey from which they are derived are subject to certain limitations. First, actual voter turnout and registration may be overestimated by the CPS, because individuals may tend to over-report electoral participation. Additionally, the CPS is a national survey, and estimates derived for smaller sub-groups within the national population may be based on relatively small sample sizes. Consequently, the margin of error associated with estimates of voting and registration for these sub-groups is greater than the margin associated with the national population or larger population sub-groups.

The Latina vote projections were derived by taking the Latina vote in 2008, and increasing it by the average of the percentage change in the Latina vote for the last three presidential elections. The Latina vote in the last three presidential elections is from *Voting and Registration in the Elections of November: 2000-2008.* Because these projections are based solely on past voting trends, they are conservative estimates that do not take into account the potential increase in Latina turnout that could result from the growth in Latina naturalizations, more robust voter engagement efforts, or other factors.

2012 NGP Voter Activation Network voter file data, August 2012.

SECTION 3: POLITICAL AND SOCIOECONOMIC PERSPECTIVES ASSESSMENT AND APPLICATION

1. Compare and contrast three aspects of Chicano history that were reinterpreted by Chicano scholars in the 1960s and 1970s.

2. How did the history of Chicanas fare initially in the process of reinterpreting Chicano history?

3. How did Chicana scholars reconcile Chicana feminism and cultural nationalism?

4. Identify the major goals of the Chicano movement and describe to what extent these have been achieved at the present time.

5. How has Chicano cultural identity changed in your community since the 1960s?

6. How did the Mexican-American and Chicano generations influence the development of the Hispanic generation?

7. According to Kim Geron, what factors tend to account for Hispanic immigration to the United States?

8. Analyze how the national battle for immigration reform affected undocumented immigrants in a given city, industry, or age group such as the "Dreamers."

9. How have contemporary border enforcement policy and practice impacted Chicanos in your community?

10. Decribe the effects of the immigration reform law and the antiethnic studies law passed in Arizona on the Chicano families in the state's climate of fear?

11. What major political party would benefit from a substantial reduction of Hispanic voters in Arizona and why?

12. How does the private prison industry benefit from Arizona's criminalization of the Hispanic population? Consult the websites of organizations like the Migration Policy Institute in appendix A.

13. What evidence supports Mortimer B. Zuckerman's assertion that new Hispanic immigrants are going to have a positive effect on American society? Feel free to consult sources like Fareed Zakaria's CNN program *Viewpoint*, available from YouTube, on how the legalization of undocumented immigrants can reduce the national debt.

14. Explain how the "politics of accommodation" affect Chicano candidates.

15. Identify five national Latino organizations and describe how each of these currently attempts to shape national public policy.

16. Identify key trends in male and female voter participation in the Latino population.

17. Analyze the political trajectory of a leading or appointed Latina elected official and identify key experiences and individuals that account for her political success.

18. According to García et al in the chapter Understanding Latina Political Leadership, Latinas are forging organizations to better shape their future. Identify a national, regional, or local Latina organization and describe how it empowers Latinas.

19. During the last election, how did Chicana/o candidates fare in your municipality and state?

20. Compare and contrast the senior citizen vote with the Chicana/o vote in your community in the last municipal and/or school bond elections.

21. Select a community with a Chicano population and determine whether there is a substantial underclass of Chicanos, and describe how they are perceived and treated by middle-class Chicanos.

22. How is current immigration from Mexico impacting communities outside the Southwest?

23. Analyze the importance of three of the social, economic, and political landscapes presented by Hipsman and Meissner.

24. How likely are the Congressional Hispanic Caucus principles on immigration reform likely to be reflected in a major immigration reform enacted into law and why?

25. What are the salient key projections listed by Taylor et al about the Latino electorate by 2030?

26. Analyze Steven Malanga's voting myths about the Hispanic vote and how ignoring them can affect electoral campaigns by each major political party.

27. Identify and describe the circumstances under which a strong Chicano voter turnout can be achieved.

28. Can Republican support for immigration reform attract Latino voters to its ranks enough to alter a presidential race?

SECTION 3: SUGGESTED READINGS

Acuña, Rodolfo. (1995). *Anything but Mexican: Chicanos in Contemporary Los Angeles*. New York, NY: Verso.

Akers Chacón, Justin & Davis, Mike. (2006). *No One Is Illegal: Fighting Racism and State Violence in the U.S.-Mexico Border*. Chicago, IL: Haymarket Books.

Amaya, Héctor. (2013). *Citizenship Excess: Latino/as, Media and the Nation*. New York: NY: New York University Press.

Balderrama, Francisco E. & Rodríguez, Raymond. (2006). *Decade of Betrayal: Mexican Repatriation in the 1930s*. Albuquerque, NM: University of New Mexico Press.

Bixler-Márquez, D. J. (2010). La Economía Política de la Aplicación de las Leyes de Inmigración por Autoridades Estatales y Municipales en Estados Unidos. In *El Cotidiano* (Vol. 164, pp. 117–122). México, DF: Universidad Autónoma Metropolitana Azcapotzalco.

Blackwell, Mayeli. (2011). *Chicana Power!, Contested Histories of Feminism in the Chicano Movement*. Austin, TX: University of Texas Press.

Border Network for Human Rights. (2013). *The New Ellis Island: Visions from the Border for the Future of America*. El Paso, TX: Border Network for Human Rights.

Calderón Cheliu, Leticia. (2013). *El Guiño de Obama*. México, DF: Observatorio de Migración Internacional OMI.

Chang, Grace. (2000). *Disposable Domestic: Immigrant Women Workers in the Global Economy*. Cambridge, MA: South End Press.

Chicago Council on Foreign Relations. (2004). *Comparing Mexican and American Public Opinion and Foreign Policy*. Chicago, IL: Chicago Council on Foreign Relations.

Chiquiar, Daniel & Salcedo, Alejandrina. (2013). *Mexican Migration to the United States: Underlying Economic Factors and Possible Scenarios for Future Flows*. Washington, DC: Migration Policy Institute.

Cisneros, Henry G. & Rosales, John. (2009). *Latinos and the Nation's Future*. Houston, TX: Arte Público Press.

De la Isla, José. (2003). *The Rise of Hispanic Political Power*. Santa Maria, CA: Archer Books.

De la Torre, Adela. (2002). *Moving from the Margins: A Chicana Voice on Public Policy*. Tucson, AZ: University of Arizona Press.

Delgado Gaitán, Concha. (2004). *Involving Latino Families in School: Raising Students Achievement Through Home-School Partnerships*. Thousand Oaks, CA: Corwin Press.

Daz, Tom. (2011). *No Boundaries: Transnational Latino Gangs and American Law Enforcement*. Ann Arbor, MI: University of Michigan Press.

Domínguez-Ruvalcaba, H. & Corona, Ignacio. (2010). *Gender Violence at the U.S.-Mexico Border: Media Representation and Public Response*. Tucson, AZ: University of Arizona Press.

Durán, Jorge & Massey, Douglas S. (2004). *Crossing the Border: Research from the Mexican Migration Project*. New York, NY: Rusell Sage Foundation.

Fry, Richard. (2006). *Gender and Migration*. Washington, DC: Pew Hispanic Center.

García, John A. (2012). *Latino Politics in America: Community, Culture and Interests*. (2nd ed.). Plymouth, UK: Rowman & Littlefield Publishers, Inc.

García, Mario T. (1995). *Rubén Salazar, Border Correspondent*. Berkeley, CA: University of California Press.

García, Mario T. (1998). *The Making of a Mexican American Mayor: Raymond L. Telles of El Paso*. El Paso, TX: Texas Western Press.

García, Mario T. & Castro, Sal. (2011). *Blowout!: Sal Castro & the Chicano Struggle for Educational Justice*. Chapel Hill, NC: University of North Carolina Press.

Geron, Kim. (2005). *Latino Political Power*. Boulder, CO: Lynne Rienner Publishers.

Gertner, Jon. (2006). What Is a Living Wage? *The New York Times* magazine. January 2006. Section 6. Pp. 38–45.

Gómez-Quiñones, Juan. (1994). *Chicano Politics: Reality and Promise, 1940–1990*. Albuquerque, NM: University of New Mexico Press.

Johnson, Kevin R. (2004). *The Huddled Masses Myth: Immigration and Civil Rights*. Philadelphia, PA: Temple University Press.

Lacey, M. (2011). Arpaio is criticized over handling of sex-crimes cases. *The New York Times*. (December 2009). Retrieved from http://www.nytimes.com/2011/12/10/us/sheriff-joe-arpaio-criticized-over-handling-of-sex-crimes-cases.html.

Lusk, Mark, Staudt, Kathleen & Moya, Eva. (2012). *Social Justice in the U.S.-Mexico Border Region*. New York, NY: Springer.

López, Mark H., Motel, Seth & Patten, Eileen. (2012). *A Record 24 Million Latinos Are Eligible to Vote, but Turnout Rate has Lagged that of Whites, Blacks*. Washington, DC: Pew Hispanic Center.

Migration Policy Institute. (2013). *Side-by-Side Comparison of 2013 Senate Immigration Framework with 2006 and 2007 Senate Legislation*. (No. 4). Washington, DC: Migration Policy Institute.

Navarro, Armando. (1998). *The Cristal Experiment: A Chicano Struggle for Community Control*. Madison, WI: University of Wisconsin Press.

Navarro, Armando. (2000). *La Raza Unida Party: A Chicano Challenge to the U.S. Two-Party Dictatorship*. Philadelphia, PA: Temple University Press.

Navarro, Armando. (2009). *The Immigration Crisis: Nativism, Armed Vigilantism, and the Rise of a Countervailing Movement*. Lanham, MD: AltaMira Press.

Navarro, Armando. (2011). *Global Capitalist Crisis and the Second Great Depression: Egalitarian Systemic Models for Change*. (1st ed.). Lanham, MD: Lexington Books.

Nguyen, Mary, Bibo, Erin Ward & Engle, Jennifer. (2012). *Advancing to Completion: Increasing Degree Attainment by Improving Graduation Rates and Closing Gaps for Hispanic Students*. Washington, DC: The Education Trust.

Orozco, Enrique C. (1996). *The Chicano Labyrinth of Solitude: A Study in the Making of the Chicano Mind and Character*. Dubuque, IA: Kendall Hunt Publishing.

Papademetriou, Demetrios G., Meissner, Doris & Sohnen, Eleanor. 2013. *Thinking Regionally to Compete Globally: Leveraging Migration & Human Capital in the U.S., Mexico, and Central America*. Washington, DC: Migration Policy Institute.

París Pombo, M. D. (2012). *Migrantes, Desplazados, Braceros y Deportados: Experiencias Migratorias y Prácticas Políticas*. (1st ed.). Tijuana, BC: Colegio de la Frontera Norte/UACJ/UAM.

Patel, L. (2012). *Youth Held at the Border: Immigration, Education, and the Politics of Inclusion*. New York, NY: Teachers College Press.

Payn, T., Staudt, K. A. & Kruszewski, Z. (2013). *A War that Can't Be Won: Binational Perspectives on the War on Drugs*. Tucson, AZ: University of Arizona Press.

Peña, Milagros. (2007). *Latina Activists Across Borders*. Durham, NC: Duke University Press.

Portes, Alejandro. (Ed.). (1996). *The New Second Generation*. New York, NY: Russell Sage Foundation.

Ramos, Jorge. (2004). *The Latino Wave: How Hispanics Will Elect the Next American President*. New York, NY: HarperCollins Publishers.

Ramos, García & José, María. (2004). *La Gestión de la Cooperación Transfronteriza México-Estados Unidos en un Marco de Inseguridad Global: Problemas y Desafíos*. México, DF: Consejo Mexicano de Asuntos Internacionales.

Rodríguez Cadavid, Fresia. (2004). *The Hispanic Role in U.S. Hemispheric Policy*. Washington, DC: Cuban American National Council/Hispanic Link Journalism Foundation.

Rosales, Arturo. (1996). *Chicano!: The History of the Civil Rights Movement*. Houston, TX: Arte Público Press.

Rosales, Francisco F. (1999). *¡Pobre Raza!: Violence, Justice, and Mobilization among México Lindo Immigrants, 1900–1936*. Austin, TX: University of Texas Press.

Rosales, Rodolfo. (2000). *The Illusion of Inclusion: The Untold Political Story of San Antonio*. Austin, TX: University of Texas Press.

Shaw, R. (2008). *Beyond the Fields: Cesar Chavez, the UFM, and the Struggle for Justice in the 21st Century*. Berkeley, CA: University of California Press.

Sisk, Christina L. (2013). *Mexico, Nation in Transit: Contemporary Representations of Mexican Migration to the United States*. Tucson, AZ: University of Arizona Press.

Skerry, Peter. (1993). *Mexican Americans: The Ambivalent Minority*. Cambridge, MA: Harvard University Press.

Staudt, Kathleen. (1998). *Free Trade? Informal Economies at the U.S.-Mexico Border*. Philadelphia, PA: Temple University Press.

Staudt, Kathleen, Payn, Tony & Kruszewski, Z. Anthony. (2010). *Human Rights Along the U.S.-Mexico Border, Gendered Violence and Insecurity*. Tucson, AZ: University of Arizona Press.

The Center for Immigration Studies. (2013). *Border Security, Economic Opportunity, and Immigration Modernization Act (s.744)*. Retrieved from http://cis.org/Border-Security-Economic-Opportunity-Immigration-Modernization-Act.

The Women Issue. *Latino Leaders: The National Magazine of the Successful American Latino*. May 2006.

Thornburgh, Nathan. (2006). Inside the Life of the Migrants Next Door. *Time* magazine. Vol. 167, (6). Pp 36–45.

Valencia, Richard R. (2013). Commentary on Jason Richwine's Dissertation, IQ and Immigration Policy: Neohereditarianism, Pseudoscience, and Deficit Thinking. Teachers College Record, http://www.tcrecord.org ID Number: 17134.

Weeks, George B. & Weeks, Joan R. (2010). *Irresistible Forces: Latin American Migration to the United States and its Effects on the South*. Albuquerque, NM: University of New Mexico Press.

Yoshino, Kenji. (2006). The Pressure to Cover. *The New York Times* magazine. January, Section 6. Pp 32–36.

SECTION 3: SUGGESTED FILMS AND VIDEOS

Across the Bridge, 2004
Rank Film Distributor of America

Bread & Roses: When You Have Nothing, You Have
Nothing to Lose, 2001
Lions Gate Home Entertainment
Santa Monica, CA

Crossing the Line/Sobrepasando la línea, 2003
Las Lineas Media Library P.O. Box 1084, Harriman,
NY 10926

Cruzando Nuestras Fronteras, 2009
HBR Productions
112 Park Avenue #3, Hoboken, NJ 07030

Cruz Reynoso: Sowing the Seeds of Justice, 2010
Berkeley Media LLC
2600 Tenth Street, Suite 626, Berkeley, CA 94710

Dying to Get In: Illegal Immigration to the E.U., 2002
Films for the Humanities and Sciences
132 West 31st Street, New York, NY 10001

El Contrato: The Contract, 2003
Films for the Humanities and Sciences
132 West 31st Street, New York, NY 10001

Farmingville, 2004
Camino Bluff Productions, Inc.,
752 W. End Ave, #2F, New York, NY 10025

Fighting for Political Power, 1996
Chicano: History of the Mexican American Movement
Series
National Latino Communications Center

Frontline: Poor Kids, 2013
PBS
2100 Crystal Drive, Arlington, VA, 22202

Hispanic Entrepreneurs: Against All Odds, 2004
Films for the Humanities and Sciences
132 West 31st Street, New York, NY 10001

Illegal, 2010
Filmworks Entertainment, Inc.
PO Box 2072, Santa Clarita, CA 91386

Immigrant Nation, Divided Country, 2006
CNN Programs

La Raza Unida Party 40th Commemoration (Part 1),
2012
http://www.youtube.com/watch?v=hw95_xaRf0k

La Raza Unida Party 40th Commemoration (Part 2),
2012
http://www.youtube.com/watch?v=RO-skj5Sk5o

La Raza: Politics, 1976
La Raza Series
Moctezuma Productions
McGraw-Hill Broadcasting

Latin and African Americans: Friends or Foes,
1998
Films for the Humanities and Sciences
132 West 31st Street, New York, NY 10001

Latino Americans: The 500-Year Legacy that Shaped a
Nation, 2013
Episode V: Prejudice and Pride (1965–1980)
PBS
2100 Crystal Drive, Arlington, VA 22202

Latino Americans: The 500-Year Legacy that Shaped a
Nation, 2013
Episode VI: Peril and Promise (1980–2000)
PBS
2100 Crystal Drive, Arlington, VA 22202

Letters from the Other Side, 2006
New Day Films
190 Route 17M, P.O. Box 1084, Harriman, NY 10926

Lost in Detention, 2012
PBS
2100 Crystal Drive, Arlington, VA 22202

Patrolling the Border: National Security & Immigration Reform, 2004
Films for the Humanities and Sciences
132 West 31st Street, New York, NY 10001

Quest for a Homeland, 1996
Chicano!: History of the Mexican American Movement Civil Rights Movement
National Latino Communications Center

Spanish in America, 2006
Films for the Humanities and Sciences
132 West 31st Street, New York, NY 10001

State of Latino America, 2013
C-SPAN
P.O. Box 2909, West Lafayette, IN 47996

The Conflict Between Blacks and Latinos, 2004
Tony Brown Productions/Insight Media
2162 Broadway, New York, NY 10024-0621

The Latino Factor, 2006
Insight Media, Inc.
2162 Broadway, New York, NY 10024-0621

The Time Has Come! An Immigrant Community Stands Up to the Border Patrol, 1996
The El Paso Border Rights Coalition
El Paso, TX

The Valley of Tears, 2005
Perry Films
135 West 29th Street #703, New York, NY 10001

The Wall Documentary, 2010
Viva Zapata Productions

The Wrath of Grapes, 1986
United Farm Workers of America
Keene, CA

Women of Hope: Latinas Abriendo Camino, 1996
Films for the Humanities and Sciences
132 West 31st Street, New York, NY 10001

Educational Perspectives

4

Education is of major importance to the Chicano community. Educational issues are commonly intertwined in public policy formulation and implementation, hence their presence in this section. American schools are the official repositories and conveyors of American values, beliefs, language, and culture. Schools are political arenas that have been historically contested by Chicanos in their quest for linguistic and cultural self-preservation, inclusion in American society, and socioeconomic and political empowerment. Therefore, the educational progress of Chicanos is an important barometer of the group's status in American society.

This section was designed to address the extant educational issues facing the Chicano community, including approaches to educate immigrant children of limited English proficiency. To gain a thorough understanding of educational issues in the nation, the reader also needs to examine some of the resources suggested at the end of this section. Additionally, we recommend the use of public school and education faculty as guest speakers, visits to educational programs and community centers, and attendance at forums in which educational issues are presented to the community.

Richard Fry and Mark Hugo López lead the section with a statistical summary of Hispanic student enrollment, which ranges from prekindergarten to higher education and examines the educational pipeline. The next two segments by Gilbert G. González and Dolores Delgado Bernal cover the educational experience of Chicanos from 1900 to 1940 and the civil rights era to the near present, respectively. The former documents the struggle for educational equality by Chicanos striving to overcome segregation, race and ethnic bias, and attempts to relegate them to an underclass status. González also describes the political and legal actions by a politically aware Mexican-American generation in its epic quest for first-class citizenship. Delgado Bernal brings to the reader a chronicle of educational change during the civil rights movement that builds on the politics of the previous decades. The social activism and social policy of the 1960s and the educational inequity of the 1970s are examined in the context of political upheaval and great society policies. Bernal Delgado covers more recent educational changes and challenges in California via an analysis of issues such as bilingual education and higher education that continue to resonate dangerously in other states.

Nicolás C. Vaca contributes an important discussion of Chicano educational emancipation in his examination of the legal role played by Chicanos in civil rights issues related to segregation. His purpose is to erase the notion prevalent in some media that Chicanos and Latinos were never or just minimally involved in civil rights litigation. To that end, he analyzes the impact of the *Méndez v. Westminster* and *Delgado v. Bastrop Independent School District* cases. Nicolás Vaca also documents the historical antecedents that shaped the legal arguments that were later heard in the *Brown v. Topeka* case, which helped deflate the structure of school segregation.

Building on Solórzano's analysis of the anti-immigrant climate in Arizona, Nolan L. Cabrera, Elisa L. Mesa, and Roberto Cintli Rodríguez tackle the much-publicized fight for Chicano Studies in Tucson, Arizona, bolstered next by Paula Beltrán's examination of the southwestern Chicano community's response to Arizona, the powerful initiative by the pen, Librotraficante. This segment depicts a Chicano community under siege fighting for its very survival. It sounds an alert to other Chicano-Mexicano communities. We strongly recommend that this segment be studied with the films recommended at the end of the section, such as *Precious Knowledge* and *Outlawing Shakespeare*, as well as information contained in the websites in appendix A, like Jesús Treviño's *Latinopia*.

Sonia Soltero examines the principal issues in education faced by Latinos, including the status of salient educational initiatives and strategies. She calls for a critical and culturally responsive education with specific recommendations for various sectors. Jason DeParle follows with a qualitative assessment of the the circumstances faced by nontraditional students making the challenging transition to higher education, particularly when they are the first ones in their familiy to do so. This segment should be perused in light of the chapter on Hispanic educational attainment statistics presented by Fry and López to gauge the educational progress of Chicanos. The Center for Educational Statistics is an excellent resource to identify national and state data, while individual states' education agencies provide data for specific school districts. Higher education systems in each state generate profiles for their universities, community colleges, and specialized institutes.

Guadalupe Valdés brings the section to a close with an ethnographic portrait that expands on the Chicano educational profiles and sociocultural dynamics in this and other sections. Explanations for the academic failure of Chicanos and other ethnic minorities are presented in a historical context, followed by an examination of educational interventions that have taken place to ameliorate said failure. Particular attention is paid to family intervention as a valid socioeducational strategy. The work of Richard Valencia listed in the suggested readings is particularly descriptive and informative on the state of Chicano education and the direction it should take.

Hispanic Student Enrollments Reach New Highs in 2011

by Richard Fry and Mark Hugo López

I. OVERVIEW

The nation's Hispanic[1] student population reached a number of milestones in 2011, according to an analysis of newly available U.S. Census Bureau data by the Pew Hispanic Center, a project of the Pew Research Center.

For the first time, the number of 18- to 24-year-old Hispanics enrolled in college exceeded 2 million and reached a record 16.5% share of all college enrollments.[2] Hispanics are the largest minority group on the nation's college campuses, a milestone first achieved last year (Fry, 2011). But as their growth among all college-age students continues to outpace other groups, Hispanics are now, for the first time, the largest minority group among the nation's four-year college and university students. And for the first time, Hispanics made up one-quarter (25.2%) of 18- to 24-year-old students enrolled in two-year colleges.

In the nation's public schools, Hispanics also reached new milestones. For the first time, one-in-four (24.7%) public elementary school students were Hispanic, following similar milestones reached recently by Hispanics among public kindergarten students (in 2007) and public nursery school students (in 2006). Among all pre-K through 12th grade public school students, a record 23.9% were Hispanic in 2011.

The new milestones reflect a number of continuing upward trends. Between 1972 and 2011, the Latino share of 18- to 24-year-old college students steadily grew—rising from 2.9% to 16.5%. During the same period, among all public school students, the Latino share grew from 6.0% to 23.9%. In both cases, rapid Latino population growth has played a role in driving Latino student enrollment gains over the past four decades.

However, population growth alone does not explain all the enrollment gains made by Hispanic students in recent years (Fry, 2011). Today, with the high school completion rate among young Hispanics at a new high, more young Hispanics than ever are eligible to attend college. According to the Pew Hispanic analysis, 76.3% of all Hispanics ages 18 to 24 had a high school diploma or a General Educational Development (GED) degree in 2011, up from 72.8% in 2010. And among these high school completers, a record share—nearly half (45.6%)—is enrolled in two-year or four-year colleges. Both demographic trends and greater eligibility have contributed to growth in the number of Hispanic young people enrolled in college in recent years.

In addition to gains in enrollment, the number of degrees conferred on Latino college students has also reached new highs.[3] In 2010, the number of Latinos who received a bachelor's degree reached a record 140,000 recipients, according to data published by the National Center for Education Statistics of the U.S. Department of Education (Snyder and Dillow, 2012). A record number of associate degrees were awarded to

Latinos in 2010 as well—112,000. In both cases, Latinos are a growing share of all degree recipients—13.2% among those with an associate degree and 8.5% among those who received a bachelor's degree in 2010. Despite these gains, the Latino share among degree recipients significantly lagged their share among 18- to 24-year-old students enrolled in two-year colleges (21.7%) and four-year colleges and universities (11.7%) in 2010.

Hispanics are the nation's largest minority group, making up more than 50 million people, or about 16.5% of the U.S. population. Among the 30 million young people ages 18 to 24, 6 million, or 20%, are Hispanics.

1. The terms "Latino" and "Hispanic" are used interchangeably in this report.
2. College enrollment refers to persons enrolled in a two-year college or a four-year college or university and includes both undergraduate and graduate students. The population of 18- to 24-year-old college students includes those enrolled at private and public colleges and universities.
3. The U.S. Department of Education reports the number of degrees conferred on graduates of all ages. While the majority is likely between ages 18 and 24, many graduates will be over age 24 and some may be under age 18.

II. HISPANIC PUBLIC SCHOOL ENROLLMENTS

Newly available data indicate that the nation's Hispanic student population continues to grow. More than 12.4 million Hispanics were enrolled in the nation's public schools pre-K through 12th grade in October 2011, according to a Pew Hispanic Center analysis of U.S. Census Bureau data. Overall, Hispanic students make up nearly one-quarter (23.9%) of the nation's public

Figure 1.1

Hispanic Share of Pre-K through 12th Grade Public School Enrollment and 18- to 24-Year-Old College Enrollment, 1972-2011

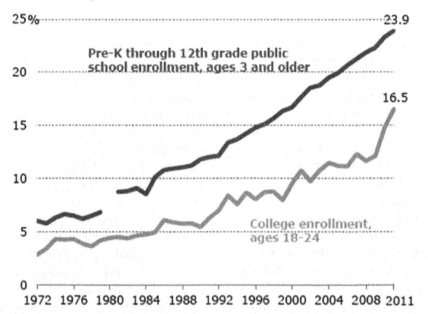

Notes: "Pre-K through 12th grade public school enrollment, ages 3 and older" shows the Hispanic share of enrollment in public schools from pre-K through 12th grade. Public school enrollment figures for 1980 are not available. "College enrollment, ages 18-24" shows Hispanic share among college students ages 18 to 24.

Source: Pew Hispanic Center analysis of the October Current Population Survey (CPS)

PEW RESEARCH CENTER

school enrollment, up from one-fifth (19.9%) in 2005 and 16.7% in 2000.

Growth in the share of Hispanics among all public school students reflects growth in their share among younger public school students. In 2011, for the first time, one-quarter (25%) of public elementary school children were Hispanic. This follows on the heels of other Hispanic student population milestones. In 2007, more than 25% of all kindergarten students were Hispanic for the first time, and in 2006 Hispanics reached the one-quarter milestone among all nursery school students.[4] Hispanic children made up 26% of public nursery school enrollments in October 2011. However, Hispanic children are less likely to enroll in nursery schools overall than other children. In October 2011, Hispanic children were only 20% of all nursery school enrollments at both private and public schools.

In 2011, Hispanics made up 21% of all public high school student enrollments. As students in nursery school progress through kindergarten and into elementary school and high school, Hispanic students will make up a rising share of public high school students and all public school students in coming years. According to the U.S. Census Bureau, by 2036 Hispanics are projected to compose one-third of the nation's children ages 3 to 17 (U.S. Census Bureau, 2008).

4. Hispanic children made up 26% of public nursery school enrollments in October 2011. However, Hispanic children are less likely to enroll in nursery schools overall than other children. In October 2011, Hispanic children were only 20% of all nursery school enrollments at both private and public schools.

III. HISPANIC COLLEGE ENROLLMENTS

Hispanics Continue to Lead Growth in College Enrollments

The ranks of the nation's young college students continue to grow. In October 2011, 18- to 24-year-old college enrollment reached a record 12.6 million students, up 3% from 2010.

Growth in the number of young Hispanics attending college accounted for the majority of the increase. Between 2010 and 2011, the number of young Hispanics enrolled in college grew by 15%, or 265,000 students, to 2.1 million. This increase follows on the heels of a 24% increase in Hispanic college enrollments between 2009 to 2010 (Fry, 2011). Alone, Hispanic college enrollment growth accounted for nearly

Figure 2.1

Racial and Ethnic Composition of Public School Enrollment, October 2011
(%)

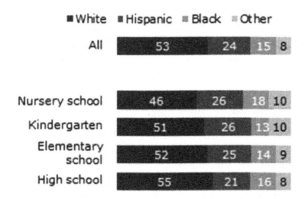

Notes: The figures above refer to the white- and black-alone populations. White, black and other include only the non-Hispanic portions of those groups.

Source: Pew Hispanic Center analysis of the October 2011 Current Population Survey

PEW RESEARCH CENTER

Table 3.1. College Enrollment of 18- to 24-Year-Olds, 2010-2011

(in thousands)

	2010	2011	Change	Percentage Change
All	*12,213*	*12,570*	*357*	*3%*
Hispanic	1,814	2,079	265	15%
White	7,663	7,882	219	3%
Black	1,692	1,639	−53	−3%
Asian	811	748	−63	−8%

Notes: "White" includes only non-Hispanic whites. The figures above refer to the white-, black-and Asian-alone populations. College enrollment refers to persons enrolled in a two-year college or a four-year college or university. It also includes those enrolled at private and public colleges and universities.

Source: Pew Hispanic Center analysis of the October 2010 and 2011 Current Population Surveys

Figure 3.1

18- to 24-Year-Old Enrollment in Four-Year Colleges, 2010-2011

(millions)

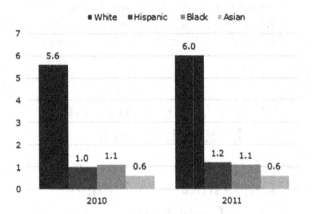

Notes: "White" includes only non-Hispanic whites. The figures above refer to the white-, black- and Asian-alone populations.

Source: Pew Hispanic Center analysis of the October 2010 and 2011 Current Population Survey (CPS)

PEW RESEARCH CENTER

three-quarters (74%) of the growth in college student enrollments over the last year.

The white non-Hispanic student population also grew between 2010 and 2011, increasing by 219,000 students, or 3%, to 7.9 million. Meanwhile, the number of blacks enrolled in college and the number of Asians enrolled in college fell, by 3% and 8% respectively between 2010 and 2011.

With fast growth in the Hispanic college student population, Hispanics now make up 16.5% of the nation's 18- to 24-year-old college students. As recently as October 2006, Hispanics were only 11% of all college students. In just five years, their share has grown by almost 50%. This is a significant milestone because for the first time Hispanic representation among the nation's traditional college student population matched Hispanics' overall population representation, also at 16.5%.[5] Even so, Hispanics' share among college students continues to lag their share (20.0%) among all young people ages 18 to 24.

Hispanics Now Largest Minority Group at Four-Year Colleges

Among 18- to 24-year-olds, Hispanic enrollment at four-year colleges and universities increased 20% from October 2010 (1.0 million) to October 2011 (1.2 million). For the first time, young Hispanic enrollments on four-year campuses exceeded young

black enrollments (1.1 million), making Hispanics the largest minority group at four-year colleges and universities. In 2011, Hispanics were 13.1% of all 18- to 24- year olds enrolled at four-year colleges and universities.

This follows a similar change since 2010 among students enrolled at two-year college campuses. Then, the number of Hispanic young people enrolled in two-year colleges was 835,000, higher than the 630,000 black students enrolled at two-year colleges (Fry, 2011). Since then, the number of Hispanics enrolled at two-year colleges has continued to grow. In 2011, some 908,000 Hispanics and 564,000 blacks ages 18 to 24 were enrolled in two-year colleges. In 2011, Hispanics made up one-quarter (25.2%) of all 18- to 24-year old students enrolled in two-year colleges for the first time.

Population Growth and Eligibility Key Reasons for Growth in Hispanic College Enrollments

Some of the growth in Hispanic college enrollments simply reflects continued growth in the nation's Hispanic population—since 1972, the number of Hispanic 18- to 24-year-olds has grown nearly five-fold, rising from 1.3 million then to 6.0 million in 2011.

However, population growth alone does not explain enrollment gains among Hispanics.

According to Pew Hispanic estimates, a record share of young Hispanics is eligible to attend college. In 2011, 76% of Hispanics ages 18 to 24 had finished high school, the highest level of Hispanic high school completion ever attained and a three-percentage-point increase over the 2010 level (73%). This record-high level of Hispanic high school completion is consistent with the recently noted strong gains in the Hispanic high school graduation rate at the nation's public schools reported by *Education Week* (Swanson, 2012).[6]

College-going among young Hispanic high school completers also reached a record level in October 2011. Nearly half (46%) were enrolled in college, eclipsing the share (45%) of black high school completers enrolled in college. By comparison, 51% of white high school completers and 67% of Asian high school completers were enrolled in college.

5. In the 2010 Census, Hispanics were 16.3% of the nation's total population (Passel, Cohn and

Figure 3.2

Hispanic High School Completion Among 18- to 24-Year-Olds

(%)

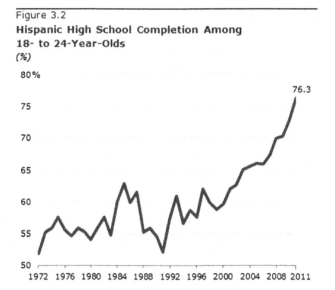

Note: High school completers are people who have completed at least four years of high school, for 1972 to 1991. Beginning in 1992, they are people who have attained at least a high school diploma (including equivalency).

Source: Pew Hispanic Center analysis of the October Current Population Survey (CPS)

PEW RESEARCH CENTER

Figure 3.3

College Enrollment Rates of Whites, Blacks and Hispanics

(% of 18- to 24-year-old high school completers)

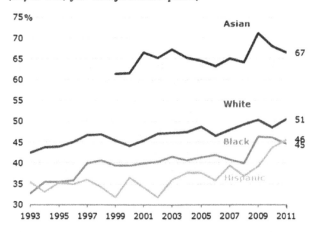

Notes: "White" includes only non-Hispanic whites. Starting in 2003, respondents could identify more than one race. The figures for 2003 onward refer to the white-, black- and Asian-alone populations. The data shown prior to 2003 consists of those identifying themselves as "Asian or Pacific Islanders."

Source: Pew Hispanic Center analysis of the October Current Population Survey (CPS)

PEW RESEARCH CENTER

Lopez, 2011). However, the college enrollment figures shown in this report are based on the U.S. Census Bureau's Current Population Survey (CPS). The population universe for the CPS is the civilian, non-institutionalized population. In the October 2011 CPS, Hispanics made up 16.5% of the civilian, non-institutionalized population.

6. The high school completion rate measure used in this report is the proportion of an age group that has completed high school by either graduating with a high school diploma or completing a GED. It does not gauge whether high school was completed on time. In the Education Week report, a different high school graduation rate measure is used. This measure uses U.S. Department of Education data and aims to measure the percentage of public high school students who graduate on time with a diploma.

IV. COLLEGE GRADUATION AND HISPANICS

Over the past four decades, the number of Hispanics graduating with either an associate or a bachelor's degree has increased seven-fold, with growth outpacing that of other groups. As a result, not only has the number of Hispanic degree recipients grown, so too has their share of all college degree recipients. Even so, the number of Hispanics awarded college degrees lags that of other groups, and their share of college graduates remains below that of all college student enrollments.

In 2010, the number of degrees conferred on Hispanics of all ages reached record levels. According to the U.S. Department of Education's National Center for Education Statistics (Snyder and Dillow, 2012), 112,000 Hispanics received an associate degree and 140,000 Hispanics were awarded a bachelor's degree—both new highs.[7]

Despite a record number of degrees conferred on Hispanic college students, they continue to lag other groups. In 2010, 1.2 million bachelor's degrees were awarded to non-Hispanic white students and 165,000 to non-Hispanic black students. Overall, some 1.7 million bachelor's degrees were awarded in 2010.

At the associate level, the number of degrees awarded to Hispanics trailed that of non-Hispanic whites (553,000), but nearly matched the number awarded to non-Hispanic blacks (114,000).

The Hispanic share among degree recipients from two-year and four-year colleges has also reached a record. In 2010, 8.5% of all bachelor's recipients were

Figure 4.1

Number of Hispanics Earning Associate and Bachelor's Degrees, 1977-2010
(thousands)

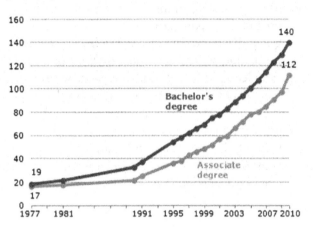

Notes: 1997 and 1981 data excludes some cases for which race/ethnicity was not available. Degree-granting institutions are those that grant associate or higher degrees and participate in Title IV federal financial aid programs.

Source: Tables 297 and 300 in U.S. Department of Education, National Center for Education Statistics, "Digest of Education Statistics, 2011"

PEW RESEARCH CENTER

Figure 4.2

Degrees Conferred, by Race/Ethnicity, 2010

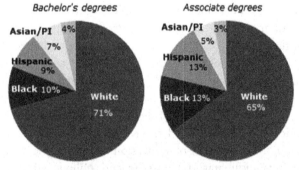

Notes: White, black, Asian and other includes only the non-Hispanic portions of those groups. Unlabeled slices include non-Hispanic American Indians/Alaska Natives and non-resident aliens. Percentages may not sum to 100% due to rounding. Degree-granting institutions grant associate or higher degrees and participate in Title IV federal financial aid programs.

Source: Tables 297 and 300 in U.S. Department of Education, National Center for Education Statistics, "Digest of Education Statistics, 2011"

PEW RESEARCH CENTER

bachelor's degrees awarded in 2010, 71% were awarded to non-Hispanic whites, 10% to non-Hispanic blacks, and 7% to non-Hispanic Asian/Pacific Islanders.

Among associate degree recipients in 2010, the share of Hispanics matched that of non-Hispanic blacks—13%—and was more than double the 5% share of non-Hispanic Asian/Pacific Islanders. Two-thirds (65%) of the 849,000 associate degree recipients in 2010 were non-Hispanic white.

7. The number of associate and bachelor's degrees conferred as reported by the U.S. Department of Education reflect all degrees awarded to graduates of all ages, not just those of traditional college age (ages 18 to 24 years).

References

Fry, Richard. 2011. *"Hispanic College Enrollment Spikes, Narrowing Gaps with Other Groups."* Washington, DC: Pew Hispanic Center.

Heckman, James J., and Paul A. LaFontaine. 2007. *"The American High School Graduation Rate: Trends and Levels."* Discussion Paper No. 3216. Bonn, Germany: Institute for the Study of Labor (IZA), December.

Passel, Jeffrey, D'Vera Cohn and Mark Hugo Lopez. 2011. *"Hispanics Account for More than Half of Nation's Growth in Past Decade."* Washington, DC: Pew Hispanic Center, March.

Snyder, Thomas D., and Sally A. Dillow. 2012. National Center for Education Statistics, Institute of Education Sciences, U.S. Department of Education. *"Digest of Education Statistics, 2011."* Washington, D.C.: June.

Swanson, Christopher B. 2012. *"Graduation Rate Keeps Climbing; Strong Gains for Latino Students."* Education Week: June 7.

U.S. Census Bureau. 2011. *"CPS Historical Time Series Tables on School Enrollment."* Washington, D.C.

U.S. Census Bureau, Population Division. 2008. *"Projected Population by Single Year of Age, Sex, Race, and Hispanic Origin for the United States: July 1, 2000 to July 1, 2050."* Washington, D.C.: August.

Hispanic, up from 8.1% in 2009. Among all associate degree recipients, 13.2% were Hispanic, also a record.

While the number of Hispanics receiving a college degree has grown, the number of degrees conferred on Hispanics trails other groups. Among the 1.7 million

Appendix A: Public School Enrollments

Appendix Table A1. Pre-K through 12th-grade Public School Enrollment of the Population 3 years old and Over, by Race and Ethnicity, October 1993 to 2011

(*thousands*)

Year	Total	White	Black	Hispanic	Asian
2011	52,026	27,440	8,267	12,445	2,280
2010	51,719	27,674	8,254	12,067	2,178
2009	51,145	28,031	8,234	11,418	1,953
2008	50,769	27,924	8,282	11,094	1,961
2007	51,082	28,356	8,232	10,866	2,110
2006	50,663	28,486	8,285	10,470	1,930
2005	50,835	29,048	8,367	10,141	1,912
2004	50,568	28,651	8,624	9,870	1,996
2003	50,654	29,394	8,612	9,512	1,856
2002	49,944	29,640	8,707	9,262	2,123
2001	49,936	29,859	8,645	8,817	2,251
2000	49,199	29,964	8,561	8,214	2,094
1999	49,338	30,259	8,556	8,081	2,254
1998	48,816	30,164	8,666	7,647	1,987
1997	49,467	30,897	8,718	7,487	1,955
1996	47,486	29,959	8,188	7,026	1,971
1995	47,320	30,788	8,257	6,751	1,087
1994	46,888	30,655	8,137	6,423	1,158
1993	46,110	30,025	7,899	6,177	1,483

Notes: Includes the civilian non-institutionalized population. "White" includes only non-Hispanic whites. Starting in 2003, respondents could identify more than one race. The figures for 2003 onward refer to the white-, black-and Asian-alone population. The "Asian" data shown prior to 2003 consists of those identifying themselves as "Asian or Pacific Islanders." Prior to 1994, total enrolled does not include the 35-and-over population.

Source: Pew Hispanic Center analysis of the October 2011 Current Population Survey (CPS) and U.S. Census Bureau, CPS, 1993 to 2010

PEW RESEARCH CENTER

Appendix Table A2.   Public Nursery School Enrollment of the Population 3 Years Old and Over, by Race and Ethnicity, October 1993 to 2011

(*thousands*)

Year	Total	White	Black	Hispanic	Asian
2011	2,904	1,332	562	766	120
2010	2,776	1,274	522	794	97
2009	2,744	1,188	640	717	107
2008	2,632	1,213	548	668	110
2007	2,570	1,225	485	711	77
2006	2,519	1,152	513	707	65
2005	2,480	1,211	542	601	80
2004	2,487	1,153	600	591	72
2003	2,567	1,382	484	561	56
2002	2,246	1,172	503	476	85
2001	2,161	1,054	537	452	91
2000	2,217	1,149	531	419	91
1999	2,269	1,146	569	458	96
1998	2,265	1,136	528	492	77
1997	2,254	1,143	582	436	59
1996	1,868	922	459	403	63
1995	2,012	1,129	478	350	28
1994	1,940	1,090	513	278	27
1993	1,258	720	320	169	38

Notes: Includes the civilian non-institutionalized population. "White" includes only non-Hispanic whites. Starting in 2003, respondents could identify more than one race. The figures for 2003 onward refer to the white-, black- and Asian-alone population. The "Asian" data shown prior to 2003 consists of those identifying themselves as "Asian or Pacific Islanders."

Source: Pew Hispanic Center analysis of the October 2011 Current Population Survey (CPS) and U.S. Census Bureau, CPS, 1993 to 2010

PEW RESERCH CENTER

Appendix Table A3.   Public Kindergarten Enrollment of the Population 3 Years Old and Over, by Race and Ethnicity, October 1993 to 2011

(*thousands*)

Year	Total	White	Black	Hispanic	Asian
2011	3,732	1,903	503	984	189
2010	3,764	1,842	682	1,002	181
2009	3,767	1,990	578	993	146
2008	3,578	1,884	545	910	119
2007	3,656	1,929	548	954	112
2006	3,552	1,940	536	798	149
2005	3,349	1,936	486	725	99
2004	3,417	1,917	535	699	152
2003	3,098	1,804	495	633	93
2002	2,976	1,585	543	688	137
2001	3,145	1,781	536	641	161

Year	Total	White	Black	Hispanic	Asian
2000	3,173	1,846	547	639	124
1999	3,167	1,839	558	594	148
1998	3,128	1,790	592	608	120
1997	3,271	1,970	571	589	110
1996	3,353	2,081	545	539	158
1995	3,174	2,047	564	465	62
1994	3,278	2,059	603	516	60
1993	3,589	2,239	649	576	125

Notes: Includes the civilian non-institutionalized population. "White" includes only non-Hispanic whites. Starting in 2003, respondents could identify more than one race. The figures for 2003 onward refer to the white-, black- and Asian-alone population. The "Asian" data shown prior to 2003 consists of those identifying themselves as "Asian or Pacific Islanders."

Source: Pew Hispanic Center analysis of the October 2011 Current Population Survey (CPS) and U. S. Census Bureau, CPS, 1993 to 2010

PEW RESERCH CENTER

Appendix Tabel A4. Public Elementary School Enrollment of the Population 3 Years Old and Over, by Race and Ethnicity, October 1993 to 2011

(*thousands*)

Year	Total	White	Black	Hispanic	Asian
2011	29,965	15,670	4,658	7,401	1,336
2010	29,841	15,960	4,498	7,052	1,358
2009	29,365	16,198	4,424	6,716	1,170
2008	29,162	16,029	4,665	6,450	1,168
2007	29,052	15,998	4,572	6,299	1,305
2006	28,975	16,332	4,608	6,109	1,105
2005	29,072	16,335	4,747	5,991	1,137
2004	29,166	16,437	4,905	5,895	1,153
2003	29,204	16,735	4,942	5,651	1,122
2002	29,658	17,495	5,210	5,585	1,237
2001	29,800	17,693	5,160	5,478	1,263
2000	29,378	17,747	5,133	5,012	1,257
1999	29,264	17,960	5,002	4,829	1,343
1998	29,124	18,107	5,031	4,568	1,190
1997	29,308	18,426	5,049	4,427	1,186
1996	28,153	17,808	4,846	4,162	1,144
1995	28,384	18,518	4,845	4,165	622
1994	28,131	18,555	4,709	3,848	707
1993	28,278	18,617	4,733	3,779	930

Notes: Includes the civilian non-institutionalized population. "White" includes only non-Hispanic whites. Starting in 2003, respondents could identify more than one race. The figures for 2003 onward refer to the white-, black- and Asian-alone population. The "Asian" data shown prior to 2003 consists of those identifying themselves as "Asian or Pacific Islanders." Prior to 1994, total enrolled does not include the 35-and-over population.

Source: Pew Hispanic Center analysis of the October 2011 Current Population Survey (CPS) and U.S. Census Bureau, CPS, 1993 to 2010.

PEW RESEARCH CENTER

Appendix Table A5. Public High School Enrollment of the Population 3 Years Old and Over, by Race and Ethnicity, October 1993 to 2011

(*thousands*)

Year	Total	White	Black	Hispanic	Asian
2011	15,426	8,535	2,545	3,294	635
2010	15,338	8,598	2,552	3,219	542
2009	15,269	8,655	2,592	3,052	530
2008	15,397	8,798	2,524	3,066	564
2007	15,804	9,204	2,627	2,902	616
2006	15,617	9,072	2,628	2,856	611
2005	15,934	9,566	2,592	2,824	596
2004	15,498	9,144	2,584	2,685	619
2003	15,785	9,473	2,691	2,667	585
2002	15,064	9,388	2,451	2,513	664
2001	14,830	9,331	2,412	2,246	736
2000	14,431	9,222	2,350	2,144	622
1999	14,638	9,314	2,427	2,200	666
1998	14,299	9,131	2,515	1,978	599
1997	14,634	9,358	2,516	2,035	600
1996	14,113	9,148	2,338	1,922	606
1995	13,750	9,094	2,370	1,772	375
1994	13,539	8,951	2,313	1,781	365
1993	12,985	8,449	2,197	1,653	390

Notes: Includes the civilian non-institutionalized population. "White" includes only non-Hispanic whites. Starting in 2003, respondents could identify more than one race. The figures for 2003 onward refer to the white-, black- and Asian-alone population. The "Asian" data shown prior to 2003 consists of those identifying themselves as "Asian or Pacific Islanders." Prior to 1994, total enrolled does not include the 35 and over population.

Source: Pew Hispanic center analysis of the October 2011 current population survey (CPS) and U.S. Census bureau, CPS, 1993 to 2010

PEW RESEARCH CENTER

Appendix B: High School Completion and College Enrollment

Appendix Table B1. Population Ages 18-24 by High School Graduate Status, College Enrollment, Attainment, Race and Ethnicity, 2010–2011

POPULATION (in thousands)		HIGH SCHOOL COMPLETERS (in thousands)				PERCENT			DROPOUTS	
Year, race/origin	All	In college	In 2-year college	In 4-year college	High school completers	In college	Of HS completers, in college	All (in thousands)	%
2011										
All	29,943	25,446	12,570	3,601	8,968	85	42	49	2,481	8.3
Hispanic	5,974	4,557	2,079	908	1,171	76	35	46	975	16.3
White	17,627	15,571	7,882	1,898	5,985	88	45	51	1,002	5.7
Black	4,503	3,666	1,639	564	1,075	81	36	45	399	8.9
Asian	1,252	1,124	748	154	594	90	60	67	65	5.2
2010										
All	29,659	25,224	12,213	3,840	8,373	85	41	48	2,590	8.7
Hispanic	5,685	4,138	1,814	835	979	73	32	44	1,050	18.5
White	17,693	15,761	7,663	2,105	5,558	89	43	49	1,003	5.7
Black	4,457	3,669	1,692	630	1,062	82	38	46	450	10.1
Asian	1,303	1,193	811	181	630	92	62	68	64	4.9

Notes: Includes the civilian non-institutionalized population. "White" includes only non-Hispanic whites.

Source: Pew Hispanic Center analysis of the October 2010 and 2011 Current Population Surveys

PEW RESEARCH CENTER

Appendix Table B2. High School Completion, Enrollment and Attainment among 18- to 24-Year-Olds, October 1967-2011

POPULATION (in thousands)		HIGH SCHOOL COMPLETERS (in thousands)				PERCENT				DROPOUTS	
	All	In college	In 2-Year college	In 4-Year college	High school completers	In college	In 2-Year college	In 4-Year college	Of HS completers, in college	All (in thousands)	%
Year											
2011	29,943	25,446	12,570	3,601	8,968	85.0	42.0	12.0	30.0	49.4	2,481	8.3
2010	29,659	25,224	12,213	3,840	8,373	85.0	41.2	12.9	28.2	48.4	2,590	8.7
2009	29,223	24,647	12,073	3,427	8,646	84.3	41.3	11.7	29.6	49.0	2,733	9.4
2008	28,950	24,568	11,466	3,425	8,040	84.9	39.6	11.8	27.8	46.7	2,702	9.3
2007	28,778	24,146	11,161	3,145	8,016	83.9	38.8	10.9	27.9	46.2	2,937	10.2
2006	28,372	23,430	10,586	2,711	7,876	82.6	37.3	9.6	27.8	45.2	3,128	11.0
2005	27,855	23,103	10,834	2,688	8,147	82.9	38.9	9.6	29.2	46.9	3,154	11.3
2004	27,948	23,086	10,611	2,616	7,995	82.6	38.0	9.4	28.6	46.0	3,836	13.7
2003	27,404	22,603	10,364	2,786	7,578	82.5	37.8	10.2	27.7	45.9	3,228	11.8
2002	27,367	22,319	10,033	2,649	7,384	81.6	36.7	9.7	27.0	45.0	3,375	12.3
2001	26,965	21,836	9,629	2,632	7,160	81.0	35.7	9.8	26.6	44.1	3,519	13.1
2000	26,658	21,822	9,452	2,508	6,944	81.9	35.5	9.4	26.0	43.3	3,315	12.4
1999	26,041	21,127	9,259	2,367	6,893	81.1	35.6	9.1	26.5	43.8	3,413	13.1
1998	25,507	20,567	9,322	2,608	6,715	80.6	36.5	10.2	26.3	45.3	3,544	13.9
1997	24,973	20,338	9,204	2,462	6,738	81.4	36.9	9.9	27.0	45.3	3,236	13.0
1996	24,671	20,131	8,767	2,332	6,436	81.6	35.5	9.5	26.1	43.5	3,147	12.8
1995	24,900	20,125	8,539	2,223	6,316	80.8	34.3	8.9	25.4	42.4	3,471	13.9
1994	25,254	20,581	8,729	2,301	6,428	81.5	34.6	9.1	25.5	42.4	3,365	13.3
1993r	25,522	20,844	8,630	—	—	81.7	33.8	—	—	41.4	3,349	13.1
1993	24,100	19,772	8,193	2,360	5,833	82.0	34.0	9.8	24.2	41.4	3,070	12.7
1992	24,278	19,921	8,343	2,414	5,928	82.1	34.4	9.9	24.4	41.9	3,083	12.7
1991	24,572	19,883	8,172	2,378	5,793	80.9	33.3	9.7	23.6	41.1	3,486	14.2
1990	24,852	20,311	7,964	2,166	5,798	81.7	32.0	8.7	23.3	39.2	3,379	13.6
1989	25,261	20,461	7,804	2,027	5,776	81.0	30.9	8.0	22.9	38.1	3,644	14.4
1988	25,733	20,900	7,791	2,253	5,539	81.2	30.3	8.8	21.5	37.3	3,749	14.6
1987	25,950	21,118	7,693	2,112	5,582	81.4	29.6	8.1	21.5	36.4	3,751	14.5
1986	26,512	21,768	7,477	2,005	5,393	82.1	28.2	7.6	20.3	34.3	3,687	13.9
1985	27,122	22,349	7,537	1,999	5,538	82.4	27.8	7.4	20.4	33.7	3,687	13.6
1984	28,031	22,870	7,591	2,048	5,544	81.6	27.1	7.3	19.8	33.2	4,142	14.8
1983	28,580	22,988	7,477	2,118	5,360	80.4	26.2	7.4	18.8	32.5	4,410	15.4
1982	28,846	23,291	7,678	2,230	5,447	80.7	26.6	7.7	18.9	33.0	4,500	15.6
1981	28,965	23,343	7,575	2,174	5,400	80.6	26.2	7.5	18.6	32.5	4,520	15.6
1980	28,957	23,413	7,400	2,059	5,381	80.9	25.6	7.1	18.6	31.6	4,515	15.6
1979	27,974	22,421	6,991	1,749	5,242	80.1	25.0	6.3	18.7	31.2	4,560	16.3
1978	27,647	22,309	6,995	1,825	5,169	80.7	25.3	6.6	18.7	31.4	4,388	15.9
1977	27,331	22,008	7,142	1,847	5,295	80.5	26.1	6.8	19.4	32.5	4,313	15.8
1976	26,919	21,677	7,181	1,734	5,447	80.5	26.7	6.4	20.2	33.1	4,276	15.9
1975	26,387	21,326	6,935	2,362	4,574	80.8	26.3	9.0	17.3	32.5	4,110	15.6
1974	25,670	20,725	6,316	1,948	4,367	80.7	24.6	7.6	17.0	30.5	4,070	15.9
1973	25,237	20,377	6,055	1,741	4,314	80.7	24.0	6.9	17.1	29.7	3,973	15.7
1972	24,579	19,618	6,257	—	—	79.8	25.5	—	—	31.9	4,068	16.6
1971	23,668	18,691	6,210	—	—	79.0	26.2	—	—	33.2	4,025	17.0

POPULATION (in thousands)			HIGH SCHOOL COMPLETERS (in thousands)				PERCENT				DROPOUTS	
		All	In college	In 2-Year college	In 4-Year college	High school completers	In college	In 2-Year college	In 4-Year college	Of HS completers, in college	All (in thousands)	%
1970	22,552	17,768	5,805	—	—	78.8	25.7	—	—	32.7	3,908	17.3
1969	21,362	16,703	5,840	—	—	78.2	27.3	—	—	35.0	3,769	17.6
1968	20,562	15,683	5,356	—	—	76.3	26.0	—	—	34.2	3,929	19.1
1967	20,009	15,114	5,100	—	—	75.5	25.5	—	—	33.7	3,967	19.8

Notes: Includes the civilian non-institutionalized populations. Starting in 2003, respondents could identity more than one race. "r" denotes revised, controlled to 1990 Census based population estimates; previous 1993 data controlled to 1980 Census-based population estimates. Prior to 1994, total enrolled does not include the 35 and over population. High school completers are people who have completed at least four years of high school for 1967 to 1991. Beginning in 1992, they are people have attained at least a high school diploma (including equivalency).

Source: Pew Hispanic Center analysis of the October 2011 Current Population Survey(CPS) and U.S. Census Bureau, CPS, 1967 to 2010

Appendix Table B3. High School Completion, Enrollment and Attainment among Hispanic 18- to 24-Year-Olds, October 1972–2011

Population (in thousands)		HIGH SCHOOL COMPLETERS (in thousands)		PERCENT			DROPOUTS	
Year		All	In college	High school completers	In College	Of HS Completers, in College	All (thousands)	%
2011	5,974	4,557	2,079	76.3	34.8	45.6	975	16.3
2010	5,685	4,138	1,814	72.8	31.9	43.8	1,050	18.5
2009	5,332	3,747	1,465	70.3	27.5	39.1	1,112	20.9
2008	5,176	3,618	1,338	69.9	25.9	37.0	1,155	22.3
2007	5,175	3,487	1,375	67.4	26.6	39.4	1,310	25.3
2006	5,006	3,301	1,182	65.9	23.6	35.8	1,313	26.2
2005	4,898	3,230	1,215	65.9	24.8	37.6	1,335	27.3
2004	4,941	3,244	1,221	65.7	24.7	37.6	1,386	28.1
2003	4,754	3,096	1,115	65.1	23.5	36.0	1,353	28.5
2002	4,918	3,078	979	62.6	19.9	31.8	1,479	30.1
2001	4,892	3,031	1,035	62.0	21.2	34.1	1,548	31.6
2000	4,134	2,462	899	59.6	21.7	36.5	1,335	32.3
1999	3,953	2,325	739	58.8	18.7	31.8	1,340	33.9
1998	4,014	2,403	820	59.9	20.4	34.1	1,383	34.5
1997	3,606	2,236	806	62.0	22.4	36.0	1,103	30.6
1996	3,510	3,019	706	57.5	20.1	35.0	1,210	34.5
1995	3,603	2,112	745	58.6	20.7	35.3	1,250	34.7
1994	3,523	1,995	662	56.6	18.8	33.2	1,224	34.7
1993r	3,363	2,049	728	60.9	21.6	35.5	1,103	32.8
1993	2,772	1,682	602	60.7	21.7	35.8	907	32.7
1992	2,754	1,579	586	57.3	21.3	37.1	936	34.0
1991	2,874	1,498	516	52.1	18.0	34.4	1,139	39.6
1990	2,749	1,498	435	54.5	15.8	29.0	1,025	37.3
1989	2,818	1,576	453	55.9	16.1	28.7	1,062	37.7

Population (in thousands)		HIGH SCHOOL COMPLETERS (in thousands)		PERCENT			DROPOUTS	
Year		All	In college	High school completers	In College	Of HS Completers, in College	All (thousands)	%
1988	2,642	1,458	450	55.2	17.0	30.9	1,046	39.6
1987	2,592	1,597	455	61.6	17.6	28.5	849	32.8
1986	2,514	1,507	548	59.9	18.2	30.4	864	34.4
1985	2,221	1,396	375	62.9	16.9	26.9	700	31.5
1984	2,018	1,212	362	60.1	17.9	29.9	691	34.2
1983	2,025	1,110	349	54.8	17.2	31.4	759	37.5
1982	2,001	1,153	337	57.6	16.8	29.2	740	37.0
1981	2,052	1,144	342	55.8	16.7	29.9	790	38.5
1980	2,033	1,099	327	54.1	16.1	29.8	820	40.3
1979	1,754	968	292	55.2	16.6	30.2	687	39.2
1978	1,672	935	254	55.9	15.2	27.2	656	39.2
1977	1,609	880	277	54.7	17.2	31.5	622	38.7
1976	1,551	862	309	55.6	19.9	35.8	566	36.5
1975	1,446	832	295	57.5	20.4	35.5	505	34.9
1974	1,506	842	272	55.9	18.1	32.3	558	37.1
1973	1,285	709	206	55.2	16.0	29.1	500	38.9
1972	1,338	694	179	51.9	13.4	25.8	541	40.4

Notes: Includes the civilian non-institutionalized population, "r" denotes revised, controlled to 1990 Census based population estimates; previous 1993 data controlled to 1980 census-based population estimates. High school completers are people who have completed at least four years of high school for 1972 to 1991. Beginning in 1992, they are people who have attained at least a high school diploma (including equivalency).

Source: Pew Hispanic Center analysis of the October 2001 Current Population Survey (CPS) and U.S. Census Bureau, CPS, 1972 to 2010

PEW REASEARCH CENTER

Appendix Table B4. High School Completion, Enrollment and Attainment among Non-Hispanic White 18- to 24-Years-Olds, October 1993-2011

Population (in thousands)		HIGH SCHOOL COMPLETERS (in thousands)		PERCENT			DROPOUTS	
Year		All	In college	High school completers	In College	Of HS Completers, in College	All (thousands)	%
2011	17,627	15,571	7,882	88.3	44.7	50.6	1,002	5.7
2010	17,693	15,761	7,663	89.1	43.3	48.6	1,003	5.7
2009	17,750	15,839	7,983	89.2	45.0	50.4	1,029	5.8
2008	17,839	16,038	7,894	89.9	44.3	49.2	960	5.4
2007	17,669	15,727	7,533	89.0	42.6	47.9	1,064	6.0
2006	17,565	15,452	7,200	88.0	41.0	46.6	1,189	6.8
2005	17,293	15,187	7,393	87.8	42.8	48.7	1,216	7.0
2004	17,326	15,224	7,228	87.9	41.7	47.5	1,313	7.6
2003	17,158	15,070	7,129	87.8	41.5	47.3	1,267	7.4

Population (in thousands)		HIGH SCHOOL COMPLETERS (in thousands)		PERCENT			DROPOUTS	
Year		All	In college	High school completers	In College	Of HS Completers, in College	All (thousands)	%
2002	17,131	14,910	7,004	87.0	40.9	47.0	1,289	7.5
2001	16,721	14,480	6,565	86.6	39.3	45.3	1,390	8.3
2000	17,327	15,187	6,709	87.6	38.7	44.2	1,316	7.6
1999	17,080	14,812	6,735	86.7	39.4	45.5	1,404	8.2
1998	16,634	14,402	6,757	86.6	40.6	46.9	1,491	9.0
1997	16,575	14,414	6,728	87.0	40.6	46.7	1,432	8.6
1996	16,339	14,288	6,447	87.4	39.5	45.1	1,303	8.0
1995	16,867	14,523	6,393	86.1	37.9	44	1,647	9.8
1994	17,114	14,916	6,521	87.2	38.1	43.7	1,505	8.8
1993	16,895	14,665	6,221	86.8	36.8	42.4	1,524	9.0

Notes: Includes the civilian non-institutionalized population, Starting in 2003, respondents could identifiy more than one race. Except as noted, the race data in this table from 2003 onward represent those respondents who indicated only one race category. High school completers are people who have attained at least a high school diploma (including equivalency).

Source: Pew Hispanic Center analysis of the October 2001 Current Population Survey (CPS) and U.S. Census Bureau, CPS, 1993 to 2010
PEW REASEARCH CENTER

Appendix Table B5. High School Completion, Enrollment and Attainment among Black 18- to 24-Year-Olds, October 1972-2011

Population (in thousands)		HIGH SCHOOL COMPLETERS (in thousands)		PERCENT			DROPOUTS	
Year		All	In college	High school completers	In College	Of HS Completers, in College	All (thousands)	%
2011	4,503	3,666	1,639	81.4	36.4	44.7	399	8.9
2010	4,457	3,669	1,692	82.3	38	46.1	450	10.1
2009	4,346	3,458	1,604	79.6	36.9	46.4	505	11.6
2008	4,265	3,387	1,349	79.4	31.6	39.8	548	12.8
2007	4,182	3,423	1,396	81.9	33.4	40.8	425	10.2
2006	4,085	3,156	1,321	77.3	32.3	41.9	532	13
2005	3,964	3,137	1,297	79.1	32.7	41.3	512	12.9
2004	3,940	3,050	1,238	77.4	31.4	40.6	596	15.1
2003	3,837	2,948	1,225	76.8	31.9	41.6	545	14.2
2002	3,924	3,040	1,226	77.5	31.2	40.3	571	14.6
2001	3,916	3,016	1,206	77	30.8	40	540	13.8
2000	4,013	3,090	1,216	77	30.3	39.4	615	15.3
1999	3,827	2,911	1,145	76.1	29.9	39.3	613	16
1998	3,745	2,747	1,116	73.4	29.8	40.6	642	17.1
1997	3,650	2,725	1,085	74.7	29.7	39.8	611	16.7
1996	3,637	2,738	983	75.3	27	35.9	581	16
1995	3,625	2,788	988	76.9	27.3	35.4	522	14.4

Year	Population (in thousands)	HIGH SCHOOL COMPLETERS (in thousands)		PERCENT			DROPOUTS	
		All	In college	High school completers	In College	Of HS Completers, in College	All (thousands)	%
1994	3,661	2,818	1,001	77.0	27.3	35.5	568	15.5
1993	3,666	2,747	897	74.9	24.5	32.7	600	16.4
1993	3,516	2,629	861	74.8	24.5	32.8	578	16.4
1992	3,521	2,625	886	74.6	25.2	33.8	575	16.3
1991	3,504	2,630	828	75.1	23.6	31.5	545	15.6
1990	3,520	2,710	894	77	25.4	33	530	15.1
1989	3,559	2,708	835	76.1	23.5	30.8	583	16.4
1988	3,568	2,680	752	75.1	21.1	28.1	631	17.7
1987	3,603	2,739	823	76	22.8	30	611	17
1986	3,653	2,795	812	76.5	22.2	29.1	617	16.9
1985	3,716	2,810	734	75.6	19.8	26.1	655	17.6
1984	3,862	2,885	786	74.7	20.4	27.2	712	18.4
1983	3,865	2,740	741	70.9	19.2	27	832	21.5
1982	3,872	2,744	767	70.9	19.8	28	851	22
1981	3,778	2,678	750	70.9	19.9	28	821	21.7
1980	3,721	2,592	715	69.7	19.2	27.6	876	23.5
1979	3,510	2,356	696	67.1	19.8	29.5	895	25.5
1978	3,452	2,340	694	67.8	20.1	29.7	850	24.6
1977	3,387	2,286	721	67.5	21.3	31.5	808	23.9
1976	3,315	2,239	749	67.5	22.6	33.5	803	24.2
1975	3,213	2,081	665	64.8	20.7	32	877	27.3
1974	3,105	2,083	555	67.1	17.9	26.6	780	25.1
1973	3,114	2,079	498	66.8	16	24	826	26.5
1972	2,986	1,992	540	66.7	18.1	27.1	782	26.2
1971	2,866	1,789	522	62.4	18.2	29.2	825	28.8
1970	2,692	1,602	416	59.5	15.5	26	897	33.3
1969	2,542	1,497	407	58.9	16	27.2	828	32.6
1968	2,421	1,399	352	57.8	14.5	25.2	799	33
1967	2,283	1,276	297	55.9	13	23.3	788	34.5

Notes: Includes the civilian non-institutionalized population. "r" denotes revised, controlled to 1990 Census based population estimates; previous 1993 data controlled to 1980 Census-based population estimates. Starting in 2003, respondents could identify more than one race. Except as noted, the race data in this table from 2003 onward represent those respondents who indicated only one race category. High school completers are people who have completed at least four years of high school for 1972 to 1991. Beginning in 1992, they are people who have attained at least a high school diploma (including equivalency).

Source: Pew Hispanic Center analysis of the October 2011 Current Population Survey (CPS) and U.S. Census Bureau, CPS, 1967 to 2010

PEW RESEARCH CENTER

Appendix C:
College Degrees Conferred

Appendix Table C1. Associate Degrees Conferred by Degree-Granting Institutions, by Race and Ethnicity, 1977 to 2010

Year	Total	White	Black	Hispanic	Asian
2010	849,452	552,863	113,905	112,211	44,021
2009	787,325	522,985	101,487	97,921	40,914
2008	750,164	501,079	95,702	91,274	38,843
2007	728,114	491,572	91,529	85,410	37,266
2006	713,066	485,297	89,784	80,854	35,201
2005	696,660	475,513	86,402	78,557	33,669
2004	665,301	456,047	81,183	72,270	33,149
2003	634,016	438,261	75,609	66,673	32,629
2002	595,133	417,733	67,343	60,003	30,945
2001	578,865	411,075	63,855	57,288	28,463
2000	564,933	408,822	60,208	51,563	27,778
1999	564,984	412,985	58,417	48,845	27,628
1998	558,555	413,561	55,314	45,876	25,196
1997	571,226	429,464	56,306	43,549	25,159
1996	555,216	426,106	52,014	38,254	23,138
1995	539,691	420,656	47,067	35,962	20,677
1991	481,720	391,264	38,835	25,540	15,257
1990	455,102	376,816	34,326	21,504	13,066
1981	416,377	339,167	35,330	17,800	8,650
1977	406,377	342,290	33,159	16,636	7,044

Notes: The figures above refer to the white¯, black¯ and Asian¯alone populations. Figures for "American Indian/Alaska Native" and "Non-resident alien" group are not shown.

Source: Table 297, U.S. Department of Education, National Center for Education Statistics, "Digest of Education Statistics, 2011"

Appendix Table C2. Bachelor's Degrees Conferred by Degree-Granting Institutions, by Race and Ethnicity, 1977 to 2010

Year	Total	White	Black	Hispanic	Asian
2010	1,650,014	1,167,499	164,844	140,316	117,422
2009	1,601,368	1,144,614	156,615	129,527	112,508
2008	1,563,069	1,122,675	152,457	123,048	109,058
2007	1,524,092	1,099,850	146,653	114,936	105,297
2006	1,485,242	1,075,561	142,420	107,588	102,376
2005	1,439,264	1,049,141	136,122	101,124	97,209
2004	1,399,542	1,026,114	131,241	94,644	92,073
2003	1,348,811	994,616	124,253	89,029	87,964
2002	1,291,900	958,597	116,623	82,966	83,093
2001	1,244,171	927,357	111,307	77,745	78,902
2000	1,237,875	929,102	108,018	75,063	77,909
1999	1,202,239	909,562	101,910	69,735	74,126
1998	1,184,406	901,344	98,251	66,005	71,678
1997	1,172,879	900,809	94,349	62,509	68,859
1996	1,164,792	905,846	91,496	58,351	64,433
1995	1,160,134	914,610	87,236	54,230	60,502
1991	1,094,538	914,093	66,375	37,342	42,529
1990	1,051,344	887,151	61,046	32,829	39,230
1981	935,140	807,319	60,673	21,832	18,794
1977	919,549	807,668	58,636	18,743	13,793

Notes: The figures above refer to the white-, black- and Asian-alone population. Figures for "American Indian/Alaska Native" and "Non-residentalien" groups are not shown.

Source: Table 300 in U.S. Department of Education, National Center for Education Statistics, Digest of Education Statistics, 2011

PEW RESEARCH CENTER

Segregation and the Education of Mexican Children, 1900–1940

Gilbert G. González

In the aftermath of the 1848 war between Mexico and the United States, the newly acquired U.S. territory in the Southwest underwent a radical social transformation. Using a variety of legal, extralegal, and generally violent means, Anglo-American capitalist society first dominated then decimated the pre-capitalist Mexican system. At the heart of the transformation was a continually expanding labor-intense production system that required an inexhaustible labor supply; this system replaced the old Mexican self-subsistence economy. As the new century opened to a national imperialist expansionism that engulfed the Caribbean, Mexico and Latin America, the entrenchment monopolistic economy of the Southwest demanded an army of cheap, mobile, unorganized, and dependable labor.

In Porfirian Mexico (1880–1910) and later in post-revolutionary Mexico, governmental policies complemented that demand and ensured the availability of labor for U.S. business. Porfirio Díaz's and revolutionary Mexico's open-door foreign investment policy (demanded by Washington), coupled with large-scale corporations' voracious appetite for Mexican labor, functioned as an international infrastructure that stabilized the Mexican immigrant community as a permanent component and

ethnicity within the U.S. working class. An incipient sector of the regional working class was formed in the early 1900s, and it continued to grow with the help of legal and illegal immigration in response to capital's requirements for workers. More often than not, "illegal" immigration constituted a form of state-sanctioned labor crossing of the border to satisfy corporate demand.

Indeed, the Mexican community emerged as a major participant in the capitalist development of the Southwest. It became integrated into the corporate industries then experiencing unprecedented growth. These same economically productive workers were segregated in terms of work, religion, occupation, recreation, housing, and education. An apparent irony was set in motion as they were integrated into a system of production dominated by monopolistic capital and yet segregated from nearly every other aspect of society. The social and economic conditions that have characterized the Mexican community in the United States throughout the twentieth century were especially evident during the first two decades, a period during which the modern Chicano community made its entrance.

IMMIGRATION AND SETTLEMENT

Well over a million Mexican migrants streamed into the United States between 1900 and 1930. The majority arrived in the 1920s to settle in mining zones, irrigated agricultural valleys, manufacturing centers, and railroad construction sites. Laborers, with families in tow, were coveted and actively recruited by employers. They entered into the lowest-wage employment in the packing houses of Southern California, the sugar beet fields of Colorado, the smelters of El Paso, the garment factories of San Antonio, the copper mines of Arizona, the cotton farms of Texas, and railroad construction across the United States. As the Mexican community in the Southwest grew, a new lexicon entered the vocabulary of the dominant community. Mexicans, it was said, were naturally suited to physical labor, as their short stature made it easier for them to pick, hoe, and lift. Nature adapted them to a subordinate status in which they took orders from a paternalistic boss and lived on meager wages. Though humble, they nevertheless enjoyed the simple pleasures of life to the fullest.

Charles Teague, longtime CEO of the Southern California Fruit Growers Exchange (the forerunner of Sunkist) in the interwar years, casually remarked that "Mexicans are naturally adapted to agricultural work, particularly in the handling of fruits and vegetables. . . . Many of them have a natural skill in the handling of tools and are resourceful in matters requiring manual ability."[1] Teague knew where the interests of the corporation lay: over 90 percent of the picking force of twenty-five thousand were Mexican laborers.[2] Although Mexicans were praised for their manual dexterity, they were seldom compensated for it. "Mexican wage" meant working for less than Anglo-American workers, and "Mexican work" meant undesirable, lowest-paid manual labor.

A settlement pattern quickly formed along the U.S.-Mexican border, where about 85 percent of migrants put down roots. They established permanent communities in company towns sponsored by mining companies, citrus associations, and cotton farms; covenants forced them to live "across the tracks," where they created *colonias* in the cities' outskirts and *campos* on the edges of agricultural towns. Throughout the Southwest, the increasing number of Mexican settlements kept pace with the economic development of the region. Mexican customs, traditions, celebrations, organizations, and activities were transplanted into the inhospitable environment. Before long, the residents established a new identity embodied in their communities and, except for leaving to work or to find some form of recreation, life was spent within the colonia or campo.

Integration into the economic sphere carried a price: segregation in theaters, parks, politics, and restaurants marked relations between Mexican society and the dominant community. In spite of the strength of community organizations and structures, Mexican barrios became associated, in the popular mind, with the outcast: Mexicans were foreigners, immigrants, transients, poor, delinquent, uncultured, and unskilled. Soon enough, the "Mexican problem," which encapsulated a host of alleged dangers to society's fundamental institutions, became a topic of widespread discussion in public policy venues. Los Angeles City Schools Superintendent Susan B. Dorsey lamented having to administer the educational mission of the schools with high enrollments of Mexican children. In one talk to district administrators she addressed the widely deplored educational problem:

> It is unfortunate and unfair for Los Angeles, the third largest Mexican city in the world, to bear the burdens of taking care educationally of this enormous group. We do have to bear a spiritual burden quite disproportionate to the return from this great number of aliens in our midst. This burden comes to us merely because we are near the border.[3]

Another complaint expressed by many educators accused Mexicans of increased crime, welfare cases, schooling problems, vice, and threats to the racial and cultural homogeneity of the nation.[4]

PUBLIC SCHOOLS AND THE SEGREGATION OF MEXICAN CHILDREN

As these communities formed, the public education system underwent a major overhaul and assumed a prominent position among the institutions shaping the political culture and social structure of the nation. In the late nineteenth century, periodic labor strikes convulsed the nation, and socialism and communism made inroads among the working classes. In response to these threats, leading social theorists cautioned that modern society contained dangerous and volatile social elements that threatened cultural disintegration, even a political revolution, if not properly controlled and neutralized.[5] Indeed, the public education system emerged transformed from a small-scale volunteer endeavor to a centralized, mass, compulsory state agency organized to indoctrinate the citizenry with a common political culture aimed at strengthening political stability, while inculcating the skills necessary for optimal economic growth and profitability.[6] At no time, however, did the schooling enterprise propose to alter existing class relations. Schools actively represented the status quo, with all of its attendant public policies, inequalities, and prejudices, and shouldered the task of creating an efficient,[7] organic, clock-like society. Across the nation, expanding public schooling placed the maintenance of the status quo high on its agenda while simultaneously assimilating and unfolding social relations, including class and racial hierarchies, dominant political ideologies, and economic operations.[8] Within this context, the Mexican problem compelled Southwestern school districts, which were enrolling significant numbers of Spanish-speaking children, to design a curriculum adapted to Mexican children. Acceptance of schooling intended to resolve the Mexican problem ensured the reproduction of the Mexican community as a source of cheap labor.

How did school systems treat the Mexican problem? What objectives guided school administrators? What methods did they employ to realize those objectives? The first administrative proposal for solving the Mexican problem was simple: segregation into all-Mexican schools. Several reasons were proffered for separating Mexican children from Anglo-American children. First, educators and academicians claimed that segregation provided a fitting environment in which to meet the educational needs of the culturally distinctive Mexican child. Administrators and educators confidently insisted that Anglo-American and Mexican children were substantially distinct culturally. Moreover, the culture of the Mexican child diminished his or her capacity to learn to such a degree that it was unwise to place both in the same school setting. The crux of the learning problem pivoted around language. Slowed by speaking Spanish, Mexican children progressively fell behind through the grades. Simultaneously, segregation unburdened the Anglo-American child from the "slower" Mexican pupils, who in turn benefited by avoiding competition with "faster students." Second, the inherited intelligence of Mexican children, as measured by IQ tests, purportedly fell well below that of the average Anglo child. This also required segregation to educate at the special ability levels of Mexican children. Third, the level of measured intelligence and the employment pattern peculiar to Mexicans (which parents seemed to pass on to their children) appeared to contain the seeds of a social inevitability. Educators

therefore implemented a strict emphasis on vocational education in the segregated environment.

THE CULTURE CONCEPT

In school districts throughout the region, a variety of segregation practices appeared. Initially, separating children into "foreign" classrooms seemed to solve the educational problem; eventually the first experiments grew into complete separation. In urban school districts such as Los Angeles, district lines created officially named "neighborhood schools" that only "foreign" (i.e. Mexican) students attended. The procedure most often applied, however, was the classic "Mexican School." In towns and cities where a Mexican colonia had been established, a separate school for Mexican children became a high priority for boards of education. Nearly all school districts separated Mexican children in one fashion or another, ostensibly because of the need to cleanse them of cultural defects by means of proper guidance and control. School bore the responsibility for teaching them the English language and American customs, values, and norms—that is, of Americanizing them. Mexicans were alleged to hold a Pandora's box of cultural dilemmas that, if allowed to escape, could move beyond the confines of the colonia and subvert the desirable and healthy cultural norms of society. If Mexicans were left to themselves, it was believed that certain destruction would threaten the superior (Anglo) culture and all that it had created. Educators and political leaders worried over Mexican habits thought to be antithetical to the national culture: uncleanliness, shiftlessness, irresponsibility, lack of ambition, unthriftiness, fatalism, promiscuity, and proneness to alcohol abuse.

E.E. Davis of the University of Texas confidently asserted in a report on illiteracy in Texas that "there is but one choice in the matter of educating these unfortunate [Mexican] children and that is to put the 'dirty' ones into separate schools till they learn how to 'clean-up' and become eligible to better society."[9] A deeply perplexed Phoenix principal argued that Mexicans' propensity to "steal cars, break windows, wreck recreational centers"[10] required that "more time should be spent teaching the [Mexican] child clean habits and positive attitudes towards others, public property, and their community in general." One Southern California teacher of Americanization wrote that "Mexican apathy . . . the infirmity of the will, forever the promise of mañana [dragged] upon the wheels of such progress as might exist."[11] An assistant supervisor in the Los Angeles city schools bluntly summarized the widely discussed Mexican problem:

> The Mexican problem . . . is principally the product of poverty in the home, which, in turn, is largely the appendage of the influx of immigrants from the Republic south of us. . . . The infusions of Spanish blood into Aztec and Maya veins has Latinized later generations since the sixteenth century. The mixture of the two is fundamentally responsible for the carefree, if not indolent, characteristic of the race.[12]

At a meeting of administrators in 1925, Susan B. Dorsey, the Los Angeles School District superintendent, recommended to her supervisors the antidote most often applied: "We have these [Mexican] immigrants to live with, and if we can Americanize them, we can live with them . . .". She, like many of her colleagues, believed that Americanization controlled the cultural defects while bringing Mexicans "to the light" so that they could embark on the process of social betterment.[13]

To fulfill the objectives of the Americanization program, however, proficiency in English and the elimination of Spanish were paramount, for language was considered the linchpin of culture. Backward cultural beliefs could be eliminated, it was claimed, once the core of the belief system, the Spanish language, was replaced by the heart of the superior culture, English. Thus, in district after district, English instruction via immersion and the forced removal of Spanish (and any traces of bilingualism) occupied the first two years of instruction in segregated schools. The first and second grades were generally known as the "Americanization" rooms, the locus of cultural change and guided entrance into American society.

Classroom rewards and punishments revolved around the child's willingness to adapt to speaking English exclusively. Schools incorporated practices that valued and rewarded proficiency in English, a practice that implicitly branded the language of the parents and the community as inferior and undesirable. Many an adult who lived through that era recalls the signs that warned "No Spanish" or "Speak English" and punishment by detention, corporal punishment, loss of privileges, or bad grades. One graduate of a segregated school bitterly recalled that "teachers warned us, 'I don't want to catch you speaking Spanish' . . . [but] we couldn't help it. That's all we knew at home. They'd

tell us 'we're going to send you back to Mexico' because they wanted to scare us that way. . . . That's about all we used to hear. . . . I forced myself to learn English."[14] The curriculum of Mexican schools correlated with the identification of the language barrier as the internal enemy arrayed against America's basic institutions.

Language, however, encapsulated a complex pedagogical equation for the education of Mexican children. Gender figured prominently. Females were considered the social "gene" that, when properly socialized, could transform Mexican colonias from islands of cultural degradation into solid, American enclaves in one generation. Towards this objective, Americanization classes for adult women and home economics for girls in school took center stage. Americanization teachers taught cooking, childrearing, housekeeping, thrift, and manners, and sponsored competitive projects like "Better Homes Week," during which women were urged to learn "acceptable" standards of housekeeping. Graduation ceremonies awarded diplomas to adult women able to speak a modicum of English. Schooling, however, did not have the interests of the women or of the community in mind.[15]

Beneath the educational surface, however, larger political issues were in command. Mexicans were alleged to harbor a culture that threatened not only to undermine prevailing norms, but also to create political mischief. The Americanization program in California, for example, initiated in 1915, targeted language because it was believed that all non-English-speaking sectors of the population held the potential to develop a class consciousness capable of evolving into radical, even communistic, organization and activities. In the Americanization agenda, more than ethnic rivalry was at stake; clear political objectives grounded the exercise.[16] Americanization, fundamental to the agenda of the segregated school, served as a preventive measure that promised the elimination of cultural disintegration and political disaster that loomed within the Mexican psyche.

THE BELL CURVE, 1920S STYLE

Justification of the selection of Mexican children for special education experiences went beyond culture to include genetic "stock." No other pedagogical device controlled classroom practice and curriculum as did the IQ test. Segregation may have accomplished the removal of Mexican children from the "normal" class, but it was the concept of intelligence and its operational contrivance, the IQ test, that "scientifically" legitimized and guaranteed unequal outcomes. Moreover, prevalent psychological theory laid the cultural "backwardness" of the Mexican immigrant community on the genetic material from which they descended.

The foremost psychologists and educators of the period, particularly in the 1920s, held that nature behaved in a most undemocratic fashion, bestowing intellectual abilities unequally. An ancillary premise of intelligence theory was that culture reflected intelligence; thus, a superior stock created a superior culture. Furthermore, a device called the IQ test could measure with great accuracy the mental variations among any population. The specter of race hovered over intelligence testing research that sought to define exactly how nature divvied up shares of intelligence. A politically saturated science that found nature's unfortunates—those endowed with degrees of intelligence below the "norm"—predominated. If the theoretical novelty had been confined there, perhaps the grosser consequences of the widespread segregation of Chicano children might have been avoided. But there were social implications in intelligence theory that affected the curriculum as well.

William James, Lewis Terman, Henry Goddard, E.L. Thorndike, and a host of social scientists who embraced the commonly accepted doctrine of the racial distribution of intelligence contended that social inequality, the division of labor, and the gross disparities in wealth and political power were passed from one generation to the next via the genes.[17] Moreover, only those with superior intelligence were capable of entering the professional occupations; the less intelligent were fitted for slots suitable to their level of mental ability in the lower quarters of the division of labor. Thus, class structure mirrored the distribution of intelligence, and neither conscious choice nor institutional practice molded the social order.

Schools across the nation rapidly adopted IQ testing and ignored all of its theoretical shortcomings and heavy-handed biases. Departments of psychological testing and research were instituted between 1910 and 1920 in the school systems of Los Angeles, El Paso, Phoenix, and San Antonio to survey the intellectual ability of students and to adjust individual school curricula to group averages. In classic doublespeak, they also embraced a new definition of democratic education: unequals could not be given the same curriculum nor expected to learn at the same pace. Differing intellectual abilities meant differing educational experiences, and therefore unequal outcomes. Educators concluded that such results were inevitable when understood in the context of prevailing theories that identified the "low-mentality" individual with low achievement (and the working class).

The principal of a Southern California school repeated the message broadcast during the 1920s by many experts when he wrote that "stupid parents are apt to have stupid children." Sensing that a critic might suggest environment as a factor, he flatly denied the environment thesis, contending that environment "never made a stupid child intelligent." So it was not unexpected that, as one Los Angeles supervisor put it, "nothing is so unequal as the equal treatment of unequals."[18] The principal at an all-Mexican school joined the broadening denunciation of the notion of equality: "The doctrine that 'all men are born free and equal' applies to man's political equality . . . In no way can this idea of equality be applied to intellectual endowment."[19] Democratizing the schools mandated an internally differentiated schooling process accommodated to the intellectual diversity contained within any student universe. An entirely new lexicon gained footing in school administrative offices, as terms like "gifted," "bright," superior," "average," "subnormal," "dull," "moron," "low grade moron," "borderline moron," "low mentality," and "feebleminded" were used to describe the children under their charge. Accordingly, a twentieth-century democratic education required unequals to be prepared differently for the inevitable reality that faced them in later life. Effective schools trained the diverse pool of children to assume the kinds of occupations that their inherited intelligence presaged. Under such a charge, school systems became training grounds not only for the superiors, but also for the slow learners and the feebleminded.

But much more was at stake. Adherents of IQ theory postulated an antidemocratic corollary: nature destined intellectual superiors to occupy positions of political power as well. The genetically less well endowed required government by their genetic superiors. Those whom nature allocated substantially fewer mental abilities required a tailored education administered by a paternal state that trained (recruited?) manual labor for employment possibilities in the Southwest's burgeoning enterprises. Although the widespread use of IQ tests appeared to have particular bearing upon Mexican children in the region, we should not ignore the national scope of the testing movement. Racialized policies enforcing the use of testing, segregation, and tracking affected children across the United States.

In segregating Mexican children, unequal education justified by a theory of inborn racial traits (and therefore inborn cultural traits) assumed center stage in the nation's state-run schools. Racial inequality—the foundation for and consequence of widespread pedagogical practices—rested on the near religious acceptance and universal application of the intelligence test. But racially inspired educational theory and practice, buttressed by scientific claims, reflected existing social relations and the division of labor in the production of commodities and sought to maintain them over generations. Moreover, dominant political and economic classes tethered those discourses and schooling practices to their interests.

Dozens of research projects simulated the scientific racism of Lewis Terman at Stanford. They were set up to identify the intellectual level of Mexican children. Over nine thousand Mexicans served as research subjects for nearly forty intelligence studies between 1915 and 1950. In survey after survey, a dismal conclusion was reached. Mexican children consistently scored lower than the norm for Anglo-American children, that mythical average 1.00. And even when the language "handicap" was controlled for, the test results hardly varied. Scores clustered around the .90 range in study after study. According to investigations in Los Angeles completed during the 1920s, about 47 percent of Mexican children scored below the .90 level, and only 22 percent scored at the normal step (a figure that paralleled general studies carried out on Mexican children by a host of psychologists). In 1932, the statistician for the Los Angeles district offered her reasons for the poor performance of Mexican children: "There is some selection in the type of Mexican family who comes to Los Angeles. Most of the children represented in the group belong to the laboring class."[20]

A 1928 investigation in California concluded that Mexican children scored on average at .86 and that 60 percent scored in the nonacademically inclined range.[21] At Belvedere Junior High in Los Angeles, with a student population that was 50 percent Mexican, 55 percent of all students scored below .90. At Lafayette Junior High School, not far from Belvedere, over half of all Mexican students were channeled into the nonacademic group. Statistics gathered for 1929 by the Los Angeles School District reported that the majority of "mentally retarded children" came from districts with the largest number of immigrants: the reverse was true for the "children of superior mentality," who were found "most frequently in the Normal Type school" or neighborhood.[22]

Many educationists and policymakers thought like the vice-principal of an urban elementary school that enrolled only "low mentality" children. He wrote that the "pupil of low intelligence" was prone to "failure, tardiness, lying, cheating, truancy." He confidently asserted that "inheritance" explained the problem.[23] California State Superintendent of Public Instruction William J. Cooper offered similar advice to the teachers under his supervision. His 1927 public policy statements on the subject added little to contemporary views of the relationship of biology and social conditions, but they demonstrate the confidence in such theoretical discourse. Like his contemporaries, Cooper contended that "we build on a biological foundation. We cannot make a black child white, a deaf child hear, a blind baby see, nor can we create a genius from a child whose ancestors endowed him with a defective brain. Within the limits set by heredity we can do much." He then recommended that "teachers should study biology."[24]

These theoretical premises and racialized cultural stereotypes had important bearing on teacher training during the period under study. In some cases, administrators were trained by leading authorities in the field of intelligence psychology. Dr. Frances Gaw, psychologist with the Los Angeles City Schools' Division of Psychology and Educational Research, earned her doctorate under Cyril Burt at the University of London. The division's director, Elizabeth Sullivan, and the agency's statistician, Alice McAnulty, were tutored by Lewis Terman at Stanford University. The clinician in charge of social service, Dorothy Henry, completed her master's degree under E.L. Thorndike at Columbia.

Of course, not all had the opportunity to study under the masters; the next best thing was to read their books. Teachers' colleges commonly used texts by leading psychological and pedagogical authorities of the day. Works by eugenicist Lathrop Stoddard and psychologists Lewis Terman and E.L. Thorndike, together with a host of others, found their way into course reading lists. Included in the lists one finds titles relating to Mexico and interpretations of Mexican culture from the perspective of these same social scientists and like-minded visitors to Mexico. Common reference texts emerged from the first cohort of scholars dabbling in Mexico, later known as Latin Americanists, which included Wallace Thompson (*The Mexican Mind*) and Edward A. Ross (*Social Revolution in Mexico*), both of whom disparaged all things Mexican, and the paternalistic and romanticized versions of Stuart Chase, Carleton Beals, Frank Tannenbaum, and Ernest Gruening, who found things of value in the Indian background and culture of Mexico. Neither the romanticized nor the racially inspired readings held any promise for enabling students to better understand Mexico and the Mexican immigrant. Both viewpoints essentially bolstered the belief in a fundamental distinction between Mexican and Anglo-American, a belief that corresponded with U.S. foreign policy in the region and provided the theoretical beginning point in the segregationist policy. One need read only a few of the dozens of master's theses on the education of Mexican children written by budding school administrators to appreciate their blind faith in the conventional pathway elaborated by the acknowledged experts.[25]

The scientific method held such sway over the education corps that the common contention that Mexican children, and the entire Mexican community, for that matter, comprised inferior genetic material appeared incontrovertible. In step with learned opinion, superintendents authoritatively cautioned principals, counselors, and teachers that the Mexican child could expect to achieve only two-thirds of the educational potential of the Anglo-American child. El Paso, Los Angeles, San Antonio, and Phoenix, like many smaller rural districts, adjusted their curriculum to the range of intelligence of the student body. All children who scored between .50 and .90 were considered "nonacademic types" who could excel with their hands but not their minds, fine material for manual labor but not the "book learning" type. In Los Angeles, the research and testing arm of the district, the Division of Psychology and Educational Research, found that at least half of all Mexican children fell into the slow-learning to feebleminded categories and were ideal material for nonacademic course work "suited to their needs." And since the remaining half still fell below the norm, it was an easy solution to the Mexican problem to design a curriculum that revolved around below-average learners. School administrators believed that the problem of the slow learner was not that he or she learned at a slower pace, but that his or her capacity to learn limited the rate of curriculum that could be adequately mastered.

INDUSTRIAL EDUCATION[26]

As segregated schools matured into the convention, a policy enforced by counselors armed with IQ tests affirmed that slow learners were quite capable of mastering the world of manual, nonacademic education; college-level preparation could never be considered for the slow learner. This conclusion became the bedrock of the education of Mexican children. In relation to

Mexican children, school officials resolved that the curriculum would comprise heavy doses of industrial education, and would derive in part from counselor surveys of the group's intelligence, the kinds of occupations open to Mexicans in the local area, and the cultural qualities attached to Mexicans.

Segregated schools resembled industrial schools, and in some districts these were (rightly) referred to as the "industrial school." These schools should not be confused with trade schools, however. Trade schools stipulated that applicants score at the norm on the intelligence test; in the trade classes of the Mexican schools, it was assumed that such courses were admirably suited to the intelligence and temperament of Mexican children. On the basis of scores on any intelligence test then in use, Mexican children found themselves placed in slow-learner tracks in numbers far out of proportion to their population. For boys, course work often included body shop, agriculture, basket weaving, upholstery, and animal husbandry. Girls learned to keep a neat house, care for children, serve as a domestic servant, keep house for an employer, and sewing and needlework.

In 1923, the copper mining enclave of Miami, Arizona, opened a school for the children of Mexican miners that was equipped "with a view to emphasizing industrial and homemaking courses for these children." Zavala Mexican School in Austin, Texas, paralleled Miami's plan; the school represented the "only elementary school in Austin . . . equipped with an industrial arts shop and home economics laboratory." Sidney Lanier Junior High School in San Antonio, Texas, attended exclusively by Mexican students, offered "special courses, flexible programs, home making, and industrial activities" based on courses in "sewing, cooking and art work for the girls; machine shop practice, auto repair, auto painting, top making, sheet metal work, plain bench and cabinet work in wood and a department in which type setting and job printing are taught to boys."[27] These examples from the 1920s and 1930s demonstrate the assumption that two goals were met simultaneously by industrial education: the cultural and intellectual needs of the Mexican community and the wider labor requirements of employers were satisfied in a single curriculum.

The assumption that Mexican children inevitably gravitated toward employment similar, if not identical, to that of their parents moved districts to begin the vocational experience in the early grades. The Arizona State Department of Education implemented early vocational curriculum because it found that "under present conditions" most Mexican children would enter unskilled or semiskilled positions, regardless of schooling; that being the case, vocational education was "to be introduced early and homemaking should be an important part of the elementary course for both boys and girls." One researcher who investigated the curriculum in Mexican schools throughout the Southwest found that the "sentiment of many teachers of Mexican children was known to favor an early introduction in the grades of these subjects [industrial education] for Mexicans."[28]

The degree and form of segregation did not end there, however. Vocational tracks absorbed the majority of children, but not all who were funneled into such classes attended the same course level. Some were judged to have an even lower mental ability than the majority of Mexican children and required a special vocational curriculum. An excessively large number of these children scored below .70, in the feeble-minded category. In Los Angeles, this group required a special education separate from their peers, which created a second level of segregation that funneled them en masse into schooling for the "mentally handicapped" (later "educationally mentally retarded") in sites named development centers and development rooms. These "less-capable" students could be trained for basic types of employment as unskilled and low-paid factory workers and workers in restaurants, hotels, laundries, private homes, agriculture, shoe-shine parlors, and the like. In 1929, some twenty-eight hundred children were assigned to ten development centers and thirty development rooms, located largely in working-class sections of the city, a substantial distance in terms of space and curriculum from the "normal" schools in Los Angeles. According to district reports, space in the centers and rooms accommodated only one-quarter of the "subnormals": many more waited for a transfer out of the normal classes.

By 1930, approximately one-fourth of the development schools and rooms were located in or near Los Angeles's Mexican colonia. One supervisor noted that "the subnormal child is apt to come from a low type home. . . . Often he comes from a foreign home," and thus the majority of recruits for the development centers and rooms attended near their neighborhoods.[29] By 1940 the population at these centers had increased to about five thousand, and throughout the era Mexican children composed approximately a quarter of the enrollees. As late as the 1960s, Chicano children still comprised one-quarter of students in the educationally mentally retarded classes, double their proportion of the school population.[30]

The Los Angeles City Schools, like most school districts administering Mexican schools, implemented a complex plan to adjust the subnormal child to the area's economic enterprises. District publications announced that at the Coronel Center, attended largely by Mexican children, courses were offered in "auto shop, tin shop, wood shop, paint shop, bakery, cookery, laundry work, power machine sewing, electric stitching, millinery, dressmaking, personal hygiene (including shampooing and manicuring), nursery maid training, cafeteria work, paper favor work, and trade ethics."[31] Every effort was made to correlate trade training with language instruction. Spelling and vocabulary words were selected from a list relating to words used in auto shops, laundries, cafeterias, and garment factories. Boys and girls received training suitable to their gender; for girls, employment in garment factories, laundries, bakeries, domestic service, and restaurants was determined adequate to their mental capacity. Beauty shop classes did not aim to prepare girls to become beauticians, but taught them grooming and personal hygiene—"to know how to keep themselves neat and clean"—which would make them more employable in their eventual search for work. Some girls were selected for training for day nursery work, not to care for children but to do the "unskilled tasks of cleaning, scrubbing, polishing, washing the dishes, etc." Particular emphasis was placed on laundry work for girls, training that, unlike beauty shop courses, had specific occupational objectives. The director of the elementary development centers reported in the 1929 *Yearbook* of the Division of Psychology and Educational Research that "several employers have told us that a dull girl makes a very much better operator on a mangle than does a normal girl. The job is purely routine and is irksome to persons of average intelligence, while subnormals seem to get actual satisfaction out of such a task. Fitting the person to the job reduces the turn over in industry and is, of course, desirable from an economic point of view."[32] Surrounded by agricultural fields, Los Angeles served as a harbor for many farmworkers, who migrated during some portion of the year. No surprisingly, enrollment in the development centers rose and fell with the harvests. According to a district publication:

> Enrollment in the Development classes is far from constant. The children enter in late Fall, due to the seasonal employment in the countryside, where the children and their parents are employed picking fruits and nuts. The enrollment reaches the peak in the Spring when many

centers and Rooms have to maintain waiting lists. The month of June usually brings an appreciable exodus when the children and their parents go out into the fields to harvest the onion crop.[33]

While IQ tests appeared to wear the mantel of infallibility, not all choices in the strict vocational regimen for Mexican children were based on testing. Some elements of Mexican culture were thought to be superior, and many a smiling educator theorized that these innate abilities redeemed Mexicans and demonstrated that not all was lost. It was believed that Mexicans enjoyed an artisanal dexterity that could turn almost anything into a work of art. Unfettered by the frenzied materialism of industrial society, Mexicans supposedly harbored a love of music, poetry, and philosophy. They did have something to offer, claimed many teachers, but nothing that was essential or of primary importance in the schooling enterprise. Moreover, in asserting that Mexicans were naturally gifted in handwork, were happy and carefree, if rather indolent despite (or perhaps because of) their poverty, educators offered more reasons for segregation and nonacademic schooling for Mexican children.

We should not be surprised that prevailing opinion among educators and employers considered Mexicans, as a group, culturally and genetically destined to perform manual labor. In 1932, the Texas Department of Education urged teachers to gauge the occupational future of Mexican children and to measure the curriculum against the findings. One Texas teacher's method was selected as a good example of an effective and appropriate approach for teaching Mexican children. In her English-language instruction, she placed "special emphasis upon the words the child will use in his work-a-day life as a tiller of the soil."[34] Later in the decade, the California State Board of Education *Bulletin* made a similar recommendation when it warned that growth in the minority population "would seem to present a problem of which educators must take cognizance, that a minority group . . . may receive appropriate instruction, *especially in reference to their probable* vocations" (emphasis added).[35] Whether by way of the IQ test or by determining "probable vocations," industrial education anchored the curriculum in Mexican schools across the Southwest. Not only did industrial course work follow the child from elementary school to junior high, but for the small minority fortunate enough to graduate from the eighth grade and enter secondary school, it also followed them. As a consequence,

many Mexican students experienced at least twelve years of manual training linked with heavy doses of Americanization.

EXCLUSION AND THE MIGRATORY CHILD

Not all Mexican children were fortunate enough to attend school. Total and partial exclusion, a third level of segregation, affected Mexican children, principally in rural areas where migrant family labor predominated. In these cases, the opportunities for schooling were rare because the family relied on children's labor for income. In districts that depended heavily on the labor of the family, as in the cotton-growing region of Texas, the sugar beet fields of Colorado, and the farming areas of some California counties, school boards in effect hung signs on schoolhouse doors to warn "No Migrant Children Allowed." One study of Hidalgo County, Texas, reported a widespread "attitude that school attendance should not be allowed to interfere with the supply of cheap farm labor." A Texas school superintendent candidly justified the practice: "Most of our Mexicans are of the lower class. They transplant onions, harvest them, etc. The less they know about everything else the better contented they are. You have undoubtedly heard that ignorance is bliss; it seems that it is so when one has to transplant onions."[36] Economist Paul S. Taylor noted that in Dimmit County, Texas, not "more than 25 percent of the Mexican scholastics, i.e., children aged 7 to 17 inclusive" were enrolled in school and that "the average number in attendance [was] undoubtedly less."[37] In 1938, a study found that in Crystal City, Texas, "the average 18 year old [Mexican] youth has not completed the third grade of school." Carey McWilliams's observation that "so far as migratory children are concerned, the compulsory school attendance laws might just as well never have been enacted" came as no surprise to those in the Southwest's agricultural belts.[38] A Texas district superintendent said as much when he testified that "the compulsory school attendance law is a dead letter—there is no effort to enforce it. Nobody cares."[39] In Texas, as late as 1945, only half of all Mexican school-age children actually attended any school, although school districts received state funds for the nonattending group. In short, Anglo-American children and corporate growers benefited from the nonenforcement of attendance laws in relation to Mexican children; meanwhile, thousands of children were denied their basic Constitutional right to equal protection of the laws.

It was not uncommon for a school district to allow migrant children into segregated schools, but this did not imply an invariable full school day. School hours, in another variation on the exclusion policy, were shortened to accommodate family labor needs during harvests. For the rural Mexican child, admission policies and the length of the school day were determined by the corporate agricultural interests. Education for the Mexican child under these conditions was a rare privilege. Obstacles to their education generated by growers shaped public policy and forced them into a kind of "hands-on" vocational education in the fields alongside their parents. The 1924 biennial report of California's superintendent for public instruction lauded the value of the special dispensation for migrant children: "There should be an adjusted school day beginning not later than the field work. This provides for the whole family leaving the camp at the same time, the adults going to the field and the children to school. . . . It also means that the school day is over when the mid-day meal is ready. It provides also that the children may work in the afternoon."[40] In school districts across Southern California, even in districts in Los Angeles County, schedules were modified throughout the 1920s to meet the demands of growers for the cheapest of all labor, that of children. County Superintendent of Schools John R. Hunt advised that the absence of Mexican children during the harvests was handled through "special migratory classes in each district whenever necessary." He continued:

> Harvesting of [walnuts] is peculiarly adapted to the Mexican family. . . . It provides them with a fine vacation, a camping experience under ideal conditions. . . . The walnut ranchers are particularly anxious to have the Mexican family do this work because of their adaptability [and because their availability] provides the rancher with the cheapest method of harvesting the crop. No other kind of labor could possibly be secured that could compete in price, and so it is an economic factor that the rancher faces.[41]

Hunt noted that students were bused to school at 8:00 a.m. and returned at noon in time to go to work in the orchards.

Despite admission into flexibly scheduled schools, the educational success of thousands of children from the migratory camps and rural colonias was affected by severe nutritional and health problems. A Depression-era study of California's migrant labor camps reported miserable wages, poor housing, irregular employment, malnourishment, and "children . . . growing up without an opportunity for normal education and recreation. . . . Medical care which they need is unavailable to them."[42] A report by the National Child Labor Committee commented that migratory "children are apt to have no schooling at all, or schooling of so poor a character and given under such adverse circumstances that it can not be effective, and the children are badly retarded."[43] Public officials, like the growers, could wash their hands of responsibility because, presumably, migrant children needed no formal preparation for the arduous agricultural tasks they would assume as adults. And if there were any doubts, IQ scores and "expert" opinion could be called upon in support of educational policy.

TEACHERS AND PHYSICAL RESOURCES

Despite the widely held contention that the Mexican school was but a temporary measure to ensure equality of opportunity, vast differences divided these schools from those attended by Anglo-American children. Teachers assigned to Mexican schools bore the stigma of the social inferiority attached to the school. Beginning teachers, older teachers, or poor teachers were commonly placed in Mexican schools. For novice teachers, their initiation into the profession required some experience before promotion "up" to a nonsegregated school. In Los Angeles, young graduates from teachers' colleges could expect to be assigned to the less-desirable sections of the city; if they proved competent, a spot somewhere in the better part of the city would be their reward. The Los Angeles assistant superintendent of assignments casually remarked in 1928 that teachers should expect a period of breaking in to demonstrate worthiness for assignment to one of the popular schools: "After two years of probation in the valley or harbor districts, the teacher transfers to the city proper. It is usually necessary to place her in the foreign, semiforeign, or less convenient schools. After a few more years of satisfactory service, she may be placed in the more popular districts."[44] The all-Mexican Miguel Hidalgo School in Brawley, California, in the fertile Imperial Valley, rotated teachers every three years. One researcher wrote that "the best teachers from the Mexican school are 'promoted' to the American school in order to provide experienced teachers there." In 1935, for example, thirty teachers taught 1,551 students, over fifty per class, at Miguel Hidalgo, but only twenty-two classrooms were available. Seasonal harvests caused some classes to expand overnight to as many as eighty students.[45]

Ambition, or status consciousness, motivated teachers to leave the Mexican schools. Administrators regularly evaluated the teaching force by school assignment and level of classes taught. Teachers at Mexican schools were considered less qualified, found little respect from their peers across town, and earned considerably less for their efforts. The best teachers were assigned to the "best" schools and taught the "bright" students. Teachers of the superior or gifted classes not only earned the greatest respect, but also were rewarded with higher salaries.

Mexican school practice eventually became tradition, ingrained in a conventional wisdom that few educators challenged. The most visible signs of educational policy were found in the quality of the physical resources available to Mexican children compared to those of the Anglo-American child. Overcrowded, poorly designed and constructed buildings, insufficient recreational space, used and repaired furniture, and books handed down from the Anglo schools plagued the Mexican schools.

In conducting research for his master's thesis, Carlos Calderón studied a district in the Lower Rio Grande Valley of Texas in 1950 to gauge the differences between a Mexican school and an Anglo school. The distinctions stood out boldly. He found the pupil-to-teacher ratio to average 32 to 1 in the Anglo schools, but 47 to 1 in Mexican schools. In eight cases a Mexican classroom held over fifty pupils, and Calderón reported that one class held seventy pupils. Nearly five hundred Mexican children were taught in inferior facilities—old frame buildings that had once served as army barracks and were badly in need of paint and repair. Classrooms were illuminated by a single light bulb, or perhaps two, and ventilated by a screen door and two transom windows. A small wooden shack housed an outdoor restroom finished with a rough cement floor and two toilets without stalls. The boys and girls used identical back-to-back restroom facilities. Drinking fountains were outdoors and unprotected for use in inclement weather. Neither medical facilities nor a cafeteria was available. Calderón then described the school for the Anglo-American community: "a modern brick structure with rest rooms, drinking fountains, book rooms, principal's office and teacher's lounge." Restrooms were finished with tile floors and six toilet stalls with doors, and the school had an indoor water cooler. The only cafeteria in the district served the Anglo school.[46]

The investigations of reformer George J. Sánchez revealed that in district after district this pattern was repeated.[47] Mexican schools were inferior in every respect, from teachers to curriculum to physical plant. Board of education policies ensured that the inequalities would remain, despite pleas for a larger share of the budget. These pleas went unheard. The principal at both La Jolla elementary and junior high in Southern California (located on the same grounds) recalled:

> They moved all the old buildings, all the old wooden shacks that they could move in and although we did get a few of the portable bungalows. . . . some of the other schools had them too, but not to the extent that we had them. And if they got rid of the furniture it was shipped down to us. After it didn't look good in the Anglo school, they would ship it down and we had no other say than to take what we were given. I was never glad to have it but we had to use it anyway.[48]

The board of education in La Jolla accepted the common belief that Mexican children were not capable of high school work and so curtailed instruction for them at tenth grade. The La Jolla school was considered a terminal school.

STRUGGLES TO DESEGREGATE THE MEXICAN SCHOOLS

If oppression is never permanent, it is only so because the victims rise up against their oppressors, and in the Southwest the Mexican community engaged in a political struggle to dismantle segregation. Despite segregation, the educational institution held a valued place within the Mexican communities, which manifested itself as a strong belief in the power of education as a means for social betterment. Bitterness arose from within the community. One observer noted, in relation to Brawley's Miguel Hidalgo School, that "Mexicans resent the crowded condition of the school, the double session, and the dearth of conveniences." A teacher commented that parents and children understood the underlying racial motives of the board of education: "Many times . . . our youngsters would say to me 'The reason they do it is because we're Mexicans.' The parents felt that way too."[49]

Formal assaults came from organizations and community leaders. In Texas, the League of United Latin

American Citizens battled long for school reform and desegregation. One member expressed a sentiment shared by many in the organization in proclaiming that "WE MUST BATTLE SEGREGATION BECAUSE OF RACE PREJUDICES!"[50] George I. Sánchez and labor leader Ernesto Galarza criticized segregation throughout the 1930s and 1940s, calling the practice arbitrary, capricious, and racially motivated. Sánchez's trenchant criticisms expressed the community's growing sentiment for reviewing the injustice of segregation. In an unprecedented legal action, incensed Mexican parents in Lemon Grove, California, boycotted their school in 1930 before suing the board of education in the first successful desegregation case in the nation's history.[51] Although the case had only local impact, the rebellion augured the resistance to come in the 1940s.

Despite the post-1920s transition to a culture-based interpretation of IQ, the curriculum remained as before; little changed in administrative procedure. The consequences of a nonhereditary theoretical basis for IQ proved meager for the Mexican community. Through the late 1930s and into the 1940s, the culture of the community was still used to explain the "Mexican problem." Gradually a philosophy, freed from scientific race theory, took shape. In the new pedagogical environment, the culture of the Mexican community was defined as the cause of the tangle of pathologies that were alleged to plague it. It was believed that nothing could be gained until there was a transformation, either coerced or voluntary, from Mexican cultural standards to American standards. Nothing appeared to indicate that segregated schooling required modification, and it remained the prescription of choice for "remedying" Mexican culture.

It is within this atmosphere that the Mexican American community engaged in its civil rights struggles of the 1940s to desegregate schools. The Mexican community joined a national political struggle to force the democratization of the nation's schools. The first round of the conflict that eventually led to the historic *Méndez v. Westminster*[52] case occurred in 1943 in Santa Ana, California, the county seat of Orange County. The school board instituted segregated classes in 1913 and established the first Mexican school in 1919. Parents at the time opposed the move and appealed to the board, but without success. For two generations, the board, with few exceptions, directed Mexican children to attend one of three segregated schools. Throughout the county, fifteen Mexican schools were maintained and attended by nearly five thousand children. Chafing under decades of segregation, several Santa Ana parents

appeared before the board of education in 1943 and vociferously demanded the right for their children to attend the school of their choice. An unbending board, upset at the strident tones of petitioners, refused.

Officials were negotiating with the politically aware second generation, however, a generation more cognizant of the injustices and harm generated by segregation. Many members of that generation had served in the armed forces during the Second World War, and many had relatives who had served. Returning veterans had tasted equality in the armed forces and were restive under the segregationist codes now governing their conduct. Leaders began to emerge and organize to challenge segregation. In Orange County, veterans founded the Latin American Organization and resolved to reform schools to serve the needs of the Mexican community. Meanwhile, parents joined the movement throughout the county.

In rural Westminster, Gonzalo and Felicitas Méndez, who had only recently moved into the area, sent their youngsters to the closest elementary school. Unknown to them, the school restricted admission to Anglos. When school officials discovered the nationality of the Méndez children, they were refused admission. Unfazed, the Méndezes took an unheard-of step and refused to send their children to the segregated school and protested to the board. The board recommended a "special admission" for the Méndezes. The Mexican parents, calling the special admission a slap in the face, refused the board's offer and organized a boycott of all parents until all children were allowed to enroll in the school of their choice. Mrs. Méndez later recalled that she and her husband organized the boycott because they got "tired of being pushed around." That sentiment became more widespread.[53]

In Garden Grove, Ruth and Cruz Barrios defied the board, and Santa Ana parents had already confronted the board in 1943. The stage was set when, in 1945, a class action lawsuit filed by five parents on behalf of five thousand children was filed in federal court to demand the desegregation of the county's schools. Assisted by the newly formed Santa Ana chapter of the League of Latin American Citizens, the plaintiffs argued that the Fourteenth Amendment's equal protection clause had been violated, as there were no laws enabling the segregation of Mexican children. The defendants answered that segregation in this case passed legal muster under the *Plessy*[54] doctrine, that is, separate but equal, and that schools for Mexican children were as good as those for Anglo children. Furthermore, argued the defendants, Mexican children required special courses in

Americanization, particularly English, to prepare them for the higher grades, and thus segregation involved strictly educational objectives.

In February 1946, U.S. District Court Judge Paul L. McCormick ruled that the school districts were guilty of violating the Fourteenth Amendment in forcing Mexican children to attend segregated schools. Judge McCormick found that a "paramount requisite in the American system of public education is social equality. It must be open to all children by unified school association regardless of lineage."[55] The judge clearly broke with *Plessy* by maintaining that separation implied inferiority, and that inferiority was obtained through arbitrary administrative practices. He wrote that the country's practices "foster[ed] antagonism in the children and [suggested] inferiority among them where none exist[ed]."[56] The county counsel appealed to the U.S. Circuit Court of Appeals, but the appeals judges upheld the lower court's ruling. The county was ordered to begin the process of dismantling segregation in the fall of 1948.

The class action suit, known by the legal title *Méndez v. Westminster*, reverberated throughout the nation, particularly in the Southwest, and led to successful challenges in Arizona and Texas. Legal analysts quickly focused on the case. An article in the *Columbia Law Review* argued that the case strongly suggested that the *Plessy* doctrine might be in for a constitutional test. The author noted that the "courts in the [*Méndez*] case breaks sharply with this approach and finds that the Fourteenth Amendment requires 'social equality' rather than 'equal facilities.'" A piece in the *Yale Law Journal* affirmed that the Méndez decision "questioned the basic assumption of the Plessy Doctrine. . . . A dual school system even if 'equal facilities' were provided does imply social inferiority."[57]

Civil rights activists understood the significance of *Méndez*. The NAACP legal defense team of Thurgood Marshall and Robert C. Carter followed the case closely and filed amicus curiae briefs during the appeals process. According to Carter, the briefs were a "dry run for the future" and contained every one of the key arguments later used in the *Brown v. Board of Education* case (which followed *Méndez* by eight years). All the documents filed by the plaintiffs' lawyer were handed over to Marshall and Carter, who read them with great interest. Clearly, the struggle to desegregate the United States has many points of origin, but one that we must not ignore is the *Méndez* case of 1947.

Many districts, particularly in rural areas, ignored the decision, and even districts that desegregated maintained many discriminatory practices. Segregation reappeared in the form of gerrymandered neighborhood school districts, and schools with a majority of Chicano students increased notably. Strong reliance on IQ testing, heavy tracking into industrial education, Americanization, English immersion, and the generally negative perception of Mexican culture continued to guide education. Continuity and change marked the transition from the era of the Mexican school to the era of integration shaped by the culture concept. Continuity, however, maintained the dominant position.

Endnotes

1. Charles C. Teague, *Fifty Years a Rancher* (Los Angeles: Ward Ritchie Press, 1944), p. 143.

2. Gilbert G. González, *Labor and Community: Mexican Citrus Worker Villages in a Southern California County* (Urban: University of Illinois Press, 1994), p. 28.

3. Susan B. Dorsey, "Problems of the Los Angeles School Board," *Los Angeles City Schools Journal*, 6 (1923), 59.

4. See Charles Clifford Carpenter, "Segregation vs. Non-Segregation of the Mexican Student," Master's thesis, University of Southern California, 1935; see also Gilbert G. González, "Educational Reform in Los Angeles and Its Effect Upon the Mexican Community. 1990–1930." *Explorations in Ethnic Studies*, 1, No 2 (1978), 5–26.

5. Edward A. Ross, *Social Control: A Survey of the Foundations of Order* (New York: MacMillan, 1912,) p. 2; also, Charles Horton Cooley, *Social Process* (New York: Scribners, 1918).

6. See Samuel Bowles, "Unequal Education and the Reproduction of the Social Division of Labor," in *Schooling in a Corporate Society*, ed. Martin Carnoy (New York: David McKay, 1972), pp. 36–64; see also, Raymond E. Callahan, *Education and the Cult of Efficiency* (Chicago: University of Chicago Press, 1962); also, David Nasaw, *Schooled to Order: A Social History of Public Schooling in the United States* (New York: Oxford University Press, 1981).

7. In the early twentieth century the term "efficient" meant "scientific management," that is, Taylorisation in all spheres of society, the controlled utilization of all available resources, human and physical, for social and economic "uplift" or progress toward a harmonious society. In practice, efficiency meant that schools (and society) were to be managed by the same principles governing the large-scale business enterprise and employ the conveyorbelt system used in factories for processing students through their courses. Further, immigrants were a drag upon progress until Americanized and able to integrate into the bureaucratic social

system. In this context, labor strikes were "inefficient" because they prevented the full and unfettered control of labor power in the production of commodities, and also because strikes "balkanized" society into classes, a great fear among adherents of efficiency.

8. See, for example, Samuel Bowles and Herbert Gintis, *Schooling in Capitalist America* (New York: Basic Books, 1976): see also, Martin Carnoy, *Education as Cultural Imperialism* (New York: David McKay, 1974).

9. Gilbert G. González, *Chicano Education in the Era of Segregation* (Philadelphia: Balch Institute, 1990), p. 37

10. H.F. Bradford, "The Mexican Child in our American Schools," *Arizona Teacher Parent*, 27 (March 1939), 199.

11. Jessie Hayden, "The La Habra Experiment," Master's thesis, Claremont College, 1934.

12. Leonard John Vandenburgh, "The Mexican Problem in the Schools," *Los Angeles School Journal*, 11, No. 34 (1928), 15.

13. Susan B. Dorsey, "Mrs. Pierce and Mrs. Dorsey Discuss Matters Before the Principals Club," *Los Angeles School Journal*, 6, No. 25 (1925), 59.

14. González, *Labor and Community*, p. 101.

15. See Gilbert G. González, "The Americanization of Mexican Women and Family During the Era of De Jure Segregation," *in Ethnic and Gender Boundaries in the United States: Studies of Asian, Black, Mexican, and Native Americans*, ed. Sucheng Chan (Lewiston, NY: Edwin Mellon Press, 1989). pp. 55–79.

16. See González, *Labor and Community*, pp. 127–129.

17. See Gilbert G. González, "The Historical Development of the Concept Intelligence," *Review of Radical Political Economy*, 11, No. 2 (1979), 44–54.

18. See González, *Labor and Community*, pp. 127–129.

19. George K. Miller, "Birds of a Feather," *Los Angeles School Journal*, 9, No. 24 (1926), 17.

20. Ellen Alice McAnulty, "Achievement and Intelligence Test Results for Mexican Children Attending Los Angeles City Schools," *Los Angeles Educational Research Bulletin*, 11, No. 7 (1932), 89.

21. See Merton Hill, *The Development of an Americanization Program* (Ontario, CA: Board of Trustees of the Chaffey Union High School District and the Chaffey Junior College, 1928), p. 110.

22. Alma Leonhardy, "Slow-Learning Groups in High Schools," in *Third Yearbook*, ed. Los Angeles City School District (Los Angeles: Los Angeles City Schools, Division of Psychology and Educational Research, 1929), pp. 187–188.

23. Joseph M. Sniffen, "The Senior High School Problem Boy," *Los Angeles School Journal*, 11, No. 32 (1928), 14.

24. William John Cooper, "Character Education," *Los Angeles School Journal*, 10, No. 26 (1927), 18.

25. This observation is based on a selected number of master's theses written by students at the University of Southern California. I used the bibliographies to gauge the typical readings covered in the course work. In all the examples consulted, conventional distortions of Mexico, Mexican culture, and immigrants permeated the works. Teacher college training programs embraced and promulgated the scientific racism of day.

26. In this article, the terms "vocational" and "industrial" are used interchangeably; however, in the materials used to prepare this article, "trade" was sometimes synonymous with the two. In Los Angeles, the district Trade School carried out training for skilled trades, whereas industrial or vocational course work implied an unskilled or semi-skilled training curriculum. The distinctions were not always consistent. In relation to Mexican children, all job-oriented curriculum, whether termed trade, vocational, or industrial, meant training for the lower skilled categories of the work force.

27. González, *Chicano Education*, p. 87.

28. González, *Chicano Education*, pp. 87, 89.

29. Mary Florence Macredy, "The Mentally Handicapped Child for Wage-Earning and Citizenship," *Los Angeles Educational Research Bulletin*, 9, No. 6 (1930), 6.

30. James Vásquez, "Measurement of Intelligence and Language Differences," *Aztlán*, 3, No. 1 (1973), 155.

31. M. Frances Martin, "Development Centers and Rooms," *Third Yearbook*, ed. Los Angeles City School District (Los Angeles: Los Angeles City School District, Division of Psychology and Educational Research, 1929), pp. 84–85.

32. Martin, "Development Centers and Rooms," p. 87.

33. "Development Centers," *Fourth Yearbook*, ed. Los Angeles City School District (Los Angeles: Los Angeles City Schools, Department of Psychology and Educational Research, 1931), p. 116.

34. González, *Chicano Education*, p. 87.

35. González, *Chicano Education*, p. 88.

36. Herschel Manuel, *The Education of Mexican and Spanish-Speaking Children in Texas* (Austin: University of Texas Press, 1930), pp. 76–77.

37. Paul S. Taylor, "Mexican Labor in the United States: Dimmit County, Winter Garden District, South Texas," *University of California Publications*, 6, No. 5 (1930), 372.

38. Carey McWilliams, *Ill Fares the Land: Migrants and Migratory Labor in California* (New York: Barnes and Noble, 1942), p. 256.

39. McWilliams, *Ill Fares the Land*, p. 256.

40. State of California Superintendent of Public Instruction, *Biennial Report of the School Years Ending 30 June*

1923 and 30 June 1924 (Sacramento: California State Printing Office, 1924), p. 35.

41. John R. Hunt, "The Problem of the Migratory School Child," *Los Angeles School Journal*, 12, No. 14 (1928), 24.

42. Bertha Underhill, "A Study of 132 Families in California Cotton Camps with Reference to Availability of Medical Care" (Sacramento: California Department of Social Welfare, Division of Child Welfare Services, 1936), p. 18.

43. González, *Chicano Education*, p. 105.

44. Jessie A. Tritt, "The Problem of Elementary Assignments," *Los Angeles School Journal*, 12, No. 1 (1928), 15.

45. Jay Newton Holliday, "A Study of Non-Attendance in Miguel Hidalgo School of Brawley, California," Master's thesis, University of Southern California, 1935.

46. Carlos Calderón, "The Education of Spanish-Speaking Children in Edcouch-Elsa, Texas," Master's thesis, University of Texas, 1950.

47. See, for example, Virgil E. Strickland and George I. Sánchez, "Spanish Name Spells Discrimination," *Nation's Schools*, 41 (1948), 22–24.

48. Interview with Chester Whitten by Robin Rodarte and Richard Gutiérrez in *Harvest: A Compilation of Taped Interviews on the Minority Peoples of Orange County*, ed. Priscilla Oaks and Wacira Gethalga (Fullerton: California State University, Fullerton, 1974).

49. González, *Labor and Community*, p. 104.

50. Guadalupe San Miguel, Jr., *"Let Them All Take Heed": Mexican Americans and the Campaign for Educational Equality in Texas, 1910–1981* (Austin: University of Texas Press, 1987), p. 76.

51. Superior Court of the State of California, County of San Diego. *Robert Alvarez v. the Board of Trustees of the Lemon Grove School District*. February 13, 1931.

52. *Méndez et al. v. Wesminster School District of Orange County et al.* Civil Action Number 4292. District Court S.D., California. Central Division February 18, 1946. 64 F. Supp. 544 (S.D. California, 1946), (C.C.A., 9th April, 1947).

53. María Newman, "Tired of Being Pushed Around," *Celebrate*, 3 (1989), 75.

54. *Plessy v. Ferguson*, 163 U.S. 537, 1896.

55. González, *Chicano Education*, p. 153; also, Gertrude Staughton, "In California's Orange County Mexican Americans Sue to End Bias in School Systems," *People's World*, 16 (March 1945), 324; Mary M. Peters, "The Segregation of Mexican American Children in the Elementary Schools of California—Its Legal and Administrative Aspects." Masters thesis, University of California, Los Angeles, 1948.

56. González, *Chicano Education*, p. 153.

57. González, *Chicano Education*, p. 154

Chicana/o Education from the Civil Rights Era to the Present

Dolores Delgado Bernal

The struggle of Chicanas/os for educational equity and the right to include their culture, history, and language in K–12 and higher education curricula predates the civil rights movements of the 1960s by decades.[1] Although Chicanas/os have made significant progress in terms of educational inclusion over the last five decades, since the late 1970s hard-won gains have eroded. Many of today's most hotly debated educational issues are very similar to those discussed in Mexican communities since before the turn of the century: improvement of inferior school facilities; removal of racist teachers and administrators; elimination of tracking; and inclusion of Mexican history, language, and culture in the curriculum. Today's conditions can be better understood within a contextual and historical analysis that connects the present to earlier periods, and links belief systems to our judicial system and social policies.

This chapter addresses educational policies and practices and judicial decisions that have affected Chicana/o education from the 1950s through the 1990s. This period encompasses the early civil rights era, including the Chicana/o Movement, which brought significant improvements in Chicana/o schooling, and the more recent neoconservative era in which we have seen the deterioration of Chicana/o educational rights. I have included several educational themes that were especially prominent throughout the Southwest from the 1950s through the 1990s: continued school segregation, bilingual education, and higher education. During this period, school segregation and desegregation efforts took on a new form, and differ greatly from the era of de jure segregation that officially ended in 1954 with the *Brown* decision.[2] The bilingual education movement is unique to this period, and Chicana/o participation in higher education was virtually nonexistent prior to the 1950s. Another common thread that weaves through this chapter (and the entire book) is the resistance and activism of Chicana/o communities, including their use of the judicial system in demanding educational equity. Though each of these themes was important throughout the Southwest, this chapter places an emphasis on California and Texas, where the majority of Chicanas/os live and where much of the research on Chicana/o education has focused. In addition, the contemporary focus on California at the end of this chapter is purposeful, as California seems to be setting a national public policy standard in regards to legislation that negatively impacts the schooling of Chicanas/os.

Starting with the 1950s and early 1960s, I examine the continued school segregation of Mexican students even after numerous court decisions found de jure segregation of Mexican students illegal. Next I turn to the social activism and social policies that positively influenced Chicana/o schooling during the late 1960s and early 1970s. Then I address the conservative retrenchment that began in the mid-1970s, specifically the tension between desegregation and bilingual education, the educational inequity in K–12 education, and the myth of meritocracy in higher education. Finally, I assess where we are today, acknowledge progress in some aspects of Chicana/o schooling, and briefly analyze recent California legislation that has or will have a negative impact on Chicana/o education.

DE FACTO SCHOOL SEGREGATION: THE 1950S TO THE EARLY 1960S

In the 1950s and early 1960s, Mexicans saw the elimination of school segregation as the key to full economic and social mobility. Throughout the Southwest, however, judicial decisions outlawing the segregation of Mexican students were ignored; instead, school boards purposely overlooked desegregation, and de facto segregation of Mexican students actually increased (Bogardus, 1949; Rangel & Alcala, 1972; Salinas, 1971). Why were these judicial decisions ignored? I argue that the White social belief system about Mexicans helped support the many political and economic reasons for their continued segregation. Indeed, the images of Mexicans held by educators and the judicial system shared a common trait during this period: both were "premised upon political, scientific, and religious theories relying on racial characterizations and stereotypes about people of color that help support a legitimating ideology and specific political action" (Tate, 1997, p. 199). The ideologies of Anglo-Saxon superiority, capitalism, and scientific theories of intelligence proved the cornerstones of de jure segregated schooling for Mexicans throughout the Southwest during the first half of this century (González, 1990; Menchaca & Valencia, 1990). These theories, along with a belief system that viewed Mexicans as "culturally deficient" and characterized them as ignorant, backward, unclean, unambitious, and abnormal were unaffected by major judicial decisions in California and Texas (see González, 1974; Taylor, 1934).

In California, the *Méndez v. Westminster* (1946) landmark case officially ended de jure segregation for Mexican students and cast doubt on the "separate but equal" doctrine. Five Mexican families, including Felicitas and Gonzalo Méndez, claimed that their children and other children of Mexican descent were victims of unconstitutional discrimination in the segregated schools of Orange County. U.S. District Court Judge Paul L. McCormick's 1946 ruling in favor of the plaintiffs, upheld in the Court of Appeals in 1947, found that the segregation of Mexican children could be considered arbitrary action taken without due process of the law (Wollenberg, 1974). In Texas, just one year later, Minerva Delgado and twenty other parents filed a suit against several Texas school districts in *Delgado v. Bastrop Independent School District* (1948). As in California, the court ruled that placing Mexican students in segregated schools was arbitrary and discriminatory, and in violation of constitutional rights guaranteed by the Fourteenth Amendment (San Miguel, 1987). However, these cases, which ended de jure racial segregation for Mexican students, did not change the existing American belief system that portrayed Mexicans as inferior.

In Texas, even after the *Méndez* and *Delgado* decisions found de jure segregation of Mexican students illegal, segregation continued to be widely practiced (Bogardus, 1949; Menchaca, 1995). When state school officials were confronted with evidence of continued school segregation, there was little interest in seriously addressing the problem. For example, representatives from the League of United Latin American Citizens (LULAC) and the American G.I. Forum found this to be true when they appeared before the State Board of Education in 1950 with a list of twenty Texas cities that were still practicing segregation in spite of the recent judicial decisions (San Miguel, 1987).[3] In response, the State Board of Education proposed a policy statement on the illegality of the segregation of Mexican schoolchildren, but allowed local districts to handle the complaints and grievances of discriminatory treatment. The Board's policy simply created a bureaucratic process that limited the number of grievances that could actually reach the state commissioner of education. As San Miguel stated, "Between 1950 and 1957 nine local school districts were brought to the commissioner of education for special hearings, although hundreds of school districts throughout the state were segregating Mexican American students" (p. 132).

Belief in the cultural deficiency of Mexicans remained in place and supported the political action that continued to segregate Mexican students. At the same time, school segregation itself perpetuated an ideology of inferiority. Critical race theorist Charles Lawrence (1993) argues that school segregation conveys an ideology of inferiority that denies equal citizenship based not just on the act of segregation (de jure or de facto), but also on the defamatory message it sends about students of color:

> *Brown* held that segregation is unconstitutional not simply because the physical separation of Black and white children is bad or because resources were distributed unequally among Black and white schools. *Brown* held that segregated schools were unconstitutional primarily because of the message segregation conveys—the message that Black children are an untouchable caste, unfit to be educated with white children. Segregation serves its purpose by conveying an idea. It stamps a badge of inferiority upon Blacks, and this badge communicates a message to others in the community, as well as to Blacks wearing the badge, that is injurious to Blacks. (p. 59)

Following this line of reasoning, the injurious message behind Mexican school segregation was that Mexican students were inferior and did not deserve society's investment in their education. For example, in the *Méndez* decision, Judge McCormick stated, "the methods of segregation prevalent in the defendant school districts foster antagonisms in the children and suggest inferiority among them where none exists" (64 Federal Supplement, 1946, cited in Harders & Gómez, 1998, p.8). In other words, school segregation itself suggested an inferiority that was greater than any attempt to provide equal school facilities, making them inherently unequal. Thus, even after the end of de jure segregation, Mexican students remained segregated in substandard schools and were labeled as members of an inferior group. The comments of a Los Angeles teacher in the 1960s reveal the cultural deficit beliefs many teachers held:

> The attitudes of my colleagues are negative toward the Mexican American. I have heard some remarks in the teachers' room made like, "I have never had a Mexican who could think for himself." I have heard others say, "These Mexican kids, why do they have to be here?" (Delgado Bernal, 1997, p. 83)

The historic devaluation of Spanish also promoted these beliefs. Prohibiting Spanish-language use among Mexican schoolchildren was a social philosophy and a political tool used by local and state officials to justify school segregation and to maintain a colonized relationship between Mexicans and the dominant society.[4] Bilingualism was seen as "unAmerican" and considered a deficit and an obstacle to learning. There were no formal bilingual programs for Spanish-speaking students prior to the late 1960s, and it was routine to segregate Mexican students into "Mexican schools" or "Mexican classrooms," using their perceived language deficiency as justification. Even after the end of de jure segregation, it was common to find Mexican students physically separated from other students within the same classroom. Los Angeles Unified School District board member Vickie Castro, who went through elementary school in the 1950s, recalls how she was physically separated from her peers:

> I do recall my first day of school. And I did not speak English. . . . I just recall being frightened and I recall not knowing what to do and I recall being told to just sit over there in the corner. And there was one other little girl and we were just scared out of our minds. (Castro, 1994, p. 2, 3)

It was also common to hold Mexican students back for several years while they learned English. This left them over age for their grade, and thereby more likely to quit school before graduating.[5] This "assimilationist" perspective viewed bilingualism as a cognitive disability that caused confusion and impeded academic development (Jensen, 1962). In other words, many educators believed that there was only so much room in the brain, and children would not be able to function if they were learning English and maintaining their native Spanish. In fact, during the 1950s and early 1960s, most educators, along with LULAC, strongly supported the idea of intensive English instruction without the maintenance of Spanish (Crawford, 1992). LULAC's motive in supporting this type of instruction was their desire for Mexican students to learn English as quickly as possible so they could be successful in the dominant society. Though the goal of LULAC leaders was not total assimilation of the Mexican population, they were drawn into the assimilationist language perspective, and only later recognized the damage this perspective had on Mexican students (San Miguel, 1987).

Some Mexican educators at the time also advocated for an English-only approach, prior to offering their support for bilingual education in the late 1960s. One interesting example is Joe Bernal, the Texas senator and former educator, who later sponsored the Bilingual Education Act of 1968. He grew up on the predominantly Mexican west side of San Antonio in the 1940s, and as a high school student leader helped enforce an English-only campus policy. Each student was given a ribbon that said, "I Am an American—I Speak English," and was urged to turn in classmates heard using Spanish. Those caught speaking Spanish faced corporal punishment, after-school detention, and other forms of discipline (Crawford, 1992). Later, as an elementary schoolteacher in the 1950s, Bernal fined his pupils a penny for each time they used Spanish, saving the proceeds for a class party. He remembers: "I used to collect a lot of money from these kids. The parents knew about it and they were supportive" because they believed that their children must learn English, whatever the cost (Crawford, 1992, p. 79). Suppressing Spanish was a way to degrade and control an entire cultural group without explicitly using force or violence. It was one strategy for sustaining a colonized/colonizer relationship between Mexicans and the dominant White society. Many Mexicans internalized these negative views of Spanish—and therefore a negative view of themselves and their families—in order to assimilate into the dominant society.

Although the relationship between Mexicans and the dominant White society is complex and beyond pedagogical issues, it was clearly a part of Mexican school segregation. Mexican boys and girls continued to be tracked into vocational classes that served an economic function and supported the unequal division of power, wealth, and status, just as in the era of de jure segregation. Young Mexican women were tracked into home economics and clerical or secretarial classes, which prepared them for low-paying domestic and subservient work. Mexican women had an additional hurdle to jump, for even if they were able to move beyond paid domestic work, their families usually did not expect them to pursue an education beyond the domestic skills they would need in their homes (García, 1997; López, 1977; Nieto Gómez, 1974). The sexist attitudes of the wider society were manifested in the Mexican culture through such common sayings as *¿Para que quieres educarte si de nada te va a servir cuando te cases?* (Why do you want to educate yourself if it will not be of any use to you when you get married?) (López, 1977).

Throughout the 1960s, the message that both Chicana and Chicano students were inferior continued to translate into overcrowded and under-financed schools, low graduation rates, and the overrepresentation of Chicana/o students in special education classes, including classes for the mentally retarded and the emotionally disturbed (California State Advisory Committee, 1968). A 1967 Chicana high school graduate remembers the deplorable educational conditions at her urban high school:

> We had severely overcrowded classrooms. We didn't have sufficient books. We had buildings that were barrack type buildings that had been built as emergency, temporary buildings during World War II, and this was the late 1960s, and we were still going to school in those buildings. (Delgado Bernal, in press)

Demographic factors such as the expanding Chicana/o school-age population, immigration, urbanization, and White flight also contributed to the increased de facto segregation of Chicana/o students. In cities such as Los Angeles, San Jose, Phoenix, Denver, San Antonio, and Houston, the picture was especially stark. By 1960, more than 80 percent of California's 1.4 million Spanish-surnamed people lived in urban areas, and the number of Spanish-surnamed children attending inferior segregated schools had increased (Wollenberg, 1974). Nearly half of all Chicana/o students in the Southwest attended elementary and secondary schools in which the Chicana/o enrollment was over 50 percent of the total student body (U.S. Commission on Civil Rights, 1971). As educational conditions worsened, tension and resentment increased, and Chicanas/os became disillusioned with the "American Dream." In response, many Chicanas/os in the 1960s embraced a nationalist perspective and a militancy to bring about educational, political, and social reform.

SOCIAL ACTIVISM AND SOCIAL POLICY OF THE LATE 1960S

The last half of the 1960s marked the first time that youth played a central role in the shaping of movements aimed against social institutions and those in power. Street politics and mass protests marked this period, and student movements helped shape larger struggles for social and political equity (Muñoz, 1989). During this period of social unrest, Chicana/o students were influenced by numerous social and political forces, such as the wider Chicana/o movement, the Black civil rights movement, the federal government's War on Poverty, anti-Vietnam War sentiments, the women's movement, and political struggles in Mexico and Latin America. At the same time, expanding economic opportunity for low-income citizens and people of color became the main focus of federal social policy, and education emerged as the fundamental mechanism for combating poverty and racial inequality (Wise, 1982).

Throughout the Southwest, Chicana/o students and their communities struggled to call attention to and improve the poor quality of public education offered to them. In March 1968, well over ten thousand Chicana/o students walked out of East Los Angeles high schools to protest inferior schooling conditions. The students boycotted classes and presented a list of grievances to the Los Angeles Board of Education. The list consisted of thirty-six demands, including smaller class sizes, bilingual education, an end to the vocational tracking of Chicana/o students, more emphasis on Chicano history, and community control of schools (McCurdy, 1968). The East L.A. walkouts focused national attention on the K–12 schooling of Chicanas/os and also set a precedent for school boycotts throughout the Southwest, including those in Crystal City and San Antonio, Texas; Denver, Colorado; and Phoenix, Arizona (Acuña, 1988).

Though their stories are often excluded in written historical accounts, Chicanas played crucial leadership roles in these mass demonstrations and were intimately involved in the struggles for educational justice. Celeste Baca, Vickie Castro, Paula Crisóstomo, Mita Cuarón, Tanya Luna Mount, Rosalinda Méndez González, Rachel Ochoa Cervera, and Cassandra Zacarías were but a few of the women who made up the East L.A. student leadership. They engaged in networking, organizing, and developing consciousness; held elected and appointed offices; and acted as spokespersons (Delgado Bernal, 1997). For example, Paula Crisóstomo and Rosalinda Méndez González both provided testimony to the U.S. Commission on Civil Rights regarding the education of Mexican American students. Méndez González described the racist curriculum and popular stereotypes of Chicanas/os in this way:

From the time we first begin attending school, we hear about how great and wonderful our United States is, about our democratic American heritage, but little about our splendid and magnificent Mexican heritage and culture. We look for others like ourselves in these history books, for something to be proud of for being

a Mexican, and all we see in books and magazines, films, and T.V. shows are stereotypes of a dark, dirty, smelly man with a tequila bottle in one hand, a dripping taco in the other, a serape wrapped around him, and a big sombrero. (California State Advisory Committee, 1968)

Chicana students resisted both racist school policies and sexist educational practices. Artist Patssi Valdez, who participated in the East L.A. walkouts, remembers what her home economics teacher told her and other Chicanas: "She would say. . . . 'You little Mexicans, you better learn and pay attention. This class is very important . . . most of you are going to be cooking and cleaning for other people'" (Valdez, 1994). The teacher's comments illustrate the intersecting forms of subordination that have historically influenced the schooling of Chicanas.[6] Because they were female, Mexican, and working class, the teacher expected Chicana students to prepare themselves for domestic labor that met the needs of White middle- and upper-class families. Chicana students struggled against sexism not only in the wider society, but also within the Chicana/o community. Within the movement and various student organizations, Chicanas had to actively reject the traditional roles to which they were often relegated by their male peers. One Chicana stated, "My male friends at the time, in the organization, would try to put me in female roles. Like be the secretary, make the sandwiches, do that. But . . . I always challenged. And when I would see that there were no women involved, boom, I made myself right there" (Delgado Bernal, in press).

Chicana/o student activism also played a crucial role in gaining access to institutions of higher education. As Chicana/o students across the Southwest demanded equitable K–12 schooling, they likewise demanded their place in colleges and universities. Prior to this time, Mexican students were virtually absent from institutions of higher education. After World War II, the G.I. Bill gave a few Chicanao servicemen access to college, and by 1958, "California enrolled nearly 36,000 college freshman of Mexican-American origin, several more than in Texas" (Weinberg, 1977, p. 341, cited in Webster, 1984, p. 42).[7] Less than a decade later, in 1967, one of the first Chicana/o college student organizations, the Mexican American Student Association (MASA), was formed at East Los Angeles Community College (Gómez-Quiñones, 1978). College student organizations rapidly formed in California and throughout the Southwest, including organizations such as United Mexican-American Students (UMAS) in California and the Mexican-American Youth Organization (MAYO) in Texas. The primary issue of these organizations was the lack of Chicana/o access to quality education, and their activities revolved around the institutionalization of Chicano Studies and support programs for Chicana/o students (López, 1977).

As a result of the development of Chicana/o student organizations, the East L.A. school walkouts in 1968, and Chicana/o student activism in general, there was a statewide student conference in Santa Barbara, California, in 1969. Rosalinda Méndez González remembers that she, like many young Chicanas, actively participated in the conference and that "the Santa Barbara conference . . . was like everybody coming together to reconceptualize the schools and higher education for our communities" (Méndez González, 1995, p. 37). At this conference, students, faculty, administrators, and community representatives produced a 150-page document called *El Plan de Santa Bárbara: A Chicano Plan for Higher Education* (Chicano Coordinating Council, 1970). *El Plan* provided the theoretical rationale for the development of Chicano Studies, a plan for recruitment and admission of Chicano students, support programs to aid in the retention of Chicano students, and the organization of Chicano Studies curricula and departments. Another significant result of the Santa Barbara conference and *El Plan* was the unification of Chicano student organizations and the creation of Movimiento Estudiantil Chicano de Aztlán (MEChA). MEChA's goal was to link all Chicano student groups throughout the Southwest and "to socialize and politicize Chicano students on their particular campus to the ideals of the [Chicano] movement" (Chicano Coordinating Council, 1970, p. 60).

El Plan offered a vision and course of action for Chicanos in higher education, one of the first of its kind among the Chicana/o community. However, it was confined in its scope, reflecting a limited consciousness by not including references to women, female liberation, or Chicana Studies (Pardo, 1984). Some have called it a "*man*ifesto" for its grounding in traditional cultural nationalism, rather than an ideology that works toward the elimination of all forms of oppression (Orozco, 1986). In the early 1970s, in response to the absence of women in the curriculum, Chicana activists at a Chicano Studies/MEChA conference at California State University, Northridge, proposed five courses on La Chicana, including The Chicana in Education, The Chicana and the Law, and Religion and la Mujer. They also proposed a requirement that all

Chicano Studies majors take at least one class on La Chicana (Nieto Gómez, 1973).

At the national level, Chicanas were also addressing the unique needs of Chicana students in attaining high school and/or higher education. At the National Women's Political Caucus Convention in 1973, the Chicana Caucus consisted of sixty women from seven states, including Texas, New Mexico, Illinois, and California. The Chicana Caucus submitted a resolution requesting that legislative efforts of the organization include: a) research on the educational needs of Chicanas; b) recruitment of Chicanas to higher education; c) financial support for the education of Chicanas; d) tutorial and counseling programs designed for Chicanas; e) incorporation of Chicana culture into educational systems and textbooks; and f) inclusion of Chicanas in all affirmative action activity (Chapa, 1973). In this way, the women of the Chicana Caucus attempted to address the unique problems that confronted Chicana students by shaping national social policy.

Throughout the 1960s and early 1970s, Chicana/o activism and Chicana feminist ideas merged with social policies to better address the needs of Chicana/o students and increase their access to institutions of higher education. During the Kennedy administration and President Johnson's War on Poverty, affirmative action attempted to equalize the playing field in the realm of higher education. Federal legislation helped facilitate Chicana/o participation in higher education. The Higher Education Act of 1965, among other things, authorized several financial aid programs, and Title VII extended the Civil Rights Act of 1964 to include all educational institutions. Federal and state programs were created, such as the Educational Opportunities Program (EOP), which played a critical role in recruiting and retaining Chicana/o students into universities and colleges. EOP and programs similar to it were the initial bridges that brought Chicana/o students into higher education in more visible numbers (Acuña, 1988). At the same time, as social activism and social policies were opening the doors to higher education, a number of social forces were also shaping bilingual education.

SOCIAL FORCES SHAPING BILINGUAL EDUCATION

The struggle by Chicanas/os to obtain bilingual education in public schools began with the social activism and policies of the 1960s. Historian Guadalupe San Miguel

(1985) proposes that two views on bilingualism came into conflict and contributed to the formation of policies on bilingual education. The "assimilationist" perspective, discussed earlier, continued to uphold the post–World War II belief that bilingualism was divisive and un-American, a disability rather than an asset. Shared by associations of school administrators and their supporters, this view held that language and culture were incidental to the teaching and learning process. It did not recognize the value or utility of incorporating the language and culture of limited-English-speaking students into the public school curriculum. As discussed earlier in this chapter, prior to the late 1960s there were no bilingual programs for Mexican students, and it was routine to segregate Mexican students based on their perceived language deficiency. In fact, during the 1940s and 1950s, LULAC and Mexican educators such as Joe Bernal did not support bilingual instruction in public schools. The assimilationist ideology left students believing that speaking Spanish in school was an evil they had to avoid at all costs. Writer and poet José Antonio Burciaga (1993) articulates the pain experienced by students when their schooling was regulated by the assimilationist beliefs that devalued Spanish:

> Perhaps the most memorable experiences one has in school are those that come into direct conflict with one's family's beliefs and traditions. . . . No learning experience was more painful or damaging than the silence imposed on our Mexican culture, history and beautiful Spanish language. To speak Spanish was not only illegal but also a sin: "Bless me father, for I have sinned. I spoke Spanish in class and during recess. . . . *Mea culpa, Mea culpa, mea máxima culpa!*" (pp. 36, 40)

A second view on bilingualism in the 1960s, the "pluralist" perspective, accepted the plurality of languages as a necessary ingredient in U.S. education. This view was embraced by most Chicana/o communities and political allies (San Miguel, 1985). Pluralists viewed the first language and culture of the child as essential to the instructional and learning process. During the late 1960s, some educators, sociolinguists, and Chicana/o communities created a philosophical force that openly challenged the commonly held assimilationist perspective. Chicana/o student activism focused on poor educational conditions, racist school policies, and the implementation of bilingual education. Chicanas/os began to regard language as a matter

of self-determination and language as a basic human right. Educator Reynaldo Macías has suggested that language rights can be based on "the right to freedom from discrimination on the basis of language" and "the right to use your language(s) in the activities of communal life" (1979, pp. 88–89). For many Chicanas/os, the right to maintain Spanish was a way of declaring some control over their lives and rejecting the colonized relationship between Chicanas/os and the dominant society. Whatever the justification, bilingual education offered some hope that Chicana/o schooling would be more meaningful and lead to educational equity.

With much political pressure from Chicana/o communities and liberal educators who held a pluralist perspective, the federal government, for the first time, funded bilingual education in 1968 through Title VII of the Elementary and Secondary Education Act of 1965 (Crawford, 1992). The 1968 Bilingual Education Act provided money to train teachers and aides, to develop instructional materials, and to establish parent-involvement projects (Loya, 1990). The Act was meant "to develop and carry out new and imaginative elementary and secondary school programs . . . [for] children of limited English-speaking ability" (Crawford, 1992, p. 85). However, the act did not impose teaching methods or even define the concept of bilingual education. In addition, the bill was viewed as a compensatory educational program in which linguistically "disadvantaged" children were assisted.

It is often argued that civil rights legislation has been very modest in its efforts to eliminate inequalities and often serves those in power as much if not more than those it is actually supposed to serve (Crenshaw, Gotanda, Peller, & Thomas, 1995; Matsuda, Lawrence, Delgado, & Crenshaw, 1993). For example, in most Chicana/o communities, bilingual education represented a way to maintain one's language and culture and was by definition a rejection of colonization. However, the official goals of bilingual education emanating from federal and state bilingual education guidelines from 1968 to the present have never included the maintenance of the student's first language. An early controversy in the House and Senate revolved around whether bilingual education was simply a better way to teach English or a means to preserve a student's first language, which might create unwanted ethnic pluralism. In fact, one of the sponsors of the original 1968 Bilingual Education Act was careful to state during the deliberation of the bill, "It is not the purpose of the bill to create pockets of different language throughout the country . . . not to stamp out the mother tongue and not to make their mother tongue the dominant language, but just to try to make these children fully literate in English, so that the children can move into the mainstream of American life" (Crawford, 1992, p. 84). Even during the mid-1970s, when bilingual education enjoyed its greatest level of support, native-language instruction was only seen as a necessary strategy that allowed a child to achieve competence in English (Roos, 1978). Never has federal or state legislation stated that bilingual education should help students maintain their first language to become bilingual and biliterate citizens. Yet, paradoxically, during the 1960s, the federal government spent millions of dollars trying to ensure a bilingual populace by calling for foreign-language requirements and well-funded foreign language departments in select high schools and most universities (Crawford, 1992; Schaller, Scharff & Schulzinger, 1992). These efforts, supported by the Cold War and the 1958 National Defense Education Act, certainly benefited middle-class Whites more than those Spanish-speaking students who started school already fluent in a "foreign" language.

In order to compel school officials to provide bilingual education, Chicanas/os have brought lawsuits under Title VI of the Civil Rights Act, which bans discrimination based "on the ground of race, color, or national origin" in "any program or activity receiving Federal financial assistance."[8] In the 1974 *Lau v. Nichols* case, non-English-speaking students of Chinese ancestry brought suit against the San Francisco Unified School District. The plaintiffs charged that where students were taught only in English, school officials had not taken significant action to provide a meaningful education. The U.S. Supreme Court unanimously found that by "failing to affirmatively overcome the English language deficiencies of national origin-minority group children with limited English-speaking ability, school officials violated Title VI of the Civil Rights Act" (Roos, 1978, p. 116). The court handed down this decision even though the school district had made an effort to remedy language difficulties by providing supplemental English instruction to about one thousand of the 2,856 Chinese students who did not speak English. About 1,800 students, however did not receive any special instruction, which was a violation of Title VI of the Civil Rights Act. The decision helped to establish a precedent, though it did not provide a specific remedy to assist students with limited English proficiency.

Chicanas/os in New Mexico used the *Lau* decision in *Serna v. Portales Municipal Schools* (1974) to seek an order requiring the district to provide bilingual and bicultural education under Title VI. Chicanas/os in the New Mexico community felt that the school district's English as a Second Language (ESL) remedy was an inadequate response to the educational needs of Chicana/o students. And expert witnesses testified that when a child "goes to school where he finds no evidence of his language and culture and ethnic group represented [she/he] becomes withdrawn and nonparticipating" (cited in Roos, 1978, p. 129). Using *Lau* as a precedent, the court held that the district's failure to offer a bilingual and bicultural educational program that provided Chicana/o students with a meaningful education deprived them of their rights under Title VI (Martínez, 1994). It is significant that the court once again decided against the school district, even though the latter was making an effort to provide a limited ESL program.

Legal indeterminacy has led to various judicial interpretations. Policies and law regarding bilingual education are indeterminate in that courts often permit a judge to exercise discretion in rendering vague standards and justifying multiple outcomes to lawsuits (Martínez, 1994). Such was the case in decisions that ignored or interpreted *Lau* and *Serna* differently. For example, *Keyes v. School District Number 1* (1973), although often thought of as a desegregation case, was similar to the *Lau* and *Serna* cases.[9] The Chicana/o plaintiffs "alleged that the Denver school board's failure to adopt a bilingual and bicultural program constituted a violation of Title VI" (Martínez, 1994, p. 608). In 1975 the 10th Circuit Court of Appeals found that the district had implemented various programs to address the needs of students with limited English proficiency (as did the school districts in *Lau* and *Serna*), and therefore was not in violation of Title VI. The *Keyes* decision, made by the same circuit that affirmed the extensive bilingual and bicultural education programs in *Serna*, failed to discuss the *Serna* and *Lau* decisions and did not explain how its ruling was consistent or inconsistent with those cases (Martínez, 1994). The *Keyes* case demonstrates that courts can and have exercised discretion to limit access to bilingual and bicultural education.[10]

CONSERVATIVE RETRENCHMENT

The sociopolitically conservative era that began in the mid-1970s and that hit hard during the Reagan and Bush administrations had a negative impact on

Chicana/o schooling conditions. A strong backlash against the social equity programs of President Johnson's War on Poverty was accompanied by increased military spending, reduced educational spending, and a growing recession. The conservatives regained a strong voice, which was reflected in social ideas, educational policy, and judicial decisions. As tension between desegregation and bilingual education intensified, the funding for bilingual education was drastically reduced and public school finance was re-stricted for Chicana/o schools. This left Chicana/o students in underfunded, segregated schools that failed to adequately prepare them for post-secondary education. At the same time, the myth of meritocracy in higher education and a growing attack on affirmative action programs also limited Chicana/o students' access to colleges and universities.

THE TENSION BETWEEN DESEGREGATION AND BILINGUAL EDUCATION

The desegregation process has usually been thought of as an issue pertinent only to African American communities, with Chicana/o students often being ignored in the process and in the educational literature. By the 1970s, more Chicana/o students attended second-rate segregated schools than at the time of the 1947 *Méndez* decision. In fact, many Chicana/o scholars and activists believe that the *Brown* decision had no effect on the schooling of Chicana/o students until the 1970s, when the courts were forced to decide how to treat Chicana/o students in the desegregation process (Acuña, 1988). *Cisneros v. Corpus Christi Independent School District* was filed in 1968 by Chicana/o labor activists in Corpus Christi, Texas, and was decided in 1970 at the federal district court level. The plaintiffs challenged the legal framework for future desegregation cases and the segregation of Chicana/o and African American school children in Corpus Christi. The court ruled that Chicanas/os were an identifiable ethnic minority and found them to be unconstitutionally segregated in the public schools. It also required that an appropriate desegregation plan that included Anglos, Chicanas/os, and African Americans be submitted (San Miguel, 1987). Prior to this case, the strategy employed in most successful school desegregation efforts was based on Chicanas/os' claim to "Whiteness."[11]

The U.S. Supreme Court reinforced how Chicana/o students were to be treated in the school desegregation process in the 1973 *Keyes v. School District*

Number 1 case. Before *Keyes*, Denver Public Schools, like many schools throughout the Southwest, integrated Chicana/o students with African American students and called it desegregation. The Court either had to define Chicana/o students as "Caucasians—and integrate them with African Americans or redefine their ethnic status (as a protected ethnic minority group) and integrate them with everyone else" (Donato, 1997, p. 124). In *Keyes*, the Supreme Court decided that Chicana/o students were an identifiable minority group and ruled that they had been denied their constitutional rights by the Denver Public Schools. The court authorized racial-balance remedies and required districts to integrate African Americans and Chicanas/os into White urban school districts.

It is important to note that after these decisions and throughout the 1970s, there was growing tension between the pursuit of bilingual education and school desegregation. During the 1930s and 1940s, Mexicans fought school segregation in the courts in such cases as *Alvarez v. Lemon Grove* (1931), *Del Rio Independent School District v. Salvatierra* (1931), *Méndez v. Westminster School District* (1947), and *Delago et al. v. Bastrop* (1948). A few decades later, Chicanas/os began to see bilingual education as key to the quest for equal education, and judicial decisions such as those in *Lau* and *Serna* placed responsibility for meeting the needs of students with limited English proficiency on the schools. After a difficult struggle to obtain the right to bilingual instruction, many Chicana/o communities were suspicious of desegregation efforts that might disperse Chicana/o students without considering their need for bilingual education.[12] Parents and policymakers argued that bilingual education and desegregation might not be fully compatible. Desegregation usually meant "scattering Black students to provide instruction in 'racially balanced' settings. Bilingual education, on the other hand, has usually meant the clustering of Spanish-speaking students so they could receive instruction through their native language" (Zerkel, 1977, p. 181, cited in Donato, Menchaca, & Valencia, 1991). By the mid-1970s, enforcement of both the *Brown* and *Lau* decisions led to more complications than policymakers originally anticipated, as Chicana/o students were resegregated based on language within desegregated schools (Donato et al., 1991). This was an ironic result of desegregation and bilingual education efforts, and depending on one's educational philosophy, either desegregation or bilingual education could be openly supported. For example, education policymakers who opposed bilingual education could avoid it by scattering limited-English-proficient students throughout their districts in the name of desegregation. At the same time, someone who opposed mixing White and Chicana/o students in the same classroom could use the opportunity to segregate Chicana/o students in bilingual classrooms, thus using the same old racially motivated rationale for separating Mexican children from White students based on their perceived language deficiency (see Donato, 1997).

By the early 1980s, the tension between desegregation and bilingual education was receiving increasingly more attention. Though some educators throughout the Southwest were optimistic that the two could work together, there was little time to successfully produce meaningful results in meeting the needs of Chicana/o students. During the 1980s, assimilationist educators and politicians gained the upper hand; bilingual education was under strong attack, and financial support for it was being drastically reduced. The 1980s provided a political climate in which community activism was difficult and bilingual education suffered many setbacks. In the words of Chicana feminist writer Ana Castillo:

> In 1980 when the Republicans and the Reagan administration came to office, their tremendous repression quashed the achievements of the Chicano/Latino Movement. . . . Community projects and grassroots programs dependent on government funding—rehabilitation and training, child care, early education and alternative schooling, youth counseling, cultural projects that supported the arts and community artists, rehab-housing for low income families, and women's shelters—shut down. (1994, p. 31)

Under the Reagan administration, while the government spent billions of dollars on the military, Title VII bilingual education funding was cut from $167 million in 1980 to $133 million in 1986, representing more than a 20 percent reduction (Loya, 1990)—this at a time when the number of English learners was greatly increasing. In California alone, students with limited English proficiency increased nearly 75 percent, from 326,000 in 1980 to 568,000 in 1986 (California State Department of Education, 1993).

EDUCATIONAL INEQUITY IN THE 1970S AND BEYOND

At the same time that bilingual education was under attack and suffering reduced financial support, the conservative retrenchment also attacked public school finance. In order to compel school officials to provide educational equity, Chicanas/os brought lawsuits under the equal protection clause. In Colorado, Josie Luján, one of the lead plaintiffs in *Luján et al. v. Colorado State Board of Education* (1979), along with a handful of parents charged that the Colorado school finance system violated the equal protection clause of the U.S. and Colorado Constitutions because of the extreme funding disparities among school districts in the state. Lower per-pupil expenditures existed in districts with high Chicana/o student enrollment. Though the district court ruled in favor of the plaintiffs, in 1982 the State Supreme Court of Colorado held that the financing system was constitutionally permissible, thus leaving the system virtually unchanged. Luján did, however, win a seat on the local school board and she became an education advocate for Chicana/o students (Espinosa, 1979).

In another key school finance case, *Serrano v. Priest* (1971), John Serrano sued the California state treasurer on the grounds that his son received an inferior education in East Los Angeles because the state school finance system was based on financing schools through local property taxes. He alleged that, due to the differential property values and resulting tax base, children were given unequal treatment and resources in poor districts that did not have as high a tax base and funding as wealthier districts (Acuña, 1988). In 1971, the California Supreme Court ruled in his favor, finding that "financing primarily through local property taxes failed to provide equal protection under the law" (Acuña, 1988, p. 389). The U.S. Supreme Court upheld the *Serrano* decision in 1976, but limited its decision to California, stating that the finance system violated the state's equal protection clause by denying equal access to education. *Serrano*, however, brought few changes to Chicana/o schools because wealthier districts still had better facilities, more experienced teachers, and less overcrowding. Soon after, in 1978, California's Proposition 13 applied a taxation cap that in effect restricted funding for all districts in California. By the late 1980s, California ranked eighth nationally in per capita income, but spent only 3.8 percent of its income on public education—placing it forty-sixth among the fifty states (Kozol, 1991). Although educators and researchers do not agree about whether there is a causal relationship between educational expenditures and the quality of education, there is widespread agreement that Chicanas/os are generally subjected to inferior educational conditions in poorly funded schools (De La Roas & Maw, 1990; Valencia, 1991).

San Antonio Independent School District v. Rodrí-guez is a class-action suit filed in 1968 by Demetrio Rodríguez and other parents on behalf of their children who were students in the Edgewood School District, which was poor and 96 percent non-White. At the time, San Antonio had several school districts segregated along class and racial/ethnic lines. Edgewood was among the poorest, while Alamo Heights, with a predominately White student population was the richest (Acuña, 1988). The Mexican American Legal Defense and Educational Fund (MALDEF) argued on behalf of the Edgewood parents that the Texas finance system taxed residents of the poor Edgewood district at a higher rate than it taxed residents of Alamo Heights. In addition, per-pupil spending was much lower in Edgewood than in the wealthier district. Even with the minimum provided by the state, Edgewood spent only $231 per pupil, while Alamo Heights was able to spend $543 on each pupil (Kozol, 1991). The state public school financing practices were challenged and presented as a violation of the federal equal protection clause of the U.S. Constitution. The district court ruled in favor of Rodríguez and the other parents, and found that Texas was in violation of the equal protection clause. However, the decision was overruled by the U.S. Supreme Court in 1973. The Court's five-to-four decision in *Rodríguez* is especially noteworthy because it signaled the end of an era of progressive change and set the tone for educational inequity during the 1980s and 1990s.

A number of other factors promoted the educational inequity of Chicana/o students in the 1980s and into the 1990s. For example, Chicana/o schools that were among the most severely underfunded were also the most overcrowded, offering a limited curriculum with few resources (Achievement Council, 1984; Assembly Office of Research, 1990). Chicana/o and other Latina/o students were disproportionately retained for at least one grade and were seldom exposed to enriched curricula or pedagogy (Achievement Council, 1984; Assembly Office of Research, 1985). There were few Chicana/o and other Latina/o teachers and administrators in California's schools (California State Department of Education, 1985, 1988). Throughout the Southwest, Chicana/o students were highly unlikely to have Chicana/o teachers to act as mentors, since Latinas/os made up only 2.9 percent of all public school teachers in the country (De La Rosa & Maw, 1990). Cassandra Zacarías, a high school counselor who went through school in the 1960s, remembers that as a student she too lacked role models in school:

When I was in high school I never felt like there was anybody that was like me who was a teacher, or counselor, or principal. I mean there was, I don't know, maybe a couple of Latinos that were teachers and it always seemed really sad to me. (Delgado Bernal, 1997, p. 160).

Chicanas/os and other high school students of color continue to report that they feel their teachers, school staff, and peers neither like nor understand them, and many of their teachers admit to not always understanding ethnically diverse students (University of California, Latino Eligibility Task Force, 1995).

In addition, the continued school tracking of Chicana/o students into vocational programs and into special education programs for learning-disabled students has prompted educational, social, and economic inequities for such students, and has limited their access to higher education (Aguirre, 1980; González, 1990; Mitchell, Powell, Scott, & McDaid, 1994; Oakes, 1985). Throughout the Southwest, Chicana/o students in K–12 schools have been systematically tracked into courses that do not provide an environment or curriculum that prepares them for the post-secondary level (Aguirre & Martínez, 1993; Oakes, 1985). Indeed, 75 percent of all Latina/o high school seniors in 1980 had been enrolled in a curricular program that made a college education improbable (Orum, 1986). For those Chicanas/os who enrolled in a post-secondary institution, half attended a community college instead of a four-year institution (Astin, 1982; Durán, 1983).

The use of a "counterstory" (Delgado, 1989) demonstrates how the secondary school context continues to promote the educational inequality of Chicana/o students and limits access to higher education.[13] Gloria Martínez, a Chicana and first-generation college student, compares her journey to higher education with the path of her White, middle-class roommate.[14] Her story describes the secondary experiences of most Chicanas/os:

One day during first semester of my freshman year, my roommate and I were sitting in our dorm room talking about our high schools. I already knew that we had very different life experiences, but I could barely believe the huge contrast between our two schools. She had attended a suburban upper middle-class high school and I went to an urban high school in a predominantly working-class Chicano community. During high school my roommate took two years of Japanese and had her choice of Spanish, French, Italian, German, and Chinese. I took Spanish in high school. I was already semi-bilingual in Spanish before I took it, but my only other choice was French, and I figured I wouldn't have much need for it. She said her high school's science department was chaired by a former NASA scientist and offered biology, chemistry, physics, geology, biochemistry, and astronomy. I was in the honors track and I was only offered biology and chemistry. Most of my friends were told to just take general science. The math department at my school was limited as the science department, while hers offered algebra, geometry, algebra II, trigonometry, calculus, and statistics. Some of these were advanced placement [AP] courses so she was able to start our freshman year with several units of university credits. There were no AP classes at my high school, only honors courses that did not carry college credit. She enjoyed great electives like journalism and computer programming, because her school had up-to-date technology and lots of computers. They also had college counselors who helped students complete college and scholarship applications, enroll and take the college entrance exams, and get information materials from various in- and out-of-state colleges. The counselors at my high school had such a heavy student load that it was impossible to get an appointment with them, and college advising just wasn't their priority. My *tía* [aunt] who'd just started going to a local community college is the one who advised me and helped me apply for college.

After that conversation with my roommate, I remember feeling like I'd been shafted, not by my roommate, but by my high school or maybe the whole educational system. It seemed really unfair that my roommate came to the university so prepared and here I was struggling with the lower division courses. I knew I was a really smart person, did really well in high school, and was dedicated to my studies. But sometimes I doubted myself, and I wondered if I really belonged in this university. I used to wonder if the only people who could actually succeed in college were the ones who had backgrounds similar to my roommate. Sometimes I questioned whether or not I deserved my spot in the university and if in fact I could succeed.

The precollege experience of Chicanas/os continues to differ vastly from that of middle-class White students, and Gloria's experience illuminates what numerous studies have found: college access and successful college participation for Chicana/o students is severely limited by an inferior secondary school education.[15] By tracking Chicana/o middle and high school students into low-ability classes, they are not given enough exposure to the academic subjects, critical thinking skills, and writing skills that are needed to do well on college entrance exams or in a college classroom (Durán, 1983). Access to college by Chicana/o students today is also limited by the myth of meritocracy and the attack on affirmative action.

MERITOCRACY AND CHICANA/O COLLEGE STUDENTS

In higher education, meritocratic values often contradict the fundamental educational mission of developing students' knowledge. Meritocracy is a system of rewards presumably based solely on ability and talent, so that rewards go to those who "perform the best." Meritocratic values drive a wide range of educational practices such as testing, grading, admissions, and ability tracking, all in the spirit of "equality." Higher education scholar Alexander Astin (1982) points out that advocates of a meritocratic higher education system often view education as an open competition, analogous to an intellectual footrace. All contestants are allowed to enter the race, and rewards go to the swiftest; however, he argues, certain realities about the competition are distorted. For example, Chicanas/os often never get to the starting line because of poor secondary school conditions. Limited school resources and tracking into vocational programs mean that Chicanas/os often fail to show up at the competition because they lack reliable information about the race. Many Chicanas/os who do start the race do not run well and struggle to remain in the race because of their inferior training and the fact that they were never given the complete rules of the game. And many Chicanas/os who participate and run well may still end up with a second-class award, since the race they have entered (community college) offers a very different trophy than the race in an Ivy League college (Astin, 1982).

It seems that most Americans do not question the myth of meritocracy in higher education, believing that admissions decisions are fair and based solely on comparing one's qualifications to a universal standard of excellence. An important and often overlooked reality in a meritocratic system, however, is the fact that "merit" is socially constructed and standards of competition are set by those in power. For example, in higher education, SAT/ACT scores and a student's high school grade point average have traditionally been the standard by which students are admitted to college. SAT/ACT scores have been used as a standard despite an abundance of research that shows that these scores are not good predictors of college success for Chicanas/os, and that standardized testing in general has had a negative impact on Chicana/o students (Aguirre, 1980; Durán, 1983; Goldman & Hewitt, 1975; Goldman & Richards, 1974; González, 1974; Valencia & Aburto, 1991). In fact, high school preparation and testing and admission standards have been cited as two of the largest barriers to higher education for Chicanas/os and other Latinas/os (Orum, 1986). In California, the SAT has been a barrier for eligibility and participation in the University of California for Chicanas/os since it was incorporated into UC admissions requirements in 1968 (University of California, Latino Eligibility Task Force, 1997). Yet, it seems that many people perceive the UC system to be a fair and meritocratic one, based on a universal standard of excellence (the SAT).

"Reverse discrimination" is only claimed by Whites and conservatives when they perceive that an allegedly fair and meritocratic system is being threatened. During the late 1970s, *Regents of the University of California v. Bakke* (1978) popularized the discourse of "reverse discrimination" and the growing public opinion that higher education had overstepped its bounds in creating opportunities for women and students of color. After Alan Bakke, a 34-year-old White engineer, applied to and was rejected by thirteen medical schools, a White administrator at the University of California, Davis, suggested he sue, as presumably less qualified students of color had been admitted. Bakke challenged the special admissions program that set aside sixteen slots out of one hundred for "disadvantaged" students. The special admissions program had been initiated just six years before his lawsuit, and prior to the program only three students of color had been admitted (Acuña, 1988). In 1978, the U.S. Supreme Court issued a somewhat ambiguous opinion in the *Bakke* case. The university's set-aside program was found to be illegal, and the university was directed to admit Bakke. Yet, the Court also ruled that race could be used in admissions provided that it was not the sole selection factor. The *Bakke* decision reflected growing public opinion

that higher education had "gone too far" in trying to accommodate the special needs of "minorities" and was a precursor of the discourse of "reverse discrimination" today (Astin, 1982).

WHERE WE ARE TODAY

Today, there is evidence that points to modest progress. More Chicanas/os and other Latinas/os are going to college; most major universities in the Southwest offer some type of Chicana/o Studies courses; and more Chicana/o scholars are writing about and documenting the life experiences of Chicanas/os. In California, more Latina/o students are graduating from high schools, more are taking the SAT and ACT tests, and more are becoming eligible for the California community college and state university system (University of California, Latino Eligibility Task Force, 1995). These improvements are modest, however, particularly when contrasted with the proportional growth of the Chicana/o population over the last fifty years. Moreover, attacks continue on the educational opportunities of and the quality of education offered to Chicana/o students. Presently, Chicanas/os are still considered to be the most unlikely racial/ethnic group to finish high school, to attend college, and to graduate from college (Chapa, 1991; Gándara, 1994). From the civil rights era to the present, it is safe to say that public schools have continued to constantly fail Chicana/o students at every point in the educational pipeline. The current anti-Latino and anti-immigrant beliefs manifested in California's Propositions 187, 209, and 227 continue to shape public policy that directly affects Chicana/o communities' educational, economic, political, and social well-being. Although such legislation and policy initiatives seem to issue primarily from California, it is significant for all Latinas/os in the United States because California appears to be setting a national public policy standard (Brownstein, 1995; García, 1995).

AN EXTENDED FORM OF SCHOOL SEGREGATION: CALIFORNIA'S PROPOSITION 187

Even the school segregation statistics of the late 1980s and the prediction that "the segregation of Chicano students will intensify in the years ahead" (Valencia,

1991, p. 7) did not prepare us for California's public referendum that attempted to push Chicana/o school segregation toward Chicana/o school exclusion. In the early 1990s, then Governor Pete Wilson and a group of "concerned" California residents tired of undocumented immigrants began the Save Our State (SOS) movement, which put Proposition 187 on the 1994 California ballot. Proponents of 187 argued that "illegal aliens" were unfairly benefiting from state resources and were crowding their children out of public schools. Proposition 187 attempted to extend the segregation of Chicana/o students by denying public education to anyone attending a public elementary, secondary, or post-secondary school who was "reasonably suspected" to be an "illegal alien" in the United States. In addition, Proposition 187 required teachers and other officials to report those who were suspected of being in this country without proper immigration documents. These educational sections of the initiative were in direct conflict with the U.S. Supreme Court's 1982 decision in *Plyler v. Doe*, which held that the state of Texas could not bar undocumented children from public elementary schools because doing so violates the Equal Protection Clause of the Fourteenth Amendment. The authors of Proposition 187 put forth the initiative knowing *Plyler* was a legal precedent that provided protection for undocumented students to attend public schools. In fact, one of the goals of the proposition's authors was to call on a more politically conservative Supreme Court to overturn the *Plyler* decision (Prince, 1994).

Supporters of Proposition 187 also contended that the measure had nothing to do with race/ethnicity, arguing that it was merely an attempt to save scarce state resources. However, opponents viewed the initiative as an attack on racial and cultural minorities, and saw it as part of a historical continuum of race-based immigration and education policies (García, 1995). For example, using the term "illegal alien" demonizes undocumented immigrants as criminals. Just as de jure segregation conveyed an idea of the inferiority of Mexican students, Proposition 187 criminalized undocumented immigrants and those who are suspected of being "illegal aliens": "If we assume that undocumented immigrants are a criminal element, then we are automatically accepting that the existing . . . laws are just and fair" (Bosco, 1994, cited in García, 1995, p. 118). Indeed, Proposition 187 was not a race-neutral law and would have disproportionately affected Chicanas/os, Latinas/os, and other people of color who are stereotyped as "illegal aliens."

Though the initiative passed by a margin of 59 percent to 41 percent, there was a tremendous amount of community action and mobilization against it. Students all over the state engaged in demonstrations, walkouts, and protests. Lilian Ramírez, a student who protested at San Francisco's city hall shortly after the passage of Proposition 187, believes that the proposition provided an "open season for racism" (Gutekunst, 1994). The 1994 student resistance to Proposition 187 was similar to the student resistance of the 1960s I have chronicled earlier in this chapter. In both cases, students were motivated to transform existing conditions (or a law) that devalued their sociocultural experiences and limited their access to quality education.

In fact, California's passage of Proposition 187 was the epitome of the educational segregation that Chicanas/os have historically resisted in their efforts to gain their constitutional right to an equal public education. The passage of Proposition 187 brought to the forefront a racist state law that attempted to dehumanize all Latina/o students and exclude them from public education. Similar measures followed in other states, as did calls for reduction in funding for bilingual education and the implementation of English-only policies (García, 1995). In California, MALDEF and the American Civil Liberties Union (ACLU) were key in pursuing legal action against the proposition, and the five lawsuits filed against the state were consolidated into one federal action. U.S. District Judge Mariana Pfaelzer recently ruled that the proposition was "unconstitutional from top to bottom" because the state has no power to regulate immigration ("Judge dumps," 1998). The 1994 student walkouts and assemblies in protest of Proposition 187 and the state and federal lawsuits filed against its passage illustrate the various actions taken by Chicanas/os to obtain equal access to public education. Certainly the legal challenges to Proposition 187, and its defeat in the courts, indicates that these grassroots and legal strategies can be successful and continue to be crucial in Chicanas/os pursuit for educational equity.

LIMITED ACCESS TO HIGHER EDUCATION: CALIFORNIA'S PROPOSITION 209

Today, the discourse of "reverse discrimination" is as strong as ever, and California leads the national movement to dismantle affirmative action programs. In

1996, California voters passed Proposition 209, the California Civil Rights Initiative. Proposition 209 appropriates the language of early civil rights legislation to, in essence, eliminate all affirmative action in California, including that in higher education. It states that California shall not use "race, sex, color, ethnicity, or national origin as criterion for either discriminating against, or granting preferential treatment to any individual or group." While the legislation outlaws considerations of race/ethnicity in university admissions, outreach, and recruitment, it also ignores current societal inequalities. The anti-affirmative action legislation and its proponents adopted a narrow interpretation of the equal protection clause, embracing a colorblind constitution and the myth of meritocracy. Therefore, supporters are able to argue simultaneously that they strongly support equal opportunity for people of all color and that affirmative action policies violate a White man's right to equal protection, resulting in "reverse discrimination."

Proposition 209 legislates restricted access for Chicanas/os and other students of color at a time when college campuses remain racially stratified. Few middle- and upper-class Whites complain that throughout the Southwest at least 50 percent of all Chicanas/os who go to college go to a community college rather than a four-year institution (Astin, 1982; Olivas, 1986; Villalpando, 1996). The proposition is a specific political action supported by the meritocracy myth, and it validates a subjective and highly selective admissions process that tracks Chicanas/os into community colleges and keeps the gate to four-year campuses guarded. The admission policies at the "gate-keeper" schools, such as the University of California system, exert a powerful and controlling influence over who enters certain professions and who has access to positions of influence and economic and social reward.

Proposition 209's attack on affirmative action policies applies to the state's system of public employment, public education, or public contracting. Astin (1982, 1995) warns, however, that we should not confuse college admissions with employment and must acknowledge that discrimination in college admissions is often based on something other than a racial/ethnic classification:

> The employer seeks to exploit talent by hiring the best applicants; the public university seeks to develop the talents of the students it admits. University admissions are inherently discriminatory anyway, simply because there are not enough places for all applicants. . . . More than 95% of the 21,445 freshman admitted to the UC system last fall met . . . eligibility requirements. The 953 who did not meet them included athletes; students with artistic, musical, or other special talents; students with disabilities, and members of underrepresented minority groups. There were just as many white students among these 953 "special action" admits. (Astin, 1995, p. B5)

Proposition 209 limits access to education just as an increasing number of Chicana/o students are attending K–12 schools. In 1995, California's Latina/o student population was 2.3 million, and it is projected to reach 3.1 million by the year 2005 (University of California, Latino Eligibility Task Force, 1997). Yet only 3.9 percent of all Latina/o high school graduates were fully eligible for admission to the University of California, and the proportion of those admitted to four-year colleges appears to be declining nationally (Kerr, 1994; University of California, Latino Eligibility Task Force, 1997). These factors combine with the passage of Proposition 209 to create a great need for an overhaul in admission standards.

Legal scholar Richard Delgado (1995) argues for "an overhaul of the admissions process and a rethinking of the criteria that make a person a deserving . . . student" (p. 51). He and many others have argued for admission standards that would result in an increased number of women and students of color gaining admission, yet he points out that these recommendations are often ignored and have never instituted. In fact, the University of California Latino Eligibility Task Force (1997) recently recommended that the university system simply eliminate the SAT in determining eligibility without reducing overall admissions standards. The Task Force argued that the eligibility of Latina/o students could be greatly increased by eliminating the SAT and relying only on grade point average. Without the SAT, the proportion of Latina/o high school graduates achieving full eligibility to the University of California would rise by 59 percent (from 3.9 to 6.2 percent). So far the University system has not acted on the Task Force's recommendation, but throughout public policy, university, and community circles, additional recommendations focusing on bringing in "educationally and economically disadvantaged" students are being proposed.

THE LATEST THREAT TO BILINGUAL EDUCATION: CALIFORNIA'S PROPOSITION 227

Even with a growing number of students with limited English proficiency and expanding global borders that call for multilingual abilities, the threat to bilingual education is as strong as ever. In June 1998, California voters passed Proposition 227, the "English Language Education for Immigrant Children" initiative. The proposition was cosponsored by Ron Unz, a wealthy Silicon Valley businessman who unsuccessfully ran for governor of California in 1994, and Gloria Matta Tuchman, who failed in her first attempt to be elected State Superintendent of Public Instruction.[16] The proposition espouses the values of a just society while calling for the elimination of all bilingual education in the state of California. The proposition mandates that within sixty days of its passage, 1.38 million limited-English-speaking students be put into separate classrooms—regardless of age, language background, and/or academic ability (Citizens for an Educated America, 1997). In these separate classrooms, these students will be taught English by a teacher who will be restricted, under the threat of a lawsuit, from speaking to them in their primary language.

Supporters of the proposition claim to have in mind the best interests of children "regardless of their ethnicity or national origins" (Article I: b, c, f). However, Article 2, the crux of the proposition, requires a 180-day English-only approach and states that "all children in California public schools shall be taught English by being taught in English during a temporary transition period not normally intended to exceed one year." This requirement counters educational research that demonstrates that English immersion is one of the least effective ways to teach children with limited English proficiency (Cummins, 1981; Gándara, 1997; Krashen, 1981; Wong Fillmore, 1991). The initiative does away with all bilingual education and English-language development programs that do not meet its rigid 180-day English-only approach. It also allows local schools "to place in the same classroom English learners of different ages but whose degree of English proficiency is similar" (Article 2). This means that twelve-year-old boys and six-year-old girls of any language group, for example, can be placed in the same classroom for a full year (180 days) to study English, without any instruction in content areas such as math,

science, and social studies. Chicanas/os know from experience that placing all English-language learners into a separate classroom, regardless of age and academic abilities, and using rote memorization to teach English without academic instruction will fail because it was the standard process that failed miserably in the era of de jure segregation. Indeed, its failure was the reason why the federal Bilingual Education Act was passed just thirty years ago.

Today, Proposition 227 represents a distinct cultural attack on Chicanas/os and other Latinas/os, and creates yet another educational barrier imposed on Chicana/o students. For example, although Ron Unz and many other Proposition 227 supporters presented themselves as the voice of Latinos, arguing that Latinos supported the measure by an overwhelming majority, the actual Latino vote on the proposition was 63 percent "No" and 37 percent "Yes" (Pyle, McDonnell, & Tobar, 1998). The proposition was carried by a two-to-one vote among Whites in an electorate in which Whites represent a larger percentage than they represent in the general population. The victory of Proposition 227 will be a victory imposed on Latinos despite their opposition. In fact, Latino students will be disproportionately affected if the new law goes into effect because 80 percent of California's K–12 limited-English-proficient students are Spanish speakers (Gándara, 1997). There is, however, hope that the new law will not be enforced as a coalition of schoolchildren, and civil rights groups filed a lawsuit in federal court to challenge Proposition 227 the day after it was passed by voters. Three of the civil rights groups participating in the lawsuit are the California Latino Civil Rights Network, Mujeres Unidas y Activas, and the National Council of La Raza. Their lawsuit, which contends that Proposition 227 violates the U.S. Equal Educational Opportunities Act of 1974, Title VI of the Civil Rights Act of 1964, and the constitutional right to equal protection (Colvin & Smith, 1998), continues the historic tradition of Chicana/o community resistance and activism in their pursuit of an equitable and just educational system.

CONCLUSION

I have provided an overview of Chicana/o education from the 1950s through the 1990s and demonstrated a relationship between popular belief systems, judicial decisions, and educational policies and practices. Bilingual education, access to higher education, K–12 school equity, and continued school segregation have all been at the forefront during this period. Schooling for Chicanas/os has indeed improved since the era of de jure segregation, yet since the late 1970s there has been a deterioration of educational gains. Many of today's most important educational issues are similar to those voiced in Mexican communities before the 1950s. In fact, Jonathon Kozol states that in the realm of public schooling, "social policy has been turned back almost one hundred years" (1991, p. 4). In reality, the improvements in Chicana/o schooling have been modest and have not really kept pace with the demographic growth of the Chicana/o population.

Chicanas/os have a rich historical legacy that includes active struggles to gain equal access to quality education. A focus of the Chicana/o student movement was improving the quality of education at various points in the educational pipeline, and Chicanas were actively involved in and offered leadership to this movement. Over the past five decades, Chicano families have used the judicial system to fight educational practices that have limited the education of their children. They have utilized the courts to fight for bilingual education and school access and to fight against school segregation and schooling inequities. Today, Chicana/o students and their families have remained active in the pursuit of quality education through grassroots resistance and legal recourse. History is re-peating itself, and exclusionary laws such as California's Propositions 187, 209, and 227 contribute to an an-tagonistic sociopolitical climate that fosters the racist practices of the de jure segregation era. Inasmuch as the education of all Latina/o students is threatened, it is crucial that educators, policymakers, and Chicana/o communities continue to engage in strategies that combat this antagonistic sociopolitical climate and work toward educational equity.

References

Achievement Council. (1984). *Excellence for whom?* Oakland, CA: Author.

Acuña, R. (1988). *Occupied America: A history of Chicanos.* New York: Harper Collins.

Aguirre, A. (1980). *Intelligence testing education and Chicanos* (ERIC/TM Report No. 76). Princeton, NJ: ERIC Clearing House on Tests, Measurement, and Evaluation, Educational Testing Service.

Aguirre, A., & Martínez, R.O. (1993). *Chicanos in higher education: Issues and dilemmas for the 21st century* (ASHE-ERIC Higher Education Report No. 3). Washington, DC: George Washington University, School of Education and Human Development.

Allsup, C. (1982). *The American G.I. Forum: Origins and evolution.* Austin: University of Texas, Center for Mexican American Studies.

Alvarez v. Lemon Grove School District (1931) Superior Court of the State of California, County of San Diego, Petition for Writ of Mandate, No. 66625.

Assembly Office of Research. (1985). *Dropping out, losing out: The high cost for California.* Sacramento, CA: Author.

Assembly Office of Research. (1990). *Education minority students in California: Descriptive analysis and policy implications.* Sacramento, CA: Author.

Astin, A.W. (1982). *Minorities in American higher education.* San Francisco: Jossey-Bass.

Astin, A.W. (1995, May 1). Perspective on affirmative action: Replace sound bites with discourse. *Los Angeles Times*, p. B5.

Barrera, M. (1979). *Race and class in the Southwest: A theory of racial inequality.* Notre Dame, IN: University of Notre Dame Press.

Biegel, S. (1994). Bilingual education and language rights: The parameters of the bilingual education debate in California twenty years after *Lau v. Nichols. Chicano-Latino Law Review*, 14, 48–60.

Bogardus, E.S. (1949, April). *School inspection report on fourteen schools* (American G.I. Forum Archives). Corpus Christi, TX: American G.I. Forum.

Brownstein, R. (1995, May 14). Immigration debate roils GOP presidential contest. *Los Angeles Times*, pp. A1, A18.

Burciaga, J.A. (1993). *Drink cultura: Chicanismo.* Santa Barbara, CA: Joshua Odell Editions.

California State Advisory Committee to the U.S. Commission on Civil Rights. (1968, April). *Education and the Mexican American community in Los Angeles county* (CR 1.2:ED8/3). Los Angeles: Author.

California State Department of Education. (1981). *Schooling and language minority students: A theoretical framework.* Los Angeles: California State University, Los Angeles, Evaluation, Dissemination and Assessment Center.

California State Department of Education. (1985). *Racial or ethnic distribution of staff and students in California public schools, 1984–85.* Sacramento, CA: Author.

California State Department of Education. (1988). *Racial or ethnic distribution of staff and students in California public schools, 1987–88.* Sacrament, CA: Author.

California State Department of Education. (1993). *R30-LC language census report.* Sacrament, CA: Author.

Castañeda v. Pickard, 648 F. 2d 989 (5th Cir. 1981).

Castillo, A. (1994). *Massacre of the dreamers: Essays on Xicanisma.* New York: Plume.

Castro, V. (1994, December). [Transcribed interview conducted by Susan Racho with Vickie Castro]. Unpublished data.

Chapa, E. (1973). Report from the National Women's Political Caucus. *Magazín,* 1 (9), 37–39.

Chapa, J. (1991). Special focus: Hispanic demographic and educational trends. In D.J. Carter & R. Wilson (Eds.), *Minorities in higher education: Ninth annual status report* (pp. 11–17). Washington DC: American Council on Education.

Chicano Coordinating Council on Higher Education. (1970). *El plan de Santa Bárbara: A Chicana/o plan for higher education.* Santa Barbara, CA: La Causa.

Citizens for an Educated America: No on Unz. (1997). Los Angeles: Citizens for an Educated America.

Cisneros v. Corpus Christi Independent School District, 324 F. Supp. 599 (S.D. Tex. 1970). appeal docketed, No. 71-2397 (5th Cir. July 16, 1971).

Colvin, R.L., & Smith, D. (1998, June 4). Prop. 227 foes vow to block it despite wide vote margin. *Los Angeles Times,* p. A1.

Crawford, J. (1992). *Hold your tongue: Bilingualism and the politics of English only.* Reading, MA: Addison Wesley.

Crenshaw, K.W., Gotanda, N., Peller, G., & Thomas, K. (Eds). (1995). *Critical race theory: The key writings that formed the movement.* New York: New Press.

Cummins, J. (1981). The role of primary language development in promoting educational success for language minority students. In California State Department of Education (Ed.), *Schooling and language minority students: A theoretical framework* (pp. 4–49). Los Angeles: California State University. Los Angeles, Evaluation, Dissemination and Assessment Center.

De La Rosa, D., & Maw, C.E. (1990). *Hispanic education: A statistical portrait 1990.* Washington, DC: National Council of La Raza.

Delgado Bernal, D. (1997). *Chicana school resistance and grassroots leadership: Providing an alternative history of the 1968 East Los Angeles blowouts.* Unpublished doctoral dissertation, University of California, Los Angeles.

Delgado Bernal, D. (in press). Grassroots leadership reconceptualized: Chicana oral histories and the 1968 East Los Angeles school blowouts. *Frontier: A Journal of Women Studies.*

Delgado, R. (1989). Storytelling for oppositionists and others: A plea for narrative. *Michigan Law Review,* 87, 2411–2441.

Delgado, R. (1995). The imperial scholar: Reflections on a review of civil rights literature. In K.W. Crenshaw, N. Gotanda, G. Peller, & K. Thomas (Eds.), *Critical race theory: The key writings that formed the movement* (pp. 46–57). New York: New Press.

Delgado et al. v. Bastrop Independent School District of Bastrop County et al., docketed, No. 388 (W.D. Tex. June 15, 1948).

Del Rio Independent School District v. Salvatierra, 33 S.W.2d 790 (Tex. Civ. App., San Antonio 1930), cert. denied, 284 U.S. 580 (1931).

Donato, R. (1997). *The other struggle for equal schools: Mexican Americans during the civil rights era.* Albany: State University of New York Press.

Donato, R., Menchaca, M., & Valencia, R.R. (1991). Segregation, desegregation, and integration of Chicano students: Problems and prospects. In R.R. Valencia (Ed.), *Chicano school failure and success: Research and policy agendas for the 1990's* (pp. 27–63). London: Falmer Press.

Durán, R.P. (1983). *Hispanics' education and background: Predictors of college achievement.* New York: College Entrance Examination Board.

Espinosa, A.L. (1979). Hispanas: Our resources for the eighties. *La Luz,* 8(4), 10–13.

Gándara, P. (1982). Passing through the eye of the needle: High-achieving Chicanas. *Hispanic Journal of Behavioral Sciences,* 4, 167–179.

Gándara, P. (1994). Choosing higher education: Educationally ambitious Chicanos and the path to social mobility. *Education Policy Analysis Archives,* 2(8).

Gándara, P. (1997). *Review of the research on instruction of limited English proficient students: A report to the California Legislature.* Davis: University of California, Linguistic Minority Research Institute, Education Policy Center.

García, R.J. (1995). Critical race theory and Proposition 187: The racial politics of immigration law. *Chicano-Latino Law Review,* 17, 118–154.

García, A. (Ed.). (1997). *Chicana feminist thought: The basic historical writings.* New York: Routledge.

Goldman, R.D., & Hewitt, B.N. (1975). An investigation of test bias for Mexican-American college students. *Journal of Educational Measurement,* 12, 187–196.

Goldman, R.D., & Richards, R. (1974). The SAT prediction of grades for Mexican-American versus Anglo-American students at the University of California, Riverside. *Journal of Educational Measurement,* 11, 129–135.

Gómez-Quiñones, J. (1978). *Mexican students por La Raza: The Chicano student movement in Southern California 1967–1977.* Santa Barbara, CA: Editorial La Causa.

González, G.G. (1974). *The system of public education and its function within the Chicano communities, 1910–1950.* Unpublished doctoral dissertation, University of California, Los Angeles.

González, G.G. (1990). *Chicano education in the era of segregation.* Cranbury, NJ: Associated University Presses.

Guadalupe Organization v. Tempe Elementary School District, 587 F.2d 1022 (9th Cir. 1978).

Gutekunst, L. (1994, November 21). Students protest passage of Prop. 187. *The Lowell,* p. 1.

Harders, R., & Gómez, M.N. (1998). Separate and unequal: *Méndez v. Westminster* and desegregation in California schools. In M. DeMartino (Ed.), *A family changes history: Méndez v. Westminster* (pp. 3–12). Irvine: University of California.

Jensen, V.J. (1962, February). Effects of childhood bilingualism, I. *Elementary English, 39,* 132–143.

Judge dumps rest of Proposition 187. (1998, March 19). *San Francisco Chronicle,* p. A15.

Kerr, C. (1994). *Troubled times for American higher education: The 1990s and beyond.* Albany: State University of New York Press.

Keyes v. School District Number 1 Denver Colorado, 413 U.S. 189 (1973), 521 F.2d 465 (10th Cir. 1975).

Kozol, J. (1991). *Savage inequalities: Children in America's schools.* New York: HarperCollins.

Krashen, S.D. (1981). Bilingual education and second language acquisition theory. In California State Department of Education, *Schooling and language minority students: A theoretical framework* (pp. 51–79). Los Angeles: California State University, Los Angeles, Evaluation, Dissemination and Assessment Center.

Lau v. Nichols, 414 U.S. 563 (1974).

Lawrence, C.R. (1993). If he hollers let him go: Regulating racist speech on campus. In M.J. Matsuda, C.R. Lawrence, R. Delgado, & K.W. Crenshaw (Eds.), *Words that wound: Critical race theory, assaultive speech, and the First Amendment* (pp. 53–88). Boulder, CO: Westview Press.

López, S. (1977). The role of the Chicana within the student movement. In R. Sánchez & R. Martínez Cruz (eds.), *Essays on a la mujer* (pp. 16–19). Los Angeles: University of California, Chicano Studies Research Center.

Loya, A.C. (1990). Chicanos, law, and educational reform. *La Raza Law Journal, 3,* 28–50.

Luján et al v. Colorado State Board of Education, 649 P.2d 1005 (Co. 1982).

Macías, R. (1979). Language choice and human rights in the United States. In J.E. Alatis (Ed.), *Georgetown University round table on languages and linguistics, 1979* (pp. 86–101). Washington, DC: Georgetown University Press.

Martínez, G.A. (1994). Legal indeterminacy, judicial discretion and the Mexican–American litigation experience: 1930–1980. *U.C. Davis Law Review, 27,* 555–618.

Matsuda, M.J., Lawrence, C.R., Delgado, R., & Crenshaw, K.W. (1993). *Words that wound: Critical race theory, assaultive speech, and the First Amendment.* Boulder, CO: Westview Press.

McCurdy, J. (1968, March 17). Frivolous to fundamental: Demands made by east side high school students listed. *Los Angeles Times,* pp. 1, 4–5.

Menchaca, M., & Valencia, R.R. (1990). Anglo-Saxon ideologies and their impact on the segregation of Mexican students in California, the 1920s–1930s. *Anthropology and Education Quarterly, 21,* 222–249.

Menchaca, M. (1995). *The Mexican outsiders: A community history of marginalization and discrimination in California.* Austin: University of Texas Press.

Méndez González, R. (1995, October). [Transcribed interview conducted by Dolores Delgado Bernal with Rosalinda Méndez González]. Unpublished data.

Méndez v. Westminster, 64 F. Supp. 544 (S.D. Cal. 1946), 161 F. 2d 774 (9th Cir. 1947).

Mitchell, D.E., Powell, R.J., Scott, L.D., & McDaid, J.L. (1994). *The impact of California's special education pre-referral intervention activities and alternative assessments on ethnolinguistically diverse students: Final report of a federal-state joint agreement evaluation feasibility study.* Riverside: University of California, California Educational Research Cooperative.

Morín, R. (1963). *Among the valiant: Mexican Americans in WWII and Korea.* Los Angeles: Borden.

Muñoz, C., Jr. (1989). *Youth identity, power: The Chicano movement.* New York: Verso.

Nieto Gómez, A. (1973). The Chicana: Perspectives for education. *Encuentro Femenil, 1,* 34–61.

Nieto Gómez, A. (1974). La feminista. *Encuentro Feminil, 1,* 34–47.

Oakes, J. (1985). *Keeping track: How schools structure inequality.* New Haven, CT: Yale University Press.

Olivas, M. (Ed.). (1986). *Latino college students.* New York: Teachers College Press.

Orozco, C. (1986). Sexism in Chicano studies and the community. In T. Córdova, N. Cantú, G. Cárdenas, J. García, & C.M. Sierra (Eds.). *Chicana voices: Intersections of class, race, and gender* (pp. 11–18). Austin, TX: Center for Mexican American Studies.

Orozco, C. (1992). *The origins of the League of United Latin American Citizens (LULAC) and the Mexican American Civil Rights Movement in Texas with an analysis of women's political participation in a gendered context, 1910–1929.* Unpublished doctoral dissertation, University of California, Los Angeles.

Orum, L.S. (1986). *The education of Hispanics: Status and implications.* Washington, DC: National Council of La Raza.

Otero v. Mesa County Valley School District Number 51, 408 F. Supp. 162 (D. Colo. 1975).

Pardo, M. (1984, March/April). A selective evaluation of El Plan de Santa Bárbara. *La Gente,* 14–15.

Plyler v. Doe, 457 U.S. 202 (1982).

Prince, R. (1994, September 6). Americans want illegal immigrants out. *Los Angeles Times,* p. B7.

Pyle, A., McDonnell P.J., & Tobar, H. (1998, June 4). Latino voter participation doubled since '94 primary. *Los Angeles Times*, p. A1.

Rangel, J.C., & Alcalá, C.M. (1972). Project report: De jure segregation of Chicanos in Texas schools. *Harvard Civil Rights-Civil Liberties Review*, 7, 348–359.

Regents of the University of California v. Bakke, 438 U.S. 265 (1978).

Roos, P. (1978). Bilingual education: The Hispanic response to unequal education opportunity. *Law and Contemporary Problems*, 42, 111–140.

Salinas, F. (1971). Mexican-Americans and the desegregation of schools in the Southwest: A supplement. *El Grito, 4*(4), 36–69.

San Antonio Independent School District et al. v. Rodríguez et al., 337 F. Supp. 280 W.D. Tex. (1971), 36 L. Ed. 2d 16, 411 U.S. 1 (1973).

San Miguel, G., Jr. (1985). Conflict and controversy in the evolution of bilingual education in the United States: An interpretation. *Social Science Quarterly, 65*, 505–518.

San Miguel, G., Jr. (1987). *Let all of them take heed: Mexican Americans and the campaign for educational equality in Texas, 1910–1981*. Austin: University of Texas Press.

Sandoval, M. (1979). *Our legacy: The first fifty years*. Washington, DC: League of United Latin American Citizens.

Schaller, M., Scharff, V., & Schulzinger, R.D. (1992). *Present tense: The United States since 1945*. Boston: Houghton Mifflin.

Segura, D. (1993). Slipping through the cracks: Dilemmas in Chicana education. In A. de la Torre & B. Pesquera (Eds.), *Building with our hands: New directions in Chicana studies* (pp. 199–216). Berkeley: University of California Press.

Serna v. Portales Municipal Schools, 499 F.2d 1147 (10th Cir. 1974).

Serrano et al. v. Ivy Baker Priest, 487 P.2d 1241 (Cal. 1971).

Solórzano, D.G., & Delgado Bernal, D. (1998). *Critical race theory and transformation resistance: Chicana/o students in an urban context*. Unpublished manuscript.

Solórzano, D.G., & Villalpando, O. (in press). Critical race theory: Marginality, and the experiences of students of color in higher education. In C.A. Torres & T.R. Mitchell (Eds.), *Sociology of education: Emerging perspectives*. Albany: State University of New York Press.

Swarts, D. (1977). Pierre Bourdieu: The cultural transmission of social inequality. *Harvard Educational Review, 47*, 545–555.

Tate, W.F. (1997). Critical race theory and education: History, theory, and implications. *Review of Research in Education, 22*, 195–247.

Taylor, P.S. (1934). *An American-Mexican frontier: Nueces County, Texas*. Chapel Hill: University of North Carolina Press.

University of California, Latino Eligibility Task Force. (1995, March). *History of responses to Latino underachievement* (Report No. 4). Berkeley, CA: Chicana/o/ Latino Policy Project.

University of California, Latino Eligibility Task Force. (1997, July). *Latino student eligibility and participation in the University of California: Ya basta!* (Report No. 5). Berkeley, CA: Chicana/o/Latino Policy Project.

U.S. Commission on Civil Rights. (1971). *Mexican American education study, report 1: Ethnic isolation of Mexican Americans in the public schools of the Southwest*. Washington: DC: Government Printing Office.

Valdez, P. (1994, December). [Transcribed interview conducted by Susan Racho with Vickie Patssi Valdez]. Unpublished data.

Valencia, R.R. (1991). The plight of Chicano students: An overview of schooling conditions and outcomes. In R.R. Valencia (Ed.), *Chicano school failure and success: Research and policy agendas for the 1990's* (pp. 3–26). London: Falmer Press.

Valencia, R.R., & Aburto, S. (1991). The uses and abuses of educational testing: Chicanos as a case in point. In Valencia, R.R. (Ed.), *Chicano school failure and success: Research and policy agendas for the 1990's* (pp. 203–251). London: Falmer Press.

Vásquez, M. (1982). Confronting barriers to the participation of Mexican American women in higher education. *Hispanic Journal of Behavioral Sciences, 4*, 147–165.

Villalpando, O. (1996). *The long term effects of college on Chicano and Chicana students: "Other oriented" values, service careers, and community involvement*. Unpublished doctoral dissertation, University of California, Los Angeles.

Webster, D.S. (1984). Chicano students in American higher education. *Integration Education, 22* (1–3), 42–52.

Wise, A.E. (1982). *Legislated learning: The bureaucratization of the American classroom*. Berkeley: University of California Press.

Wollenberg, C. (1974). *Westminster v. Méndez*: Race, nationality, and segregation in California schools. *California Historical Quarterly, 53*, 317–332.

Wong-Fillmore, L. (1991). Language and cultural issues in early education. In S.L. Kagan (ed.), *The care and education of American's young children: Obstacles and opportunities, the 90th yearbook of the National Society for the Study of Education* (pp. 39–50). Chicago: University of Chicago Press.

Zambrana, R. (1994). Toward understanding the educational trajectory and socialization of Latina women. In L. Stone & G.M. Boldt (eds.), *The education feminism reader* (pp. 135–145). New York: Routledge.

Zavella, P. (1991). Reflections on diversity among Chicanas. *Frontiers: A Journal of Women Studies, 12*, 73–85.

Endnotes

1. "Chicana/o" is used when referring to both females and males of Mexican origin living in the United States, irrespective of immigration or generation status. Chicana/o is meant to be inclusive of females and males, rather than using the Spanish masculine gender, Chicano, to refer to both genders. Terms of identification vary according to context, and Chicana/o is used here as a political term of self-determination and solidarity that was popularized during the Chicano Movement in the 1960s, and are used interchangeably with "Mexican" when referring to pre-1960s history. "Latina/o" is sometimes used when referring to contemporary issues in order to be more inclusive of all mestizo peoples whose families might originate in Central America, South American, the Caribbean, and Mexico, and who share geographic and sociopolitical space with Chicanas/os. Latina/o is also used when data on "Hispanics" has not been desegregated specifically for Chicanas/os.

2. "De jure" segregation refers to that which is supported by official policy or law, while "de facto" segregation refers to that which exists in reality, but without lawful authority.

3. LULAC was founded in Texas in 1929 by middle-class English-speaking Mexican Americans who stressed American patriotism. As a civil rights organization, LULAC led the fight for school desegregation in the 1930s and 1940s (see Sandoval, 1979; San Miguel, 1987; Orozco, 1992). In 1948, the American G.I. Forum was founded in Texas as a Mexican American veteran's organization that was interested in the welfare of veterans and their families. The organization became interested in fighting discriminatory practices in all public institutions, and educational issues were of primary importance (see Allsup, 1982; San Miguel, 1987). Today, LULAC and the G.I. Forum are national organizations that have often joined forces in their struggles for educational and social equity.

4. A colonized relationship in general is one of economic, political, and cultural domination and subordination of one group by another. The dominant and subordinate groups are defined along ethnic and/or racial lines, and the relationship is established to serve the interests of the dominant group. See Mario Barrera (1979) for a theoretical discussion of Chicanas/os and internal colonialism—a form of colonialism in which the dominant and subordinate groups are within a single society and there are no clear geographic boundaries of a "colony."

5. For historical and contemporary discussions of Chicana/o grade retention and risk factors for dropping out, see California State Advisory Committee (1968), Assembly Office of Research (1985), and De La Rosa and Maw (1990).

6. See Segura (1993), Gándara (1982), and Vásquez (1982) for studies that examine barriers to education experienced by various groups of Chicanas.

7. The Servicemen's Readjustment Act of 1944, or the G.I. Bill, provided veterans and their families with various employment, health, economic, and educational benefits until the program ended in 1956. Veterans pursuing a college education received $110 a month, plus allowance for dependents and payment of tuition, fees, and books. Nationally, the G.I. Bill opened up a selective higher education system to working-class people by assisting over two million new students. Chicano servicemen also took advantage of the G.I. Bill's educational benefits (see Morín, 1963). However, because of the relatively small number of women who had served in the military and of active discrimination (i.e., women did not receive full benefits), Chicanas and other women received few direct educational benefits (see also Schaller, Scharff, & Schulzinger, 1992).

8. These lawsuits include Serna v. Portales Municipal Schools (1974); *Otero v. Mesa County Valley School District* (1975); *Guadalupe Organization v. Tempe Elementary School District* (1978). For more on these cases see, Martínez (1994).

9. In *Keyes v. School District Number 1*, plaintiffs alleged that the school board was practicing de jure segregation. The U.S. Supreme Court ruled that the school board had an unconstitutional policy of deliberately segregating Park Hill schools, one segment of the Denver school district, and mandated a desegregation plan. The Keys case did not address the issue of de facto segregation (see Martínez, 1994; San Miguel, 1987).

10. Later in 1981, the *Castañeda v. Pickard* case put forth a three-pronged test that the federal courts continue to follow today when evaluating a school districts' actions in overcoming the language barriers of students. In *Castañeda,* a group of Chicana/o children and their parents challenged the practices of a Texas school district under the Fourteenth Amendment, Title VI, and the Equal Educational Opportunity Act. The plaintiffs charged that the district failed to offer adequate bilingual education to overcome the linguistic barriers of students. The court ruled in favor of the plaintiffs and set forth the three-pronged analysis for courts to follow: 1) Ea court must determine whether the district is pursuing a program that is based on sound educational theory; 2) the court must establish whether or not the programs and practices effectively implement the educational theory adopted; and 3) the court must determine if the school's program actually results in overcoming language barriers of students (see Biegel, 1994).

11. In other words, since federal and state policies prior to 1954 had allowed for the segregation of Blacks and Whites and had not referenced Mexicans, the strategy

had been to have Mexicans classified as part of the White race. If Mexicans were declared White, then segregating Mexican students from White students in the absence of a law allowing for their separation would be illegal. The Cisneros case was the first time a court officially recognized Mexicans as an identifiable minority group, thereby allowing them to use the equal protection strategy used in Black desegregation cases, rather than the claim to "Whiteness" strategy (see San Miguel, 1987).

12. See Donato (1997) for documentation of the tension between bilingual education and desegregation.

13. Critical race theorist Richard Delgado (1989) describes "counterstorytelling" as both a method of telling the story of those experiences not often told, and a tool for analyzing and challenging the dominant discourse and the stories of those in power.

14. Gloria Martínez is a composite character based on data from focus group interviews, individual conversations, and personal experiences. She was first introduced as an undergraduate student in an article by Daniel G. Solórzano and Octavio Villalpando (in press) and also appears in an article by Solórzano and Dolores Delgado Bernal (1998). In these articles, Gloria facilitates a technique of counterstorytelling.

15. The complex relationship between race/ethnicity, class, and gender, and how each of these categories contributes to the marginalization of Chicana/o students, cannot be fully dealt with here. However, it should be noted that even middle-class Chicana/o college students often experience a sense of marginalization, particularly when they are first-generation college students. These students may lack the kind of "cultural capital" valued by higher education systems. As Bourdieu has stated, "academic performance is linked to cultural background . . . and is more strongly related to parents' educational history than to parents' occupational status" (Swarts, 1977, p. 547). See Gándara, this volume, for a discussion of class, gender, and Chicana/o college students, and see Zavella (1991), Castillo (1994), Zambrana (1994), and García (1997) for a general discussion on how institutional and cultural differences based on sexism, racism, and classism create a different range of choices and options for Chicanas in particular.

16. In California's June 1998 primary election, Gloria Matta Tuchman once again ran for the position of State Superintendent of Public Instruction. She came in second with 25.5 percent of the votes, behind the incumbent Delaine Eastin with 43.3 percent of the votes. The two will face a run-off in the November 1998 election.

Who's the Leader of the Civil Rights Band?

Latinos' Role in Brown v. Board of Education

Nicolás C. Vaca

The fruits of the African American battle for civil rights are positions of power held by African Americans in the public and private sectors. And now we find ourselves in the position of defending that power against other people pushing for inclusion. Though we pride ourselves on our leadership role in civil rights, paradoxically, we guard the success jealously. "We're the ones who marched in the streets and got our heads busted. Where were they? But now they want to get in on the benefits."

Brenda Payton
Columnist for the *Oakland Tribune*

There is a Black perception that Latinos have not suffered discrimination to the same degree and in the same manner as they and are thus are not entitled to the benefits of the civil rights movements. African Americans often assume that they were the pioneers in the area of civil rights. The actions of Martin Luther King, Roy Innis, and myriad other Black leaders would tend to confirm this belief. In addition to these inspirational leaders of the civil rights movement, Blacks reference the NAACP, the Congress of Racial Equality, and the Southern Christian Leadership Conference as leading examples of organizations that pushed for civil rights in the 1960s.

More specifically, African Americans point to their role in the passage of the Voting Rights Act of 1965 and the benchmark case of *Brown v. Board of Education* as demonstration of their leadership in the area of

civil rights. While it is true that the historical deprivation of Black suffrage in the South was the impetus for passage of the Voting Rights Act of 1965, Latino civil rights litigation presaged the *Brown* decision by some eight years. Unfortunately, ignorance of Latino activism around this issue has led one scholar to conclude that the role of Latinos has been reduced to little more than a sidebar.[1]

The discrimination suffered by Mexican Americans in California and Texas and their response in the form of pioneering litigation gives Latinos a legitimate claim to being pioneers in the area of civil rights, as *Méndez v. Westminster* and *Delgado v. Bastrop Independent School District* make clear.

CALIFORNIA: *MÉNDEZ V. WESTMINSTER*

The insatiable appetite for cheap Mexican labor in the Southwest did not come without social consequences. In the beginning most Mexican workers were single

Pages 62–84 from *The Presumed Alliance: The Unspoken Conflict Between Latinos & Blacks & What It Means for America* by Nicolás C. Vaca. Copyright © 2004 by Nicolás C. Vaca. Reprinted by permission of HarperCollins Publishers.

men who came to the United States with the goal of earning money and sending it back to Mexico. But later immigrant male workers arrived with their families. Inevitably, this had an impact on social service agencies and the education system as well. The impact was two-way. Historian George J. Sánchez writes: "In the 1930s, three institutions most clearly framed the experience of Mexican American adolescents and young adults in Los Angeles: the family, the school, and the workplace."[2] Mexican Americans, Sánchez argues, had accepted that education was the path to success in American society. In 1938 the Mexican American Movement (MAM), an organization comprised of second-generation Mexican Americans, published a piece in its newspaper, the *Mexican Voice*, that stressed the significance of remaining in school. "Education is the only tool which will raise our influence, command the respect of the rich class, and enable us to mingle in their social, political and religious life. . . . EDUCATION is our only weapon."[3]

But education facilities for Mexican American students were not only separate but also unequal—this was the harsh reality. The creation of separate schools for Mexican American children existed throughout southern California. In 1913, Pasadena established a Mexican school. In 1921, the city of Ontario built its own Mexican school, and by 1928, the school was so overenrolled that another "Mexican" school had to be built. In 1924, Riverside built another "Mexican" school to accommodate the wishes of white parents to separate their children from Latino children.[4]

As the number of Mexican children who enrolled in school continued to increase, so did the degree of segregation. By 1927 over 65,000 Mexican American children were enrolled in California schools, and 88 percent were located in southern California with 50 percent concentrated in Los Angeles County. A study conducted in 1926 found that 80 percent of the Mexican American children were enrolled in 3 of the 14 elementary schools in East L.A. and 3 others had an enrollment of approximately 60 percent. The numbers had increased by 1939: each of the 6 schools enrolled more than 80 percent of their students from the Mexican American community. A survey conducted in 1931 discovered that 80 percent of school districts with significant Mexican student enrollment were segregated.[5]

The creation of separate schools for Latino children was not based on any statute or legal ruling. Up to 1947 California provided for the establishment of separate schools, but they were reserved for children of Native American, Chinese, Japanese, and Mongolian descent. Curiously, the statute did not mention Blacks or Mexicans. But even without a statutory basis, the school districts accomplished their goal of de facto segregation by two methods. The first was to gerrymander the school district. Gerrymandering was accomplished by arbitrarily creating school zone boundaries designed to include Mexicans only within those boundaries, thus assuring that the school that fell within that zone became a Mexican school. An example of how this gerrymandering was accomplished is reflected in a letter written by a "supervisory official" of the city of Los Angeles in 1933.

> Our educational theory does not make any racial distinction between the Mexican and native white population. However, pressure from white residents of certain sections forced a modification of this principle to the extent that certain neighborhood schools have been placed to absorb the majority of the Mexican pupils in the district.[6]

Such gerrymandering was not only the result of protest by white parents but also fit nicely into the pedagogy of the time. The segregation of Mexican American children was justified on several grounds, one being that they were naturally happier with their own kind. One educator described Mexican American students who sat in the same classroom as white students as "dull, stupid and phlegmatic." She contrasted this with the atmosphere in an all-Mexican American classroom, where the faces of the children "radiated joy, they had thrown off the repression that held them down when they were in school with other children."[7]

Another argument used by educators for segregated schools was the need to Americanize Mexican children. This push to assimilate the Mexican children could best be accomplished, educators argued, by segregating the students so that the special "assimilation" training that Mexican students needed would not hinder the white students' educational progress.[8]

An additional, and to many educators persuasive, argument for segregating Mexican children in separate classrooms or separate schools was the use and acceptance of standardized intelligence tests which ostensibly established that Mexican children were duller and slower than white students. The literature on the education of the Mexican-American in the early part of the 20th century emphasized their sub-normal intelligence. Study after "scientific" study established that Mexican children simply were not as intelligent as white students.

In 1931 B. F. Haught conducted a study that concluded that the "average Spanish child has an intelligence quotient of .79 compared with 1.00 for the average Anglo child." O. K. Garretson concluded that "retardation of the Mexican child . . . is from three to eight times as great as that of the American child. . . ."[9] Leo M. Gamble conducted a study on Mexican-American children and found that "the average intelligence quotient for the Mexican was 78.75"[10] William Sheldon of the University of Texas administered the Cole-Vincent and Stanford-Binet tests to Mexican and American students in Texas. His results "scientifically" established that Mexicans had only 85 percent of the I.Q. of the white students. Thomas Garth, a professor at the University of Denver, administered the National Intelligence Test to more than 1,000 Mexican and Mexican-American students in Texas, New Mexico and Colorado and discovered that the median I.Q. was 78.1.[11]

This group was joined by numerous other scholars—Helen L. Koch, Rietta Simmons, Kimball Young, Ellen A. McAnulty, F. C. Paschal, C. R. Sullivan, and Florence L. Goodenough—in concluding that the intelligence of Mexican children was inferior to that of American children.

By the late 1920s and early 1930s the segregation of Mexican and Mexican American children was a fact of life. As Charles M. Wollenberg, a scholar who has examined the segregation of Mexican children in California schools, observed, "In Orange County . . . over 4,000 students, a quarter of total school enrollment, were Mexicans or Mexican-Americans in 1934. About 70 percent of the Spanish-surnamed total attended the fifteen Orange County elementary schools which had 100 percent Mexican enrollment."[12] It is this background of de facto segregation of Mexican children in Orange County that led to the groundbreaking case of *Méndez v. Westminster*—a case that helped lay the groundwork for the ruling in *Brown v. Board of Education* eight years later.

THE SOCIAL CONTEXT OF *MÉNDEZ V. WESTMINSTER*

Orange County's economy in the early 1930s and 1940s was almost exclusively based on agriculture. Crops such as oranges, lemons, nuts, beans, and vegetables dominated the region's industry. And like the rest of Southwest agriculture, the preferred labor for these crops was Mexicans. Over time the Mexican population, instead of remaining migratory, established

permanent residency in various cities in Orange County. González notes that in 1930, 17,000 Mexicans resided in these towns and cities.[13]

The Mexican population made an impact on the educational system as early as 1913 when a report revealed that school administrators had set aside a special room for "Spanish" children at one of the elementary schools. In time the number of Mexican children flowing into the school district forced the construction of a separate school building. Accompanying the physical segregation of Mexican children from white children was the creation of a separate curriculum for Mexican children. The school district emphasized manual training for the Mexican children, while it maintained academic preparation for white students.

In 1916, the Committee on Buildings recommended that a six-room building be constructed near the existing Fifth Street building, and that a separate two-room building be constructed to be used exclusively by Mexican children. Not only was there to be a separate physical facility for the Mexicans, and a different curriculum, but different criteria were used for selecting teachers assigned to the Mexican school and those assigned to the Anglo school. Responding to this resolution, the school board instructed the president to obtain bids for the construction of the building where all Mexican children would attend.

The proposed construction of the separate facility for Mexican children was criticized by both white and Mexican parents. The white parents did not believe that the construction was moving quickly enough, while the Mexicans demanded that it not proceed at all. In 1918, the all-Anglo Lincoln School PTA passed a resolution urging the school board to do something about the Mexican problem and advised that "segregation is eminently desirable from moral, physical and education standpoints." For its part, the Mexican community objected to the construction of the Mexican school. Pro Patria Club, a Mexican organization, objected strongly to the segregation of Mexican children and demanded they be returned to their respective schools.

Confronted with the two opposing parties, the superintendent of schools asked the city attorney to issue a legal opinion addressing the legal basis on which segregation of Mexican children could be justified. The city attorney conceded that the existing education statute did not provide for any basis for the creation of segregated schools for Mexican children. However, his opinion justified the creation of separate educational facilities for Mexicans based on language differences, age, and regularity of attendance. Based on this incorrect interpretation of the statute, the Santa Ana Board of Education passed a resolution that read, in part, "agreed that for the best interest of the Schools and especially for the great benefit to the Mexican children, to continue the Mexican school work at the present."[14] In other words, the school facilities would continue to be segregated.

Armed with what they believed was legal justification for segregating Mexican children, the Santa Ana Board of Education subsequently identified three schools as Mexican schools. González writes:

> On 5 June 1919, the "plans and specifications for the [just permanent] Mexican school buildings were approved and the secretary was instructed to advertise for bids. . . ." The temporary arrangement evolved into the first Mexican school building in Santa Ana, named the Santa Fe School. Thus, the process of segregation, begun in 1912 with separate classroom, reached its completed form in 1920 with the establishment of a separate Mexican school. In 1921 the district added Logan, another Mexican school, and incorporated a third, Delhi, in 1924.[15]

Mexican children were not only relegated to separate school buildings, but the teachers hired to instruct them also were paid anywhere from $90 to $100 less per year than teachers assigned to the Anglo schools.

The unequal nature of the education provided to the Mexican children was exemplified not only by the separate curriculum developed for them (emphasis on manual training for the boys and homemaking for the girls) and the lower-paid teachers assigned to them, but also by the decrepit structures in which they received their segregated instruction. In 1928 Osman R. Hull and Willard S. Ford, two University of Southern California professors, conducted an educational survey of the Santa Ana school district at the behest of the school district. Hull and Ford described the Mexican schools as follows:

> The Delhi school is a wooden structure which is a fire hazard and poorly constructed [and] provides less than one-third of the required amount of light. . . .
> The Grand Avenue School . . . is a two story frame structure entirely unsuited to school use . . . it has been condemned for years.
> The most unsatisfactory school that is now being used . . . is the Artesia school. . . . It is a frame building with no interior finish. It has a

low single roof with no air space, which makes the temperature in many of the rooms almost unbearable. Since no artificial light is provided in the building, it is impossible to do satisfactory reading without serious eye strain on many days of the year."[16]

Based on these findings, they recommended that two of the Mexican schools be demolished and new schools be constructed. The reaction of the Anglo community to this recommendation was swift and forceful. Harvey Gardner, a member of the advisory committee of the Chamber of Commerce, objected to the monies that would have to be used to build two new Mexican schools when, he argued, there were not "proper facilities for the American school children." The board, cowed by the fierce reaction of the Anglo citizens, rejected Hull and Ford's recommendation and instructed them to provide a new set of recommendations.

Ford and Hull, in compliance with the board's request, provided a revised plan: they recommended that only one school be torn down instead of two, and they reduced from $170,000 to $112,000 the amount of money designated for repairs to the Artesia school. However, even these reduced figures did not satisfy the board, so Ford and Hull were instructed to provide a third revised plan.

Once again, the plan proposed by Ford and Hull did not meet with the approval of the board and advisory committee, and the contract with Ford and Hull was then terminated. In their stead a committee was appointed to decide what to do about a Mexican school. Ultimately, the committee recommended a new Artesia school building with a budget of $65,000; a new kindergarten for Delhi at a cost of $500; and instead of building a new Grand Avenue school, the committee recommended that the vacant Logan school be restored and an addition be appended at a cost of $32,000.

After considerable debate and input from Anglo citizens, who objected to the proposal for a variety of reasons, not the least of which was a desire to relocate the Artesia school within the boundaries of a Mexican neighborhood, the committee's plan was adopted. In the 1929–1930 school year, the new Artesia school (which was renamed Fremont School) opened: Logan enrolled 232 students and Delhi enrolled 319 students. The total number of Mexican children enrolled in these schools represented more than one-quarter of the district's total enrollment.

While segregation of Mexican children continued into the 1940s, by the early 1930s theories regarding the benefits of segregation were coming under attack. George I. Sánchez, at that time director of information and statistics for the New Mexico Department of Education, argued that the results of intelligence tests administered to Mexican children had to take into consideration the child's environment. Wollenberg notes that "California educator Simon Treff asserted that Mexican students in mixed schools seemed to be less 'retarded' than those in segregated schools. Herschel T. Manuel of the University of Texas claimed that reading and arithmetic problems of Mexican-American children were caused primarily by poverty and bilingualism."[17] By 1937, some educators were "calling for an end to 'emotionalism' on the question of segregation; what was needed was more research."

It is generally accepted that soldiers who fought in World War II and returned to their towns were the impetus for many of the significant changes that occurred during the late 1940s in Mexican communities. Guadalupe San Miguel Jr., a Latino historian, writes:

> Despite these tremendous social and economic changes wrought by World War II, the status of Mexican Americans in the United States changed little . . . the majority continued to be denied equal opportunities, discriminated against, and treated as second-class citizens. . . .
>
> But change . . . was brewing within the Mexican American community. Much of this change was due to their experiences in the defense of American institutions and ideals. . . .
>
> The war experience gave Mexican Americans a new sense of dignity and responsibility. For the first time many of them were treated as first-class citizens and recognized for their contributions to the war effort.[18]

One of the issues that returning veterans confronted was the ongoing segregation in the school system. In 1943 Mexican veterans who returned to Santa Ana formed an organization, the Latin American Organization, whose main goal was combating school segregation. One of the first confrontations occurred on October 25, 1943, when Mrs. Leonides Sánchez and Mrs. Frank García appeared at a meeting of the Santa Ana Board of Education and argued that their children should be allowed to attend Franklin School, a largely Anglo school. The school board rebuffed the request, stating that while admitting that Anglo students were frequently transferred out of Mexican schools, the

reverse was seldom the case. A year later Sánchez and García enrolled their children in the Franklin School, even though they had not been granted authorization to do so. The enrollment of the students was accomplished through a subterfuge, using false addresses that would allow the students to fall within the Franklin School zone. When this was discovered, the school board decided that, once the correct addresses for the two children were verified, they would be placed in the proper school—the Mexican school.

No sooner was the school board confronted with the Sánchez-García demand than an attorney representing Mr. and Mrs. William Guzmán and their son Billy Guzmán, along with several other parents, appeared before the board and requested leave to send Billy to the Franklin School. While the board initially indicated that it would study the problem and provide a response within 90 days, there was no change in the board's policy.

The struggle in which the Sánchez, García, and Guzmán families were engaged in Santa Ana was also going on in the town of Westminster. There, in 1944, Gonzalo and Felicitas Méndez attempted to enroll their three children in the school nearest their home—Westminster Elementary School. The school prevented them from enrolling on the basis of language deficiency. The Méndez family could have pursued the matter for their children alone, but the political atmosphere had changed by then. Instead, they organized a group of parents and petitioned the school board to end the segregation of Mexican children.

The superintendent maintained that Mexican children belonged in the Mexican schools, but that an exception would be made for the Méndez children: they would be allowed to enroll in Westminster Elementary School. Mr. and Mrs. Méndez rejected the offer and refused to allow their children into the school until such time as they could "regularly" enroll in the school. They were already of a mind to institute legal action, not only for the benefit of their own children but to challenge—and perhaps end—the existence of Mexican schools.

David Marcus, a Black attorney, represented the Méndez family. Marcus came to the Méndez case with an impressive résumé of court victories. In addition to having prevailed in litigation to desegregate the San Bernardino public parks and pools, he also handled matters for the Mexican consulates in Los Angeles and San Diego.

On March 2, 1945, Gonzalo Méndez, William Guzmán, Frank Palomino, Thomas Estrada, and

Lorenzo Ramírez filed a class-action suit in Federal District Court, Southern District, against the Westminster, Garden Grove, and El Modeno school districts, the Santa Ana city schools, and the respective trustees and superintendents of the school districts (*Méndez et al. v. Westminster School District of Orange County et al.*).[19] The American Civil Liberties Union and the National Lawyers Guild filed amicus briefs, attesting to the importance of the case.

The complaint alleged that the school districts had engaged in a systematic and purposeful segregation of Mexican children whereby the Mexican children "are now and have been segregated and required to and must attend and use certain schools . . . reserved for and attended solely and exclusively by children and persons of Mexican and Latin descent, while such other schools are maintained, attended, and used exclusively by and for persons and children purportedly known as White or Anglo-Saxon children."[20] The plaintiffs in the action argued that such segregated schools violated the Mexicans' constitutional rights under the Fourteenth Amendment and asked, as part of their relief, that the court issue an injunction abating the segregation of the schools.

Both parties to the lawsuit stipulated to the court that while the segregation was not based on race, segregation per se was practiced by the defendant school districts beginning with the time that the Mexican children entered school and advanced through the grades. The parties further stipulated that this was the case even though the children were qualified to attend public schools in their own school zone.

Having stipulated that the segregation of Mexican children was not based on race, the defendant school districts justified their actions on the special educational needs of the Mexican children. The court noted that the Mexican children were "required to attend schools designated by the boards separate and apart from English-speaking pupils; that such group should attend such schools until they had acquired some proficiency in the English language."[21]

The Méndez family responded that the use of language as a basis for segregation of Mexican children was a subterfuge used by the school districts to arbitrarily discriminate against children of Mexican descent.

The court was careful to note that the "separate" educational facilities provided to the Mexican children were "equal" to if not superior to that offered to the Anglo children. The court noted, "The record before us shows without conflict that the technical facilities and physical conveniences offered in the schools housing entirely the segregated pupils, the efficiency of the teachers therein and the curricula are identical and in some respects superior to those in the other schools in the respective districts."[22] By so noting, the court dismissed any potential argument that its decision was influenced by "separate but unequal" educational access for the Mexican children.

Having set the record regarding the various stipulations by the parties and the "separate but equal" nature of the educational facilities provided to the segregated Mexican children, the court then framed the question before it as follows: "Does such official action of defendant district school agencies and the usages and practices pursued by the respective school authorities as shown by the evidence operate to deny or deprive the so-called non-English-speaking school children of Mexican ancestry or descent within such school districts of the equal protection of the laws?"

In presenting their case, plaintiffs relied heavily on social scientists who testified that segregation of Mexican children had a detrimental effect on them. The social science testimony was persuasive, leading the court to write:

> The evidence clearly shows that Spanish-speaking children are retarded in learning English by lack of exposure to its use because of segregation, and that commingling of the entire student body instills and develops a common cultural attitude among the school children which is imperative for the perpetation of American institutions and ideals. It is also established by the record that the methods of segregation prevalent in the defendant school districts foster antagonism in the children and suggest inferiority among them where none exists.[23]

In addressing the districts' principal defense argument that the segregation of Mexican children was based on their lack of English, the court acknowledged that segregation of Mexican children could be justified on this basis, but that the facts before it did not warrant such a conclusion and sided with the plaintiff's position that language skills was a ruse for arbitrarily segregating Mexican children. As to the facts before it relating to the Santa Ana city schools, the court noted that "The tests applied to the beginners are shown to have been generally hasty, superficial and not reliable." In other instances, the court noted, the Santa Ana city schools simply used the "Latinized or Mexican name of the child" to determine the child's language skills.

Such methods "of evaluating language knowledge are illusory," the court wrote.

The court went further to undermine the districts' argument that segregation of Mexican children in the elementary schools could be justified because of deficiency in English, by first stating that such deficiency had to be established by "credible examination by the appropriate school authority of each child." Furthermore, the court noted, if the segregation of a child was based on English-language deficiencies, then "such segregation must be based wholly upon indiscriminate foreign language impediments in the individual child, regardless of his ethnic traits or ancestry." Meaning, apparently, if children of Italian descent or German descent were appropriately tested and found to be deficient in English, then they too could be segregated for the sole purpose of improving their English.

At the end of the day, the court found that the school districts had, by virtue of arbitrarily segregating Mexican children, violated their rights under the Fourteenth Amendment and concluded that "the allegations of the complaint [petition] have been established sufficiently to justify injunctive relief affianced all defendants, restraining further discriminatory practices against the pupils of Mexican descent in the public schools of defendant school districts."[24]

The decision by Judge Paul McCormick was hailed as groundbreaking. *La Opinión*, a Los Angeles Spanish-language newspaper, reported that McCormick's decision was a "brilliant judicial exposition." And Marcus hailed the results as "one of the greatest judicial decisions in favor of democratic practices granted since the emancipation of the slaves."[25]

The celebration was short-lived because the defendants decided to appeal. The appeal to the Ninth Circuit attracted the attention of a number of major organizations: the NAACP, the American Jewish Congress, the Japanese-American Citizens League, and the State of California attorney general, in addition to the ACLU and the National Lawyers Guild. Not only did the NAACP submit an amicus brief, but it considered the case to be of such significance that it sent Thurgood Marshall to argue before the court. The *New York Times* reported that the case was being closely watched and considered a test case for addressing the constitutional validity of the "separate but equal" doctrine.

The *Times* was correct. Christopher Arriola, an attorney who has written on the *Méndez* case, notes that the civil rights organizations saw *Méndez* as a test case to attack the separate but equal underpinning of *Plessy v. Ferguson*. The amicus brief filed by the NAACP argued that "fundamental law" invalidated racial classification. It also argued that segregation prevents the achievement of due process and equal protection. Finally, it argued that *Plessy v. Ferguson* did not prohibit a finding that school segregation was invalid since that case was restricted to public transportation."[26]

The court of appeals did not take the NAACP bait and refused to rule on the "separate but equal" issue. The court wrote, "We are not tempted by the siren who calls to us that the sometimes slow and tedious way of democratic legislation is no longer respected in the progressive society."[27]

The school districts did not choose to appeal the case to the United States Supreme Court and the education commissioner of Orange County ordered that there be "some Anglo and Mexican children in every class." In the fall of 1947 the schools in Westminster, Garden Grove, El Modeno, and Santa Ana integrated their schools with few problems.[28]

While the impact of *Méndez was* not national in scope, its effect in California was both apparent and dramatic. In January 1947, a bill was introduced into the state legislature to repeal the state statutes that provided for the creation of segregated schools for Chinese, Japanese, Native Americans, and Mongolians. Some opposition was raised to the bill but it eventually passed, and on June 14, 1947, the bill was signed into law by Governor Earl Warren.

In Riverside, the school board members, reading McCormick's decision as writing on the wall, capitulated to the demands from the Mexican American community and integrated schools in the section of the city called Bell Town. Riverside closed an "all-white" school near a Mexican neighborhood, thus integrating a school that had previously been all Mexican. And the Ontario school board integrated a school in 1946.

Even though the effect of *Méndez* was not national in scope, its significance in preparing the ground for *Brown v. Board of Education* cannot be overemphasized. The use of social science testimony had a significant impact on McCormick and his decision. González writes that Robert Carter, one of the NAACP attorneys, was so impressed with the effective use of social science testimony that he suggested to Thurgood Marshall that such an approach would be the only way to "overturn segregation in the United States." González further notes:

> Later attorneys for the NAACP employed with success this particular strategy in the 1954 Supreme Court decision, *Brown v. Board of*

Education. Carter . . . also felt that the *amicus curiae* that he and Marshall filed in the appellate court in support of the district court's *Méndez* decision was a "dry run for the future." [29]

A note in the *Yale Law Journal* concurred: "However, a recent District Court decision, affirmed by the Ninth Circuit Court of Appeals, has questioned the basic assumption of the *Plessy* and may portend a complete reversal of the doctrine."[30] This conclusion was given further credence by Lester H. Phillips in an article published in the Black journal *Phylon*: "The observations of the judges in both the district and the appellate courts relative to segregation suggest that this case must be ranked among the vanguard of those making a frontal attack upon the 'equal separate' canon of interpretation of the equal protection clause."[31]

It is, therefore, not an exaggeration to state that *Méndez* was the first stage in the process of overturning the "separate but equal" doctrine in the 1896 *Plessy v. Ferguson* case.

TEXAS: *DELGADO V. BASTROP INDEPENDENT SCHOOL DISTRICT*

The discrimination and segregation that Mexicans experienced was not confined to California, as Chicano historian David Montejano makes clear in his highly acclaimed book *Anglos and Mexicans in the Making of Texas: 1836–1986*.[32] The parallels between California and Texas are clear. Like California, Texas had no state statute that provided for the creation of separate schools for Mexican children. In the absence of a statutory basis on which to segregate Mexican children, educators in Texas relied on administrative decrees. Reminiscent of statements in California, Texas school officials—administrators, school boards, trustees, superintendents—justified the creation and maintenance of separate Mexican schools because Mexicans suffered from mental retardation, did not speak English, had poor hygiene, did not really appreciate education, and, frankly, were just inherently inferior. And when a well-meaning school administrator happened to ignore the common lore regarding Mexican children, he was reminded by Anglo parents of the imperative to keep Mexican and Anglo children separate. As an example, in 1919 Mexican children in the town of Pharr-San Juan in Hidalgo County were initially allowed to attend school with Anglo children. However, they were quickly transferred to a "Mexican church" for separate instruction after Anglo parents protested the mingling of the Mexicans with Anglo children.[33]

Herschel T. Manuel, a professor of educational psychology at the University of Texas, conducted a study of Mexican children in Texas and published the results in 1930. He found that Mexican children were segregated into inferior schools. He describes one school for Mexican children as a run-down building that had previously been a church, and in southwest Texas he found four Mexican children using one tablet and one pencil, which they rotated among themselves.[34]

By the late 1920s and early 1930s segregation of Mexican children was widespread and institutionalized in areas of Texas. For example, during the 1930s it was believed that more than 40 school districts had created separate schools for Mexicans, and by 1942 it was estimated that 122 districts in 59 counties operated separate schools for Mexican American children.[35]

While there had been individual challenges to segregation, the legal challenges were made with the help and support of a new statewide Mexican organization, the League of United Latin American Citizens, generally referred to by its acronym, LULAC. LULAC's membership was uniquely different from other Mexican organizations in that all of its members were either born in the United States or naturalized citizens. Its goals were also different. While the other organizations existed primarily to provide social services to the Mexican community, LULAC's goal was to enable Mexicans to take advantage of U.S. political, social, and cultural institutions. This was reflected in LULAC's constitution, which had as one of its goals: "to assume complete responsibility for the education of our children as to their rights and duties and the language and customs of this country." Conjoined with this goal was LULAC's avowed purpose of eliminating all discriminatory practices based on race.[36]

The 1928 claim of Amanda Vela was one of the first challenges to the segregation of Mexican children in Texas. In the case of *Vela v. Board of Trustees of Charlotte Independent School District*, Felipe Vela, a Mexican American, had adopted Amanda Vela, a girl whose "race" was undetermined. Vela attempted to enroll Amanda in a school with white children. She was denied enrollment and transferred to the "Mexican school" by the board of trustees. Vela bypassed the local school board and made a direct appeal to the state superintendent of public instruction for a decision allowing his daughter to attend the "white school."

Much like the *Méndez* case, though not in a legal context, both sides agreed to certain facts. First, the parties agreed that the school district did not have any legal authority on which it could bar Amanda from attending the "white school." Second, the parties stipulated that Amanda did not live within the zone designated for the Mexican school, and that she was placed in the "Mexican school" simply because her parents were Mexican. Also, much like in the *Méndez* case, the local school officials defended their actions on pedagogical grounds, stating, "It is well understood that non-English-speaking children should be given special instruction and it is probably to the best interests of such children that they be placed in one room or in one school in order that the character of instruction given will be different from that given to English-speaking children."[37]

Like Judge McCormick in the *Méndez* case, the state superintendent of public instruction, S. M. N. Marrs, agreed that separation of Mexican children based on language difficulties could be used to justify segregating them into separate classes. In the case of Amanda, however, Marrs found that she not only spoke English well but was able to translate from Spanish to English and English to Spanish with great facility. As a consequence, he concluded, placing Amanda in the "white school" would not interfere with the progress of the white children and placing her in the "Mexican school" would disadvantage Amanda, since so many of the Mexican children did not speak English or, if they did, they did not speak it well. The school district, dissatisfied with the decision, appealed to the state board of education, but the board declined to reverse the state superintendent.

The first legal challenge to the practice of segregating Mexican children in the Texas education system was fostered by LULAC in 1930, two years after the Vela matter was resolved. *Independent School District v. Salvatierra* was a class-action suit filed against the Del Rio school district.[38] *Salvatierra* was also significant because it was a case of first impression, a fact the court acknowledged when it wrote, "The question of race segregation, as between Mexicans and other white races, has not heretofore found its way into the courts of the state, and therefore the decision of no Texas court is available in the disposition of the precise question present here." [39] Thus, its decision, if favorable to the plaintiffs, could be used to further challenge segregation in other school districts, but if favorable to the defendants could be devastating to any future challenges.

The Del Rio school district was composed of four school buildings and an athletic field, all of which were located on the same parcel of land. The white high school and two white elementary schools were at one end of the field and the Mexican school was located at the other end.

In 1930 the residents of Del Rio approved the sale of $185,000 in bonds to be devoted to the improvement of the existing school facilities. The school trustees earmarked the money to be used for constructing a new senior high school building, remodeling and enlarging the white elementary schools, and enlarging the Mexican school by adding five rooms, including an auditorium.

Mexican parents immediately objected to the plan not because of the quality or nature of the renovations to the Mexican school, but because such construction ensured the separation of the Mexican children from the white students.

The court, in deciding the case, concluded that the school district had not exceeded its administrative powers because the school board was not "arbitrarily" assigning Mexican children to the Mexican school. It also found that how Mexican students were identified as non-English-speaking for purposes of placing them in the Mexican school was not arbitrary or unconstitutional. Finally, it held that placement of Mexican children in the Mexican school was justified for additional pedagogical reasons. The first was the late enrollment and spotty attendance of the Mexican children. The second was, as in the *Méndez* case, the language issue. The school district argued that placing the Mexican children in the white school handicapped the Mexican students and thus they were better served by placing them in the Mexican school where their fellow students were more like them. Based on these grounds the court found that the school district had not violated any of the Mexican schoolchildren's constitutional rights.

The decision was a critical blow to LULAC and its zeal to eliminate segregation in the Texas school system. So devastating was the decision that LULAC concluded that, for the foreseeable future, the legal arena was not where the battle to end segregation in the school system should be fought. LULAC urged its members to take the battle to a different level and work informally with the various school districts to eliminate the discriminatory practices that they challenged in Del Rio.

While LULAC and the American G.I. Forum, another Mexican American organization that had as one of its goals the education of Mexican American children, continued to militate for equal educational opportunities for Mexican children, legal challenges to segregation in the Texas school system lay dormant until after the *Méndez* decision.

On April 8, 1947 the attorney general of Texas issued an opinion that prohibited segregation of Mexican children when such segregation was based solely on race. However, the decision provided an out to the local school districts by providing that separate placement of children could be justified based on language deficiencies and other needs, but only after these deficiencies and needs were determined by the administration of unbiased tests.

The attorney general's opinion turned out to be a paper tiger. It not only provided the school districts with an easy out—it also did not set forth a procedure to force compliance. The toothless nature of this decision was demonstrated when, several months after its passage, numerous challenges to school districts that continued to segregate Mexican schoolchildren were dismissed. A study of the Texas school system conducted by Virgil E. Stickland and George I. Sánchez found that segregation was practiced on "a purely arbitrary basis, determined solely by local custom, tradition and prejudice."[40]

Inspired by the *Méndez* case and assessing that the social and legal environments had changed, LULAC in 1948 assisted in filing a class-action suit against the Bastrop Independent School District. In *Delgado et al. v. Bastrop Independent School District of Bastrop County, Texas. et al.*[41] the complaint listed five arguments:

1. The defendants acted beyond the authority provided to them under the Texas constitution and laws of the state by separate placement of Mexican children.

2. Nothing in the Texas constitution permitted the segregation of Mexican children into separate schools and/or classes.

3. The segregation of the Mexican children was based on custom, usage and/or common plan.

4. The segregation of the Mexican children was condoned by the state superintendent of public education and state board of education.

5. The segregation of Mexican children denied them due process and violated their rights under the Fourteenth Amendment.[42]

As in *Méndez*, the court found that placing Mexican students in separate buildings was arbitrary, discriminatory, and illegal. The judge further wrote, "The plaintiffs, as aforesaid, by the acts of the defendants complained of, were deprived of their rights under the Constitution of the United States and the Laws of the United States to be free from discrimination solely because of their ancestry."

The *Méndez* decision, rendered in 1946, presaged the *Brown v. Board of Education* decision rendered by the U.S. Supreme Court in 1954 by approximately eight years, and the *Delgado* case rendered in 1948 presaged it by approximately six years. While *Brown v. Board of Education* provided the Supreme Court with the factual basis and legal arguments to declare state-imposed de jure segregation in public schools a violation of the Fourteenth Amendment, Mexicans in California and Texas had fought similar battles and laid much of the legal groundwork for *Brown*'s eventual victory.

One plausible reason can be advanced to explain why *Méndez* and *Delgado* have received so little attention from legal scholars and historians. The decision in *Brown v. Board of Education* was rendered by the Supreme Court, making it the law of the land. So while *Méndez* and *Delgado* had significant regional impact, the ruling in *Brown v. Board of Education* blanketed the United States, radically altering the educational policies of every state of the Union. It was therefore reasonable for the general public, and scholars as well, to view *Brown v. Board of Education* as the natural reference point for the elimination of the "separate but equal" doctrine in *Plessy v. Ferguson*. All other decisions were regarded as having lesser significance.

However, the struggle by Mexican Americans in the Southwest to overcome the pernicious effect of segregated schools was no less significant and meaningful than was the parallel struggle of African Americans in the South. And the detrimental, and in some instances devastating, effect that segregated schools had on Mexican American students was no less than their impact on Blacks in the South. On these grounds alone, the Latino struggle to eliminate the insidious quality of the "separate but equal" doctrine should receive the recognition that it deserves.

Endnotes

1. Kenneth J. Meier and Joseph Stewart, Jr., *The Politics of Hispanic Education: Un paso pa'lante y dos pa'tras* (Albany: State University of New York Press, 1991), p. xvii.

2. George J. Sánchez, *Becoming Mexican-American*, New York: Oxford University Press, 1993, p. 255.

3. Ibid., p. 257.

4. Charles Wollenberg, *All Deliberate Speed: Segregation and Exclusion in California Schools, 1855–1975*

(Berkeley: University of California Press, 1976), p. 112.

5. Sánchez, *Becoming Mexican-American*, p. 258.

6. Wollenberg, *All Deliberate Speed*, p. 112.

7. Ibid., p. 113.

8. Ibid.

9. Gilbert G. González, *Chicano Education in the Era of Segregation* (Cranbury, NJ.: Associated University Press, 1990), p. 72.

10. Ibid.

11. Wollenberg, *All Deliberate Speed*, p. 115.

12. Ibid., p. 116.

13. González, *Chicano Education in the Era of Segregation*, p. 137.

14. Ibid., p. 141.

15. Ibid., p. 142.

16. Ibid., p. 143.

17. Wollenberg, *All Deliberate Speed*, p. 120.

18. Guadalupe San Miguel Jr., *Let All of Them Take Heed: Mexican Americans and the Campaign for Education Equality in Texas, 1910–1981* (Austin: University of Texas Press, 1987), pp. 114–115.

19. *Méndez et al. v. Westminster School District of Orange County et al.* (1946), 64 F. Supp. 544.

20. Ibid., p. 545.

21. Ibid., p. 546.

22. Ibid.

23. Ibid., p. 549.

24. Ibid., p. 551.

25. Wollenberg, *All Deliberate Speed*, p. 128.

26. Christopher Arriola, "Knocking on the Schoolhouse Door: *Méndez v. Westminster:* Equal Protection, Public Education and Mexican Americans in the 1940s," *La Raza Law Journal* 8, no. 2 (1995): pp. 166–207.

27. *Westminster School District of Orange County et al. v. Méndez et al.*, 161 F. 2nd 774 (9th Cir., 1947), 780.

28. Wollenberg, *All Deliberate Speed*, p. 132.

29. González, *Chicano Education in the Era of Segregation*, p. 28.

30. "Segregation in Public Schools—A Violation of 'Equal Protection of the Laws'," *Yale Law Journal* 56, no. 6 (1947): 1059–1067; see also, "Segregation in Schools as a Violation of the XIVth Amendment," *Columbia Law Review* 47, no. 1 (1947): 325–329.

31. Lester H. Phillips, "Segregation in Education: A California Case Study," *Phylon* 10, no. 4 (1949): 407–413, p. 407.

32 David Montejano, *Anglos and Mexicans in the Making of Texas: 1836–1986* (Austin: University of Texas Press, 1987).

33. Ibid., p. 191.

34. Herschel T. Manuel, *The Education of Mexican and Spanish-Speaking Children in Texas* (Austin: University of Texas Press, 1930), p. 60.

35. Guadalupe San Miguel, *Let All of Them Take Heed*, p. 56.

36. Ibid., p. 71.

37. Ibid., p. 77.

38. *Independent School District v. Salvatierra*, 33 S.W.2d 790 (Tex. Civ. App. 1930), cert. Denied, 284 U.S. 580 (1931).

39. Guadalupe San Miguel, *Let All of Them Take Heed*, p. 78.

40. Ibid., p. 121.

41. *Minerva Delgado et al. v. Bastrop Independent School District of Bastrop County, Texas, et al.* (D.C. Texas Western District), June 15, 1948, Civil Action No. 388.

42. Guadalupe San Miguel, *Let All of Them Take Heed*, p.123.

The Fight for Mexican-American Studies in Tuscon

Nolan L. Cabrera, Elisa L. Meza and Dr. Roberto Cintli Rodríguez

May 3 was a Surreal Day at the Tucson Unified School District (TUSD). That afternoon, the entire neighborhood surrounding the district's headquarters was blocked off by Tucson police officers. K-9 units were on the prowl for bombs, snipers were stationed on the building's roof, a bomb squad patrolled the front of the building, and a helicopter hovered above. Dozens of officers lined the streets, and there were police vehicles as far as the eye could see. Near the entrance stood a makeshift altar set up by local clergy. By 4:30 p.m., two hours before the start of the school board meeting, several hundred people gathered outside, in the 90-degree desert heat. The building was locked down. Why this high level of "security" usually associated with militarized societies?

One week earlier, nine students had chained themselves to chairs at the April 26 TUSD board meeting in an act of civil disobedience in protest of the banning of Mexican American Studies. On December 30, 2010, Arizona State Superintendent of Public Instruction Tom Home declared the school district's Mexican, American Studies program out of compliance with A.R.S. § 15-112 (introduced as HB 2281)—a law enacted in May 2010 that effectively banned the teaching of ethnic studies in Arizona's K–12 schools and primarily targeted TUSD Mexican American Studies.[1] Rather than wait for Home to destroy the highly successful Mexican American Studies program, the TUSD School Board began dismantling it internally by removing Mexican American Studies classes from core curricula and demoting them to elective status.[2]

This led to the April 26 action. The hoard reacted by militarizing the next meeting with as much security as possible, claiming it was for the safety of the students and community members. Loudspeakers were put on the roof top for the hundreds of people outside, since it is against boardroom policy to prevent the community from hearing the meeting's agenda. As each minute passed, more supporters of Mexican American Studies arrived; a troupe of nearly 50 people showed up on bicycles with megaphones and flags. At the TUSD entrance, dozens of officers frisked and scanned everyone who entered with metal-detecting wands. Inside, many more heavily armed officers roamed the sealed-off building. Shortly before the meeting commenced, a number of officers in riot gear marched up the aisle in the boardroom. At least 50 officers were inside the building. Perhaps 150 were outside (estimates vary).

The board members sat in their designated chairs, waiting attentively to convene the meeting and seemingly oblivious to the unprecedented militarization

Dr. Nolan L. Cabrera is an Assistant Professor in the University of Arizona's Center for the Study of Higher Education, and an ethnic studies graduate from Stanford University. Elisa L. Meza is a fourth-year undergraduate at the University of Arizona studying English and Mexican American Studies, and is a member of UNIDOS. Roberto Dr. Cintli Rodriguez is an Assistant Professor at the University of Arizona in the Mexican American Studies Department and a member of the Mexican American Studies Community Advisory Board.

NACLA Report on the Americas, Copyright © 1995 by the North American Congress on Latin America, 38 Greene Street, New York, NY 10013.

surrounding them. After the meeting began, District Superintendent John Pedicone recommended tabling the proposal that would make Mexican American Studies classes, electives (establishing a path to elimination), but it was never clear whether the board would follow this recommendation. TUSD's usual 30-minute "call to audience" portion began the, meeting, allowing select individual to speak for three minutes, each. The last speaker, Raquel Rubio-Goldsmith, a respected professor and community activist, reminded the board that no matter how much they tried to dismantle Mexican American Studies, the community of Tucson would exist well beyond their tenure and the collective fight would continue.

After a rousing standing ovation, there was a motion from the floor for additional time to speak. The' motion was denied, but an audience member boldly stood up and approached the podium. She was promptly arrested and escorted out by eight security officers. A second audience member, Lupe Castillo, a 69-year-old disabled woman, began to read Dr. Martin Luther King Jr.'s, "Letter From a Birmingham Jail." Several officers in full riot gear approached her from behind, escorted her out, and arrested her. There was bedlam. About a dozen students took off their sweatshirts and, with fists in the air, revealed their T-shirts, which read: "You can silence our voices, but never our spirits." Amid chaos, riot police threw several elderly people and a cameraman out of the building. After Castillo was escorted out, five others were arrested for speaking. After much community outcry, the board finally adjourned the meeting and tabled the proposal, but not before many Mexican American Studies supporters and students were assaulted outside by Tucson police officers.[3] With the proposal tabled, Mexican American Studies was left intact after the May 3 meeting.

The struggle for equitable, relevant education through Mexican American Studies has been occurring for years. Since 2006, TUSD's Mexican American Studies program has come under political attack on a statewide level in particular from Tom Horne. From 2006 to 2010, Horne wrote three separate pieces of legislation to eliminate Mexican American Studies in TUSD. In the summer of 2009, hundreds of community members ran from Tucson to Phoenix in 115-degree heat as a visible social protest meant to raise awareness and ultimately defeat the proposed anti-Mexican American Studies law. As Horne continued his campaign, the students in the district responded with a series of meetings, protests, marches, rallies, vigils, and more runs. All of this changed in 2010, when growing

fears around immigration, a recession, and a midterm election made Mexican American Studies a perfect wedge issue to feed the Arizona Republican base. The proposed legislation did not stand alone. The draconian SB 1070 (legalizing racial profiling) and Prop 107 (banning affirmative, action) were also introduced by Arizona Republicans during this election cycle.

When Horne introduced HB 2281, he reminded the public that he had participated in the 1963 March on Washington. Invoking Dr. King, Horne attacked Mexican American Studies as antithetical to "the Dream," in an obvious attempt to avoid being labeled a racist. The law mandates that a school district can lose 10% of its state funding (about $15 million) if curricula violate any of the following, criteria: that classes (1) advocate ethnic solidarity rather than treating pupils as individuals, (2) promote resentment toward a race or class of people, (3) are designed primarily for pupils of a particular ethnic group, and (4) promote the overthrow of the U.S. government.[4]

These provisions were problematic for a number of reasons. The first tenet (ethnic solidarity) has almost no tangible meaning. What does ethnic solidarity look like? The vagueness allows Horne to misinterpret and misuse the term *la raza,* equating it with ethnic chauvinism ("the race") as opposed to ethnic pride ("the people").[5] There is a certain irony in Horne citing Dr. King and the March on Washington, a race-based collective, as a way of framing ethnic solidarity as inherently negative. The second tenet (promoting racial resentment) is an attack on even teaching about racism because this contradicts Horne's view that students should be "taught that this is the land of opportunity, and that if they work hard, they can achieve their goals: They should not be taught that they are oppressed."[6] Horne rejects the notion that racism still exists and equates the teaching of racism with victimizing white people. This fits well within contemporary racial theory whereby racism is so systemically ingrained in society that color-blindness actually becomes a form of racism.[7]

With respect to the charge of ethnic grouping, one could argue that the disproportionate representation of white students in advanced-placement high school courses means they are designed for a particular ethnic group. However, these classes will never be the targets of HB 2281, since Horne only finds ethnic clustering problematic when minorities do it. Finally, the tenet about overthrowing the U.S. government relies on a racist framing of Latinas and Latinos as foreign "others" worthy of increased scrutiny and suspicion.[8] Sedition is an extremely serious charge, and the inclusion of this criterion in HB 2281 plays to the popular racist view that Latinas and Latinos are not fully American, that their, national loyalty is in question, and that they might even try to reconquer Aztlán—the name given by Chicano activists to the territories seized in the Mexican-American War (1846–48).

On May 11, 2010, Arizona governor Jan Brewer signed HB 2281 into law after it was approved by a margin of 32 to 26, and it eventually became A.R.S. § 15-112. The next day, Horne came to Tucson a victory lap.[9] He had planned to hold a press conference at the TUSD headquarters to announce the bill's passage. However, middle and high school students formed a human chain around the building, and Horne retreated to the Arizona federal building in downtown Tucson. Several hundred students followed him there, filled the building, and waited to address him after the press conference. Instead, Home left through the rear entrance, avoiding the community at all costs. In the end, 15 people were arrested at the federal building for refusing to leave until they could meet with Horne.

During his time as state superintendent, Horne never set foot in a Mexican American Studies classroom or conducted a systematic audit of the program. He said that if he did attend a class, it would likely be tailored to avoid controversial subjects in his presence.[10] On his last day in office, Horne found TUSD out of compliance on all four tenets of A.R.S. § 15-112, arguing, "In view of the long history regarding that program, the violations are deeply rooted in the program itself, and partial adjustments will not constitute compliance."[11] In other words, there was no way for the Mexican American Studies program to meet the state requirements; it could only be eliminated.

Although Horne became the Arizona attorney general before he could fully enforce A.R.S. § 15-112, his successor, John Huppenthal's, has carried the torch. This was not "surprising, since Huppenthal's campaign advertisements specifically said that if elected he would "stop la raza."[12] He did not say he would stop Mexican American Studies, ethnic studies, or raza studies. Rather, he would stop la raza—that is, the people of Mexican descent in Arizona.

The tusd school board capitulated to the pressure applied by Huppenthal and the school district under A.R.S. § 15-112. First, the board voted not to challenge the constitutionality of the law.[13] Second, board president Mark Stegeman introduced what has become known as the Stegeman Resolution.[14] The resolution was couched in the language of valuing diversity—"The traditional high school core curriculum substantially

ignores the experiences and contributions of ethnic minorities," it reads—yet it demoted Mexican American Studies courses from being part of the core curricula to electives, slowly bleeding the program from the inside out. On top of students' already packed schedules, taking an additional elective literature or history course would be overbearing. Although this proposal made no sense to the students, Stegeman insisted he knew best.

Disregarding vocal, consistent community opposition, Stegeman introduced his resolution for a vote, at the April 26 board meeting. Most board members including Stegeman, believed he had the necessary votes to pass his resolution.[15] For many in the community, the vote seemed to be a foregone conclusion and the dismantling of Mexican American Studies seemed imminent. It was no secret which school board members supported Mexican American Studies and which did not, but the vote never happened.

April 26 began with high attendance, in part because students had rallied community support for Mexican American Studies. The boardroom was so packed, many community members had to stand outside. While the hallway filled, chanting began, despite new TUSD regulations meant to eliminate demonstrations during meetings. Fifteen minutes before the meeting started, group of nine students seated inside stood up, moved past the numerous news cameras, and ran up behind the TUSD board dais: The students belonged to a group called United Non-Discriminatory Individuals Demanding Our Studies (UNIDOS), a grassroots, radical youth collective founded in January 2011 to defend ethnic studies, and Mexican American Studies in particular. The first student ran straight into a security guard. As he attempted to grab her, the other eight revealed hidden chains around their waists and locked themselves to the board members' seats. The students began to chant with fists raised high, "Our education is under attack! What do we do? Fight back!"

The community immediately piled into the board room, megaphones held in the air, while several more students ran up to the dais to hang up a hand-painted canvas banner that read, "UNIDOS Presents the Youth School Board." Police were waiting outside but the TUSD board ordered them not to enter the room. The demonstration continued peacefully. The chanting only lowered when the students' media team read from their Ten Point Resolution, demanding the repeal of HB 2281, an end to school closures, an accountable school board, and the preservation of Mexican American Studies.

In most areas throught the country, teenagers are trying to avoid going to school. In Tucson we have the opposite: students risking everything for their education.

There was still tension in the air as the police presence grew outside, but the students continued their peaceful act of civil disobedience. The room responded with thunderous applause when it was announced that the board meeting, was postponed. Three hours later, TUSD Superintendent John Pedicone negotiated with adult allies in the audience and ultimately decided not to press charges against the students. The demonstration evolved into a community celebration. Two youth mariachi musicians climbed onto the TUSD dais to play music for the room. Everyone danced, laughed, chanted. No one was hurt. No arrests were made. There was no official board meeting and therefore no vote, which meant Mexican American Studies remained intact for the time being.[16]

The student organizing that led up to april 26 began as an offshoot of Save Ethnic Studies, a teachers' group that filed a lawsuit on October 18, 2010, challenging the constitutionality of HB 2281.[17] In December 2010, students began to question why their voice was not part of the discussions surrounding Mexican American Studies, especially since it was their education that was at stake. These students formed UNIDOS in the first week of 2011, and they began a political discussion group that met each Saturday, creating their own autonomous space to discuss how to defend their education. The students began to organize themselves. They wanted to be at the forefront of the struggle, to remind the school district who the classes were for.

After the April 26 action, numerous commentators both locally and nationally weighed in. *The Arizona Republic* ran an editorial titled, "Who's in Charge at Tucson Unified?" It described April 26 as "chaotic political theater" and called on adults to "reassert themselves."[18] Glenn Beck called the action an instance of juvenile "rage."[19] Pedicone wrote an editorial claiming, with scant evidence, that the protest occurred because "adults used students as pawns."[20] These commentators all made problematic assumptions: that students do not possess social agency, that their action was spontaneous—akin to throwing a temper tantrum—and that "restoring order" involves adults regaining control of the situation. These discussions were devoid of the notion that the students on April 26 were thoughtful, intentional, and purposeful in their actions. Interviews with student activists contest the assumptions. As one participant in the April

26 action explains (because of continued police harassment, we are maintaining the students' anonymity):

I hoped that the school board would stop ignoring us and stop treating us as if issues discussed in school board meetings were not of our concern and should be left up to the adults to handle. In fact, every decision made in that room is of huge concern for us as students. I also hoped to make them realize we're not just kids hollering outside buildings for the heck of it. When we say we're defending our classes, we mean business.

This passion was tempered with a critical analysis of both the district and the state's anti-Latino atmosphere within which the attacks on Mexican American Studies occurred. The students began educating themselves on grassroots organizing. They met on the weekends and studied the teachings of the Zapatistas, the Black Panthers, and Dr. King. They focused on redefining the term *resistance,* and worked to become, critical analysts and media strategists who could create the space for other youth to become politically engaged. The UNIDOS members publicly asserted their political voice at a February 8 press conference outside of TUSD headquarters, just before a board meeting. They told the community that they were a youth collective fighting for Mexican American Studies. UNIDOS utilized a unique style of political expression that evening as they were joined by a DJ, MCs, and live bands.

At the February 8 board meeting, UNIDOS representatives demanded to meet with all school board members to discuss HB 2281. Due to TUSD's many regulations, however, not all could meet at once. As a result, UNIDOS was able to meet with only two school board members: Adelita Grijalva and Judy Burns, who have been the only consistent", public supporters of Mexican American Studies classes. On March 8, UNIDOS requested a public statement from TUSD that it would protect Mexican American Studies courses. TUSD refused. For UNIDOS, the choices were clear: do nothing and allow Mexican American Studies classes to be dismantled, or respond through alternative means. One student offered the following analysis:

We felt that if we didn't do something [on April 26], then our history would be erased. This action was needed to stop the vote and to save our roots from being slashed away. We knew what this action entailed when we decided to go through with it. Arrest was definitely something we knew could happen, but we felt this action was needed. If we didn't stand up for what we believed in, then who would? Our job as citizens is to stop unjust laws or be pushed around unjustly. And we chose to take a stand no matter the consequences.

Displaying more moral courage than most of the adults at the April 26 board meeting, the students knew they had one chance to keep their classes intact. Instead of capitulating to the overtly racist HB 2281, they decided to fight back, putting themselves at great risk physically, emotionally, and academically. The students' demeanor during the action was self-assured, but inside, many felt trepidation:

[I felt] a mixture of emotions: anxious, nervous; scared, but very hopeful. The reason for this was because everyone up there was risking something. I for example didn't know the reaction my parents would have after they found out; that was scary. The overall experience was all of the above because that moment was do or die. Without our actions, the right to our history would be taken.

Another student put it this way:

We wanted to show we are not tired, we will not be moved, we will fight for education. Because as scholars of today and of the future, we are critical thinkers that will not have our essential history that connects us to who we truly are be taken away from us.

One student noted the hypocrisy of the TUSD board, a group of adults who continually preach the importance of civic engagement, and their reaction to UNIDOS student act of civil disobedience:

You have education figures telling students to take charge and become active for their education, to be heard and create change. Then you have youth and community alike act in civil and responsible ways for over a year and still be ignored. Then to have those same figures become angry with the youth for standing up and taking radical action that was youth led, youth empowered, youth organized is absurd. Not only was [April 26] worth it, it was necessary!

Without the UNIDOS students' efforts, the Stegeman Resolution would have passed and Mexican American Studies would have been dismantled. In most areas throughout the country, teenagers are trying to avoid going to school. In Tucson, we have the opposite: students fighting for their rights, risking everything for their education. The struggle continues, and as one student said:

Our classes are still being attacked to this day, but UNIDOS will not stop till there is equitable education for all.

In response to the April 26 action, the community was met with the militarized rescheduled board meeting of May 3 described at the beginning of this article. Instead of celebrating the civic engagement of students fighting for their education, the TUSD School Board viewed them as a threat. There was never an analysis of how TUSD systematically ignored the student voice or how the Stegeman Resolution vote brought about the actions of April 26. Instead, the students were framed as uncivil, out of control, and unproductive. Their example, however, motivated a number of adult community members at the May 3 board meeting to put themselves at the same physical risk to defend Mexican American Studies. For now, the classes are still intact, but the struggle continues. The lawsuit from the TUSD teachers is still tied up in the courts. The TUSD School Board appealed the Huppenthal ruling which found TUSD out of compliance with A.R.S. § 15-112, despite the findings of Huppenthal's $110,000 hand-picked external audit concluding the opposite (i.e., that Mexican American Studies was in compliance with A.R.S. § 15-112).[21] The community was awaiting the judge's decision in mid-November. Regardless of the outcome, the actions of UNIDOS serve as continual inspiration throughout the community, as this group of informed, dedicated, insightful, and above all brave students reignited the movement in the fight for ethnic and Mexican American Studies.

The Librotraficante Behind the Movement to Smuggle "Wetbooks" Back Into Arizona

Paula Beltrán

Manuel Muñoz's book, *Zigzagger*, is banned at the high school right across from the University of Arizona campus where he is a professor of creative writing. Munoz graduated from Harvard, received his MFA from Cornell University, and is the recipient of a fellowship from the National Endowment from the Arts. Apparently, the Tucson Unified School District (TUSD) has found that all of that literary pedigree only led him to *"promote the overthrow of the United States government."* His collection of short stories was also found to be promoting the "resentment toward a race or class of people," and "ethnic solidarity." The book was among the titles blacklisted last month by TUSD, who say they're only looking to be in compliance of Arizona's HB 2281. The district maintains that the books were not "banned," but merely "confiscated" and/or "cleared" from classrooms.

Houston-based novelist Tony Diaz said he was more than a little baffled by the TUSD's decision. "There are schools across the country that would covet having Manuel Muñoz in their vicinity, yet Tucson squanders his talents, and puts at risk the education of our young. The school's student body is predominantly Mexican-American," he said. "His writing would have an incredible impact on the children in those classrooms."

Diaz is the author of *The Aztec Love God* and a graduate of the University of Houston's MFA program. He teaches English and Mexican-American lit at Houston's Community College. He is also the founder of *Nuestra Palabra: Latino Writers Having Their Say* - a Houston-based literary nonprofit established in 1998 to "promote Latino Literature and culture."

And Diaz is behind the *Librotraficante* movement, arguably the most creative of responses to the Tucson's School District's controversial decision.

The Librotraficantes believe it is "the cause of our generation" to protest Arizona's HB 2281, the law which *bans ethnic studies and the books used to teach them.*

It should be noted that despite the "ethnic" tag, Mexican-American studies is the only course prohibited. Ninety-nine percent of the books boxed by school authorities were the works of literature and critical theory by respected MexAm authors and activists. Though a few Amer Indian authors are among the banned/boxed/or unwelcome texts, despite the fact that the Arizona statute on prohibited courses clearly states "This section shall not be construed to restrict or prohibit: 1. Courses or classes for Native American pupils that are required to comply with federal law." The rest of the wording goes on to describe—more or less—several federally protected classes. So far African-American and Asian American studies remain alive in Arizona. (Someone double-check!)

The mission and vision of the Librotraficantes? The "smuggling" of "wet books" across state lines. The plan is for a caravan of "mind-altering prose," activists, and writers to make their way from Houston to Tucson for a mass reading. The caravan will be on the road for about a week and on the way they will stop in cities across the Southwest for readings by emerging literary talent and some of the authors allegedly banned. They plan to arrive in Tucson by March 18.

I asked Diaz to chat with me about his trade in "illegal literature."

PB: **As the founder of Nuestra Palabra (NP), did you ever think the day would come when there would be a ban on the very books your organization has done so much to bring to the awareness of the reading public?**

TD: This really is stunning. At this moment, in Tucson, Arizona, it is illegal to teach Sandra Cisneros's young adult novel, House on Mango Street. For the past thirteen years, I've brought to Houston, or interviewed on our radio show many of the writers who are on the Tucson Banned List, including *Sandra Cisneros, Dagoberto Gilb*, Manuel Muñoz, Jimmy Santiago Baca, and *Luis Alberto Urrea*. We crossed state lines with them, maybe handling these contraband books is now a matter for the FBI? This is the cause of our generation.

PB: **Unlike TUSD board member, *Adelita Grijalva*, most TUSD administrators have insisted that there is no such "ban" and that the titles were merely "cleared" from the classrooms and "stored" but remain available in libraries district-wide. Banned or cleared, what do you think is the not-so-subtle message that is being given to students?**

TD: George Orwell lives. Double Speak exists. The TUSD administrators have actually pushed back hard to play with words to make this atrocity palatable to Americans. But let's make this clear, in Tucson public school classes it is against the law right now to teach Manuel Munoz's book. If his book is taught, the

district loses 10% of its funding. That's hyper-banning. We must speak up for the well-being of our community. Books changed my life. I didn't read a book by a Latino until I was a junior in college. That book was *Down These Mean Streets* by Piri Thomas. Before then, I didn't know I could write about my background.

If that first book by a Latino had not come into my hands, I would not have gone on to leave Chicago to attend the University of Houston's Creative Writing program and become only the 3rd Latino to complete an MFA there. I would not have gone on to begin Nuestra Palabra. I would not have been able to unite the talented writers I have been blessed to work with. I can honestly say, our words have transformed Houston. We made the world a better place. Tucson is preventing this from happening to all our young.

PB: **In the press release posted on your website it states "Children of the American Dream must unite to preserve the civil rights of all Americans." Who do you hope to hear from at this time? Who do you see joining NP's cause?**

TD: I am shocked at how many people do not know about this happening. When people do find out about it, they are skeptical. Some think that the books are being eliminated because they are published in Spanish. All the books are in English. Some people think that this is being done because the students are undocumented. This is being done to American Citizens. When people realize that, they do get mad. But we need them to get involved. We will be extolling quantum demographics during our caravan. This means we will celebrate not just our culture, not just other cultures, but we will pinpoint and celebrate the bridges the already exist between us. All other groups need to unite behind us to protect the first amendment for all Americans.

Immigrants, Latinos, and Education in the United States

By Sonia Soltero

Sonia Soltero is director of the Bilingual-Bicultural Education Program and associate professor of education at DePaul University, where she works in the Department of Leadership in Education, Language, and Human Services. Soltero's research covers the fields of bilingual and dual-language education, language planning, and language minority rights and policy, and she has taught courses on curriculum development, sociopolitical and historical perspectives in bilingual education, and emergent reading and language arts. Soltero's works in progress address the determinants of native language development in school among Chinese immigrant families in Chicago and the support and opposition to bilingual education, official English, and undocumented immigrants' rights in the United States.

ABSTRACT

Today's educational leaders face an unprecedented challenge to improve the quality of public education while simultaneously accommodating the educational needs of children who come from recently immigrated families, most of whom are Mexican and Latin American. Soltero examines the principal issues that pertain to the education of Latino students who come from non-English-speaking backgrounds. The paper offers brief synopses of the historical, demographic, political, and legal contexts of language-minority education in the United States, tracing factors influencing positive and negative conceptions of bilingual education. It outlines the debates surrounding additive and subtractive methods of bilingual education, analyzing their theoretical and pedagogical underpinnings. There is no federal mandate for bilingual education, but civil rights laws do require educational programs that offer equal opportunities for English-Language Learners (ELLs). Many ELLs have long been marginalized and too often segregated into programs that suffer from inadequate attention. The extent to which schools affirm and promote ELLs' language and cultural backgrounds produces either empowering or disabling educational frameworks. The demographic changes in the United States have generated increasing challenges for educators and policy-makers on how best to address ELLs' educational experiences and outcomes. Calling for a critical and culturally responsive education system, Soltero's essay concludes with a section that presents both broad and specific recommendations at the federal and state government, boards of education, school district, school, and classroom levels for improving these experiences and outcomes.

INTRODUCTION

This paper examines the principal issues that pertain to the education of Latino students who come from non-English-speaking backgrounds. The paper offers brief synopses of the historical, demographic, political, and legal contexts of language-minority education in the United States, analyzes its theoretical and pedagogical underpinnings, and discusses implications for the advancement of linguistic-minority student achievement.

The demographic changes in the United States have generated increasing challenges for educators and policymakers on how best to address the educational needs of children who come from recently immigrated families, most of whom are Mexican and Latin American. Federal and state laws require that all children residing in the United States have access to quality education, including children who are not proficient in the English language and who may or may not be legal residents. However, providing education services to recently immigrated children from developing countries has been a contentious political and educational issue for some time.

In the United States the education of non-English-speaking children has been closely tied to the sociopolitical context of anti-immigration movements, xenophobic sentiments, and assimilationist ideologies. These nativist principles favor the interests of the natives over those of foreigners, often leading to hostility toward immigrants (Fry 2007). Part of the nativist approach is for the natives to control foreign access to valued resources such as employment, the *lingua franca* (English), citizenship, and education.

In response to the continued and increasing influx of immigrants from Spanish-speaking countries, anti-immigrant sentiment has surged in many parts of the United States. Two popular stances govern the ideology of anti-immigration: abolish bilingual education and make English the official language of the United States. In response, many Latino communities create stronger social bases by resisting language and cultural assimilation in favor of acculturation models of integration. This acculturation model results in bicultural groups that can function in two spheres by maintaining their native language and culture and at the same time adopting the language and culture of the host country. However, maintaining a non-English language in the United States is especially difficult due to societal pressures to assimilate, a proclivity for monolingualism, legal and funding restrictions on bilingual education, and a collective desire to increase the status of English as the official language of the land.

Education for non-English-speaking children in the United States is provided in one of two mediums: bilingual or English-only instruction. English-only instruction offers the academic curriculum through immersion in English with no native language support, whereas bilingual instruction presents the academic curriculum in students' mother tongue while they are learning English. On the surface, bilingual education appears to be merely a choice of language of instruction, but a closer look reveals that it is heavily politicized and contentious. The controversial nature of bilingual education is fed by lack of public support, misconceptions about the language acquisition process, a shortage of qualified teachers, and lack of appropriate instructional materials and assessment measures, all factors that have contributed to negative attitudes toward bilingual education not only on the part of the mainstream population but also on the part of immigrant communities.

Several studies have examined the public's opinion of bilingual education in the United States (Huddy and Sears 1990; Shin and Gribbons 1996). Shin and Kim (1996) found that most Korean immigrant parents support the general principles of bilingual education, but when asked specifically if the use of Korean in the classroom allowed their children to be at the same level as their peers academically while they developed English, only 32 percent of the parents agreed. The findings point to a lack of understanding among immigrant parents about the workings of bilingual education.

Conflicting views of bilingual education are common among immigrant groups residing in the United States. Opposition to bilingual education is most pronounced when an extreme view (only native-language instruction) of bilingual education is presented, but when subjects are asked about using both languages or are asked about bilingual education in general, responses are more positive (Krashen 1996). Shin and Gribbons (1996) found that Latino parents tend to support the general principles of bilingual education. Similarly, De la Garza et al. (1992) found strong support for bilingual education among Mexican, Puerto Rican, and Cuban parents. The majority of Latino parents felt that reading, writing, and basic subjects should be taught in both English and Spanish.

Several conditional characteristics shape attitudes and perceptions toward bilingual education. Elements that contribute to negative attitudes include:

- immigrants' desire to succeed in an English-dominant society that requires English proficiency to access better educational and employment opportunities;
- an emphasis on assimilating into the mainstream society;

- fear of discrimination and prejudicial treatment due to lack of English proficiency;
- belief that bilingualism is a liability;
- supposition that bilingual education retards English-language development and stigmatizes children who participate in bilingual programs; and
- assumptions that bilingual education programs are of inferior quality in comparison to English-only education programs.

Factors that contribute to favorable attitudes toward bilingual education include:

- immigrants' desire to maintain and pass on the native language and culture to the second and third generations;
- belief that bilingualism is an asset;
- recognition that a bilingual person has better employment opportunities;
- aspirations to eventually return to the native country;
- circular migration and close ties to the native country; and
- fear of discrimination and prejudicial treatment due to lack of language proficiency in the native country.

Bilingual education in the United States has typically been implemented as a corrective and subtractive program that aims to assimilate linguistic minorities into the mainstream culture and produce monolingual English speakers. Although bilingual education models originated as enrichment programs intended to develop fluency in two languages and promote cultural pluralism, the focus has shifted to remedial efforts designed to help *disadvantaged* children overcome their *handicap* of limited English proficiency. The most detrimental elements of this type of subtractive education are both the loss of the home language and the resulting alienation from the home culture.

Cummins's (2000) notion of *coercive vs. collaborative relations of power,* in which society's micro-and macro-structures are configured by dominant-subordinated group relationships, helps to explain the influences on how educators define their roles, expectations, and assumptions in the education of Latino children. For English-language learners (ELLs), *coercive* relations of power are manifested in assimilationist practices that promote the rejection of the home culture and language as a necessary condition to succeed in the mainstream

society. Conversely, *collaborative* relations of power value and recognize the sources of knowledge that minority students possess even though they are outside the dominant discourse of schools. For ELLs, the extent to which schools affirm and promote their language and cultural backgrounds produces either empowering or disabling educational frameworks.

DEMOGRAPHIC CONTEXT

The number of students who are not proficient in English in the United States has surpassed the overall growth in school enrollments and created additional challenges for schools to meet the demands for adequate bilingual programs and English as a second language (ESL) services. According to the 2000 Census, the total K–12 enrollment in the United States grew 12 percent in a decade (from 45,443,389 in 1993 to 49,619,090 in 2003). Of the 53.2 million children currently enrolled in K–12 classrooms, 3.8 million children are not proficient in English. In contrast, ELLs' enrollment increased by 65 percent from 3,037,922 students to 5,013,539 between 1993 and 2003. Almost 70 percent of ELLs live in California, Florida, Illinois, New York, and Texas. According to Kominski, Jamieson, and Martinez (2001), who examine seven at-risk conditions for school-age populations, ELLs are more likely to live in families with incomes below 185 percent of the federal poverty threshold and come from new immigrant backgrounds. Children who do not speak English well, or have family incomes less than $10,000, or have parents who have recently immigrated, are at risk for poor life outcomes. Kominski, Jamieson, and Martinez identify the seven risk factors as:

> at least one disability; retained in grade at least once; speaks English less than 'very well'; does not live with both parents; either parent emigrated in past 5 years; family income below $10,000; and neither parent/guardian employed. Generally, these conditions are thought to be characteristics of the individual, or situations of the context they are a part of, that are believed to create higher likelihoods of undesirable life outcomes (e.g., completing high school, avoiding premarital births), or to impact overall quality of life. (Kominski, Jamieson, and Martinez 2001)

The essential risk factors facing many Latino children in the United States (poverty, lack of English proficiency, and lack of access to social support systems) are well researched and broadly reported (Suarez-Orozco, Suarez-Orozco, and Todorova 2008). Latino children face many challenges related to family income and structure, parental work patterns, educational attainment, English proficiency, and health insurance coverage. Students of Mexican descent have the largest high school dropout rate in the United States and have experienced an alarming rate of school failure. According to the final report of the President's Advisory Commission on Educational Excellence for Hispanic Americans (2003), 61 percent of recently immigrated Mexican students drop out of high school. According to census data, Latino immigrants' graduation rates are well below those of native-born groups such as African Americans and whites. Only 34 percent of Mexican immigrants have a high school diploma, compared to 90 percent for whites and 74 percent for African Americans (National Center for Education Statistics 2002).

Although measures to address the educational needs of Latino students have been adopted, the educational attainment of this group continues to be a source of concern. In 2005, among Latinos aged 25, 7.9 percent had less than five years of elementary school; 58.5 percent had high school completion or higher, and 12 percent had a bachelor's or higher degree, compared to 0.5 percent, 90 percent, and 30.5 percent in respective categories for the white non-Hispanic population (National Center for Education Statistics 2007).

Because students who are considered 'at risk' commonly underperform academically, they require access to qualified educators and quality language education services to address their linguistic and academic needs. In the United States most teachers and administrators lack basic knowledge about factors that impact the education of ELLs, such as understanding bilingual education and second-language acquisition as well as how poverty and immigration impact educational attainment. To compound this lack of knowledge, Latino teachers and administrators are underrepresented in schools nationwide. According to the National Center for Education Statistics (2006a), only 6 percent of all teachers in the United States are Latino (compared to 83 percent who are white) and only 5 percent of school principals are Latino (compared to 82 percent who are white). The lack of relevant knowledge among administrators and teachers and the under-representation of Latino teachers and principals affect schools, school districts, and language-minority populations:

Americas ethnic profile is rapidly changing. In 2000, 1 of every 3 children in the United States is from a racial or ethnic minority group, 1 in 7 speaks a language other than English, and 1 in 15 was foreign born ... Minority children comprise an increasing percentage of public school students ... The limited English proficient population is the fastest growing in our nation. (United States Code Service; Title 20, Education, 2007)

Although the urgency to address the academic needs of Pre K–12 students from non-English-speaking backgrounds is clear, institutions of higher education that prepare educators for the realities of a diverse student population have not responded with adequate teacher preparation programs. Compounding the difficult practical issues that schools face with respect to teaching ELLs, the current mechanisms for preparing teachers and administrators have failed to produce enough educators who possess the knowledge and skills required to address more effectively the needs of ELLs and their families. Existing education leadership programs fall short in preparing school administrators to deal with the complexities of an increasingly diverse school population (Darling-Hammond et al. 1995). A nationwide survey of 417 higher education institutions reported the following:

Only a small number of higher education institutions surveyed offer a teacher preparation program in bilingual education or TESOL [Teachers of English to Speakers of Other Languages]. Few preparation programs require that mainstream teacher candidates are prepared to teach English language learners. The study found fewer than 1/6th of the higher education institutions studied require preparation of mainstream elementary and secondary teachers regarding the education of limited English proficient students ... The population of English language learners in our public schools continues to rise exponentially, such that half of all teachers may expect to teach an English language learner during their career. [So] the dearth of programs that exist to prepare teachers to work with this population of students is staggering. (Menken and Antunez 2001)

Only the states of Florida and New York require that all university students who are earning teacher certification complete courses related to the education of students who are not yet proficient in the English language. Such courses cover ESL instructional methods, second-language acquisition theories, legal requirements for ELL education, and socio-cultural aspects of educating language-minority students.

In addition to the shortage of qualified teachers and administrators and the lack of appropriate teacher education coursework and programs in institutions of higher education, other institutional and societal at-risk factors contribute to the underachievement of minority-language students: underfunded schools and programs; overcrowded schools with predominantly minority students; over-representation of novice teachers in high-risk and 'combat zone' schools; lack of extracurricular activities for students; segregated and unsafe schools; inadequacy of services such as health and counseling; and deteriorating school buildings.

The Chicago metropolitan area, which includes six counties, is reflective of the challenges faced by school systems across the United States. According to the Chicago Council on Global Affairs report, *A Shared Future: The Economic Engagement of Greater Chicago and its Mexican Community* (2006), of the 1.6 million Latinos in the Chicago metropolitan area, about 1.3 million, or 80 percent, are Mexican or of Mexican origin, followed by 149,000 Puerto Ricans and 17,000 Cubans. According to Paral (2006), "the Latino population of metropolitan Chicago has become arguably less 'Latino' and increasingly more 'Mexican'" (105). In 2004 Mexicans accounted for 41 percent of all immigrants in the city of Chicago and 16 percent of the surrounding area. Mexicans constitute the largest ethnic group in the Chicago metropolitan area, and their population is expected to double by 2030. According to the Chicago Council on Global Affairs report, the role of the Mexican community in the Chicago and Illinois economy is critical: "Mexicans constitute 80 percent of the Chicago Latino community ... Mexico is Illinois' second largest trading partner ... Mexicans' bilingual and bicultural capabilities represent opportunities for business and cultural exchanges with the $2.4 trillion market of the world's Spanish-speaking countries" (ll).

The Chicago metropolitan area has one of the largest and fastest-growing populations of students of Mexican origin. Latino children under 18, who are mostly born in the United States, make up 35 percent of the total Latino population in the Chicago metropolitan area. Between 1990 and 2004 every county in the Chicago metropolitan area except Cook County experienced more than a 150 percent increase in the population of Mexican descent. Chicago Public Schools (the third largest public school system in the United States

after New York City and Los Angeles) educate a total of 430,000 students; 38 percent of these students come from Latino backgrounds, mostly from Mexican families.

BILINGUAL EDUCATION

Broadly defined, bilingual education includes any educational program that uses two languages for instruction. Unlike foreign-language education, where students study the target language and culture as a subject, bilingual education usually entails the study of literacy and/or content areas (math, science, and social studies) through two languages, the majority language (English) and a minority language (such as Spanish). In the United States bilingual education programs may be offered in early childhood, elementary, or high school settings and sometimes in colleges and universities. The feasibility of offering bilingual education programs for second-language learners depends on several factors: sufficient numbers of students from the same language group; availability of certified bilingual teachers; and state and local policies.

Bilingual education is a multidimensional concept used to refer to numerous types of program designs that have divergent linguistic goals (bilingualism or monolingualism), differences in the length of implementation (short-term or long-term), variations in the amount of use of each language, and distinctions in programmatic composition (Crawford 2004). According to the *Encyclopedia of Bilingualism and Bilingual Education* (Baker and Jones 1998) "Bilingual education is a simple label for a complex phenomenon." Mackey (1978) categorized 90 variations of bilingual education around the world. Nevertheless, all programs in which ELLs participate fall under two basic paradigms:

1. *Additive programs.* The goal is to develop full bilingualism, biliteracy, and biculturalism by adding the second language and maintaining and developing the first language. Additive program models include *maintenance, developmental bilingualism, heritage language,* and *dual language* or *two-way immersion.*

2. *Subtractive programs.* The goal is to become monolingual in the majority language by abandoning the native language. Subtractive models include *transitional bilingual education* and *newcomer programs.* Other program models for ELLs that do not fall under the category of

bilingual education because they generally only use English as the medium of instruction are *structured English immersion* and *English as a second language* (ESL).

Transitional bilingual education temporarily supports students' academic development by providing native-language instruction as they acquire English through ESL for a period ranging from one to eight years. The principal objective is to facilitate students' academic progress through the language they understand while they acquire proficiency in the second language to function academically in English. Transitional bilingual education consists of two program types: 1) *Early-exit* is the model most widely implemented in the United States, where ELLs are exited into the general English education program after one to four years, once they have achieved proficiency in English. 2) In *late-exit* students continue to receive instruction in the native language for a few more years after having achieved proficiency in English. The primary goal in late-exit is to continue to develop students' literacy and oral language skills in the native language as well as in English for a longer period of time.

Maintenance bilingual education is sometimes known as *developmental* or *enrichment* education. In this model ELLs maintain and develop their native languages after they have acquired English, usually through eighth grade or beyond. The primary aim of maintenance bilingual education is for students to develop bilingual and biliterate proficiencies and to achieve academically at grade level. Maintenance bilingual programs are culturally responsive because they value and build on students' home cultural and linguistic knowledge (Cummins 2000).

Heritage language programs are designed for students who come from homes where a language other than English is used, including people of indigenous ancestry, colonized groups, new immigrants and refugees, and children and grandchildren of immigrants. These programs aim either to maintain the language and culture of the home or to revitalize the native language and culture that is no longer used fluently by the younger generation of its speakers.

Newcomer centers programs provide academic, linguistic, and social support to recently immigrated students typically in middle or high school settings and are designed to address the needs of recent arrivals who have interrupted schooling or no schooling (Castro Feinberg 2002). Newcomer centers were created to address the special needs of ELLs that bilingual or ESL

programs are not adequately equipped to manage because these students are not proficient in English and they are not academically prepared to deal with grade-level work. A key feature of most newcomer centers is the provision of an emotionally safe learning environment that supports rapid second-language learning, adaptation to the host culture, and development of a positive self-image (Diaz-Rico and Weed 2002).

Dual-language education, also known as *two-way bilingual immersion,* is the only bilingual program that integrates English native speakers with speakers of another language in the common pursuit of continuing to develop their native language and culture while acquiring a second language and culture (Soltero 2004). The major goals of this model are to develop full biliteracy and bilingualism, high academic achievement, and multicultural competencies. Dual-language education in the United States was adapted from the Canadian educational program that began in 1965 in Montreal, where English-speaking children initially received all curriculum instruction in French and gradually added English (Lambert and Tucker 1972).

Researchers and educators differ in their conceptions and definitions of bilingual education. Nevertheless, the descriptions of the models presented above provide general characteristics of the types of educational programs offered to ELLs in the United States. Unfortunately, not all ELLs have the benefit of participating in specialized instruction programs such as ESL and bilingual education. Many ELLs throughout the United States end up in submersion or 'sink or swim' contexts, where ELLs are simply placed in mainstream classrooms with no specialized support.

SECOND-LANGUAGE THEORIES AND PROGRAM MODELS

One of many incorrect assertions used against bilingual education is the notion that second-language learners can acquire English in less than one year. Decades of research both in the United States and abroad have demonstrated that the acquisition of *academic language* for second-language learners takes between five and seven years in comparison to the length of time to learn *conversational language,* which can take from one to two years (Cummins 2000).

In the United States English is a fundamental tool to achieve in school and to have the potential to become a successful member of society. Bartolome (1994) points to the contradictory disparities in the status of languages in the United States'. "[W]hile we discourage the maintenance of linguistic minority students' native language throughout their education, we require English-speaking students to study a foreign language as a prerequisite for college ..." (207). In other words, monolinguals should become bilinguals and bilinguals should become monolingual.

The loss of the home language and culture is often seen as necessary for the appropriate development of English. Hence, linguistic minorities not only experience loss of personal identity and emotional bonds with their communities but also rejection from the mainstream society. Ada (1995) asserts that:

> Despite its widespread acceptance, the subtractive model of bilingualism, in which mastery of the second language is achieved at the expense of proficiency in the first, need not be the framework on which bilingual education rests. Additive bilingualism, in which a second language is acquired while maintaining and continuing to develop the first, is a healthy and viable alternative to subtractive bilingualism (237).

Research has shown that cognitive skills are best acquired through the primary language and then transferred to the second language. The use of the home language helps children develop critical thinking abilities and cognitive skills. This cognitive structuring is not only shaped by linguistic knowledge but also by cultural knowledge and the context in which that knowledge is obtained (Trueba 1991).

Cummins (2000) proposes three principles relevant to bilingual development and language teaching. First, the *additive bilingual enrichment principle* contends that "the development of additive bilingual and biliteracy skills entails no negative consequences for children's academic, linguistic or intellectual development the evidence points in the direction of subtle metalinguistic and intellectual benefits for bilingual children" (21). Numerous studies have reported findings that indicate that bilingual children demonstrate a greater awareness of linguistic meanings and seem to be more flexible in their thinking than monolingual children. Bilingual children must decipher much more linguistic input through the effort of gaining command of two languages than monolingual children who are exposed to only one language system.

Second, the *interdependence principle* is based upon the premise that there is an underlying cognitive and academic proficiency common across all languages regardless of their distinct surface features. Cummins maintains that first-and second-language academic skills are interdependent and that there is no relationship between the amount of instructional time spent in the second language and academic achievement. According to Cummins, the *common underlying proficiency* makes possible the transfer of literacy-related skills between languages.

Third, the *interactive pedagogy principle* subscribes to Krashen's (1996) assertion that language is acquired more easily when it is comprehensible. The key factor in Krashen's theoretical model is *comprehensible input*: messages in the second language that make sense when modified and facilitated by visual aids and context. He contends that we acquire grammatical structures in their natural order when sufficient amounts of high-quality input are present. Rules are then generalized from verbal stimuli according to innate principles of grammar. The principle of comprehensible input is based on the idea that the main function of language use is meaningful communication. The importance of meaningful language use at all stages in the acquisition of second-language skills has become recognized as a critical and determining factor for the successful development of a second language and the maintenance of the first language.

BILINGUAL EDUCATION IN THE UNITED STATES; HISTORY, LEGISLATION, AND POLICY

Following the United States Supreme Court ruling in *Brown v. Board of Education* of 1954 abolishing school segregation, as well as the Civil Rights Act of 1964 prohibiting discrimination on the basis of race, color, or national origin, the federal government passed the Bilingual Education Act of 1968. This legislation provided federal funding to encourage local school districts to implement native-language instruction and other types of support services for students not yet proficient in English (Crawford 2004).

The Bilingual Education Act was enacted as Title VII of the Elementary and Secondary Education Act and remained in force until 2002, when it was replaced by the English Language Acquisition Act under the new federal No Child Left Behind Act (NCLB). Title VII became Title III of the Elementary and Secondary Education Act, which no longer gave funding priority for native-language instruction and instead turned the choice of how to spend federal funds for ELLs to the discretion of each state. The NCLB Act requires that schools address the educational needs of students who are not yet proficient in English regardless of whether they are documented or not. The law defines limited-English-proficient students as: "ages 3 to 21, enrolled in elementary or secondary education, often born outside the United States or speaking a language other than English in their homes, and not having sufficient mastery of English to meet state standards and excel in an English-language classroom."

In the 1974 landmark case *Lau v. Nichols,* the United States Supreme Court ruled that "there is no equality of treatment merely by providing students with the same facilities, textbooks, teachers and curriculum; for students who do not understand English are effectively foreclosed from any meaningful education" (Baker 2006). The court's decision in the *Lau v. Nichols* case required schools to take "affirmative steps" to overcome language barriers impeding children's access to the curriculum. Congress immediately endorsed this principle in the Equal Educational Opportunity Act of 1974. Neither the Bilingual Education Act nor the Lau decision requires any particular method for teaching students who are not yet proficient in English. That is, there is no federal mandate for bilingual education (although a few states mandate it under certain circumstances). What civil rights laws do require are educational programs that offer equal opportunities for ELLs.

The federal law stipulates that schools are responsible for ensuring that all students, including ELLs, have equal access to a quality education that enables them to progress academically while learning English. Furthermore, in its 1974 decision in *Lau v. Nichols,* the United States Supreme Court upheld the 1970 memo issued by the Office of Civil Rights. The basis for the case was the claim that students could not understand the language in which they were being taught; therefore, they were not being provided with an equal education. The case reaffirmed that all students in the United States, regardless of native language, have the right to receive a quality education. It also clarified that equality of opportunity does not necessarily mean the same education for every student but rather the same opportunity to receive an education. An equal education is only possible if students can understand the language of instruction.

Administrative, judicial, and legislative policies tend to favor bilingual programs that are remedial, compensatory, and transitional in nature (those that try

to 'fix' children's deficiencies of not knowing English), rather than supporting bilingual programs that are additive and enrichment-oriented (those that add English and maintain the native language). Interwoven in the debate on how to best meet the academic and linguistic needs of ELLs in schools have been basic ideologies and beliefs about linguistic diversity, immigration, and immigrant rights. Ruiz (1994) delineates three broad orientations on language diversity that have driven policy and politics in the United States:

- *Language as a Problem.* Subscribes to the notion that language diversity results in social conflict, divisiveness, and ethnic strife.
- *Language as a Right.* Views language as a basic human right challenging language prejudice and discrimination.
- *Language as a Resource.* Considers the diverse linguistic capital of a society as a cultural, social, personal, and national resource, both in terms of its economic potential and also of fostering social unity.

Since the early 1980s a resurgence of the "language as a problem" orientation has paved the way for the Official English movement that aims to legislate English as the official language of the United States. As a result of this movement two opposing organizations emerged: U.S. English—driving the push to make English the official language of the United States, a move that would restrict government-supported services in non-English languages, including bilingual education; and English Plus—countering the necessity to make English the official language and promoting linguistic pluralism. To date, bills introduced to congress to make English the official language of the United States have failed. Nonetheless, 28 states have passed Official English laws.

Language restrictionism policies are closely tied to language-minority education. The passage in 1998 of California's Proposition 227, *English Language Education for Children in Public Schools Initiative,* made it law to disband bilingual education and institute compulsory one-year English-immersion programs for ELLs. Similarly, Arizona passed Proposition 223 in 2000, which also virtually eliminated bilingual education for linguistically diverse students, and voters in Massachusetts approved a referendum to discontinue bilingual education in 2002.

Claims about the ineffectiveness of bilingual education coupled with the media's predisposition against it have allowed for the dissemination of inaccuracies and misinformation (Crawford 2001). The inadequate implementation of many bilingual programs has further cultivated the notion that bilingual education is a failure. The causes of low performance for most bilingual education programs are closely correlated to the lack of adequate funds, scarcity of qualified educators, large class size, and the absence of proven teaching methodology (Dicker 2000). Solidly designed bilingual programs that address these fundamental factors have proven to be highly effective for linguistically diverse students. Numerous studies (August and Hakuta 1997; Ramirez 1992; Thomas and Collier 1997, 2002) have demonstrated that students who participate in well-implemented programs that use the native language for instruction for more than three years show better academic performance and mastery in English and have lower drop-out rates.

IMPLICATIONS AND RECOMMENDATIONS

For many years the predominant and accepted means of explaining the educational failure of linguistic minorities has been in the context of *deficit theories,* based on the notions of *cultural deprivation and genetic inferiority.* Deficit theories perpetuate the notion that some minority students experience school failure due to "limited educability, poor motivation, and inadequate familial socialization for academic competence" (San Miguel and Valencia 1998, 368). These perspectives of limitations subscribe to the popular 'blame the victim' approach while dismissing any consideration of how schools are structured to prevent students from learning.

Research studies reveal the kinds of critical thinking and inference-making that culturally and linguistically diverse students exercise and express given the opportunity and motivation. They also show how the motivations that deficit theories claim to be lacking in minority students need only be activated by a transformative and culturally responsive pedagogy that incorporates the topics that are most relevant to students' lives. Preire (2000) argues that students will only acquire real ownership of their learning when they are invited to ask their own questions on subjects that are important to them. The educational outcomes of ELLs are meaningful and successful only when the assumptions behind deficit theories are challenged and replaced (Nieto 2000). Bilingual education in its additive

and culturally responsive form provides a vehicle for linguistically diverse students to reach their potential and in turn exposes and discredits the deficit theory.

Ruiz (1997) contends that native-language instruction goes beyond the development of language proficiency and cognitive growth. He argues that sociopolitical and sociolinguistic ramifications extending from bilingual education provide the means to break from established social inequity constructs. That is, the use of the native language and culture in the curriculum catapults minority students from their subjugated positions by sharing the power with the dominant group. Macedo (1997) concurs in that educators must demystify the standard dominant language and the old assumption about its inherent superiority. Educators must develop liberatory and critical bilingual programs informed by a radical pedagogy so that the minority language will cease to provide its speakers with the experience of subordination ... (276)

However, Ruiz cautions that often the *inclusion* of the *language* of a group has coincided with the *exclusion* of its *voice,* which is the central ingredient of critical pedagogy; without its consideration, there is no radical reform in curriculum.

Improving the academic outcomes of language-minority children in the United States requires a broad reconfiguration of the many factors that impact the quality of education for this population. The National Association of State Boards of Education's recently published report (2007) on the education of language learners recognizes the urgency to address the "unprecedented challenge for today's education leaders to simultaneously improve the quality of public education while accommodating the largest number of ELLs the nation has ever seen" and speaks to the "widespread recognition that ELLs have long been marginalized and too often segregated into programs that suffer from inadequate attention" (8). The large body of research on language-minority education points to some key micro-and macro-level elements and approaches that show promise in improving academic outcomes for ELLs. Moving toward implementation of these recommendations will facilitate the restructuring of ELL policy and instruction and align practice to current research and theory in the field. The following section presents some broad as well as specific recommendations for improving the educational experiences and outcomes of ELLs.

CONSIDERATIONS FOR THE BROADER CONTEXT

- Teacher preparation and educational administration licensure programs in higher education must include coursework for all teachers and administrators that address the special needs of ELLs.
- Federal and state government education agencies should provide financial support and incentives to increase the pool of qualified bilingual and ESL-endorsed/certified teachers and administrators.
- State Boards of Education must recognize the urgent national imperative to address language education policies and enact research-based mandates that support the educational attainment of ELLs.
- State Boards of Education should include early childhood education mandates for providing language support services in the preschool setting.
- State Boards of Education and school districts should include alternatives to high-stakes testing for ELLs and design appropriate evaluation methods for second-language learners.
- School districts should improve placement and reclassification tests for ELLs to more adequately monitor their progress and placement in ESL, bilingual, or general English programs.
- School districts should monitor and guide teachers' use of proven successful instructional approaches and techniques for ELLs.

CONSIDERATIONS FOR THE SCHOOL CONTEXT

- Implement additive bilingual programs that maintain and develop both the native language and English and when possible institute dual-language programs to benefit both ELLs and native English speakers.
- Implement high-quality transactional-oriented programs for ELLs rather than remedial transmission-oriented programs.
- Create safe and supportive school environments to promote higher levels of academic engagement that value the linguistic and cultural capital of all their students.
- Avoid segregating ELLs and instead integrate them in mainstream school activities and course offerings with specialized support. Hire experienced and qualified teachers who hold positive attitudes toward language-minority students.
- Hire administrators who enforce policies and practices that foster the success of ELLs' academic development.
- Increase professional development requirements and offerings that specifically address the needs of ELLs.
- Have high expectations for ELLs' academic achievement.
- Design culturally relevant curricula for language-minority students.
- Utilize constructivist and transactional approaches to teaching and learning (such as cooperative learning, thematic-based instruction, flexible grouping, differentiated instruction, literature-based, student-centered classrooms, inquiry-based approach, etc.).
- Focus on developing high levels of language and literacy as a basis for achievement on all academic content.
- Educate teachers and administrators about students' and their families' cultural beliefs and norms, migratory experiences, economic and employment conditions, etc.

CONSIDERATIONS FOR THE PARENT AND FAMILY CONTEXT

- Communicate with parents in ways that show them respect and appreciation.
- Create a welcoming school environment for parents and families.
- Educate parents and families about the benefits of maintaining bilingualism and developing biliteracy.
- Inform parents and families about their rights and responsibilities (which may be different from those in their countries of origin), as well as the policies and responsibilities of the school system.

- Involve parents in governance and advocacy activities.
- Show parents how to access information and navigate the educational system in the United States.
- Provide language support and translation for parents and family members.

CONCLUSION

Enacting more effective instructional practices for ELLs calls for a shift in perspective. This paradigm shift must be from "a narrow and mechanistic view of instruction to one that is broader in scope and takes into consideration the sociohistorical and political dimensions of education" (Bartolome 1994, 176). This perspective should compel educators to critically analyze the sociocultural and political realities in which subordinated students find themselves at school and the implicit and explicit antagonistic relations between students and teachers, as well as between communities and education systems. Demographic changes coupled with more stringent legal requirements and continued academic underachievement of language-minority students require urgent attention from educators and policy-makers alike.

In maintaining a certain coherence with the educational plan to reconstruct new and more democratic educational programs for linguistic minority students, educators and political leaders need to create a new school grounded in a new educational praxis ... with the principles of a democratic, multicultural, and multilingual society (Macedo 1997, 276).

Critical and culturally responsive education and transformative modes of teaching and learning enable students and teachers to break away from these adverse relationships and negative beliefs and allow for the creation of learning environments that are informed by both participatory action and critical reflection. Educating children of culturally and linguistically diverse backgrounds is an inescapable challenge for school systems across the country.

References

Ada, A. F. 1995. "Creative Education for Bilingual Teachers." In O. Garcia and C. Baker, eds., *Policy and Practice in Bilingual Education: A Reader Extending the Foundations,* 237–43, Clevedon, England: Multilingual Matters.

August, D. and K. Hakuta, 1997. *Improving Schooling for Language Minority Children.* Washington DC: National Academy Press.

Baker, C. 2006. *Foundations of Bilingual Education and Bilingualism.* Clevedon, England: Multilingual Matters.

Baker, C, and S. Jones. 1998. *Encyclopedia of Bilingualism and Bilingual "Education.* Clevedon, England: Multilingual Matters.

Bartolome, L. I. 1994. "Teaching Strategies: Their Possibilities and Limitations." In B. McLeod, ed., *Language and Learning: Educating Linguistically Diverse Students,* 199–223. New York: State University of New York Press.

Castro Feinberg, Rosa. 2002. *Bilingual Education: A Reference Handbook.* Contemporary education issues. Santa Barbara, CA: ABC-CLIO.

Chicago Council on Global Affairs. 2006. *A Shared Future: The Economic Engagement of Greater Chicago and Its Mexican Community.* Chicago: Chicago Council on Global Affairs.

Crawford, J. 2001. *At War with Diversity.* Clevedon, England: Multilingual Matters.

——. 2004. *Educating English Language Learners: Language Diversity in the Classroom.* Los Angeles: Bilingual Educational Services.

Cummins, J. 2000. *Language, Power and Pedagogy. Bilingual Children in the Crossfire.* Clevedon, England: Multilingual Matters.

Darling-Hammond, L., D. J. Holtzman, S. J. Gatlin, and J. Vasquez Heilig. 1995. "Does Teacher Preparation Matter? Evidence about Teacher Certification, Teach for America, and Teacher Effectiveness." Education Policy Analysis Archives 13, no. 42 (October 12).

De la Garza, R., L. DeSipio, F. C. Garcia, J. Garcia, and A. Falcon. 1992. *Latino Voices: Mexican, Puerto Rican, and Cuban Perspectives on American Politics.* Boulder, CO: Westview Press.

Diaz-Rico, Lynne T, and Kathryn Z. Weed. 2002. *The Crosscultural, Language, and Academic Development Handbook: A Complete K-12 Reference Guide.* Boston: Allyn and Bacon.

Dicker, S. J. 2000. "Official English and Bilingual Education: The Controversy over Language Pluralism in US Society." In J. K. Hall and W. G. Eggington, eds., *The Sociopolitics of English Language Teaching,* 45–66. Clevedon, England: Multilingual Matters.

Freire, P. 2000. *Pedagogy of the Oppressed.* New York: Continuum International Publishing.

Fry, B. N. 2007. *Nativism and Immigration: Regulating the American Dream,* New York: LFB Scholarly Publishing.

Huddy, L., and D. Sears. 1990. "Qualified Public Support for Bilingual Education: Some Policy Implications."

Annals of the American Academy of Political and Social Science 508, no. 1:119–134.

Kominski, R., A. Jamieson, and G. Martinez. 2001. "At-risk Conditions of US School-age children." US Bureau of the Census. Working Paper Series no. 52 (June). http://www.census.gov/population/www/documentation/twps0052.html (accessed February 25,2008).

Krashen, S. 1996. *Every Person a Reader: An Alternative to the California Task Force Report on Reading.* Culver City, CA: Language Education Associates.

Lambert, Wallace E., and G. Richard Tucker. 1972. *Bilingual Education of Children: The St. Lambert Experiment.* [Rowley, MA]: Newbury House Publishers.

Lee, S. K. 1999. "The Linguistic Minority Parents' Perceptions of Bilingual Education." *Bilingual Research — Journal* 23, nos. 2–3:113–24.

Levine, R. 2007. Assimilation, Past and Present. In P. McCaffrey, ed., *Hispanic Americans,* 55-66. New York: H. W. Wilson.

Macedo, D. 1997. "English Only: The Tongue-Tying of America." In A. Darder, R. D. Torres, and H. Gutierrez, eds., *Lathios in Education. A Critical Reader,* 269–78. New York: Routledge.

Mackey, W. F. 1978. "The Importation of Bilingual Education Models." In J. Alatis, ed., *Georgetown University Roundtable: International Dimensions of Education.* Washington DC: Georgetown University Press.

Menken, K., and B. Antunez. 2001. "An Overview of the Preparation and Certification of Teachers Working with Limited English Proficient (LEP) Students." Washington DC: The ERIC Clearinghouse on Teaching and Teacher Education. http://eric.ed.gov/ERICDocs/data/ericdocs2sql/content storage_01/0000019b/80/29/cb/0e.pdf (accessed February 25, 2008).

National Association of State Boards of Education. 2007. *E Pluribus Unum: English, Language Education, and America's Future.* The Report of the NASBE Study Group on Language and Learning. Alexandria, VA: National Association of State Boards of Education.

National Center for Education Statistics, US Department of Education. 2002. Education Longitudinal Study, http://nces.ed.gov/surveys/els2002/.

——. 2006a. *Characteristics of Schools, Districts, Teachers, Principals, and School Libraries in the United States: 2003–04 Schools and Staffing Survey,* http://nces.ed,gov/pubsearch/pubsinfo.asp?pubid = 2006313 (accessed February 25, 2008).

——. 2006b. "Percentage of Persons Age 25 and over and 25 to 29 by Race/Ethnicity, Years of School Completed, and Sex: Selected Years 1910 through 2005." http://nces.ed.gov/programs/digest/d05/tables/dt05_008.asp (accessed February 25, 2008).

——. 2007. *The Condition of Education 2007.* NCES 2007–064.

Nieto, S. 2000. *Affirming Diversity: A Sociopolitical Context for Multicultural Education.* 3rd ed. Boston: Longman.

Paral, R. 2006. "Latinos of the New Chicago." In J. Koval, L. Bennett, M. Bennett, F. Dimissie, R. Garner, and K. Kim, eds., *The New Chicago: A Social and Cultural Analysis,* 105–14. Philadelphia: Temple University Press.

President's Advisory Commission on Educational Excellence for Hispanic Americans. 2003. *From Risk to Opportunity.* Final Report, http://www.yic.gov/paceea/finalreport.pdf (accessed on February 25, 2008).

Ramirez, J. D. 1992. "Longitudinal Study of Structured English Immersion Strategy, Early-exit and Late-exit Transitional Bilingual Education Programs for Language Minority Children (Executive Summary)." *Bilingual Research Journal* 16 (1 & 2): 1–62.

Ruiz, R. 1994. "Language Policy and Planning in the United States." *Annual Review of Applied Linguistics* 14:111–25.

——. 1997. "The Empowerment of Language-minority Students." In A. Darder, R. D. Torres,

and H. Gutierrez, eds., *Latinos and Education. A Critical Reader,* 320–28. New York: Routledge.

San Miguel, G., and R. R. Valencia. 1998. "From the Treaty of Guadalupe Hidalgo to Hopwood: The Education Plight and Struggle of Mexican Americans in the Southwest." *Harvard Educational Review* 68, no. 3 (fall): 353–412.

Shin, F., and B. Gribbons. 1996. "Hispanic Parent Perceptions and Attitudes of Bilingual Education." *The Journal of Mexican American Educators* 6: 16–22.

Shin, F., and S. Kim, S. 1996. "Korean Parent Perceptions and Attitudes of Bilingual Education." In R. Endo, C. Park, J. Tsuchida, and A. Abbayani, eds., *Current Issues in Asian and Pacific American Education.* Covina, CA: Pacific Asian Press.

Soltero, S. W. 2004. *Dual Language: Teaching and Learning in Two Languages.* Boston: Allyn and Bacon.

Suarez-Orozco, C, M. Suarez-Orozco, and I. Todorova. 2008. *Learning a New Land: Immigrant Students in American Society.* Cambridge: Harvard University Press.

Thomas, Wayne P., and Virginia P. Collier. 1997. *School Effectiveness for Language Minority Students.* Washington DC: Disseminated by National Clearinghouse for Bilingual Education, the George Washington University, Center for the Study of Language and Education.

——. 2002. *A National Study of School Effectiveness for Language Minority Students' Long-term Academic*

Achievement. Center for Research on Education, Diversity and Excellence. http://crede.berkeley.edu/research/llaa/l.l_final.html (accessed February 25, 2008).

Trueba, H. T. 1991. "The Role of Culture in Bilingual Instruction: Linking Linguistic and Cognitive Development to Cultural Knowledge." In O. Garcia, ed., *Bilingual Education. Focuuschrift in Honor of Joshua A. Fishmanon the Occasion of His 65 th Birthday,* 43–55. Philadelphia: John Benjamins.

United States Code Service; Title 20, Education; Chapter 33, Education of Individuals with Disabilities General Provisions. Approved 6/15/2007.

For Poor, Leap to College Often Ends in a Hard Fall

Jason DeParle

GALVESTON, Tex.—Angelica Gonzales marched through high school in Goth armor—black boots, chains and cargo pants—but undermined her pose of alienation with a place on the honor roll. She nicknamed herself after a metal band and vowed to become the first in her family to earn a college degree.

"I don't want to work at Walmart" like her mother, she wrote to a school counselor.

Weekends and summers were devoted to a college-readiness program, where her best friends, Melissa O'Neal and Bianca Gonzalez, shared her drive to "get off the island"—escape the prospect of dead-end lives in luckless Galveston. Melissa, an eighth-grade valedictorian, seethed over her mother's boyfriends and drinking, and Bianca's bubbly innocence hid the trauma of her father's death. They stuck together so much that a tutor called them the "triplets."

Low-income strivers face uphill climbs, especially at Ball High School, where a third of the girls' class failed to graduate on schedule. But by the time the triplets donned mortarboards in the class of 2008, their story seemed to validate the promise of education as the great equalizer.

Angelica, a daughter of a struggling Mexican immigrant, was headed to *Emory University*. Bianca enrolled in community college, and Melissa left for Texas State University, President Lyndon B. Johnson's alma mater.

"It felt like we were taking off, from one life to another," Melissa said. "It felt like, 'Here we go!' "

Four years later, their story seems less like a tribute to upward mobility than a study of obstacles in an age of soaring economic inequality. Not one of them has a four-year degree. Only one is still studying full time, and two have crushing debts. Angelica, who left Emory owing more than $60,000, is a clerk in a Galveston furniture store.

Each showed the ability to do college work, even excel at it. But the need to earn money brought one set of strains, campus alienation brought others, and ties to boyfriends not in school added complications. With little guidance from family or school officials, college became a leap that they braved without a safety net.

The story of their lost footing is also the story of something larger—the growing role that education plays in preserving class divisions. Poor students have long trailed affluent peers in school performance, but from grade-school tests to college completion, the gaps are growing. With school success and earning prospects ever more entwined, the consequences carry far: education, a force meant to erode class barriers, appears to be fortifying them.

"Everyone wants to think of education as an equalizer—the place where upward mobility gets started," said Greg J. Duncan, an economist at the University of California, Irvine. "But on virtually every measure we have, the gaps between high- and low-income kids are widening. It's very disheartening."

The growing role of class in academic success has taken experts by surprise since it follows decades of equal opportunity efforts and counters racial trends, where differences have narrowed. It adds to fears over recent evidence suggesting that low-income Americans have lower chances of upward mobility than counterparts in Canada and Western Europe.

Thirty years ago, there was a 31 percentage point difference between the share of prosperous and poor Americans who earned bachelor's degrees, according to Martha J. Bailey and Susan M. Dynarski of the University of Michigan. Now the gap is 45 points.

While both groups improved their odds of finishing college, the affluent improved much more, widening their sizable lead.

Likely reasons include soaring incomes at the top and changes in family structure, which have left fewer low-income students with the support of two-parent homes. Neighborhoods have grown more segregated by class, leaving lower-income students increasingly concentrated in lower-quality schools. And even after accounting for financial aid, the costs of attending a public university have risen 60 percent in the past two decades. Many low-income students, feeling the need to help out at home, are deterred by the thought of years of lost wages and piles of debt.

In placing their hopes in education, the Galveston teenagers followed a tradition as old as the country itself. But if only the prosperous become educated—and only the educated prosper—the schoolhouse risks becoming just another place where the fortunate preserve their edge.

"It's becoming increasingly unlikely that a low-income student, no matter how intrinsically bright, moves up the socioeconomic ladder," said Sean Reardon, a sociologist at Stanford. "What we're talking about is a threat to the American dream."

HIGH SCHOOL

No one pictured the teenagers as even friends, much less triplets. Angelica hid behind dark eyeliner, Melissa's moods turned on the drama at home, and Bianca, in the class behind, seemed even younger than she was. What they had in common was a college-prep program for low-income teenagers, Upward Bound,

and trust in its counselor, Priscilla Gonzales Culver, whom everyone called "Miss G."

Angelica was the product of a large Mexican-American family, which she sought both to honor and surpass. Her mother, Ana Gonzales, had crossed the border illegally as a child, gained citizenship and settled the clan in Galveston, where she ruled by force of will. She once grounded Angelica for a month for coming home a minute late. With hints of both respect and fear, Angelica never called her "Mom"—only "Mrs. Lady."

Home was an apartment in a subdivided house, with relatives in the adjacent units. Family meals and family feuds went hand in hand. One of Angelica's uncles bore scars from his days in a street gang. Her grandmother spoke little English. With a quirky mix of distance and devotion, Angelica studied German instead of Spanish and gave the fiesta celebrating her 15th birthday a Goth theme, with fairies and dragons on the tabletop globes. "Korn chick," she fancifully called herself, after the dissonant metal band.

But school was all business. "Academics was where I shined," she said. Her grandmother and aunts worked at Walmart alongside Mrs. Lady, and Angelica was rankled equally by how little money they made and how little respect they got. Upward Bound asked her to rank the importance of college on a scale of 1 to 10.

"10," she wrote.

Melissa also wanted to get off the island—and more immediately out of her house. "When I was about 7, my mom began dating and hanging around a bunch of drunks," she wrote on the Upward Bound application. For her mother, addiction to painkillers and severe depression followed. Her grandparents offered her one refuge, and school offered another.

"I like to learn—I'm weird," she said.

By eighth grade, Melissa was at the top of her class and sampling a course at a private high school. She yearned to apply there but swore the opposite to her mother and grandparents. Protecting families from their own ambition is a skill many poor students learn. "I knew we didn't have the money," Melissa said. "I felt like I had no right to ask."

New to Upward Bound, Melissa noticed that one student always ate alone and crowded in beside her. "She forced her friendship on me," Angelica said.

Bianca joined the following year with a cheerfulness that disguised any trace of family tragedy. As the eldest of four siblings, she had spent the years since her father's death as a backup mother. To Bianca, family meant everything.

She arrived just in time for the trip at the heart of triplets lore—the Upward Bound visit to Chicago.

While they had known they wanted more than Galveston offered, somewhere between the Sears Tower and Northwestern University they glimpsed what it might be. The trip at once consecrated a friendship and defined it around shared goals.

"We wanted to do something better with our lives," Angelica said.

Ball High was hard on goals. In addition to Bosco, a drug-sniffing dog profiled in the local paper, the campus had four safety officers to deter fights. A pepper spray incident in the girls' senior year sent 50 students to the school nurse. Only 2 percent of Texas high schools were ranked "academically unacceptable." Ball was among them.

Melissa now marvels at what a good parent her mother has become to her younger brother after she stopped drinking and was treated for her depression. But when she returned from the high school trip to Chicago, the conflicts grew so intense that Miss G. took her in one night. "I really put her through a lot," said Melissa's mother, Pam Craft. "Everything she did, she did on her own—I'm so proud of her." Miss G.'s notes variously observed that "there are limited groceries," "student is overwhelmed" and "she's basically raising herself."

While faulting her mother's choices in men, Melissa made a troubling choice of her own with her ambitionless boyfriend. Among the many ways he let her down was getting another girl pregnant. Yet as many times as they broke up, they got back together again. "He is going to bring her down," Miss G. warned.

Despite the turmoil, Melissa earned "commended" marks, the highest level, on half her state skills tests, edited the yearbook and published two opinion articles in the Galveston newspaper, one of them about her brother's struggle with autism. Working three jobs, she missed so much school that she nearly failed to graduate, but she still finished in the top quarter of her class. It was never clear which would prevail—her habit of courting disaster or her talent for narrow escapes.

Returning from Chicago, Bianca jumped a grade, which allowed her to graduate with Melissa and Angelica.

Angelica kept making A's on her way to a four-year grade-point average of 3.9. "Amazingly bright and dedicated," one instructor wrote. A score of 1,240 on the math and reading portions of her SAT ranked her at the 84th percentile nationwide. When the German teacher suddenly quit, the school tapped her to finish teaching the first-year course.

Outside school, Angelica's life revolved around her boyfriend, Fred Weaver, who was three years older and drove a yellow Sting Ray. Fred was devoted—too devoted, Mrs. Lady thought, and she warned Angelica not to let the relationship keep her from going to college. Fred's father owned a local furniture store, and everyone could see that Fred's dream was to run it with Angelica at his side.

Senior year raced by, with Miss G. doing her best to steer frightened and distracted students though the college selection process. Despite all the campus visits, choices were made without the intense supervision that many affluent students enjoy. Bianca, anchored to the island by family and an older boyfriend, chose community college. Melissa picked Texas State in San Marcos because "the application was easiest."

Angelica had thought of little beyond Northwestern and was crestfallen when she was rejected. She had sent a last-minute application to a school in Atlanta that had e-mailed her. Only after getting in did she discover that she had achieved something special.

Emory cost nearly $50,000 that year, but it was one of a small tier of top schools that promised to meet the financial needs of any student good enough to be admitted. It had even started a program to relieve the neediest students of high debt burdens. "No one should have to give up their goals and dreams because financial challenges stand in the way," *its Web site says.*

Plus an unseen campus a thousand miles away had an innate appeal. "How many times do you get the chance to completely reinvent yourself?" Angelica said.

RICH-POOR GAP GROWS

If Melissa and Angelica felt that heading off to university set them apart from other low-income students, they were right. Fewer than 30 percent of students in the bottom quarter of incomes even enroll in a four-year school. And among that group, fewer than half graduate.

Income has always shaped academic success, but its importance is growing. Professor Reardon, the Stanford sociologist, examined a dozen reading and math tests dating back 25 years and found that the gap in scores of high- and low-income students has grown by 40 percent, even as the difference between blacks and whites has narrowed.

While race once predicted scores more than class, the opposite now holds. By eighth grade, white students surpass blacks by an average of three grade levels, while upper-income students are four grades ahead of low-income counterparts.

"The racial gaps are quite big, but the income gaps are bigger," Professor Reardon said.

One explanation is simply that the rich have clearly gotten richer. A generation ago, families at the 90th percentile had five times the income of those at the 10th percentile. Now they have 10 times as much.

But as shop class gave way to computer labs, schools may have also changed in ways that make parental income and education more important. SAT coaches were once rare, even for families that could afford them. Now they are part of a vast college preparation industry.

Certainly as the payoff to education has grown—college graduates have greatly widened their earnings lead—affluent families have invested more in it. They have tripled the amount by which they outspend low-income families on enrichment activities like sports, music lessons and summer camps, *according to* Professor Duncan and Prof. Richard Murnane of Harvard.

In addition, upper-income parents, especially fathers, have increased their child-rearing time, while the presence of fathers in low-income homes has declined. Miss G. said there is a reason the triplets relied so heavily on boyfriends: "Their fathers weren't there."

Annette Lareau, a sociologist at the University of Pennsylvania, argues that the affluent also enjoy an advocacy edge: parents are quicker to intervene when their children need help, while low-income families often feel intimidated and defer to school officials, a problem that would trail Melissa and Angelica in their journey through college.

"Middle-class students get the sense the institution will respond to them," Professor Lareau said. "Working-class and poor students don't experience that. It makes them more vulnerable."

Matthew M. Chingos of the Brookings Institution *has found* that low-income students finish college less often than affluent peers even when they outscore them on skills tests. Only 26 percent of eighth graders with below-average incomes but above-average scores go on to earn bachelor's degrees, compared with 30 percent of students with subpar performances but more money.

"These are students who have already overcome significant obstacles to score above average on this test," Mr. Chingos said. "To see how few earn college degrees is really disturbing."

TRIPLETS START COLLEGE

Melissa lasted at Texas State for all of two hours. As soon as she arrived, her car battery died, prompting a tearful call to Miss. G., who arranged a jump. Her dorm mates had parents to haul boxes and hover. Melissa unpacked alone. With four days left until classes began, she panicked and drove 200 miles back home.

For all the talk of getting away, her tattoo featured a local boast: she was "B.O.I."—born on the island. Her grandparents ordered her back to school. "I really didn't want to leave" the island, she said.

Midway through the semester she decided she had made a mistake by going to Texas State. She had picked the wrong time to leave home. She would move back to Galveston, join Bianca at community college and transfer to a four-year school later. But when she tried to return the financial aid to Texas State, she discovered it was too late. A long walk across the hilly campus led to an epiphany.

"I realized there was nothing in Galveston for me," she said. "This is where I need to be."

Angelica had a costlier setback. For an elite school, Emory enrolls an unusually large number of low-income students—22 percent get Pell grants, compared with 11 percent at Harvard—and gives them unusually large aid packages. But Angelica had failed to complete all the financial aid forms.

Slow to consider Emory, she got a late start on the complex process and was delayed by questions about her father, whom she did not even know how to reach. Though Emory sent weekly e-mails—17 of them, along with an invitation to a program for minority students—they went to a school account she had not learned to check. From the start, the wires were crossed.

As classes approached, she just got in the car with Mrs. Lady and Fred and drove 14 hours to Atlanta hoping to work things out. But by then Emory had distributed all of its aid. Even with federal loans and grants, Angelica was $40,000 short. The only way to enroll was to borrow from a bank.

Forty thousand dollars was an unfathomable sum. Angelica did not tell Mrs. Lady, to protect her from the worry. She needed a co-signer, and the only person she could ask was Fred. That would bind her future to her past, but she feared that if she tried to defer, she might not have a future—she might never make it back.

"I was like, 'I don't care what kind of debt it puts me in—I've got to get this done,'" she said.

Fred answered her request with his. They got engaged.

A few weeks later, *Hurricane Ike hit Galveston*, with Katrina-like consequences. About a sixth of the population never returned. Mrs. Lady lost her apartment and much of what she owned. Fred, consumed with rebuilding the store, reduced the modest sums he had promised to send Angelica.

Social life was awkward. She often felt she was the only one on campus without a credit card. Her roommate moved out, with no explanation. But one element of college appealed to Angelica and Melissa alike: the classes. Other debt-ridden students might wonder why the road to middle-class life passed through anthropology exams and lectures on art history. But Melissa was happy to ponder tribal life in Papua New Guinea and Angelica stepped off the 18-hour bus ride home and let slip an appreciative word about German film.

"My family said 'O.K., now you go to some big fancy school,' " she said.

With A's, B's, C's and D's, her report card looked like alphabet soup. "I was ready for Galveston College—I wasn't ready for Emory," Angelica said. But she salvaged a 2.6 GPA and went home for the summer happy.

"I thought the hard part was over," she said.

At the end of the summer, Angelica and Melissa marked their ascent as college women with the perfect road trip. Melissa had decided to become a speech therapist. Angelica would practice child psychology. Somewhere between the rainbow in Louisiana and the blues bar in Orlando, they talked of launching a practice to help poor children. Fortune smiled all week.

"We were where we should be and we had the world at our feet," Melissa said.

MELISSA

She returned to a campus that was starting to feel like home. She had a roommate she liked and a job she loved, as a clerk in a Disney store. But despite the feeling of deep change—or perhaps because of it—she got back together with her high-school boyfriend. "That was one of the stupidest things I've ever done," she said.

In the middle of Melissa's sophomore year they became engaged. He moved near the campus to live with her, and Melissa charged most of their expenses on her credit cards. He was enrolling in the Job Corps program, and they agreed they would pay down the bills together after he became an electrician.

Melissa hit an academic pothole —a C in a communications course, which kept her out of the competitive speech therapy program. But she decided to aim for graduate-school training, and her other grades soared, placing her on the dean's list both semesters her junior year. When her mother made a rare campus visit, Melissa hurried to show her the prominent display on the student center wall.

"That was one of the proudest moments of my life," Melissa said.

Just before her senior year, Melissa planned a trip to celebrate her 21st birthday. Preparing to leave, she discovered her money was missing. Only one person had her bank code. After finishing Job Corps, her boyfriend was jobless once again and acting odd—as if he were using drugs.

No one but Melissa was surprised. Although she returned the engagement ring, she could not return the $4,000 in credit card debt he had promised to help pay. With her finances and emotions in disarray, she started her senior year so depressed she hung up black curtains so she could sleep all day. She skipped class, doubled her work hours, and failed nearly every course.

"I started partying, and I was working all the time because I had this debt," she said.

If the speed of her decline stands out, so does her lack of a safety net. It is easy to imagine a more affluent family stepping in with money or other support. Miss G. sent her the names of some campus therapists but Melissa did not call. She waited for an internal bungee cord to break the fall. She came within one F of losing her financial aid, then aced last summer's classes.

She is now a fifth-year senior, on track to graduate next summer, and her new boyfriend is studying to be an engineer. At home, she had a way of finding the wrong people. "I haven't found any wrong people out here," she said.

With more than $44,000 in loans, she can expect to pay $250 a month for the next quarter century, on top of whatever she may borrow for graduate school. She hides the notices in a drawer and harbors no regrets. "Education—you can't put a price on it," she said. "No matter what happens in your life, they can't take your education away."

BIANCA

Bianca missed the Florida road trip, though no one remembers why. She liked to talk of getting away, until it came time to go.

Among the perils that low-income students face is "under-matching," choosing a close or familiar school instead of the best they can attend.

"The more selective the institution is, the more likely kids are to graduate," said Mr. Chingos, the Brookings researcher. "There are higher expectations, more resources and more stigma to dropping out."

Bianca was under-matched. She was living at home, dating her high-school boyfriend and taking classes at

Galveston College. A semester on the honor roll only kept her from sensing the drift away from her plan to transfer to a four-year school.

Her grandfather's cancer, and chemotherapy treatments, offered more reasons to stay. She had lived with him since her father had died. Leaving felt like betrayal. "I thought it was more important to be at home than to be selfish and be at school," she said.

The idea that education can be "selfish"—a belief largely alien among the upper-middle class—is one poor students often confront, even if it remains unspoken. "Family is such a priority, especially when you're a Hispanic female," Miss G. said. "You're afraid you're going to hear, 'You're leaving us, you think you're better.' "

In her second year of community college, Bianca was admitted to a state university a hundred miles away. Miss. G. and her mother urged her to go. Her mind raced with reasons to wait.

"I didn't want to leave and have my grandfather die."

"I had to help my mom."

"I think I got burned out."

Bianca stayed in Galveston, finished her associate degree, and now works as a beach-bar cashier and a spa receptionist. She still plans to get a bachelor's degree, someday.

"I don't think I was lazy. I think I was scared," she said. In the meantime, "life happened."

ANGELICA

After the financial aid disaster in her first year, Angelica met the next deadline and returned as a sophomore with significant support. Still, she sensed she was on shakier ground than other low-income students and never understood why. The answer is buried in the aid archives: Emory repeatedly inflated her family's income without telling her.

Angelica reported that her mother made $35,000 a year and paid about half of that in rent. With her housing costs so high, Emory assumed the family had extra money and assigned Mrs. Lady an income of $51,000. But Mrs. Lady was not hiding money. She was paying inflated post-hurricane rent with the help of Federal disaster aid, a detail Angelica had inadvertently omitted.

By counting money the family did not have, Emory not only increased the amount it expected Angelica to pay in addition to her financial aid. It also disqualified her from most of the school's touted program of debt relief. Under the Emory Advantage plan the school replaces loans with grants for families making less than

$50,000 a year. Moving Angelica just over the threshold placed her in a less-generous tier and forced her to borrow an additional $15,000 before she could qualify. The mistake will add years to her repayment plan.

She discovered what had happened only recently, after allowing a reporter to review her file with Emory officials. "There was no other income coming in," she said. "I can't believe that they would do that and not say anything to us. That seems completely unfair."

Emory officials said they had to rely on the information Angelica provided and that they will not make retroactive adjustments.

"The method that was used in her case was very standard methodology," said J. Lynn Zimmerman, the senior vice provost who oversees financial aid. "I think that what's unusual is that she really didn't advocate for herself or ask for any kind of review. If she or her mother would have provided any additional information it would have triggered a conversation."

Unaware she had any basis for complaint, Angelica found a campus job she loved, repairing library books. It was solitary and artistic work, and it attracted a small sisterhood of women who appreciated her grandmother's tamales and her streak of purple hair. One day her boss, Julie Newton, overheard her excitedly talking about Hegel.

"She was an extremely intelligent woman and an unusual one," she said.

Yet even as Angelica's work hours grew, so did the rigor of her coursework. Meetings with faculty advisers were optional and Angelica did not consult hers. When it came time to declare a major, she had a B-plus average in the humanities and D's in psychology. She chose psychology.

By the end of her second year, she felt exhausted and had grades to show it. Her long-distance love life was exhausted, too, and she briefly broke up with Fred. She went home for the summer to work at Target and dragged herself back to a troubled junior year.

She moved off campus to save money but found herself spending even more. "I would sit and debate whether I could buy a head of lettuce," she said. Fred was no longer helping, and her relationship with him snapped. That he had backed a $40,000 loan only made the split harder. They had been together since she was 15.

"It was days of back and forth, crying," she said.

This was no time to tackle Psychology 200, a course on research methods required of majors. The devotion of the professor, Nancy Bliwise, had earned her a campus teaching award. But her exacting standards and brusque manner left student opinion divided.

"Quite possibly the greatest professor at Emory," wrote one contributor to the Web site Rate My Professor. Others found her "condescending," "horribly disrespectful," and "plain out mean."

Midway through the semester, Angelica just stopped coming to class. Professor Bliwise called her in and found her despondent. "She was emotionless and that scared me," the professor said in an interview. Angelica said she had to work too much to keep up, but could not drop the course without losing her full-time status and her aid. So she planned to take an "F."

Alarmed, Professor Bliwise raised other options, then asked—empathetically, the professor thought— if Angelica had considered cheaper schools. She herself had worked her way through Cleveland State then earned a doctorate at the University of Chicago.

Angelica sat stone-faced, burning. All she could hear was someone saying she was too poor for Emory. "It was pretty clear if I couldn't afford to be there, I shouldn't waste her time," she said.

That was the beginning of the end. Angelica failed that course and three others her junior year, as her upside-down circumstances left her cheating a $200,000 education for a $9-an-hour job. She was not one to make it easy, but Emory never found a way to intervene. "Is there a way to reach out to her?" Professor Bliwise asked in an e-mail to the dean's office.

The dean's office left messages. Angelica acknowledged that she was slow to respond but said she got no answer when she did. The school did an electronic key card check to verify whether she was still on campus. More professors expressed concerns. "Personal issues are interfering with her ability to concentrate," one warned. Angelica contacted campus counseling but said all the appointments had been taken.

Emory can hardly be cast as indifferent to low-income students. It spends $94 million a year of its own money on financial aid and graduates its poorest students nearly as often as the rest. Its failure to reach Angelica may have come up short, but that is partly a measure of the sheer distance it was trying to bridge.

When Angelica finally found a way to express herself, she did so silently. Her final piece for a sculpture class was a papier-mâché baby, sprouting needles like a porcupine. No one could mistake the statement of her own vulnerability.

"It was a shocking piece," said her professor, Linda Armstrong. "She had a way of using art to tap into her deepest emotions and feelings. I don't think she understood how good she was."

Angelica spent the next summer waiting for an expulsion letter that never came. Another missed deadline cost her several thousand dollars in aid in her senior year, and Emory mistakenly concluded that Mrs. Lady had made a $70,000 down payment on a house. (In describing the complicated transaction with a nonprofit group, Angelica failed to note that most of the money came from a program for first-time home buyers.) Emory officials said the mistake did not affect her aid, but the difference between the school's costs and her package of loans and grants swelled to $12,000—a sum she could not possibly meet.

She skipped more classes and worked longer hours.

"I felt, I'm going to be on academic probation anyway, I might as well work and pay my rent until they suspend me."

Finally, Emory did—forcing her to take a semester away with the option of reapplying.

The tale could be cast as an elite school failing a needy student or a student unwilling to be helped, but neither explanation does justice to an issue as complicated as higher education and class.

"It's a little of both," said Joanne Brzinski, a dean who oversees academic advising. "We reached out to her, but she didn't respond. I always fault myself when students don't do as well as we'd like them to."

"It's such a sad story," she added. "She had the ability."

Ms. Newton, Angelica's former supervisor at the library, wondered if her conflict went beyond money, to a fear of the very success she sought. "I wouldn't go as far as to say she was committing self-sabotage, but the thought crossed my mind," she said. "For someone so connected to family and Grandma and the tamales, I wondered if she feared that graduating would alienate her."

A long bridge crosses the bay to Galveston Island. Angelica returned a year ago the way she had left, with Mrs. Lady and Fred at her side. She is $61,000 in debt, seeing Fred again, and making $8.50 an hour at his family's furniture store. No one can tell whether she is settling down or gathering strength for another escape.

A dinner with Melissa and Bianca a while back offered the comfort of friends who demand no explanations. Melissa suggested they all enroll at Texas State. But Bianca does not know what to study, and Angelica said that she had gone too far to surrender all hopes of an Emory degree.

"I could have done some things better, and Emory could have done some things better," she said. "But I don't blame either one of us. Everyone knows life is unfair—being low-income puts you at a disadvantage. I just didn't understand the extent of the obstacles I was going to have to overcome."

Kitty Bennett contributed research.

School Failure: Explanations and Interventions

Guadalupe Valdés

Mexican-origin children have not fared well in American schools. Their problems have been documented by many researchers (e.g., Arias, 1986; Bean & Tienda, 1987; Carter, 1970; Carter & Segura, 1979; Durán, 1983; Keller et al., 1991; Matute-Bianchi, 1986; Orfield, 1986; Olivas, 1986; Orum, 1986; U.S. Commission on Civil Rights, 1972a, b, c; 1973; 1974; Valencia, 1991a, 1991b). Many attempts have been made both to explain the reasons for the poor school performance of this particular group of children and to intervene in meaningful ways in their educational experiences. Within the last 20 years, for example, much attention has been given, by both the research and the policy communities, to the study of factors that appear to contribute to the school failure of Mexican-background students. In general, research on the condition of education for Mexican-origin students has focused on issues such as segregation, attrition, school finance, language and bilingual education, and testing.

Reprinted by permission of the publisher from Valdés, Guadalupe, Con Respeto: *Bridging the Distance Between Culturally Diverse Families and Schools*, (New York: Teachers College Press, © 1984 by Teachers College, Columbia University. All rights reserved.), pp. 15–40.

includes the disadvantaged, the at-risk, and the underprivileged. A discussion of the school failure of Mexican-origin students must, therefore, be framed by a broader discussion that examines why other children who share similar backgrounds have also failed. It is important to first outline the causes of school failure among all children whom the educational establishment does not serve well and then to examine how the specific status of the Mexican-origin population might contribute in unique ways to this group's lack of educational success and achievement.

In general, explanations of poor academic achievement by non-mainstream children can be grouped into a number of categories. The three categories used by Bond (1981) are

1. the genetic argument,
2. the cultural argument, and
3. the class analysis argument.

EXPLANATIONS OF SCHOOL FAILURE

Mexican-origin individuals are, in terms of their school performance, a part of a much larger population that

THE GENETIC ARGUMENT

In the United States, the genetic argument—the view that certain groups are genetically more able than others (Eysenck, 1971; Herrnstein, 1973; Jensen, 1969)—had been out of favor for a number of years. Revisited recently by Herrnstein and Murray (1994), the genetic argument holds that academic talent is largely inherited and that society rewards these genetically inherited abilities. Supporters for this position argue that, given unequal innate capabilities, children of different ethnic or racial groups perform differently in school.

Strong views about the relationship between heredity and intelligence—which are largely based on the analysis of group performance on IQ tests—have been criticized by a number of scholars. Such scholars question the premises underlying psychometric testing (Figueroa, 1983, 1989; Gould, 1981; Kamin, 1977; Morrison, 1977; Schwartz, 1977; White, 1977; Zacharias, 1977), and specifically challenge the entire notion of IQ, a notion that is based exclusively on psychometric procedures and practices. A number of individuals (e.g., McClelland, 1974) have pointed out that IQ tests do not measure important features of intelligence. Others (e.g., Samuda, 1975) argue that efforts to produce culture-free tests have been disappointing. Still others (Roth, 1974) present evidence that procedures and practices in test administration may negatively affect the performance of minority children.

It is important to note that the genetic argument has failed to convince scholars within the research community who themselves may accept the assumptions underlying ability testing. Some individuals (Goldberg, 1974a, b; Kamin, 1974), for example, have challenged specific aspects of research carried out by Jensen, one of the most prominent proponents of the genetic argument. Both Goldberg and Kamin question Jensen's findings based on available twin studies. Additionally, a number of scholars (e.g., Lewontin, Rose, & Kamin, 1984) have attacked the entire concept of race. They argue not only that from a biological perspective "race" is a fuzzy concept, but also that studies focusing on adoption across racial and class lines failed to separate the genetic from the social. More recently, a number of scholars (e.g., Sternberg, 1982, 1985; Sternberg & Detterman, 1986) have attempted to move "beyond IQ" and have endeavored to examine conceptions of intelligence from a variety of different perspectives.

The Cultural Argument

As opposed to the genetic argument, the cultural explanation is currently still drawn upon by many researchers and practitioners. In its strongest form, proponents of this position (e.g., Lewis, 1966) argue that poor children are trapped in a "culture of poverty" and locked into a cycle of failure that is, in essence, self-perpetuating. Those who subscribe to this position maintain that children succeed in school only if their many

deficiencies are corrected and if they are taught to behave in more traditionally mainstream ways in specially designed intervention programs.

The less extreme forms of the cultural argument do not see poor children as directly playing a role in perpetuating their own circumstances. They nevertheless consider children who historically performed poorly in school to be either culturally deprived (Bereiter & Englemann, 1966; Deutsch et al., 1967; Hess & Shipman, 1965; Hunt, 1961; McCandless, 1952) or culturally different and therefore mismatched with schools and school culture (Baratz & Baratz, 1970). Language in particular has been used as a primary example of the ways in which children are mismatched with schools and school personnel (Au & Mason, 1981; Bernstein, 1977; Drucker, 1971; Erickson & Mohatt, 1982; Heath, 1983; Michaels & Collins, 1984; Philips, 1982).

Although the line between theories of cultural difference and cultural deprivation is a fine one, it can generally be said that advocates of the cultural difference or mismatch perspective ordinarily attribute value to the backgrounds of non-mainstream children. They do not speak of deprivation, but hold, instead, that rich and rule-governed as these children's experiences may be, they are not what educational institutions value and expect. Examples of work carried out from this perspective are those on Black English (Labov, 1973) and on children's socialization for literacy in the Appalachian region of the United States (Heath, 1983).

Closely related to the research on differences between mainstream and disadvantaged children is research on parents and their ability to "support" their children's education. This work has primarily focused on parental involvement in education, parental attitudes toward schools and education, and maternal teaching styles. In general, this research takes the perspective that at-risk children do poorly in school because of their parents' beliefs and behaviors. Non-mainstream parents either do not have the "right" attitudes toward the value of education; or they do not prepare their children well for school; or they are not sufficiently involved in their children's education. During the 1960s and early 1970s, much of this research focused on Black American families. Descriptions of the supposedly inadequate home environments of Black children were used by well-meaning social scientists to refute the arguments made by geneticists about the causes of school failure. In a review of the several streams of research on the achievement of Black children, for example, Baratz and Baratz (1970) discussed the findings of this research. Black children were found by some researchers (e.g., Hunt, 1961) to suffer from too little stimulation, while other researchers found them to be victims of too much stimulation (Deutsch, Katz, & Jensen, 1968). Others defined the problem as rooted in the inadequacy of parenting skills by Black mothers (Hess et al., 1968) and advocated compensatory programs that would teach Black women how to become "good" parents from the perspective of the majority society.

While perhaps less popular with theorists, cultural difference arguments continue to undergird a variety of practices currently being implemented in schools and communities around the country.

The Class Analysis Argument

The final explanation of school failure involves the analysis of the role of education in maintaining class differences, that is, in maintaining the power differential between groups. Proponents of this view argue that non-mainstream children do poorly in school because of the class structure of capitalist society. They argue that educational institutions function to reproduce the structure of production and that schools serve as sorting mechanisms rather than as true avenues for movement between classes. For these theorists, it is not accidental that the children of the middle classes are primarily sorted into the "right" streams or tracks in school and given access to particular kinds of knowledge (e.g., technology). The role of schools is to legitimize inequality under the pretense of serving all children and encouraging them to reach their full potential. The genius of the system resides in the fact that although the cards are clearly stacked against them, students come to believe that they are in fact given an opportunity to succeed. They leave school firmly convinced that they could have done better, perhaps achieved as much as their middle-class peers, if only they had tried harder or worked more. They are then ready to accept low-paying working-class jobs, and the working class is thus reproduced.

Explanations of school failure from this particular perspective, however, are more complex than I have outlined above. Essentially, as Giroux (1983) has argued, there are three different theories or models of reproduction: the economic-reproductive model

represented by the work of Bowles and Gintis (1976), Althusser (1969), and Althusser and Brewster (1971); the cultural reproductive model represented by the work of Bourdieu and Passeron (1977, 1979, and Bourdieu, 1977); and the hegemonic-state reproductive model represented by the work of Dale and Macdonald (1980), David (1980), and Sarup (1982) and based largely on the work of Gramsci (1971).

The economic-reproductive model focuses on the relations between the economy and schooling and argues that schools reproduce labor skills as well as relations of production. The cultural reproductive model, on the other hand, attempts to link culture, class, and domination and argues that culture is itself the medium through which the ruling class maintains its position in society. Schools validate the culture of the ruling class and at the same time fail to legitimize the forms of knowledge brought to school by groups not in power. Finally, the hegemonic-state reproductive model focuses on the role of the state in organizing the reproductive functions of educational institutions.

A particular concern for a number of theorists has been the role of human agency in explaining societal reproduction. A number of individuals—although willing to agree that macro-level factors lead to a reproduction of class relations and that schools play an important role in such reproduction—seek to understand exactly how individual members of society in particular institutions actually bring about such reproduction. These scholars hypothesize that the relationship between schooling and the perpetuation of class status is recreated at the interpersonal level in the school setting and that students actively contribute to the perpetuation of their situation by viewing mainstream students and the life choices valued by this group as worthy of contempt. "Working-class" students thus band with others of their same background and present an oppositional stance to that of the "good" or successful student. This "resistance," however, rather than allowing them to break out of the "working-class" cycle, results in the replication and reproduction of their class status. This particular trend in the investigation of the ways in which schools reproduce class membership is an attempt to understand the contents of the "black box," that is, to understand what actually goes on in educational institutions in order to bring about "failure" for certain groups of individuals. Work in this tradition is represented by the investigations carried out in Great Britain by McRobbie and McCabe (1981), Robins and Cohen (1978), and Willis (1977).

UNDERSTANDING SCHOOL FAILURE

From a theoretical perspective, the understanding of the difficulties surrounding the education of non-mainstream children must of necessity involve, as Persell (1977) argued, the integration of four levels of analysis: the societal, the institutional, the interpersonal, and the interpsychic. According to Persell, an adequate theory of educational inequality must take into account the distribution of power within a particular society and the ideology that supports that distribution. It must then link these macro-concerns to both existing ideologies about education and the nature of educational institutions. As Cortes (1986) maintains, moreover, such a theory must also take into account the educational process itself. It must consider factors such as the knowledge, skills, and attitudes of teachers, administrators, and counselors and individual student qualities and background, as well as instruction and the instructional context.

Unfortunately, as the discussion above suggests, to date examinations and explorations of school failure by non-mainstream students in school settings have been explored primarily from a single perspective.

School Failure and the Education of Immigrants

Current discussions of differential achievement by "new" American immigrants (e.g., Asians and Latinos) have tended to suggest that the difficulties encountered in schools by these newcomers were surmounted easily by the immigrant groups that arrived in this country during earlier historical periods. Vehement arguments against special compensatory programs such as bilingual education, for example, are frequently couched in the supposition that non-English speakers who entered the United States in the early part of the century managed to succeed in school without special attention given to their language or cultural differences.[1]

A review of the work carried out on the educational experiences of those immigrants who came into this country in the mid-19th century as well as in the early 20th century, however, presents a very different picture. It is evident that school failure or lack of school success was common and that Italian, Irish, Polish, and many Jewish children left school early and did not enter high school. Recent work on New York public schools (Berrol, 1982), for example, points out that until the 1950s,

immigrant and even first generation children in New York City received a very limited amount of formal education. This was the case not only for the "ignorant" Irish, but also for children (e.g., Jewish children) whose parents have consistently valued formal education. Indeed, the picture that emerges from the work of most researchers who have focused on the education of turn-of-the-century immigrants (e.g., Berrol, 1982; Bodnar, 1982; Fass, 1988; Handlin, 1982; LaGumina, 1982, Mathews, 1966; Olneck & Lazerson, 1988; Perlmann, 1988; Weiss, 1982; Williams, 1938/1969) is one that does not support idealistic views about the power of education to help all children succeed. Instead, what emerges is a sense that between 1840 and 1940, immigrants, rather than immediately availing themselves of the "opportunities" offered by educational institutions, made choices for their children that were framed by their views about education in general, their economic position, and the success or failure experienced by their children in school.

As has been the case in the examination of school failure in general, numerous explanations have been offered to account for the differences in academic and economic achievement of the various ethnic groups represented among turn-of-the-century immigrants. In particular, much attention has been given to accounting for the differences between generally "successful" groups such as the Jews and generally "unsuccessful" groups such as the Italians, the Irish, and the Slavs. As Perlmann (1988) points out, however, most of these explanations have had a long and ugly history in American intellectual life. As was the case in the late 1960s and early 1970s, for example, there was much concern in the early 20th century about genetic differences. Indeed, interest in ethnic differences reflected a profound suspicion of new immigrants that took on what Fass (1988) has characterized as a "racist slant." For many individuals who wrote during the early part of this century and even as late as the 1930s, differences in economic achievements (and educational achievements) by new immigrants were considered to be the result of inborn "race traits." As Fass (1988) argues, however, race was confused with what we now would consider to be culture, and many discussions about race focused on the habits and values of immigrant families. According to Fass, the eager acceptance of IQ testing in this country after World War I occurred in response to educators' concerns about the "retardation" of large numbers of pupils. IQ testing supposedly provided a means for ranking individuals according to their innate and unchanging talent and for ordering a hierarchy of groups. It offered a "scientific" rationale for existing views about inherited endowment and provided educators with justification for creating different "opportunities" for different students.

For early-20th-century immigrants, the genetic argument was used not only to account for differences in school performance, but to argue for the development of differentiated curricula suited to the particular talents of the less able members of the population. As a result, children with lower IQs (largely children of foreign parentage who were also poor) were placed in vocational or commercial programs. According to Fass (1988), in New York City high schools, "as early as 1911–12, about one third of the population was enrolled in commercial tracks or in the two special commercial high schools." Moreover, "educators did not believe that the new masses were smart enough to benefit from traditional academic subjects" (p. 67).

The cultural difference or deficit argument has also figured prominently in discussions about educational attainment among immigrant/ethnic groups in the United States. As Perlmann (1988) points out, variations in the attainment levels of different ethnic groups have been attributed in large part to their pre-migration histories. Much attention has been given both to the occupational skills, resulting from the positions they occupied in their countries of origin, and to the cultural attributes (attitudes, habits, values, and beliefs) that newcomers brought with them. A number of scholars, for example, have argued that certain groups (e.g., Italians) did not improve their lot as rapidly as others because their cultural background did not allow them to take advantage of the opportunities offered to them by the educational system. These scholars generally maintain that other groups (e.g., the Jews) did indeed bring with them views and attitudes about education that were congruent with the focus on the importance of schooling present in this country. Dinnerstein (1982), for example, argues that the cultural heritage of the Jews (what he considers to be "their high regard for learning") was vital to their achieving social mobility through education. Agreeing with this general view of cultural deficit, LaGumina (1982) stresses that Italians did not enjoy similar rapid mobility through education because southern Italian peasants who immigrated to the United States were conservative, fatalistic, and family-oriented. A parallel argument is made by Sowell (1981) and others about the Irish and their cultural orientation. Miller (1985, cited in Perlmann, 1988) views the traditional Irish peasant culture as communally dependent and

fatalistic, and Irish people as "feckless, child-like, and irresponsible" (p. 53).

For those individuals who support the cultural background explanations of differences in school attainment, the issues are straightforward. Certain groups of immigrants did not bring with them life experiences and cultural values that would have allowed or encouraged them to take advantage of the opportunities offered to them by American educational institutions. These immigrant parents failed because cultural "differences" prevented them from expecting their children to persevere and to succeed in school .

Scholars who take this perspective do not generally ask questions about the ways in which children of different groups were treated in schools, about whether the curriculum responded or failed to respond to these children's needs, or about the ways in which extreme poverty might have impacted on families' decisions to withdraw their children from school. The root of the problem is seen to reside in the shortcomings of the immigrants themselves.

Other scholars offer a different perspective. Steinberg (1981), in particular, argues that cultural explanations of differences in attainment are based on a "New Darwinism" in which cultural superiority and inferiority have replaced biological measures of superiority. For New Darwinists, he maintains, there are certain cultural traits associated with attainment and achievement (e.g., frugality, temperance, industry, perseverance, ingenuity), while others (e.g., familism, fatalism) are associated with limited success and social mobility. Steinberg contends that Horatio Alger stories about success and hard work are based primarily on New Darwinism and glorify the effect of tenacity and hard work without taking into account the many other factors that impact on people's lives. Specifically, such myths discount the importance of the structural locations in which new immigrants find themselves in their new society.[2]

More recently, Perlmann (1988), in his work on ethnic differences in schooling among the Irish, Italians, Jews, and Blacks in Providence, Rhode Island, between 1880 and 1935, has presented evidence that supports the argument that differences in attainment among ethnic groups are the results of social processes that have long histories. He contends that an understanding of such differences involves "determining the specific manner in which these general factors—the pre-migration heritage, discrimination, and the place of the migrants in the new class structure—operated, and interacted, in the history of a given ethnic group" (p. 6).

From the data that he examined, Perlmann concluded that "neither culture nor discrimination nor class origins in the American city can alone provide a credible summary" (p. 219). He further argues that there is not a single consistently primary factor or a single generalization that will account for differences in individual ethnic histories.

In sum, explorations of differences in school success among the various immigrant groups that entered this country between 1840 and 1940 have in general terms attempted to account for the inequality of their educational outcomes by using the same three arguments used to explain the educational failure of non-mainstream children in general. The genetic argument coupled with the cultural difference argument appears to have been used most frequently. However, it also appears that the cultural argument, with its perspective on desirable cultural traits and characteristics, was the most influential. To date, beliefs about desirable individual and family characteristics continue to be reflected in both research and practice.

Recent Immigrants, Minorities, and School Achievement

In present-day American society, the success or lack of success experienced by turn-of-the-century immigrants is often contrasted with that experienced by African-Americans as well as with that experienced by Latinos. While there are some parallels between the position occupied by African-Americans in this country with the positions occupied by both Latinos and earlier "problem" immigrant groups, there are also many significant differences.

A few scholars have attempted to understand these differences by focusing on the economic-reproductive effects of societal arrangements and taking into account the responses of oppressed or exploited populations to these societal arrangements. Ogbu (1978, 1983, 1987a, b), for example, has sought to identify important distinctions between different groups of present-day minorities" in the United States. He discusses *immigrant minorities* and *caste minorities* and shows that there is a clear difference, for example, between newly arrived Korean immigrants (an immigrant minority) and Black Americans (a caste minority), who have suffered generations of discrimination and racial prejudice. He argues that immigrant minorities frequently achieve success in ways that caste minorities do not, because they are both not conscious of the limits the

majority society would place upon them, and content to do slightly better than their co-nationals who remained at home. Caste minorities, on the other hand, are quite aware of the reality in which they live, of the jobs they will never get, and of the kinds of lack of success they will experience. Arguing that caste minorities develop folk theories of success based on the options available to them in that society, Ogbu suggests that these individuals justifiably reject education because they also reject the common view that it can provide them with true alternatives.

For Ogbu, the question of why different groups of non-mainstream children succeed while others fail is answered within the tradition of the class analysis argument and in particular from the economic-reproductive perspective. For Ogbu and for theorists who work in this tradition, premigration factors are of less importance than the discrimination that is experienced by different groups in this society, their particular location within the class structure, and their awareness or perception of the permanency of that location.

THE MEXICAN-ORIGIN POPULATION

The Mexican-origin population of the United States, as opposed to other recently arrived immigrant groups, includes individuals who have been here for generations and who see themselves as the original settlers of parts of the United States as well as individuals who have arrived here relatively recently as both legal and illegal immigrants. Generalizations about the Mexican-origin population with regard to educational success or failure are difficult to make because there are important and significant differences (generational, regional, experiential, linguistic) among the various groups that make up the Mexican-origin population.

There is evidence to suggest, however, that a large majority of Mexican persons who emigrate to the United States do not come from the groups that have obtained high levels of education. There are problems, however, in generalizing about the class origins of both early and recent Mexican immigrants. According to Bean and Tienda (1987), Jasso and Rosenzweig (1990), Portes et al. (1978), and Portes and Bach (1985), Mexican-origin immigrants are poor and have low levels of educational attainment. However, Duránd and Massey (1992) have argued that generalizations about Mexican migration to the United States are inconsistent and contradictory. They maintain that case studies (e.g., Cornelius, 1976a, b, 1978; Dinerman, 1982; Massey et al., 1987; Mines, 1981, 1984; Mines & Massey, 1985; Reichert & Massey, 1979, 1980) of Mexican "sending" communities (communities from which large numbers of Mexican nationals have emigrated) have yielded very different views about a number of questions. Among other topics, these studies present contradictory evidence about the class composition of U.S. migration. Duránd and Massey (1992) argue that a few community factors, including age of the migration stream, the geographic, political, and economic position of the community within Mexico, and the distribution and quality of agricultural land, affect the class composition of migration. The authors stress the difficulties surrounding attempts at generalization, and they suggest that such generalizations can only be made when a number of communities are studied using a common analytical framework. What this means is that educational researchers must use caution in interpreting findings about Mexican immigrants and persons of Mexican background.

As might be expected, a number of researchers have attempted to be sensitive to intragroup differences when working with Mexican-origin populations in educational settings. Matute-Bianchi (1991), for example, proposes five different categories for students:

1. "recent Mexican immigrants," who have arrived in the United States within the last three to five years;
2. "Mexican-oriented" students, who are bilingual but retain a *Mexicano* identity and reject the more Americanized Mexican-origin students;
3. "Mexican-American" students, who are U.S.-born and highly acculturated;
4. "Chicanos," who are U.S.-born, generally second generation, and frequently alienated from mainstream society; and
5. "Cholos," who dress in a distinct style and are perceived by others to be gang-affiliated.

Consistently clear differentiations between members of these several categories are difficult to make, and because of this, the study of the causes of school failure for the different segments of this population becomes complex. The Mexican-American group does not fit neatly into the categories proposed by a number of researchers. For example, the Mexican-origin population cannot be classified adequately using Ogbu's (1978, 1983, 1987a, b) two categories, *immigrant and caste*

minorities. The problem is that there are simultaneously both *immigrant* minorities and *caste* minorities within this single population. The former group includes those individuals who have recently entered the United States and cyclical immigrants who have worked in this country for years at a time, but who return to Mexico for extended periods. The latter group could include children of recently arrived *Mexicanos* whether U.S.-born or not, as well as first-, second-, third-, fourth-, and fifth-generation residents of several regions of the country. In several areas (e.g., Texas), persons of Mexican origin were already residing in the area when the area was annexed by the United States. While these individuals were not indigenous to the areas, they were certainly more "indigenous," for example, than persons who have arrived in the area within the last 20 years.

In this book, I take the position that the distinction between Mexican-origin persons who can still be categorized as immigrants and those persons who must be considered "hyphenated Americans" (Mexican-Americans/Chicanos/Cholos) has to do with a number of factors. Those persons who can be categorized as "immigrants" from Mexico (whether born in this country or not) still have what can be termed an "immigrant mentality," that is, they are oriented toward the home country, identify with Mexico, and measure their success (as Ogbu has suggested) using Mexican nationals in Mexico as their reference group. Mexican-Americans or Chicanos, on the other hand, no longer look to Mexico for identification. Their ties with Mexico have weakened and they see their lives as being carried out exclusively in this country. In general, these persons consider themselves to be different from white Americans as well as from Mexican nationals. More importantly, however, members of this group have often experienced discrimination in this country as members of a low-status and stigmatized minority. They have frequently developed an "ethnic consciousness" and have a sense of sharing the same low status as other Mexican-origin people. Mexican immigrants are immigrant minorities, while Mexican-Americans/Chicanos are caste minorities. This latter group is conscious of discrimination and prejudice by the majority group directed at Mexican-origin people *in particular* rather than at new immigrants or at outsiders in general.

What I am suggesting is that the development of an awareness of being both different and unacceptable to the majority society is a key factor in the shift in identification from immigrant to caste minority by Mexican-Americans/Chicanos. I would argue that Mexican immigrant individuals can be considered full members of the caste minority group in the United States when they:

1. become conscious that they are no longer like Mexican nationals who have remained in Mexico,
2. feel little identification with these Mexican nationals,
3. self-identify as "Americans"
4. become aware that as persons of Mexican origin they have a low status among the majority society, and
5. realize the permanent limitations they will encounter as members of this group.

Mexican-Origin Students and Explanations of School Failure

According to a number of researchers (e.g., Arias, 1986; Durán, 1983; Fligstein & Fernández, 1988; Meier & Stewart, 1991; Rumberger, 1991), Mexican-origin students have experienced a long history of educational problems, including below-grade enrollment, high attrition rates, high rates of illiteracy, and under-representation in higher education. As might be expected, a coherent theory that takes into account the many factors that impact on the poor school achievement of Mexican-origin students has not been proposed. However, a number of factors have been identified as influencing the school achievement of Mexican-origin children. These include: family income, family characteristics, and language background (Macías, 1988; Nielsen & Fernández, 1981; U.S. Department of Education, 1987); teacher/student interaction (Buriel, 1983; So, 1987; Tobias, Cole, Zinbrin, & Bodlakova, 1982; U.S. Commission on Civil Rights, 1972b); school and class composition (i.e., segregation and tracking) (Espinosa & Ochoa, 1986; Fernández & Guskin, 1981; Haro, 1977; Oakes, 1985; Orfield, 1986; Orum, 1985; Valencia, 1984); and school financing (Domínguez, 1977; Fairchild, 1984).

As will be noted, of the factors that have been identified as influencing the school achievement of Mexican-origin students, one factor (family income) can be said to be indicative of the family's location in the social structure. Two factors (school composition and school financing) can be identified as involving the school or institutional context, and two other factors (family characteristics and language background) can be considered to refer to a set of "cultural traits" not unlike those discussed by the literature on immigrants written in the early part of this century.

Not surprisingly—given that the cultural difference explanation of school failure is still drawn upon—much attention has been paid by researchers and practitioners to both language differences and family characteristics. Although most researchers working on the language problems of Mexican-origin children do not see themselves as working primarily within the deficit/difference paradigm, language issues have come to dominate the debate surrounding the education of today's "new" immigrants. The literature that has concentrated on language background issues as they relate to Mexican-origin children is immense and encompasses the study of a number of different areas, including the investigation of the process of second-language acquisition, the sociolinguistic study of language use in Mexican-American communities, the study of the relationship between teacher behaviors and second-language acquisition, the instructional use of two languages (e.g., bilingual education, two-way immersion), and the effects of various types of language intervention programs on Mexican-origin children.[3]

As compared to the literature on language background, the study of family characteristics as they relate to the education of Mexican-origin children has, in general, attempted to discover whether and to what degree these characteristics are like or unlike those found in mainstream American families. One important trend in this research (e.g., Laosa, 1978; McGowan & Johnson, 1984) has been the study of socialization practices within Chicano families. Interestingly enough, in spite of clear evidence that research conducted in this country on child development and on "desirable" socialization practices is biased (Laosa, 1984b; Ogbu, 1985), recent implementation efforts focusing on parent involvement include family education components that are directly based on a deficit-difference paradigm. I will return to this point below.

In addition to the study of socialization practices, research on family characteristics has included work on the relationship between family constellation (size and sibling structure) and children's development, and on the relationship between single-parent families and children's development and scholastic performance (Henderson & Merritt, 1968; Laosa, 1984a; LeCorgne & Laosa, 1976; Valencia, Henderson, & Rankin, 1985).

In comparison to the work that has been carried out from the deficit difference paradigm, much less work has been carried out from the class analysis perspective on the causes of the low school attainment in the Mexican-origin population. Increasingly, however, broad examinations of the educational experiences of this population are being written that include attention to the power relationships between the dominant majority population and the Mexican or Chicano minority. These analyses (Meier & Stewart, 1991; San Miguel, 1987) take the perspective that policies resulting in segregation practices and in unequal school financing reflect the structural location of the Mexican-origin population.

Work in the tradition of the economic-reproduction model has been carried out by Ogbu and Matute-Bianchi (1986), Matute-Bianchi (1986, 1991), and Foley (1990). This work has been concerned with trying to understand differences in performance by Mexican-origin students of different generational backgrounds and has included an attempt to link factors such as premigration educational experiences, attitudes toward education, attitudes toward the majority group, and the like with academic achievement. Foley (1990), in particular, examined high school students' behaviors in school against a parallel study of discrimination and prejudice present in a Texas border city. For these researchers, societal arrangements themselves as reflected in teacher-student and student-student interactions in the classroom result in their reproduction.

In sum, research carried out on the causes of school failure in Mexican-origin students has followed the principal trends present in the research on non-mainstream populations in general. Less attention has been given to examining the genetic argument among this population, although interest in testing and test bias has been high.[4] For the most part, the research on this population can be categorized as falling within the cultural deficit-difference paradigm in that it attempts to explain low scholastic achievement by focusing on differences brought to school by the children themselves. What is evident is that single-factor explanations of school failure among the children of first-generation Mexican immigrants are inadequate and cannot account for the complexity of the experience. To attribute to language factors alone, for example, what is inextricably linked to elements such as children's non-mainstream behavior, teacher perceptions, and assumptions made by the schools about parents and by parent about schools, is simplistic. In order to account for the academic failure of Mexican-origin

students from, for example, the perspective of theories of reproduction, researchers are faced with the challenge of having to account for the elements that lead to this reproduction using a binational framework.

FIXING THE PROBLEM: EDUCATIONAL INTERVENTIONS

In spite of the complexity of the problem of school failure for non-mainstream children, those concerned about its remediation have focused on attempting to change particular aspects of the institutional and instructional contexts in the hope that such changes will bring about increased school success. While aware of the structural factors that frame the problem, these researchers and practitioners represent the tension that Carnoy and Levin (1985) have described as existing between "the unequal hierarchies associated with the capitalist workplace" and "the democratic values and expectations associated with equality of access to citizen rights and opportunities" (p. 4).

In comparison to theorists who have sought to explain the nature and circumstances of educational failure, practitioners and policymakers have focused on breaking the cycle of low educational achievement or bringing about change in schools and in school outcomes. It is interesting to note, however, that programs that have endeavored to alter or reverse educational outcomes for poor, disadvantaged, or at-risk children have reflected the thinking of theorists who have worked within the deficit-difference paradigm. Many of these theorists have tended to address single micro-level factors such as English language fluency, standardness of spoken English, or the blend and mix of students of different racial groups within a given school. These research and theoretical foci, in turn, have led to the implementation of programs that offer narrow solutions to far broader problems (e.g., bilingual education programs, desegregation programs, Head Start) and that have been marginally successful. Ironically, even though the theories that held that problems experienced by at-risk children were their own "fault" or responsibility have been called into question, program implementation still responds to this fundamental view. With few exceptions, programs aimed at at-risk children are designed to address key shortcomings or "deficits" in these students in order to assist them in succeeding in the school environment.

It is not surprising that researchers working within the class analysis paradigm argue that such programs leave existing institutions largely untouched and that these institutions continue to reflect the power realities of the larger society. For that reason, they point out, compensatory programs have failed to meet the expectations of those policymakers and practitioners who sincerely hoped that correcting or compensating for key factors would bring about significant changes in total educational outcomes.

In the case of Mexican-origin students, the absence of a sound underlying perspective that brings together explanations with interventions is particularly evident. Not only is there a lack of a coherent theory about macro-level factors that can adequately explain the failure and success of these children in American schools, but there is also a lack of coherence among the many theories that have focused on micro-level variables. In general, the work of both policymakers and practitioners involved in the education of Mexican-origin children also reveals a very practical and problem-oriented focus. The focus for such individuals has been finding solutions, establishing policies, funding programs that will address the needs of these children, and implementing promising programs in spite of heavy local and national political fire.

While from the perspectives of class analyses of schooling and society the educational problems of Mexican-origin children cannot be alleviated without a major change in the societal structure that impacts on every level of students' lives, from the perspective of many policymakers and practitioners, what is needed is the right kinds of instructional solutions, the right kinds of school programs in order to bring about meaningful, if not lasting, change. Single and partial solutions, then, often take on extraordinary meaning, and these interventions become the focus of intense debate. The politics of bilingual education (a solution designed to focus on children's inability to profit from instruction carried out exclusively in English), for example, have been particularly acrimonious. Many practitioners, parents, and policymakers are convinced that good bilingual education programs *by themselves* will impact significantly on educational outcomes.[5]

The fact is that current educational outcomes—high drop-out rates, grade delay, low test scores, and low college enrollments by Mexican-origin students—demand solutions. Whatever the realities of the structures of inequality in this country may be, practitioners feel a strong pressure to find ways of helping their students to succeed in school.

THE CONCEPT OF FAMILY INTERVENTION

In this book, I am concerned primarily with those examples of educational intervention that focus on families and their young children. I will argue throughout this book that this focus is problematic, and I will point out that this particular approach to equalizing educational outcomes is based directly on the deficit-difference paradigm.

In the section that follows, I will discuss a recently popular educational intervention perspective that has focused specifically on parents and families. This strategy, currently known as *parent involvement,* is considered by some researchers (e.g., Becker & Epstein,1982; Bennett, 1986; Díaz-Soto, 1988; Epstein, 1982, 1985, 1986b, 1991; Epstein & Dauber, 1991; Henderson, 1987; Simich-Dudgeon, 1986; Walberg, 1984) to result in various kinds of positive benefits for both parents and children. As I will point out below, this strategy is currently being implemented around the country, and its use is being advocated by both policymakers and practitioners.

The position I will take here is that, like many of the family intervention programs that came before it, parent involvement is an attempt to find small solutions to what are extremely complex problems. I am concerned that this new" movement—because it is not based on sound knowledge about the characteristics of the families with which it is concerned—will fail to take into account the impact of such programs on the families themselves.

In order to provide a context for this position, which I will elaborate further in later chapters, I will discuss current thinking about parent education and provide a brief review of the literature that has focused on this notion.

Parent Education Programs for Mexican-Origin Families

Within the past decade, there has been a renewed interest in the impact of families and homes on children's education. Concern about parent "involvement" in children's learning has been expressed by educators, legislators, and religious leaders. The generally held view, as the publication *What Works* (U.S. Department of Education, 1987) made evident, is that schools depend directly on parents for assistance in educating children, and that without parental help the schools cannot carry out their work as effectively. The tone and direction of this publication reflects the thinking underlying many current attempts to solve what is perceived to be a serious problem. The section on the home within *What Works* (p. 5) makes the following statement:

Curriculum of the Home

Research: Findings: Parents are their children's first and most influential teachers. What parents do to help their children learn is more important to academic success than how well-off the family is.

Comment: Parents can do many things at home to help their children succeed in school. Unfortunately, recent evidence indicates that many parents are doing much less than they might. For example, American mothers on average spend less than half an hour a day talking, explaining, or reading with their children. Fathers spend less than 15 minutes.

They can create a "curriculum of the home" that teaches their children what matters. They do this through their daily conversations, household routines, attention to school matters, and affectionate concern for their children's progress.

Conversation is important. Children learn to read, reason, and understand things better when their parents:

- read, talk, and listen to them,
- tell them stories, play games, share hobbies, and
- discuss news, TV programs, and special events.

In order to enrich the "curriculum of the home," some parents:

- provide books, supplies, and a special place for studying,
- observe routine for meals, bedtime, and homework, and
- monitor the amount of time spent watching TV and doing after-school jobs.

Parents stay aware of their children's lives at school when they:

- discuss school events,
- help children meet deadlines, and
- talk with their children about school problems and successes.

Research on both gifted and disadvantaged children shows that home efforts can greatly improve student achievement. For example, when parents of disadvantaged children take the steps listed above, their children can do as well at school as the children of more affluent families.

At first glance, this statement appears to be straightforward and unproblematic. For middle-class practitioners, for middle-class parents, and for those who are familiar with middle-class standards and practices and who aspire to be middle class, there is not much to quarrel with in this set of recommendations. Of course parents should spend time with their children. Of course they should talk to them and engage them in conversations.

There are many activities on this list, however, that poor and newly arrived immigrant parents do not engage in. Moreover, there are assumptions in this seemingly innocuous statement about how families should live their lives. As I will endeavor to make clear in the descriptions of the 10 families that I will present here, for various important reasons, some families do not observe routines or discuss school events, or even tell their children stories. They cannot provide books or supplies, and they do not have hobbies. Many parents do not know how to read. Many others work late. Most have little understanding about school deadlines or about how to "monitor" their children's homework.

What is evident, however—given the above position about the role of families in education—is that many educators and policymakers believe that attention must be directed at educating or changing what I term here "nonstandard" families, that is, families that are non-mainstream in background or orientation (e.g., nonwhite, non-English-speaking, non-middle-class). This concern about nonstandard families and the widely held belief that these families—for the good of their children—must be helped to be more like middle-class families has led to a strong movement in favor of family intervention or family education programs.

In the case of Hispanic families, and in particular in the case of Mexican-origin families, the perception that these families must be brought into the mainstream is particularly strong. For example, while in office, the former Education Secretary, Lauro Cavazos, strongly criticized Hispanic families (Suro, 1990). Arguing that neither the language barrier nor economic difficulties completely explain the problems of Hispanic students, he stated that Hispanic parents deserve much of the blame for the high dropout rate among their children. According to Cavazos, Hispanics have stopped placing a high value on education. They have not acknowledged the problem, and they have not cared that youngsters have dropped out of school. For Cavazos, then, the first vital step in improving education for Hispanics involves, not obtaining increased funding for programs at every level, but obtaining a commitment from Hispanic parents that they will work to educate their children.

Inflammatory as Cavazos's remarks were, they simply echoed what has been generally believed by many American educators to be true: Hispanic parents are neither committed to nor involved in their children's education. These educators—because they have neither the experience nor the information that might help them make sense of the lives of people different from themselves—feel both angry and indignant at the seeming indifference of Mexican-origin parents.

Not surprisingly, many well-meaning educators have decided to intervene and to try to interrupt the pattern of failure. And like many educators, social workers, and policymakers in the past, they have decided to implement programs that have as their purpose teaching Mexican-origin mothers how to help their children succeed in school. As a result, many kinds of programs have been established around the country.[6] Most focus on mothers, and most hope to teach what middle-class professionals believe are valuable parenting skills: for example, how to prepare nutritional meals, how parents should talk to their children, how little ones should and should not be disciplined, and how everyday household objects and activities can be used to teach children valuable school-related skills.

In one well-known and well-funded program established in the Southwest, for example, 2,000 low-income Mexican-origin families are being served under an umbrella of subprograms. In the parent-child education segment, mothers are visited at home and taken to receive instruction at a central program office while their children from birth to two years are cared for by others in a pleasant and well-designed child care center. They learn how to be "better" parents while they make toys for their children. They network with other parents, and they are encouraged to go to school, to learn English, and to aim for better jobs for themselves and for their children.

In another program established on the West Coast, the focus is home literacy in Spanish. Program organizers teach parents to read to their children and to encourage their writing of stories. Parents begin to write,

too, and they take great pride in their children's stories. The program brings parents together to share their children's efforts and to support their "involvement" in their children's education. The aim of the organizers is to build parents' self-esteem and confidence, to develop their literacy skills, and to break the cycle of school failure for their children.

Initially, even without empirical evidence of their effectiveness, few would want to fault such programs. Indeed, as historians of education (e.g., Schlossman, 1976, 1978, 1983, 1986) have made clear, the tendency to solve perceived problems affecting families in this country by "educating" parents goes back to the turn of the century. As Schlossman (1986) has pointed out, the family-in-crisis motif is perennial and has led to a tendency "to see parent education as a solution for deeply rooted social problems" (p. 39).

A Brief Overview of Changing Goals and Purposes of Parent and Family Education

In this country parent education has been known by very different names and has had many goals. Movements to implement parent education programs have responded to varying perceptions about the existence of different problems and have been influenced by a wide variety of values or ideals about what should be. As Florin and Dokecki (1983) and Dokecki and Moroney (1983) have pointed out, an overview of the changing goals and purposes of parent and family education reveals that concern about families has periodically shifted its focus between "mainstream" and "troubled" families. From 1600 through 1800, for example, educational programs aimed at families sought to instill moral values and to combat immorality and corruption. From 1850 to 1880 and again from 1900 to 1920, the goal of parent education programs was to socialize new immigrants to this society's dominant values. During certain periods (e.g., 1880–1900 and 1920–1940), parent education programs were aimed at the middle class and were mainly concerned with political corruption and moral responsibility. Beginning in the late 1950s, in an attempt to redress social inequalities, parent education programs were directed at the disenfranchised urban poor. The goals of such programs included the equalization of opportunities, the promotion of school success, and the early cognitive development of at-risk children. In the 1980s, in part as a result of the activities of the Barbara Bush

Foundation for Family Literacy (1989), funding was made available to parent education programs that focused on developing the literacy skills of both parents and children.

According to Dokecki and Moroney (1983, pp. 56–59), the knowledge bases and theoretical/philosophical underpinnings as well as the specific purposes of parent education programs have shifted in important ways. Beginning in the early part of this century, for example, practices were directly influenced by theories about child development. According to Schlossman's (1983) overview of the first three decades of the 20th century, the nascent science of child development had a "tremendous popular appeal." In particular, "scientific" support for parent education was helped along by the efforts of foundation funding. Schlossman (1983) carefully documents how the Laura Spelman Rockefeller Memorial enlisted university researchers in the cause of child development research, in the publication of *Parents Magazine,* and in the cause of instructing women on how best to raise their children. Similarly, Laosa (1984b) traces the close relationship between these activities and the establishment of several government agencies: the National Institute of Mental Health in 1946, the National Institute of Child Health and Human Development in 1963, and the Office of Child Development in 1969. He comments that during the 1960s the public concern about children in particular led to an expansion of support for research in child development as well as to an expansion of funding for children's programming. Belief in the importance of education as well as in the need to equalize opportunities for the children of poor and immigrant families led to the implementation of compensatory programs. Early childhood intervention, according to Laosa (1984b), "was seen as having an unlimited potential not only for breaking the cycle of poverty, but also as a possibility for forging revolutionary changes in the entire educational system" p. 54). However, as Laosa also points out, professional knowledge and scientific expertise often greatly exceeded the available supply [of reliable data]." Sheldon White (1968, P. 204, cited in Laosa, 1984b, p. 54), for example, stated that "Placed in the uncomfortable role of experts without expertise, we are all in the business of trying to supply educated guesses about the nature of children's cognitive development.

During the 1960s and 1970s, that is, during the period in which the deficit-difference paradigm was widely supported, research on child development was designed to inform policies and practices that might improve educational opportunities for disadvantaged children. However, as Ogbu (1982) has argued, the underlying assumption of this research (e.g., Bloom, Davis, & Hess, 1965; Hunt, 1969; White et al., 1973) was that poverty, unemployment, and low attainment were caused by the inadequate childrearing practices of the poor themselves. Criticizing the process-product research paradigm, Ogbu (1982) contended that these studies were designed to show "causal relationships between family processes, especially parent-child interaction on the one hand and child rearing outcomes—generally the language cognitive, motivation and social competencies—on the other" (p. 253). For the most part, these studies compared particular kinds of skills and competencies found in minority parents with those found among middle-class white parents.

The problems with this particular orientation are more evident today than they were when this research was first conducted. Nevertheless, the view that there exists a universal model of human development and a set of particular competencies that all children should acquire if reared adequately still influences both policy and practice. Evidence from cross-cultural research on child socialization has had little impact on the notion that, as Ogbu (1981) maintains, sets up "white middle-class child rearing practices and competencies as the standard upon which all others are measured." Even though this research documents the fact that children around the world are socialized to develop those skills and competencies that are necessary for them to live as competent adults in their particular societies, child rearing strategies of minority populations have not generally been seen from that perspective. The socialization practices of these populations are seen as deficient or limited, rather than as based directly on the family and community's experience in providing their children with the competencies they will need in order to survive.

There is evidence, moreover, that in this country, notions about maternal competence and appropriate care for young children have changed dramatically during the last 85 years. Indeed, as Wrigley (1989) has demonstrated, the increasing emphasis on the cognitive stimulation of young children is not only recent but also rooted in the social context of the times. Her analysis of 1,017 articles drawn from the literature directed at parents written between 1900 and 1985 revealed that between 1900 and 1910, experts were concerned about hygiene, regular routines for baby management, and babies' physical care. Between 1900 and 1935, many articles argued that stimulation harmed babies and recommended leaving children strictly alone. By the 1930s, when child development had become a nascent science, experts began to be concerned about children's social and emotional development. Finally, in the 1960s, as poor children were targeted for special compensatory programs, interest in stimulating children's intellectual growth increased sharply. As a result, Wrigley (1989) argues, "middle-class families soon became interested in stimulating their young children's learning" (p. 65). By 1980, what Wrigley (1989) terms "better babies" were children "who were geared to perform academic feats at an unusually early age" (p.71). She argues that because education has become even more important in sorting people into different occupations and class locations parents must strive to foster in their children those competencies and skills that they will need in order to enter high-prestige professions.

Unfortunately for those who have worked to equalize opportunities for disadvantaged children by involving their parents in parent education, what emerges from the scholarship on parent education programs in general—especially those that were designed as part of an effort to equalize opportunities—is that there are no clear answers or formulas for providing early educational advantages for disadvantaged children. Research carried out on the effectiveness of many programs designed to provide an early start for non-mainstream children is contradictory. Different reviews of the literature (e.g., Boger et al., 1986; Bronfenbrenner, 1974; Goodson & Hess, 1975; Lazar, 1988; Lazar et al., 1977) provide different interpretations of the findings. Florin and Dokecki (1983), for example, present the findings of evaluations of parent education programs and begin by pointing out that the cross-study comparison of projects is exceedingly difficult. Using only studies that had a true or quasi-experimental design, they concluded that "as a group, parent education programs have demonstrated moderate to high immediate IQ gains in program children" (p. 41). They emphasize, however, that these gains gradually decrease over time but do persist into the elementary school years. They also report that evidence from objective measures of school achievement, special education placement, and grade retention is also not altogether consistent. They point out that even though results of evaluations focusing on both child and parent outcomes demonstrate a number of positive effects, "unbridled enthusiasm" should be tempered because of the possibility of biases in self-selected program samples, effects produced by non-treatment variables, and the lack of representation of the programs included in evaluation comparisons.

The Parent Involvement Movement

The currently popular term for family intervention/parent education programs appears to be *parent involvement*. Parent involvement in schools is being strongly advocated by both researchers and practitioners. Claims about the positive effects of such involvement (Becker & Epstein, 1982; Bennett, 1986; Clark, 1988; Díaz-Soto, 1988; Epstein, 1982, 1985, 1986a, 1991; Epstein & Dauber, 1991; Henderson, 1987; Simich-Dudgeon, 1986; Walberg, 1984) maintain that parent involvement results in raising student achievement among low-income and minority youngsters, developing parents' abilities to help their children, fomenting positive attitudes by children and parents toward teachers and schools, reducing absenteeism and dropout rates, and increasing home–school communication. McLaughlin and Shields (1987) suggest, however, that the involvement of disadvantaged parents may not have achieved what educators had hoped.

According to the NEA publication *Schools and Families: Issues and Actions,* the four currently popular parent involvement models are: (1) parents as volunteers, (2) parents as receivers of information about the school, (3) parents working at the school, and (4) parents working with their own children at home. Recent research, however, suggests that teachers' views about parent involvement seem to center around the notion that parents should receive training so that they can adequately work with their children at home. Olsen et al. (1994), for example, documented in their study of reform efforts in 32 schools in California that the "prevalent belief was that for teachers to do their job at school parents need to do their job at home" (p. 95). Teachers primarily wanted parents to support their children's school work. They had less interest in parents' becoming genuinely involved in restructuring efforts and only valued their ability to help out as volunteers, as advocates of the school, and or as fundraisers. Moreover, teachers generally expressed negative views about parents and thought of them as uneducated, poor, and dysfunctional.

Similarly, Lareau (1989) found in her research on parental involvement that there are important contrasts in home–school relationships between white middle-class and white working-class parents that raise questions about both the effectiveness of involvement and the degree to which teachers welcome such involvement. Lareau argues that rather than a question of degree or amount of involvement, it is the middle-class parents' ability to mobilize their cultural capital that accounts for differences in achievement between their children and the children of working-class whites. Even though white working-class mothers were found by Lareau to have high aspirations for their children, and even though they spend time working with their children, they do not have the resources available to middle-class mothers. They often do not know how to respond when their youngsters complain that their attempts at helping them are "all wrong," and they do not have friends who are members of the teaching profession. When talking to their children's teachers, working-class mothers often feel insecure and apprehensive.

According to Lareau's view of the middle-class "home advantage," children from this background succeed in school because their parents have power (social and occupational status), competence (knowledge about schools and school learning), education, income and material resources, a vision of the interconnectedness of home and work, and networks of individuals who have information about schools and school practices.

Working-class mothers' involvement is never quite satisfactory. Working-class parents must, therefore, depend much more on both teachers and schools. They cannot serve in the role of co-teachers as the schools would hope that they could. Lamentably, because of this, their home-school relationships will fall short of what school personnel have currently concluded is desirable for *all* families. Indeed, if teachers use the middle-class family as a standard, teachers will generally assume that all parents who are "committed to their children's education" will engage in the same kinds of activities and behaviors. They will often surmise quite erroneously that parents who do not do so are unsupportive of their children's academic performance.

Parental involvement, then, may not quite be what its supporters would hope. Relationships between parents and schools do, in fact, reflect the structural locations of these individuals in the wider society. Simply bringing parents to schools will not change the racist or classist responses that teachers may have toward them and their behaviors. Parenting classes alone will not equalize outcomes.

THE VIEW FROM INSIDE TEN FAMILIES

In the chapters that follow, my objective is to bring into focus the everyday lives of 10 women whose energies were primarily involved with the survival of their families and who viewed themselves as successes or failures in terms of their ability to contribute to that survival. By showing how these 10 families lived, what they thought about, believed in and aspired to, I hope to raise serious questions about current family education programs that seek to teach immigrant adults how to parent. What my data will show is that Mexican parents do indeed know how to parent, but that because their parenting styles are the product of their class, culture, and experiences, they are unlike those of the American model of the "standard" family.

As will be clear in my description of the parents and their children, I am not arguing here that their patterns of living and of socializing their children are unique or different from those found among people in many parts of the world. Instead, it is my contention that the Mexican-origin families that I followed are similar in many ways to the turn-of-the-century immigrants who were considered to be familistic, fatalistic, and otherwise unacceptable by the mainstream members of the population.

It is my position also that a view from inside the families may help to put into perspective old cultural-deficit theories in new clothing. By inviting readers to come to know 19 adults and 12 children, I want to offer a basis for examining and weighing carefully efforts ultimately designed to change stable, successful, and functioning households. By presenting the lives of 10 families, I hope to offer insights about how their lives and the lives of other people like them might be altered by well-intentioned intervention movements designed to help non-mainstream children to succeed in school. Very specifically, I contend that to date, we still lack the kinds of knowledge that Bronfenbrenner (1979) referred to when he wrote:

I shall presume to speak for the procession in pointing out what we do know and what we don't. We know a great deal about children's behavior and development, and quite a bit about what can and does happen inside of families-parent child interaction, family dynamics, and all that. But we know precious little about the circumstances under which families live, how these circumstances affect their lives, and what might happen if the circumstances were altered. . . . Before we can engage in parent education of the kinds here proposed, we have to learn a good deal more than we know at present about the actual experience of families in different segments our society. (p. 220)

Endnotes

1. For a discussion of these arguments as they relate to bilingual education policy, the reader is referred to Crawford (1989, 1992a, 1992b).

2. Steinberg (1981) directly refutes the myth of Jewish intellectualism and Catholic anti-intellectualism and argues that many poor Jews in this country did not rapidly ascend the social ladder. He coincides with Berrol (1982) in his claim that poor Jews (like poor Italians, poor Irishmen and poor Slavs) dropped out of school quite early. He contends that cultural values were not the major or primary cause of school success and social mobility among Jews, but that the economic success of the first and even second generation led to the educational success of succeeding generations.

3. The literature on the research carried out on the effectiveness of bilingual education is voluminous. For excellent reviews of this research, the reader should refer to Cazden and Snow (1990) and Casanova and Arias (1993). Both Hakuta (1986) and August and García (1988) include comprehensive overviews of language research as it relates to the education of linguistic minority students.

4. Two recent volumes contain excellent bibliographies on testing and Mexican-origin students; Keller et al. (1991) and Valdés and Figuerosa (1994).

5. For a discussion of the bilingual education debate in this country, the reader is referred to Crawford (1989), Cazden and Snow (1990), Porter (1990), and Hakuta (1986).

6. Because it is not my intention to criticize particular programs, I am deliberately not referring to these various efforts by name. I will point out, however, that many "parent education" programs focus on such areas as family literacy, family involvement in education, early learning, care and feeding of newborn children, etc. A general search of the ERIC system, for example, using the descriptors *Mexican and family education* yields an impressive number of articles describing such efforts.

SECTION 4: EDUCATIONAL PERSPECTIVES
ASSESSMENT AND APPLICATION

1. Identify the major enrollment trends for Chicanos in higher education and determine to what extent your college or university is representative of those trends.

2. Select a community with a substantial Chicano population and identify key K–12 "educational pipeline" leaks in its school system.

3. Are you facing major obstacles in higher education like those listed in Jason DeParle's article? If so, how do you plan to overcome them?

4. Analyze a major legal decision that has affected the educational standing of Chicanos.

5. What role has intelligence testing played in the education of Chicanos?

6. Give your reaction to the 2013 Heritage Foundation's report on the IQ of Hispanics and their desirability as immigrants to the United States. The report is available at that organization's website and LULAC has issued a position statement on it.

7. Identify and analyze the major changes in the education of Chicanos from the civil rights era to the present.

8. Select a major court decision on Chicano education and explain its educational importance.

9. How did legal decisions on Latinos relate to the *Brown v. Board of Education* decision by the Supreme Court in 1954?

10. Analyze the validity of three leading explanations for the school failure of Mexican-origin students.

11. Identify a "family intervention" program in the schools of your community and describe its structure, aims, rate of success, and replicability or transportability potential.

12. Determine the demand and availability of English-as-a-second-language programs for adults in a predominantly Hispanic community.

13. Compare and contrast additive and subtractive bilingual education programs.

14. How do you foresee the standing of bilingual education in your state in the next five years?

15. Based on the article by Bernal on the fight for Mexican American Studies and the films suggested in this section, *Precious Knowledge* and *Outlawing Shakespeare,* write a description of the role played by students and faculty in resisting cultural agression.

16. How effectively did the Librotraficante initiative described in Paula Beltrán's chapter promote resistance to the Arizona ban on Chicano Studies texts in public schools? Consult the Librotraficante website listed in appendix A for additional information.

SECTION 4: SUGGESTED READINGS

Acuña, Rodolfo F. (2011). *The Making of Chicana/o Studies: In the Trenches of Academe.* Piscataway, NJ: Rutgers University Press.

Bennet, Christine I. (2007). *Comprehensive Multicultural Education* (6th ed.). Boston, MA: Allyn and Bacon.

Bermúdez, Andrea B. (1994). *Doing Our Homework: How Schools Can Engage Hispanic Communities.* Charleston, WV: ERIC Clearinghouse on Rural Education and Small Schools.

Bigelow, Bill. (2006). *The Line Between Us: Teaching about the Border and Mexican Immigration.* Milwaukee, WI: Rethinking Schools.

Bixler-Márquez, Dennis J. (1988). *Chicano Speech in the Bilingual Classroom.* New York, NY: Peter Lang Publishing.

Bixler-Márquez, Dennis J. (2005). La Preparatoria Bowie versus la Patrulla Fronteriza. *Aztlán: A Journal of Chicano Studies.* Vol. 30, (2). Pp.157–168.

Bixler-Márquez, Dennis J. (2010). The Schools of Crystal City: A Chicano Experiment in Change. In M. Perales & R. A. Ramos (Eds.), *Recovering the Hispanic History of Texas* (1st ed., pp. 92–110). Houston, TX: Arte Público Press.

Bixler-Márquez, Dennis J. & Seda, Milagros. (1994). The Ecology of a Chicano Student at Risk. *The Journal of Educational Issues of Language Minority Students.* Vol. 13. Pp. 195–208.

Cockroft, James D. (1995). *Latinos in the Struggle for Equal Education.* New York, NY: Franklin Watts.

De Ortego y Gasca, Felipe. (2008). Why Chicano Studies? *Hispanic Outlook in Higher Education*, October, *19*, 34–37.

Donato, Rubén. (1997). *The Other Struggle for Equal Schools: Mexican Americans During the Civil Rights Era.* Albany, NY: State University of New York Press.

Figueroa, Richard A. (1999). *A Report to the Nation on Policies and Issues on Testing Hispanic Students in the United States.* Washington, DC: President's Advisory Commission on Educational Excellence for Hispanic Americans.

Foley, Douglas E. (1990). *Learning Capitalist Culture Deep in the Heart of Texas.* Philadelphia, PA: University of Pennsylvania Press.

Gándara, P. C. & Contreras, F. (2010). *The Latino Education Crisis, the Consequences of Failed Social Policies.* Cambridge, MA: Harvard University Press.

García, John A. (2012). *Latino Politics in America: Community, Culture and Interests.* (2nd ed.). Plymouth, UK: Rowman & Littlefield Publishers, Inc.

Genesee, Fred. (1999). *Program Alternatives for Linguistically Diverse Students.* Washington, DC: Center for Research on Education, Diversity and Excellence.

Gibson, Margaret A., Gándara, Patricia & Koyama, Jill Peterson. (2004). *School Connections: U.S.-Mexican Youth, Peers and School Achievement.* New York, NY: Teachers College Press.

Ginorio, Angela & Huston, Michelle. (2001). ¡Sí, Se Puede! Yes, We Can: Latinas en la Escuela. Washington, DC: American Association of University Women Educational Foundation.

González, Gilbert G. (1990). *Chicano Education in the Era of Segregation.* Philadelphia, PA: Bach Institute Press.

Gutiérrez, José Angel. (2010). The Chicano Movement: Paths to Power. *The Social Studies, 102*(1), 25–32.

Guzmán-DuVernois, Laura. (2013). *From Plyler to Daca: Policy Guiding Undocumented Students' Rights in a K-12 Compulsory System and Its Pipeline to Higher Education.* (Doctoral dissertation). El Paso, TX: University of Texas at El Paso.

Harvey, William B. & Anderson, Eugene L. (2005). *Minorities in Higher Education: Twenty-First Annual Status Report.* Washington, DC: American Council on Education.

Hill, Jane D. & Flynn, Kathleen M. (2006). *Classroom Instruction that Works with English Language Learners.*

Alexandria, VA: Association for Supervision and Curriculum Development.

Jones, Toni Griego & Fuller, Mary Lou. (2003). *Teaching Hispanic Children*. Boston, MA: Allyn and Bacon.

MacDonald, V. (2004). *Latino Education in the United States: A Narrated History from 1513–2000*. (1st ed.). New York, NY: Palgrave Macmillan.

Madrigal González, Lizely. (2012). *Still "Unfinished Education": Latino Students Forty Years After the Mexican American Education Study*. (Doctoral dissertation). El Paso, TX: University of Texas at El Paso.

Montemayor, Robert & Mendoza, Henry. (2004). *Right Before Our Eyes: Latinos Past, Present & Future*. Tempe, AZ: Scholargy Publishing.

Moreno, José F. (Ed.). (1999). *Elusive Quest for Equality: 150 Years of Chicano/Chicana Education*. Cambridge, MA: Harvard Educational Review.

Noguera, Pedro. (2003). *City Schools and the American Dream: Reclaiming the Promise of Public Education*. New York, NY: Teachers College Press.

Oakes, Jeannie & Lipton, Martin. (2006). *Learning Power: Organizing for Education and Justice*. New York, NY: Teachers College Press.

Ochoa, Gilda. (2007). *Learning from Latino Teachers*. (1st ed.). San Francisco, CA: Jossey-Bass.

Orfield, Gary. (2004). *Dropouts in America: Confronting the Graduation Rate Crisis*. Cambridge, MA: Harvard Education Press.

Ortega, Carlos. (2012). *The Struggle for Inclusion: The Chicano Educational Experience in a Diverse Society*. San Diego, CA: Cognella Academic Publishing.

Otto, Santa Anna. (2004). *Tongue Tied: The Lives of Multilingual Children in Public Education*. Lanham, MD: Rowman & Littlefield Publishers.

Reyes, Pedro, Scribner, Jay D. & Scribner Paredes, Alicia. (1999). *Lessons from High-Performing Hispanic High Schools: Creating Learning Communities*. New York, NY: Teachers College Press.

Reyes III, Reynaldo. (2013). *Learning the Possible: Mexican American Students Moving from the Margins of Life to New Ways of Being*. Tucson, AZ: University of Arizona Press.

Reyes, Rogelio. (1988). The Sociolinguistic Foundations of Chicano Caló: Trends for Future Research. In Jacob L. Ornstein-Galicia, George K. Green & Dennis J. Bixler-Márquez, (Eds.). *Research Issues and Problems in United States Spanish*. Brownsville, TX: University of Texas at Brownsville.

Rippberger, Susan J. & Staudt, Kathleen A. (2003). *Pledging Allegiance: Learning Nationalism at the El Paso-Juárez Border*. New York, NY: Routledge.

Rosales, Arturo. (1996). *Chicano!: The History of the Mexican Civil Rights Movement*. Houston, TX: Arte Público Press.

San Miguel, Guadalupe, Jr. (1987). *Mexican Americans and the Campaign for Educational Equality in Texas, 1910–1981*. Austin, TX: University of Texas Press.

Sánchez, Rosaura. (1992–96). Mapping the Spanish Language Along a Multiethnic and Multilingual Border. *Aztlán: A Journal of Chicano Studies*. Vol. 21, (1,2). Pp 49–104.

Soldatenko, Michael. (2011). *Chicano Studies: The Genesis of a Discipline*. Tucson, AZ: University of Arizona Press.

Soltero, Sonia W. (2011). *Schoolwide Approaches to Educating ELLS: Creating Linguistically & Culturally Responsive K–12 Schools*. Portsmouth, NH: Heinemann.

Suárez-Orozco, Carola, Suárez-Orozco, Marcelo M. & Todorova, Irina. (2010). *Learning a New Land, Immigrant Students in American Society*. Cambridge, MA: Belknap Press of Harvard University Press.

Trujillo, Armando. (1998). *Chicano Empowerment and Bilingual Education: Movimiento Politics in Crystal City, Texas*. New York: Garland Publishing.

Vaca, Nicolás C. (2004). *The Presumed Alliance: The Unspoken Conflict Between Latinos and Blacks and What it Means for America*. New York, NY: HarperCollins Publishers.

Valencia, Richard. R. (2011). *Chicano School Failure and Success: Past, Present and Future*. (3rd ed.). New York, NY: Routledge.

Valenzuela, Angela. (1999). *Subtracting Schooling: U.S.-Mexican Youth and the Politics of Caring*. Albany, NY: State University of New York Press.

Valenzuela, Angela. (2005). *Leaving Children Behind: How "Texas-Style" Accountability Fails Latino Youth.* New York, NY: State University of New York Press.

Valdés, Guadalupe. (1996). *Con Respeto: Bridging the Distance Between Cultrally Diverse Families and Schools.* New York, NY: Teachers College Press.

Vázquez, Carmen Inoa. (2004). *Parenting with Pride, Latino Style: How to Help Your Child Cherish Your Cultural Values and Succeed in Today's World.* New York, NY: HarperCollins Publishers.

White, Michael J. & Glick, Jennifer E. (2009). *Achieving Anew: How New Immigrants Do in American Schools, Jobs, and Neighborhoods.* New York, NY: Russell Sage Foundation.

SECTION 4: SUGGESTED FILMS AND VIDEOS

Bilingualism: A True Advantage, 1992
Heritage Series
Films for the Humanities, Inc.
132 West 31st Street, New York, NY 10001

Brown vs. Board Jubilee Anniversary, 2010
Microtraining and Multicultural Development
141 Walnut Street Hanover, MA 02339

Cada Cabeza es un Mundo/Every Mind Is a World, 2001
AIMS Multimedia
9710 DeSoto Avenue, Chatsworth, CA 91311

Closing the Achievement Gap: A Vision for Changing Beliefs and Practices, 2004
ASCD
1703 North Beauregard Street, Alexandria, VA 22311

Culture, Politics & Pedagogy
Media Education Foundation
60 Masonic Street, Northampton, MA 01060

Dropout Nation, 2012
PBS
2100 Crystal Drive, Arlington, VA 22202

Education in Resistance, 2000
Chiapas Media Project

Education Under Arrest, 2012
PBS
2100 Crystal Drive, Arlington, VA 22202

English Only in America?, 1995
Films for the Humanities and Sciences
132 West 31st Street, New York, NY 10001

La Raza: Education, 1976
La Raza Series
Moctezuma Productions
McGraw-Hill Broadcasting

Latino Education and Counseling, 1992
Heritage Series
Films for the Humanities, Inc.
132 West 31st Street, New York, NY 10001

Latino Parents as Partners in Education, 1992
Films for the Humanities and Sciences
132 West 31st Street, New York, NY 10001

Moyers & Company: Between Two Worlds—Life on the Border, 2012
Films for the Humanities and Sciences
132 West 31st Street, New York, NY 10001

No Saco Nada del Escuelín, 1972
El Teatro Campesino
San Juan Bautista, CA

Our Hispanic Heritage—Strategies for Educators, 1986
Multicultural Media Corp.

Outlawing Shakespeare, 2012
The Nonprofit Network
4018 City Terrance Drive, Los Angeles, CA 90063

Precious Knowledge: Arizona's Battle for Ethnic Studies, 2011
Dos Vatos Productions, Inc.

Race to Nowhere, 2010
Reel Link Films
3527 Mt. Diablo Blvd, Lafayette, CA 94549

School: The Story of American Public Education, 2001 (Episode 2), 2001
PBS Home Video
2100 Crystal Drive, Arlington, VA 22202

Speaking in Tongues, 2009
Patch Works Films
663 7th Avenue, San Francisco, CA 94118

So They May Speak…, 2003
California Tomorrow
1904 Franklin Street, Suite 300, Oakland, CA 94612

Taking Back the Schools, Part 3, 1996
Chicano: History of the Mexican American Civil
Rights Movement
Series National Latino Communications Center
Los Angeles, CA

The Lemon Grove Incident, 1985
The Cinema Guild
115 West 30th Street, Suite 800, New York, NY 10001

The War on Kids, 2009
Spectacle Films, Inc.
2 East Broadway Suite 901, New York, NY 10038

Tavis Smiley Reports: Education Under Arrest, 2013
PBS
2100 Crystal Drive, Arlington, VA 22202

Walkout, 2006
HBO Films
New York, NY

5

Literature, Art, Folklore, Music, and Cinema

This section addresses literature, art, folklore, music, and cinema as dynamic avenues for cultural expression among Chicanas and Chicanos. Literature encompasses the rich, stimulating voices and histories of the Chicano people and their struggles for cultural affirmation. It also encompasses language, its application, and the creation of a multiplicity of subjectivities, which are written and expressed through oral tradition and folklore.

The literature of the Chicano goes back in time to the conquest and colonization of the Southwest. Chicanas and Chicanos, through their diverse narratives, continue to challenge and resist historical and economic forces of domination and subjugation. They address the dialectics of liberation and oppression through a process of *"conscientización"* or social awareness. Hence, literature, in its many genres, becomes a multiplicity of lenses through which Chicanos confront, challenge, and transcend their daily situational limitations.

Literature by Chicanos and Chicanas writes "visible" the historical "invisibility" of a people's struggles for self-determination and political empowerment. Multiple identities emerge, spiraling from within the prose, poetry, theater, novel, essays, journal entries, diaries, and historical accounts of "Chicanismo," "Xicanisma," Mexicanness, and bilingualism. Chicano literature includes Mexican and US dominant eurocentric values and a complex separate identity formation emanating from the confluence of social and historical contexts.

Literature, while historically and socially situated, transcends time and space. It serves as a vehicle for cultural awareness, identity formation, and political power. Felipe de Ortego y Gasca provides a panoramic view of Chicano literature through a historical trajectory from the Spanish colonial environment to the Mexican independence and the Mexican-American War, which ended in 1848. This date marks, for some, the birth of the Chicano in the United States. Ortego traces Chicano letters from the beginning to the Chicano movement and its concomitant cultural renaissance. He views the 1960s as a period of spiritual rebirth for Chicano literature that encompasses distinct historical stages or developmental phases of Chicano literature. He also addresses the interface of race, ethnicity, and nationality in constructing Chicano-based identities, which embrace their Indo-Hispanic roots partially with oral tradition and folklore. Yarbro-Bejarano provides an overview of the literary output of Chicanas. The feminist perspective is an important component to Chicano literature because Chicanas have taken gender and sexuality to shape voices that for a time had largely been ignored.

George Vargas provides an insightful historical overview of Chicano art and an analysis of its current status and directions. He reveals the various facets of Chicano art and traces its historical foundations and lines of development in a hemispheric framework. He employs portrayals of salient exponents of Chicano and Chicana art such as Gaspar Enríquez, Grunk, Mago Gándara, and Nora Mendoza to illustrate contemporary trends in Chicana/o art in various regions of the United States, including the borderlands.

Amalia Mesa-Bains depicts the participation of Chicanas in redefining social and sexual roles, focusing on border and deconstructing "otherness" through artistic cultural representation. She introduces resistance as a characteristic of Chicana artistic expression, which also encompasses issues of cultural identity formation. Her well-documented and structured essay compiles an introduction to the Chicana aesthetic forms and narratives, where women are featured as figures of power and control that challenge a patriarchal system.

Mesa-Bains characterizes Chicana art as social defiance through the use of "inversion, satire, reversals, and juxtapositions of resistant feminine commentary." The author provides an introduction to and critical analyses of the works of Chicana artists Judith Baca, Santa Barraza, Carmen Lomas Garza, Ester Hernández, Yolanda López, Patricia Rodríguez, and Patssi Valdez. These Chicana artists have challenged the established social and sexual role norms that yield gender inequalities between women and men in Chicano communities.

The piece by María Herrera-Sobek on Chicano folklore examines oral traditions that have been handed down from generation to generation, such as narratives, folk songs, folk speech, proverbs and proverbial expressions, folk drama, children's songs and games, riddles, beliefs and folk medicine, folk festivities, folk arts and crafts, folk dance, and folk gestures.

Carlos F. Ortega examines the development of Chicano music. By utilizing a working concept, he first discusses the foundations of the Chicano music then builds on the role of the Chicano movement as the key architect of what we call Chicano music. He also examines how popular musicians and styles were influenced by the *Movimiento* in the late 1960s so as to broaden the base of this musical style.

Finally, Chon Noriega discusses how the Chicano movement also played a role in the development of Chicano cinema. He takes the reader through the stages that comprised the development of professional filmmakers as well as stylistic views.

Mexican-American Literature: Reflections and a Critical Guide

Felipe de Ortego y Gasca

PROLOGUE

Literature is not the product of a vacuum, nor is a literary text a divine inspiration as John Milton rhapsodized. Literature is *work*. It's a strand in a bundle of strands that comprise human activity. As such it is engendered by factors in a complex matrix of cultural production. And equally complex factors determine a reader's response to a text, depending on cultural affiliation or association. No one reader is privy to *the reading* of a text.

To understand a literature, a text, one must consider the backgrounds out of which a literature emerges. Writing is a cultural act surrounded and impacted by historical forces. What is written depends on the motivations of the writer. As readers and critics, we cannot accurately discern those motivations, we can only approximate them.

More to the point, however, is the question: What is Mexican American Literature? Simply, it's literary production by Mexican Americans, literary production which before the Chicano era had been marginalized by the hegemonic forces of the American literary establishment and its minions.

In the Summer of 1969, toward the end of the first decade of the Chicano era, I was on sabbatical at the University of New Mexico at Albuquerque from New Mexico State University at Las Cruces. Louis Bransford, Director of the fledgling Chicano Studies Program at the University of New Mexico at Albuquerque, asked me to organize a course in Mexican American literature for the Fall of 1969. I agreed, little realizing it would be the first course in Mexican American literature taught in the country, or so I have come to believe.

What was needed for the course were texts I naively assumed would be easy to find. Many of the Mexican American literary works I found and surveyed for that course were in various libraries whose nooks and crannies I scoured diligently, but many were in private collections difficult to get to. The wonder, though, is why no one before had looked at Mexican American writing as a literary tradition, studied it and given it a taxonomical structure from which to discuss it critically and historically as an integral part of the Mexican American experience and of American literature. There were bits and pieces of study but not an overview.

The course was successful beyond my expectations despite the paucity of works readily available for instruction. Many of the historical texts I thought suitable for the course were woefully out of print. Contemporary works were difficult to secure in quantities sufficient for the enrollment of the course since many of them were published ephemerally by "small" presses or in garage presses like Raymond Barrios' *The Plum Plum Pickers*.

After teaching that course I found validity for the proposition that there existed a body of Mexican American literature, in places amorphous in literary structure but there nevertheless. As a consequence of that course I undertook the study of *Backgrounds of Mexican American Literature* (University of New Mexico, 1971) in which I sought to provide some historical and taxonomic shape to Mexican American literature, a preliminary scaffold from which to start.

In the Preface of that study I pointed out that what was proffered therein represented but a skeletal view of Mexican American literature, that it was an exploration in literary archaeology akin to the representations we see of dinosaurs in museums, made lifelike from inductions and deductions of the animal remains found here and there. We don't really know what woolly mammoths or mastodons looked like. Or saber-toothed tigers. Or pterodactyls. Or early man. The taxidermic models we see in museums are what we think they looked like from the way we've pieced together the scant evidence we've found.

In literary history, as in archaeology, there is always a lacunae (discontinuity) in need of exploration and interpretation. By and large, in 1969 our view of Mexican American literature was nominal. We know more about Mexican American literature in the year 2006 than we did in 1969. Thirty-seven years after Kitty Hawk we knew considerably more about heavier-than-air flight than when Wilbur and Orville Wright undertook their first flight.

INTRODUCTION

Mexican American literature begins in 1848 with the signing of the Treaty of Guadalupe Hidalgo on February 2, ending American hostilities against Mexico and ceding more than half of Mexico's territory to the United States including Mexican citizens living in the wrested area which now includes the states of Texas, New Mexico, Arizona, California, Nevada, Utah, Colorado, and parts of Wyoming, Kansas, and Oklahoma.

But that beginning did not mean Mexicans in the dismembered territory had no literature. Mexicans who became Americans by conquest had been nurtured by a literary tradition that stretched back hundreds of years. That was what I learned from the course and what I sought to infuse in my study.

Backgrounds of Mexican American Literature was not exhaustive. It was *a first effort* at a chronology of Mexican American literary history. Taxonomically I

conceptualized Mexican American literature as a continuum of two pasts, welded together by the Treaty of Guadalupe Hidalgo. I dichotomized Mexican American literature into *Roots* and *Traditions*, pointing out that both the Spanish Colonial literature between 1527 (the year of Cabeza de Vaca's shipwreck on what is now Galveston, Texas) and 1821 (end of the war for Mexican independence) and the literature of the dismembered Mexican territory between 1821 and 1848 were part of the literary roots of Mexican American literature. As well as the indigenous works of greater Mexico (what is left of them), like the *Popul Vuh* of the Maya, for example. Most of the literary codices of indigenous Mexico were destroyed by zealous Spanish friars who thought them the works of the devil because of their pictographs. Ironically, no original works of indigenous Mexico are extant in the country; only copies.

What followed in the development of Mexican American literature after 1848 were the *traditions* the people developed in a series of periods which I proffered: the *Period of Transition,* 1848–1912, early Mexican American literature written mostly in Spanish by "the conquest generation" as Mario García identifies it (*Mexican Americans: Leadership, Ideology & Identity, 1931–1960,* 1989: 295); the *Period of Americanization,* 1912–1960, later Mexican American literature written in both Spanish and English; and the *Period of the Chicano Movement and the Chicano Renaissance,* 1960–1971/present, written in English, some Spanish, or a blend of both as a trans-border phenomenon.

In *Backgrounds of Mexican American Literature,* I contended that just as the English-language literature of New England and the Atlantic Frontier between 1607 and 1776 constitutes the British Colonial roots of American literature, so too the Spanish-language literature of New Spain and Mexico in what is now the United States constitutes the Spanish Colonial and Mexican National roots of American literature.

I also explained that the literary citations of the Spanish Colonial and Mexican National Periods which I referred to therein were just baseline citations, that future research would yield a trove of literature whose size would astonish us, as the University of Houston project in *Recovering the Hispanic Literary Heritage of the United States* has borne out in the last fifteen years. My rationale for bringing into American literature the Spanish Colonial and Mexican National roots of Mexican American literature emerged from the contention that, properly speaking, American Literature begins not with the founding of Jamestown in 1607 but with the Declaration of Independence in 1776: ergo, the literature of the British Colonies from 1607 to 1776 is really British Colonial literature. American literature is everything after 1776.

In the periodization of American literature there needs to be room for the literatures of populations which have been absorbed into the American hegemony by conquest. That includes the literatures of Native Americans (including Aleuts), of Mexican Americans, of Puerto Ricans, and of Pacific Islanders, all of them *territorial minorities.*

The histories of these *territorial minorities* did not begin *sui generis* at the moment of their conquest. They came into the American fold with a history, with customs, with roots. As I have already pointed out, in 1848 when the Mexicans of the Mexican Cession became Americans, they had been nurtured by a long literary tradition. The same is true of Puerto Ricans, of Native Americans, and of Pacific Islanders. In the case of Mexican Americans brought into the American fold in 1848 and Puerto Ricans brought into the American fold in 1898, their literary roots were in Spanish.

In large part, resistance to incorporating the literary traditions of *territorial minorities* has been because of language. But language should not be a bar to that incorporation as Thomas M. Pearce, professor of English at the University of New Mexico, argued in 1942 ("American Traditions and Our Histories of Literature," *American Literature*, November, 279).

In the history of the United States, not all American writers produced works in English. In the ethnic enclaves of America, there were publications in myriad languages. The Germans in America produced literary works in German; they produced newspapers and other information venues in German. The Italians of New York, the Poles and the Ukrainians of the Ohio Valley Crescent all produced literatures, respectively, in Italian, in Polish and in Ukrainian. The Jews of America, especially in New York, produced literature in Yiddish. The Norwegians and Swedes of the Midwest produced literature in their respective languages.

The American writer from Minnesota, Ole Rølvaag, wrote *Giants in the Earth* (1929) in Norwegian and was published in Norway for distribution there and in the Norwegian communities of the United States. Isaac Bashevis Singer, the Jewish writer from New York and a Nobel Prize winner for Literature, wrote principally in Yiddish. We know his works in English through translations. So too, Mexican American writers produced literary works by necessity in Spanish both during the Period of Transition (1848–1912) and by choice

during the Period of Americanization (1912–1960) and the Chicano Period (1960 to the Present).

Foreign language venues have flourished from the beginning of the American experience, catering to the linguistic diversity of the American people. There are still large linguistic communities in the United States producing non-English language newspapers for scores of non-English language readers.

PERIOD OF TRANSITION

The Period of Transition covers a span of 64 years, from 1848 to 1912, at least two generations. These were difficult years for Mexicans now Americans. Whatever social and political conditions wracked Mexico before 1848, its citizens had an identity with the country. Between 1527 and 1810, for example, most of the inhabitants of New Spain thought of themselves as Spaniards though not a few of them were called *criollos* (Spaniards born in the New World). And those who were not Spaniards in the Spanish caste system understood their political identity, nevertheless, as Spanish subjects.

Solomonically, hostilities severed their country, creating all at once a political diaspora that would stigmatize Mexican Americans into the 21st century. They would be strangers in their own land. But unlike noncontiguous immigrants to the United States, Mexican Americans were right next to their motherland. The 1800 mile U.S.-Mexico border was in large part a river of history from the Gulf of Mexico to the edge of Texas and only a line in the earth the rest of the way to the Pacific.

Though cut off politically from Mexico, the first Mexican Americans of the *conquest generation* continued to be succored linguistically, culturally, and intellectually by the motherland while participating in the activities of their new political context. The Chicano historian, Armando Alonzo, calls this *in situ* participation "agency." According to Leonard Pitt, between 1850 and 1856 in the Hispanic borderlands, Mexican Americans "obtained practically every imaginable public office, important or otherwise" (*Decline of the Californios*, 1966: 147).

Unfortunately, Mexican Americans were unprepared for the holocaust that was to befall them. The brutality of that holocaust caused them to cleave all the more to the motherland. And to remember, and pass on to their heirs, that the land they lived on had been their homeland before the conquest.

The force of that memory surged to consciousness a hundred years later during the Chicano Period when the sins of the Anglos would be called to account.

Despite the historical characterization of wholesale illiteracy in the Spanish and Mexican Southwest, the fact of the matter was that from the beginning Mexican Americans were a highly literate people as the inventories of personal and church libraries attest (Aurora Lucero-White Lea, *Literary Folklore of the Hispanic Southwest*, 1953: 4). There were scores of newspapers in the northern border states of New Spain, later Mexico. The Hispanic bent for documentation, suggests a substantial literate Spanish language public in Hispanic settlements.

Literary inventories affirm that Spanish language literature was read and written in Hispanic America. For example, the Spanish playwrights Calderón de la Barca and Lope de Vega extended their literary influence in Spanish America as did the Mexican playwright Juan Ruiz de Alarcón, the Mexican humanist-scholar Carlos de Sigüenza y Góngora, and the Mexican literary nun, Sor Juana Inez de la Cruz, often referred to as the 10th Muse of Mexico.

Mexicans who became Americans continued the Hispanic literary traditions not only by preserving the old literary materials but by creating new ones in the superimposed American political ambience. For example, in the Mexican and, later, Mexican American Southwest, liturgical pastorals depicting the creation and fall of man and of Christ's resurrection evolved into "cycle plays" similar to those of Spain and England.

By the time of the Civil War, there were a number of Mexican Americans engaged in the work of newspapers. In New Mexico alone, ten out of eighty journalists of the period were Mexican Americans (Porter A. Stratton, *The Territorial Press of New Mexico 1834–1912*, 1969: 12). Most Anglo American newspapers in the Hispanic Southwest published bilingual editions for their Spanish-language readers. And bilingual Mexican Americans were employed to translate English language news into Spanish.

There was a ferment of literary activity among Mexican Americans. Donaciano Vigil, editor of the newspaper *Verdad*, compiled a *History of New Mexico to 1851*. In 1859 Miguel Antonio Otero, who had been Assistant Professor of Latin and Greek at Pingree College at Fishkill-on-the-Hudson, essayed *The Indian Depredations in the Territory of New Mexico*. In California, Juan Bautista Alvarado completed a *History of California* which dealt chiefly with the Spanish and Mexican periods of California, its settlement, development, and commerce with the Indians. In Northern California, Mariano Guadalupe Vallejo wrote prolifically on a number of topics, composing sonnets for his children and for special occasions, culminating his literary activities with a five-volume *History of California* that became the source for Hubert Bancroft's *History of California* (Nadie Brown Amparan, *The Vallejos of California*, 1968: 131). In Arizona, Estevan Ochoa reflected on his election as Chairman of the 1859 convention to organize the Arizona territory (Frank Lockwood, *Life in Old Tucson 1854–1864*, 1959: 237). When the Civil War came, men like Ochoa, Vallejo, Otero, and Vigil remained loyal to the Union. During the war, the bilingual *New Mexican* newspaper published accounts of Mexican American Union officers like the Diary of Major Rafael Chacón in both Spanish and English (September 24, 1864). It was common for Southwestern newspapers with large audiences of Spanish-language readers to publish letters bilingually from and for their Mexican American readers.

Between 1880 and 1890, some forty new Spanish-language newspapers were introduced in the territory of New Mexico, with similar growth in Texas, Arizona, and California. Most of these Spanish-language newspapers carried a literary page or cultural supplement that contained poetry, short stories, and 'serial' novels (Tey Diana Rebolledo, *Women Singing in the Snow: A Cultural Analysis of Chicana Literature*, 1995: 20).

Political conditions in Mexico during the latter part of the 19th century caused many Mexican intellectuals to flee the country, finding refuge in Southwestern American cities like Los Angeles, El Paso, Laredo, San Antonio, and Brownsville. There was a special historical relationship between Mexicans and Mexican Americans that a border did not sunder. They were all members of *la raza*, the people.

Mexican writers like Ricardo Flores Magón, fleeing difficulties with Porfirio Díaz in Mexico, found ready sympathy in cities like El Paso and San Antonio. The presence of these writers in the United States significantly influenced Mexican American thought, particularly during the Chicano Period. The tremors of political stress in Mexico reached all the way to the American Southwest. And, indeed, it was from the Mexican American Southwest that Mexican leaders like Benito Juárez, Porfirio Díaz, and Francisco Madero launched their political careers.

So close were the ties between Mexicans and Mexican Americans that when Benito Juárez sought help in ousting the French puppet Maximilian, from Mexico, he contacted such Mexican Americans as Víctor Castro, Agustín Alviso, and Mariano Vallejo for help.

During the Period of Transition, Mexican Americans continued to bear the brunt of injustice after injustice in the American Southwest. Their lands were craftily secured by squatters, shyster lawyers and con artists who bilked them because of their disadvantage with the English language and American law. For example, in 1877 for $15 an Anglo American purchased from the Sheriff of Hidalgo County in Texas 3,027 acres of land confiscated from a Mexican American for back taxes. When the Mexican American Lugo family of southern California lost its wealth, Benjamin Hayes quickly suggested it was the finger of providence that was responsible for the decay of Mexican Americans (*Pioneer Notes 1849–1875*, edited by Marjorie Tisdale Wolcott, 1929: 280). The providence of Anglos was fraught with peril for Mexican Americans despite the fact that Anglos had guaranteed Mexican Americans full citizenship and had agreed to regard them as equals rather than a conquered people. Anglo rationalization for broken promises was that Mexican Americans were culturally unsuited to the new order and that they had brought misfortune on themselves. According to Leonard Pitt, the American pretense at ethical behavior "appears all the more reprehensible because of the blatant bigotry" (284).

Despite the fact that Mexican Americans constituted the majority population in the Southwest at first, they were quickly eased down the social ladder with the increase of Anglos in the area. During these years, Mexican American literature was undergoing the rigors of change from one social order to another. Mexican American writers like Vallejo, Alvarado, Pico, and others, continued writing in Spanish, their sentiments and outlook still rooted in the literary tradition from which they sprang.

The transition from writing in Spanish to writing in English was a process encompassing the latter half of the 19th century. Only an occasional Mexican American writer like María Amparo Ruiz de Burton (1872), Andrew García (1877) or Miguel Antonio Otero (1896) wrote in English, although García and Otero's works did not appear until the 20th century.

How many works in English by Mexican American writers appeared in the last half of the 19th century is difficult to ascertain only because comprehensive efforts like the University of Houston Project have,

thus far, yet to make that determination. What the University of Houston Project has made us aware of is that there were more Mexican Americans writing during the Period of Transition than we had been aware of.

In the meantime, American writers mischievously stereotyped Mexican Americans in their writings, casting them as indolent and afraid of hard work, adjudging a Mexican American's wealth as the product of connivance rather than of fortitude and application. One particularly mischievous work was *Ramona* by Helen Hunt Jackson, published in 1884. During the Chicano Period, Mexican Americans repudiated her portrait of their forebears just as Blacks repudiated their portrait in *Uncle Tom's Cabin* and *Huckleberry Finn*. The most objectionable aspect of *Ramona* is that it perpetuated the "pastoral fallacy" of nostalgia for a kind of life that never really existed. In *North From Mexico*, Carey McWilliams called that fallacy "the Templar Tradition." *Ramona* stressed the pintoresque at the expense of reality, for the fact of the matter is that life in the American Southwest during the days of the Dons was as strenuous as it was under American rule.

Unfortunately, the works of Anglo American writers "have glorified the heroic at the expense of the mundane" (Pitt, 290), the Spanish tradition at the expense of the Mexican, so much so that many of the descendants of the early Mexican Americans prefer to identify with the Spanish Templar Tradition (however fictitious) rather than with their Mexican-Indian roots. Why this dysphoria? one might ask. Was there anything in the existing literature of the Mexican Americans which might have reinforced an Anglo novelists's inaccurate picture of life in the Hispanic Southwest? Those were accepted by some Mexican Americans because, in retrospect, they saw the American occupation and annexation of their homeland as nothing more than broken promises.

Mariano Vallejo himself, last of the military governors of Mexican California who most eagerly welcomed the American takeover, asked bitterly:

> What has the state government done for the Californians since the victory over Mexico? Have they kept the promises with which they deluded us? I do not ask for miracles; I am not and never have been exacting; I do not demand gold, a pleasing gift only to abject peoples. But I ask and I have a right to ask for an answer ("At Six Dollars an Ounce" in *California: A Literary Chronicle*, edited by W. Storrs Lee, 1968: 183).

In the face of disappointment, Mexican American writers looked favorably and nostalgically upon their past ties with Mexico and Spain. Dysphorically, however, many Mexican Americans today insist on their Spanish ancestry, eschewing their Indian past even when they look more Indian than Spanish.

Toward the end of the 19th century there was a growing awareness about cultural pluralism in the United States. On July 20, 1883, for example, Walt Whitman wrote to New Mexico officials who had asked him for a poem commemorating the 333rd anniversary of the founding of Santa Fe. In response, Whitman wrote that Americans had yet to really learn about their own antecedents, to sort them, and to unify them. Whitman's reference was to the great diversity of the American experience and to the wide-ranging sources of its people. Whitman was responding positively to the New Mexicans when he reminded them that "impressed by New England writers and schoolmasters, we tacitly abandon ourselves to the notion that our United States have been fashion'd from the British Island only" (*Complete Poetry and Prose*, Deathbed Edition, 402–403). A decade later, in 1892, two short novels in Spanish by Eusebio Chacón were published in New Mexico but were to remain "undiscovered" until the Chicano era.

The strongest evidence for racial discrimination in the territorial Southwest occurred in 1904 in Arizona over an incident involving Anglo American foundlings from New York placed in Mexican American foster homes in the mining towns of Clifton and Morenci. The Anglo American residents of the two communities became so incensed at the thought of Anglo American children being placed in "half-breed Indian" families that they forcibly restrained placement of the children, taking them into their own homes instead, over the protests of the Foundling Hospital. The Territorial Supreme Court ruled in favor of the action by the Anglo American citizens of Clifton and Morenci, a decision later upheld by the U.S. Supreme Court.

It would be an egregious error to conclude that Mexican Americans were passive in defending themselves against Anglo American "aggressions." From 1848 to 1853, Father Martínez, a Catholic priest in New Mexico, led furious guerrilla resistance to Anglo American occupation of the state. In the 1880s, militia groups like *Las Gorras Blancas* (the White Caps), strenuously defended themselves against Anglo American depredations like that which in 1904 took the life of Colonel Francisco J. Chaves, a surgeon and Civil War veteran who had become a Mexican American

spokesman, leader and territorial superintendent of Public Instruction. For their efforts they were called *marauders*.

In 1883, Mexican American agriculture workers struck for better wages and working conditions in the Panhandle of Texas, and in 1903, Mexican American sugar-beet workers struck for similar reasons in Ventura, California. To counter their exclusion from Anglo American schools, Mexican Americans formed private and parochial schools like *El Colegio Altamirante* in Hebbronville, Texas, in 1897. To overcome rural depredations, Mexican Americans founded the Knights of Labor in 1890, a mutual assistance and protective organization.

In 1894, a decade before formation of the NAACP, Mexican Americans in Tucson, Arizona, founded the *Alianza Hispano Americana*, a *mutualista* civil rights organization that persisted until the 1960s. In 1896 Manuel Cabeza de Baca published *Historia de Vicente Silva* as a commentary on another Mexican American "marauder" from New Mexico. In the last decade of the Period of Transition, Juan Caballería published in 1902 a *History of San Bernardino Valley, 1810–1851*, a nostalgic reminiscence of the Mexican national period of California through the early days of the American annexation. The story of *La Piedra Pintada* (a California legend) by Myron Angel in 1910 suggests the extent the allure of the mythic past of Mexican Americans still had on Mexican American writers.

For some years, Professor Aurelio M. Espinosa had been collecting Mexican American folklore at Stanford University. As early as 1910 one of his pieces on New Mexican folklore appeared in the *Journal of American Folk-Lore*. In the article, professor Espinosa pointed out the paucity of Mexican American folklore studies. Even earlier, in 1907, while he was professor of Romance languages at the University of New Mexico, he had edited a critical edition of *Los Comanches*, a dramatic composition of the latter half of the 18th century and very popular through the 1890s. In 1907, Professor Espinosa also undertook a study of New Mexican Spanish which was published by the University of New Mexico Press (December 1909). One could see in the steady progression of works by Mexican American writers during the Period of Transition that they were becoming American, shifting their texts from Spanish to English.

In summing up the *fin de siècle*: Mexican American labor helped forge and link the principal western rail lines and helped develop the Texas cotton and cattle industry. More than half of Teddy Roosevelt's Rough

Riders were Mexican Americans. In 1897, Miguel Antonio Otero was appointed Governor of the New Mexico territory. Mexican Americans had served at Manila Bay and Guantanamo Bay. In the Hispanic Southwest, Mexican water and mining laws had been retained by Anglo American settlers and governments, Spanish words developed English equivalents: *la riata* became lariat; *juzgado* became hoosegow; *calabozo* became calaboose; *chapas* became chaps, and so on. While the American language absorbed Mexican vocabulary, Mexican Americans themselves were kept at arms length as outsiders, to be marginalized for another 60 years.

I chose 1912 as the end year for the Period of Transition instead of 1900 because the history of the American Southwest and the conquest generation comes to closure, it seems to me, with the admission of New Mexico and Arizona in 1912 as the final states of the forty-and-eight. Also, in 1910 the election and subsequent nullification of Francisco Madero as president of Mexico, ignited the Mexican Civil War of 1910–1921, creating so much turmoil in the country that one-and-a-half million Mexicans migrated to the United States between 1910 and 1930 in an exodus of unparalleled proportions in human history.

New Mexico and Arizona did not become states until 1912 owing to the vehement opposition of Senator Albert Beveridge of Indiana, a Catonist and an outright anti-Hispano, who led the resistance to statehood on grounds that Mexican Americans were unaspiring, easily influenced, and totally ignorant of American ways and mores; that despite the passage of more than fifty years since the Mexican War, Mexican Americans were still aliens in the United States, most of them having made no effort to learn English. The actual reason was based on racial prejudice and the number of Mexican Americans comprising the populations of New Mexico and Arizona. When the population shifted to Anglo Americans majority by 1912, Senator Beveridge dropped his objections, thus ushering in the era of the forty-and-eight, a nation that stretched from sea to shining sea. American euphoria endorsed manifest destiny.

PERIOD OF AMERICANIZATION

The Period of Americanization starts in 1912 and ends in 1960, covering 48 years. But it did not begin automatically in 1912. The process of Americanization had been steady since 1848, becoming particularly noticeable during the first decade of the 20th century. The period of Americanization begins with the closing years of the presidency of William Howard Taft, a one-term president who left the turmoil of the Civil War in Mexico to his successor, Woodrow Wilson.

Not only did political conditions in Mexico force the flight of a million-and-a-half Mexicans to the United States, but World War I caused such severe manpower shortages in industrial and agricultural sectors of the United States that the U.S. government contracted for Mexican labor to ease the crunch. Once the war was over, the U.S. government hurried the return of those workers back to Mexico, as it did in the 1930s to repatriate almost a million Mexicans in the United States. Unfortunately, among the repatriated were American citizens of Mexican descent. That detail seemed to matter little to zealous immigration officers for whom all "Mexicans" looked alike in their racial profiling.

The U.S. battled with the border problem from 1912 to 1921 in an effort to contain the hostilities of the Mexican Civil War on the Mexican side of the border. The situation along the U.S.-Mexico border was perceived by Americans as so bad and the threat to American life and property in Mexico so grave that President Wilson ordered the occupation of Veracruz by United States Marines. That act of belligerency has been adjudged by both Mexican and American historians as hasty and indicative of the roughshod manner in which the United States has always dealt with its sister Republic.

After the 1916 raid on Columbus, New Mexico, by Pancho Villa, Wilson dispatched General Pershing to Mexico in pursuit of Villa. Public opinion against Mexico and Mexicans (including Mexican Americans) had been so whipped up by the American press that many factions in the United States clamored for war with Mexico and for further annexation of Mexican territory. Only the war in Europe prevented further hostility against Mexico.

Interestingly, sometime between 1910 and 1920 American literature 'came of age' (Robert E. Spiller, *The Cycle of American Literature*, 1955: 158). Before then only English literature was worthy of study in American colleges and universities. At the same time Mexican American literature was also coming of age. Mexican American scholars and writers like Aurelio M. Espinosa were seriously engaged in preserving the literary roots of their heritage. Mexican American creative writers were attempting poetry in both English and Spanish, nothing at all like the experimentally vibrant poetry of the Chicano Renaissance in the late 60s and early 70s where Spanish and English were used in binary syntactic structures. Still, this poetry was a harbinger of literary creativity to come.

In 1916, one year after his death, a collection of Vicente Bernal's poetry was edited and published under the title *Las Primicias* (First Fruits). Bernal, born in Costilla, New Mexico in 1888, was only 27 at the time of his death. What was particularly impressive about Bernal's poetry was his command of the English language. As was to be expected, Mexican American writers were becoming Americanized.

Throughout the country, however, Mexican Americans fared badly with their public image. In 1917, Edith Shatlo King wrote in *The Survey* magazine (March 3), "When there is no occasion for personal loyalty, the Mexican is bitter in hatred. He is supersensitive to insults and slights, quick tempered, proud and high spirited. He lacks a habit of sustained industry and a practical sense which Americans cannot accept" (626). And in *The Century Magazine*, almost a dozen years later in 1928, Erna Fergusson wrote patronizingly, "The Mexican frankly hates work and refuses to be bullied into believing that he loves it" (438). In 1930, a particularly vicious piece by C.M. Goethe describes Mexicans: "His standards are those of a Chinese coolie . . . his code of morals increases his undesirability . . . he is superstition-bound and has the revengeful instinct of the savage" (*The World's Work*, July-December, 47–48).

Avarice and prejudice did not distinguish between Mexicans and Mexican Americans. Avarice saw them as cheap, exploitable, and therefore necessary; prejudice saw them as alien, unnatural, and therefore undesirable. Both won, for Mexicans and Mexican Americans were discriminated as much as they were exploited. Many Mexican Americans were unaware that they too were contributing to their own oppression. In 1927, Emilie M. Baca contributed to the stereotypes about Mexicans and Mexican Americans. In a piece entitled "Pachita," she wrote: "Embued [sic] with the futile philosophy of the peon, she yields to whatever emotion is uppermost in her mind, taking her sorrows without much complaint as she takes her pleasures without comment—her outlook on life utterly apathetic" (*The Family*, April 1927: 44). So completely had the spurious profiles of Mexicans and Mexican Americans gained acceptance in the United States by the end of the 1920s that even Mexican Americans themselves had come to reiterate their assigned characteristics as articles of faith.

Unfortunately, these stereotypes were contributing to a pernicious theory of cultural determinism—"Mexicans" were the way they were because of their culture. Their improvement lay in changing their culture. The deficiencies of Mexican Americans could be eliminated simply by wringing all their Mexican culture out of them. But brave Mexican American voices were beginning to murmur their dissent and to express their disapproval of the distorted images of Mexican Americans being purveyed by Anglo American writers.

In 1929, some of those brave voices succeeded in forming the League of United Latin American Citizens (LULAC) in Corpus Christi, Texas, in the days when the law both east and west of the Pecos very much discriminated against Mexicans and Mexican Americans. The aim of LULAC was not only to improve the tarnished image of Mexican Americans but to hasten the process of Americanization, which to them seemed doubly slow for Mexican Americans. To this end LULAC advocated the primacy of the English language and special classes in citizenship. Americanization seemed to LULAC members to merit the emphasis.

But 40 years later the problem of Mexican Americans were as acute as they had always been. However, the great migration north from Mexico had just about come to an end by 1930. Indeed, Mexicans continued to emigrate to the United States in the 30s and 40s but not in the phenomenal numbers of the previous two decades. Later, during World War II, Mexicans were again courted to fill up the labor shortage of the United States, but this time the influx was more systematically controlled by what came to be known as "bracero pacts," that is, "labor agreements" between the United States and Mexico.

Perhaps the most important work by a Mexican American writer in the decade prior to the Second World War was George I. Sánchez' *Forgotten People: A Study of New Mexicans* (1939), a study undertaken for the Carnegie Corporation. At the time, his was almost the only voice in the American ethnic wilderness pointing out the special needs of Mexican Americans: "In this nation, there is no excuse for human misery . . . good intentions cannot substitute for good deeds" (viii). Another gifted Mexican American writer of this period is Josephina Niggli, whose plays from the 1930s have transcended time and space.

Prose works like *Mexican Immigration to the United States* (1930) by Manuel Gamio and *Old Spain in Our Southwest* (1936) by Nina Otero reflected the kinds of sociocultural perspectives held by some Mexican American writers during the 30s. Unwittingly, Dr. Gamio wrote:

The majority of immigrants [Mexicans] continue to talk Spanish, but since they generally belong to the lower classes of Mexico and since in the United States they come in contact with the same grade of people, their poor Spanish becomes deformed and incrusted with English, and the result is a barbarous jargon which could not be understood in any Spanish-speaking country (231).

But linguistic science was still in the future, and Dr. Gamio was uttering what was commonplace about the mixture of languages among the linguistic elite. Prophetically the very language Dr. Gamio eschewed, *intrasentential alternation* or code switching (using Spanish and English words in the same sentence), would become the language of choice for Chicano poets. More importantly, though, in Dr. Gamio's day, most people did not recognize the centrality of language in the lives of human beings, and that languages in contact are like consenting adults, creating new language wherever that contact occurs. That's how Latin produced Spanish, French, Italian, Portuguese and Romanian. Like human genealogy, linguistic genealogy is equally diverse.

As people still do today, Dr. Gamio equated *poor* Spanish with *poor* Mexican immigrants. For him, *good* language went with *good* breeding and background. It seems he was unaware that *good* and *bad* language are value judgments predicated on where one is on the socioeconomic scale. Fortunately, since then, works by linguists like Benjamin Whorf and Edward Sapir have dramatically enlightened our notions of linguistic propriety, as well as works by Rosaura Sánchez.

In the 1930s there were essentially two principal Mexican American literary outlets for Mexican American writers since, by and large, Anglo American literary outlets excluded them. The first was *Alianza Magazine* founded in 1907, published by the *Alianza Hispano-Americana* in Tucson; the second was *Lulac News* founded in 1933. The two publications differed in scope and purpose. The former dedicated itself to maintenance of Hispanic culture and language, running almost half, if not more, of its pieces in Spanish. The latter emphasized articles in English and was concerned with issues of citizenship and discrimination. Of the two, *Alianza Magazine* was the more literary. Occasionally, it published poetry and fiction, although *Lulac News* published poetry occasionally also. Interestingly, *Alianza Magazine* reported on events in Arizona and California while *Lulac News* covered Texas

and New Mexico. Though *Lulac News* was radical from the beginning, the radicalization of *Alianza Magazine* did not occur until the 1950s. In general, both publications stressed the intense loyalty of Mexican Americans to the United States.

The 1930s also saw the emergence of such Mexican American writers as Arturo Campa, Juan Rael, Cleofas Jaramillo, and Jovita González, all of whom contributed significantly to the corpus of Mexican American literature as well as American literature. Campa, Rael, and González were avid collectors of folklore, but Campa also wrote fiction. One of his most celebrated short-stories, "The Cell of Heavenly Justice" (*New Mexico Quarterly*, August 1934) has been widely anthologized, particularly since the Chicano period. Though written in English, Campa's story is in the best tradition of the Hispanic *cuento* which stresses characterization over plot as in the Anglo American short story. Other Mexican American writers of the period were Bert Baca and Ely Leyba whose works appeared in the *New Mexico* magazine.

While Mexican American writers like Ernesto Galarza ("Without Benefit of Lobby," *Survey Graphic*, May 1, 1931) and George I. Sánchez were trying to break down the pernicious structures of stereotype, other Mexican American writers like Nina Otero and Emilie Baca only reinforced those structures.

Mexican American fiction of the 30s was generally characterized by themes and motifs of the past in which the characters are cast as gentle, peace-loving, and wise with the knowledge of things of the earth like Juan Sedillo's "Gentleman of the Río en Medio" (*New Mexico Quarterly*, August 1939: 183). In 1939 Robert Félix Salazar's poem "The Other Pioneers" about the Hispanic pioneers of the United States appeared in the July issue of *Lulac News*. The poem is noteworthy in view of the fact that Salazar had published poetry in such prestige magazines as *Esquire*, one of the few Mexican Americans poets who achieved that distinction.

World War II was a turning point for Mexican Americans as it was for Americans in general. On far-flung battlefields Mexican Americans were dying in their search for America. The tragedy for Mexican Americans was that even though they responded to the colors during the war, they were still considered as "foreigners" by so many of the Anglo American population, many of whom had themselves "recently" arrived from elsewhere, particularly Europe. But the irony of the Mexican American's situation was that the first draftee of World War II was Pete Despart, a Mexican American from Los Angeles.

In 1943 *Alianza Magazine* spoke out forcefully against what it called "the Mayflower Complex" of Anglo Americans, "a strange malady which may be contracted in the Northeastern section of the United States if one is not well inoculated against it by travel and study." Continuing the editorial, *Alianza Magazine* pointed out that Anglo Americans appear "surprised when a 'Martínez' or an 'Urías' brings down a Jap plane, sinks a Nazi U-Boat, or is promoted in rank" (January, 8).

In mid-century America, Mexican Americans were to emerge as the American ethnic group having won more medals of honor (17 altogether in World War II and Korea) than any other group of Americans except Anglos. Yet at the height of the war, just one month after Private José P. Martínez (U.S. Army) had been killed at the battle of Attu in the Aleutians, an action for which he was the first American awarded the Medal of Honor (posthumously), Mexican Americans were fleeing for their lives in Los Angeles in what came to be known nationally as "the Zoot-Suit Riots." American sailors didn't like the attire of Mexican Americans so they beat up on them. Sparked innocently enough, the roots of the incident lay deep in the strata of American racism of the kind that sent Japanese Americans to "detention" camps for the duration of the war and which kept African Americans segregated.

In 1942, on fabricated evidence 17 Mexican American youths were indicted for a murder that occurred in what was called "the Sleepy Lagoon" area of Los Angeles. The case became notorious for the manner in which the Mexican American defendants were treated by the police and the California judicial system. Carey McWilliams, who served as Chairman of the Sleepy Lagoon Defense Committee, described the proceedings as "more of a ceremonial lynching than a trial in a court of justice" (*North From Mexico*, 1948: 231). The defendants had served two years in San Quentin before their convictions were reversed unanimously by the District Court of Appeals.

The events of the Sleepy Lagoon case and the Zoot-Suit Riots helped create an awareness on the part of Mexican Americans in California (as well as elsewhere) about the need for effective organizations capable of protecting their interests. The first such organizations to be founded in the wake of this awareness were the Unity Leagues, intended to achieve political objectives and to protect its members from harm.

The war years were to affect Mexican Americans as no other period in American history had, save the U.S. War with Mexico. While no accurate figures are available as to the number of Mexican Americans who served in the armed forces during World War II, estimates suggest that perhaps as many as half-a-million Mexican Americans were in uniform during the war years (McWilliams, 259).

Not only did Mexican Americans distinguish themselves on the battlefield, but for the first time they moved in large numbers into the industrial occupations made available by the war economy. At heart, the change in Mexican American attitudes was brought about by the fact that having fought to preserve the ideals of American democracy abroad, they would expect nothing less back home than first-class citizenship. The war sparked a growing resentment of all forms of discrimination.

The war rhetoric of "the good neighbor policy" and "hands across the border" quickly evaporated after the war. American amnesia obscured the fact that during the war Mexico had been an ally of the United States, declaring war on Germany, Italy, and Japan on May 22, 1942, and sending its troops to the principal theaters of war, including a Mexican air squadron in the Pacific. German and Italian prisoners of war interned in the United States received better treatment than Mexicans and Mexican Americans.

In the post-war years from 1946 to 1960, Mexican Americans discovered there were two Americas. The America of the 30s, 40s, and 50s had become a land of contradiction for them. Were they Mexicans or Americans? In 1946 Arturo Campa offered this explanation:

> Mexican Americans are not Mexicans, and they have not been since 1848; neither are they natives exclusively. Few can prove conclusively to be of Spanish descent, and none of them are Spanish-Americans, considering that such an adjective applies to people in Spanish-America, although legally and nationally they are Americans; linguistically Spanish; Spanish-Americans, geographically; culturally Mexican (*Spanish Folk Poetry in New Mexico*, 15).

The dilemma would not be resolved until the efflorescence of the Chicano Renaissance. That event helped them understand they were both and need not be ashamed of either. But the post-war years were a struggle.

At every turn Mexican Americans had to go to the courts or establish alternative organizations for their well-being. On April 14, 1947, the Ninth Circuit Court ruled in *Méndez v. Westminster* (California) that it was unconstitutional to segregate

Mexican American students. This was a precedent case for Thurgood Marshall's argument in *Brown v. Board of Education*. In 1947 the city of Three Rivers, Texas, refused to bury a Mexican American veteran in its municipal cemetery. The brouhaha led to the creation of a Mexican American veterans organization, the American GI Forum, by Dr. Héctor P. García in order to protect the rights of Mexican American veterans. A decade later an official of the Daughters of the American Revolution in Denver refused to let a Mexican American youth carry the American flag in a parade on grounds that only "American boys" should carry the flag, adding "I wouldn't want a Mexican to carry Old Glory, would you?" (*Alianza Magazine*, March 1957: 11).

In the meantime, Mexican American literature changed hardly at all in character from what it had been prior to World War II. With some exceptions, the emphasis was still on reflective pastoral themes highlighting "the hacienda syndrome," as Raymond Paredes called it. ("The Evolution of Chicano Literature" in *Three American Literatures*, 1982: 52). *We Fed Them Cactus* (1954) by Fabiola Cabeza de Baca and *Romance of a Little Village Girl* (1955) by Cleofas Jaramillo signaled the end of pastoral themes in Mexican American literature.

One cannot fault the writers (male or female) of these idyllic accounts for seeking refuge in their culture. They were writing about the verities they knew: about the loss of a Hispanic Eden as they remembered it. Rebolledo regards this writing as acts of resistance to Anglo domination (*Women Singing in the Snow*, 29). I can see that, but what is important is that they were writing and that their works demonstrated not just mastery of literary techniques, but comprehension of the historical dynamics engulfing them.

Not all works during this period dealt with the Spanish Templar Tradition. Arnold Rojas was writing about the equestrian tradition in the Hispanic Southwest with works like *California Vaquero*, 1953. During this time, Fray Angélico Chávez was a master of technique in poetry, prose, and fiction. His eye may have been on the past but his grasp was on the future. In *New Mexico Triptych*, 1959, a trio of stories, he weaves for us the meaning of perseverance and faith. The story abounds with sensitivity and *gravitas*.

On occasion short stories like Mario Suárez' "Señor Garza" appeared in such literary publications as the *Arizona Quarterly* (Summer 1947), stories which reflect more realistically the actuality of Mexican American life in the *colonias* and *barrios* of the Southwest.

At the close of the Period of Americanization, a seminal work of scholarship on the *corrido* in the Southwest, *With His Pistol in His Hand: A Border Ballad* by Américo Paredes (1958), appeared and transcended this period to become a key work in the development of Mexican American thought during the Chicano period. Paredes was more than a folklorist. "Throughout his early writings," Leticia Garza-Falcón explains, "Paredes gives voice to experiences of characters who had never been written into [Walter Prescott] Webb's story," supplying "the text missing from Anglo histories" of Mexican Americans (*Gente Decente: A Borderlands Response to the Rhetoric of Dominance*, 1998: 164–165).

Harbingers of things to come were on the horizon. Few, if any, Mexican Americans could foresee just how dramatic a change was in the offing. But it was not a change without consequences.

PERIOD OF THE CHICANO MOVEMENT AND THE CHICANO RENAISSANCE

No one can say with certainty when the Chicano Movement began, but most commentators trace its beginnings to 1960 and the political ferment of presidential elections that year. Some memoirists point to the founding of the United Farm Workers Association by César Chávez in 1962 as the beginning of the Chicano Movement. According to Alfredo Cuellar, "there is some evidence that [it] grew out of conferences held at Loyola University in Los Angeles in the summer of 1966" ("Perspectives on Politics," in *Mexican Americans* by Joan Moore, 1970: 149). The movement was happening everywhere.

Mexican Americans certainly honed their political skills in the election year of 1960. Viva Kennedy clubs sprang up everywhere as Democrats forged ties with Mexican American communities, recognizing their potential political strength. Though the election of 1960 produced little political patronage, it provided Mexican Americans with the expertise to get Edward Roybal elected to the U.S. House of Representatives in 1962, making him the first Mexican American to be elected to the federal legislature from California. That same year, Mexican Americans in Crystal City, Texas, captured the city government. In New Mexico, Reies López Tijerina founded the Alianza Federal de Mercedes as a means to reclaim land promised sacrosanct per the Treaty of

Guadalupe Hidalgo. In Denver, Corky Gonzales was laying the foundation of his Crusade for Justice.

Chicano literature began, more or less, in tandem with the Chicano (Civil Rights) Movement of the 1960s as a reaction to exclusion by the American literary mainstream. Before 1960 few Mexican American writers were published by mainstream literary outlets. Concerned by that exclusion, in 1966 Octavio Romano, professor of anthropology at the University of California at Berkeley, gathered a cohort of Mexican Americans to organize *El Grito: Journal of Mexican American Thought*, a publication that was a manifesto and a shot across the bow of the American literary juggernaut that Mexican American writers would no longer look to the American literary mainstream for intellectual validation. *El Grito* (the cry) was a line in the sand.

Before *El Grito*, the literature of Mexican Americans was what the American literary mainstream said it was; after *El Grito*, Mexican Americans would say what Mexican American literature was. *El Grito* would be dedicated solely to the Mexican American experience. Chicano readers would be judges of Chicano literature which would create its own critical strictures and its own critical aesthetic.

Discourse-specific, Chicano texts would generate their own dynamics from which a critical criteria would emerge. That was a radical departure. And yet, necessary. For *El Grito* was the manifesto of Chicano liberation from Anglo American intellectual traditions that marginalized non-privileged perspectives. Publication of *El Grito* in the Spring of 1967 ushered in "The Chicano Renaissance"—a period of literary ferment that forever changed the intellectual relationship between Mexican Americans and the American literati. The promise of *El Grito* was that it would be the forum for Mexican Americans to articulate their own sense of identity.

Prior to the Chicano Renaissance, the American literary mainstream perceived Mexican American literary production as little more than folklore (like the folktale of *La Llorona)* and ballads of banditry (like the *Corrido of Gregorio Cortez)*. In 1967, I was asked to submit a short story for an anthology of fiction, only to have it returned with the explanation that it wasn't the kind of story they were expecting from me. Along with the explanation they sent me a copy of J. Frank Dobie's "The Straw Man" as an example of the kind of story they wanted. They wanted a quaint story about the stereotypical culture of Mexican Americans. I had sent them "Chicago Blues," a story about a contemporary Mexican American jazz musician in Chicago. The story had won an international story competition in 1957 judged by Richard Wright.

The dynamics of the stereotypes about Mexican Americans have been engendered by pernicious Anglo characterizations of Mexican Americans, especially men, as untrustworthy, villainous, ruthless, tequila-drinking, philandering *machos,* indolent and afraid of hard work or else as courteous, devout and fatalistic peasants who were to be treated more as pets than as people. More often than not Mexicans were cast as either bandits or loveable rogues; as hot-blooded, sexually animated creatures or passive, humble servants.

In one report to Washington, DC in the 19th century, Mexican Americans were described as "thoroughly debased and totally incapable of self-government," with "no latent quality about them that can ever make them respectable." Adding that "they have more Indian blood than Spanish, and in some respects are below the Pueblo Indians, for they are not as honest or as industrious" (*Congressional Globe*, 32nd Congress, 2nd Session (January 10, 1853), Appendix, p. 104). The pejorations and generalizations were deplorable, and the Chicano Renaissance gave rise against the perpetuation of such slanderous stereotypes.

Perhaps the main significance of the Chicano Renaissance lay in the identification of Chicanos with their Indian past. Chicanos cast off the meretricious externally imposed identification with the Spanish Templar tradition foisted on them by Anglo American society because of its preference for things European. In the 1930s, Mexican Americans turned to the label "Latin Americans" because Anglo America blanched at the word "Mexican."

Significantly, a literature draws from the history and myths of its people's past; and Chicanos turned to their Indian past for their most meaningful symbols and metaphors. For example, one of the key symbols of the Chicano Movement was the icon of the 5th Sun celebrated by the Aztecs in the form of the great calendar stone. The Aztecs considered themselves people of the Fifth Sun (*Quinto Sol*). According to their mythology, there had been four previous epochs, each governed by a sun. The first epoch ended with the inhabitants of earth devoured by ocelots; the second world and sun were destroyed by wind; the third by a rain of fire; and the fourth, by water. According to the Aztecs, the sun and world in which they lived—the fifth sun—was destined to perish as a result of earthquakes, famine, and terror.

The publishing enterprise that would produce *El Grito* was named *Quinto Sol* Publications. At the same time, the name of the publication, *El Grito*, celebrated the essence of the Mexican War for Independence, the start of which was initiated by the literal cry of Dolores by Father Hidalgo, spiritual leader of Mexican resistance against the Spaniards. Cuauhtémoc, not his brother Moctezuma, was apotheosized as the champion of indigenous resistance to Cortez and the Spaniards who vanquished Mexico City in 1521. That was not the conquest of Mexico as is popularly accepted, only the conquest of the city. Indigenous resistance to Spanish hegemony persisted into the 19th century ushering in the Mexican war for independence.

In the same manner, the Chicano Movement elevated Pancho Villa and Emiliano Zapata to the pantheon of Chicano populist heroes instead of any person or persons from the victorious cohort of the Mexican Civil War (1910–1921). Chicano mural painters depicted the "common folk" of Mexico and greater Mexico in their art, splashed vibrantly across any available wall. Chicano art was art for the people; just as Chicano literature was literature for the people. However, beyond the goal of equity, the significance of the Chicano Movement and the Chicano Renaissance was, as I have pointed out, the identification of Chicanos with their Indian past. They would be who they said they were, not who the mainstream said they were.

In 1969 Quinto Sol Publications brought out its first book entitled *El Espejo—The Mirror: Selected Mexican American Literature* edited by Octavio Romano. *El Espejo* was a brown paperback book reflecting "brown" literary hopes and aspirations in the United States. *El Espejo* represented the first efforts of a nascent literary boom, probing for its relevance in the Mexican American experience which had theretofore been articulated only at the margins of American literature, if at all. Explanation of the title of the anthology was given in the preface:

> To know themselves, to know who they are, some need nothing more than to see their own reflection. Therefore . . . *The Mirror—El Espejo*. May this book serve as a mirror for the many who see themselves herein.

From the beginning, Mexican American literature was a body of intellectual production looking for a form. I offered a form in *Backgrounds of Mexican American Literature*, to my knowledge, the first historical inquiry in the field and out of which grew my concept of "The Chicano Renaissance" a term that may, indeed, have been premature, as Juan Bruce Novoa has pointed out, considering the scarcity of Chicano materials available. For me, the term "Chicano Renaissance" signified the beginning of a boom in the literary production of Mexican Americans. That I contrasted it to other historical renaissances was a way of validating it as a historical movement.

In the 1960s Chicano literature emerged as a means by which Chicanos could find their own voice, their own sense of being Chicano, not Spanish, not Mexican, not American, but Chicano. As it emerged from the cauldron of cultural nationalism, the role of Chicano literature was to reflect Chicano life and Chicano values, drawing from an imagination distinctively Chicano.

That during this *incunabula* many of the early works of Chicano literature were inspired by ideological needs did not lessen the expectations that the responsibilities of Chicano writers were ultimately to create a literature so essentially Chicano that it stood on its own merits apart from other literatures. Chicano literature was to free Chicanos from the burden of American history and its libelous account of Chicanos and their ancestors. Like the disciples of Senchan Torpeist, the fabled Irish poet of myth, who were sent out to recover the whole of the *Tain*—the great Irish saga—which none of them could remember entirely, Chicano writers were the "disciples" through whom the lost inheritance of Chicanos would be recovered.

Literature means many things to many people. In literature as in other human endeavors there are problems with definitions. A piece of literature is not just a speech act—it's a social act; it has cultural connotations that reveal a writer's relation to his or her group and to the entire fabric of society. As a cultural manifestation, a literary work inheres a sense of audience, its language (whether English, Spanish or a combination of both) is part of a *weltanschauung* shared by a community of readers. The significance of a literary work lies not only in the social reality in which the writer participates but grows out of the culture which nourishes him or her.

What most characterized Chicano literature, early on, were its countertexts—the textual backgrounds against which Chicano literature was superimposed, the texts of Chicano reality. Chicano writers were expositing not just Chicano views but countertexts of Anglo views by which Chicanos were judged socially; countertexts which showed how Chicanos were contained within the apodictic value framework of mainstream culture and subjected cruelly and brutally to it.

Through countertexts, Chicano writers showed the insidious ways by which mainstream culture exercised hegemony over the Chicano community. Chicano countertexts pointed out how having been subjected to coercive Anglo texts and having internalized the values inherent in them, Chicanos had inadvertently been instruments in their own oppression. It was this ploy of text and countertext that provided Chicano literature with its most enduring quality—process. Chicano literature was a process, not an outcome, a process of imagining and figuring out the world, as Henry Louis Gates would have put it (*Black Literature and Literary Theory*, 1984: 71).

As products of process, Chicano texts were not finalities of truth but limns by which Chicano liberation could be achieved. Chicano literature was thus envisioned in the service of the cause, the people. It was not an end in itself. This meant Chicano texts were not self-sufficient but required the help of Chicano readers to actualize their meanings.

In 1971 when Tomás Rivera, José Reyna, and I took part in the first national symposium on Chicano Literature and Critical Theory at Pan American University, our presentations were not as arbiters nor as *dicta* in the development of Chicano literature. Chicano literature was a barely emerging field then. My essay on "The Chicano Renaissance" had just appeared in the May 1971 issue of *Social Casework*. Our presentations sought to show how Chicano writers were looking for forms discrete to the Chicano experience by which to articulate that experience; that Chicano writers were searching for textual structures of meaning unique to the Chicano experience through which the meaning of the Chicano experience would be validated—by Chicanos, not Anglos. Or as Ramón Saldívar has put it:

> the function of Chicano narrative is . . . to produce creative structures of knowledge to allow its readers to see, feel, and understand their social reality (*Chicano Narrative: The Dialectics of Difference*, 1990: 6).

In this sense, the Chicano Renaissance functioned for Chicano writers much the way the Irish Renaissance functioned for Irish writers who cut their ties to British literature and turned to the roots and traditions of Irish literature for sustenance. Chicanos cast adrift the privileged norm of Anglo American literature. At that moment, Chicano literature embodied what Georg Simmel identifies as that process in life by which it generates forms demanding "a validity which

transcends the moment" (*On Individuality and Social Forms*, 1971: 346).

What we can say about Chicano literature is that it's a literature in process, drawing from different literary traditions (American, Mexican, global), sometimes from one or the other, and sometimes in a unique synthesis of Mexican and American that is truly startling and innovative.

The earliest manifestation of that synthesis appeared in what has since come to be called "the first Chicano novel"—*Pocho* by José Antonio Villarreal, published in 1959. It's a "coming of age" novel in which the boy, Richard Rubio, experiences growing up in two cultures, feeling rejected by both because in both he's an outsider: in the United States, he's a "Mexican" and to the Mexicans he's a *pocho*, a Mexican who lives beyond the pale of Mexican culture, a Mexican who has become Americanized, foregoing his patrimony. Interestingly, the word *pocho* comes from the Nahuatl word *pochteca*, which means "he who wanders abroad." For the Aztecs this identified the trader who sold and bought wares in regions beyond the borders of their homeland which they called *Aztlán*.

The novel *Pocho* begins in Mexico at the end of the Mexican Civil War (1921) and traces the flight of Juan Rubio, ex-revolutionary colonel, from Mexico to the United States. Having killed a man in a brawl over a prostitute in *Ciudad Juárez*, Juan Rubio seeks safety north of the border, first in Texas then in California where he suffers silently the debilitating effects of acculturation upon his children, especially Richard, the *pocho* of the novel. Ambivalent about his identity, at the end of the novel, Richard Rubio goes off to war and to an uncertain future.

The novel received scant attention initially and lay in remainders until the early 1970s when it was used extensively in Chicano literature courses. A slew of novels by Mexican American writers appeared during the 60s, some of which ran into ideological quagmires. Were they Chicano novels consistent with the aims of Chicano literature as first advanced by the cultural nationalism driving the Chicano Movement? Not all of those novels passed muster. John Rechy's novel *City of Night* (1963) ran into ideological difficulties because of its homosexual implications. There was some question about Floyd Salas' *Tattoo the Wicked Cross* (1967). Ray Barrios' novel *The Plum Plum Pickers* (1969) became a favorite Chicano novel of the 60s principally because the author drew his characters lifelike as migrant workers. But it was an experimental novel looking for an audience.

The Chicano novels of the 70s ran the gamut of thematic diversity but the majority of them were actuated by the mnemonic impulse, that is, their autobiographic thrust was linked to the collective memory of a displaced people, scratching out a living in a land dismembered from its self. Like Villarreal's *Pocho*, Richard Vásquez' novel *Chicano* (1970) details the odyssey of Héctor Sandoval from Mexico to the United States during the Mexican Civil War (1910–1921) and the travails of his children, Neftalí, Jilda, Hortencia, and their heirs in California. Like Chicano novels that were to follow, *Chicano* is a novel about a family, an immigrant Mexican family striving to survive in a place that does not welcome them.

In 1970, Tomás Rivera (now deceased) won the first *Premio Quinto Sol* for his episodic novel *And the Earth did not Part*, a work which has grown in stature over the last 30 years because of its enduring qualities. In 1972, Rolando Hinojosa won the *Premio Quinto Sol* and in 1976 the *Premio Casa de las Américas* for his novel *Klail City*. In 1973, Estela Portillo Trambley (now deceased) won the *Premio Quinto Sol* for fiction though she is better known for *Day of the Swallows*, a powerful play about strong women. She went on to publish other plays, collections of short fiction, and the novel *Trini* (1986). That same year one of the most enigmatic of the Chicano novelists, Oscar Zeta Acosta, published *Autobiography of a Brown Buffalo*, and like Ambrose Bierce disappeared from public view not long thereafter. The most successful novelist of the 70s still writing is Rodolfo Anaya whose novel, *Bless Me, Ultima* (1973), has become a landmark of Chicano literature. Another landmark novel of Chicano literature is *Peregrinos de Aztlán* (1974) by Miguel Méndez. *The Road to Tamazunchale* (1975) by Ron Arias was the first novel by a Chicano to employ the literary techniques of *magical realism*; that same year Alejandro Morales' novel *Caras Viejas y Vino Nuevo* (1975) was published in Mexico in Spanish; also that year Aristeo Brito's novel *El Diablo en Tejas* appeared in Spanish, later in a bilingual edition; another work of magical realism appeared in 1976 with Orlando Romero's *Nambé-Year One*. And in 1977, Nash Candelaria published *Memories of the Alhambra*.

During the 80s, Chicanos and Chicanas produced a range of novels. By and large, though, the novels produced by Chicanos and Chicanas during the 80s and early 90s still dealt with the verities of Chicano life in a hostile American environment. Significantly, during the 80s a surge in Chicana literary production engendered a wave of creativity that regenerated the Chicano Renaissance.

From the start, Mexican American women played prominent roles in literary production but, unfortunately, their texts have been "inaccessible" as Annie Eysturoy has pointed out (*Daughters of Self-Creation: The Contemporary Chicana Novel*, 1996: 35). Also, their contributions were little bruited in the masculine tsunami of early Chicano letters. That situation has been put aright by scores of Chicana writers who in the 1990s seem to have eclipsed their male counterparts.

In Chicana fiction, Sandra Cisneros, *The House on Mango Street*, 1985, has become the most visible and equally visible in public controversy. Other Chicana novelists include Isabella Ríos, *Victuum*, 1976; Sheila Ortiz Taylor, *Faultline*, 1982; Cecile Piñeda, *Face*, 1985; Ana Castillo, *The Mixquiahuala Letters*, 1986; Mary Helen Ponce, *The Wedding*, 1989; Roberta Fernández, *Intaglio*, 1990; Lucha Corpi, *Eulogy for a Brown Angel*, 1992; Beatriz de la Garza, *The Candy Vendor's Boy*, 1994; and Helena María Viramontes, *Under the Feet of Jesus*, 1995.

Chicano novels since the 70s include Ed Vega, *The Comeback*, 1985; Lionel García, *Hardscrub*, 1990; Víctor Villaseñor, *Rain of Gold*, 1992; Graciela Limón, *The Memories of Ana Calderón*, 1994; Alejandro Grattan-Domínguez, *Breaking Even*, 1997; and others.

Scores of Chicanos have written short (stories) fiction, starting with cuentos during the Period of Transition and the Period of Americanization. But the genre exploded among Chicanos during the Chicano Period. In 1967, Felipe de Ortego y Gasca won the NEA-Reader's Digest Foundation award for fiction with "Soledad," a short story about Mexican American high school students and their first experience with a Mexican American teacher of English. In 1968 his short story "The Coming of Zamora," a fictive rendering of the trial of Reies López Tijerina appeared in *El Grito* (Spring 1968), "Chicago Blues," *ARX Magazine* (Spring 1969), "The Dwarf of San Miguel," *New England Review*, April–May 1970, and "Rosemary, For Remembrance," *La Luz*, October and November 1974. Collections of short stories/cuentos by Chicano writers have appeared less often than novels by Chicano writers. In 1971, Sabine Ulibarrí published *Tierra Amarilla*; other short story collections include Alonso M. Perales, *La Lechuza: Cuentos de Mi Barrio* in Spanish, 1972; *Cachito Mío* by José Acosta Torres, 1973; *Blue Day on Main Street* by J. L. Navarro, 1973; *Rain of Scorpions* by Estela Portillo Trambley, 1975; *Requisa Treinta y Dos* edited by Rosaura Sánchez, 1979; *There are no Madmen Here* by Gina Valdés, 1981; *The Adventures of the Chicano Kid and Other Stories* by Max Martínez, 1982;

Tales of Huitlacoche by Gary Keller, 1984; *The Iguana Killer* by Alberto Ríos, 1984; *The Last of the Menu Girls,* by Denise Chávez, 1986; *Days of Plenty, Days of Want* by Patricia Preciado Martin, 1988; and *Weeping Woman* by Alma Luz Villanueva, 1994.

In prose, one of the most influential books of the 70s was Marta Cotera's *Diosa y Hembra*, an exposition of the Hispanic woman as both goddess and *female.* There have been many Mexican American writers of prose over the years; but many more, it seems, during the Chicano period, many of them producing counter-texts to dispel the protocols of racism that characterized Mexican Americans.

A text of profound significance, "The Space of Chicano Literature" by Juan Bruce Novoa in 1974 would become the standard for the expansion of Chicano Literature. In an open letter to me when I was Editor and Associate publisher of *La Luz* magazine in Denver (September 1973), he called for the space of Chicano literature to include the sum of its parts without canonical restrictions. I argued for that same inclusion.

Having written extensively on the educational condition of Mexican Americans since the 60s, the *Center Magazine* published my piece on "Montezuma's Children" as a cover story in its November/December issue of 1970. The piece was an exposé on the deplorable conditions of Mexican American education. In 1972, *The Saturday Review* ran a follow up piece of mine on "Schools for Mexican Americans" (April 17). In 1974, I teamed up with Marta Sotomayor for the study on *Chicanos and American Education* funded by the Ford Foundation through the National Council of La Raza. The study was released in 1976.

Richard Rodríguez' *Hunger of Memory* appeared in 1982 and quickly encountered a firestorm of controversy for its lack of political correctness. In 1987, Gloria Anzaldúa's *Borderlands*, a text of remarkable proportions, swept the emerging field of Chicana studies, staking out new markers in the intellectual field traversed by Chicanos and Chicanas. That same year, Al Martínez, the *Los Angeles Times* columnist, published *Ashes in the Rain (Selected Essays).* And in 1990 the gifted theoretician, Ramón Saldívar published *Chicano Narrative*, a work that brought into sharper focus the narratology of Chicano texts. In autobiographic prose, *Barrio Boy* (1971) by Ernesto Galarza continues its preeminence. Anthony Quinn's *The Original Sin* (1972) has held up equally well. However, Chicano autobiographic prose is scant, although much of Chicano prose has biography embedded in it. See, for example, Richard Rodríguez' *Hunger of Memory* and

Days of Obligation; or Linda Chávez' *Out of the Barrio.* Also, many Chicano novels are thinly veiled biographies. One biography of some years ago but only published recently is *The Rebel* (1994) by Leonor Villegas de Magnón, edited by Clara Lomas.

In addition to Estela Portillo Trambley in drama during this period, Luis Valdez is by far the most renowned both for his plays (*actos*) and for creation of *El Teatro Campesino*, the agitprop arm of César Chávez' United Farmworkers Organization. From plays like *Los Vendidos* (The Sellouts), Valdez went on to produce films like *Zoot Suit* and *La Bamba.* The playwright Carlos Morton came into drama out of the Chicano generation of the 70s. Prolific, Morton is nevertheless identified with *The Many Deaths of Danny Rosales* (1983), a message play about Anglo oppression of Chicanos in the criminal justice system. Other Chicano/a playwrights include Denise Chávez (who studied with Mark Medoff, author of *Children of a Lesser God*) and Felipe de Ortego y Gasca whose play about Cortez, Moctezuma, and the *Virgin de Guadalupe, Madre del Sol/Mother of the Sun*, premiered in San Antonio in 1981 and was performed at the Teatro Antonio Casso in Mexico City in 1982. His play *Voces de Mujeres* was presented in 1993 at the 5th International Conference on Women at the University of Costa Rica in San José.

The work, *Mexican American Theatre: Then and Now (Revista Chicano Riqueña*, Spring 1983) edited by Nicolás Kanellos advances our historical understanding of Mexican American theater. And the works of drama critic and teacher, Jorge Huerta, extend our comparative knowledge of Chicano theater and its relationship to Latin American theater. Huerta was one of the principal organizers of TENAZ (*Teatro Nacional de Aztlán*), an international coalition of *teatros.*

Chicano/a poets abound. Some of the early poets were Felipe de Ortego y Gasca, *Sangre y Cenizas*, 1964; "the Poet Laureate of Aztlán," Abelardo Delgado, "Stupid America," 1968; Luis Omar Salinas, *Crazy Gypsy*, 1970; "the Walt Whitman of the Chicano Movement," Ricardo Sánchez, *Canto y Grito mi Liberación*, 1971; José Montoya, *El Sol y los de Abajo*, 1972; Raymundo "Tigre" Pérez, *The Secret Meaning of Death*, 1972; Juan Felipe Herrera, *Rebozos of Love*, 1974; and Reyes Cárdenas, *Chicano Territory*, 1975. Though not as productive in poetry as his compatriots, Rodolfo "Corky" Gonzales is best known for *I am Joaquín* (1968), perhaps the most celebrated poem of the early Chicano era, full of sound and fury signifying everything. Chicano poets vented the anger of the Chicano community in a range of protest poetry which Francisco Lomelí calls "instigative poetry with strong political overtones" ("An Overview of Chicano Letters: From Origins to Resurgence" in *Chicano Studies: Survey and Analysis*, 1997: 289).

Poets like Alurista (Alberto Urista) experimented with binary lines of poetry in "Mis Ojos Hinchados," for example, using English and Spanish in non-standard syntactic structures, intrasententially alternating Spanish and English—code switching. Rosaura Sánchez' work in linguistics (*Chicano Discourse: Sociolinguistic Perspectives*, 1983) illuminates this sphere of Chicano cultural production.

Other poets of the early Chicano renaissance include Tino Villanueva, *Hay Otra Voz Poems*, 1972; Sergio Elizondo, *Perros y Antiperros*, 1972; Nephtali De León, *Chicano Poet*, 1973; José Antonio Burciaga, *Un Torero*, 1974; Juan Gómez Quiñones, *5th and Río Grande*, 1974; Angela de Hoyos, *Arise, Chicano and Other Poems*, 1975; Dorinda Moreno, *La Mujer es la Tierra*, 1975; Ricardo Aguilar, *Caravana Enlutada*, 1975; Bernice Zamora, *Restless Serpents*, 1976; Leroy Quintana, *Hijo del Pueblo*, 1976; Gary Soto, *The Elements of San Joaquín*, 1977; Jesús Rafael González, *El Hacedor de Juegos*, 1977; Ana Castillo, *Otro Canto*, 1977; Juan Bruce-Novoa, *Inocencia Perversa*, 1977; and Marina Rivera, *Sobra*, 1977.

In the 80s, a new wave of Chicano/a poets emerged which included Raúl Salinas, *A Trip Through the Mind Jail*, 1980; Olivia Castellano, *Blue Mandolin, Yellow Field*, 1980; Evangelina Vigil, *Thirty an' Seen a Lot*, 1983; Carmen Tafolla, *Curandera*, 1983; Cheri Moraga, *Living in the War Years,* 1983; Teresa Palomo Acosta, *Passing Time*, 1984; Rosemary Catacalos, *As Long as it Takes*, 1984; Leo Romero, *Celso*, 1985; Naomi Quiñónez, *Sueños de Colibrí*, 1985; Francisco Alarcón, *Tattoos*, 1985; Pat Mora, *Borders*, 1986; Ray González, *Twilights and Chants*, 1987; Jimmy Santiago Baca, *Black Mesa Poems*, 1989; and Alfred Arteaga, *Cantos*, 1991.

FIN DE SIECLE AND THE NEW MILLENNIUM

Toward the end of the 20th century, the esthetic philosophy of the pioneer activist writers of the Chicano Renaissance had given way to a wave of Chicano/a writers with tempered views of Chicano life mitigated by legal and social victories that made access to the American literary mainstream less difficult than it had been. This did not mean, however, that Chicano/a

writers were swept up *en masse* by mainstream presses. On the contrary, while more Chicano/a writers were being published by mainstream presses, the competition for those writers focused on works that satisfied the institutional standards of those presses. In other words, nothing much changed. For Chicano/a writers seeking mainstream literary recognition, they had to pass the literary muster of mainstream presses. This had been the situation that had activated the Chicano Renaissance in the first place: in order to be published by a mainstream press, Chicano/a writers had to write in the public mould acceptable to mainstream publishers. The aspirations of the Quinto Sol writers to be free from the strictures of mainstream presses which suppressed the realities of Chicano life ebbed. The need for Chicano/a literary independence made the presence of Arte Público Press, the Bilingual Review Press, and other independent Chicano/a presses all the more necessary. This is not to diminish the artistry of those Chicano/a writers who have found outlets for their works with mainstream presses. But those outlets are finite, sustaining only a small number of Chicano/a writers. That is to say, Chicano/a literary voices are more numerous than mainstream presses seem able to handle—or are willing to handle.

What redeems this whole process of selection by mainstream presses is that, by and large, the Chicano/a works published by mainstream presses represent the high quality of writing produced by Chicanos and Chicanas and heretofore published elsewhere—oftentimes ephemerally in those garage presses of the 60s and 70s now transformed electronically into desktop publishing. The need for Chicano/a literary outlets as Octavio Romano foresaw in 1967 continues. While many Chicano/a writers are being featured by mainstream publishers, many more Chicano/a writers are being featured by a still lingering thread of "pick-up presses" established for the purpose of publishing a particular book—much the way Mictla Press was organized in El Paso in 1971 to publish *Canto y Grito mi Liberación* by Ricardo Sánchez. Interestingly, university presses have stepped in to provide outlets for Chicano/a literary production. A quick survey reveals the significance of university presses to Chicano/a writers.

In this period of the last 16 years (1990–2006) the most surprising surge of literary production among Chicano/a writers has been in expository/argumentative prose and what the Mayborn Institute of Journalism at the University of North Texas calls "literary non-fiction." More Chicano/a scholars have turned to the production of critical works in Chicano Literature like *Decolonial Voices: Chicana and Chicano Studies in the 21st Century* (2002), edited by Arturo J. Aldama and Naomi Helena Quiñónez.

The works that have most inspired Chicano/a literary non-fiction are Gloria Anzaldúa's *Borderlands/La Frontera: The New Mestiza* (1987) and an earlier work (with Cherrie Moraga) *This Bridge Called my Back* (1981). Both are "bridge" works where the "bridge" becomes an enthymeme of hope in bridging two borderland cultures and a bridge of communal knowledge "where our paths converge." Anzaldúa's work is in the vein of "countertexts," which came into being early in the Chicano Renaissance as contestatory texts, refuting the historical images of Chicanos in mainstream texts and also setting the record straight about Chicanos in the United States.

In the main, the most notable Chicano/a writers of this *fin de siecle* phase and the start of the new millennium are those Chicano/a writers who started writing in the 80s, hitting their stride in the 90s and maturing in their art in the first decade of the new millennium. Among others, the newest Chicano/a novelists and novels of this period are Demetria Martínez (*Mother Tongue*, 1994), Benjamín Alire Sáenz (*Carry Me Like Water*, 1994 and *In Perfect Light*, 2005), Denise Chávez (*Loving Pedro Infante*, 2001), and Manuel Luis Martínez (*Drift*, 2003). From a nominal beginning of some nine novels in the first Chicano decade (1960–1969), Chicano/a novelists burst into flower in the second (1970–1979) and third (1980–1989) Chicano decades. That boom in the Chicano novel diminished somewhat in the fourth (1990–1999) and millennial (2000–2010) Chicano decades.

As a genre, the short story receives short shrift as fiction, but the exception is a superb collection of short stories *Mirrors Beneath the Earth: Fiction by Chicano Writers* (1992) edited by Ray González who is often compared with Raymond Chandler as a master of the genre. Some representative short story writers of this period are Luis Rodríguez (*Republic of East L.A.: Stories*, 2002), Rick Yáñez (*El Paso del Norte: Stories on the Border*, 2003) who also appears in *Mirrors Beneath the Earth*, and Daniel Chacón (*And the Shadows Took Him*, 2004). Chicano *literateurs* opine that the short story is the strongest genre of Chicano writers of fiction. Writers of the genre contend that it is the toughest of the literary genres to control and to master because of Aristotelian strictures defining its architecture and Edgar Alan Poe's successful formula for the genre.

A remarkable book that challenges generic classification but bearing a resemblance to *Like Water for Chocolate* is *Voices in the Kitchen: Views of Food and the World from Working-class Mexican and Mexican American Women* (2006) by Meredith Abarca.

Poetry is the most enduring genre for Chicanos though the least remunerative. Among the earliest Chicano poets still at the plough is Tino Villanueva who won an American Book Award for *Scene From the Movie Giant* (1993). One of the most overlooked Chicano pioneer poets whose productivity is prodigious is Rafael Jesús González from the San Francisco Bay Area but originally from El Paso, Texas. While his poems have appeared in countless reviews, journals, and anthologies he has produced only one tome *El Hacedor de Juegos* (1977). Many of the Chicano novelists, short-story writers, and literary non-fictionists (prose) also publish individual poems here and there, no books or chapbooks.

In drama and theater, Carlos Morton is still the most productive Chicano playwright, though a crop of Chicano playwrights have emerged as scriptwriters and directors for film and television, among them Jesús Treviño (*Raíces de Sangre*, film, 1976), Octavio Solís (*Man in the Flesh*, play, 1988), and Josefina López (*Real Women Have Curves*, play, 2002). No Chicano Neil Simon looms in the wings, though a plethora of Chicano actors now appear on screens.

TRENDS AND THE FUTURE OF MEXICAN AMERICAN LITERATURE

Two trends are discernable in Mexican American literature at the moment: (1) the mnemonic impulse generating scores of memoirs, autobiographies, and biographies like *Capirotada: A Nogales Memoir* by Alberto Ríos, 1999; *Thirteen Senses: A Memoir* by Víctor Villaseñor, 2001; *Man of Aztlán: A Biography of Rudolfo Anaya* by Abelardo Baeza, 2001; and (2) works like Denise Chávez's *Loving Pedro Infante* (2001) that deal more explicitly with borderland themes, locales, and issues. There is a growing corollary trend in works of social and literary history and criticism. It's in this corollary trend that I sense the vulnerability of Mexican American literature. Current critical analysis of Mexican American literature seeks to validate its presence and legitimacy by subjecting it to critical templates of other literatures or esoteric formulas not engendered from Mexican American literature. When Chicano literature emerged from the cauldron of Chicano nationalism in the 60s there was an expectation on the part of Chicano writers and critics that Chicano literature would develop *sui generis* an esthetic and criticism uniquely Chicano. In other words, Chicano literature would be what Chicanos said it was, not what others said it was. Chicanos would validate their own texts. What has emerged in Chicano literary studies is a critical elitism that judges Chicano literature in terms of over-arching strictures advanced by literary theoreticians like Derrida, Foucalt, DeMan, Bhabha, et al, a new form of Edward Said's orientalism but now practiced by Chicano/a scholars and critics unaware they are aiding in their own literary oppression.

My hope for Chicano literature today, as it was 30 years ago, is its integration into the body of American literature. About those early aspirations of mine for Chicano literature, José Aranda, Jr. writes: "[Ortego] foresaw what would become by the 1990s, a whole industry from editors to academic scholarship redefining 'American literature as a fabric woven not exclusively on the Atlantic frontier by the descendants of New England Puritans and southern Cavaliers'. . . Ortego imagined the day this politically awakened ethnic group would participate more directly in the nationalist revision of American literature and culture. Ortego's generation of Chicano/a scholars thus fashioned a literary history faithful to a broad Chicano social politic" (*When We Arrive: A New Literary History of Mexican America*, 2005: 59).

I still think that revision of American literature is an important objective, though it's no longer as pressing as it once was despite the fact that not long ago I received a desk copy of an anthology purporting to be *The American Tradition in Literature* from McGraw Hill. It's a text of some 2300 pages. It seems to reflect the diversity of the American mosaic with the exception of Mexican Americans. Not till page 2199 do we see a Hispanic writer, Isabel Allende, a Chilean who now lives and writes in the United States. This is the editorial myopia so prevalent in mainstream presses: they don't see the distinctions among Hispanics. This is not to depreciate Isabel Allende's art but she is not a Mexican American and for the editors of the McGraw Hill anthology to offer her as the token U.S. Hispanic is tantamount to offering Chinua Achebe as the token African American.

The most disturbing development in Mexican American literature is the divide that distinguishes Chicana literature from Chicano literature. That divide was precipitated, of course, by Chicanos in the early days of the Chicano Renaissance when Chicanas were excluded from the initial literary burst—not all of them, but the disparity was evident. The backlash was inevitable. To tell their stories, Chicanas rallied around the rubric of Chicana literature. The strategy was effective. By the 1990s Chicana writers had so revitalized Mexican American literature that by the end of the decade they eclipsed their male counterparts and reignited the smoldering fire of the literary renaissance of the 60s and 70s, pushing its spike to an apogee surpassing the pioneer Chicano writers, a spike still sustained and climbing. It seems to me the future of Chicano/a literature lies in the hands of Chicanas whose current productivity is prodigious. But the situation creates a bifurcation that keeps the two strands of Chicano/a literature identifiably separate and confounds presentation. Despite cooperative efforts in the field, the division poses considerations not only for teaching the conspectus of Chicano/a literature vis-a-vis texts but for developing an integrated perspective of the field that enfolds the bifurcation. This is not an insurmountable task but it will require genuine intra-ethnic deliberations to establish a historical baseline for Mexican American literature that recognizes and acknowledges both Chicano and Chicana writers as *trabajadores de la raza*. In the film *The Dark Crystal*, wholeness embraces all the parts.

Chicano literature has transcended the bounds of American literature. It is studied in Paris, Munich, Rome, Moscow, and Mexico City. It is part of a new world order in which the Eurocentric view of literary canon is being scrutinized for its relevance to non-European-based literatures.

This is a critical juncture for Chicano literature. No longer necessary now is the need to juxtapose Chicano text and countertext, no need to identify the enemy, praise the people and promote the revolution. Chicano texts must manifestly stand on their own—not for the benefit of Anglo mainstream readers but for the benefit of Chicano readers with whom Chicano literature has a pact of long-standing. For it is Chicano literature, after all, whose responsibility it is to proffer the verities of Chicano life to Chicano readers and, ultimately, to a universal audience.

There are many Chicanos who argue that Chicano literature is so much of a piece that it has a distinctive center of gravity as well as its own ground of being and, therefore, its own esthetic. There are norms and patterns in Chicano writing that are common to mainstream American literature and to world literature while at the same time different. Not because of innate Chicano characteristics but because Chicano writers, by and large, have emerged from a distinctive group experience in the United States.

This is not to say that that experience is uniquely different. Most writers, I daresay, have emerged from comparable group experiences: Jewish writers, Black writers, and others. While each group experience may be comparable (and thus not unique), the experiences of each group are different. For instance, Jews have not been slaves in the United States nor did their ancestors lose a war to the United States. Blacks have not suffered religious pogroms in the United States nor have they been prohibited from speaking their home language in the schools. Yet Jews, Blacks, and Chicanos have suffered outrageous bigotry and discrimination in the United States. But that is not enough to say that their group experiences have been the same.

Chicano readers have come to understand intellectually what they knew all along intuitively: that Chicano literature is not value-free; that language and culture—what Taine called *moment, race, and milieu*—are key factors in literary (cultural) production. The Anglo American mainstream lost sight of that, believing that its appointed mission was to pass on to generation after generation of Americans of all colors the "truths" embedded in the literary works of the Western Tradition: what is fitting for us is fitting for them. Thomas Macaulay's words about the literature of India and Arabia reverberate in our consciousness as words about black and Chicano literature spoken by or subscribed to by white heirs of Macaulay's literary imperialism:

I have no knowledge of either Sanskrit or Arabis, but I have done what I could to form a correct estimate of their value. I have read translations of the most celebrated Arabic and Sanskrit works. I have conversed both here and at home, with men distinguished by their proficiency in the Eastern tongues. I am quite ready to take the oriental learning at the valuation of the orientalists themselves. I have never found one among them who could deny that single shelf of a good European library was worth the whole native literature of India and Arabia. The intrinsic superiority of the Western literature

is indeed fully admitted by those members of the committee who support the oriental plan of education . . . It is, I believe, no exaggeration to say that all the historical information which has been collected in the Sanskrit language is less valuable than what may be found in the paltry abridgements used at preparatory schools in England. (*Selected Writings*, 1972: 241).

The distinguished men identified by Macaulay as proficient in the Eastern tongues were non-Easterners. The Orientalists were non-Oriental, as Edward Said has pointed out. They were all English, expounding on the Eastern and the Oriental from the perspective of British imperialism.

The import of this perspective is that, with the exception of the Heath Anthology of American Literature, in the United States information about the literary accomplishments of Mexican Americans has been nil in literary texts. Like Macaulay's non-Easterners and non-Orientals, editors and writers of American literary texts have excluded and marginalized the literary achievements of Mexican Americans, first, and Chicanos, later, for reasons ranging from jingoism and racism to ignorance, disdain, and imperialism.

EPILOG

Much research remains to be undertaken in Mexican American letters. For example, there is yet no comprehensive study of the Mexican American press or Mexican American journalists, showing their contributions to the development of Mexican American thought. My role in that area was the 10 year stint I put in *La Luz* magazine from 1972 to 1982 as Associate Publisher. At its peak, *La Luz* (first national Hispanic public affairs magazine in English published in Denver) reached a readership of 500,000. Our editorial aim was to represent the diversity that made up Hispanics in the United States. When Dan Valdés, founder and publisher died in 1982 I withdrew from the enterprise. I went on to be Editor-in-Chief and Publisher of the *National Hispanic Reporter* from 1983 to 1992, first national Hispanic newspaper in English published in Washington, DC. Again, our aim was to represent the diversity of American Hispanics. There are many Hispanic publications in the United States now but so many of them lack the bite of their activist predecessors as they paddle to stay afloat in the Anglo mainstream. Only *Hispanic Link*, a weekly newsletter out of Washington, DC continues the journalistic tradition of Hispanic representation.

But the still greater work remaining is the reconstruction of American literary history. For only then will the literature of *los de abajo* (the marginalized) be available for all Americans and the world. In 1973, José Carrasco and I argued for that reconstruction in our piece "Chicanos and American Literature" published in *Searching for America* by the National Council of Teachers of English. What I marvel at today is how much each generation of Mexican Americans progresses because of the work of the previous generation. The panorama of Mexican American literature gives me hope.

Endnotes

This work includes some commentary that also appears in "The Labyrinth and the Minotaur" by the author published in *Aztlán*, Spring 2001.

The absence of some Mexican American writers herein does not mean their works are not worthy of inclusion or discussion. There are many Mexican Americans who have contributed significantly to Mexican American letters mention of whom was a question of length limitations for this presentation. Most of the authors cited have produced considerably more works than cited.

Chicana Literature from a Chicana Feminist Perspective

Yvonne Yarbro-Bejarano

What are the implications of a Chicana feminist literary criticism? The existence of a Chicana feminist literary criticism implies the existence, first of all, of a tradition or body of texts by Chicana writers, which in turn implies the existence of a community of Chicanas and ideally of a Chicana feminist political movement. In other words, I do not see the development and application of a Chicana feminist literary criticism as an academic exercise. Like white feminism, Chicana feminism originates in the community and on the streets as political activism to end the oppression of women. This political movement is inseparable from the historical experience of Chicanos in this country since 1848, an experience marked by economic exploitation as a class and systematic racial, social and linguistic discrimination designed to keep Chicanos at the bottom as a reserve pool of cheap labor.

Within this collective experience, the facts and figures concerning Chicanas' education, employment categories and income levels clearly delineate the major areas of struggle for Chicana feminist movement.[1] There have always been Chicanas involved in political activism aimed at the specific situation of Chicanas as working-class women of color, objectified by economic exploitation and discrimination. Lucy González

Parsons, the Liga Femenil Mexicanista, Dolores Hernández, Emma Tenayuca, the miners' wives in the strike in Santa Rita, New Mexico, in the early 50s, Alicia Escalante and many, many more—these names evoke community, Chicanas who have laid the groundwork for a contemporary movement.

The Chicana feminist critic, then, does not work in isolation, alone with her texts and word processor, typewriter or pad and pencil. She is a Chicana-identified critic, alert to the relationships between her work and the political situation of all Chicanas.[2] The exclusion of Chicanas from literary authority is intimately linked to the exclusion of Chicanas from other kinds of power monopolized by privileged white males. Their struggle to appropriate the "I" of literary discourse relates to their struggle for empowerment in the economic, social and political spheres.

The term "Chicana feminist perspective" also implies certain similarities with and differences from either an exclusively "feminist" or "Chicano" perspective. While sharing with the feminist perspective an analysis of questions of gender and sexuality, there are important differences between a Chicana perspective and the mainstream feminist one with regard to issues of race, culture and class. The Chicano perspective, while incorporating these important facets of race, culture and class, has traditionally neglected issues of gender and sexuality. The Chicana feminist is confronted with a dilemma, caught between two perspectives which appeal strongly to different aspects of her experience. In 1981, the publication of This Bridge Called My Back documented the rage and frustration of women of color with the white women's movement, not only for the racism, the tokenism, the exclusion and invisibility of women of color, but also for ignoring the issues of working-class women of color (such as forced sterilization).[3] The creative way out of this dilemma is the development of a Chicana feminism in coalition with other women of color dedicated to the definition of a feminism which would address the specific situation of working-class women of color who do not belong to the dominant culture. While recognizing her Chicana cultural identity and affirming her solidarity with all Chicanos and other Third World men and women to combat racial and economic oppression, the Chicana feminist also spearheads a critique of the destructive aspects of her culture's definition of gender roles. This critique targets heterosexist as well as patriarchal prejudice. Above all, Chicana feminism as a political movement depends on the love of Chicanas for themselves and each other as Chicanas.

Perhaps the most important principle of Chicana feminist criticism is the realization that the Chicana's experience as a woman is inextricable from her experience as a member of an oppressed working-class racial minority and a culture which is not the dominant culture. Her task is to show how in works by Chicanas, elements of gender, race, culture and class coalesce. The very term "Chicana" or "mestiza" communicates the multiple connotations of color and femaleness, as well as historical adumbrations of class and cultural membership within the economic structure and dominant culture of the United States. While this may seem painfully obvious, the assertion of this project in Chicana writing is crucial in combatting the tendency in both white feminist and Chicano discourse to see these elements as mutually exclusive. By asserting herself as Chicana or mestiza, the Chicana confronts the damaging fragmentation of her identity into component parts at war with each other. In their critique of the "woman's voice" of white feminist theory, María C. Lugones and Elizabeth V. Spelman suggest that being invited "to speak about being 'women' . . . in distinction from speaking about being Hispana, Black, Jewish, working-class, etc." is an invitation to silence.[4] The Chicana-identified critic also focuses on texts by Chicanas that involve a dual process of self-definition and building community with other Chicanas. In these works, Chicanas are the subjects of the representations, and often relationships between women form their crucial axes. In the 70s and especially the 80s, their works explore the full spectrum of Chicanas' bonds with Chicanas, including lesbianism. The process of self-definition involves what Black critic bell hooks calls moving from the margin to the center.[5] White male writers take for granted the assumption of the subject role to explore and understand self. The fact that Chicanas may tell stories about themselves and other Chicanas challenges the dominant male concepts of cultural ownership and literary authority. In telling these stories, Chicanas reject the dominant culture's definition of what a Chicana is. In writing, they refuse the objectification imposed by gender roles and racial and economic exploitation.

Chicana writers must overcome external, material obstacles to writing, such as limited access to literacy and the means of literary production, and finding time and leisure to write, given the battle for economic survival. But they must also overcome the internalization of the dominant society's definition of women of color. As Black writer Hattie Gossett phrases it, "who told you anybody wants to hear from you? you ain't nothing but a black woman!"[6] In her essay "Speaking in Tongues: A Letter to Third World Women Writers," Gloria Anzaldúa affirms that they must draw power from the very conditions that excluded them from writing in the first place, and write from what she calls the deep core of their identity as working-class women of color who belong to a culture other than the dominant one.[7]

By delving into this deep core, the Chicana writer finds that the self she seeks to define and love is not merely an individual self, but a collective one. In other words, the power, the permission, the authority to tell stories about herself and other Chicanas comes from her cultural, racial/ethnic and linguistic community. This community includes the historical experience of oppression as well as literary tradition. In spite of their material conditions, Chicanas have been writing and telling their stories for over a century. The Chicana writer derives literary authority from the oral tradition of her community, which in turn empowers her to commit her stories to writing.

Since this specific experience has been traditionally excluded from literary representation, it is not surprising that writing that explores the Chicana-as-subject is often accompanied by formal and linguistic innovation. In her essay "Speaking in Tongues," Anzaldúa stresses the need for women of color writers to find their authentic voice, to resist "making it" by becoming less different, to cultivate their differences and their tongues of fire to write about their personal and collective experience as Chicanas (166). The search is for a language that consciously opposes the dominant culture. Poet Cherríe Moraga has written: "I lack language. / The language to clarify / my resistance to the literate. / Words are a war to me. / They threaten my family." This search for an authentic language may include the fear of incomprehensibility, as the poem goes on to articulate: "To gain the word / to describe the loss / I risk losing everything. / I may create a monster . . . / her voice in the distance / unintelligible illiterate. / These are the monster's words."[8] "Visions of Mexico . . .," by poet Lorna Dee Cervantes, also speaks of the urgent need to dominate the written word in order to smash stereotypes and rewrite history from the perspective of the oppressed:

"there are songs in my head I could sing to you
songs that could drone away
all the mariachi bands you thought you ever heard
songs that could tell you what I know
or have learned from my people
but for that I need words
simple black nymphs between white sheets of paper
obedient words obligatory words words I steal
in the dark when no one can hear me."[9]

As evidenced by the poems quoted above by Moraga and Cervantes, the theme of writing itself may appear as mediator between individual and collective identity in works by Chicanas.

Writing is central to Sandra Cisneros' work of fiction *The House on Mango Street*.[10] *Mango St.* and Helena María Viramontes' collection of stories *Moths*,[11] are innovative in opposite directions—Moths characterized by formal experimentation, *Mango St.* by a deceptively simple, accessible style and structure. The short sections that make up this slim novel, *Mango St.*, are marvels of poetic language that capture a young girl's vision of herself and the world she lives in. Though young, Esperanza is painfully aware of the racial and economic oppression her community suffers, but it is the fate of the women in her barrio that has the most profound impact on her, especially as she begins to develop sexually and learns that the same fate might be hers. Esperanza gathers strength from the experience of these women to reject the imposition of rigid gender roles predetermined for her by her culture. Her escape is linked in the text to education and above all to writing. Besides finding her path to self-definition through the women she sees victimized, Esperanza also has

positive models who encourage her interest in studying and writing. At the end of the book, Esperanza's journey towards independence merges two central themes, that of writing and a house of her own: "a house as quiet as snow, a space for myself to go, clean as paper before the poem" (100).[12]

Esperanza's rejection of woman's place in the culture involves not only writing but leaving the barrio, raising problematic issues of changing class:

I put it down on paper and then the ghost does not ache so much. I write it down and Mango says goodbye sometimes. She does not hold me with both arms. She sets me free. One day I will pack my bags of books and paper. One day I will say goodbye to Mango. I am too strong for her to keep me here forever. One day I will go away. Friends and neighbors will say, what happened to Esperanza? Where did she go with all those books and paper? Why did she march so far away? (101–02)

But Esperanza ends the book with the promise to return: "They will not know I have gone away to come back. For the ones I left behind. For the ones who cannot get out" (102).

The House on Mango St. captures the dialectic between self and community in Chicana writing. Esperanza finds her literary voice through her own cultural experience and that of other Chicanas. She seeks self-empowerment through writing, while recognizing her commitment to a community of Chicanas. Writing has been essential in connecting her with the power of women and her promise to pass down that power to other women is fulfilled by the writing and publication of the text itself.

Mango St. is not an isolated example of the importance of writing in Chicana literature. The *teatropoesía* piece *Tongues of Fire*, scripted by Barbara Brinson-Pineda in collaboration with Antonio Curiel (1981), broke new ground in focusing on the Chicana subject as writer, drawing from Anzaldúa's essay which gave the play its title. The text did not privilege one Chicana voice, but created a collective subject through the inclusion of many individual voices speaking to multiple facets of what it means to be Chicana. The tongues of fire of the Chicana writers in the play exposed oppression from without as well as from within the culture, denouncing exploitation and racism but also the subordination of Chicanas through their cultures rigid gender roles and negative attitudes towards female

sexuality. Writing emerged as the medium for the definition of the individual subjectivity of the Chicana
writer through the articulation of collective experience
and identity.

In *The Mixquiahuala Letters*,[13] Ana Castillo plays
with the conventions of the epistolary novel, undermining those conventions by inviting the reader to
combine and recombine the individual letters in Cortá-
zar fashion. At the same time, the epistolary form calls
attention to the role of writing in sifting through and
making sense of experience. The narrative voice not
only engages in a process of self-exploration through
writing, but the form of the writing-letters-foregrounds
an explicit exchange with a reader to whom the writing is directed. The novel defines subjectivity in relation to another woman, and the bond between the two
women further cemented by the epistolary examination of their relationship is as important as the exploration of self through writing.

In *Giving Up the Ghost*, Cherríe Moraga broke a
twenty-year silence in the Chicano theater movement
by placing Chicana lesbian sexuality center stage. The
text explores the ways in which both lesbian and heterosexual Chicanas' sense of self as sexual beings has
been affected by their culture's definitions of masculin-
ity and femininity. The theme of writing emerges at
the end of the play. Marisa's writing is both provoked
and interrupted by her memories of Amalia and sexual
desire, just as the text itself. Marisa's secular "confession"
to the audience is the product of her need to exhume
and examine her love for this woman and all women.
The text presents both the failures and the promises of
building community. Just before Marisa speaks of her
"daydream[s] with pencil in . . . mouth," she articulates
the need for "familia," redefined as women's community: "It's like making familia from scratch / each time
all over again . . . with strangers / if I must. / If I must,
I will."[14]

The love of Chicanas for themselves and each
other is at the heart of Chicana writing, for without
this love they could never make the courageous move
to place Chicana subjectivity in the center of literary
representation, or depict pivotal relationships among
women past and present, or even obey the first auda-
cious impulse to put pen to paper. Even as that act
of necessity distances the Chicana writer from her oral
tradition and not so literate sisters, the continuing

commitment to the political situation of all Chicanas
creates a community in which readers, critics and writers alike participate.[15]

Endnotes

1. Elizabeth Waldman, "Profile of the Chicana: A Statistical Fact Sheet," in *Mexican Women in the United
States*, Eds. Adelaida del Castillo & Magdalena Mora
(Los Angeles: Chicano Studies, U.C.L.A., 1980),
195–204.

2. My understanding of the similarities and differences between Black and Chicana feminist criticism
is indebted to Barbara Smith's "Towards Black Feminist Criticism" (1977), reprinted in *The New Feminist Criticism*, Ed. Elaine Showalter (N.Y.: Pantheon,
1985), 168–85.

3. *This Bridge Called My Back. Writings by Radical Women
of Color*, Eds. Cherríe Moraga & Gloria Anzaldúa
(Watertown, Ma.: Persephone Press, 1981).

4. "Have We Got a Theory for You! Feminist Theory,
Cultural Imperialism and the Demand for 'the Woman's Voice,'" *Women's Studies International Forum*, 6:6
(1983), 574.

5. *Feminist Theory: From Margin to Center* (Boston: South
End Press, 1984).

6. *This Bridge Called My Back*, 175–76.

7. In *This Bridge*, 165–74.

8. "It's the Poverty," in Anzaldúa, *This Bridge*, 166.

9. *Emplumada* (Pittsburgh: University of Pittsburgh
Press, 1981), 45–46.

10. *The House on Mango Street* (Houston: Arte Público
Press, 1985).

11. *The Moths and Other Stories* (Houston: Arte Público
Press, 1985).

12. Sonia Saldívar-Hull includes a discussion of *Mango St.*
in "Shattering Silences: The Contemporary Chicana
Writer," forthcoming in *Women and Words: Female
Voices of Power and Poetry*, Ed. Beverly Stoelbe (University of Illinois Press).

13. (Binghamton, N.Y.: Bilingual Press, 1986).

14. (Los Angeles: West End Press, 1986), 58.

15. The concept of a "Black writing community" is devel-
oped by Hortense J. Spillers in "Cross-Currents, Dis-
continuities: Black Women's Fiction," in *Conjuring.
Black Women, Fiction and Literary Tradition*, Eds.
Marjorie Pryse and Hortense J. Spillers (Bloomington:
Indiana University Press, 1985).

Adelante! The Progress of Chicano Art: An Overview of Chicano Art History

George Vargas

The Spanish word *adelante* has many uses to give direction or encouragement: "Forward!" "Come on!" "Keep at it!" "Get ahead!" Among Mexican Americans or Chicanos in the United States, *adelante* literally describes social and economic progress in the historical development of Chicano peoples as Americans.

From coast to coast, the U.S. Latino population numbers over 50 million. Chicanos, the largest subgroup of Latinos, comprise over half the Latino population. Chicanos mainly live in urban areas and in the U.S. Southwest where they dominate the border zone. This fast growing ethnic group and its history have been largely ignored in academia. Chicano artists still are excluded from most mainstream museums decades after the demise of the Chicano political movimiento of the 1960s and 1970s when artists primarily created political art. Over time Chicano art has evolved with the changing demographics and psychology of the Chicano community. Today's Chicano art is an open model, clearly multifaceted in idea, medium, content and style, with many more artists exploring alternative art forms. Chicano art is a people's art, as diverse as the larger Chicano community or pueblo. Unequivocally, Chicano art is art by, for and about Americans.

Many Chicano artists act as historians by portraying the truth about living and working in America, the backdrop of their lives and art. "I believe strongly that

the artisan has been and still is the historian of people's culture," affirms premier Chicano artist Amado M. Peña. Chicano art represents the joys and despairs, triumphs and tragedies of everyday reality. Contextualized within broader American culture, Chicano art calls forth wide aesthetic meaning with social implications for audiences on a universal level. In this essay, we will review Chicano art history to better understand the Chicano experience of American culture as interpreted by contemporary artists.

CHICANO ART HISTORY

The Aesthetic

In constructing Chicano art history, it is crucial to note that the aesthetic includes issues of identity and self determination, a main thrust in early Chicano art of the late 1960s to the 1970s. The Chicano majority was and is concerned with its right to proper identification and place in American culture, keystone elements that shaped the philosophy of Chicanismo. Chicano artists protested issues by promoting Chicanismo on behalf of their respective communities, largely underrepresented and under-developed. Searching their own Mexican roots, Chicano artists modeled themselves after Mexican modern artists of post-Revolutionary Mexico, innovating signs and symbols into a new expression of aChicano Revolution to communicate their community's socio-economic needs. Other interests were interwoven as common threads and articulated in Chicano art:

- Mestizaje (mixed culture) based on mestizo ancestry (of mixed races, Spanish, Mexican Indian and African). The mestizo populace signifies the largest racial/ethnic. trunk in the Americas, with Spanish being the dominant language in the hemisphere.
- Nativism (or neo-indigenism) explored Amerindian or indigenous influences, particularly Mexican Indian cultures (from Olmec to Aztec). Many Chicano artists interpreted the legend of Aztlán, drawing comparisons between the Aztecs and Chicanos as the "chosen people."
- Nationalism (associated at times with separatism) toward the formation of a Chicano nation, popularly espoused in the 1960s and 1970s among activists. Even the use of the term Chicano denoted ethnic pride and activism. "A Chicano is a Mexican American with a non-Anglo image of himself," declared Los Angeles Times journalist Ruben Salazar (who later was "accidentally" killed by L.A. police during the Chicano Moratorium).

Meanwhile, Chicano art became a cause unto itself. The artists called for cultural equality and urged other artists to make works reflective of non-Western styles. In time, scholars Jacinto Quirarte and Raymond Barrio began to document the Chicano art phenomenon. Tomás Ybarra-Frausto and Shifra M. Goldman would also initiate new scholarship.

By the 1980s, the Chicano aesthetic progressed with the shift in the socio-political climate and artists began to practice multiculturalism. From the 1990s and into the 21st century, Chicano art grew more complex. Artists injected a sense of universality into their expressions. Once serving as propaganda, Chicano artists became interested in being more humanistic, less confrontational. Today, the term "Chicano" is used interchangeably with Mexican American, more as a descriptive term and less a political one.

The Emergence of Chicano Art, 1960s and 1970s

Chicano art intertwines Mexican and American history into a perspective that by nature is political, therefore provocative. Artists interpret the story of countless Mexicans and Chicanos who have lost land, language and culture because of the European Conquest, the Mexican American War and the Mexican Revolution. Not all Mexican American artists believed in the concept of ethnic art. Numerous modern artists of Mexican ancestry successfully worked in the mainstream in this period, using explicit and implicit references to their Mexican background without demanding attention to ethnicity or political identity.

Painter Melesio Casas (born 1929, El Paso, Texas) and sculptor Luis Jiménez (born 1940, El Paso) were prolific Pop artists working in the national art scene, but at home in El Paso, they proudly identified themselves as Chicano artists and were role models to younger Chicano artists. In the late 1960s, they joined ranks with other artists to form a people's art that would not only carry the message of a growing Chicano political movement, but also would carry the message of a larger liberation movement that included women and people of color primarily through the production of mural art, posters and prints.

Murals

Ideologically linked to the broader People's Art Movement, early Chicano artists were influenced by the Mexican Mural Renaissance (1920–1930) that followed the Mexican Revolution (1910–1917), especially by Los Tres Grandes—José Clemente Orozco, Diego Rivera and David Alfaro Siqueiros. Ironically, all three muralists received big commissions for murals in the U.S. that were either unfairly criticized or whitewashed in the 1930s. These Mexican muralists nonetheless inspired the creation of the Public Works of Art Project (PWPA, Franklin D. Roosevelt's New Deal program initiated in 1933), which not only provided work for countless unemployed American artists but also recorded the idealism of the New Deal era on walls of public buildings throughout America.

Chicano murals helped revive America's interest in public art. Now murals were more accessible and demystified—a people's expression that engaged the community. Murals exploded like piñatas in urban centers throughout the U.S. in the late 1960s and 1970s. Neighborhood artists and residents planned and executed murals, literally taking their social issues to the streets by painting on public walls. Most early murals were produced on a shoe-string budget independent of governmental funds, underscoring their revolutionary intent. Painted mainly in cities with substantial Chicano populations, Chicano murals were invigorated by the civil rights movement, anti-war protest, student activism, women's rights, labor and politics, and counter-culture. Creativity became a metaphor for personal freedom and public expression guaranteed to all Americans. Eventually, Chicago and Los Angeles became hubs of the mural movement, where many visually striking murals were created in Chicano barrios.

Early Chicano murals communicated contemporary themes of race, class and ethnicity that spoke specifically to the Chicano experience but also addressed topics relevant to poor and working class Americans of all colors. Artists tended to use figurative and representational styles easily read by the masses. To accentuate their indigenism, artists portrayed images taken from pre-Columbian history. Pictures of heroic figures (Adelita, Ché, César Chávez, Virgin of Guadalupe, Zapata) from popular culture were also used to address current issues. These early muralists retold the past while capturing the exciting times of the present.

Manuel Gregorio Acosta, a proficient easel painter, produced what may have been El Paso's first mural. He painted *Iowa Jima* at the Veterans of Foreign Wars office in 1966. It documented the often overlooked Chicano presence in the Armed Forces.

Chicano artists painted murals in Estrada Courts, a low-income housing complex in east-side Los Angeles. Charles "Cat" Felix organized neighborhood youth, including gang members, to paint the earliest murals in Estrada. By 1973, two or three murals existed; by 1978 there were over 50 murals, attracting world-wide media attention.

In 1975, José Gamaliel González organized youth of Westtown, Chicago, to paint *Raza de Oro*. Exploiting neo-indigenism, González utilized the form of a Mayan relief lintel (AD 725) in Yaxchilán to produce a vision of the plumed serpent, which symbolized the common struggle of Chicanos as an emerging golden race related to the Aztecs, a new "people of the sun."

Interestingly, Chicano artists symbolically claimed Aztlán, the Mexica/Aztec Indians' ancestral homeland. The Aztecs left Aztlán, perhaps somewhere in the U.S. Southwest, and undertook a long and dangerous quest for a new home base and special identity. The migratory Aztec finally settled in central Mexico, borrowing ideas from others to forge their own mythology and identity, eventually building one of the world's biggest empires. The legend of Aztlán served as a metaphor for the Chicano's own search for history, self and place in U.S. society.

Much like the Aztecs, migratory Chicanos constructed their own peculiar history by blending reality and myth. Chicano artists transformed the Indian into a symbol of cultural achievement and consciousness.

By painting their people's symbolic exodus, artists hoped to reclaim a place of honor in the American landscape on behalf of Chicanos deprived of land and civil rights. For example, Emilio Aguayo's 1971 mural *Somos Aztlán* in the Ethnic Cultural Center at University of Washington, Seattle, envisioned a new Chicano nation geographically reclaimed from the U.S. Southwest, part of the old Aztec empire.

Artists soon became community leaders and arts administrators to advance their art. Judith Baca directed a massive mural project beginning in 1976, *The Great Wall of Los Angeles*, which featured the multicultural history of California, as well as the history of the U.S. pertaining especially to Chicanos. Measuring 2,400 feet in length by 13 feet in height, Baca invited various community members and professional artists to paint the mural in 1978, 1980, 1981 and 1984. Baca stressed the organic creative process, rather than the end product, when training neighborhood artists. Working together on murals was a spiritual experience of self and community.

Over time, Chicano muralists began to study more forms of world art. More sophisticated and contemporary styles began to appear like classical representation, photo-realism, expressionism and abstraction. They also discovered more permanent materials and advanced technologies. Some artists introduced portable murals (moveable panels first innovated by the Mexican muralists), making it possible to carry visual messages into new spaces.

Graphic Art (Posters and Prints)

Satirical newspaper illustrations by turn of the century Mexican printmakers José Guadalupe Posada and Manuel Manilla inspired a long-standing tradition in Mexican graphic art, and later in Chicano graphic art. In 1937, the Taller de Gráfica Popular (TGP) was borne, a Mexican graphic arts collective whose purpose was to produce art devoted to social realism and to teach graphic techniques, both traditional and new.

Borrowing directly from TGP members such as Posada, Diego Rivera and Mexican photographer Agustin Casasola, Chicano artists portrayed Mexican revolutionary figures as heroes of the Chicano revolution as well. For instance, Casasola's famous photograph of Zapata was copied by the United Farm Workers (UFW) Graphic Center in a 1970 poster, with the declaration "Viva la Revolución." The Royal Chicano Air Force used skeletons in their posters, inspired by Mexican printmaker Posada, who popularized calaveras in his social satire.

Printmaking offered artists a means to mass produce art, fast and cheap. Creating multiple prints meant more viewers. More viewers meant increased dissemination of artistic and social ideals to the Chicano community and beyond. For example, Jose Montoya glorified the zoot suiter or pachuco of 1930s and 1940s. Until then, historians only mentioned pachucos in reference to California's infamous zoot suit riots of World War II. Artists saturated communities with a different vision of this historical "rebel," causing a rediscovery of the pachuco's language, fashion and music.

Chicano posters and flyers announced important exhibitions, mural unveilings and rallies and were distributed free or at a nominal charge. In Austin, Texas Luis Guillermo Guerra (born in Mexico and raised in Texas) produced the 1977 serigraph *Hasta La Gloria* to commemorate the famous "Texas Farmworkers March" to Washington, D.C. (1977).

Other artists celebrated family traditions in prints, such as native Texan Carmen Lomas Garza. Influenced by Mexican bingo and lottery games, she featured her family in Loteria-Tabla Llena (intaglio, 1972) enjoying these popular games of chance.

The Emergence of Chicana Art

The early Chicano art movement was overwhelmingly male-dominated. When the Chicana art movement emerged in the 1970s, it was nothing short of a miracle. Chicanas still identified with traditional Chicano values but also fostered principles of empowerment, independence and feminine unity. Chicana art proved to be an instant forum for Chicanas, a way to express themselves in their respective communities. The emergence of the Chicana art movement was soon documented by Sybil Venegas and others in publications of the 1970s, such as *ChismeArte*, which had special issues devoted to investigating feminism and the Chicana aesthetic.

Chicanas experienced particular difficulty breaking into the mural scene, a few succeeded. Barbara Carrasco and Yolanda M. López were among the first women to enter the mural scene in California. Carrasco helped to train emerging muralists. López guided a group of high school girls who painted one of the first Chicana murals at Chicano Park in San Diego, a "people's park" heavily decorated with mural art throughout the 1970s.

Many Chicanas excelled in printmaking and produced challenging, interesting images of. In 1979, Isabel Castro (Santa Monica, California) made the provocative *Women Under Fire*. The viewer looks through the cross-hairs of a rifle that is pointed at a young Latina, symbolizing scores of Chicanas and other Latinas who were involuntarily sterilized while undergoing delivery in hospitals nationwide during the 1970s.

More artists contributed to a new Chicana aesthetic that strived to create nonwestern models of feminine beauty. Amalia Mesa-Bains, Delilah Montoya and Celia Rodriguez explored heroines such as the Virgen of Guadalupe, La Llorona, La Malinche and Frida Kahlo to illustrate a feminist perspective. Yreina D. Cervántes in *Homenaje a Frida Kahlo*, a 1978 watercolor, featured a pregnant (with twins) and sensuous-looking Kahlo in a lush fantastic garden, sitting nude on top of a living Aztec statue of a jaguar (a cuauhxicalli, receptacle in which human hearts were possibly placed as part of a sacrificial ritual). At her feet, a fat, smiling "frog-toad" (Rivera's own nickname for himself) serves as a fertility symbol from pre-Columbian times.

Californian Patssi Valdez and Texan Kathy Vargas experimented in mixed media to create a new version Chicana art. Muse-artist, Patssi Valdez contributed her artistic genius to ASCO, producing avant-garde performances/installations, such as ASCO's 1974 *The First Supper (After a Major Riot)*, which celebrated the history of Chicano demonstrations in Los Angeles. A member of C/S Con Safo, Kathy Vargas, specializing in black and white photography and installation, beautifully documented viejitos as in her 1974 portrait *Tio Gregorio y Tia Luisa*.

Chicanas fought to gain greater exposure and began to consolidate their power by forming groups that promoted women's art. Organized in the early 1970s, San Francisco-based Mujeres Muralistas was one of the earliest Chicana mural groups to paint community murals using a women's perspective. Fresno-based Las Mujeres Muralistas del Valle followed their lead in the mid-1970s. In 1977, Chicanas formed Mujeres Artisticas del Suroeste (MAS, co-founded by Nora Gonzales Dodson and Santa Barraza) in Austin to represent women artists from central and south Texas.

1980s: Expansion into the Contemporary Art Movement

Mainstream America became aware of Chicano culture in the 1980s, the so-called "decade of Hispanics" (label preferred by the government). Shifting from poor and working class to middle class, Hispanics were becoming educated and economically mobile and for the first time were recognized as an emerging consumer group. The face of Chicano art also changed. More Chicano artists were academically trained, exploring new theories and mediums. They recognized, and sometimes rejected, postmodernism, and yet supported the radical aspect of the vanguard—not refuting history but (re)discovering it by inventing and constructing new American art for a new American society. Artists extended their focus beyond the Chicano struggle. Their art proudly affirmed their dual (Mexican and American) identity, increasingly contextualized within a global perspective.

Much of Chicano art in the 1980s challenged description. Labels like neo-Chicano and nueva onda were applied to conceptual and performance art, mixed-media sculpture, assemblage, video, film-making and anti-art. Carlos Almaraz, Rupert Garcia, Teddy Sandoval, Linda Vallejo and others were reshaping the face of Chicano art in Los Angeles and throughout California.

Chicanos especially advanced in photography and film/video. In Oakland, California, Aztlán Cultural Center organized an exhibit of 18 Chicano photographers that toured West Germany in 1983. The San Antonio Chicano Film Festival was established to fill a gap left by traditional film festivals. Latina video/film makers Sylvia Morales, Lourdes Portillo and Susan Racho were breaking into the male-dominated medium.

Chicano artists continued to make murals, promoting Chicano pride, correcting cultural ignorance about Chicanos and simply beautifying neighborhoods. In Denver, Colorado, Chicano and non-Latino artists joined forces with local and state organizations to produce a series of mural projects throughout the area. In the early 1980s, the City Walls Project produced murals on courthouses, high schools, migrant labor offices, social services agencies and a Girls Club. For some artists, their success in wall painting led to other successes. Photographic reproductions of Al Sanchez's murals became part of Exxon Corporation's S.W. Barrio Art Collection.

Because community murals had greatly increased in scale and cost, more artists formed highly visible coalitions to seek broader community support since competition was tough for public art funding. Directed by Judith Baca, the Citywide Mural Project (CMP), produced over 250 murals in Los Angeles by 1984. Baca also helped to found the Social and Public Art Resource Center (SPARC), which sponsored 46 murals beginning in 1989 through its Great Walls Unlimited: Neighborhood Pride program, thus elevating mural painting to higher ground.

Mural art continued to rise as a popular public expression in the 1980s, but Chicano muralists still encountered censorship problems. On the eve of the 1984 Summer Olympics in Los Angeles, city officials banned Barbara Carrasco's *The History of Los Angeles—A Mexican Perspective* (1981–1983). Carrasco's portable 16-by-80-foot mural featured the artist's own face, her braids interwoven with various scenes representing a people's history, which critics charged as historically inappropriate. Though Carrasco received favorable public support, officials would not budge, ordering her to whitewash the "offensive" images. Instead of self-censorship, Carrasco found an alternative site to display her work.

Meanwhile, more Chicano artists smartly packaged original art to alert Latino and non-Latino audiences alike about hot-button issues. In 1986, UFW leader César Chávez commissioned Nora Mendoza (Detroit, Michigan) to create a series of paintings to be reproduced as greeting cards honoring migrant workers. Mendoza rendered expressionistic images of UFW marchers waving banners, women harvesting grapes from arbors sprayed by pesticides and children laboring alongside their parents. Afterwards, Mendoza exhibited her original paintings at the George Meaney Labor Center in Silver Springs, Maryland, underscoring the contributions made by Chicanos to U.S. labor and economy.

Increasingly, Chicano artists worked old and new mediums in unusual ways. Jerry Dreva presented performance pieces (including tattooing his body on February 14, 1980) to celebrate the 200th anniversary of the founding of Los Angeles; Diane Gamboa (Los Angeles) constructed *Snow Queen* (a paper fashion installation, 1984) to comment on beauty in fashion; performance/body artist Sylvia Salazar Simpson (born, Santa Fe) wore a headdress of living green plants and flowers populated by earthworms in her piece *Antes/Before*. And computer/video artist Rene Yañez (San Francisco) produced animated hologram art in *Pachuco*, about a young girl flirting with a pachuco.

A model of diversity, Chicano art naturally blended with a trend in U.S. art toward pluralism and universality. Chicano artists dialogued and exhibited with artists from Latin America and Asia, many of them in exile, searching for new identity and a renewed sense of historical presence in the New World; and to better conceptualize the role of art in politics, and politics in art.

In the 1980s key exhibitions were sponsored by major corporations: "Mira!" the Canadian Club Hispanic Art Tour; AT&T's "Hispanic Art in the United

States;" and Philip Morris' "The Latin American Spirit." These kind of black-tie affairs scored high by introducing Latino and Chicano art to new audiences, but were too few in number to benefit the majority of Chicano artists during the "decade of the Hispanic," an era of false promises.

New artists appeared on the scene, some faded away and others matured moving in new directions. Founding members of the Los Angeles group ASCO, for instance, headed down different paths. By 1987, they no longer worked together as ASCO and a chapter in Chicano vanguard art closed. Looking historically at the "face" of Chicano art, "ASCO [was] the jawline, because we could take the punches!" Gronk explains. With ASCO now dismantled, according to the group's historian Gamboa, "[T]here was no oasis in the urban desert."

New Chicano Art, 1990s and Beyond

The fact that Chicano art (or post Chicana/o art) survived into the 1990s and beyond should be no surprise, given the extraordinary surge in the Chicano population and its increasing socio-economic impact on U.S. society. New Chicano art flourished through the 90s, expanding with the burgeoning community from which it flowed. Individual artists began to exhibit in major spaces outside their immediate community, reaching new viewers. Chicano art was becoming a fresh and progressive American expression within the scope of North American art. The cross-over of a handful of Chicano artists was significant, underscoring the interest of Chicanos as consumers in mainstream society. For instance, a photographic image of Gronk was used to advertise the California Lottery.

Even more Chicano artists transcended their communities to work in transnational forums, relating to audiences beyond borders by addressing global issues such as poverty, famine, genocide, AIDS, mass exile, immigration and terrorism. Some were exhibiting their works to savvy European and Latin American audiences that perceived the expression as new American art, free of preconceived notions from its "political" past. These overseas admirers took Chicano art at face value, despite or because of its provocative nature.

Public Art (Murals & Sculpture)

The urge for public expression persisted after the passing of the Chicano political movement. Chicano murals and more sculpture continued to evolve into the 1990s despite debates involving predictable issues of content and quality. A new interest in community oriented art was brought on by urban renewal and a heightened concern to preserve local history and ethnic culture.

Respected sculptor and art professor, Luis Jiménez juxtaposed Chicano and mainstream popular images in giant fiberglass statues of Aztec gods and warriors, undocumented workers, vaqueros (cowboys), lowriders and cholos (Chicano youth), thus enlarging the definition of monumental public art while describing a new American borderland culture. Jiménez and his public works were sometimes attacked, due to his insistent expression of social realism via his choice of subject matter. For instance, as in *Crossing the Rio Bravo* (1989), and *El Chuco/El Paso* (1993), Jiménez explored the theme of immigration, a volatile subject in the borderlands where undocumented Mexican immigrants continue to enter the U.S. Jiménez's oeuvre of monumental art is well represented by *Vaquero* (1990), a cast fiberglass and epoxy statue standing prominently at the Smithsonian in Washington, D.C. No doubt, he is the most important figure in the Chicano public art movement, despite his demise in an accident in 2006.

Public artists have continued to fine-tune their technical approaches, while learning the business of finance to make more permanent monumental art. Deep in the heart of Austin, Texas, Ambray Gonzales and David Santos have organized public art projects through ALTA (American League of Tejano Artists), a collaboration of muralists, metal workers and sculptors creating public art with the support of the city's public art program. Meanwhile in Michigan, Grand Rapids artist Jose Narezo is engaged in decorating business interiors with tile and glass; his new interest in public art includes the study of Mexican mosaic and tile work, as well as the architectural decoration of Frank Lloyd Wright.

In El Paso, murals are a major attraction in this popular border town. Murals speak to Texas borderland history and culture. Garspar Enriquez' 1994 *History of the Mission Valley* is painted on a farm silo near a Big-8 Supermarket and documents the Indian, Spanish, Mexican and Euro-American presence in the region. Margarita "Mago" Gandara received a series of prestigious mural commissions in El Paso's sister city, Juarez, Mexico. Gandara lately has been planning a public art project to memorialize the hundreds of young women that were abducted and murdered in Juarez.

Together, public art of the larger Chicano pueblo represent a new expression in contemporary American art and reflect a dynamic picture of U.S. culture in transition. These powerful vehicles of environmental communication act to identify the very "heart and soul" of the community-at-large. Presenting history, religion or landscape themes, mural painting is familiar to most Mexicans and Chicanos because they frequently find themselves surrounded by public art, whether visiting ancient ruins, the marketplace or church. Adding a distinct character to America's urban environment, these mural/sculptural portraits present Americans with a "bigger picture" of American history.

Graphic Art

In the 1990s Chicano graphic art, much like mural art, continued to be a popular vehicle of visual communication in the community. The 1995 touring print exhibition "Chicano Connection" presented a group vision of the Chicano community and the world. Featuring a variety of subjects and approaches, the collection included Pat Gomez' War Stories, a family narrative, beautifully framed with roses and sacred hearts. Mario Calvano's Portrait with Text depicts a human figure with indirect references to Columbus and the Conquest, forcing the viewer to ponder personal and political realities.

Old fashioned printmaking collectives or workshops are still in popular demand, perpetuating the communal spirit of the Mexican graphic art tradition. In Austin, Sam Coronado, high school art teacher and master printmaker, directs printmaking workshops at Coronado Studios, an off-shoot of Self-Help print studio in Los Angeles, which was started by Sister Karen Boccalero. Since 1993, Coronado has coordinated print-making activities through his "Serie Project" involving Texas Chicano artists such as Santa Barraza, Gaspar Enriquez, Benito Huerta, Luis Jimenez and José Treviño

Performance Art

American performance art in the 1990s became more sophisticated and multi-layered in form and content. Chicano performance artists examined social issues, self-identity, feminism and urban life. Whether called performance art, street theatre or anti-art, Luis Alfaro, Ruebén Martínez, Vito Valdez, Mary "Laredo" Herbeck, the Chicano Culture Club and the Chicano Secret Service crossed new borders to unify performance with the evolving Chicano aesthetic.

California became a center of performance art. The bi-national arts collective Border Arts Workshop/Taller de Arte Fronterizo probed social issues, like identity, nationality, immigration and war, in a series of works involving the international border in San Diego. Performances included *Oh George, Oh Panama Performance* (1990), protesting the U.S. invasion of Panama.

In San Francisco Chicana artist Nao Bustamente used performance art to question the artificiality of the western notion of feminine beauty in her satirical 1995 piece *America the Beautiful.*

Chicana poet/performance artist Tammy Gómez and artist Marisa Nuñez of Austin, Texas, in collaboration with the Mexic-Arte Museum and the city's Summer Youth Employment Program (SYEP), helped students present a multimedia performance *Loud and Large: Image & Sound Under Construction* in 1997. Their performance installation demanded great teamwork and commitment to the community, and brought positive attention to the young students of color who are usually portrayed in a negative light.

1990s Exhibitions

With Chicanos slowly entering into mainstream art, overall acceptance of Chicano art has improved only slightly. Cultural wars of previous decades continued through the 1990s, affecting the exhibition of Chicano art in the 21st century as well. However, the 1990–1993 touring exhibition "Chicano Art: Resistance and Affirmation" (CARA) proved to be a blockbuster in the history of Chicano art. Attendance records were broken at many of the sponsoring museums, including those in Albuquerque, Denver, El Paso, Fresno, Los Angeles, New York City, San Francisco, San Antonio and Tucson. Excited crowds viewed a kaleidoscope survey of Chicano art produced from 1965–1985, displayed in an historical context. The collection's volume and diversity was awesome, with works including paintings, prints, photographs, sculptures, installations, *altarcitos* (altar installations), graffiti-inspired art and hologram art.

Here and there, Chicano artists received favorable reviews in small exhibitions mounted by mainstream museums and galleries. Among the handful of institutions that exhibited Chicano art as a part of American contemporary expression:

- Chicago's Department of Cultural Affairs presented group shows of Chicano and Latino artists together, such as "In the Heart of the

Country" (1991) with artists like Michigan's, Ed Fraga and Mel Rosas, and Chicago's Marcos Raya.

- The City of San Francisco organized "The Chicano Codices: Encountering Art of the Americas" (1992), an exhibition curated by Marcos Sanchez-Tranquilino, and hosted a series of panel discussions dealing with issues such as shattering the "glass-ceiling" in mainstream museums and "Replenishing Our Ancestral Archive."

- The Phoenix Art Museum presented "Contemporary Identities: 23 Artists—The 1993 Phoenix Triennial," highlighting artists of color and women, including Chicano artists.

- The "Latino Artists, Michigan U.S. A." (1991) exhibition toured Europe for three years, featuring 17 Latino and Chicano artists.

Recent Exhibitions

The 2001 touring exhibition "The Road to Aztlán: Art from a Mythic Homeland" repositions Meso American myth in American art and demonstrates its influence in development of Mexican, American Southwestern and Chicano cultures. Presented at Los Angeles County Museum of Art (also in Austin, Texas and Albuquerque, New Mexico), the exhibition is thematically organized around art inspired by the mythic Aztlán, homeplace of the ancient Aztec. Intertwining myth and history, this exhibition traces the image or concept of Aztlán in art throughout native, European and mestizo cultures, focusing particularly on its fluorescence in Chicano visual expression. The myth speaks to countless Americans and new immigrants who also seek the Promised Land.

The highly touted touring exhibition "Chicano Visions: American Painters on the Verge" (2001–06) marked a change in the museum business because it contextualized Chicano art within the western aesthetic and American art. Thus, Chicano art was categorized as a valid "school" of art, even compared to the French school of Impressionism because of its revolutionary vision, which conceptually resembles early Impressionism when it challenged the outdated approaches of salon art. Organized largely from Hollywood actor Cheech Marin's collection of contemporary art, the five-year exhibition toured 14 major U.S. cities and represented 26 artists of several generations. It debuted at the San Antonio Museum of Art (SAMA) in December 2001. The show opened as two stand-alone exhibitions presented simultaneously at different locations: the actual exhibition "Chicano Visions" and a multimedia extravaganza "Chicano Now: American Expressions" that showed how Chicano culture influences American pop culture through music, dance, film and cuisine., the exhibition received civil and corporate support at each of its exhibition sites.

Chicano artists still turn to alternative spaces such as community centers, schools or churches to exhibit their work. In larger cities, specialized museums such as the Mexic-Arte Fine Art Museum in Austin, Texas, Mexican Art Center in Chicago and the Mexican Art Museum in San Francisco have been created, directed and staffed by professionals who generally are knowledgeable about both the Western aesthetic and Latino aesthetic. People's galleries fill gaps left by traditional museums. Mainstream museums can certainly empower themselves to "do the right thing" rather than waiting for political pressure to unlock museum doors to multiculturalism.

New Historicity

Chicano art continues to expand into new territories. "Trailblazers" in art history have matured over time and are joined by younger scholars who bring a new sense of historicity to aesthetics, theory and criticism. Many of them seek new strategies to better analyze and exhibit Chicano art. Rising scholars in the new historicity, Victor Zamudio-Taylor, Charlene Villaseñor Black and Alicia Gaspar de Alba call for a new language and methodology to examine Chicano art, particularly in analysis and discourse of Chicana expressions.

Alicia Gaspar de Alba, author of *Chicano Art: Inside/Outside the Master's House, Cultural Politics and the CARA Exhibition*, presents the most comprehensive historical overview of the analysis and exhibition of Chicana art. Alba constructs an historical chronology of Chicana art, dating from the 1960s into the 1980s, defining the Chicana aesthetic as derived from themes of "motherhood, regeneration, and female ancestry," inspired by pre-Columbian symbolism and Catholic ritualism, and politicized with working class sensibility. She places Chicano culture outside the "master's house" describing through metaphor how Chicana/o art remains standing outside the museum. She methodically takes the CARA exhibition to task for its under-representation of Chicanas and challenges both community leaders and museum curators to develop better methods by which to bring a fair balance in exhibitions of Chicana artists.

CONCLUSION

To honestly judge it and in turn better understand it, we must expand definitions of Chicana/o art. Certainly, Chicano art features all forms of expression, a diversity of content and imagery and an abundance of styles or approaches made by artists who are individual visual authors contributing to the richness of the collective experience of America. More than ethnic or nationalistic expression, Chicano art is a peoples' art that has many purposes, as manifested by a new collective mind looking globally. Art has the power to communicate, educate, enlighten and heal while advancing the precious American ideal of individual freedom and the unalienable right to creative speech. As such, the new, open model of Chicano art will serve as a visual mirror reflecting social and spiritual changes in popular culture in a new, open American frontier of the future. The images reflected in the mirror of change must also include more women and immigrants, to show a more realistic portrait of our diverse American character. Parallel to the growth of a universality or world view in Chicano art, U.S. mainstream art will greatly expand beyond the confines of a strict Euro-American aesthetic, in part due to the rising influence of Latin(o) American culture and emergence of a global community.

Chicano artists by and large have already met and exceeded the criteria in postmodernism, but still are judged by class and race rather than on artistic merit by the museum gatekeepers. Yet, not withstanding a new paradigm in postmodernism, Chicano artists are at the cutting-edge of contemporary American expression, searching for their own postmodernity, but on their own terms as they invent a new plastic language for a new plastic age in American art. Some of their art speaks beyond formal concerns, dealing with spiritual values in the common search among artists and their audiences for deeper meaning in life. Increasingly, Chicana/o art is as much about other Americans as it is about Chicano peoples for the expression is a result of the great American experiment. Chicana/o artists reveal a dynamic vision of America searching inward for the Great American Dream, in the best and worst of times, now and tomorrow. *Adelante!*

El Mundo Femenino: Chicana Artists of the Movement—A Commentary on Development and Production

Amalia Mesa-Bains

Cultural transformation requires an expansion of an aesthetic language. Consequently, in the search for new concepts to describe America's broadening cultural diversity, we critics, scholars, and historians must begin to address those groups whose artistic production challenges old labels and limits. In particular we must try to understand the conditions and concerns that shape the work of Chicana artists, as well as the means by which these issues constitute a specificity of gender expressiveness.

Heritage, origin, family values, and cultural practices reside deep within the world view of Chicanas. Chicanas have renegotiated the domestic and community roles they fulfill as they migrate, become educated, and interact with their culture and the larger society. Their social roles are often in conflict, and this collision has recast the borders and boundaries of geography and identity. To begin to describe the cultural production and aesthetic language of Chicana artists, we must be willing to view their visual voice as a multiple text composed of shifting layers of meaning. This multiple text asserts a relationship between form and content. The work of these artists during the Movement was the result of the historical moment in which they found themselves; as such, it reflects an intention born of the social, cultural, and sexual realities of their lives.

Chicano Art: Resistance and Affirmation, 1965–1985, edited by Griswold del Castillo, McKenna and Yarbo-Bejarano. Reprinted by permission of Wight Art Gallery-University of California.

To understand the aesthetic production of Chicanas, we must place their cultural development in its historical framework. The twenty-five years following the mid-1960s were an era in which all Chicanos sought to define themselves and to understand the sources of their identity. The sense of alienation and struggle that marked the discrimination experienced by Chicanos also fueled the resistance so characteristic of Chicano and Chicana art.

THE CHICANA FOCUS ON CULTURAL IDENTITY

During the Chicano Movement, the resistance of Chicanas to the cultural oppression of the majority was matched by their resistance to the intracultural roles through which males dominated many aspects of family life and the arts community. Chicana artists focused on their cultural identity using the female lenses of narrative, domestic space, social critique, and ceremony, which filtered these nutrient experiences, contradictory roles, and community structures.

Narrative

Broad categories of cultural content provide a context for examining the work of specific Chicana artists. Narration is particularly significant in the artistic effort of Chicanas to restate family histories. The feminist critic

Griselda Pollock asserts that through language women are continually produced as elements in the social and economic structure of patriarchy.[1] Consequently, the narrative in Chicana art alters the relationship of women to domination by affirming positive histories so often denied in the larger society and by relocating women in a central, emancipated position.

The telling of family tales and the recording of daily events through recuerdos, diaries, letters, and home altars call upon women to remember the details of a personal and familial reality. Since their roles center on relationships, women are entrusted with teaching values through the oral traditions of storytelling, sayings, songs, and family histories. These are the sources of the cultural narration found in the work of many Chicana artists.

Within an emancipated dialogue, Chicanas positioned women as figures of power and control, while maintaining some of the familial and regional elements that affirmed the culture of the larger Chicano community. Rural and urban settings produced widely varying narratives that were often linked only by the role of women.

Domestic Space

In addition to the narrative intention, the need to circumscribe space in the community is a driving force in the work of women artists, who have, for example, used neighborhood walls for their murals. Another kind of reappropriation of territory is found in works that spring from a domestic space. The day-to-day experience of working-class Chicanas circumscribes space within the domestic sphere through home embellishments, home altars, healing traditions, and personal feminine poses or styles. The phenomenon of the home altar is perhaps the most prevalent.

Established through pre-Hispanic continuities of spiritual belief, the family altar functions for women as a counterpoint to male-dominated rituals within Catholicism. Often located in bedrooms, the home altar presents family history and cultural belief systems. Women arrange bric-a-brac, memorabilia, devotional icons, and decorative elements, and in doing so exercise a familial aesthetic. Constant formal elements include images of saints, flowers (plastic, dried, natural, and synthetic), family photographs, mementos, historic objects (military medals and flags), candles, and offerings. Characterized by accumulation, display, and abundance, altars allow history, faith, and personal objects to commingle. Formal structures and

techniques include nichos (niches), retablos (box-like containers highlighting special icons), innovative uses of Christmas lights and reflective material, and miniaturization.

Like the family life of women, the box form occupies space. If so-called feminine space seeks to gather, encircle, bind, link, and therefore circumscribe site, location, and activity, then box art and installation work break feminine space and refashion domestic enclosures.

Chicana rasquache, which I call domesticana, is like its male counterpart, the product of resistance to the majority culture and affirmation of other cultural values.[2] It also grows out of women's restrictions within the culture. Female rasquachismo defies the cultural identity imposed by Anglo Americans and defies the restrictive gender identity imposed by the Chicano culture. In the work of Chicana artists, techniques of subversion play with traditional imagery and cultural material, and together they characterize domesticana.

Social Critique

The social defiance that characterizes Chicano art in general finds a unique gender expression among Chicanas. Through the use of inversion, satire, reversals, and juxtapositions, Chicanas express a kind of resistant feminine commentary. These devices of subversion take benign symbols of North American culture and present them as signs of exploitation. The resulting social indictment is driven by women's political consciousness, desire for social change, and maternal sense of responsibility for the generations to come.

In an intracultural critique, artists take shared female images of everyday family life and manipulate them to question the limits of the feminine. In this sense, the work of many Chicanas does not simply reflect ideology, it constructs ideology. Their social critique provokes the viewer to see the benign and often domesticated versions of the feminine in new ways.

The Ceremonial

Spirituality, religiosity, spectacle, and pageantry are a prevailing aesthetic dimension of the work of many Chicana artists, who use, in particular, the shrine, ofrenda, altar, retablo, and nicho box forms. This ceremonial aspect highlights belief, healing, and celebration as elements in the ongoing lexicon of women's work. Maintaining the traditional place of women in spiritual practices, artists use ceremonial forms to expand their painting and mixed-media work. For example, the need to mediate death and transform the spiritual in celebrating El Día de los Muertos (the Day of the Dead) inspires a new body of work reflecting ritual and pageantry. The sources and sensibilities of folk practices, curanderismo, and the Catholic Baroque are fragments of the ceremonial intention expressed by Chicana artists.

CHICANA ARTISTS

The elements of the narrative, the circumscription of domestic space, the social critique, and the ceremonial are never discrete and monodimensional influences. They are, instead, memories and experiences, layered and scattered in a multiple text within each work. Overlapping and polysemous references permeate the work of Chicana artists.

Signifiers of their era, the following artists represent different outlooks and generations within the Chicano Movement. Despite their differences they are artistic pioneers of their epoch and, as such, cross boundaries. Their production lends insight into the major themes, aesthetic vocabulary, and multiple realities that characterize the larger Chicano identity and struggle for rights. Their personal development is complex and must be viewed within a historical framework. Their world view, cultural practices, social context, and early artistic influences thus determine and reflect their particular aesthetic. The nutrient experiences and sensibilities that express their intention as artists must be located in the historical moment of their group. The following women are but a few of the Chicanas whose presence as leaders, activists, and artists has been critical to achieving large-scale social change.

Judith Baca

Judith Baca's work, primarily the production of murals, is part of a large-scale, publicly engaged process that employs both narration and social critique. Baca's methods of solving problems and involving the community in her work arise from her early collective struggles in the family and neighborhood. Raised in a strong female household, Baca uses her family of women as a model for structures of feminist empowerment. The family model also inspires her to involve youth gangs in her work as a public muralist. Her conceptualization and production of murals involve historians, cultural informants, storytellers, neighborhood residents, young artists, and others in a collaborative venture to identify issues, images, and narratives.

The Great Wall of Los Angeles, located in the Tujunga Wash Drainage Canal in the San Fernando Valley, California, began in 1967 as the project of an artists' collective and became over many years the longest mural in the world (over half a mile long). In its portrayal of the history of Los Angeles the mural presents a panorama of the social struggle and disenfranchisement of diverse racial and ethnic groups. Each year youths of all races, under Baca's direction, learned about events such as the Japanese American Internment, the Freedom Bus Rides, and the Dust Bowl Journey as they worked on the mural.

Baca is committed to engaging gang youth in work that helps them define themselves and their culture because she was challenged as a youth growing up in Chicano barrios in the Pacoima area to define her self. Her installation piece *Las Tres Marías* (1976; cat. no. 33) plays on the multiple roles that the pachuca of the 1940s (proper left panel) and the chola or ruca of the 1970s (proper right panel) have assumed over time. This piece, whose title recalls the Three Marys of the crucifixion, sets up a good woman/bad woman satire by positioning a mirror so that it captures the viewer in the center of these extremes. Baca, seen dressed in a pachuca costume in the proper left panel, used this work as a performance piece in 1976.

Through her work, Baca focuses primarily on redefining social history and repositioning women in roles of power. She founded the Social and Public Art Resource Center in 1976, a center organized and run by women to document and preserve mural images, in part as a response to the male exclusivity of much of the mural movement. Baca's artistic association with Suzanne Lacy and Judy Chicago was at that time one of the few instances in which Chicana artists were in direct contact with the White feminist art movement. In general, Chicana artists were located within the broader cultural reclamation movement of the Chicano community while espousing a critical discourse related to women's issues. As artists deeply imbedded in their own communities, women disagreed with their male counterparts within the greater cultural dialogue. *Uprising of the Mujeres,* (1979; cat. no. 106), a sketch for a larger mural project, reflects the concerns of Chicanas in an emblematic construction of images of women.

In the largest perspective, Baca's contribution has been to develop structures and ideology using the mural. The *Great Wall* project is a multiracial, not just a Chicano, chronicle of history. Strong social critique. investigative indictment, and a cine-documentary perspective characterize her work. Baca applies her style of mural painting to socially charged theories, but her murals are only one product of her art; the process of empowering Chicanos and reclaiming neighborhood space is equally important.

Santa Barraza

Santa Barraza was raised in Kingsville, Texas, which is located on the vast King Ranch of southern Texas. Her ancestors have lived in this region for generations, an area known for its historic oppression of Mexican and Chicano communities. Her personal experience of continuity and history placed Barraza in the pivotal role of cultural chronicler. Her early photorealist work, which forms an archive of cultural narrative, provides Chicanos with strong visual support affirming their own reality in the face of a hostile Anglo culture. In depicting the characters and events of her region in painstaking detail, Barraza traces the events and memories of her own life and family: first holy communions, healing ceremonies, and familiar figures, landscapes, and neighborhoods. Barraza's *Renacimiento* is a classic Chicano work that blends myth, spirituality, and family sustenance in a symbolically coded layering.

Her pastel on paper, *El Descanso Final o la Entrada* (1980–84; cat. no. 81), narrates her grandmother's death by overlapping the memories of generations and fusing the icon of Zapata with the Chicano soldier boys and the image of la Abuelita. Barraza's grandmother, an emancipated figure, was the first person to drive a Model-T on the ranch. Her family relationships formed the basis of her healing world view.

> My father's sister, a curandera, would go to Mexico the first Tuesday of each month to see her master. She would train, and it was an all day thing. I would go with her to keep her company. This master curandera was about four feet tall and very heavy, with real short, black hair. There was an energy about her. She had this separate mud house, and she was always sitting on her bed. In the main house lived her daughters and husband, but she lived in this little hut. There was one bed right in the center of the room and then her altar. They would talk for hours, and I could see all this incense going out through the doors, burning up. Then once they invited me in. Though I never understood why, they performed a ritual on me. I think it was like going into womanhood because I was at that age. They dug a hole in the center, of the room. She summoned one of the little boys to go out to the field and get some plants to burn. She put some coal in the pit and had the smoke going, and I had to stand over it and open my legs. I would rotate around it, and she would perform the chants. I didn't understand what was going on, but when they finished, they took the ashes and buried them so I knew it was a very important ritual.[3]

Barraza internalizes this world view within the context of a folk belief that joins the mind, body, and soul and does not distinguish clearly between the natural and the supernatural. Objects of power, herbs, and talismans are the common currency of such healing. The blending of this often secret curing with the maintenance of home altars stands as a powerful parallel to the allegory of the mass and the ritual of Catholicism.

These themes remained part of Barraza's work even as she shifted from photorealism to expressionism. Like many Chicanas, she moved away from collective and historical imagery and toward a personal visual representation as an organic part of her own development. In the 1980s she began to work in mixed media and printmaking, using an intimate and highly charged feminine imagery. Dreams, healing gestures, death, and sexuality permeate her later work. The mixed-media folding book *Una Vida,* for example, presents and preserves the deep continuity of the generations of women of her family: the spirituality that links cultural practices, religiosity, and curanderismo and that centers her world view as an artist.

Carmen Lomas Garza

The distinctive monitos paintings of Carmen Lomas Garza depict stylized figures in a South Texas community. These cultural narratives present her childhood in a Kingsville, Texas, barrio. As in Barraza's work, the historical element is felt intimately and personally in Lomas Garza's paintings. Her visual storytelling offers varied groupings of characters engaged in the everyday events and festivities, of their community. Images of the cakewalk, la cena, and el curanderismo form the memories of a generation of rural Chicanos. The details of Lomas Garza's narratives signify the collective memories that make up an important regional Chicano experience. Along with Barraza, Lomas Garza has brought to a wider audience her remembrances of a rural Texas landscape of community pastimes like the cumpleaños party, the loteria games, and the healing traditions of important figures such as Don Pedrito Jaramillo, a curandero known for his legendary cures.

In her paintings she also recreates the folk-ethos of everyday life. She incorporates popular art forms, such as papel picado, in her paintings and reclaims her regional history by affirming the artistic legacy of artesanías. The multiple voices of her experience help us to understand the universe of her paintings and to renew our own memories.

In the sociopolitical sense, Lomas Garza's use of memory stands against the historical erasure of Chicano culture. Within the greater society, her cultural narrative recreates the lived reality of a community. She remembers what we can never forget and thereby subverts the dominance of Anglo society. As critic Víctor Zamudio-Taylor reminds us, the alternative chronicle only has power in the anecdote, or chisme. Walter Benjamin refers to the power of the anecdote when he writes:

> Anecdote brings them closer to us in space, allows them to enter our lives. Anecdote represents the extreme opposite of History . . . the true method of making things present is to image them in our own space.[4]

As an alternative chronicler, Lomas Garza offers a history that is an antidote to the institutional Texas histories. She creates in her paintings the sense of another time and uses this device to jar our memory and declare her resistance. Hers is not the history of the Alamo or Sam Houston; hers is the community record of the American G.I. Forum, the miraculous apparitions of the Virgen de Guadalupe, and the healing cures of Don Pedrito Jaramillo. Throughout this litany of recuerdos, Lomas mother, and curandera attest to Garza's grandmother, mother, and curandera attest to the powerful attributes of women. In many respects, the sequence of Lomas Garza's paintings resembles the pages of a family album or a young woman's diary.[5] They are the events that marked her. Hers is an alternative chronicle where culture and gender interpenetrate. Lomas Garza's device of flattening the figures is often perceived to be part of an unconscious, naive folk style. It is, instead, a deliberate technique that reduces the external, formal elements that might distract from the storytelling itself.

Both Ybarra-Frausto and Zamudio-Taylor note that the setting of Lomas Garza's paintings is often tinged with the sinister and the disquieting, with details such as knives and traces of blood. Most prevalent is what Zamudio-Taylor refers to as the "uncanny": the presence of a temporal reality magnified through minute details.[6]

Her gouache painting *Camas para Sueños* (1985: cat. no. 123) uses a somber palette to depict a remembered vignette of Carmen and her sister Margie lying on the roof under the moon while their mother prepares their bed in the house below. The painting commemorates the dreams and aspirations in which their mother encouraged them to indulge while she provided protection and sustenance. In this sense her narratives tell of both a sociocultural and internal psychology of gender identity.

Throughout Lomas Garza's chronicle we glimpse the artist as a young girl struggling against a world filled with discrimination and hostility. She has recalled:

> They would make snide remarks about your dresses and your being dirty. "Look at you, your dress is torn and hand-me-down. Why don't you ever set your hair? Don't you ever carry a purse?"[7]

Reconciling the past history and the anticipated future is the great task of each individual seeking to create an inner identity. Lomas Garza, like others of her generation, has had to mediate vastly disparate worlds. Beyond that she has had to locate her potential as a woman and as an artist within the cultural roles assigned to females. *Camas para Sueños* shows how that reconciliation was made possible within the family context.

Ester Hernández

Ester Hernández is of both Yaqui and Mexican descent. The influences of her parents, and particularly her grandmother, infuse her work with an ongoing set of images. Although imbued with the familial, her works provoke and defy the viewer. From her earliest association with the Mujeres Muralistas in the 1970s through her portraits in serigraphy and oil pastels, Hernández has consistently indicted society through her powerful and memorable images. Her classic print, *Sun Mad,* (1982; cat. no. 115). which transforms the smiling Sun Maid of the commercial raisin box into a skeleton, is a stinging and disturbing icon of death. *Sun Mad* not only recalls the satirical tradition of Mexican artists, such as the nineteenth-century printmaker Guadalupe

Posada, but also conveys her own rage at having been unknowingly contaminated by poisonous pesticides used in the fields where she worked.

The serigraph *Tejido de los Desaparecidos* (1984; cat. no. 121) potently blends an innocent pattern of folkloric weaving with the subtle but alarming images of calaveras, helicopters, and blood. Hernández has mastered the disquieting technique of juxtaposing the seemingly benign domestic symbol with horrifyingly unexpected elements.

Equally important is how she reworks the female image. Marked by the early family models of mother and grandmother as well as the festivities of the local Guadalupana society, she has articulated the gender issue in a series of portraits, such as those of Lydia Mendoza and Frida Kahlo as calaveras. Her Guadalupe karate fighter in the print *La Virgen de Guadalupe Defendiendo los Derechos de los Xicanos* (1975; cat. no. 100), in particular, breaks the traditional role of the Virgen de Guadalupe as icon and repositions her as a feminist assertion. Her Guadalupe karate fighter and *La Llorona* are two of the signature pieces of her generation.

Crucial to her visual commitment to the issues of empowerment is her lived commitment to social service among the elderly, the disabled, and the farmworkers within the cultural institutions of her community. Like most of her Chicana peers, she produces works of art and is of service within the community. Hernández, along with Yolanda López, restructures the feminine through social critique. She subverts, recontextualizes, and thus transforms culturally traditional images into a series of feminist icons.

Yolanda López

The potential of feminine images to emancipate women is best realized in the landmark Guadalupe series by Yolanda López (1978; cat. nos. 103, 104, 105). López restates the Virgin of Guadalupe by removing the traditional figure from the halo of rays and replacing it with powerful images of family and self. The traditional icon is customarily portrayed as a passive and submissive figure. López's Guadalupes are mobile, hardworking, assertive, working-class images of the abuela as a strong, solid nurturer, mother as a family-supporting seamstress, and daughter as a contemporary artist and powerful runner. This repositioning becomes both satire and provocation, while retaining the transfigurative liberation of the icon. By breaking the bonds of Guadalupe and setting her free, López attests to the internal

familiarity of the image and the powerful influence of her own family members. The art in this series does not simply reflect an existing ideology; it actively constructs a new one. It attests to the critique of traditional Mexican women's roles and religious oppression in a self-fashioning of new identities.

López works with a variety of forms, including prints, posters, drawings, videos, and installations Throughout this range of forms, her intent is to indict, analyze, and critique. From her earliest commitment to the farmworkers' struggle, to the cause of Los Siete—the seven political activists from San Francisco's Mission District who were charged with and later aquitted of killing a policeman in 1969—to examining conditions existing along the border, López melds her personal and political activism in the aesthetic of her community.

Her early experience with cultural conflict, Anglo discrimination, and even adolescent conflict itself sets the stage for her efforts to redefine the feminine in a feminist context. López has stated:

> The ideal was white, and I was not. I didn't understand it in those terms as such, but I knew very well that I didn't look like that. So I never considered myself pretty or anything like that. Like all thirteen and fourteen-year-olds, I worked very hard at grooming myself.[8]

López's close relationship with her grandmother connected her with a cultural memory unavailable through her young working mother. The family tales of migration and change were gifts of history from her abuela and later served as text for her installation work. Becoming a mother herself also heightened and expanded her concern with and focus on, the family and the future. López uses cultural memory to connect the generations of her family, and this adds a new dimension to socially charged work. Currently, she has moved into both community and domestic discourse on object and image, politics and power in her analysis of Mexican kitsch and her video work on Mexicana stereotypes.

Patricia Rodríguez

Early in the Chicano Movement, Rodríguez, like others, was mentored by artists such as Esteban Villa and José Montoya. Nevertheless, Rodríguez, like many other Chicanas, recognized an element of male exclusivity that required women to form their own collectives. The impulse to make a collective commitment was great in the early period of the Movement. Rodríguez recalled:

> You understood what discrimination was about. . . . I felt that I had a responsibility. I had a duty as part of this younger generation with this kind of consciousness to try and correct some of those things. It was like enlisting in the army. If I had to have art become part of that duty for X amount of time, then it would, because it was simply something that I would have felt terrible if I had not done.[9]

For Rodríguez, as for many other artists, el Movimiento offered hope for a generation raised within discrimination and conflict. It created new models and a new sense of their potential as artists. The Movement focused on collective, publicly accessible, and socially committed work, and Las Mujeres Muralistas was driven by these values. The traditional male model of the individual artist was too limiting, and Rodríguez turned to women's traditions for a model that could strengthen her life as an artist and cultural worker. Las Mujeres Muralistas was formed to give working artists a support structure and only included women. Together, Irene Pérez, Graciela Carrillo, Consuelo Méndez, and Rodríguez worked as a team on the arduous and sometimes hazardous task of painting murals in public spaces. Circumscribing public space was rarely associated with the work of women, and Las Mujeres Muralistas was a revolutionary effort. Their structure resembled that of other organizations in the Movement whose work was publicly accessible, antielitist, and collective in nature. Their formula was feminist, however, and therefore unique. Although short-lived as a collective force, Las Mujeres Muralistas exerted a considerable impact on Chicano and Chicana art and artists.

In the years after Las Mujeres Muralistas, Rodríguez turned to a more private and intimate form of art, yet one deeply marked by the ceremonial and enduring memories of her rural childhood: her retablo box pieces. In these boxes, Rodríguez represents private space within public discourse. She elaborates and retells stories of childhood festivities, rural celebrations, and patterns of kinship and community in satirical stagings within the small box tableau. She persistently uses memory as device of emancipation.

Rodríguez's *Sewing Box* includes the predictable elements of feminine portraiture, such as threads, bits of fabric, milagros, and toy doll limbs. Compartmentalized in distinct enclosures with drawers partially opened, small plastic soldiers, representing the dominant patriarchy, are offered in juxtaposition to the feminine materials. She reminds us of the segregated roles of girl and boy and of nurturing and aggression through these phenomena of discarded experience. Tokens of love and narratives of domesticity and ruin are presented as a secret exposed to us, but from which we are ultimately excluded.

Retablo, or box art, has a strong tradition among both Chicano and Chicana artists, due in part to the persistence of the venerated pre-Hispanic and Catholic reliquaries. As Tomás Ybarra-Frausto writes:

> These sacred objects were venerated religious items such as a supposed thorn from the crown of the crucifixion, a piece of the true cross or vials of blood or mummified anatomical parts of a holy personage displayed behind glass in elaborate containers. As worshipers touched or venerated them, their aura or power was transferred to the supplicant.[10]

The creative reconstruction of these reliquaries through domesticana retrieves memory and captures in permanent imagery the ephemeral and temporal remembrances of things past. In assemblage, bricolage, miniaturization, and small sculpture, Rodríguez creates a mimetic worldview that retells her feminine past from a new position. The rasquache attitude of making the most from the least in dazzling displays of popular decorative art marks much of Rodríguez's work, including the box portrait *José Montoya,* (1973; cat. no. 60). Similar to the function of home altars, Rodríguez's ceremonial works document, accrue, and detail events of family relations through arrangements often characterized by a subtle sense of the seductive, the veiled, and the contained. Like small stage sets they present themes of passion, death, healing, ancestry, and the everyday, and serve as narrative junctures for broader cultural themes.

Patssi Valdez

The early work of Patssi Valdez was integrally tied to the urban conceptual group Asco. Raised in Los Angeles, Valdez faced many of the problems common to urban life: poverty, violence, alienation, and family fragmentation. Detached from traditional rural experiences, Valdez and the other members of Asco sought the meaning of the Chicano experience in their own inner-city environment.

Along with Gronk, Harry Gamboa, Jr., and Willie Herrón, Valdez articulated a visual and conceptual language of her own urbanism. Like a tierra incognita, the Los Angeles context inspired works such as *The Instant Mural* (1974), *The Walking Mural* (1972), the No Movies, and other satirical, iconoclastic gestures of impermanence. Valdez, the only woman participating in Asco's aesthetic of alienation, developed a feminine iconography out of her own need to create instant glamour in an impoverished world. Using herself as an object of art, she collaborated on producing a series of images of her own persona through the media of pageantry, urban spectacle, and photomontage. Like other artists who shared her Los Angeles experience, she used fragments of television, film, fashion, and theater to produce satirical statements on America's throw-away society.

Asco produced a counterpoint to the traditional regional cultural politics of the Chicano Movement. Their alienated urban focus often clashed with the more idealized family and community narratives of the Southwest. Valdez began to construct her own ephemeral installations composed of urban discards, party materials, and her own photographic studies. Through her installations Valdez contributed to an urban feminine rasquache that could only be created from the remnants of a metropolis. Her reference points were the glamorous industries of cinema, television, and fashion and their spontaneous obsolescence. In the company of the other members of Asco, who were much like a family, Valdez formed part of a larger social indictment of the violent, disturbing conditions facing Chicanos: la Migra, police harassment, homelessness, and psychological isolation.

In her installation work Valdez reminds us of the sincere and innocent longing for an inaccessible world of beauty and festivity that contrasts with the lived reality of ruination, destruction, and loss. In site-specific homages to the Black Virgin, she uses the discards of pop culture, the remnants of party materials, and the hyperfeminine gestures of the glamorous to represent the polarities of purity and debasement. She combines and recombines jewelry, kitchenware, toiletries, saints, holy cards, and milagros to create the spectacle of the modern metropolis. She juxtaposes the patriarchal polarities of the good woman and the bad woman and thus transgresses the controlling masculine gaze. This transgression brings redemption and enunciates the language of domesticana as both the product and the pose of rasquachismo.

In her later development, Patssi Valdez turned to a more intimate and private domain. Images of her domestic world include introspective and provocative selfportraits. Her details of private landscapes present a kind of feminine diary and replace the instant glamour of her earlier works. She now presents a more permanent perspective of the enduring objects of her everyday world.

SUMMARY

These artists continuously negotiate the narrative in their work, an effort that binds their strikingly diverse work. The diversity of region and generation, which directly affects their choice of themes, materials, and forms, brings richness to their output. In the 1960s and 1970s, working within the demands of the larger Chicano Movement to produce socially charged work, many of these artists also redefined their own roles within Mexican/Chicano culture. They reorchestrated, for example, the positive strengths of mother and grandmother to emancipate the roles of women. The idiom of feminist Chicanas inhibited the traditional roles and images, a change that called for negotiation within the cultural group. This reorchestration was problematic. The balancing of enduring, sustaining aspects of cherished cultural roles and practices, and the strengthening of emancipatory devices is never accomplished easily. Tradition and innovation are intertwined and reflected in the degree to which Chicanas drew images, themes, and content from the apparently constricting and contradictory roles. Armed with a contemporary understanding of the struggles facing them, these artists used ancestry, ceremony, mass media, social subversion, and critique to fashion an aesthetic and reconstruct ideologically a new language of liberation for themselves. Perhaps the greatest hallmark is that disparate views of a single cultural phenomenon, such as Yolanda López's representation of the Virgen de Guadalupe and the traditional Virgen image, have been able to coexist in Chicana art.

Exploring a new aesthetic vocabulary is the first step in establishing a context for Chicana artists, although that vocabulary is neither fixed nor singular. Narration, the circumscription of domestic space and spirit, indictment, and ceremony are often fissured in a constantly shifting language. These artists move freely within broad sensibilities and intentions, breaking the preexisting categories and enlarging the vocabulary of the feminine. Reclaiming our past and marking our experiences through our culture and lives have been the real contributions of Chicana artists. Their work continually recasts an open identity where tradition and innovation must live together.

Endnotes

1. See Griselda Pollock, *Vision and Difference—Femininity, Feminism and the Histories of Art* (London and New York: Routledge Press, 1988).

2. For an introduction to the concept of rasquache from the larger cultural perspective, see essay by Tomás Ybarra-Frausto, "Rasquachismo: A Chicano Sensibility."

3. Santa Barraza, interview with the author, 1982.

4. Walter Benjamin, *Illuminations* (New York: Harcourt, Brace & World, 1968).

5. Lomas Garza has in fact recently published a selection of her paintings as a children's book with short bilingual narratives, *Family Pictures* (San Francisco: Children's Book Press, 1990).

6. Víctor Zamudio-Taylor, "Allegory, Memory & History," lecture presented at the Museum of Hispanic Art, New York, 1990.

7. Carmen Lomas Garza, interview with the author, 1982.

8. Yolanda López, interview with the author, 1982.

9. Patricia Rodríguez, interview with the author, 1982.

10. Tomás Ybarra-Frausto, "Cultural Context," in *Ceremony of Memory* (Santa Fe, New Mexico: Center for Contemporary Arts of Santa Fe, 1988), ll.

Chicano Literary Folklore

María Herrera-Sobek

Up to the present the formulation of an exact definition for the term "folklore" has been a difficult and elusive goal. The *Standard Dictionary of Folklore, Mythology and Legend* incorporates no less than twenty-one separate definitions submitted by experts in the field. A cursory examination of these definitions, however, does show a certain consistency in the general framework of their constructs. We note, for example, that certain key words are repeatedly utilized in the descriptions of this cultural phenomenon. Scholars generally agree that folklore encompasses the *oral traditions* (as opposed to the written traditions) of a people that have been handed down from generation to generation. Traditions considered under the field of folkloristics include:

1. prose narratives (myths, folktales, legends, memorates, *casos,* jests);
2. folksongs (ballads, *canciones, décimas, coplas);*
3. folk speech;
4. proverbs and proverbial expressions;
5. folk drama;
6. children's songs and games;
7. riddles;
8. beliefs and folk medicine;
9. folk festivals;
10. folk arts and crafts;
11. folk dance; and
12. folk gestures. In this study we focus on the first eight genres subsumed under the category of literary folklore.

We define Chicano folklore as that folklore belonging to the group of people of Mexican-American descent residing in the United States; the majority living mainly in the American Southwest: Texas, California, Arizona, New Mexico, and Colorado. Interest in Chicano folklore scholarship began early in the twentieth century with the efforts of Aurelio M. Espinosa (from New Mexico) who collected, analyzed, and published articles and books related to Hispanic folklore. Espinosa contributed serious articles and books on New Mexican-Spanish romances, folktales, children's songs and games, and other related areas. Generally regarded as an "Españolista," Espinosa was principally concerned with demonstrating that the folklore evidenced in New Mexico was a direct descendant of the folklore the original Spanish settlers introduced in the area and that it had not been "contaminated" by Mexican influences. This thesis was of course debunked by later scholars, but his collections and studies nevertheless first pointed out the richness of oral traditions extant in the Southwest. Espinosa is particularly remembered for his studies on the New Mexican romance. In his

Andándome yo paseando	While I was traveling
por las orillas del mar	along the seashore
me encontré una chaparrita	I met a petite woman
y me puse a platicar	and we started to talk
¡Mi marido, mi marido!	My husband, my husband!
¡Válgame Dios! ¿Qué haré yo?"	O my God! What shall I do?
"Siéntese aquí en ese catre.	Sit down on this cot.
Déjeme ir a conversar yo?"	I will talk to him.
"¿De quién es ese caballo	Whose horse it that
que en mi corral relinchó?"	Which hee-hawed in my corral?
"Ese es de un hermano tuyo	It belongs to your brother.
que tu padre te lo mandó	Your father sent it to you,
pa que vayas al casorio	so you could attend the wedding
de un hermano que se casó."	of one of your brothers.
"Ya me puedes ir diciendo	You can tell me now
que caballos tengo yo."	which horses belong to me.
La mujer murió a la una	The wife died at one o'clock,
y el hombre murió a las dos.[1]	the man died at two.

collections are included such famous romances as "La aparición," "Gerineldo," "Estaba señor don Gato," "El piojo y la liendre," and others. The following is a short version of "La esposa infiel":

Other scholars from New Mexico, such as Arthur León Campa and Aurora Lucero-White Lea, continued to collect and analyze the folklore of New Mexico in the decades that followed. Succeeding authors, however, began to acknowledge the great influence Mexican folklore has had on Chicano folklore. Research activity also flourished in Texas with such publications as J. Dobie's *Puro Mexicano* and Mody C. Boatright's *Mexican Border Ballads and Other Lore* in the 1930s and 1940s.

The foremost Chicano folklore scholar, however, is no doubt Américo Paredes from Texas, who has been at the forefront of folklore scholarship in general and Mexican-American folklore research in particular since the publication in 1958 of his book *With His Pistol in His Hand: A Border Ballad and Its Hero*. In the three decades since then, Paredes has published close to one hundred articles and books dealing specifically with Mexican-America folklore. His expertise and intimate knowledge of the Chicano experience led him to examine such wide ranging topics as the *corrido*, the *décima*, folk speech, folk medicine, the jest, the proverb, as well as other Chicano-related issues. His clarity of thought, perceptiveness, and incisive logic provided him with the proper tools to make serious, original contributions to the field in general and to Chicano studies in particular.

In recent years the turbulent 1960s and 1970s initiated a new awareness of the Chicano experience. The social upheavals and confrontations of this era were no doubt directly responsible for stimulating research related to and dealing with Mexican-American issues. Chicano folklore benefited directly from this upsurge in interest; the numerous books and articles published in the 1960s in various genres of folklore attest to this fact. In an issue of *Aztlán* dedicated to Mexican-American folklore and art, Américo Paredes elaborates in no uncertain terms that:

> folklore is of particular importance to minority groups such as the Mexican Americans because their basic sense of identity is expressed in a language with an "unofficial" status, different from the one used by the official culture. We can say, then, that while in Mexico the Mexican may well seek lo mexicano in art, literature, philosophy, or history—as well as in folklore—the Mexican American would do well to seek his identity in his folklore.[2]

No doubt Chicano folkloristics will continue to prosper in the future and will prove profitable in the understanding and elucidation of the Chicano character and experience.

PROSE NARRATIVE

The categories subsumed under the broad umbrella of "prose narratives" include myths, folktales, legends, *casos*, memorates, and jests. There are no true"

Chicano myth narratives as such; myths evidenced in Chicano literature derived mainly from Aztec and Mayan sources. These myths proved vitally important in the Chicano's quest for self-definition and identity in the past twenty years. It should not be surprising that Aztec myths found fertile ground in the creative thought processes of Chicanos, who, having been denied their Indian heritage in previous decades, suddenly felt a renovated affiliation with that heritage. Thus, a new political meaning was grafted into the old myth of Aztlán, the land of the Chicanos' mythic Aztec ancestors who dwelled in the American Southwest before migrating south, to Tenochtitlán (Mexico City). Early Chicano political activists and creative writers renovated these Aztec myths in their groping for a reaffirmation of their centuries-old roots in America, sense of identity which they perceived to be not wholly Mexican, not wholly American, but Chicano. *Lo indio, lo azteca, lo maya* was no longer a source of embarrassment or something to be ashamed of, but a source of pride. Through the breathtakingly beautiful myths of the Ancients, one could perceive that brown was indeed beautiful. Alurista, one of the most prominent poets of the Chicano literary renaissance, liberally sprinkles his verses with the themes of Quetzalcóatl, priest-god of the Toltecs; Kukulcán, Mayan god; Coatlicue, an Aztec mother goddess; and many other Aztec and Mayan deities to effectively convey this new-found pride.

The folktale, on the other hand, bears the stamp of both an Indian and Spanish heritage and is a rich source of Chicano folklore. The European-Spanish heritage surfaces in the fairytale or märchentype of narratives. *María Cenicienta, Caperucita Roja, Blancanieves, The Little Horse of Seven Colors, Juan y las habichuelas,* and others of this type are obviously of European origin having migrated with the Spaniards to the New World. It was inevitable, however, that contact with a large Indian population would eventually produce a syncretism of European tales with Native American ones. In addition, a significant number of Meso-American Indian tales integrated themselves into the general Mexican and Mexican-American folktale repertoire. Thus an important number of animal tales such as those pertaining to the coyote cycle originate from Native American stock.

A similar statement can be formulated for the legends. Although many came from Europe, particularly the religious legends, a good number derive from Meso-American Indian lore. Others demonstrate a decided syncretism in the type of motifs found in the structural framework. A good example of this process is evident in the *La Llorona* legend. Two strands exist and intermingle in this legend: one Mexican and one Aztec. According to the former version, *Llorona* was originally a beautiful young mestizo woman madly in love with a wealthy Spanish caballero. The fruit of this love resulted in various children (one to nine, the number varies) out of wedlock; the Spaniard having promised to eventually marry her. It came to pass that one night the young mestizo's mother was informed of her caballero's impending wedding. On the night of her lover's wedding, after peeking through the window of her lover's house witnessing the wedding scene, she returns to her own home intensely distraught. There, in a fit of rage and/or insanity, she kills all her children. Having realized her deed, she madly rushes out of her house screaming "¡Ayyyyy, mis hijos!" As punishment for this barbaric deed, she roams the waterways, any dark street or road screeching, "¡Ayyyyy, mis hijos!" forever in search of her lost children. According to the Aztec version, on the other hand, *La Lórona* was a woman who, before the conquest, predicted the fall of the Aztec empire and was seen in the streets of the Aztec capital in a white dress, long hair in disarray and screaming in anguish, "¡Ayyyy, mis hijos!" in anticipated pain of the loss to come.

Some excellent work has been done on the Mexican/Chicano legend and folktale. Juan Rael published a large collection of tales from Colorado. Stanley L. Robe from UCLA has done extensive research on tales and legends from various parts of Mexico and the Southwest. Elaine Miller published a collection of folktales from the Los Angeles area called *Mexican Folk Narrative from the Los Angeles Area* (1973). Her collection includes religious narrative such as La Virgen de Talpa and El Santo Niño de Atocha, devil narratives, the return of the dead-that is, legends depicting the apparition of dead persons, another very popular type being the dead person that returns to pay a *manda* (promise) to some saint—buried treasure, *duendes,* as well as traditional tales (animal tales, tales of magic, stupid ogre tales, and others).

Américo Paredes amply explains the usefulness of legends in exploring the character of Mexicans and Mexican Americans. In an incisive article entitled Mexican Legendry and the Rise of the Mestizo" published in 1971,[3] Paredes proposes that the "rise of the mestizo as representative of the Mexican nationality may be illuminated by the study of Mexican legendry" (p. 98). According to the author, before the "rise of the mestizo" (prenineteenth-century Mexico), legends dealt generally with supernatural, miraculous events such as the apparition of saints. As the mestizo seized power, legend content leaned toward the recounting of the deeds of flesh and blood heroes such as Heraclio Bernal, Gregorio Cortez and later, during the Mexican Revolution of 1910, the deeds and actions of the revolutionary heroes such as Pancho Villa, Emiliano Zapata, Francisco I. Madero, and others.

Recently, scholars are grappling with the new concepts of caso and memorate. These new terms are designed to meet the ever-increasing problem of defining in more precise terms the large corpus of prose narrative present in all cultures. More and more scholars are realizing that the old terminology (folktale, legend, märchen) is inadequate and too broadly based to meet the needs of rigorous scientific analysis. The terms caso, memorate, and personal experience narrative are currently used to classify a large body of narratives extant in the Mexican/Chicano folklore. The above terms generally encompass narratives that happened to the informant or to someone the informant knows. Joe Graham provides the following definition:

a relatively brief prose narrative, focusing upon a single event, supernatural or natural, in which the protagonist or observer is the narrator or someone the narrator knows and vouches for, and which is normally used as evidence or as an example to illustrate that "this kind of thing happens."[4]

Graham offers fourteen types of casos discernible by their theme and structure in Chicano folklore. The following is an example:

Caso Type I

A Mexican American becomes ill and is taken to a doctor, who either treats him, with no visible results, or says that the person is not ill. The person is taken to a *curandero* or folk practitioner, who provides the proper remedy, and the patient gets well. (p. 31)

These new areas of endeavor in folklore, such as the caso, memorate, and personal experience narrative, illustrate the richness and complexity of Mexican/Chicano culture.

An equally significant area of folklore is the *chiste* or jest. Again, Américo Paredes undertook seminal research in this genre and provided a theoretical construct for understanding the underlying basis of much of Chicano folklore in general, and Chicano jokes in particular. Paredes' basic thesis underscores the element of cultural conflict as the principal moving force generating Chicano folklore.

Much of Chicano humor derives from the confrontation of two cultures: one Mexican, Catholic, Spanish-speaking; the other Anglo, Protestant, English-speaking. A large corpus of jokes, for example, relies on Mexican-Anglo conflicts using the linguistic differences between the two cultures as points of departure. Notice the following:

A gringo was traveling on a rural Mexican road in his Cadillac when suddenly a man and his burro block his path. The gringo gets down from his car, takes off his glove, and slaps the Mexican in the face with the glove yelling, "Son-of-a-bitch!" Whereupon' the Mexican takes off his huarache, slaps the gringo in the face and yells, "B.F. Goodrich!"[5]

Here, although the Mexican does not understand the insult, he manages to outsmart the Anglo by striking the hardest blow. It is typical of Chicano humor in general that the Mexican/Chicano protagonist comes out the best in the exchange.

There is a cycle of jokes, however, where the protagonist (a Mexican immigrant) is the butt of the joke. This cycle of jokes portrays the difficulties recently arrived Mexicans have due to the differences in language. A good example of this type of joke follows:

A recently arrived Mexican immigrant who cannot read English wants to buy a coke. He sees a coke machine and takes the smallest coin he has which is a dime and inserts it in the slot. A red light flashes out reading *DIME*. The man reads it in Spanish with its equivalent meaning of "Tell me!" So the fellow looks around and whispers: "¡Dame una coca!" ("Give me a coke!)[6]

These jokes told by immigrants themselves to other immigrants serve cathartic function of relieving the stress and anxiety concomitant with moving to a foreign country.

A second basic factor that characterizes many Chicano jokes is the bilingualism expressed within the jokes as evidenced in the two examples given above. Many Chicano jokes require an understanding of both Spanish and English due to the fact that the structure of the jokes utilizes the misunderstanding of one or both languages to deliver its intended humor and punch line.

FOLKSONGS

Two of the most researched genres of Chicano folksongs are corrido and the décima. Both Arthur L. Campa and Américo Paredes have contributed substantial scholarly articles and collections of these two types of folklore.

The corrido or ballad has been and continues to be an important means of self-expression for the Chicano community. In fact, the corrido, according to Américo Paredes' theory on the renaissance of this genre, experiences its rebirth as a result of the bloody conflict between Mexicans and Anglos in the Mexican-American War of 1848. A conquered people, having been denied access to the printing press of the dominant culture, seized the corrido as a valid form of self-expression, historical documentation, and information dissemination.[7]

Most scholars agree that the corrido originally derived from the Spanish romances. Imported to America during the fifteenth and sixteenth centuries, it languished in the area until the nineteenth century; at this point in time historical events propelled it to the center stage where it became the literary instrument of protest and revolt par excellence. Paredes posits that it was the clash of cultures in the Lower Rio Grande Valley where men of Mexican descent were forced "defender su derecho con su pistola en la mano" (to defend their right with a pistol in their hand). The heroic deeds and actions of these valiant, fearless men were duly recorded in the oral history and expressive folklore of the people. Corridos were lustily and proudly sung from ranch to ranch and pueblo to pueblo, the lyrics of these depicting the exploits of Chicanos who resisted the encroachment and heavy hand of the Anglo settlers.

Paredes incisively analyzes one of these corridos in his seminal book *With His Pistol in His Hand: A Border Ballad and Its Hero*. The corrido examined in this work depicts the legend of Gregorio Cortez who, having been unjustly accused of killing a Texas sheriff, was hunted down through the state of Texas until he voluntarily surrendered to the Texas Rangers (after realizing his family had been imprisoned).

Another example of the Chicano/Anglo conflict-type corridos that vividly portrays this state of affairs is the "Corrido de Joaquín Murieta."

Yo no soy americano
pero comprendo el inglés.
Yo lo aprendí con mi hermano
al derecho y al revés.
A cualquier americano
lo hago temblar a mis pies.

Cuando apenas era un niño
huérfano a mí me dejaron.
Nadie me hizo ni un cariño,
a mi hermano lo mataron.
Y a mi esposa Carmelita,
cobardes la asesinaron.

Yo me vine de Hermosillo
en busca de oro y riqueza.
Al indio pobre y sencillo
lo defendí con fiereza.
Y a buen precio los sherifes
pagaban por mi cabeza.

A los ricos avarientos,
yo les quité su dinero.
Con los humildes y pobres
yo me quité mi sombrero.
Ay, que leyes tan injustas
fue llamarme bandolero.

A Murieta no le gusta
lo que hace no es desmentir.

I am not an American
but I understand English.
I learned it with my brother
forwards and backwards.
And any American
I make tremble at my feet.

When I was barely a child
I was left an orphan.
No one gave any love,
they killed my brother,
And my wife Carmelita,
the cowards assassinated her.

I came from Hermosillo
in search of gold and riches.
The Indian poor and simple
I defended with fierceness
And a good price the sheriffs
would pay for my head.

From the greedy rich,
I took away their money.
With the humble and poor
I took off my hat.
Oh, what laws so unjust
to call me a highwayman.

Murieta does not like
to be falsely accused.

Vengo a vengar a mi esposa,
y lo vuelvo a repetir,
Carmelita tan hermosa,
como la hicieron sufrir.

I come to avenge my wife,
and again I repeat it,
Carmelita so lovely
how they made her suffer.

Por cantinas me metí,
castigando americanos.
"Tú serás el capitán
que mataste a mi hermano.
Lo agarraste indefenso,
orgulloso americano."

Through bars I went
punishing Americans.
"You must be the captain
who killed my brother.
You grabbed him defenseless
you stuck-up American."

Mi carrera comenzó
por una escena terrible.
Cuando llegué a setecientos
ya mi nombre era temible.
Cuando llegué a mil doscientos
ya mi nombre era terrible.

My career began
because of a terrible scene.
When I got to seven hundred [killed]
then my name was dreaded.
When I got to twelve hundred
Then my name was terrible.

Yo soy aquel que domina
hasta leones africanos.
Por eso salgo al camino
a matar americanos.
Ya no es otro mi destino
¡pongan cuidado, parroquianos!

I am the one who dominates
even African lions.
That's why I go out on the road
to kill Americans.
Now my destiny is no other,
watch out, you people!

Las pistolas y las dagas
son juguetes para mí.
Balazos y puñaladas,
carcajadas para mí.
Ahora con medios cortados
ya se asustan por aquí.

Pistols and daggers
are playthings for me.
Bullets and stabbings
big laughs for me.
With their means cut off
they're afraid around here.

No soy chileno ni extraño
en este suelo que piso.
De México es California,
porque Dios así lo quiso.
Y en mi sarape cosida
traigo mi fe de bautismo.

I'm neither a Chilean nor a stranger
on this soil which I tread.
California is Mexico's
because God wanted it that way,
And in my stitched serape,
I carry my baptismal certificate.

Que bonito es California
con sus calles alineadas,
donde paseaba Murieta
con su tropa bien formada,
con su pistola repleta,
y su montura plateada.

How pretty is California
with her well-laid-out streets
where Murieta passed by
with his troops,
with his loaded pistol,
and his silver-plated saddle.

Me he paseado en California
por el año del cincuenta.
Con mi montura plateada,
y mi pistola repleta.
Y soy ese mexicano
de nombre Joaquín Murieta.

I've had a good time in California
through the year of '50 [1850].
With my silver-plated saddle
and my pistol loaded
I am that Mexican
by the name of Joaquín Murieta.[8]

Early corridos from the Lower Rio Grande Valley in Texas served as paradigms for the *guerrillero,* rebel corridos that surfaced in Mexico during Porfirio Díaz's repressive regime, one of the most famous of these corridos being "El corrido de Heraclio Bernal." The events of the Mexican Revolution of 1910 provided further material for corrido productions. The heroes of the revolution were immortalized in the lyrics of the corrido: Pancho Villa, Emiliano Zapata, Benjamín Argumedo, Francisco I. Madero, Venustiano Carranza, La Adelita, and many others.

The ever-present stream of Mexican immigrants to the United States in search of work continually replenishes the general repertoire of Chicano folk songs with Mexican corridos. Thus, literally thousands of corridos exist in the southwestern part of the United States with as varied themes as Mexican immigrant corridos ("El deportado," "Corrido de Pennsylvania," "Corrido de Texas"), corridos whose main subject is horses ("El potro lobo gatiado"), those depicting the exploits of drug and tequila smugglers ("El tequilero"), love-tragedy corridos ("Rosita Alvírez," "La 'Güera' Chavela," "Rafaelita"), those extolling the life and death of political figures such as the Kennedy corridos, and those dealing with protest. During César Chávez's farmworkers' union movement of the 1960s and 1970s, numerous songs appeared depicting the hardships and aspirations of the farmworkers. These are frequently sung at protest rallies and serve as an effective means of uniting the people in a common cause. At present the corrido is very much a vital force in ethnic identification and in expressing through its lyrics the continuing struggle for achieving social justice in America.

La décima, on the other hand, experienced its apogee in the eighteenth and nineteenth century in both Mexico and the Southwest. Américo Paredes has several articles on the décima in Texas and Arthur L. Campa has a significant collection of décimas from New Mexico. Its rigid form, however (in contrast to the flexible form of the corrido), doomed it to be discarded in favor of the more flexible corrido.

FOLK SPEECH

Chicano Spanish has recently been the focus of intense study, particularly by linguists and those interested in bilingual education. The realization by American schools and by linguists that the Spanish spoken in the Southwest differed markedly from that spoken in Spain, Mexico, and other Latin-American countries, led to a flurry of research. The most comprehensive bibliography on Chicano speech is Richard V. Teschner, Garland D. Bills, and Jerry R. Craddock's *Spanish and English of United States Hispanos: A Critical, Annotated, Linguistic Bibliography* (1975), which cites 675 items. The most fruitful work undertaken is on the aspect of code-switching (switching in the middle of a phrase, sentence, or paragraph from English to Spanish or vice versa), but the most outstanding area of research from a folklorist's point of view has been neglected. Thus, little in-depth research is available on *caló* (the jargon of the underworld or the pachuco) or other areas of folk speech. A seminal work by George C. Baker "Pachuco: An American-Spanish Argot and Its Social Function in Tucson, Arizona" (1975) [9] is still one of the best works in the field. Baker studied the speech of *pachucos* from Tucson and related this speech to the social function it played within the in-group and the out-group. Some of these words include: *carnal* (brother*), jaina* (girlfriend*), chante* (house*), ruca* (girl*), birrea* (beer*), cantón* (house*), chale* (no*), lisa* (shirt*), simón* (yes) and *refinar* (to eat). The lack of studies in this genre is indeed deplorable. José Limón, a scholar on folklore, has amply demonstrated the importance of this area in his article "The Folk Performance of 'Chicano' and the Cultural Limits of Political Ideology." Limón analyzes the failure of the folk term *Chicano* to gain widespread acceptance in the community and posits the thesis that *"in part* this failure may be attributed to the unintentional violation of the community's rules about the socially appropriate use of the term—rules keyed on the community's definition of the performance of the term as belonging to the folklore genres of nicknaming and ethnic slurs."[10] It is fairly easy to deduce from this study that if political movements are to succeed, the leaders of these movements must have an intimate and working knowledge of the people they propose to represent. One way to accomplish this is through an in-depth understanding of the cultural vectors (such as folklore) operative in the community.

PROVERBS AND PROVERBIAL EXPRESSIONS

Proverbs and proverbial expressions, entities intimately related to folk speech, form an integral part of Chicano folklore. Although used most frequently by the older generation, a recent study undertaken by Shirley Arora[11] demonstrates that the younger generations of Chicanos are indeed aware of proverbs, having been raised by a mother, father, or other family member who interspersed their speech with these colorful expressions.

A proverb may be defined as a short, succinct expression that encompasses within its words a philosophical wisdom. Examples include:

1. Más vale pájaro en mano que ver un ciento volar. (Better a bird in hand than two in the bush.)
2. Dime con quién andas y te diré quién eres. (Tell me who your friends are and I'll tell you who you are.)
3. De tal palo tal astilla. (A chip off the old block.)
4. El que con lobos anda a aullar se enseña. (He who runs around with wolves will learn how to howl.)
5. En boca cerrada no entran moscas. (In a closed mouth no flies can enter.)
6. Todo cabe en un jarrito sabiéndolo acomodar. (All can be filled in a mug if you know how to place things right.)
7. Al que madruga Dios lo ayuda. (He who rises early God helps.)
8. Dios dice: "Ayúdate que yo te ayudaré." (God helps those who help themselves.)
9. El que con niños se acuesta mojado se levanta. (He who sleeps with children wakes up wet.)[12]

The proverb, as other folklore genres prove to be, is yet another important area in which the philosophy or worldview of a people can be profitably explored. Américo Paredes, however, advised extreme caution when attempting to analyze the character of a people and warns against literal interpretation of proverbs and/or deducing Mexican/Chicano traits when taken out of context. Analysis of proverbs must be undertaken in the context in which these expressions are uttered. Otherwise, the social scientist or folklorist may be, albeit unwittingly, misled to make totally false and harmful generalizations about the character of a people. Valuable information regarding the Chicano experience can be gleaned from careful research of these entities and their use in Chicano households as demonstrated by Shirley Arora's article "Proverbs in Mexican American Tradition." Her study provides key insights into status and usage of proverbs by Chicanos in Los Angeles. For example, Arora found that frequent use of proverbs is most noticeable in the area of child-rearing, "from the inculcation of table manner—El que come y canta loco se levanta, la mano larga nunca alcanza—to the regulation of social relationships and dating behavior" (p. 59). Arora also indicates that proverbs have

a potential and may indeed be already employed for purposes of ethnic identification and group solidarity. Needless to say, more in-depth studies on proverb usage need to be undertaken to better comprehend this particular aspect of Chicano folklore.

Shirley Arora has also undertaken extensive research on proverbial comparisons in the Los Angeles area in her work *Proverbial Comparisons and Related Expressions in Spanish*. The comparison may be defined as a phrase in which the following formulaic structures appear:

> está como . . .
> tan . . . como
> tan . . . que

The exaggeration likewise employs the formulaic structures of:

> más . . . que

Arora interviewed 517 informants and collected thousands of entries. Some examples follow.

1. Más aburrido que un abogado (more boring than a lawyer) (p. 37).
2. Tan flaca que si se traga una aceituna parece que está preñada (so skinny that if she swallows an olive she looks pregnant) (p. 38).
3. Más alegre que un día de pago (as happy as payday) (p. 172).
4. Es tan avaro que no da ni los buenos días (he's so stingy that he doesn't even give a good morning) (p. 172).
5. Se repite como disco rayado (he repeats himself like a scratched record) (p. 179).

The humorous nature and originality of many of these proverbial expressions, together with the large number collected within a relatively small geographic area (greater Los Angeles), indicate the amazing creativity present in the speech of the Chicano community. It is evident in the large number of entries of both proverbs and proverbial expressions collected by Arora that a great premium is placed on language skills and language dexterity by Chicanos. Arora found in her study that more often than not people with a large repertoire of proverbial expressions elicited admiration and respect from the community.

Proverbs and proverbial expressions provide a strong affectivity factor toward the Spanish language and are no doubt one important reason for the high premium placed on preserving the Spanish language.

The wealth of Spanish proverbs and the witticism inherent in proverbial expressions contribute to the widespread folk belief that Spanish is one of the most delightful languages in the world. This folk belief in turn brings us to closer understanding of why a conquered people, after one hundred years of political and cultural domination, tenaciously clings to one of their cultural manifestations-the Spanish language.

FOLK THEATRE

The folk theatre of the Chicano, like Mexican- and Latin-American theatre, traces its roots to the Spanish *conquistadores* and their religious plays. The early missionaries, interested in converting the Indians of the New World, discovered that, due to the differences in language representations of biblical and religious stories, drama provided an effective means of indoctrinating them into the Catholic faith. Thus, early theatrical works in the western hemisphere were religious plays in which the Indians themselves played major roles and which were extremely popular with the faithful. These plays generally took place in the church atrium and were presented to the populace on specific holy days such as Christmas or Easter Sunday. When New Mexico was settled in the seventeenth century, works that had been successful in Mexico migrated with the Spanish and Mexican settlers into what is now the American Southwest. Arthur Campa and Aurora Lucero-White Lea have both collected folk plays from this region. Among those collected is *Coloquio de los Pastores*, which, according to Lea, "represents that older type of traditional Nativity play which was presented in the village church on Christmas Eve in lieu of Midnight Mass when that village had no resident priest."[14]

Other popular plays collected include: *La aurora del nuevo día, Adán y Eva, Los tres reyes, El niño perdido, Las cuatro apariciones de Nuestra Señora de Guadalupe, and Los moros y cristianos.* One should also mention the pastorelas or shepherd's plays performed during the Christmas season and which are still being enacted today. Folk theatre influenced to some extent present-day Chicano theatre, particularly that of Luis Valdez. Like the corrido, present-day Chicano theatre is being effectively used as a vehicle to convey and express the injustices perpetuated on the Mexican/Chicano by Anglo society.

CHILDREN'S SONGS AND GAMES

As is true of most of the other genres of folklore, children's songs and games from the Chicano Southwest evidence basically the same categories and specimens as those from Spain. A rather flexible division of songs and games played or sung by or for children is attempted in the following major categories:

1. *canciones de cuna* (lullabyes) "Duérmete mi niño";
2. *canciones de manos y dedos* "Tortillitas" (hand and finger games);
3. *rondas* "Naranja dulce";
4. *retahilas* "El castillo de Chuchurumbel";
5. *canciones* "La muñeca";
6. *conjuros* "Sana, sana colita de rana"; and
7. miscellaneous "escondidas," "matatena," "los encantados," "rayuela."

Those of us who grew up in a Spanish-speaking environment can nostalgically remember songs and games of yore such as:

Duérmete mi niño
que tengo que hacer
lavar los pañales
ponerme a coser.

Tortillitas de manteca
pa mamá que está contenta.
Tortillitas de cebado
pa papá que está enojado.

Naranja dulce
limón partido
dame un abrazo
que yo te pido.

Go to sleep my child
I have work to do
wash the diapers
and some sewing too.

Little tortillas made of lard
for mommy, for happy is she.
Little tortillas made of barley
for daddy, for angry is he.

Sweet orange
lemon is cut
Give me a hug
I ask of you.

Doña Blanca está encerrada
en pilares de oro y plata
romperemos un pilar
para que salga Doña Blanca.

Doña Blanca is imprisoned
within pillars of gold and silver
let us break one of these pillars
so Doña Blanca can be free.[15]

Paredes made a revealing observation with regard to children's songs, and games and cultural conflict—the basic thread that runs throughout Chicano folklore. As innocuous and free from anxiety and conflict as children's games may appear, the opposite state of affairs is discovered upon close analysis. Experts agree that children oftentimes express their fears and anxieties through play. Paredes pointed this out in a game played by Chicano children that exemplifies the point. The game is "la roña" also known as "la mancha" (tag). In this game children flee from the one that has "la roña" and the latter in turn tries to "touch" or "tag" the others. In Texas the game is known as "la correa," a name given to immigration officers. Thus, by implication, the Texas children enact the real-life situation of Immigration and Naturalization Services officers trying to capture undocumented workers.[16]

RIDDLES

Riddles comprise another area of Chicano folklore. Archer Taylor, a folklorist from Berkeley, provides us with the classic definition of a "true riddle:" "questions that suggest an object foreign to the answer and confound the hearer by giving a solution that is obviously correct and entirely unexpected."[17]

More recently, Elli Kongas-Maranda has suggested that "the riddle is a structural unit, which necessarily consists of two parts: the riddle image and the riddle answer. In a riddling situation, these two parts are 'recited' by two different parties."[18] *La adivinanza,* as it is called in Spanish, is an integral part of the expressive culture of the Chicano. However, few studies have been undertaken on Chicano riddling habits. An exception is John M. McDowell's *Children's Riddling* (1979). McDowell's in-depth study offers extremely relevant conclusions as to the function of riddles in children's ludic activities. For McDowell,

> Riddles in the modern, industrial society serve as models of synthetic and analytic thinking. They encourage children to discover the archetypical set of commonalities binding diverse experimental realms into a single, coherent world view; and at the same time, they require children to confront the tentative status of conceptual systems, thereby fostering a flexibility of cognition evidently of some utility in a great many cultural settings.[19]

The following are some popular examples of riddles common throughout Mexico, Latin America, and the Southwest:[20]

As is apparent, the adivinanza challenges the intellect and the reasoning processes by offering descriptions that are close enough to resemble the objects yet so hidden between the texture (metaphors, similes) of the words as to yield them difficult to answer. The riddle, a thoroughly social act in itself in that at least two people are required for it to function, provides the players with an excellent instrument to play with language. Different opportunities are offered: rhyming schemes (nos. 1–5); disconnecting and connecting various morphemes (nos. 1 and 5); deceiving metaphorical images (nos. 2 and 3) and alliterative, onomatopoetic sounds (no. 4).

Agua pasa por mi casa
cate de mi corazón.
Si no me adivinas ésta
eres puro burro cabezón.
                    (aguacate)

Water passes through my house
my beloved.
If you do not answer this one
you are a thick-headed donkey.
                    (avocado)

Adivíname esta adivinanza
que se pela por la panza.
                    (la naranja)

Answer this riddle for me:
You peel it from the tummy.
                    ([navel] oranges)

Una vieja larga y seca
que le escurre la manteca.
                    (la vela)

A tall, skinny old lady
that drips lard.
                    (the candle)

Tito, Tito capotito
sube al cielo
y tira un grito.

(el cohete)

Tito, Tito, little cape
fly up in the sky
and give out a scream.

(the firecracker)

McDowell perceived two different sets of riddles in the repertoire of the children interviewed (Chicano children from a barrio in Austin, Texas in 1972).

1. a collection of riddles learned at school, from Anglo children, from the media (television, radio) and
2. a set of more traditional ones learned at home from parents, relatives, and/or peers.

One significant function deduced in this Texas study is the proposition that riddles serve enculturation purposes, (enculturation being defined as "the process of induction, wherein the individual acquires competency in his own culture, or the kinds of knowledge requisite to fulfillment of recognized social roles."[21]) In the acquisition of the riddling/habits of the dominant society one is also being acculturated into this dominant culture. The riddle, then, aside from serving the pleasure function manifest in all ludic play, equally serves other cognitive endeavors.

FOLK BELIEF AND FOLK MEDICINE

The folk-belief system of the Chicano community, particularly as it deals with folk medicine and curanderismo, is one of the most controversial areas of scholarship in Chicano folklore. In a revealing article by Beatrice A. Roeder, "Health Care Beliefs and Practices Among Mexican Americans: A Review of the Literature,"[22] the author identified four stages in the trajectory of folk, belief scholarship vis-à-vis Mexican Americans. These stages include:

1. works dealing with the sources and historical development of Mexican folk medicine,
2. pioneer works of documentation—that is, collections done between 1894–1954,
3. the 1950–1960s—Lyle Saunders and his follower's era (who seek to understand Mexican American health practices by placing them in their cultural context), and
4. the 1970s—includes revisionist Chicano scholars who vigorously challenge previous research findings and take a socioeconomic approach

to understanding Mexican medical practices as opposed to a "cultural context" approach.

The basic controversy between the last two major groups centers upon the question of whether the Mexican-American folk belief system is largely responsible for the Chicano's "inability" or reluctance to utilize and take advantage of modern "scientific" medical services. In other words, this perspective posits that it is the Chicanos' own cultural restraints that hamper them in obtaining adequate medical services. Chicano revisionists such as Nick C. Vaca, Miguel Montiel, and Armando Morales argue on the other hand that the culture-as-culprit thesis, or "cultural determinism" as they label it, is a "myth" propagated by and used as a rationalization tool by the Anglo-dominant society, which, through institutionalized racism (such as segregated schools, lack of bilingual personnel), prevents Chicanos from attaining proper medical care. A glaring example is found in Joe S. Graham's article "The Role of the *Curandero* in the Mexican American Folk Medicine System in West Texas." In his introductory remarks he states:

In West Texas the term "scientific medicine" became almost synonymous with "Anglo medicine"—and still is. To my knowledge, there is not one licensed Mexican American doctor practicing in the whole rural region between Del Rio and El Paso, separated by over four hundred miles—this in spite of the fact that over half of the population is Mexican American.[23]

What Graham failed to do in this otherwise sensitive article was to point out

1. that Texas has had a de facto segregated system (Chicano schools are generally much inferior to all white schools),
2. that medical schools in the United States previous to the 1970s had racial quotas and it was next to impossible for a black, Mexican American, or a woman to be admitted, and
3. that border-area residents in Texas did heavily utilize Spanish-speaking Mexican doctors from Mexico (who in addition tend to be less expensive than their American counterparts).

The above issues were totally neglected in the article, which instead zeroed in on the culture-as-culprit theory.

As can be deduced from the expressed concerns of the above investigators, folk medicine has been largely studied from a social scientist's perspective and is very much the concern of the anthropologist and sociologist.

The inclusion of belief and folk medicine in this study, however, is due to their close proximity to the legend, the caso, the memorate, and personal-experience narrative. Folk beliefs cover a wide range of cosmological and human experiences and are perceived by some scholars as man's attempt at "scientific" explanation for an otherwise incomprehensible event. Beliefs are interconnected with prose narratives in the sense that for any, given belief there may be a "story" explaining this belief. In addition to a narrative explicating the belief, additional narratives corroborating the truthfulness or efficacy of this belief may be present. These narratives may surface in

1. the form of a personal experience,
2. an experience that happened to a close relative or acquaintance, or
3. an experience that happened to some unknown person.

For example, numerous folk beliefs are associated with the Catholic religion.

A common belief is the following:

A *manda* (promise) to a saint is sacred. One must always keep these promises or suffer the consequences.

Generally, when the above belief is stated, a narrative or series of narratives will illustrate this specific point. The casos described earlier are frequently corroborating stories of a belief. There are literally thousands of beliefs. The following are but a few examples:

1. belief in the existence of witches *(brujas)*
2. belief in *curanderas (os)* or folk healers
3. belief in the devil
4. belief in la Llorona
5. belief in ghosts, evil spirits, *duendes,* werewolves, vampires, headless riders, *espantos* (supernatural beings both good and bad), poltergeists, kobolds, bewitched areas or places *(lugares encantados)*
6. belief in buried treasures
7. belief in objects to put hexes or prevent bewitchment

8. belief in folk medicine and folk ailments such as *susto* (shock*), empacho, aire* (air*), caída de la mollera* (fallen fontenelle)*, mal puesto* (bewitched)

For each of the above entities there are thousands of narratives in existence detailing how in fact such an event was witnessed by someone or how it actually happened to a specific individual. All of these narratives, of course, are jewels in the rough that when discovered by a literary genius can transform them into, veritable gems. For example, the Colombian novelist Gabriel García Márquez utilized hundreds of folk beliefs in the process of constructing the magical-fantastic universe of his masterpiece *One Hundred Years of Solitude (1967).* One needs to mention only three well-known Chicano works—" . . . *y no se lo tragó la tierra*" by Tomás Rivera; *Bless Me, Ultima* by Rudolfo Anaya; and *El diablo en Texas* by Aristeo Brito—to realize the impact of folk beliefs on Chicano literature. Folk beliefs, then, are an integral and significant element in Chicano folklore (and of course in the folklore of all cultures) and certainly merit continued investigation.

This necessarily short introduction to Chicano folklore provides the reader with a greater appreciation of the cultural phenomenon called folklore and with a better understanding of the richness of Chicano culture.

Endnotes

1. Aurelio M. Espinosa, *Romancero de Nuevo México* (Madrid: Consejo Superior de Investigaciones Científicas, 1953), P. 66.

2. Américo Paredes, "Folklore, Lo Mexicano and Proverbs," *Aztlàn*, vol. 13, nos. 1 and 2 (Spring and Fall 1982), p. 1.

3. Américo Paredes, "Mexican Legendry and the Rise of the Mestizo," in Wayland D. Hand, ed., *American Folk Legend: A Symposium* (Los Angeles: University of California Press, 1971), pp. 97–107.

4. Joe Graham, "The Caso: An Emic Genre of Folk Narrative," in Richard Bauman and Roger D. Abrahams, eds., *"And Other Neighborly Names" Social Process and Cultural Image in Texas Folklore* (Austin: University of Texas Press, 1981), p. 19.

5. Collected from the personal repertoire of a student in my folklore class at the University of California at Irvine in 1980.

6. María Herrera-Sobek, "Verbal Play and Mexican Immigrant Jokes," *Southwest Folklore*, vol. 4 (Winter 1980), p. 16. See also María Herrera-Sobek, *The Bracero Experience: Elitelore Versus Folklore* (Los Angeles: UCLA Latin American Center Publications, 1979).

7. For further discussion on the topic, see Américo Paredes, "The Mexican Corrido, Its Rise and Fall," in Mody C. Boatright, Wilson M. Hudson, and Allen Maxwell, eds., *Folk Travelers* (Austin: Texas Folklore Society Publications, 1957), pp. 91–105.

8. "Corrido de Joaquín Murieta," collected by Philip Sonnichsen and printed in "Texas-Mexican Border Music," vols. 2 and 3, corridos 1 and 2, Arhollie Records, 1975.

9. This particular study appears in Eduardo Hernández-Chávez, A. D. Cohen, and A.F. Beltrano, eds. *El lenguaje de los chicanos* (Arlington: Center for Applied Linguistics, 1975).

10. José Limón, "The Folk Performance of 'Chicano' and the Cultural Limits of Political Ideology," in Bauman and Abrahams, eds., "*And Other Neighborly Names*, p. 197.

11. Shirley Arora, "Proverbs in Mexican American Tradition," *Aztlán*, vol. 13, nos. 1 and 2 (Spring and Fall 1982), pp. 43–69.

12. Collected from my grandmother Susana Escamilla de Tarango.

13. Shirley Arora, *Proverbial Comparisons and Related Expressions in Spanish* (Berkeley: University of California Press, 1977).

14. See Aurora Lucero-White Lea, *Literary Folklore of the Hispanic Southwest* (San Antonio: Naylor Company, 1953), p. 5.

15. Collected from my grandmother Susana Escamilla de Tarango.

16. Américo Paredes, "El folklore de los grupos de origen mexicano," *Folklore Americano*, no. 14, año 16 (1966), p. 158.

17. As quoted in John Holmes McDowell, *Children's Riddling* (Bloomington: Indiana University Press, 1979), p. 18.

18. Elli Kongas-Maranda is quoted in McDowell, *Children's Riddling*, p. 20.

19. McDowell, *Children's Riddling*, p. 20.

20. Collected from my grandmother Susana Escamilla de Tarango.

21. McDowell, *Children's Riddling*, p. 222.

22. This article appears in *Aztlán*, vol. 13, nos. 1 and 2 (Spring and Fall 1982), pp. 223–56.

23. Joe S. Graham, "The Role of the *Curandero* in the Mexican American Folk Medicine System in West Texas," in Wayland D. Hand, ed., *American Folk Medicine* (Berkeley: University of California Press, 1976), p. 176.

On Chicano Music in the United States

Carlos F. Ortega

A term long in use and applied to music and artists with a connection to the Chicano community, can the idea of Chicano music be defined and qualified? Growing up in Los Angeles, my experience is linked to Chicano music: As a musician, a teacher in Chicano Studies, developing musical projects on radio, and finally, writing on the subject itself. Over the years I have questioned the exactness of the term 'Chicano music.' There has always been a sense of ambiguity. Is there an exact definition or is it a working concept? Are there reference points? Does it refer to an era? Is it a sound? The scrutiny of these questions may answer or attempt to answer what Chicano music can mean; not just to musicians but also to the audience. I am no longer surprised, for example, when students enrolled in my Chicano/Latino music course refer to Chicano music as "pocho" music, low rider music, a narco-corrido or any music with Spanish lyrics. The list is extensive. Yet, I can also understand because what we call Chicano music is something not taught in public schools. And even if students listen to Chicano music at home, I doubt if an academic discussion of what is being listened to will take place. The goal of this essay then is to bring some clarification on Chicano music as a form of cultural expression.

The most obvious of my concerns is the manner by which the term Chicano music is used. Some authors use the term in a broad context and without clear definitions or clear parameters for locating the term within its historical and political context, at times rendering the term confusing. José Angel Gutiérrez, for example, writing on the roots of Chicano music paints a broad canvass of what appears to be every musical influence from the indigenous, to European, and African experience in Mexico and the Southwest United States as a source of Chicano music.[1] He starts with indigenous music, beginning with the Olmecs who lived in the present day Mexican states of Veracruz and Tabasco almost 1,200 years ago. Gutiérrez acknowledges the significance of this group as the first civilization in the Americas and devotes space in discussing their social organization. Musically, there are two primary instruments mentioned in his essay: The conch or *caracol*, made from a seashell and the drum. The caracol was used primarily for signaling others and not music per se. Later the Olmecs did develop a drum and over time it became an integral part of Mesoamerican religious functions.

From this vantage point, Gutiérrez moves linearly as he discusses African and Spanish influences (drumming and guitar/song styles respectively). Into the present era, key artists are discussed who presumably help to develop Chicano music. I say presumably, because he never really says who or when this occurred. He refers to the great Tejana singer, Lydia Mendoza, for example, as a "Chicana recording star." Not wanting to nitpick, I wonder if Mrs. Mendoza, who began recording in the 1920s, saw herself as a Chicana in the decades of the

1930s, 40s, 50s, or even 60s; though Lydia Mendoza most likely referred to herself as Tejana. What made Mendoza so important, besides her voice, was here connection to her audience: working-class Mexicans. In those turbulent decades, especially during the Great Depression, her music spoke to the experience and spirit of those excluded by society.[2]

While we can identify musical influences in contemporary music, indigenous roots (in terms of instrumentation) are not clearly evident in Chicano music - played traditionally or with new arrangements. Perhaps the closest we come is with Los Lobos, who's recording of 'La Bamba,' as close to the Ritchie Valens version as one can find, segues into *son jarocho* as the rock version fades out. Or listen to 'Be Still,' which uses the *huapango* style effectively.[3] Yet even these renditions reflect the fusion of European instruments and African rhythms by indigenous peoples and not the pre-Columbian rhythms played by groups such as the Olmecs. On the other hand, in his live review, Rubén Guevara, would include a ballet folklorico performing pre-Columbian dances.

In reading Gutiérrez's essay, I searched for a location where one could say, "This is where Chicano music begins," a point never made clear. Chicano music simply exists.

Another essay, which moves with broad strokes, is by Robert Rivera-Ojeda. He writes: "The history of musica Chicana dates back to the mid 1800s; prior to and after the Mexican American War. In reality, it dates back to the landing of Cortez at Veracruz in 1519.[4] He cites Américo Paredes as his source and I went back to check what Paredes said. In fact, Paredes was speaking of Mexico as a "cultural entity" that began with the arrival of Cortez, though not necessarily in the context of music.[5] The rest of Ojeda's essay addresses the emergence of Tejano music and for the most part he covers this history quite well, but like Gutiérrez, Rivera-Ojeda subtly gives this entire history the moniker of Chicano music. The problem I feel is his use of the term Chicano music within the historical context of Tejano conjunto music. His perspective defines Chicano music as early as the 1920s.[6] While the need to categorize social phenomena is a feature of academic writing, I cannot help but wonder how Narciso Martínez, Bruno Villareal and Santiago Jiménez, Sr. identified themselves. And while there was a stage in Tejano music referred to as *La Onda Chicana*, it did not emerge until the late 1960s. Now some Tejanos might agree (with his assessment) that Chicano music is a Texas creation, but Chicanos in California would say otherwise.

In addition to using Chicano music in a broad context, the term can also be contradictory and ambiguous, depending to whom you speak. In general, many are in agreement that Chicano music is a dynamic fusion of musical influences, or an attempt to reclaim the past, especially in musical genres. Connected to Chicano music is the use of language. That is, the use of English, Spanish and Spanglish within the lyrical context of a song. I will explore these possibilities further on in the essay. Reyes and Waldman, for example, add to this concern when they write:

> While not all these musicians and bands - and their audiences - called or call themselves 'Chicanos,' they come from Mexican American backgrounds or offer a blend of American and Latino sound that we call Chicano rock 'n' roll.[7]

Another insight comes from Rafael Pérez-Torres who writes that according to some critics: "Cultural mestizaje at times has been viewed as a type of assimilation." He cites Manuel Peña's notion of how Tejano music "oscillates" between 'authenticity' and 'assimilation.'[8] In Peña's 1985 book, *The Texas-Mexican Conjunto,* he depicts the conjunto style as a resilient cultural product of the working class and orquesta music as an "example of assimilationist desires" sought by the Tejano middle class. In other words, Peña believes conjunto music (made up of the accordion, bajo sexto, upright bass or tololoche, and drums) is more 'organic' and rooted in the lives of the working class. On the other hand, the upscale orquesta (consisting of a fifteen to twenty piece orquestra, without accordion and bajo sexto, and rooted in the styles of American swing bands), represents a form of cultural disloyalty.[9] Pérez-Torres writes: This disloyalty stems from the contradictory position of an emergent Chicano middle class that does not identify with the working class but that, in turn, is not accepted by a xenophobic American society.[10] But why would Pérez-Torres even refer to a 'Chicano' middle class when Peña refers to this group as Tejano? Here again: Is 'Chicano' a generic term or is there a specific definition?

Instead of cultural disloyalty let's consider other possibilities. Are musical forms ascribed ideological positions as Peña asserts? Or is it also possible to conceive that cultural influences shape the ideological contours of a musician's choice to play certain types of music?[11] The notion of cultural change is the subject of literature too extensive to address here. The question should be: Can change be the result of conquest, accident or choice. To say disloyalty is to draw a picture of something planned an attempt to abandon an aspect of culture. For some time now, anthropologists and sociologists have worked with the concept of 'transculturation' as a means of understanding what or why change occurs.

Ethnomusicologist Margaret Kartomi has defined 'transculturation' as a "process of cultural transformation marked by the influx of new cultural elements and the loss or alteration of existing ones."[12] For many, the "alterations" are real; felt from generation to generation. Yet, depending on the individual it is possible to situate oneself between those changes in order to create a bicultural experience. Let us also define our terms. Gutiérrez places music within its cultural context. He writes: "Each succeeding generation and civilization builds upon that of the previous one in such areas as musical form, rhythm, instrumentation, composition, arrangement, and utility."[13] There is no disloyalty here, just a process felt in all cultures. Another term that needs clarification is 'Chicano.' It is a concept, an expression of a people's history. In Mexico, the word 'Chicano' would refer to the poor and/or uneducated. But 'Chicano,' according to musician Rubén Guevara, became a "statement of pride and defiance by student activists in the sixties."[14]

We'll come back to this notion momentarily, but for now let us assume that if Guevara is right, and I believe he is, then this definition (of Chicano) clearly visualizes the concept of Chicano music. While one can say Chicano music is "anything that has to do with Mexicans" or based on 'lo mexicano,' or is an 'East L.A. thing,' we still need a better sense of the term.

THE DIMENSIONS OF CHICANO MUSIC

Determining what constitutes Chicano music requires a sound concept enabling the student researcher to zero in on the parameters of the subject of study. Pérez-Torres has come as close to anyone I know at achieving this level of exactness. He uses the term Chicano music:

...to indicate music that thematically - in terms of both lyrics and music - situates itself within a context of Chicano cultural production. The music forms a kind of hybrid creation, one that acknowledges both African American and Latino art forms and that evokes a cultural as well as at times, historical and political connection to Chicano and Latino social communities.[15]

From this vantage point we can begin to narrow down our search for meaning in Chicano music. Pérez-Torres uses the word, hybridity, a tendency to absorb musical influences while at the same time expressing a unique Chicano sound and connection to Chicano identity and place. He points to Los Lobos in their 1978 debut album *Just Another Band from East L.A.* ' or Kid Frost in his 1992 album' *East Side Story.*' In each case the artists utilize influences as diverse as Tejano, rock, and the blues, as did Los Lobos, or hip hop and rap, as did Kid Frost. In the latter, language use by Kid Frost demonstrates a concern with "the naming and placing of self through linguistic mixture." As such Chicano artists have used English, Spanish, Caló, and street slang in order to accomplish this connection.

If characterized by the fusion of music to create a synthesis, Chicano music also reflects how language is used; whether straight ahead English, Spanish, slang, or Caló. There is also language mixing within a song, a process referred to as code- switching, the practice of using two languages simultaneously. Thematically, Chicano music contains social and/or political lyrics, which speak to concerns affecting the Chicano community. Pérez-Torres analyzes the work of numerous groups, such as Rage Against the Machine and determines that within the context of their lyrics, musical influences and political positions, they constitute Chicano music.[16]

Add to this the idea of the word 'Chicano' referring to a statement of pride and defiance, then we have, a situation where musical artists strive to create a sound reflecting their community and the use of language that leads to a cultural connection. No one else may get it, but within the community, the music speaks loud and clear. However, whereas Pérez-Torres speaks to contemporary musical developments and examples like Los Lobos and Kid Frost in determining what he means by Chicano music, it is just as important to turn back the pages and search those locations directing us to the creation of Chicano music.

CORRIDOS AND SONGS

I begin my music course with an examination of the corrido; its history and evolution but also a textual analysis of the lyrics. We analyze *El Corrido de los Oprimidos* (Ballad of the Oppressed). Composed in 1821, as Mexico gained its independence, students delve into the ideas of the unnamed composer and his take on the independence movement. The lyrics enable them to see and understand the power of this genre and understand why the corrido reflects the 'editorial pages of the poor' as Merle Simmons once wrote. The composer concludes independence was a sham for indigenous people because they never achieved equality. According to Luis Leal, Professor of Chicano Studies at the University of California, Santa Barbara and Américo Paredes, Professor of English and Folklore, University of Texas, Austin, the corrido has a long and diverse history in the American Southwest. Early Spanish explorations saw the creation of settlements providing a cultural base for individuals to create different forms of cultural expression. In his study of the corrido, Leal makes mention of the 'corrido in Aztlán, no doubt reflecting his understanding of the concept within the literature of the Chicano movement.[17] Aztlán meant more than just the legendary homeland of the Aztecs; in the Chicano Movement, Aztlán came to mean the Southwest, but more importantly, a homeland. That is, he distinguishes between the Mexican corrido and the Chicano corrido.

The Chicano corrido has all the characteristics of the Mexican corrido but, now and then, slight changes emerge reflecting the experiences of Chicanos and Anglos, which help lay the foundation for the use of hybridity that Pérez-Torres writes about. One corrido, 'La Guerra Mundial' ('The World War') from the early 20th century shows the effects of this encounter:

Cantando desde el 'number one'
Cantando hasta el 'number two'
No era el 'Spanish influenza'
Era el 'American flu.'

Paredes wrote numerous studies regarding the border corrido. One example concerned the "corrido of intercultural conflict," a corrido that focused on the Mexican experience with Anglo Americans in Texas. This particular corrido took on many themes and whether the individual Mexican was guilty or not, within the text of these corridos became a hero. Paredes writes:

Not all border men who shot it out with the law were completely blameless individuals defending their rights. But so keen was the Mexican sense of injustice against Anglo domination, so vivid the pattern of intercultural in the corrido, that sometimes an outlaw with no conscience of social or political justice was elevated into a hero of border conflict.[18]

This style of corrido becomes the hallmark for capturing the Chicano experience of the twentieth century.

Another type of corrido that Paredes collected was one that addressed the issue of assimilation. These songs were usually humorous but also reflected the experience of culture change. The use of the word *pocho,* especially in the 1950s reflected a particular disdain for U.S.-born Mexican Americans. In *Los Mexicanos que Hablan Inglés,* however, the composer captures the experiences of Mexican immigrants who attempt to use English:

Y *jau-dididu mai fran*
En ayl si yu tumora
Para decir 'diez reales'
Dicen *dola yene cuora.*
And 'how-dee-do, my friend,
And I'll see you tomorrow.'
When they want to say 'diez reales,'
They say 'dollar and a quarter'[19]

Corridos were at their greatest peak in the late nineteenth century and early twentieth century. Thematically, corridos of intercultural conflict reflected a sense of resistance and a stand against the perceived or real injustice that existed at the time. The late Guillermo Hernández, professor of English at the University of California, Los Angeles, collected songs for a study that illuminated the diversity of the Chicano experience. Urbanization, effects of culture change through language, cultural transitions from oral traditions to written composition, effects of war, pachucos, and the war hero were some of the themes one might hear in the first half of the twentieth century. He writes:

The effects of culture change can be clearly observed in the linguistic varieties employed in the two dialogues that form part of this collection ('Street Dialogue' and the 'Pachuco and the Tarzan'). In both of these, standard Spanish speech alternates with regionalisms, archaisms, slang, and Anglicisms; in their bilingual humor they convey interesting examples of attitudes towards languages and cultures in contact.[20]

Do the songs illustrated by Hernández constitute Chicano music? I am not sure. However, these themes are important for they capture events affecting the community - all driven by politics, economics, and culture. Here again is a clear attempt to capture the conditions faced by Chicanos as seen through culture change and intercultural conflict. Some of these issues would again emerge during the Chicano movement. Perhaps such themes then set the stage for what was to come during the decade of the sixties and seventies. It does make sense since during the period under review Chicano exclusion from the larger U.S. society was the accepted practice of the data.

One thing is clear as we look back to the early examples of the corrido: Its lyrical content is tied to the epic poetry of Europe. As this structure made its way into the Americas, it began to take shape as a chronicle of events reflecting the history of Mexico, the border and later, Chicanos. The fact that corridos are still composed in the 21st century attests to its power as a document of current events and cultural expression.

THE FOUNDATIONS OF CHICANO MUSIC

During the 1940s, music had a tremendous impact on Latino communities but also on the larger musical community. From the standpoint of commercial radio and recordings, music was as popular and diverse as one could imagine. In different ways, the Chicano community borrowed and reshaped these musical trends, and a close look at these developments highlights the strengthening of the musical foundations that created Chicano music two decades later. From the east coast came the emerging orchestra of Machito and His Afro-Cubans. From the start of the decade, Machito and his musical director Mario Bauza developed a unique orchestra sound that pushed the mambo onto dance floors around the country. Rooted in a West African Congolese cult, Machito developed a powerful rhythm section that was Afro Cuban at heart, added strong brass arrangements still heard in salsa music today, and perfected the *son montuno,* an improvisational section that came to influence jazz musicians of the day. The popularity of the mambo was evident throughout the decade and in the fifties was still going strong thanks to the efforts of Tito Puente and Pérez Prado.[21]

U.S. musicians were also riding high on the popularity of swing music and a piano style that made its way from New Orleans, called boogie woogie. Both of these developments were to capture dancing audiences throughout the country, although for a time, the boogie was more rooted to the Black musical experience. The swing bands of Benny Goodman and others hit stages in Los Angeles. Their recordings were available. Even segregated Los Angeles, however, could not keep this music away from young Mexican Americans and Afro Americans. They went deep into this music as a form of cultural expression. On the boogie side of things, a brilliant saxophonist named Louis Jordan

landed in Los Angeles after playing some years with the Count Basie Orchestra in Kansas City. He was looking for a sound not as big as that of an orchestra, but effective enough to cause the audience to jump and dance. Because he was long connected to the blues, Jordan began to experiment with his new five piece band, the Tympani Five, and ended up creating what is known as 'jump blues,' a style that many now believe was the forerunner to rock 'n' roll in the 1950s.[22] His recording of *Caldonia* in 1945 clearly demonstrates the influence of Jordan's innovation.

Another popular form emerging from the east coast was a street style known as doo-wop. Grounded in harmony and acapella singing, this sound remained popular throughout the early sixties. It should be noted, what some writers characterize as a Black sound, many east coast groups were racially mixed, Blacks, Latinos and Whites. They were not bothered by the segregationist attitudes of the day and joined together to form very hip music for young people.

All these ingredients need to be mentioned because they formed the base of sounds young Mexican Americans would begin to fuse and synthesize during the late 1940s. As music progressed into the 1950s, the next generation of Mexican Americans would continue the mix, and rock music, which was now popular, would become part of the fusion. Thus, when Pérez-Torres speaks of hybridity, musically or linguistically, we can see a process that has been at work through much of the twentieth century, and with this knowledge we can now move into the early stages of what we know as Chicano music.

During the 1940s, Los Angeles was awash in bitter racial battles with young Mexican Americans who called themselves Pachucos as seen in the Sleepy Lagoon Murder Case (1942) and the Zoot Suit Riots (1943). Strident in their cultural space they did not fit into the world of their parents. They had seen too much of 'the other side' -the world of popular music, dance, and film. They were part of a world were English seemed to be everywhere; if not at home then at school, magazines, radio and the movie house. This is not to say they did not speak Spanish because the great majority did. They were bilingual and now bicultural. Not accepted by the larger society, and segregated in school, from popular dance halls, and restaurants in Hollywood. So, they created their own form of expression, manifested through the zoot suit, linguistically through the use of Caló - unfortunately characterized as criminal speech. Then, there was the music. While Pachucos could sit with anyone and sing rancheras or corridos, they began to express their musicality through their tastes in swing music, the mambo and, as Pachucos shared more of their experiences with young Afro Americans (who also knew something about being segregated), they learned the blues and boogie woogie.

Musicians Lalo Guerrero and Don Tosti began organizing bands in order to compose, record and perform music that would speak to the Mexican-origin community in Los Angeles.[23] This would eventually find expression in different parts of the Southwest. Lalo Guerrero, for example, had been in Los Angeles for over a decade and during this time sang with Mexican trios, usually in restaurants or at cultural activities. He found it confining to be a musician relegated to the same style, the same venues. He wanted to explore other avenues of style and interest, in spite of segregation and racial attitudes. In the early forties, Jack Teagarden asked Don Tosti to join his jazz band. Because of his skill with the upright bass, toured for almost eight years and heard on hundreds of recording. He also played with the orchestras of Charlie Barnett, Les Brown and Jimmy Dorsey. But he returned to Los Angeles tired of the road and looking for other possibilities. The L.A. club scene provided an avenue for jazz expressions. Both of these men knew of the Sleepy Lagoon Murder Case, which in 1942 had caused great fear in the community due to the scandalous trial that ensued. They also understood the fallout that existed in the city following the Zoot Suit Riots in 1943. To be Pachuco was to be viewed as a pariah. The city even went so far as to ban the wearing of the Zoot Suit in order to keep things calm.

Yet both of these men formed bands that in the late 1940s went into studios to record songs that would put a unique slant on the social realities of Los Angeles. Both artists borrowed from the popularity of the mambo, swing, boogie, and jump blues. Lyrically, both utilized Pachuco Caló and also lyrics considered risque by the morally upstanding community of the day. Lalo Guerrero y Sus Cinco Lobos released 'Chicas Patas Boogie,' which was later heard in Luis Valdez's play and film, Zoot Suit. 'Muy Sabroso Blues,' and 'Mambito' all demonstrate Guerrero's ability to fuse various styles of music and arranged each in such a way so as to speak to young and old. Don Tosti and his Pachuco Boogie Boys recorded 'Pachuco Boogie' (1948).[24] 'Pachuco Boogie' eventually sold 2 million copies, unique for a record that upheld the Pachuco experience five years after the Zoot Suit riots and six years after the Sleepy Lagoon Murder Case. Besides the use of Caló, Don Tosti used scat-singing and blues harmonies. While some Spanish-language radio stations refused to play

the song, Anglo DJ's programmed black R & B aimed at White teenagers, put the song on their play lists.[25]

By the mid-fifties, the development of Chicano rock was about to begin. Since the previous decade, Afro Americans and Mexican Americans had worked together in bands, had been influenced by their own music, so the fusion continued at a very natural gait. Chicanos listened to doo-wop performers like Johnny Ace and the Drifters. Groups forming in Los Angeles in the 1950s fused doo-wop, R&B, and rock. This should be no surprise. The level of segregation created an environment where blacks and Chicanos attended similar dance halls and continued to borrow musically from each other. Songs like 'Hey Senorita' by the Penguins and 'Pachuko Hop' by Chuck Higgins made reference to Chicano culture and language.[26] Both Guerrero and Don Tosti were still working in Los Angeles; the mambo was stronger than ever in California and the Southwest thanks to the touring of Pérez Prado. The next foundational stage in Chicano music was about to take place.

In 1956, Johnny Otis discovered Lil' Julian Herrera and they began to work together. Otis had moved to Los Angeles from Oakland, California in 1943, where he worked with African American bands playing the music he so dearly loved. His association with boogie and blues covered sixty years. He has been a band leader, composer, DJ, author and mentor. Herrera grew up in East Los Angeles. Together they composed 'Lonely Lonely Nights'. It was a local hit. Guevara writes: "It's an elegant doo-wop ballad, very much in the black style, but something about it -the accent, the voice, the 'attitude' -made it different. It was Chicano rock."[27] I'm not sure if doo-wop can be linked to rock because of the style's musical roots, but be that as it may, Guevara was pointing to a beginning that was to have a key impact on musicians on the east side of Los Angeles.

If Lil' Julian Herrera was about attitude, then Ritchie Valens was about fusion at its best. Much has been written about his life and work so I will summarize key points regarding his influence on Chicano music. In his short life Valens had learned from numerous styles: traditional Mexican, country, black R & B, and rock; influences partly shaped by the musical environment that was post-war Los Angeles. Many of my teaching colleagues have always mentioned, when the subject comes up, at how impressed they are at Ritchie's composition of 'La Bamba.' And I'm always amused when they go into shock upon learning that Valens did not write the song but in fact recorded a treasured piece of Mexican folklore. John Storm Roberts found that 'La Bamba' was performed in Mexico City by *a jarocho* group from the Mexican state of Veracruz in 1775.[28] What's more, it is in the state of Veracruz that Africans rhythms are nurtured by the Mexican community, thanks to the musical influence of African slaves, as well as, early Afro Cuban rhythms from the Caribbean. Indigenous groups and mestizo musicians borrowed from European-stringed instruments by developing the harp, a four-stringed, guitar-shaped instrument called the *requinto* as well as a rhythm instrument called the *jarana*. Valens took the lyrics of the song, arranged a brilliant rock rhythm and lead-solo part to create the first Chicano rock song: 'La Bamba.' And if one listens carefully, they will hear the Cuban 2–3 reverse clave rhythm.[29]

Finally, in Texas, Tejano groups were themselves going through musical changes that would eventually tie into Chicano music. Stylistically, traditional conjunto, characterized by the group's instruments, the accordion, the bajo sexto, the upright bass or tololoche, and drums, remained unchanged. But as early as the late 1940s, musicians began to form orquestas, influenced by the big band sound of the day and began to perform popular swing music of the time. Peña has discussed this development as reflecting the assimilation and upwardly mobile status of Tejanos during the war years. This process led audiences to demand a newer music, something that left conjunto in the past. Eventually orquestas began to include Tejano music, but without the traditional instruments. The music of Beto Villa and Isidro López provided the key development of the Orquesta mosaic at the time. Essentially, one could attend a dance and hear Tejano music in a very different light. By the late fifties, younger musicians, better trained musically, began to merge into the Orquesta tradition but brought different influences to the table: The influence of rhythm and blues. Ozuna, who preferred to sing in English hit the big time with his 1963 hit, "Talk to Me."[30] Little Joe Hernández and Sunny Ozuna are the prime movers of this tradition. Little Joe, while occasionally recording in English stuck to Tejano after being influenced by the Chicano Movement.[31]

These developments, already influenced by the hybridity of musical growth that began in the 1940s, bring Chicano music into its own.

CHICANO MUSIC HITS ITS STRIDE

The Chicano Movement emerged in the mid 1960s when César Chávez began the grape boycott in California. The actions of Chávez, Dolores Huerta and others galvanized the community against the tactics of grape growers, but also set off political activity in urban areas as well. The work of Reies López Tijerina and his struggles to reclaim land grants lost in the 19th century, the Crusade for Justice in Denver, Colorado, and La Raza Unida in Crystal City, Texas, were the key areas of work throughout the Southwest.[32] It is a misconception, however, to leave the impression these were the only areas of work. The energy of the movement affected all areas of the Southwest. Slates of political, social and cultural issues became the foci of organizational work. Armando Navarro writes:

> The Chicano Movement was a heterogeneous political reform movement comprised of 'multiple' leaders, organizations, competing ideologies, and protest mobilization strategies and tactics. While some organizations within its ranks perceived themselves as revolutionary, ultimately its modus operandi proved to be essentially reformist in orientation.[33]

When Rubén Guevara wrote that Chicano was a term reflecting pride and defiance, he expressed the influence nationalism within the Chicano Movement. In recent years writers have criticized the movement's failure to be more revolutionary because of its reformist tendencies and clinging nature to nationalism. Manuel Peña has characterized the *movimiento* as driven by romantic nationalism, with a developed political and cultural agenda, with a focus on creating a separatist community, centered and shaped by a cultural renaissance found in literary, musical, theatrical, and filmic expressions. Peña refers to the Chicano agenda as 'ethnocentrist', which connects to the notion of romantic nationalism.[34] But as opposed to what?

The impression Peña, and other critics leave, is of a movement entirely naive and lacking in political maturity, yet fails to offer examples of the perfected political activism he (and others) so admire but have yet to demonstrate. From this vantage point the only nationalism one can embrace is romantic. On the other hand, Anthony D. Smith writes:

> Romance, mystery, drama - this is the stuff of any nationalist salvation - drama. It is important because it helps to teach us 'who we are,' to impart the sense of being, a link in a chain which stretches back over the generations to bind us to our ancestors and our descendents.[35]

Add to this the historical context: As Rodolfo Acuña has expressed, it was okay to be anything but Mexican.[36] What the Chicano Movement illustrated was the importance of first accepting oneself. This stage was a necessity; call it romantic or naive. Moreover, nationalism was a vehicle, a strategy and, in some degree, essential. Remember, Chicanos were responding to pressures to assimilate, to social injustice, exclusion and outright disdain. The pressure to eliminate one's culture, felt in the schools, among academics and other spokespersons who felt Mexicans were just in the way. The Chicano Movement and its nationalism was a reaction to this experience. Nationalism was able to direct Chicanos towards the question of identity and self-determination. Thus, the movement created a strategy to redefine who we are as a people. More important, critics fail to understand that political change takes time. Only then might the student move forward to embrace a more progressive set of ideas.

This perspective also leads to the Chicano Renaissance in literature, art, film, and music.[37] For musicians, choice of style was dictated by influence and preferences, but always with a connection to the community. While the movement may have been reformist, naive, and lacking in political maturity, in many cases there was a strong leadership, commitment to the Chicano community, and a desire to see change occur.

Thus when Los Lobos played a show and focused on traditional Mexican music, it became a wake-up call to young people: this is what we come from. Folkloric or commercial, people made the connection. Or take the experience of Danny Valdez – brother of playwright, Luis Valdez. Though never achieving the commercial success of other composers or singers, Valdez stuck to his guns by composing and playing music rooted in the corrido and ranchera tradition. His lyrics though, spoke to the contemporary issues of the day and related clearly to farm workers. But when he composed 'Primavera' and went on tour, his band delivered an Afro Cuban set of rhythms along with the more traditional Mexican ones. Clearly, while delivering a political message, the music reflected multiple influences that had been present in the Chicano community for some time. As Estevan César Azcona writes:

It was the activist nature of movimiento music -and the groups linked to it - that ultimately defined it from its brethren in the commercial realm. This was not music for the market or for its critics but rather music for and from an emerging 'Chicano public sphere.'[38]

The insight from Azcona is made stronger when placed in its historical context: Music, according to Dorothea E. Hast, James R. Cowdery, and Stan Scott, has provided vehicles for presenting political messages. From the Psalms of David, the epics of Homer, from the Yugoslavian nationalist whose songs capture the glory of past heroes against ethnic groups who were viewed as enemies, to a Chicano activist whose songs speak to social injustice. Music also serves to critique government: The songs of Robin Hood, to outlaw ballads celebrating Pretty Boy Floyd and Jesse James, to the punk anthems by the Clash and Rage against the Machine, all speak to injustice and oppression at the hands of social institutions. Songs of protest and resistance, topical songs, which thematically have covered subjects such as anti-rent wars in the 19th century, the abolition of slavery, the labor movement, the civil rights movement, and the anti-war movement, serve to illustrate the power of music to inspire and encourage people to take a stand.[39]

I discuss the Chicano Movement because its energy was great and made a significant impact on Chicano musicians. But then they also expressed this influence in different ways. Azcona makes clear that the Chicano Movement gives birth to Chicano music. Viewed in this way, we can eliminate some of the confusion with what we call Chicano music: Besides hybridity, the Chicano Movement lends inspiration to the influences that shape the perspectives of Chicano musicians on the more commercial side of industry. The rest of this section will be devoted to examining how the Chicano Movement influenced music in the late 1960s and early 1970s, specifically, I will examine music of the Chicano Movement, rock music in the late 60s and 70s, and *La Onda Chicana* from Texas. Building on what happened in the decades of the forties and fifties; we can then determine how Chicano music emerged as a genre all of its own; with different forms of instrumentation, style, and lyrical content.

MUSICA DEL MOVIMIENTO

The Chicano Movement was more than mass political struggle. There was also a need for cultural expression, which found its home in different realms: Literature, art (particularly, the mural movement), theatre, film and music. All provided a way for Chicanos to express the realities, cultural and political, encountered within the movement. Three different styles of Movement music were prominent. Huelga songs addressing the experience of farm workers in California and Texas; corridos, the narrative ballads that stylistically centered on heroes of the movement and experiences of inter-cultural conflict; and Movimiento music, which were protest songs written by Chicanos participating in the movement but also influenced by larger struggles such as those of Viet Nam and Mexico.[40]

Daniel Valdez, as a member of El Teatro Campesino, the Farm Worker Theatre, began adding musical themes that related to the struggle in the fields. By using the corrido and the ranchera rhythms, he was able to utilize lyrics that spoke to the striking members of the union. 'Huelga en General', 'El Picket Sign', 'El Corrido de Dolores Huerta', and 'El Corrido de César Chávez' were sung at rallies, marches, and protests that were not even tied to the farm workers struggle.

In urban areas like Los Angeles, 'Yo Soy Chicano' became an important anthem for organizing youth and spear energy at marches. 'Yo Soy Chicano' was musically borrowed from 'La Rielera,' one of the more famous corridos of the Mexican Revolution. Ramon "Chunky" Sánchez wrote some memorable pieces like 'Trilingual Corrido', 'Chorizo Sandwich' and 'Chicano Park Samba.'[41]

Movimiento music reflects the numerous struggles that took place in the Southwest by Chicanos in the mid 1960s to 1980. Each piece collects an event, an individual or issue that Chicanos took to heart. Like the hymns, which energized the African American Civil Rights struggle, such as 'We Shall Overcome,' Chicanos used music to propel the nature of their struggle. In fact, on the 1977 recording of the album, *Si Se Puede*, a key song is 'No Nos Moveran,' (We Shall Overcome), Chicano style.[42]

The lyric found in a Movement song is a clear cry, a reaching out to the community: A call to organize and confront the institutions responsible for our oppression! Political lyrics over the centuries have had the same goal: inform and get people involved. From this perspective, songs of the Chicano Movement literally reflect the idea of Chicano music. And it is the energy of the music and the *movimiento* in general that inspires commercial musicians to borrow ideology, image, language and sensibility, then fuse it with their own form of musical expression.

Rockin' in the Southwest

Chicano artists between the 1950s and 1968 -with the probable exception of Ritchie Valens -did not draw attention to their ethnicity, or so say Reyes and Waldman. Perhaps there was pressure to adapt to industry desires, such as when Bob Keane told Ritchie Valens his given name, Ricardo Valenzuela, will not do. Hence, his stage name 'Ritchie Valens.' But Lipsitz sees clearly that these groups also came to taste the vicious nature of discrimination and segregation. During the 1960s, as Black and Anglo artists composed and recorded numerous songs with a clear political content, nothing of the sort existed within the Chicano community. Chicano artists who did have hit records, were largely of the pop variety. René and René, for example, saw their Spanish language hit song, "Lo Mucho Que Te Quiero," receive substantial airplay. Sonny (Ozuna) and the Sunglows had a national hit with "Talk to Me" and Chan Romero, following in the footsteps of Ritchie Valens, with a minor hit titled, "The Hippy Hippy Shake." Guevara tells us that this changed or began to change in the late 1960s when a local group, the VIP's, changed their name to El Chicano.[43] There is some confusion here. Bobby Lespron, guitarist for the band stated in two separate interviews that the label changed the band's name at the release of their first album, while in the other he states it was his manager who pushed the band to change their name. After 1968, there was a deliberate change. Bands now chose Spanish names (for their bands), used Mexican dress, or sang songs about conditions in the barrio, police brutality, the INS, or the Vietnam War. The source of this change was the emphasis on ethnic nationalism, which was in opposition to assimilation. Also, the criticism of the Mexican American generation placed the Chicano Movement within the context of the generational revolt evident in the 1960s.[44]

While Chicano rock was developing in the East side, developments were also shaping music in Texas. But while these groups did not build on the imagery or political themes often used by Chicano groups in the East side, they too fused with different musical styles. Specifically, they borrowed from the Tejano conjunto sound. While they did not use the accordion, the Vox farfisa organ carried the same melodic movement and the bass lines played on the farfisa reflected the bass lines played on the bajo sexto. The important groups in this regard were the Sir Douglas Quintet (She's About a Mover), led by Doug Sham, and? and the Mysterians, young musicians whose parents worked the migrant trails, actually recorded their hit song '96 Tears' in Michigan; and Sam the Sham and the Pharaoh's 'Wooly Bully.' The intro to that song has Sam (Samudio) saying, "one, two, one, two, tres, cuatro . . ."[45] Artists such as the late Freddy Fender, recorded country-inspired songs that became popular: 'Wasted Days and Wasted Nights' and 'Before the Next Teardrop Falls' were regularly heard on radio and the latter tune was aided in its popularity because it was sung bilingually.

La Onda Chicana

As previously mentioned, the orquesta tradition in Texas emerged as a response to the process of assimilation. The early stage was an attempt to mimic the music of swing bands popular in the 1940s. In the 1950s orquestas led by Isidro López provided a spin on the original orquestas by developing a new Tejano sound that came to define the nature of Tejano music. By the late fifties, the third generation of *orquesta* leaders began to emerge. Little Joe and Sunny Ozuna took the helm of their respective groups and by the mid 1960s each brought his own form of expressing the *orquesta* sound. Little Joe and the Latinaires utilized R & B, while Sunny focused his act on English-language covers and originals; all within the *orquesta* sound.

By the early sixties it appeared as if Sunny and the Sunglows would be the top *orquesta* group. His rendition of 'Talk to Me', a song he learned from San Antonio bluesman, Randy Garibay, and originally recorded by Little Willie John, shot into the top 10, garnered him incredible exposure and a spot on the American Bandstand lineup. His success further drove home the point that Tejano would not be part of his musical career. But by the late sixties, Sunny was doing Tejano songs, especially in the local performances and Little Joe and the Latinaires were touring California. For Little Joe, the political activity and mobilization within the Chicano Movement had an effect on him. Little by little, he began to reflect on the issues addressed by activists and in 1968 the climate was intense. By the time he returned to Texas he was already planning to reinvent himself.

As early as 1967, Johnny González of Zarape Records used the label, *La Onda Chicana,* as a way of linking the new style of Little Joe and the Latinaires to the ethnocentric consciousness emerging among Mexican Americans.[46] The connection to *La Onda Chicana* is what Manuel Peña refers to as 'compound bimusicality,' a process "interacting with politico-ideological activity" and evident in Little Joe with an aesthetic transformation beginning with a Chicano look, a new name (La Familia), a counterculture lifestyle and a shift toward the ideology of Chicanismo. This led to a

unique display of music by Little Joe, which has yet to be equaled. Peña writes:

> *Para la Gente* (1970) was the first LP by any Texas group to exploit what I earlier called a 'compound' form of bimusicality - where styles identifiable as Mexican ranchero and those identifiable as sophisticated American swing-jazz were yoked together within the same musical piece to create, in effect, a hybrid or synthetic music in a relation homologous to compound bilingualism. Several of the tunes prominently displayed 'intrasentential code-switching' between ranchero and sophisticated.[47]

This bimusicality, alternating ranchero with American 'jaiton' styles within the same musical piece - is at the center of hybridity and synthesis. It was also heard on 'Las Nubes,' which led off Little Joe's *Para la Gente.*

Much of the success of *La Onda Chicana* was helped by the exposure gained through the Johnny Canales Show. Popular in the southwest, Mexico and parts of the U.S., Canales brought exposure to Tejano music by presenting new and established artists such as Al Hurricane from New Mexico and Selena from South Texas. He promoted *La Onda Chicana* and the use of code-switching.

CHICANO CULTURAL PRODUCTION

In the end, what we call Chicano music is a musical style with roots in the intercultural conflicts and experiences between Mexicans and Anglos. A review of what Leal calls Chicano corridos and other song forms provide insight with respect to what was on the minds of composers. Whether social in content or linguistically mixed, this was the first stage of development.

By the middle of the 20th century, we see Mexican Americans borrowing from diverse styles such as the mambo, jazz, swing, the blues, boogie-woogie, doo-wop and rock. Forms such as Pachuco Boogie, R & B stylings and rock interpretations by Ritchie Valens signal the development musical fusion or bimusicality and linguistic playfulness. But it is still not Chicano music but rather musical forms embraced by the Mexican American community. It is not until the rise of the Chicano Movement and concurrently, the renaissance in literature, the arts, music and film, that we begin to see the influence of a Chicano perspective in these fields. With these fusions, one relates to the lyrics, styles, as well as the use of traditional musical forms like the corrido and ranchera. These elements influence Little Joe, El Chicano, Thee Midnighters, Los Lobos, and others to adopt a Chicano image in music. According to George Lipsitz:

> (Chicanos) were neither assimilationist nor separatist, they drew on 'families of resemblance' - similarities to the experiences and cultures of other groups - to fashion a 'unity of disunity.' In that way, they sought to make alliances with other groups by cultivating the ways in which their particular experiences spoke with special authority about the ideas and alienations felt by others.[48]

Moreover, the emphasis of popular music "supports the contention of ethnic studies scholars who see cultural production not only as an integral part of oppositional politics, but as an 'important register' of social and political change."[49] The socio-historical relationships between Blacks and Chicanos in Los Angeles are joined by political, economic and culture change. When we listen to Los Lobos, Rage Against the Machine and Ozomatli, we become the beneficiaries of this relationship. For Gayle Johnson, it represents the development of multi ethnic identities, gender, and geographic space that leads to the development of cross border music.[50]

The role of Chicano cultural production is a vast array of genres, attitudes, experiences and solidarity with the community. The individual expressions by artists reflect their understanding and depth of connection to Chicano music. I have tried to show that understanding Chicano music as a concept requires the student and listener to grasp characteristics of fusion, tradition, lyrical expression, whether political or cultural, sound, and attitude. It is tied to political movements such as the Chicano Movement; it is tied to generational expression whether in rock, punk or hip-hop. Cajun musician Jo-El Sonnier, who I remember well during his stint in Los Angeles, once commented to a journalist:

> I've sold myself as French, as R & B, as country, and as rock. But I want to do it all if I can. I think we could open doors for this music. Look at what Los Lobos has done for ethnic music, and they got signed without really changing. It can't just be that all people want is Madonna and punk music! All I've ever wanted to do is bring my music and my culture to the people.

I have a message about the preservation of it. I feel like if I let my culture die, I die with it.[51]

CONCLUSION

Bonnie Wade writes: "Worldwide integration through technology and market exchange is the hallmark of globalization, and we are beginning to understand that many, if not most, music has emerged from processes of hybridization or fusion."[52] She is of course addressing the idea of transnationalization. It is a process that is taking us to other places or bringing other places to us and the more we open up to influences from the outside, we will see changes culturally and in our forms of cultural expression.

But this is not new; it is only more evident, more powerful and more encompassing. Guevara writes:

> There are now many sounds, many subcultures, from hip-hop to traditional Mexican, from sixties soul traditionalists in the car clubs to punk bands that helped to start the whole L.A. punk scene. From Spanish to English and all shades in between.[53]

In the end, what makes Chicano music a unique set of sounds, genres, linguistic mixing, political thought and poetry, historical insight, and cultural capital, is the fact that it moves people - to sing and dance, to higher levels of analysis, to emotional power. The quality of Chicano music is that it reigns in the collective identity of Chicanos, as diverse as that may be. Again: "Memories tell us who we are, and music is one of the most powerful tools for evoking memory. Music helps us to recall ideas and events, and serves to make particular occasions memorable."[54] Thus researchers who study the issue of immigration can find a wealth of musical material that clearly details the experience of crossing borders. This type of data connects us to experiences that to date continue to educate. Memory shapes identity within groups, within nations, around ethnic and cultural communities that live within and across political borders. At the personal level, friends and family members help us to understand how culture and memory are linked.

So Chicano music then draws from the past. It is our foundation; expressed through political lyrics and content with respect to the Chicano experience. And for those not always engaged at the political level, consider *La Onda Chicana* or East L.A. rock bands, where Chicano music, expressed through ideological symbolism, captures the realities of the larger Mexican community. There is the experience of Mark Guerrero, son of Lalo Guerrero, who majored in Chicano Studies at California State University, Los Angeles, who continues to perform and has written songs like, 'Pre-Columbian Dreams.' Tierra, a band utilizing jazz, Mexican melodies and R & B, becomes a stable at political events in East L.A. As we journey through the twenty-first century, Chicano music will continue to evolve. Historical styles will always be there. The oldies and *La Onda Chicana* will continue to be emotional connections, the political verve will inspire as long as the community is affected by social injustice. As styles make their impact, Chicano music will continue to hybridize and synthesize new sounds for new generations.

"Go on; tírame una rola."

Endnotes

1. José Angel Gutiérrez, "Chicano Music: Evolution and Politics to 1950," in *The Roots of Texas Music*, eds. Laurence Clayton and Joe W. Specht. (College Station: Texas A & M Press, 2003), 146–174.

2. See, Yolanda Broyles-González, *Lydia Mendoza's Life in Music.* (New York: Oxford University Press, 2001), 182–85. This life story also includes a Spanish language version of the text. Also, Gloria Anzaldua, *Borderlands/ La Frontera: The New Mestiza.* (San Francisco: Aunt Lute Books, 1987), 61.

3. Los Lobos, "La Bamba, "La Bamba Soundtrack, LP, Slash Records, 1987 and, Los Lobos, "Be Still," The Neighborhood, CD, Slash Records, 1990.

4. Robert Rivera-Ojeda, "Chicano Music: A Perspective," Mexican and Chicano Music, ed. José "Pepe" Villarino, 2nd ed. (New York: Primus Custom Publishing, 1999) 93.

5. Américo Paredes, *A Texas-Mexican Cancionero* (Urbana: University of Illinois Press, 1976), 3.

6. Ojeda, *Chicano,* 94.

7. David Reyes and Tom Waldman, *Land of a Thousand Dances: Chicano Rock 'n' Roll from Southern California* (Albuquerque: University of New Mexico Press, 1998),viii.

8. Rafael Pérez-Torres, *Mestizaje.* (Minneapolis: University of Minnesota Press, 2006), 93.

9. The orquestas emerged during the 1940s as a growing Tejano middle class sought to move away from the traditional sound of conjunto. The middle class Tejano sought to become more Americanized by distancing themselves from their working class brethren. This is what Peña means by cultural disloyalty.

10. In fact, Peña does mention that upwardly mobile Mexican American never quite broke away from their conjunto roots. See Manuel Peña, *A Texas-Mexican Conjunto.* (Austin: University of Texas Press, 1996), 10–14.

11. Pérez-Torres, *Mestizaje,* 94.

12. As quoted in Bonnie C. Wade, *Thinking Musically: Experiencing Music, Expressing Culture.* (New York: Oxford University Press, 2004), 146.

13. Gutiérrez, *Chicano Music,* 14

14. Rubén Guevara, "The View from the Sixth Street Bridge: The History of Chicano Rock," in *The Real World of Rock and Roll*, ed. Dave Marsh (New York: Pantheon, 1984), 113.

15. Pérez-Torres, *Mestizaje,* 87–88.

16. Pérez-Torres does not examine lyrics in terms of context, such as those relating to violence.

17. Luis Leal, "El Corrido" *Xalman* (1980): 24. Paredes, 30.

18. Paredes, *Canciones,* 163–64.

19. Paredes, *Canciones,*

20. Guillermo Hernández, *Canciones de la Raza: Songs of the Chicano Experience.* (Berkeley: El Fuego de Aztlán, 1978), 2.

21. John Storm Roberts, *The Latin Tinge,* 2nd. ed. (New York: Oxford University Press, 1998), 101.

22. On boogie woogie piano styles, see Marshall Stearns, *The Story of Jazz.* (New York: The New American Library, 1958), 122–23. On jump blues, see Steve Loza, *Barrio Rhythm: Mexican Music in Los Angeles.* (Urbana: University of Illinois Press, 1993), 80–81.

23. Ed Morales, *The Latin Beat.* (New York: De Capo Press, 2003), 283. Also, *Pachuco Boogie*, CD, Arhoolie Records, 2002.

24. George Lipsitz, "Chicano Rock: Crusing Around the Historical Bloc," in *Rockin the Boat: Mass Music and Mass Movements,* ed. Reebee Garofolo (Boston: South End Press, 1992), 271.

25. Ed Morales, *Latin Beat,* 284.

26. Rubén Guevara, *View From,* 127. Rubén Guevara, *View From,* 11.

27. Rubén Guevara, *View From,* 118.

28. George Lipsitz, *Chicano Rock,* 273. Also see, Beverly Mandheim, *Ritchie Valens: the First Chicano Rocker* (Tempe: Bilingual Review Press, 1987).

29. John Storm Roberts, *Latin Tinge,* 20.

30. Ed Morales, *Latin Beat,* 284. Only later when the hits stopped coming, at least nationally, Ozuna reinvented himself by performing and recording Tejano music with his orquestas sound. He learned 'Talk to Me' from Randy Garibay, a San Antonio bluesman. Little Willie John composed, and originally recorded 'Talk to Me.'

31. See chapters 3 and 4 in Manuel Peña, *The Mexican American Orquesta* (Austin: University of Texas Press, 1999).

32. See, Rodolofo F. Acuña, *Occupied America: A History of Chicanos,* 6th edition. (New York: Pearson/Longman, 2007).

33. Armando Navarro, *Mexicano Political Experience in Occupied Aztlán: Struggle and Change.* (Walnut Creek: Altamira Press, 2005), 303–04.

34. Manuel Peña, *Musica Tejana.* (Austin: University of Texas Press, 1999), 160.

35. Anthony D. Smith, *The Ethnic Origins of Nations.* (New York: Blackwell Publishers, Inc., 1998), 180.

36. Rodolfo F. Acuña, *Anything But Mexican: Chicanos in Contemporary Los Angeles.* (New York: Verso Press, 1996).

37. Phillip D. Ortego, "Chicano Renaissance."

38. Esteban César Azcona, *Rolas de Aztlán,* Liner Notes, CD Recording. (Washington: Smithsonian Folkways Recording, 2005), 3.

39. Dorothea E. Hast, et.al., *Exploring the World of Music.* (Dubuque: Kendall-Hunt Publishers, 1999) 38.

40. Esteban C. Azcona, *Rolas,* 4–6.

41. Jose "Pepe" Villarino, "The Blending of Two Cultures Through Music," in *Mexican and Chicano Music,* ed. Jose "Pepe" Villarino, 2nd ed. (New York: Primus Custom Publishing, 1999) 105.

42. *Si Se Puede*, LP, Brown Bag Records, 1977.

43. Rubén Guevara, *View From,* 122.

44. *Chicano Rock, DVD Release.*

45. David Reyes and Tom Waldman, *Land of,* 112; George Lipsitz, *Chicano Rock,* 275; and, Ed Morales, *Latin Beat,* 290–91.

46. Manuel Peña, *Música,* 162.

47. Manuel Peña, *Música,* 168 and George Lipsitz, *Chicano Rock,* 270.

48. George Lipsitz, *Chicano Rock.*

49. Gaye T. M. Johnson, "A Sifting of Centuries: Afro-Chicano Interaction and Popular Musical Culture in California, 1960–2000," *Decolonial Voices: Chicana and Chicano Cultural Studies in the 21st Century* (Bloomington: Indiana University Press, 2002), 317.

50. Gaye Johnson, *Shifting,* 327.

51. Judy Raphael, "Ragin Cajun: Jo-El Sonnier's Last Stand," *LA Weekly* 8 (15) (1985): 57 as quoted by George Lipsitz, *Chicano Rock,* 278.

52. Bonnie Wade, *Thinking Musically,* 148.

53. Rubén Guevara, *View From,* 125.

54. Dorothea Hast, et.al., *Exploring,* 52.

Imagined Borders: Locating Chicano Cinema in America/América

Chon A. Noriega

In this essay, I will examine the articulation and development of a "Chicano cinema" as an expression of the Chicano civil rights movement. To some extent, this is a history that has been told a number of times already, first by the filmmakers themselves, and later by programmers and scholars.[1] And it is a history that has been told within a metanarrative of cultural resistance that defines *lo chicano* according to its oppositional "experience," "expression," and "identity." Nonetheless, in these accounts, my own included, Chicano cinema inevitably occupies an ambiguous location within the national culture, caught between the conflicting egalitarian and communitarian goals of both its practitioners and its academic critics.[2] This conflict marks the underlying conditions for the production of both Chicano films and the critical discourse on them (in short, race relations), while the metanarrative of cultural resistance requires that, as a practical matter, such social contradictions be addressed at the allegorical level. Although an institutional critique of either Chicano cinema or Chicano studies is beyond the scope of this essay, I do want to raise the ambiguous location of Chicano cinema to the level of historiographic operation. One can find a precursor in Coco Fusco's writings on Black and Latino media in the late 1980s.[3] Working not as an academic but as a media professional actively involved in the object of her study—curator, writer, and program officer—Fusco voiced pragmatic concerns as she sought to define a historical moment of "minority" intellectual or cultural production. If more academic accounts necessarily diverted these concerns to an allegorical level, Fusco bristled against her location as the representative for the underrepresented, as the insider for the outsiders, and, consequently, as the outsider who was inside. This ambiguous or dual location, then, became the very methodology by which she read against the grain of oppositional thinking and of "minority" texts. In a similar fashion, I want to raise several questions about the function of "Chicano cinema" within various discourses—nationalist, postnationalist and American, pan-American—in order to make a distinction between the idea of "Chicano cinema" (as category) and its practice. In some respects, the category preceded the practice insofar as it created the possibilities for special admissions, trainee programs, public affairs series, production grants, distribution agencies, exhibition slots, and so on. From this discursive origin, "Chicano cinema" constructed itself in opposition to Hollywood and in alliance with New Latin American Cinema.[4] Although framed as a matter of either/or choice, this strategy actually provided new terms within which access could be negotiated. As a final matter, I want to suggest that "Chicano cinema" developed not just vis-à-vis Hollywood and New Latin American Cinema (as well as cinema and television), but through the disavowal of an avant-garde tradition within Chicano cultural production. The focus of this essay will be on the period of the Chicano civil rights movement (1965–75), during which the first generation of Chicano filmmakers went from student activists to film and television professionals. I will pay special attention to Jesús Salvador Treviño and his pivotal role as filmmaker, organizer, advocate, and polemicist.

THE CHICANO CIVIL RIGHTS MOVEMENT

As the story is told, the first generation of Chicano filmmakers emerged out of the context of the farmworkers' struggle and the student movement. In the first years of the Chicano movement, the farmworkers' struggle would in some sense define its political, class, and rhetorical orientations, providing the basis for a categorical shift away from the perceived middle-class, accommodationist, and integrationist strategies of the Mexican American Generation.[5] Under the leadership of César Chávez, the United Farm Workers (UFW), founded in 1962, gained national attention when it joined the grape strike in Delano, California, on September 16, 1965, the anniversary of Mexican independence from Spain in 1810. Both Mexican-based historical references and cultural production played a pivotal role in these social protests (and their political resonance), incorporating more subtle allusions to American political history. Luis Valdez, writer and director of *Zoot Suit* (1981) and *La Bamba* (1987), was especially important in developing this bicultural political rhetoric in the mid-1960s. In 1965, he founded El Teatro Campesino in order to rally striking farmworkers, developing collaborative agit-prop *actos* (skits) that were performed on the flatbeds of trucks. Then, in March 1966, he wrote the influential "Plan of Delano," a manifesto that announced the grape strike as the start of a "social movement"—done in the rhetorical style of the U.S. Declaration of Independence and Black gospel à la Martin Luther King Jr.—which it then rooted in the Virgin of Guadalupe, Benito Juárez, and the Mexican Revolution of 1910.[6] In this manner, Valdez created a unique expression that coupled together seemingly opposed egalitarian and communitarian goals, so that the call for equal justice within the United States justified an affirmation of a Mexican past and culture that then made such equality its inevitable outcome. As a Chicano rhetorical strategy, Valdez's "Plan of Delano" would have a direct impact on other plans ("El Plan Espiritual de Aztlán"

and "El Plan de Santa Barbara"), epic poems ("I Am Joaquín"), films (in particular, Valdez's *I Am Joaquín* [1969] and *Los Vendidos: The Sellouts* [1972]), and—in a more indirect fashion—film manifestos.[7]

By the late 1960s, the emphasis of the Chicano movement shifted from rural to urban issues, and from farmworkers to students, and Los Angeles became a major focal point. In East Los Angeles, some ten thousand high school students undertook a series of "Blow Outs" (or walkouts) in March 1968 to protest institutional racism and poor education. The Blow Outs were initiated by high school teacher Sal Castro, who joined the students, and were coordinated by members of United Mexican American Students (UMAS), including UCLA students and future filmmakers Moctesuma Esparza and Francisco Martínez. In June, Castro and Esparza were among the "L.A. Thirteen" indicted on conspiracy charges for their organizational role in the Blow Outs, an act that resulted in increased Chicano student activism and radicalism within the next year.[8] In March and April 1969, student conferences in Denver and Santa Barbara consolidated the student movement, uniting the four major Mexican American student groups under one banner: M.E.Ch.A., or El Movimiento Estudiantil Chicano de Aztlán (The Chicano Student Movement of Aztlán). The rejection of the self-designation "Mexican American" in favor of "Chicano," and the fact that *mecha* is vernacular Spanish for "match," underscored the student movement's militant nationalism.

The first Chicano film, *I Am Joaquín* (1969), embodies these transitions in the Chicano movement and represents the culmination of an intertextual dialogue between the movement's rural and urban visionaries: Luis Valdez and Rodolfo "Corky" Gonzales. Like Valdez, Gonzales had been actively involved in the Democratic Party, but became disenchanted in the early 1960s. In 1965, Gonzales resigned from the party and founded the Crusade for Justice, a civil rights organization located in Denver. The film is Valdez's adaptation of Gonzales's epic poem of the same title, written in 1967, and widely distributed through chapbooks and mimeograph copies.[9] The poem itself, however, draws upon the rhetorical style of Valdez's "Plan of Delano," ending with the first person singular expression of phrases that punctuate the earlier manifesto: "I SHALL ENDURE. I WILL ENDURE."[10] The major shift between plan and poem occurs in terms of the subject of their "poetic consciousness."[11] The "Plan of Delano," although grounded in key figures and moments from Mexican history, addressed a multiethnic membership (mostly Mexican and Filipino), then focused on one class-based social movement rooted in the farmworkers' struggle, but ultimately aimed at uniting "all of the races that comprise the oppressed minorities in the United States," including "poor whites." Furthermore, in defining the role of theater and other cultural expressions within that movement, Valdez himself made a clear-cut distinction between its symbolic politics (both theater and demonstrations) and "actual hard-ass, door to door, worker to worker organizing."[12] If community had to be imagined for a national audience, local politics required an interpersonal expression and organization of that community. In contrast to the "Plan of Delano," Gonzales's "I Am Joaquín" envisioned a mestizo historical genealogy for the broad-based Chicano movement, articulating a series of bipolar parameters for Chicano identity—of race, religion, class, and, more insidiously, gender—that could be subordinated to nationalism. For Gonzales—as echoed in the words of "El Plan Espiritual de Aztlán"—"nationalism as the key to organization transcends all religious, political, class, and economic factions" within the Chicano community.[13] Nationalism, then, gave a singular political meaning to *mestizaje*. Whereas Valdez used nationalist icons in order to argue for historical justification as well as internal unity within a working-class struggle, Gonzales turned nationalism itself into the "key" for uniting an admittedly heterogeneous group of Mexican descent.

By the time "I Am Joaquín" was written, Valdez had realized the need to develop the aesthetic and political dimensions of El Teatro Campesino beyond direct involvement with the United Farm Workers. At stake for Valdez was a question of professionalism and the potential for a national audience for an artistic practice that had begun as a component within grassroots politics. Valdez's film adaptation exemplifies his own artistic shift from community-based organizing to addressing a mass audience for which community must be imagined. Before the adaptation, El Teatro Campesino had developed a slide show that combined the photographs of George Ballis, who worked with the United Farm Workers, with a dramatic reading of the poem. Shortly thereafter, Ballis's photographs were shot and edited together into a film, with Luis Valdez's narration and Daniel Valdez's improvised music recorded in a sound studio in Los Angeles.[14] The film was shown at both farmworkers' rallies and within the urban barrio (as with earlier dramatic readings of the poem and the slide show), but it also reached classrooms, festivals, and a national television audience. Thus, the film—like

the poem—brought together the diverse aspects of the Chicano movement, while it also expanded the domain for Chicano expressions into the mass media of film and television.[15] In this manner, the film adaptation of "I Am Joaquín" signaled both the professional reorientation of El Teatro Campesino (and Chicano arts in general), Luis Valdez's own shift from rural/local/grassroots to mass media forms, and "a new era in Chicano self-determination in film and television."[16]

FROM PROTESTS TO TRAINEE PROGRAMS, 1967–69

Although *I Am Joaquín* is symptomatic of the struggle for Chicano self-representation within film and television—both as an organizing tool and as a means of representing the Chicano movement to a national audience—more structural changes would come about as a result of the combined efforts of social protests, federal regulation, and foundation initiatives. From these efforts emerged a number of industry trainee programs and film school admissions policies that brought in the first generation of would-be Chicano filmmakers. In the summer of 1968, for example, the U.S. Office of Economic Opportunity funded a program called New Communicators that was designed to train minorities for employment in the film industry. With a board of directors comprised of various progressives within Hollywood, the program "recruited about twenty students, largely Blacks and Chicanos, with a few Indians and one or two token hippie-type white guys."[17] Through intensive hands-on training with film graduates from the University of Southern California, the students were to advance from Super-8 to 16mm over the course of one year. Although the program fell apart within eight months because of internal conflicts, it nonetheless provided several Chicanos with their first exposure to the film industry: Jesús Treviño, Esperanza Vásquez, Francisco Martínez, and Martín Quiroz. Treviño, who by this time had become involved in the Educational Issues Coordinating Committee (EICC) formed within the Chicano community after the Blow Outs of March 1968, used a Super-8 (and later a 16mm) camera from the New Communicators to document subsequent Blow Outs as well as EICC activities. In particular, he documented the Sal Castro hearings before the board of education, and the EICC sit-in and arrests after the board refused the appeal to reinstate Castro.[18] In addition to the ten to twelve hours of unedited footage collected, Treviño edited together several films in early 1969 as part of his training at New Communicators. These include *La Raza Nueva* (The new people), on Super-8 with sound and narration on a separate tape cassette, and *¡Ya Basta!* (Enough already!), on 16mm. *La Raza Nueva* documents the March 1968 Blow Outs, the conspiracy trial of the "L.A. Thirteen," and the Castro hearings and sit-in. In *¡Ya Basta!*, Treviño experiments with jump cuts, dramatic recreations, and multiple story lines, which reemerge in Treviño's later television documentaries such as *Yo Soy Chicano* (1972). The "free-form" docudrama intercuts blown-up footage from *La Raza Nueva* with a dramatic sequence about a teenage boy with troubles at home and school. By the end of the film the boy's death is coded as a direct outcome of the board of education's refusal to reinstate Castro. Although these films appear "primitive" and incoherent according to mass-media conventions, their effective use within the EICC and the Chicano community at the time suggests another way of understanding early artistic expressions within the movement. As Treviño himself argues, the "free-form" style of *¡Ya Basta!* relied upon the fact that "so much of this was self-evident to the audience."[19] Thus, the film served the needs of an audience whose main concern was the organization of a "community" and not the craft of an autonomous, objective, or artistic statement. To that extent, watching a "Chicano" film about an event experienced firsthand by many of the audience members played a role in community building, becoming more important than the actual form and content of the film, and more important than its ability to function within the mass media.

CHICANO PUBLIC AFFAIRS SERIES, 1970–74

The limited or distorted media coverage of social protests and community concerns motivated a number of student activists to become filmmakers able to work within the mass media itself. Meanwhile, Chicano media advocates and activist groups, including Carissma and Justicia, aggressively pushed for Chicano-produced local television shows in the Los Angeles area.[20] Overall, these local television shows or specials provided initial, albeit contested, outlets for Chicano-produced film related to the issues, protests, and goals of the Chicano movement. But as producers attempted to address these issues within the television industry, they confronted both economic and ideological constraints. In fact, program budgets did not provide for more than a "talking heads" format, while station managers suppressed their efforts to use television for social critique. An examination of two series produced by Treviño reveals the extent to which Chicano filmmakers were able to subvert these constraints.

The *¡Ahora!* series—funded by the Ford Foundation as part of an initiative at PBS affiliate KCET in Los Angeles—was perhaps the first television show to document and discuss current issues within the Chicano community. Given the prior absence of local media coverage on Chicanos, members of the community were hostile to the series, then in development, even though politically active Chicanos were in the role of producers. Various community meetings were held, and at one such meeting some two hundred people voted on whether or not to support the program. Treviño attempted to intervene: "I gave this impassioned plea, like, at least give us a chance, don't you trust me, et cetera. And the vote . . . there were four people who voted for me: my wife, two friends and myself! [Laughing] It was really tense in those days."[21] In the first week, the program featured "every single major [Chicano] group," and by the end of the year, "whenever we would have a major news event happening, the local news stations would come to our studio, because we would have the people there. We would get them before anyone else."[22] Because of the close relationships Treviño established within the community, *¡Ahora!* could also provide immediate coverage for planned protests and other events. Treviño quickly became the associate producer, writer, and on-air host for the show, which aired live weeknights at 7:00 p.m. for 175 episodes. In addition to the political issues dealt with in talk-show format or documented through live remotes, *¡Ahora!* scheduled regular episodes on cultural and historical dimensions of the Chicano experience. These included a three-part series on Mexican Americans in Hollywood.[23] Treviño also hired Luis Torres, a high school senior (later a producer for the National Latino Communications Center), to research and write a weekly episode on "la raza history." On Fridays, the show usually aired live performances of Latino music and drama. In this manner, in its weekly programming, *¡Ahora!* wove together current events, history, culture, and entertainment, providing an integrated vision of the Chicano community and its political struggle.

Taken as a whole, Treviño's programming on *¡Ahora!* can be seen as congruent with "El Plan Espiritual de Aztlán" and its demand for cultural expressions that would "strengthen our identity and the moral backbone of the movement." The Plan made explicit the movement's assumption about the role of cultural production within political struggle, and, more generally, the way in which cultural nationalism mediated between the Chicano family and dominant society: "our culture unites and educates the family of La Raza towards liberation with one heart and one mind." The Plan then articulated seven "organizational goals" for the movement, calling upon "writers, poets, musicians, and artists" to assist this process by defining the "cultural values" of the family and home as a "powerful weapon" against the "gringo dollar value system." But while the role of cultural expression was central to the organization of the movement, it was also the only "organizational goal" that was absent from the "action" or public sphere portion of the Plan. To some extent, this can be explained by the way in which the Plan equated cultural expression with the private domain of the family and home. Thus, although the Chicano family served as a model for political organization and "nation" building, its patriarchal and hierarchical structure served to keep the issues associated with family *entre familia* (literally, "between family members," or not for public discussion). These issues were, namely, those of gender, generation, and sexuality. Within the terms of the Plan, cultural production was expected to maintain this status quo—to reaffirm the traditional family—as a central element within an oppositional Chicano politics.

Despite its location within mass media, *¡Ahora!* worked within the terms of the Plan, since the public affairs series used broadcast television to reach the homes of Chicano families just after dinner, informing that audience about political events, but also cultivating cultural and historical awareness that was, in the words of the Plan, both "appealing" and "revolutionary." As an example of prime-time access programming, *¡Ahora!* was situated between the six o'clock news and prime-time entertainment, drawing upon both forms of television discourse, but serving a specific segment of the station's market. Thus, although ratings were generally above average for its time slot, the viewership was constituted along the lines of local and ethnic needs (what would now be called narrowcasting). As such, this type of show was at odds with commercial television, which sold advertising time based on reaching a percentage of a broadcast audience. This narrowcasting strategy would typify minority public affairs series throughout the 1970s until deregulation brought an end to prime-time access, shifting the few remaining shows to Sunday mornings.

When Ford Foundation support ended in 1970, Treviño had to apply activist strategies within the station in order to secure another show that addressed the concerns of the Chicano community. He organized the fifteen to twenty "Spanish surnamed" employees of the station—janitors, secretaries, and various technicians—"to sign a petition that said, unless the Chicano community had a weekly television show, we were all going to resign en masse. . . . and that was the birth of *Acción Chicano* [sic]."[24] By the time *Acción Chicano* first aired in 1972, Treviño had decided that "the problem with our programming was that it kept being ghettoized and relegated to the corner." His response was to reproduce the "high production values" of the station's other shows, even though this meant that he had to stick to a talk-show or performance format given the limited budgets (about fifteen hundred dollars per week/episode). Even with these limitations, however, Treviño and other Chicano filmmakers could draw upon various strategies in order to introduce political commentary, and to find alternative ways to "run the whole spectrum of programming."[25]

One effective strategy used by Treviño and others was to speak from behind the mask of a "folk" ethnicity, in particular through *teatro* performances that included variations on the folk music of the Mexican Revolution. In this manner, the "folkloric" appearances satisfied station managers who might otherwise have been concerned about the unsubtitled Spanish. In one episode of *Acción Chicano*, Treviño featured a performance by Los Mascarones (The Masquers), a Mexican *teatro* group similar in style and politics to El Teatro Campesino. The episode was sent to PBS for national release, and, "they thought this was a nice folkloric kind of stuff . . . and went along with it." It was during the national airing that PBS discovered the content of the Spanish-language episode (with no subtitles), since numerous Cuban exiles in Miami called in to protest. The Los Mascarones performance ends with the theme song of the Cuban Revolution, with added lines that place the civil rights struggles of Chicanos, Puerto Ricans, and Blacks within its radical framework.[26] In the 1970s, many of the Chicano and Latino television series and specials would use Spanish as a way to communicate ideas and information that might have been censored in English.[27] Other examples of *teatro*-based programs that relied on Spanish-language dialogue and code switching, included *Los Vendidos: The Sellouts* (1972), *Guadalupe* (1976), and *El Corrido* (1976).

Using *Acción Chicano* as a base from which to pool resources and expand his audience, Treviño was also able to produce some of the first film documentaries. "I would tape two or three shows and make them all talk shows so that I could take that budget and invest it in film stock." These films included *La Raza Unida* (1972), *Yo Soy Chicano* (1972), *Carnalitos* (1973), and *Somos Uno* (1973). Treviño also used these films as a way to train other Chicano filmmakers, such as Bobby Páramo, who coproduced *Carnalitos*.[28] Finally, in a move that would have national repercussions, in 1972 *Acción Chicano* pooled resources with a new Puerto Rican series in New York City, *Realidades*, wherein the two shows traded five episodes each for local rebroadcast. This became a first step in the development of pan-Latino advocacy and organization at the national level.

"OUR OWN INSTITUTIONS"

In 1975, *Realidades* became the first national Latino television series, and subsequently commissioned numerous Chicano films, including Severo Pérez's *Cristal* (1975), Susan Racho's *Garment Workers* (1975), José Luis Ruiz's *Guadalupe* (1976), Bobby Páramo's *Salud and the Latino* (1976), Ricardo Soto's *Cosecha* (1976), *Migra* (1976), and *Al Otro Paso* (1976), and Adolfo Vargas's *Una Nación Bilingüe* (1977). The program stood in contrast to the earlier occasional national feeds of local material, and provided a pan-Latino forum for Chicano and Puerto Rican films. Several works dealt with national Latino issues, with footage shot on both coasts and in the Midwest: *Garment Workers,* Jay Ojeda's *De Colores* (1975), *Salud and the Latino. Realidades* was created in 1972, when members of the Puerto Rican Education and Action Media Council took over the studio of PBS affiliate WNET-TV (New York) during the station's pledge drive. In its first two years, the series was similar to the concurrent *Acción Chicano* (also created through protest), with which it exchanged programs.[29] In 1974, the Corporation for Public Broadcasting (CPB) awarded *Realidades* sixty thousand dollars to produce a one-hour pilot for national broadcast. In its two years as a national series, *Realidades* received $553,687 from the CPB, and produced twenty-three half-hour programs. The monies from CPB represented less than 3 percent of the CPB total production budget; after the series ended, that level dropped to 1 percent for Latino projects.[30]

Despite its short-lived success, *Realidades* revealed the need for a national pan-Latino organization in order to secure greater continuity of reforms, while it also provided a national network of producers associated with the series. With the waning of public protests in the early 1970s, Chicano/Latino filmmakers began to develop national institutions within the industry. These included the Latino Consortium (since 1974; now, National Latino Communications Center), which syndicates Latino-themed and -produced works on public television; the Chicano Film Festival in San Antonio, Texas (since 1975; now, CineFestival), which provides a national forum for public exhibition, as both a community-based event and a professional one; and the National Latino Media Coalition (1975–80), formed by Humberto Cintrón, executive producer of *Realidades*, which lobbied for federal funding. Echoing "El Plan Espiritual de Aztlán," Treviño identified these various efforts as an attempt to create "our own institutions."[31] These were, however, institutions that attempted to speak on behalf of both the community and media professionals from within the mass media, rather than institutions whose domain was that of the community itself. In contrast to *¡Ahora!* and other eclectic-format series whose primary audience was the Chicano community, these "institutions" worked at the crossroads of a Chicano/Latino audience and a national one, primarily within the domain of educational programming rather than that of entertainment. Overall these efforts represented a significant shift from social protest strategies to professional advocacy within the industry and the independent sector. But, as Trevino and other filmmakers have noted, Hollywood studios and television networks remained intransigent in the face of these internal pressures.[32]

LOCATING CHICANO CINEMA

The move to professionalism, however, did not occur in a political vacuum; rather, despite limited success with studios and networks, it represented a significant maneuver within a larger strategy to locate Chicano culture. Throughout the 1960s and 1970s, contacts with Latin America via postrevolutionary Cuba provided an essential framework for the development of the movement's radical politics as well as its reformist achievements. Even before the Chicano movement, in 1964 Luis Valdez traveled to Cuba as a member of a Progressive Labor Party delegation. Valdez, like many Chicano student activists, had been involved in reformist efforts directed at the Democratic Party, such as the Mexican American Political Association (MAPA), and had been active in the "Viva Kennedy!" clubs. Upon his return from Cuba, however, Valdez coauthored one of the first radical student manifestos, "Venceremos! Mexican American Statement on Travel to Cuba," which anchored its rejection of reformist politics in a pan-American solidarity.[33] Chicano political discourse continued to look to Mexico, Cuba, and, more generally, the "Bronze Continent" as the necessary backdrop of its efforts to imagine an ethnic community within the political, socioeconomic, and legal structures of the United States. This "imagined" location in the Americas became the context for local political action as well as professional reform within the U.S. film and television industries.

Perhaps the most lasting impact has been the result of Treviño's involvement with New Latin American Cinema. In 1974, Treviño was recruited into the Cuban-sponsored Comité de Cineastas de América Latina (Latin American Filmmakers Committee), an international committee of a dozen filmmakers committed to the advancement of New Latin American Cinema. The committee met six mimes between 1974 and 1978, and worked toward the organization of the Annual Festival of New Latin American Cinema, which premiered in December 1979 in Havana, Cuba. At its sixth meeting (in Havana, July 12–17, 1978), the committee issued a declaration about the festival, and, in the second paragraph, spelled out the relationship of the Chicano filmmakers to New Latin American Cinema:

> We also declare our solidarity with the struggle of Chicano cinema, the cultural manifestation of a community that combats the oppression and discrimination within the United States in order to affirm its Latin American roots. This reality remains almost or entirely unknown by most of our people, or reaches them through the distortions of the imperialist news media. Yet today the Chicano community has its own filmmakers and films, and demands of us the commitment to strengthen the cultural-historical ties that join us together, by contributing to the dissemination of their films, their experiences, and their struggles.[34]

Treviño and the Chicano Cinema Coalition led a delegation of Chicano filmmakers and media advocates to the first festival. As he explains, "It was a real eye-opener experience for a lot of Chicanos that went, because for the first time they were seeing a lot of Latin American, not just Cuban, cinema."[35] Although the experience seemed to confirm the predictions of the earlier film manifestos, the social context for racial and radical politics in the United States had changed quite a bit since the heyday of the Chicano movement and New Latin American Cinema. Nonetheless, the contacts with Cuba and Latin America did foster an increased international political perspective in the 1980s, although it is difficult to separate this from the filmmakers' increased awareness of and attention to the international film market and festival circuit.[36] In this respect, the festival served an important symbolic role in doubling the "location" of Chicano cinema, making it into a movement that was at once reformist and revolutionary. But rather than constitute a contradiction, this dual location provided Chicano filmmakers with an effective political strategy within the United States. Clearly, many of the early successful reforms came about as a result of shifting the center leftward during public protests and press statements, providing filmmakers with a vantage point from which to negotiate.

By the late 1970s, this strategy rang hollow after national and international "movement" politics came to a violent end. Chicano filmmakers would, for the most part, shift to a politics of "professionalism" within the industry and the independent sector. Still, "Chicano cinema" persists as a quasi-national category within international film festivals in Latin America and Europe, and is generally tied to a "minority" cultural politics.[37] Since the late 1970s, Chicano filmmakers have continued to articulate and develop connections to New Latin American Cinema as well as Spanish-language cinema in general. These filmmakers also initiated various efforts to integrate both Hollywood and the independent sector in order to produce and distribute Chicano-themed feature films and documentaries. Thus, if Treviño and others located "Chicano cinema" within both New Latin American Cinema and Hollywood, it was as the functional synthesis of ostensible contradictions, one that allowed the practice to follow upon the idea and the possibilities it created.

What stands outside these efforts to walk the line between reform and revolution—the bipolar terms of the Chicano movement—was the simultaneous emergence of a Chicano avant-garde in the mid-1960s and early 1970s, one split between the modernist aesthetics of a personal, visionary cinema and the postmodern parody of an alienated television generation.[38] Taking this work into account challenges the prevailing history of Chicano cinema with its equivalence between body, politics, and aesthetics as well as its ambivalence about institutional location. Indeed, *I Am Joaquín* is not the "first" Chicano film in the strict sense of the word, since there are at least two earlier avant-garde films: Ernie Palomino's *My Trip in a '52 Ford* (1966), also a film poem, but one that follows in the tradition of Beat counterculture rather than the neo-indigenist *floricanto* (Chicano poetry); and Severo Pérez's *Mozo: An Introduction into the Duality of Orbital Indecision* (1968), a pot-induced send-up of the trance film that circulated as part of the Texas Underground National Tour. Most filmmakers and critics, however, continue to identify *I Am Joaquín* as the "first" Chicano film, in the same manner that poets and literature scholars identify Gonzales's "I Am Joaquín" as the "first" Chicano poem: both are seen as the first articulations of a political, historical, and poetic consciousness about the "Chicano experience." Unlike the experimental films with their interracial, cross-cultural, and transcendental concerns, *I Am Joaquín* contributed to the idea of a "Chicano cinema" that operated within clearly marked borders (for community, for identity) that were defined by the exigencies of the Chicano civil rights movement. Like Gonzales's poem, which recontained its ambivalence within stable bipolar terms, Chicano cinema both juxtaposed and straddled two locations: America and América. Again, this was not so much a matter of an either/or choice (even though it was presented as such), but rather an attempt to define tightly coupled oppositional terms—nationalism and assimilation; revolution and reform—so that the one would inevitably produce the other. Without a doubt, such a strategy put Chicano cinema on the map in both a literal and a figurative sense, constructing an alternative to Hollywood. But it was an alternative in both senses of the word, something different from Hollywood, yet something that also aspired to take its place.

Endnotes

1. Of the filmmakers, Jesús Salvador Treviño has been the most prolific and influential, publishing in Europe and the Americas, and in some ways setting the terms for subsequent scholarship. See, for example, Treviño's articles "Cinéma Chicano aux Etats-Unis," in *Les Cinémas de l'Amérique Latine*, ed. Guy Hennebelle and Alfonso Gumucio-Dagron (Paris: Nouvelles Editions Pierre Lherminier, 1981), 493–99; "Chicano Cinema," *New Scholar* 8 (1982): 167–80; and "El desarrollo del cine chicano," in *Hojas de cine: testimonios y documentos del nuevo cine latinoamericano* (México: Fundación del nuevo cine latinoamericano, 1986), n.p. Books on Chicano cinema include Gary D. Keller, ed., *Chicano Cinema: Research, Reviews, and Resources* (Binghamton, N.Y.: Bilingual Review/Press, 1985); Chon A. Noriega, ed., *Chicanos and Film: Representation and Resistance* (Minneapolis: University of Minnesota Press,

1992); Rosa Linda Fregoso, *The Bronze Screen: Chicana and Chicano Film Culture* (Minneapolis: University of Minnesota Press, 1993); and Gary D. Keller, *Hispanics and United States Film: An Overview and Handbook* (Tempe, Ariz.: Bilingual Press, 1994).

2. I draw upon Mario Barrera's insightful analysis of the historical role of egalitarian (integrationist) and communitarian (cultural nationalist) goals in the Mexican-origin community. See Mario Barrera, *Beyond Aztlán: Ethnic Autonomy in Comparative Perspective* (Notre Dame, Ind.: University of Notre Dame press, 1988), chapters 1–6.

3. Coco Fusco, "Fantasies of Oppositionality: Reflections on Recent Conferences in Boston and New York," *Screen* 29 (autumn 1988): 80–93; and "Ethnicity, Politics and Poetics: Latinos and Media Art," in *Illuminating Video: An Essential Guide to Video Art*, ed. Doug Hall and Sally Jo Fifer (New York: Aperture/BAVC, 1990), 304–16.

4. Chon A. Noriega, "Between a Weapon and a Formula: Chicano Cinema and Its Contexts," in Noriega, ed., *Chicanos and Film*, 141–67.

5. See Carlos Muñoz Jr., *Youth, Identity, Power: The Chicano Movement* (New York: Verso, 1989).

6. The "Plan of Delano" is reprinted in Armando B. Rendón, *Chicano Manifesto* (New York: Macmillan, 1971), 327–30. Rendón reprints the "Plan of Delano" with three other manifestos under the appendix title "Four Declarations of Independence."

7. As I discuss later, this can be seen in the use of specific phrases as well as rhetorical strategies. The "Plan Espiritual de Aztlán" is reprinted in Rudolfo A. Anaya and Francisco Lomelí, eds., *Aztlán: Essays on the Chicano Homeland* (Albuquerque, N.M.: Academia/El Norte Publications, 1989), 1–6. The "Plan de Santa Barbara" is reprinted in Muñoz, *Youth, Identity, Power*, 191–202. Three film manifestos from the 1970s are reprinted in Noriega, ed., *Chicanos and Film*, 275–307.

8. The charges against the "L.A. Thirteen" were dismissed as unconstitutional after two years of appeals (Rodolfo Acuña, *Occupied America: A History of Chicanos*, 3d ed. [New York: HarperCollins, 1988], 388).

9. *I Am Joaquín* was later annotated and reissued by Bantam Books in 1972. Film and poem appear in Spanish and English versions.

10. "I/WE SHALL ENDURE" appears in capital letters in both texts.

11. See Tomás Ybarra-Frausto, "The Chicano Movement and the Emergence of a Chicano Poetic Consciousness," *New Scholar* 6 (1977): 81–109.

12. Luis Valdez, "Notes on Chicano Theater" (1970), in *Luis Valdez—Early Works* (Houston: Arte Público Press, 1990), 8.

13. "El Plan Espiritual de Aztlán," in Anava and Lomelí, eds., *Aztlán,* 2. See also Gonzales, "Chicano Nationalism: The Key to Unity for la Raza," *Militant*, March 30, 1970.

14. The production dates cited for the film range from 1967 to 1970. In his article "Cinéma Chicano aux Etats-Unis," Treviño—based on interviews with the Valdez brothers—states that the film was shot and recorded "[o]n a hot summer evening in 1967," the same year the poem was written. The film itself has a 1969 copyright, which may indicate that the film was shown before it was copyrighted, or that it took over a year to edit the film.

15. See Rolando Hinojosa's comments on the changes made in the film in order to make it more commercial (Hinojosa, *"I Am Joaquín:* Relationships between the Text and the Film," in Keller, ed., *Chicano Cinema,* 142–45). The United Farm Workers Service Center continued to document events on film, and produced at least two Spanish-language documentaries for internal use: *Nosotros Venceremos* (1971; *We Will Overcome*), which uses photographic stills to relate UFW struggles and goals; and *Sí, se puede* (1973; *Yes, We Can*), on César Chávez's hunger strike in Arizona.

16. Jesús Salvador Treviño, "Chicano Cinema Overview," *Areíto* 37 (1984): 40.

17. Personal interview with Treviño, May 28, 1991.

18. Ibid.

19. Ibid.

20. Treviño, "Chicano Cinema": 170–71; and Harry Gamboa Jr., "Silver Screening the Barrio," *Equal Opportunity Forum* 6.1 (November 1978): 6–7.

21. Personal interview with Treviño, May 28, 1991.

22. Ibid.

23. An unauthorized reprint appears in Cine-Aztlán, "The Treviño/Ahora Survey: A Historical Profile of the Chicano and Latino in Hollywood Film Productions," in *La Raza Film Bibliography* (Santa Barbara, Calif.: Cine-Aztlán, 1974), 9–16.

24. Personal interview with Treviño, May 28, 1991. In Spanish, adjectives usually conform to the gender of the noun. Thus, the correct title would be *Acción Chicana.* Treviño, however, "purposely changed it to *Chicano*," since "I basically, at that time, thought that *Chicana* would read that it was a show only for women, and I wanted to make it clear that this was for the whole community." That there would have been such confusion owes more to the decreased Spanish-language maintenance within the Chicano generation than to sexism. In fact, Treviño himself was not fluent in Spanish at the time.

25. Ibid.

26. Ibid.

27. In Lubbock, Texas, for example, the Spanish-language series *Aztlán* (1976–79), produced by Héctor Galán, "got away with murder, because the station didn't understand" (statement by Héctor Galán during the roundtable "In the Public Eye: A Dialogue on Chicano Media Arts," Dialogues in Movement: A Chicano Media Arts Retrospective, San Antonio, Texas, July 13, 1991).

28. Bobby Páramo, "*Cerco Blanco, The Balloon Man,* and *Fighting City Hall:* On Being a Chicano Filmmaker," *Metamorfosis* 3.2 (1980–81): 77–82.

29. José García Torres, "José García Torres & *Realidades*," interview by Aurora Flores and Lillian Jiménez, *Centro Bulletin* 2.8 (spring 1990): 30–43.

30. "Pensamientos: Latinos and CPB," *Chicano Cinema Newsletter* 1.6 (August 1979): 2–3, 2.

31. Quoted in Antonio José Guernica, "Chicano Production Companies: Projecting Reality, Opening the Doors," *Agenda: A Journal of Hispanic Issues* 8.1 (January-February 1978): 12–15, 13.

32. Jesús Salvador Treviño, "Lights, Camera, Action," *Hispanic* (August 1992): 76.

33. Luis Valdez and Roberto Rubalcava, reprinted in Luis Valdez and Stan Steiner, eds., *Aztlán: An Anthology of Mexican American Literature* (New York: Alfred A. Knopf, 1972): 215–16.

34. "Declaración del Comité de Cineastas de América Latina," *Cine Cubano* 8.3 (1977–78): 45–46; translation mine. The declaration was translated by Ralph Cook and reprinted in *Cineaste* 9.1 (fall 1978): 54. In Cook's version, he inserts references to the Chicano movement. The original text, however, refers to the Chicano "community," and not the "movement," whose militant phase had already come to an end.

35. Personal interview with Treviño, May 28, 1991.

36. See, for example, David Rosen's chapter on *The Ballad of Gregorio Cortez* in *Off-Hollywood: The Making and Marketing of Independent Films* (New York: Grove Weidenfeld, 1990), 1–22.

37. See my forthcoming article, "On Curating," *Wide Angle* 17.1–4.

38. These two tendencies are exemplified by the work of Willie Varela and Harry Gamboa Jr., respectively. See Chon A. Noriega, "Willie Varela," *New American Film and Video Series* 72, program note (New York: Whitney Museum of American Art, 1994); and the section on Gamboa in my article "Talking Heads, Body Politic: The Plural Self of Chicano Video," in *Resolutions: Contemporary Video Practices,* ed. Michael Renov and Erika Suderburg (Minneapolis: University of Minnesota Press, in press.). For the filmmakers' own accounts, see Gamboa, "Past Imperfecto," *Jump Cut* 39 (June 1994): 93–95, and Varela, "Chicano Personal Cinema," *Jump Cut* 39 (June 1994): 96–99.

SECTION 5: LITERATURE, ART, FOLKLORE, MUSIC, AND CINEMA ASSESSMENT AND APPLICATION

1. Identify and describe each of Ortego's historical developmental stages of Chicano literature and provide examples of each period.

2. Name the four principal reasons why literary production was limited during the pre-Chicano period.

3. How is Chicano literature different from Mexican, Latin-American, or Euro-American literature?

4. Discuss the importance of gender and sexuality in Chicano feminist literature according to Yarbro-Bejarano.

5. Identify the major differences between literature, oral history or tradition, and folklore.

6. Provide various examples of Chicano folklore that would be useful to providers of social services, educators, or business persons in your community.

7. Contrast and compare the images, cultural icons, norms, values, and beliefs manifested by a Chicana and a Chicano author.

8. After reading Vargas's essay, identify and describe the themes in some salient murals in your community.

9. Take photographs of selected murals in your community and produce a twenty-minute socio-ethnographic presentation illustrating each mural, its painter, and the themes addressed by each mural. Preface your presentation with a socioeconomic and historical overview of the areas where these murals are found. What cultural messages do you find? How is ethnic identity depicted by the murals?

10. How does Amalia Mesa-Bains define the political and feminist work of Chicana artists?

11. How does Chicana art differ from Chicano art?

12. Select two Chicano and two Chicana artists from your community and organize a panel presentation in which they can discuss their artistic contributions and relevant gender issues.

13. Interview your parents and identify traditions in your home that are listed by Herrera-Sobek. Explain why the traditions are still maintained in your family.

14. According to Ortega, what are some of the key conceptual features of Chicano music?

15. Why is the Chicano movement a catalyst for Chicano music, especially with the use of lyrics?

16. Describe how Noriega links the expression of Chicano cinema with the Chicano movement.

SECTION 5: SUGGESTED READINGS

Abarca, Meredith E. (2006). *Voices in the Kitchen: Views of Food and the World from Working-Class Mexican and Mexican American Women*. College Station, TX: Texas A&M University Press.

Aldama, Frederick Luis. (2006). *Spilling the Beans in Chicanolandia: Conversations with Writers and Artists*. Austin, TX: University of Texas Press.

Anzaldúa, Gloria. (1998). Chicana Artists: Exploring Nepantla, el Lugar de la Frontera. In Antonia Darder & Rodolfo Torres, (Eds.). *The Latino Studies Reader: Culture, Economy and Society*. Maiden, MA: Blackwell Publishers.

Agrasánchez, Rogelio, Jr. (2006). *Mexican Movies in the United States: A History of the Films, Theaters and Audiences, 1920–1960*. Jefferson, NC: McFarland.

Arrizón, Alicia. (1999). *Latina Performance: Traversing the Stage*. Bloomington, IN: Indiana University Press.

Broyles-González, Yolanda. (1994). *El Teatro Campesino: Theater in the Chicano Movement*. Austin, TX: University of Texas Press.

Byrd, Bobby & Mississippi Byrd, Susannah. (Eds.). (1996). *The Late Great Mexican Border: Reports from a Disappearing Line*. El Paso, TX: Cinco Puntos Press.

Cantú, Norma E. & Nájera-Ramírez, Olga. (2002). *Chicana Traditions: Continuity and Change*. Champaign, IL: University of Illinois Press.

Castro, Rafaela G. (2001). *Chicano Folklore: A Guide to the Folktales, Traditions, Rituals and Religious Practices of Mexican Americans*. New York, NY: Oxford University Press.

Chacón, Corinne. (2006). *The Mystics of Reyesville*. New York, NY: Universe Inc.

Chacón, Daniel. (2013). *Hotel Jurez: Stories, Rooms and Loops*. Houston, TX: Arte Público Press.

Chávez, Denise. (2006). *A Taco Testimony, Meditations on Family, Food and Culture*. (1st ed.). Tucson, AZ: Rio Nuevo Publishers.

Chew Sánchez, Martha I. (2006). *Corridos in Migrant Memory*. Albuquerque, NM: University of New Mexico Press.

Clayton, Lawrence & Specht, Joe W. (2003). *The Roots of Texas Music*. College Station, TX: Texas A&M University Press.

Cortez, Sarah & Troncoso, Sergio. (2013). *Our Lost Border: Essays on Life Amid the Narco-Violence*. Houston, TX: Arte Público Press.

Cull, Nicholas J. & Carrasco, David. (2004). *Alambrista and the U.S.-Mexico Border: Film, Music, and Stories of Undocumented Immigrants*. Albuquerque, NM: University of New Mexico Press.

Delgado, Abelardo. (2011). *Here Lies Lalo: The Collected Poems of Abelardo Delgado*. Houston, TX: Arte Público Press.

Edberg, Mark Cameron. (2004). *El Narcotraficante: Narcocorridos and the Construction of a Cultural Persona on the U.S.–Mexico Border*. Austin, TX: University of Texas Press.

Flores, Carlos N. (2006). *Our House on Hueco*. Lubbock, TX: Texas Tech University Press.

Gaspar de Alba, Alicia. (1998). *Chicano Art Inside/Outside the Master's House*. Austin, TX: University of Texas Press.

Gaspar de Alba, Alicia. (2003). *Velvet Barrios: Popular Culture & Chicana/o Sexualities*. New York, NY: Palgrave Macmillan.

Gilb, Dagoberto. (2011). *Before the End, After the Beginning: Stories*. New York, NY: Grove Press.

Gilb, Dagoberto. (2006). *Hecho en Tejas: An Anthology of Texas Mexican Literature*. Albuquerque, NM: University of New Mexico Press.

Gladstein, Mimi R. & Chacón, Daniel. (2008). *The Last Supper of Chicano Heroes: Selected Works of José Antonio Burciaga*. Tucson, AZ: University of Arizona Press.

Griswold del Castillo, Richard, McKenna, Teresa & Bejarano, Yvonne. (1991). *Chicano Art: Resistance and*

Affirmation, 1965–1985. Los Angeles, CA: Wight Gallery, University of California, Los Angeles.

Guerrero, Lalo & Mente, Sherilyn Meece. (2002). *Lalo: My Life and Music.* Tucson, AZ: University of Arizona Press.

Gutiérrez-Jones, Carl. (2004). *Rebellious Reading: The Dynamics of Chicana/o Cultural Literacy.* Santa Barbara, CA: Center for Chicano Studies, University of California, Santa Barbara.

Hatfield Daudistel, M. (2009). *Literary El Paso.* Fort Worth, TX: Texas Christian University Press.

Hernández, Guillermo. (1978). *Canciones de la Raza: Songs of the Chicano Experience.* Berkeley, CA: El Fuego de Aztlán.

Hernández-Gutiérrez, Manuel de Jesús & Foster, David William. (Eds.). (1997). *Literatura Chicana, 1965–1995: An Anthology in Spanish, English, and Caló.* New York, NY: Garland Publishing.

Herrera-Sobek, María. (1993). *Northward Bound: The Mexican Experience in Ballad and Song.* Bloomington, IN: Indiana University Press.

Herrera-Sobek, María. (1996). *Chicana Creativism and Criticism: New Frontiers in American Literature.* Albuquerque, NM: University of New Mexico Press.

Hernández, Tim Z. (2013). *Mañana Means Heaven.* Tucson, AZ: University of Arizona Press.

Huerta, Jorge A. (1982). *Chicano Theater: Themes and Forms.* Tempe, AZ: Bilingual Review Press.

Islas, Arturo. (1991). *The Rain God.* New York, NY: Avon Books.

Joysmith, Claire. (Ed.). (1995). *Las Formas de Nuestras Voces: Chicana and Mexicana Writers in México.* México, DF: Centro de Investigaciones sobre América del Norte, Universidad Autónoma de México.

Kanellos, Nicolás, et al. (2002). *En Otra Voz: Antología de la Literatura Hispana de los Estados Unidos.* Houston, TX: Arte Público Press.

Keller, Gary D. (1997). *A Biographical Handbook of United States Film.* Tempe, AZ: Bilingual Review Press.

Keller, Gary D., et al. (2002). *Contemporary Chicana and Chicano Art, Vol. I: Artists, Works, Culture and Education.* Tempe, AZ: Bilingual Review Press.

Keller, Gary D., et al. (2002). *Contemporary Chicana and Chicano Art, Vol. II: Artists, Works, Culture and Education.* Tempe, AZ: Bilingual Review Press.

Keller, Gary D. (2005). *Triumph of Our Communities: Four Decades of Mexican American Art.* Tempe, AZ: Bilingual Review Press.

López, Miguel R. (2001). *Chicano Timespace: The Poetry and Politics of Ricardo Sánchez.* College Station, TX: Texas A&M University Press.

Loza, Steven. (1993). *Barrio Rhythm: Mexican American Music in Los Angeles.* Urbana, IL: University of Illinois Press.

Loza, Steven. (1993). *Mexican American Music in Los Angeles.* Urbana, IL: University of Illinois Press.

Maciel, David R., Ortiz, Isidro D. & Herrera-Sobek, María. (2000). *Chicano Renaissance: Contemporary Cultural Trends.* Tucson, AZ: University of Arizona Press.

Malagamba-Ansótegui, A. (2006). *Caras Vemos, Corazones No Sabemos: The Human Landscape of Mexican Migration.* Notre Dame, IN: University of Notre Dame.

McFarland, Pancho. (2008). *Chicano Rap: Gender and Violence in the Postindustrial Barrio.* Austin, TX: University of Texas Press.

Méndez-Negrete, Josie. (2002). *Las Hijas de Juan: Daughters Betrayed.* Durham, NC: Duke University Press.

Mendoza, Louis Gerard. (2001). *Historia: The Literary Making of Chicana & Chicano History.* College Station, TX: Texas A&M University Press.

Morton, Carlos. (1994). *The Many Deaths of Danny Rosales and Other Plays.* Houston, TX: Arte Público Press.

Noriega, Chon A. & López, Ana M. (1996). *The Ethnic Eye: Latino Media Arts.* Minneapolis, MN: University of Minnesota Press.

Peña, Manuel. (1985). *The Texas-Mexican Conjunto: History of a Working-Class Music.* Austin, TX: University of Texas Press.

Peña, Manuel. (1999). *Música Tejana: The Cultural Economy of Artistic Transformation.* College Station, TX: Texas A&M University Press.

Perezdíaz, Roberto. (2012). *Más Sabe El Diablo.* Mexico, DF: Ediciones y Gráficos Eón.

Pérez-Torres, Rafael. (1995). *Movements in Chicano Poetry: Against Myths, Against Margins*. New York, NY: Cambridge University Press.

Pérez-Torres, Rafael. (2006). *Mestizaje: Critical Uses of Race in Chicano Culture*. Minneapolis, MN: University of Minnesota Press.

Portales, Marco. (2000). *Crowding Out Latinos: Mexican Americans in the Public Consciousness*. Philadelphia, PA: Temple University Press.

Quirarte, Jacinto. (Ed.). (1984). *Chicano Art History: A Book of Selected Readings*. San Antonio, TX: Research Center for the Arts and Humanities.

Rebolledo, Diana Tey & Rivero, Eliana S. (1993). *Infinite Divisions: An Anthology of Chicana Literature*. Tucson, AZ: University of Arizona Press.

Rebolledo, Diana Tey. (2005). *The Chronicles of Panchita Villa and Other Guerrilleras: Essays on Chicana/Latina Literature and Criticism*. Austin, TX: University of Texas Press.

Reyes, David & Waldman, Tom. (1998). *Land of a Thousand Dances: Chicano Rock 'n' Roll from Southern California*. Albuquerque, NM: University of New Mexico Press.

Richmond Ellis, Robert. (1997). *The Hispanic Homograph: Gay Self-Representation in Contemporary Spanish Autobiography*. Urbana, IL: University of Illinois Press.

Rodríguez Kessler, E. & Perrin, Anne. (2007). *Chican@s in the Conversations*. (1st ed.). New York, NY: Longman.

Rohrleitner, Marion & Ryan, Sarah. (2012). *Dialogues Across Diasporas: Women Writers, Scholars, and Activists of Africana and Latina Descent in Conversation*. Lanham, MD: Lexington Books.

Sáenz, Benjamín A. (2005). *In Perfect Light*. New York, NY: HarperCollins.

Sáenz, Benjamín A. (2012). *Everything Begins and Ends at the Kentucky Club*. (1st ed.). El Paso, TX: Cinco Puntos Press.

Sheey, Daniel. (2006). *Mariachi Music in America: Experiencing Music, Expressing Culture*. New York, NY: Oxford University Press.

Shirley, Carl R. & Shirley, Paula W. (1988). *Understanding Chicano Literature*. Columbia, SC: University of South Carolina Press.

Smithsonian Latino Center. (2006). *Hispanic Heritage at the Smithsonian: A Decade of Latino Initiatives*. Washington, DC: Smithsonian Latino Center.

Stavans, Ilan. (1996). *Oscar "Zeta" Acosta: The Uncollected Works*. Houston, TX: Arte Público Press.

Stavans, Ilan. (Illustrated by Lalo Alcaraz). (2000). *Latino USA: A Cartoon History*. New York, NY: Philip Lief Group, Inc.

Storm Roberts, John. (1979). *The Latin Tinge: The Impact of Latin American Music on the United States*. New York, NY: Oxford University Press.

Tejeda, Juan & Valdez, Avelardo. (2001). *Puro Conjunto: An Album in Words & Pictures*. Austin, TX: University of Texas Press.

Torres, René. (2011). Narciso "Chicho" Martínez incubated the conjunto sound in the RGV. *The Rrun Rrun*.

Treviño, Jesús Salvador. (2001). *Eyewitness: A Filmmaker's Memoir of the Chicano Movement*. Houston, TX: Arte Público Press.

Vargas, Deborah R. (2012). *Dissonant Divas in Chicana Music: The Limits of La Onda*. Minneapolis, MN: University of Minnesota Press.

Vázquez, Francisco H. & Torres, Rodolfo D. (2003). *Latino/a Thought: Culture, Politics and Society*. New York, NY: Rowman & Littlefield Publishers.

Vila, Pablo. (1996). Catholicism and Identity on the U.S.-Mexico Border. *Occasional Papers in Chicano Studies*. (8). El Paso, TX: Chicano Studies, University of Texas at El Paso.

Yáñez, Richard. (2003). *El Paso del Norte: Stories on the Border*. Reno, NV: University of Nevada Press.

Yáñez, Richard. (2011). *Cross Over Water*. Reno, NV: University of Nevada Press.

Yorba, J. (2001). *Arte Latino: Treasures From the Smithsonian American Art Museum*. New York, NY: Watson-Guptill Publications.

SECTION 5: SUGGESTED FILMS AND VIDEOS

A Language of Passion, 2002
Joie de Vivre Productions
3010 Highview Ave., Atadena, CA 91001

Al Otro Lado/To the Other Side, 2006
Natalia Almada/Altamura Films
50 South 4th St., Suite 402, Brooklyn, NY 11211

Border Brujo/The Shaman, 1990
Cine West
Coronado, CA
New York, NY

Brown Is the New Green: George López and the
American Dream, 2007 PBS
2100 Crystal Drive, Arlington, VA 22202

Casting Calls: Racial and Ethnic Stereotypes on
Screen, 2004
Discovery Channel

Chicano Park, 1989
Cinema Guild
115 West 30th Street, Suite 800, New York,
NY 10001

Chicano Rock! The Sounds of East Los Angeles,
2008 PBS
2100 Crystal Drive, Arlington, VA 22202

Chulas Fronteras, 1976
Rower Films
El Cerrito, CA

Concurso de Tribal Sonido Projector Texano
http://www.youtube.com/watch?v=aFuVXhtxNk4

Corridos!: Tales of Passion and Revolution, 1987
KQED, Inc./El Teatro Campesino
San Juan Bautista, CA

Countdown: Reflections of a Life Dance, 2005
American Public Television
55 Summer Street, Boston, MA 02110

Crossing Arizona, 2006
The Cinema Guild
115 West 30th Street, Suite 800, New York,
NY 10001

Diego Rivera: Art and Revolution, 1999
Films Media Group
132 West 30th Street, 17th Floor, New York,
NY 10001

El Contrato/The Contract, 2003
Films for the Humanities and Sciences
132 West 31st Street, 17th Floor, New York,
NY 10001

El Corrido Mexicano: Música y Cuernos de
Chivo, 2007
Films Media Group
132 West 30th Street, 17th Floor, New York,
NY 10001

El Día de Los Muertos/Day of the Dead, 1991
Institute of Texan Cultures
San Antonio, TX

Exploring Borderlands, 2003
Insight Media
2162 Broadway, New York, NY 10024-0621

Fandango, 2006
Los Centzoles Mexican Arts Center
13108 San Pablo Ave., San Pablo, CA 94805

Hispanic Art & Culture
An instructional unit that includes a video, a book,
fourteen slides, and a bilingual guide.
Produced by the Smithsonian National
Museum of Art
Social Studies School Service
10200 Jefferson Blvd., Room 1611
P.O. Box 802
Culver City, CA 90232-0802

Hispanic Excellence: Arts and Entertainment, 1993
Conrad & Associates Inc./Tuoka Productions, Inc.

Hispanics in the Media, 1994
Films for the Humanities and Sciences
132 West 31st Street, 17th Floor, New York, NY 10001

Lalo Guerrero: The Original Chicano, 2006
Original Chicano Productions
P.O. Box 2558, Palm Springs, CA 92263

La Mission, 2009
Screen Media Films
757 Third Ave., Third Floor, New York, NY 10017

La Ofrenda: The Days of the Dead, 1989
Direct Cinema, LTD

La Pastorela: The Sheperd's Tale, 1991
El Teatro Campesino
San Juan Bautista, CA

Latin Music U.S.A. & Chicano Rock, 2009 PBS
2100 Crystal Drive, Arlington, VA 22202

Latinos Beyond Reel, 2012
Media Education Foundation
60 Masonic Street, Northampton, MA 01060

Limón: A Life Beyond Words, 2005
Dance Conduit
35 5th Street, Frenchtown, New Jersey 00825

Los Four (Documentary on Key Moments and Figures in Chicano Art), 1974
Chicano Cinema and Media Art Series (UCLA)
193 Haines Hall, Los Angeles, CA 90095-1544

Los Vendidos, 1972
El Teatro Campesino
San Juan Bautista, CA

Madres Unidas: Parents Researching for Change, 2003
Berkeley Media LLC
2600 Tenth St., Suite 626, Berkeley, CA 94710

Mariachi High, 2012 PBS
2100 Crystal Drive, Arlington, VA 22202

Mujeres, 1989
Women Make Movies
New York, NY

Murals of Aztlán: The Street Painters of East Los Angeles, 1981
Chicano Cinema and Media Art Series (UCLA)
193 Haines Hall, Los Angeles, CA 90095-1544

My Family, 1995
New Line Home Entertainment/Warner Bros.
4000 Warner Blvd., Bldg. 154, Burbank, CA 91422

Paño Arte: Images from Inside, 1996
About Time Productions
Los Angeles, CA

Pilots of Aztlan: The Flights of the Royal Chicano Air Force, 1995
KVIE Public Television
2030 W. El Camino Ave., Sacramento, CA 95833

Quinceañera: Princess for a Day, 1993
Mexicana Imágenes de México
México, DF

Rancho California (Por Favor), 2003
Berkeley Media LLC
2600 Tenth St., Suite 626, Berkeley, CA 94710

Real Women Have Curves, 2002
HBO Independent Productions
Rivera in America, 1999
Alturas Films
2403 Main Street Santa Monica, CA 90405

Rolas de Aztlán, 2005
Smithsonian Folkways Recordings
750 9th St. NW, Suite 4100, Washington DC 20560-0953

Salt of the Earth, 1953
Independent Productions and the
International Union of Mine, Mill & Workers
Oak Forest, IL

Selena, 1997
Warner Bros.
4000 Warner Blvd., Bldg. 154, Burbank, CA 91422

Sing and Don't Cry: The Mariachis, 2005
Films Media Group
132 West 31st Street, 17th Floor, New York, NY 10001

Songs of the Homeland: History of Tejano Music, 1995
Films for the Humanities and Sciences
132 West 31st Street, 17th Floor, New York, NY 10001

Tapestry II, 1996
Martin Recording
El Paso, TX

The Bronze Screen: 100 Years of the Latino Image in Hollywood, 2002
Insight Media
2162 Broadway, New York, NY 10024-0621

The Piñata Makers, 1988
Barr Films
Irwindale, CA

Visiones, Latino Art & Culture, 2004
Galán, Inc.
5524 Bee Caves Rd., Suite B-5, Austin, TX 78746

Walls that Speak: A Video about El Paso's Murals, (1994)
The Junior League of El Paso
The El Paso Hispanic Chamber
El Paso, TX

Zoot Suit, 1981
Universal Pictures

Appendix A:
Organizations and Entities
Concerned With
The Mexican Origin Population

Advanced Research in Latin American Studies: latcar.rutgers.edu/lauria/advanced/index.htm

Aztecanet: www.azteca.net

Chicanopedia: Mexican American Library and Encyclopedia: http://Chicanopedia.org

Classic Mexican Cinema Online: www.brill.com/publications/online-resources/classic-mexican-cinema-online

Congressional Hispanic Caucus Institute (CHCI): www.chci.org

Digest of Education Statistics: 2011: nces.ed.gov/programs/digest/d11/index.asp

El Colegio de la Frontera Norte (El Colef): www.colef.mx

Environmental Defense Fund (EDF): www.edf.org

Farmworker Movement Documentation Project: www.farmworkermovement.org\

Great Minds in Stem: www.greatmindsinstem.org

H-Borderlands: research.utep.edu/borderlands

Hispanic Association of Colleges and Universities (HACU): www.hacu.net

Hispanic Business Inc.: www.hispanicbusiness.com

Hispanic Federation: www.hispanicfederation.org

Hispanic National Bar Association (HNBA): www.hnba.com

Inter-University Program for Latino Research (IUPLR): www.nd.edu/~iuplr/

Julián Samora Legacy Project: www.samoralegacymedia.org

Labor Council for Latin American Advancement: www.lclaa.org

Las Comadres Para Las Américas: www.lascomadres.org

Latinopia: www.latinopia.com

Latino Point of View: www.latinopov.com

Latino Policy Forum: www.latinopolicyforum.org

Latinos in Higher Ed: www.latinosinhighered.com

Latinoteca: www.latinoteca.com

League of United Latin American Citizens (LULAC): www.lulac.org

Librotraficante: http://librotraficante.com

Mexican American Coalition: www.mxac.org

Mexican American Legal Defense and Educational Fund (MALDEF): www.maldef.org

Mexican American Library and Encyclopedia: http://Chicanopedia.org

Mexican American National Association: A National Latina Organization: (MANA): www.hermana.org

Mexican Fine Arts Center Museum: www.nationalmuseumofmexicanart.org

Mexico-North Research Network, Inc.: www.mexnor.org

Mexmigration: History and Politics of Mexican Immigration: www.mexmigration.blogspot.com

Migrantólogos: Los que estudian la migración: http://mograntologos.mx

Migration Policy Institute: www.migrationpolicy.org

Mujeres Activas en Letras y Cambio Social (MALCS) *Women Active in Letters and Social Change:* www.malcs.org

National Association for Bilingual Education (NABE): www.nabe.org

National Association for Chicana and Chicano Studies (NACCS): www.naccs.org

National Association of Hispanic Federal Executives (NAHFE): www.nahfe.org

National Association of Hispanic Journalists (NAHJ): www.nahj.org

National Association of Hispanic Publication (NAHP): www.nahp.org

National Association of Latino Arts and Cultures (NALAC): www.nalac.org

National Association of Latino Elected and Appointed Officials (NALEO): www.naleo.org

National Association for Multicultural Education (NAME): www.nameorg.org

National Center for Children in Poverty (NCCP): www.nccp.org

National Coalition for Parent Involvement in Education (NCPIE): www.ncpie.org

National Council of La Raza (NCLR): www.nclr.org

National Hispana Leadership Institute (NHLI): www.nhli.org

National Hispanic Council on Aging (NHCOA): www.nhcoa.org

National Hispanic Cultural Center (NHCC): www.nhccnm.org

National Hispanic Environment Council (NHEC): www.nheec1.org

National Hispanic Foundation for the Arts (NHFA): www.hispanicarts.org

National Hispanic Leadership Agenda (NHLA): www.lulac.net/nhla/

National Hispanic Media Coalition: www.nhmc.org/

National Hispanic Medical Association: www.nhmamd.org

National Institute for Latino Policy (NiLP): www.nilpnetwork.org

National Latino Education Network: nlen.csusb.edu

National Museum of the American Latino Commission: www.americanlatinomuseum.gov

National Network for Immigrant and Refugee Rights (NNIRR): www.nnirr.org

National Park Service: American Latino Heritage Projects: www.nps.gov/latino/

National Puerto Rican Coalition, Inc. (NPRC): www.bateylink.org

New Carpa Theater Company: www.newcarpa.org

Pan American Health Organization (PAHO): www.paho.org

Pew Research Hispanic Center: www.pewhispanic.org

Raza Unida Progresista: www.razaunidaprogresista.org

Red Internacional de Migración y Desarrollo: www.migracionydesarrollo.org

REFORMA: The National Association to Promote Library and Information Services to Latinos and the Spanish Speaking: www.reforma.org

Smithsonian Latino Center: www.latino.si.edu

Society for Advancement of Chicanos and Native Americans in Science (SACNAS): www.sacnas.org

SouthWest Organizing Project: www.swop.net

Southwest Voter Registration Education Project (SVREP): www.svrep.org

Texas Association of Chicanos in Higher Education (TACHE): www.tache.org

The Tomás Rivera Policy Institute (TRPI): www.trpi.org

UCLA Chicano Studies Research Center (CSRC): www.chicano.ucla.edu

U.S. Hispanic Leadership Institute (USHLI): www.ushli.org

U.S. Latino & Latina WWII Oral History Project: www.lib.utexas.edu/voces/

United States Hispanic Chamber of Commerce Foundation (USHCC): www.ushccfoundation.org

United States–México Border Health Commission: www.borderhealth.org

University of California Institute for Mexico and the United States (UC MEXUS): www.ucmexus.ucr.edu

William C. Velásquez Institute (WCVI): www.wvci.org